Encyclopedia of
CHRISTMAS
and New Year's
Celebrations

2nd Edition

Encyclopedia of
CHRISTMAS
and New Year's
Celebrations

2nd Edition

*Over 240 Alphabetically Arranged Entries Covering
Christmas, New Year's, and Related Days of
Observance, Including Folk and Religious Customs,
History, Legends, and Symbols from Around the World.
Supplemented by a Bibliography and Lists of Christmas
Web Sites and Associations, as well as an Index*

Tanya Gulevich

Illustrated by Mary Ann Stavros-Lanning

615 Griswold • Detroit, Michigan 48226 • 313-961-1340
2003

Henderson, *Copy Editor*
Barry Puckett, *Research Associate*
Allison A. Beckett and Linda Strand, *Research Assistants*

Omnigraphics, Inc.

* * *

Matthew P. Barbour, *Senior Vice President*
Kay Gill, *Vice President — Directories*
Kevin Hayes, *Operations Manager*
Leif Gruenberg, *Development Manager*
David P. Bianco, *Marketing Consultant*

* * *

Peter E. Ruffner, *Publisher*
Frederick G. Ruffner, Jr., *Chairman*

Copyright © 2003 Omnigraphics, Inc.
ISBN 0-7808-0625-5

Library of Congress Cataloging-in-Publication Data

Gulevich, Tanya.
  Encyclopedia of Christmas and New Year's celebrations : over 240 alphabetically
arranged entries covering Christmas, New Year's, and related days of observance,
including folk and religious customs, history, legends, and symbols from around the
world / Tanya Gulevich ; illustrated by Mary Ann Stavros-Lanning.
    p. cm.
  Rev. ed. of: Encyclopedia of Christmas. 2000.
  Includes bibliographical references and index.
  ISBN 0-7808-0625-5
    1. Christmas—Encyclopedias. 2. New Year—Encyclopedias.   I. Gulevich, Tanya.
Encyclopedia of Christmas. II. Title.

GT4985.G79 2003
394.261—dc21

                                                                                    2003040580

The information in this publication was compiled from the sources cited and from other
sources considered reliable. While every possible effort has been made to ensure reliability, the
publisher will not assume liability for damages caused by inaccuracies in the data, and makes
no warranty, express or implied, on the accuracy of the information contained herein.

This book is printed on acid-free paper meeting the ANSI Z39.48 Standard. The infinity symbol
that appears above indicates that the paper in this book meets that standard.

Printed in the United States

Contents

To my Yiayia, Evdokia, with love and admiration

Introduction

ike a river winding its way to the sea fed by countless tributaries, the festival we call Christmas has rolled down to us over the course of two millennia. It has taken many twists and turns on its journey across the rugged landscape of the ages, thereby gaining and losing a range of meanings, legends, customs, and symbols. It has been fed along the way by such sources as the Bible, pre-Christian calendar customs, Christian lore and tradition, and a wide range of folk practices, beliefs, and symbols. The interventions and innovations of many individuals — be they saints, kings, queens, musicians, writers, business men and women, manufacturers, scholars, clergy, or politicians — have also swelled the flow. Today, standing at the mouth of the river, the yearly phenomena we call Christmas roars past us each December, a joyous tumult composed of all these influences.

In western cultures the celebrations surrounding Christmas and New Year's have unified into a single holiday season. Hence, the second edition of the *Encyclopedia of Christmas* has expanded its coverage of New Year's Eve and Day. For this reason, the second edition has been retitled *Encyclopedia of Christmas and New Year's Celebrations*.

The *Encyclopedia of Christmas and New Year's Celebrations* addresses this sprawling holiday, tracing its history back to ancient times and describing its observance in countries spanning six continents. The encyclopedia format allows the user to locate sought-for information quickly, or to browse. The diverse range of material presented offers the reader the opportunity to gain a new appreciation of the breadth and depth of this ancient, international festival.

Audience

The *Encyclopedia of Christmas and New Year's Celebrations* is intended for general audiences, including students and teachers, as well as interested adults. Those researching various aspects of the history and celebration of Christmas will find pertinent information, and general readers will find engaging historical narratives, descriptions, tales, and facts.

Scope and Organization

The *Encyclopedia of Christmas and New Year's Celebrations* contains 247 entries on all facets of Christmas arranged in alphabetical order. Topics covered include folk customs and beliefs, religious practices, symbols, legends, mythological and historical figures, foods, beverages, and major artistic and popular works associated with the celebration of Christmas and New Year's Eve and Day. Entries also provide information on related days and celebrations, such as the Annunciation, Candlemas, and Epiphany. Because many of the entries include material on a range of subjects, the reader is strongly urged to consult the index in order to locate all available information on any given topic.

The *Encyclopedia* traces the history of Christmas and New Year's Day from antiquity to the twentieth century. It contains a number of essays on ancient celebrations which bequeathed some of their customs to this holiday season, such as the Roman festivals Kalends and Saturnalia. It also traces the origins and development of Christmas as a Christian holiday. To this end it includes essays exploring the controversy over the date of Jesus' birth, explaining the selection of December 25 as the date of the new festival, and describing the development of the many Christian holidays and celebrations related to the Nativity.

Many essays touch on the blossoming of Christmas customs, legends, symbols, and foods in medieval and Renaissance Europe, as well as the expansion of the Christmas season that took place during that era. Further essays outline the decline of Christmas following the Protestant Reformation, as well as examine its resurgence in the Victorian era. The *Encyclopedia* also covers the continuing evolution of the holiday in the twentieth century, noting the development of new symbols and customs, such as those represented by the Christmas seal and the Christmas club, as well as the growing popularity of Santa Claus, the Christmas tree, the Christmas gift, and other modern Christmas customs.

The book is international in scope, offering 39 entries dealing wholly or mostly with the Christmas season in other countries. These essays cover Christmas celebrations in European, Asian, Middle Eastern, African, and Latin American countries. Additional information about foreign Christmas customs appears throughout the volume. For example, there is no entry on Jamaica or the Bahamas, but the "Jonkonnu" entry describes an important Jamaican and Bahamian Christmas custom. Therefore, readers are encouraged to use the index to locate all pertinent information on a geographic location, ethnic group, or any other subject.

New to the Second Edition

The second edition adds 60 new entries to the *Encyclopedia*. These entries greatly expand coverage of New Year's Eve and Day, Christmas in the United States, and Christmas celebrations in foreign countries.

The *Encyclopedia* now offers 21 entries treating New Year's customs, observances, and symbols. Additional information can be found in Christmas-centered entries throughout the *Encyclopedia* and is easily located with the aid of the index. The expanded coverage of New Year's Eve and Day celebrations focuses on the western New Year's Day, falling seven days after Christmas on January 1. Other New Year's holidays—such as Chinese New Year—that are unrelated culturally, religiously, or calendrically to Christmas have not been covered.

Readers interested in American Christmas and New Year's celebrations may now consult 49 entries dealing wholly or in good part with the customs, history, and symbols of these holidays as they are celebrated in the United States. For a complete listing, see **United States of America, Christmas and New Year's Celebrations in the**. These entries expand the historical coverage of the holiday and detail, for example, how American slaves celebrated Christmas as well as discuss the history of Christmas in the White House. They also survey pop culture contributions to the American holiday season, such as football bowl games, Christmas villages, and a number of the nation's favorite Christmas movies and television specials. New entries also discuss Christmas observances in several distinctive American towns and cities such as Williamsburg, Virginia, Bethlehem, Pennsylvania, and New York City.

Seventeen new entries increase the book's coverage of Christmas in foreign countries. Four describe Christmas in Middle Eastern countries, and five cover Christmas in African countries. New entries on Christmas in India, Australia, and the Marshall Islands shed further light on Asian, Pacific, and Pacific Islands Christmas celebrations. Several other new entries enhance the book's coverage of eastern European Christmas celebrations.

Entries and References

Entries range in length from about 100 words to well over 2,500 words. Suggestions for further reading follow each essay. The *Encyclopedia of Christmas and New Year's Celebrations* is thoroughly cross-referenced. Within each article words in boldfaced type and see-also references guide the reader to further entries containing information on the same or related subjects.

Each entry is followed by one or more sources for further reading. In some instances, sources consulted in writing the entry were not listed after the text of the entry, especially if the work contained little pertinent information, was especially scholarly, difficult to obtain, or out of print. A full bibliography of all sources consulted appears at the end of the book. Though not included in the further reading lists, *Colliers Encyclopedia, Encyclopedia Britannica, Webster's New Universal Unabridged Dictionary, Microsoft Encarta 2001 Standard Encyclopedia,* and the *Oxford English Dictionary* were freely consulted in the writing of a number of entries.

Appendices

Three appendices supplement the *Encyclopedia*:

Appendix 1: Bibliography—Contains a complete listing of books and articles consulted.

Appendix 2: Web Sites—Furnishes addresses for more than seventy web sites offering information on a wide variety of Christmas-related topics. Countless Christmas sites populate the World Wide Web. Those appearing in the *Encyclopedia*, either in further reading lists or this appendix, were chosen for inclusion because they were deemed to offer substantial information presented by reliable sources.

Appendix 3: Associations—Lists groups whose missions relate to Christmas in some way. A brief summary of the group's purpose, available publications, and full contact information accompanies each listing.

Index

The index provides the reader with an important tool for getting the most out of this book. It covers customs, symbols, legends, historical and mythological characters, ethnic groups, musical and literary works, foods, beverages, religious groups and denominations, geographical locations, keywords, alternate names, and other subjects mentioned in the entries.

Acknowledgments

Several people aided me in the long process of researching and writing this manuscript. First and foremost I would like to thank my editor, Helene Henderson, for bringing her excellent editorial skills to bear on all aspects of this book. Her faith in this project has been much appreciated. I am also grateful to Joseph A. Lane, Katherine Lehman, Jane McDougle, and Judith Reuss for their feedback on various aspects of the manuscript. I would also like to acknowledge George and Elizabeth Gulevich for their unfailing enthusiasm for this enterprise and the editorial staff of Omnigraphics for their confidence in my work.

The illustrations appearing in the *Encyclopedia of Christmas and New Year's Celebrations* were created using images from the following sources: Corel Draw; Image Club Graphics' Art Gear Visions of Christmas and Festive Occasions; and Dynamic Graphics' Artworks Series. You may copy the designs and illustrations for classroom and library use free of charge and without special permissions. Electronic or mechanical reproduction, including photography, recording, or any other information storage and retrieval system for the purpose of resale is strictly prohibited without permission in writing from the publisher.

Advisors

This project was reviewed by an Advisory Board comprised of librarians to assist editorial staff in assessing its usefulness and accessibility. They evaluated the title as it developed, and their suggestions have proved invaluable. Any errors, however, should be attributed to the author and editors. The Omnigraphics editorial staff would like to list the Advisory Board members and thank them for their efforts.

Gail Beaver
Ann Arbor Huron High School Library and the
University of Michigan School of Information and Library Studies
Ann Arbor, Michigan

Linda Carpino
Detroit Public Library
Detroit, Michigan

Helen Gregory
Grosse Pointe Public Library
Grosse Pointe, Michigan

Rosemary Orlando
St. Clair Shores Public Library
St. Clair Shores, Michigan

Encyclopedia of

CHRISTMAS

and New Year's
Celebrations

2nd Edition

Adam and Eve Day

According to the Bible's Book of Genesis, God created the first man and woman and invited them to live in a heavenly place called the Garden of Eden. This couple, known as Adam and Eve, lived there in bliss until they took the advice of a serpent and disobeyed God's command not to eat the fruit of the tree of knowledge of good and evil. As punishment for their disobedience, God expelled them from the Garden, thus compelling them to work for their living, suffer pain, and eventually die. Medieval Christians honored Adam and Eve as the father and mother of all people and commemorated their story on December 24, the day before Christmas.

Eastern Christians, that is, those Christians whose traditions of belief and worship developed in the Middle East, eastern Europe, and north Africa, were the first to honor Adam and Eve as saints. Their cult spread from eastern lands to western **Europe** during the Middle Ages, becoming quite popular in Europe by the year 1000. Although the Roman Catholic Church never formally adopted the pair as saints, it did not oppose their veneration.

Commemorating the lives of Adam and Eve on December 24 promoted comparison of Adam and Eve with **Jesus** and the Virgin **Mary**. Medieval theologians were fond of making such comparisons, the point of which was to reveal how Jesus and Mary, through their obedience to God's will, rescued humanity from the consequences of Adam and Eve's disobedience. Indeed, the Bible itself refers to Jesus as the "second Adam" (Romans 5:14). Whereas humanity inherited biological life from the first Adam, it would imbibe spiritual life from Jesus, the second Adam (1 Corinthians 15: 22, 45, 49). Some theologians took this to mean that Jesus' coming could restore humankind to a state of grace lost when Adam and Eve were exiled from Eden. In like manner, Mary would undo the effects of Eve's disobedience. When the **angel** Gabriel visited Mary and delivered the message that she would bear a divine son, Mary replied, "Behold, I am the handmaid of the Lord; let it be to me according to your word" (Luke 1:38; *see also* **Annunciation**). Medieval commentators relished the fact that in Latin, Eve's name, *Eva*, read backwards spelled *Ave*, meaning "hail." *Ave Maria*, or "Hail Mary" were the first words that the angel **Gabriel** spoke to the Virgin Mary. The spelling of these two short words seemed to them to symbolize God's plan to reverse the consequences of Eve's deed by bring a savior into the world through the Virgin Mary.

Medieval Christians celebrated Adam and Eve's feast day with a kind of mystery play referred to as the paradise play (*for more on the paradise play, see* **Paradise Tree**). This little folk drama retold the story of Adam and Eve in the Garden of Eden. It ended with the promise of the coming of a savior who would reconcile humanity with God. The paradise play was often staged around a single prop called a paradise tree. Actors adorned an evergreen tree with apples and sometimes also with communion wafers. Decked out in this way it served to represent the two mystical trees in the Garden of Eden: the tree of knowledge of good and evil and the tree of life. Although the church officially banned the performance of mystery plays in the fifteenth century, the people of **France** and **Germany**'s Rhine river region kept on decorating paradise trees for Christmas. Some writers believe that the paradise tree evolved into what we now know as the **Christmas tree**. Indeed, as late as the nineteenth century people in some parts of Germany customarily placed figurines representing Adam, Eve, and the serpent under their Christmas trees. In some sections of Bavaria, people still hang apples upon their evergreens at Christmas time and refer to the decorated trees as paradise trees.

As the Middle Ages receded into history, so too did the western European feast of Adam and Eve. Adam and Eve have retained a bit more of their ancient importance among certain Eastern Christians. The Greek Orthodox Church still honors Adam and Eve on the Sunday before Christmas.

Further Reading

Cross, F. L., and E. A. Livingstone, eds. "Adam" and "Eve." In their *The Oxford Dictionary of the Christian Church*. Second edition, revised. Oxford, England: Oxford University Press, 1983.

Ryken, Leland, James C. Wilhoit, and Tremper Longman, III, eds. "Adam." In their *Dictionary of Biblical Imagery*. Downers Grove, Ill.: InterVarsity Press, 1998.

Weiser, Francis X. *Handbook of Christian Feasts and Customs*. New York: Harcourt, Brace and World, 1952..

Advent

Christmas Lent, Little Lent,
St. Philip's Fast, Winter Lent

The word "Advent" comes from the Latin word *adventus*, which means "coming" or "arrival." The Advent season serves as a period of spiritual preparation for the coming of Christmas. Advent calls Christians to reflect on both the birth of **Jesus** and on the Second Coming of Christ (*see also* **Jesus, Year of Birth**). In Western Christianity Advent begins on the Sunday closest to November 30, St. Andrew's Day, and lasts till December 24, thereby extending over a period of 22 to 28 days. In the Orthodox Church Advent begins on November 15. The Roman Catholic, Orthodox, Anglican, and Lutheran traditions view Advent as the beginning of the Church year.

The liturgical color for Advent is purple, reflecting the repentant mood characteristic of early Church Advent observances. By contrast, many popular customs associated with this period joyfully anticipate the coming of Christmas.

History

In 490 A.D. Bishop Perpetuus of Tours, France, established a period of penance and preparation for Christmas in his diocese. He advocated fasting on Mondays, Wednesdays, and Fridays for a forty-day period preceding Christmas. This fast period began on the day after **Martinmas**, November 11, thereby acquiring the name "St. Martin's Lent" or "The Forty Days' Fast of St. Martin." The observation of a period of penance in preparation for Christmas gradually spread throughout **France**, and on to **Spain** and **Germany**, though it may have been largely restricted to monastic communities. In Spain groups of Christians were already fasting in preparation for **Epiphany**. In the early years there was little agreement regarding the dates and length of this pre-Christmas fast period. In some areas the fast began on November 11. In others, September 24, November 1, or December 1 might be the starting date. In 581 A.D. the Council of Mâcon ordered the laity throughout France to observe the forty-day period of fasting. Two hundred years later the Advent fast was adopted in England as well.

Advent was not observed in Rome until the sixth century. Pope Gregory I (590-604 A.D.) developed much of the Roman Advent liturgy and shortened the period of observance from six to four weeks. The joyous, festive spirit with which the Romans celebrated Advent clashed with the somber, penitential mood established in Gallic observances. For a number of centuries Advent celebrations throughout western Europe varied in tone, length, and manner of observance. Sometime after 1000 A.D. Rome accepted the practice of fasting during Advent, which in those times meant abstaining from amusements, travel for purposes of recreation, and marital relations, as well as certain foods. In addition, no weddings were permitted during fast periods.

By the thirteenth century the observance of Advent in western Europe had stabilized. It combined the Roman tradition of a four-week observance, the Gallic custom of fasting, and a liturgy that mingled the themes of penance and joy. In recent centuries the Roman Catholic Church reduced, and eventually eliminated, Advent fasting.

The Orthodox Church

The Orthodox churches of eastern Europe developed different traditions. Since the eighth century Orthodox believers have fasted in preparation for Christmas. Orthodox believers fast by eliminating meat, fish, dairy products, wine, and olive oil from their diets for a set period of time. A common Orthodox term for Advent is "Little Lent." In the Greek tradition, Advent is often called "Christmas Lent," a period that lasts from November 15 until the eve of December 24 and is observed with fasting, prayer, and almsgiving (*see also* **Greece, Christmas in**). The Orthodox period of preparation before Christmas may also be called "St. Philip's Fast" because it begins the day after St. Philip's Day. Armenian Orthodox believers fast for three weeks out of a seven-week Advent period, which runs from November 15 till January 6. Orthodoxy does not maintain a special liturgy for this period (*see also* **Armenia, Christmas in**).

Folk Customs

The folk customs of Advent reflect the anticipation and joy that characterize the weeks preceding Christmas in many countries. In many lands **Nativity scenes** are constructed and displayed. Advent may also be a favorite time of year to attend special Christmas concerts and performances. Many customs connected with the season feature the lighting of **Advent candles**. Indeed, the candle has become a symbol of the season. Some Christians fashion and display **Jesse trees** and **Chrismon trees** in observance of Advent. Others attend special church services, such as the Anglican **Ceremony of Lessons and Carols**. The **Advent wreath** keeps adults focused on the spiritual message of Advent. The **Advent calendar** offers children a toy to help them count the days until Christmas. Other children's customs include writing letters to the child Jesus or **Santa Claus** (*see also* **Children's Letters**) and participating in the Hispanic folk play called Las **Posadas**, in which children and adults recreate the Holy Family's search for a place to spend the night in **Bethlehem**.

Frauentragen, or "woman carrying," is a German Advent custom which closely resembles Las Posadas. Children carry a picture or figurine representing the Virgin **Mary** to a neighborhood home. Once there, they sing or enact a brief scene from the Nativity story, say a prayer, and place the picture or figurine near the family crucifix. The children return for the image the following evening and carry it to a new home. In this way they act out Mary and **Joseph**'s search for lodging in Bethlehem. On Christmas Eve the children carry Mary back to the church, where she takes her place in the Nativity scene. Musical folk plays were once a popular Advent custom in Germany. Known as *Herbergsuchen,* or "search for the inn," this folk drama also reenacted Mary and Joseph's search for shelter in Bethlehem. The play ended happily with the birth of the baby Jesus in a stable.

In Latin America and central Europe the nine days before Christmas take on a special character. In Latin America many people participate in a popular novena in honor of the Christ child. A novena is a series of special religious services or private devotions held on nine consecutive days. In Europe the nine days before Christmas were sometimes called the "Golden Nights," as many of the religious observances and popular celebrations that characterized the period occurred after dark.

Further Reading

Henderson, Helene, and Sue Ellen Thompson, eds. *Holidays, Festivals, and Celebrations of the World Dictionary.* Second edition. Detroit, Mich.: Omnigraphics, 1997.

Metford, J. C. J. *The Christian Year.* London, England: Thames and Hudson, 1991.

O'Shea, W. J. "Advent." In *New Catholic Encyclopedia.* Volume 1. New York: McGraw-Hill, 1967.

Russ, Jennifer M. *German Festivals and Customs.* London, England: Oswald Wolff, 1982.

Slim, Hugo. *A Feast of Festivals.* London, England: Marshall Pickering, 1996.

Thompson, Sue Ellen, ed. *Holiday Symbols.* Detroit, Mich.: Omnigraphics, 1998.

Weiser, Francis X. *Handbook of Christian Feasts and Customs.* New York: Harcourt, Brace and Company, 1952.

Web Site

The German Embassy in Washington, D.C., offers a page describing Advent customs in Germany: http://www.germany-info.org/xmas/ch_16.html

Advent Calendar

Advent calendars help children count the days between the beginning of Advent and Christmas. By furnishing a treat for each day of **Advent**, these one-page calendars help curb the impatience of countless children in many countries who long for the arrival of Christmas Day. The history of the Advent calendar is uncertain, although some writers believe that it was invented in **Germany** around the turn of the twentieth century.

Advent calendars may take many forms, but each offers a playful method for checking off the days between December first and twenty-fifth. In the United States one often finds the calendars printed onto double layers of paperboard (*for a list of entries treating American history and customs, see* **United States of America, Christmas in**). A Christmas scene with the numbers one through twenty-five incorporated into the design decorates the surface of the calendar. Perforations around the numbers allow children to fold back or remove a number each day, revealing the tiny images printed on the bottom layer below. These images generally depict a Christmas or Advent theme.

Some calendars attach chocolates or other sweets behind the fold-back dates on the calendar. In Germany cardboard houses may serve as the basis for homemade Advent calendars. Behind doors and windows children find edible goodies. Creative German crafters may even use matchboxes or walnut shells as devices for marking off the days of Advent and delivering tiny treats to children. The less inventive may press regular wall calendars into service by gluing candy, pictures, or verses to each of the December days before Christmas. Finally, in recent years one can find a variety of interactive Advent calendars posted on the World Wide Web (*see* Appendix 2).

Further Reading

Del Re, Gerard, and Patricia Del Re. *The Christmas Almanack*. Garden City, N.Y.: Doubleday, 1979.

Russ, Jennifer M. *German Festivals and Customs*. London, England: Oswald Wolff, 1982.

Thompson, Sue Ellen, ed. *Holiday Symbols*. Detroit, Mich.: Omnigraphics, 1998.

Advent Candle

A number of different **Advent** customs require the lighting of candles. Some writers believe that the use of candles during Advent may have been adopted from the fires and lights that illuminated pre-Christian midwinter festivals. Before the widespread use of electric lighting, the twinkling candles not only served to dispel the gloom of the long winter nights, but also represented the hope of light and life to come. In Christian terms, the flame of the Advent candle represents the coming of **Jesus**, "the light of the world" (John 8:12).

Placing a lighted candle in the windowsill is perhaps the simplest Advent candle custom. In Europe during centuries past, a flickering candle in the window symbolized the offer of hospitality to nighttime wayfarers. Some believed the glowing light might even attract the Christ child. The Irish brought with them the tradition of placing a lighted candle in the windowsill at Christmas time when they emigrated to the United States (*see also* **Ireland, Christmas in**). In the late nineteenth century groups of carolers popularized the custom in Boston. From there the practice spread to other American cities. The citizens of **Bethlehem, Pennsylvania**, keep candles in their windows at Christmas time, though they trace their tradition back to the town's Moravian founders (*for more on Moravian Christmas customs, see* **Christingle; Lovefeast; Watch Night**). Christmas time candles also twinkle in the windows of historic **Williamsburg, Virginia**. The custom there developed as a means of decorating historic district homes in a manner consistent with the town's colonial architecture and décor.

In the American Southwest people decorate the exteriors of their homes with **luminarias**, candles placed in brown paper bags filled with sand. This custom originated in **Mexico**.

Many churches hold special candle-lighting services sometime during Advent. Often, each person attending is given a candle (*see also* Christingle). The lighting of these candles then becomes part of the service.

Advent wreaths may be found in both home and church Advent observances. These wreaths contain four candles, one for each of the four Sundays of Advent. One is lit on the first Sunday of Advent. One more candle is lit on each of the following Sundays until on the fourth Sunday of Advent all four candles burn in unison. These four Advent candles may also be used without a wreath. (*See also* **Christmas Candles**.)

Further Reading

Augustine, Peg, comp. *Come to Christmas*. Nashville, Tenn.: Abingdon Press, 1993.

Thompson, Sue Ellen, ed. *Holiday Symbols*. Detroit, Mich.: Omnigraphics, 1998.

Weiser, Francis X. *Handbook of Christian Feasts and Customs*. New York: Harcourt, Brace and World, 1952.

Advent Wreath

Many Christians enhance their observance of **Advent** with an Advent **wreath**. Although **Germany**'s Lutheran community is credited with popularizing this custom sometime in the nineteenth century, its ultimate origins may lie in the pre-Christian practice of fashioning winter festival decorations from evergreen boughs. Whatever its origins, the symbols and customs connected with today's Advent wreath represent the spiritual significance of the Christian Advent season. Advent wreaths are used in both home and church observances.

Advent wreaths are usually fashioned out of **greenery** and are meant to lie on a flat surface or to hang horizontally from the ceiling. Four candles are incorporated into the wreath. They symbolize eternal life, as does the circular design of the wreath (*see also* **Christmas Candles**). Purple candles are often found in wreaths designed for church use, since purple is the liturgical color of the Advent season. Finally, a larger white candle, known as the Christ or Christmas candle, is placed in the center of the wreath or off to one side. The white color of this candle coincides with the liturgical colors for Christmas Day, white or **gold**. Some churches do not follow the liturgical color scheme, however.

Wreaths made for home observances employ candles of various shades. For example, red and white candles are often found in European Advent wreaths.

On the first Sunday of Advent, the first of the four candles in the wreath is lit. On the second Sunday, the second candle joins the first. By the fourth Sunday in Advent all four candles glow in unison. Finally, on Christmas or Christmas Eve, the Christ candle flickers alongside the others. The ever increasing amount of light given off by the candles represents the spiritual illumination hoped for in the Advent season. The Christ candle, bigger and brighter than the rest, symbolizes the arrival of **Jesus**, "the light of the world" (John 8:12), and Christmas, the culmination of the Advent season. This lighting of candles at the darkest time of year may also stand for commitment to one's faith in times of darkness. In some home observances, family and friends pray, sing, or read spiritual texts by the light of the Advent wreath. An old German custom suggests adding one paper star to the wreath for each day in Advent. The star carries an Old Testament verse on one side and a New Testament verse on the other. Children might then be expected to memorize these verses.

Many assign special significance to each of the four wreath candles. Some say they represent the four gifts of the Holy Spirit: hope, joy, peace, and love. Others use them to represent the themes of the Advent season. Thus they may signify hope, preparation, joy, love, or light. Still others tell the story of Jesus' birth with the candles, allowing each to stand for some of the important figures associated with the Nativity, such as the prophets, **angels**, **shepherds**, and the **Magi**.

Further Reading

Augustine, Peg, comp. *Come to Christmas*. Nashville, Tenn.: Abingdon Press, 1993.

Slim, Hugo. *A Feast of Festivals*. London, England: Marshall Pickering, 1996.

Thompson, Sue Ellen, ed. *Holiday Symbols*. Detroit, Mich.: Omnigraphics, 1998.

Weiser, Francis X. *The Christmas Book*. 1952. Reprint. Detroit, Mich.: Omnigraphics, 1990.

Web Site

A site sponsored by the Evangelical Lutheran Church in America on the meaning and use of the Advent wreath in the Lutheran tradition of worship: http://www.elca.org/dcm/worship/worship_planning/church_year/christmas_cycle.html

America, Christmas in Colonial

The religious upheaval known as the Reformation divided sixteenth-
and seventeenth-century Europeans on many religious issues, including the celebration of Christian feast days. The European immigrants who settled in the thirteen American colonies brought these
controversies with them. Among colonial Americans, attitudes towards Christmas depended largely on religious affiliation. In general,
Puritans, Baptists, Presbyterians, Congregationalists, and Quakers
refused to celebrate the holiday. In areas of the country settled primarily by people of these religious affiliations, Christmas withered.
By contrast, those who belonged to the Anglican (or Episcopalian),
Dutch Reformed, Lutheran, and Roman Catholic traditions generally approved of the holiday. Communities composed primarily of
people from these denominations planted the seeds of Christmas in
this country.

The First American Christmas

The first Christmas celebration in what was later to become the continental United States took place in St. Augustine, Florida, in 1565
(*for a list of entries treating American history and customs, see* **United
States of America, Christmas in**). Old documents inform us that
Father Francisco Lopez de Mendoza Grajales presided over a Christmas service held at the Nombre de Dios Mission in that year. The
Shrine of Nuestra Señora de la Leche now marks this location. The
town of St. Augustine boasts of being the oldest settlement founded
by Europeans in what is now the United States. Still, residents of
Tallahassee, Florida, suspect that an even earlier Christmas celebration may have been held near the site of their town. In 1539 a party
of Spanish colonists, led by explorer Hernando de Soto (c. 1500-
1542), camped near the place where Tallahassee now stands. Since
the Spaniards stayed from October 1539 to March of the following
year, some Floridians speculate that they must have celebrated
Christmas there.

The First Christmas in the English Colonies

In Jamestown, Virginia, a ragged band of Englishmen huddled together on Christmas morning in the year 1607. Although one hundred hopeful settlers had left England in order to found this, the first American colony, less than forty were still alive to celebrate their first Christmas in the New World. Their leader, Captain John Smith, was gone. He had left them to barter for food with the local Indians, and, according to legend, returned alive thanks only to the intervention of a young Indian woman named Pocahontas. Although the settlers had little food with which to rejoice, they still observed Christmas Day with an Anglican worship service.

Virginia and the South

In Virginia, Maryland, and the Carolinas the majority of early settlers were Anglicans of English descent. In the second half of the seventeenth century, as their way of life grew more secure, they began to reproduce the festive Christmas they had known in their homeland (*see also* **Williamsburg, Virginia, Christmas in Colonial**). They celebrated with feasting, drinking, dancing, card playing, horse racing, cock fighting, and other **games**. Although Anglican churches offered Christmas worship services, these apparently did not play a large role in colonial Christmas celebrations. Wealthy plantation owners who lived in large houses aspired to fill the **Christmas season** with lavish entertainments of all sorts. For many, this festive period lasted until **Twelfth Night**. By the eighteenth century these wealthy southerners studded their holiday season with balls, fox hunts, bountiful feasts, and openhanded hospitality. One year guests at a Christmas banquet hosted by a wealthy Virginia planter named George Washington, who later became the first president, dined sumptuously on the following dishes: turtle soup, oysters, crab, codfish, roast beef, Yorkshire pudding, venison, boiled mutton, suckling pig, smoked ham, roast turkey, several dishes of vegetables, biscuits, cornbread, various relishes, cakes, puddings, fruits, and pies. Wines, cordials, and a special holiday drink known as **eggnog** usually rounded out the plantation Christmas feast. Although wealthy parents might give a few presents to their children on Christmas or **New Year's Day**, this practice was not widespread. More common was the practice of making small **gifts** to the poor, to one's servants, or to one's **slaves**.

The less well-off could not reproduce the splendor of a plantation Christmas, but they could still celebrate with good food and good cheer. In addition, southerners of all classes saluted Christmas morning by **shooting** off their guns and making all sorts of noise. Those who did not own muskets banged on pots and pans or lit fireworks. Slaves were usually given a small tip or gift and some leisure time at Christmas. Since they had to prepare the parties and feasts for everyone else, however, their workload increased in certain ways at this time of year.

Southern colonists transported a number of old English Christmas customs to the New World including **Christmas carols**, **Yule logs**, kissing under the **mistletoe**, and decking homes with **greenery**. Southern schoolboys of this era sometimes resorted to the Old World custom of **barring out the schoolmaster** in order to gain a few days off at this festive time of year.

New England

The first bands of settlers to colonize New England were mostly made up of Puritans, members of a minority religious sect in England. They advocated a simplified style of worship and the elimination of many religious holidays, including Christmas. Although they came to America in search of religious freedom, once here, the Puritan settlers established rules and laws favoring their religion above all others, as was the custom in Europe at the time. In Plymouth colony, the first European settlement in New England, Puritan leaders frowned upon Christmas from the very beginning. In 1621, one year after their arrival from England, Governor William Bradford discovered young men playing ball games in the streets on Christmas Day. He sent them back to their work, remarking in his diary that while he may have permitted devout home observances, he had no intention of allowing open revelry in the streets. In 1659 Massachusetts Bay Colony made Christmas illegal. Any person found observing Christmas by feasting, refraining from work, or any other activity was to be fined five shillings. In 1681, however, pressure from English political authorities forced colonists to repeal this law. The anti-Christmas sentiment continued, though, and most people went on treating Christmas like any other workday. Many Puritan colonists resented the presence of the few Anglicans in their midst, especially if they were British officials. On Christmas Day in 1706 a Puritan gang menaced worshipers at the King's Chapel in Boston, breaking windows in protest against the Anglican worship service taking place inside.

The very fact that Puritan leaders passed a law against the holiday suggests that some New Englanders were tempted to make **merry** on that day. Historic documents record a few instances of seventeenth-century Christmas revelers and mummers being cold-shouldered by their more severe neighbors. The late seventeenth and eighteenth centuries witnessed a slight thawing in Puritan attitudes towards Christmas, as the New England colonies began to fill with people from a wider variety of religious backgrounds. Many still criticized drinking, gaming, flirting, feasting, and **mumming** as unholy acts of abandon that dishonored the Nativity of Christ, but some now accepted the idea of marking the day of Jesus' birth with religious devotions. Nevertheless, noted Puritan minister Cotton Mather (1663-1728) clearly warned his congregation against secular celebrations of the holiday in his Christmas Day sermon of 1712:

> Can you in your conscience think that our Holy Saviour is honored by Mad Mirth, by long eating, by hard Drinking, by lewd Gaming, by rude Revelling? . . . If you will yet go on and do Such Things, I forewarn you That the Burning Wrath of God will break forth among you [*Christmas in Colonial and Early America*, 1996, 12].

In eighteenth-century New England, Christmas services could be found in Anglican, Dutch Reformed, Universalist, and other churches representing pro-Christmas denominations.

New York and Pennsylvania

New York and Pennsylvania hosted significant numbers of Dutch and German immigrants. Denominational differences divided many of these immigrants on the subject of Christmas. In general, the Mennonites, Brethren, and **Amish** rejected Christmas. The Lutherans, Reformed, and Moravians cherished the holiday and honored it with church services as well as folk celebrations (*see also* **Lovefeast** and **Bethlehem, Pennsylvania, Christmas in**). Like their English counterparts in the South, the pro-Christmas communities in New York and Pennsylvania ate and drank their way through the Christmas holiday. In addition, both the Dutch and the Germans brought a rich tradition of Christmas baking to this country, including the making of special Christmas cookies, such as **gingerbread**. In fact, the American English word "cookie" comes from the Dutch word *koek*, meaning "cake." This in turn gave rise to the term *koekje*, meaning "cookie" or "little cake."

German immigrants brought other Christmas customs with them as well. As early as the mid-eighteenth century Moravian communities in Pennsylvania were celebrating the day with Christmas **pyramids**. Other early German communities imported the beliefs and customs surrounding the German folk figures **Christkindel** and **Knecht Ruprecht,** whose gift-giving activities delighted children at Christmas time. Although the Germans probably also introduced the **Christmas tree**, no records of this custom can be found until the nineteenth century.

In addition to its large German population, Pennsylvania became home to many Scotch Irish and Quakers. Both the Scotch Irish, most of whom were Presbyterians, and the Quakers disapproved of Christmas celebrations in general. The Quakers adamantly opposed all raucous street revels, including those of German belsnickelers, mummers, and masqueraders of all kinds. In the nineteenth century, when Quakers dominated Philadelphia and Pennsylvania state government, they passed laws to prevent noisy merrymaking in the streets at Christmas time (*see also* **America, Christmas in Nineteenth-Century**).

The German Christmas blended lively folk customs with devout religious observances. This combination eventually became typical of American Christmas celebrations. At least one researcher has concluded that increased immigration from the German-speaking countries in the second half of the eighteenth century profoundly influenced the American Christmas. The increasing number of Germans permitted their balanced approach to Christmas to spread among the wider population and so encouraged the festival to flourish in the United States.

Conclusion

The colonial American Christmas differed significantly from contemporary American Christmas celebrations. Many religious people completely ignored the day. Even after the founding of the United States no state recognized Christmas as a legal holiday. Those people who celebrated it anyway did so without **Santa Claus**, **Christmas cards**, Christmas trees, and elaborate Christmas morning gift exchanges. Instead, the most common ways to observe the holiday featured feasting, drinking, dancing, playing games, and engaging in various forms of public revelry. Although the colonies attracted people from many different countries, English, German, and Dutch settlers exercised the strongest influence on early American Christmas celebrations.

Further Reading

Barnett, James. *The American Christmas.* New York: Macmillan, 1954.

Christmas in Colonial and Early America. Chicago: World Book, 1996.

Kane, Harnett. *The Southern Christmas Book.* 1958. Reprint. Detroit, Mich.: Omnigraphics, 1998.

Lizon, Karen Helene. *Colonial American Holidays and Entertainments.* New York: Franklin Watts, 1993.

Nissenbaum, Stephen. *The Battle for Christmas.* New York: Alfred A. Knopf, 1996.

Restad, Penne. *Christmas in America.* New York: Oxford University Press, 1995.

Shoemaker, Alfred L. *Christmas in Pennsylvania.* Kutztown, Pa.: Pennsylvania Folklore Society, 1959.

Snyder, Phillip. *December 25th.* New York: Dodd, Mead, and Company, 1985.

Young, Joanne B. *Christmas in Williamsburg.* New York: Holt, Rinehart and Winston, 1970.

America, Christmas in Nineteenth-Century

At the beginning of the nineteenth century American Christmas celebrations varied considerably from region to region. These variations reflected religious and ethnic differences in the population. In **Puritan** New England, for example, many people ignored the holiday (*see* **America, Christmas in Colonial**). In Pennsylvania German-American communities reproduced a number of German Christmas traditions. Prosperous Southerners, especially those of Anglican English or French descent, hosted lavish Christmas meals and parties. All across the country many of those who celebrated Christmas in nineteenth-century America did so with noisy, public, and sometimes drunken, reveling. By contrast, non-observers tried to ignore the noise and the festivities. They treated the day as any other workday, since it was not a legal holiday in most of the century.

During the second half of the nineteenth century, however, more and more people began celebrating Christmas. Regional and religious differences faded as new American Christmas customs emerged. These customs helped to transform the American Christmas into the tranquil, domestic festival we know today. As the century rolled on, larger numbers of people incorporated customs and myths surrounding the **Christmas tree**, **Santa Claus**, and family **gift** exchanges into their Christmas celebrations. The Civil War (1861-65) served as a watershed in American Christmas observances, after which time the **commercial** trappings of the holiday—especially **Christmas cards**, store-bought gifts, **store window displays**, and **wrapping paper**—took on greater importance.

New York and Pennsylvania

In the early nineteenth century some New Yorkers and Pennsylvanians celebrated Christmas with **mumming** and other forms of noisy, public merrymaking. Young men of German extraction carried out their own variation of mumming known as "belsnickeling" (*see*

19

Knecht Ruprecht). In Pennsylvania Dutch country, students sometimes celebrated Christmas by **barring out the schoolmaster**. In New York brazen parties of drunk men sang, played instruments, and shouted in the streets on Christmas Eve, disturbing the sleep of more serious-minded citizens. On **New Year's Day** custom dictated that ladies stay at home to exchange New Year's greetings with a string of gentlemen callers, all of whom were entertained with food and drink. For gentlemen with a wide range of female acquaintances, this custom presented yet another opportunity to consume large quantities of alcohol. Christmas mumming occurred in both New York and Pennsylvania, to the dismay of those who favored a more solemn observance of the season.

In addition to those customs it shared with New York, Pennsylvania boasted its own highly developed noisemaking traditions during this era. In Philadelphia young men wandered the streets during the **Christmas season**, drinking, shooting off firecrackers, shouting, and sometimes fighting with one another. Some even strutted about in costume and were referred to as "fantasticals." Many of these celebrants wandered about the downtown blowing horns on Christmas Eve. Those who could not lay their hands on horns added to the pandemonium with tin whistles, sailors' hornpipes, tin pans, hand-held **bells**, sleigh bells, or homemade instruments. In the year 1861 these mock minstrels raised such a racket that they reduced the center of the city to chaos.

The city government, dominated by those who did not celebrate Christmas, made two attempts to outlaw parading, masquerading, and horn playing on Christmas Eve, once in 1868 and again in 1881. The practice proved too deeply rooted to stamp out, however. Eventually, the city instituted the New Year's Day **Mummers Parade**, which modified these activities and channeled them into a controlled format. This popular parade continues today. (*For other nineteenth-century Pennsylvania customs, see* **Amish Christmas**.)

The South

Southerners also celebrated Christmas by making noise. Men shot off guns both on Christmas Eve and Christmas Day. Firecrackers and gunpowder explosions added to the din. Children without access to either of these items sometimes celebrated by popping inflated hog bladders, the nineteenth-century farm equivalent of a balloon. Southern Christmas celebrations featured so many bangs and explosions that some witnesses said they rivaled Independence Day celebrations. In 1902 an article printed in a New York newspaper claimed that New York manufacturers had sold $1 million worth of fireworks to Southern buyers during the Christmas season.

In addition to noisemaking, residents of many Southern cities also enjoyed dressing in costume on Christmas Eve. In some places they were referred to as "fantasticals," like their fellow celebrants in Pennsylvania. Baltimore, Savannah, Mobile, and St. Augustine hosted versions of this Christmas Eve masquerade. Arrayed in costumes ranging from funny to frightening, residents sallied forth to promenade up and down the main streets of the town. Something similar survives today in New Orleans' Mardi Gras celebrations. Lastly, many residents of the former French territories, which became the states of Louisiana and Missouri, celebrated Christmas with French customs. These customs included assembling **Nativity scenes**, attending **Midnight Mass**, cooking up sumptuous **réveillon** suppers, and hosting parties in honor of New Year's Eve and **Twelfth Night**.

The Slaves

The **slaves** developed Christmas customs of their own. In North Carolina some celebrated **Jonkonnu**. Some slaves observed an all-night vigil on Christmas Eve during which they sang, danced, and prayed. Throughout the South slaves greeted white folk on Christmas morning with the cry of "Christmas gif'!" According to custom, the white person responded by giving them a present, either a coin or a gift. In addition, slaveowners often distributed presents of clothing, shoes, blankets and other necessities to their slaves at Christmas time. Some slaveowners provided their slaves with extra rations of food at Christmas, including meat, which was something the slaves rarely ate during the rest of the year. Slaveowners frequently provided ample portions of liquor as well. At many plantations slaves celebrated Christmas by dressing in their best clothes, feasting, and dancing. At other plantations slaves worked through the Christmas holidays. Sometimes slaveowners withheld the privilege of celebrating Christmas from those slaves who had displeased them during the year. Others gave presents only to women who had borne babies or to the most productive workers. Abolitionist Frederick Douglass (1817-1895) later looked back on the customs of the plantation Christmas as mechanisms for controlling the slaves. He argued that days of drunken carousing subtly convinced some slaves that they were incapable of productive behavior if left to their own devices.

After Slavery

In the late nineteenth century African-American Christmas celebrations varied quite a bit. Some African Americans celebrated a modest Christmas, exchanging gifts of homemade food and clothing and attending church. Visitors to the Indiana State Museum's Freetown Village, a permanent, living-history exhibit, can watch a play that reenacts an 1870s African-American Christmas of this type. Others reproduced some of the old customs of the plantation Christmas. The children greeted any adult they could find with the cry of "Christmas gift!" and the adults danced, drank to excess, and refrained from work. African-American educator Booker T. Washington (1856-1915) observed these conditions in Tuskegee, Alabama, in the 1880s. As head of the town's newly founded school for African Americans (now Tuskegee University), he made it a point to teach his students to celebrate a sober Christmas, dedicated at least in part to religious observance and to aiding the less fortunate.

The West

Out on the Western frontier men celebrated Christmas by **shooting** off their guns and banging on tin pans in noisy and often drunken processions. In Minnesota settlers of Swedish descent attended *Julotta* services on Christmas morning (*see also* **Christmas Carol**). Texans celebrated with Christmas Eve balls. Throughout the Southwest many of Hispanic descent staged Las **Posadas** and Los **Pastores**, traditional Christmas folk plays.

Christmas Becomes a Legal Holiday

After the Revolution the newly established American government revoked all British holidays. This act left the United States without any national festivals. In 1838 Louisiana was the first state to recognize Christmas as a legal holiday. One by one, the other states followed suit. Finally, on June 26, 1870, in recognition of the large number of people who already observed the day, Congress declared Christmas to be a national holiday.

Protestants Embrace Christmas

Just as the states of the nation began to declare Christmas a legal holiday, many Protestant denominations that had previously rejected Christmas began to accept the festival. Between the years 1830 and 1870 Christmas slowly crept into Sunday school curriculums. The middle of the century also witnessed the publication of new American Christmas hymns. A number of these, such as "O Little Town of Bethlehem," "It Came Upon a Midnight Clear," and "We Three Kings" — all composed by clergymen — have become Christmas standards. By the end of the century Presbyterian, Baptist, Methodist, and Congregationalist churches were offering Christmas services on the Sunday nearest Christmas. Perhaps this change signified that the passage of time had finally severed the connections made by many Protestants between Christmas, Roman Catholicism, and the religious oppression of past eras.

A Festival of Home and Family

The Christmas celebrations that the Protestant denominations were now embracing were not quite the same ones their ancestors had rejected. Several researchers of nineteenth-century American Christmas customs point out that as the century progressed many of the more boisterous elements of the festival diminished. These elements included mumming, belsnickeling, public drinking, and noisemaking. Americans increasingly viewed these activities as unworthy of the season. Instead, they began to create a tranquil celebration that focused on home and family ties. These changes probably encouraged former non-celebrants, including many previously hostile Protestant denominations, to adopt the new version of the holiday. Several new Christmas customs helped to facilitate this transition to a more peaceful, domestic festival, including the Christmas tree, Christmas cards, the family gift exchange, and the new American gift bringer, Santa Claus.

23

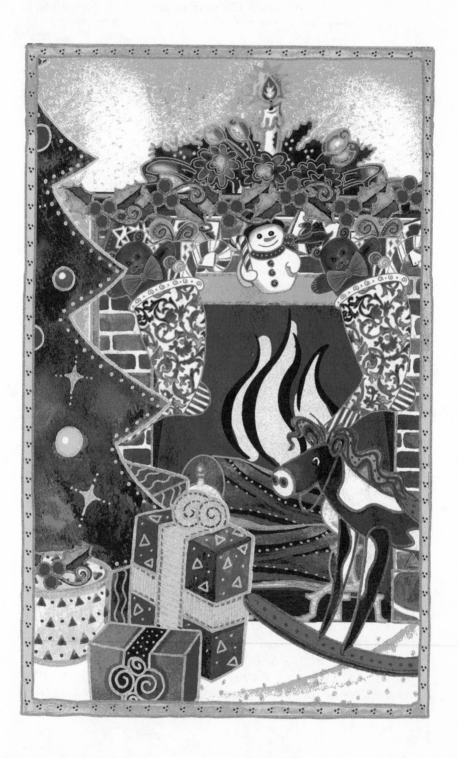

Christmas Trees and Gift Giving

Most colonial Americans who observed the day did not give Christmas gifts to their children. Eighteenth-century Americans were more likely to give gifts to servants or to those who performed services for them during the year (*see* **Boxing Day**). Likewise, many nineteenth-century Americans resisted the idea of exchanging Christmas gifts with friends and family because they viewed Christmas gifts as something one gave to social inferiors. At the turn of the nineteenth century those who did give presents to family members and neighbors frequently gave simple, homemade gifts, such as handsewn or knitted articles of clothing, wooden toys, or homemade preserves. Family gift giving appears to have been somewhat more frequent in German-American and Dutch-American communities. In these areas children might receive fruits, nuts, and sweets from **Christkindel** or the local belsnickelers. Some adults in these communities also exchanged small gifts, such as handkerchiefs, scarves, or hats. Of those adult Americans who exchanged gifts during the winter holiday season, many did so on New Year's Day rather than on Christmas.

Christmas gifts started to become more common about mid-century. Several factors contributed to this rise in popularity. First, people began to adopt the German custom of installing a Christmas tree in their parlors as a holiday decoration. The Germans covered their trees with good things to eat and small gifts. Hence, the tree focused everyone's attention on giving and receiving. In addition, because it stood at the center of the household, the tree showcased the family gift exchange. Whereas, in the past, some parents may have stuffed a few sweets into their children's **stockings**, they now could hang little gifts from a tree branch. Liberated from the tight quarters of the Christmas stocking, the gifts parents gave to children grew in size and substance. Before 1880 people usually hung their unwrapped gifts from the tree with thread or string. After that time, wrapping paper and fancy decorated boxes slowly became fashionable. As Christmas presents grew too large or heavy to hang on the tree, people began to place them beneath the tree.

Although charity had been an element of Christmas celebrations for centuries (*see also* **Europe, Christmas in Medieval**), it became a more prominent theme of the festival during the nineteenth century. Some writers credit the Christmas stories of English author Charles Dickens (1812-1870), especially *A Christmas Carol*, with significantly increasing public interest in Christmas charity. In addition, many ministers preached to their congregations about giving to those less fortunate. The **Salvation Army** took this message to heart in the 1890s, mounting a successful campaign to raise funds to provide the poor with bountiful Christmas dinners in large public halls.

Santa Claus and Children's Gifts

Santa Claus played an important role in the popularization of Christmas gift giving. This American folk figure became widely known in the second half of the nineteenth century, consolidating and replacing the lesser-known, ethnic gift bringers Christkindel (also known as Kriss Kringle), Belsnickel, and **St. Nicholas**. This bit of American folklore did not spring up from the masses of the American folk, however. Literary and artistic figures, such as Clement C. Moore (1779-1863), the author of "A Visit from St. Nicholas," and illustrator Thomas Nast (1840-1902), developed the myth and image of Santa Claus that became popular through their works. Nevertheless, the American people quickly adopted him as their own. Santa delivered gifts to youngsters by visiting their homes on Christmas Eve. The increasing popularity of Santa Claus boosted the importance of gifts, especially gifts for children, in American Christmas celebrations.

Commerce and Cards

The decade following the Civil War witnessed a sudden rise in store-bought gift giving. Researchers have traced this upsurge to two complementary factors: consumer demand and commercial promotion. Although some people objected to the impersonality of store-bought gifts, others desired the new, manufactured goods. Moreover, retailers set about enticing the public into spending money on Christmas with such innovations as lavish store window displays, wrapping paper, and special advertising campaigns (*see* Commercialism). Stores began to schedule special holiday season hours to accommodate the seasonal increase in customers. In **New York City** shop doors remained open until midnight during the Christmas season, generating concern in some quarters for the plight of overworked shop assistants.

Christmas cards achieved widespread popularity by the 1880s, about the time when Americans began celebrating Christmas by exchanging store-bought gifts. According to one researcher, nineteenth-century cards replaced more personal yet more time-consuming ways of sending seasonal greetings, such as writing letters and visiting (*see also* **Children's Letters**). The cards anchored themselves more firmly among America's Christmas customs after the turn of the twentieth century, when people began to use cards to replace cheap gifts for more distant friends and relatives.

Conclusion

During the nineteenth century American Christmas celebrations began to coalesce around customs that promoted symbolic exchanges of love and good will both between family members and in the wider community. These customs—the night visit of Santa Claus, Christmas trees, family gift exchanges, Christmas cards, and Christmas charity—still stand at the center of today's festivities. Throughout the nineteenth century regional differences in the celebration of Christmas diminished, although they never quite disappeared. The twentieth century would witness the further erosion of these regional customs.

Further Reading

Barnett, James. *The American Christmas*. New York: Macmillan, 1954.

Bigham, Shauna, and Robert E. May. "The Time O' All Times? Masters, Slaves, and Christmas in the Old South." *Journal of the Early Republic* 18, 2 (summer 1998): 263-88.

Dipeiro, Diane. "Together at Christmas (Christmas Traditions of African-American Slaves)." *Colonial Homes* 20 (December 1, 1994): 28(2).

Kane, Harnett. *The Southern Christmas Book*. 1958. Reprint. Detroit, Mich.: Omnigraphics, 1998.

Nissenbaum, Stephen. *The Battle for Christmas*. New York: Alfred A. Knopf, 1996.

Restad, Penne. *Christmas in America*. New York: Oxford University Press, 1995.

———. "Christmas in Nineteenth-Century America." *History Today* 45 (December 1995): 13-19.

Shoemaker, Alfred L. *Christmas in Pennsylvania*. Kutztown, Pa.: Pennsylvania Folklore Society, 1959.

Snyder, Phillip. *December 25th*. New York: Dodd, Mead, and Company, 1985.

Web Site

Freetown Village, a living-history museum located in Indianapolis, Indiana, offers a brief description of the reenactment of an 1870s Christmas in a settlement of newly freed African Americans on its web site at: http://www.freetown.org/ (click on "special events")

Amish Christmas

The Amish observe Christmas but do not share many mainstream, American Christmas customs. For example, they don't set up **Christmas trees** in their homes, tell their children about **Santa Claus**, and buy lots of expensive presents (*see also* **Commercialism**). Few decorate their homes in any way for the holiday, and those that send **Christmas cards** generally send them to their non-Amish friends. Instead, the Amish Christmas revolves around a few simple, homespun pleasures.

The Amish

The Amish are Protestant Christians who maintain a lifestyle many Americans associate with centuries past. They reject most modern industrial and technological developments. Amish families continue to work their own farms without the aid of tractors or other motorized farm equipment, ride in horse-drawn buggies, and wear clothes popular two hundred or more years ago. The Amish came to this country in the eighteenth century to escape religious persecution in Europe. Here they found the freedom to worship as they wished and live in the manner they chose. Today's Amish speak English but also preserve the German dialect of their ancestors. Many Amish live in the state of Pennsylvania, but they can also be found in Ohio and other Midwestern states, as well as Canada.

The Amish faith emerged from the Protestant Reformation, a sixteenth-century religious reform movement that gave birth to Protestant Christianity. Like the English and American **Puritans**, the Amish initially rejected the celebration of Christmas as a non-biblical, frivolous, and sometimes even decadent holiday. A touch of this attitude remains today in their restrained observance of Christmas.

Amish Christmas Customs

Most Amish schools prepare Christmas pageants. Since Amish children attend school right up till Christmas Day, the pageant is generally set for the afternoon of December 24. Parents and other relatives attend and watch with pride as their young people recite poems and take part in skits — many of which contain moral teachings about Christmas charity, faith, and love — and sing **Christmas carols**. Earlier that day the children may have taken part in a **gift** exchange in which each child, having drawn a slip of paper with another child's name on it, brings a present for that boy or girl.

For most Amish, Christmas morning begins with farm chores. Afterwards the family gathers for breakfast and Christmas gifts in the kitchen. In nineteenth-century Amish families, parents set out plates on the kitchen table and piled their children's presents on top. They usually gave their children things like nuts, raisins, cookies, candy, and rag dolls and other homemade toys. Other Pennsylvania Dutch families also set out Christmas plates in past times. The custom of setting out Christmas presents on the kitchen table seems to have died out among other groups, however. Today Amish families exchange a few useful gifts on Christmas morning. Typical gifts include simple toys such as skates and sleds, books, homemade candies and cookies, kitchenware, and household items. A large Christmas dinner completes the day's activities.

On December 26 the Amish celebrate "second Christmas." This custom, once common in Pennsylvania Dutch country, came into being so that those who devoted much of **December 25** to religious observance did not miss out on all the Christmas fun. It's a popular day for family outings, visits, **games**, and other leisure activities. (*For more on Pennsylvania Dutch Christmas customs, see* **America, Christmas in Nineteenth-Century; Barring Out the Schoolmaster; Bethlehem, Pennsylvania, Christmas in; Knecht Ruprecht.**)

Further Reading

Ammon, Richard. *An Amish Christmas*. New York: Atheneum Books, 1996.
Shoemaker, Alfred L. *Christmas in Pennsylvania*. Kutztown, Pa.: Pennsylvania Folklore Society, 1959.

Web Site

"An Amish Christmas," by Brad Igou, posted on the web site of *Amish Country News*, a monthly visitors guide to Lancaster, Pennsylvania's Amish Country: http://www.amishnews.com/amisharticles/amishChristmas.htm

Angels

Images of angels adorn **Nativity scenes, Christmas cards,** Christmas trees, and many other Christmas displays. These popular **Christmas symbols** boast an ancient pedigree. They play a prominent role in the New Testament accounts of **Jesus'** birth (*see also* **Gospel Accounts of Christmas; Gospel According to Luke;** and **Gospel According to Matthew**). Angels also appear in many Old Testament stories.

Biblical Angels

The Hebrew scriptures (the Christian Old Testament) often use the term *malakh,* meaning "messenger," to refer to the beings we call angels. Writing in Greek, the authors of Christian scripture called these beings *angelos,* a Greek term meaning "messenger" or "herald." This word eventually passed into the English language as "angel." Although the word "angelos" denoted an ordinary, human messenger, biblical authors selected it over another available Greek term, *daimon*, which referred to a guardian spirit. Perhaps they discarded this term because Greek lore taught that the daimon exercised both good and evil influences over people. Eventually, the Greek word "daimon" passed into the English language as "demon."

The angels of biblical tradition frequently acted as messengers. In fact, angels served this function in both scriptural accounts of Jesus' birth. In Matthew's account of the Nativity an angel appeared to **Joseph** on three separate occasions. The first time the angel came to explain the nature of **Mary**'s pregnancy. Later, an angel warned Joseph of **Herod**'s evil intentions concerning Jesus and advised him to flee into **Egypt** (*see also* **Flight into Egypt; Holy Innocents' Day**). An angel returned one final time to inform Joseph of Herod's death and to command his return to Israel. In Luke's account of the Nativity, the angel **Gabriel** visited Mary to inform her that she would bear a child by the Holy Spirit. On the night of Jesus' birth an angel appeared to **shepherds** in a nearby field to announce the glorious event. Then a "multitude" of angels suddenly materialized behind the first angel, singing praises to God.

What Angels Look Like

With so many angels involved in orchestrating the events surrounding Jesus' birth, it is no wonder that they became a symbol of the Christmas holiday. Today's Christmas angels frequently appear as winged human beings in flowing white robes with somewhat feminine faces and haloes. This image evolved over the course of two millennia.

The very first Christian depictions of angels date back to the time of the Roman Empire. Early Christian paintings of angels rendered them as ordinary men rather than as winged, spiritual beings. Some artists, however, garbed their angels in white robes, resembling a Roman senator's toga, in order to symbolize their power and dignity. The first winged angels appeared in the fourth century. Some scholars believe that early Christian artists patterned the image of winged angels after the Greek goddess Nike, the winged, female spirit of victory. Others trace this image back even further to winged spirits associated with the religion of ancient Babylon. By the fifth century Christian artists from the Byzantine Empire began to depict angels with a disk of light, called a nimbus, behind their heads. This nimbus, or halo, signifies holiness, purity, and spiritual power.

In medieval times most western European artists portrayed angels as masculine in face and form. This trend reversed itself from the fourteenth to the sixteenth centuries. After that time, western European angels acquired softer, more feminine, or androgynous, looks. Sometimes they appeared as chubby children or toddlers. Artists often depicted angels with harps or other musical instruments. These emblems signify what some consider to be the primary occupation of angels—praising God.

Further Reading

Cross, F. L., and E. A. Livingstone, eds. *The Oxford Dictionary of the Christian Church*. Second edition, revised. Oxford, England: Oxford University Press, 1983.

Efird, James M. "Angels." In Paul J. Achtemeier, ed. *The HarperCollins Bible Dictionary*. Revised edition. San Francisco, Calif.: HarperSanFrancisco, 1996.

The Glory and Pageantry of Christmas. Maplewood, N.J.: Time-Life Books, 1963.

Lang, Judith. *The Angels of God*. London, England: New City Press, 1997.

Lewis, James R., and Evelyn Dorothy Oliver. *Angels A to Z*. Detroit, Mich.: Visible Ink Press, 1996.

Ward, Theodora. *Men and Angels*. New York: Viking, 1969.

Annunciation

Annunciation means "announcement." When spelled with a capital "A," the word refers to the announcement made by **Gabriel**, God's messenger **angel**, to the Virgin **Mary**, telling her that she would bear a son by the Holy Spirit whom she should call **Jesus** (Luke 1:26-28). By the early Middle Ages the Church had established a feast day to commemorate this angelic announcement.

In the middle of the fourth century, Church officials in Rome created a new festival to honor the birth of Jesus. They scheduled this festival, which we now call Christmas, on **December 25**. Eventually December 25 gained widespread acceptance as the actual date on which Jesus had been born, implying that Mary must have become pregnant nine months earlier, on March 25. According to the astronomical calculations used by the ancient Romans, the spring equinox also fell on that day (*see also* **Winter Solstice**). By the eighth century the Feast of the Annunciation of the Blessed Virgin Mary, celebrated on March 25, was firmly established in western Europe.

As Mary's pregnancy marked the beginning of a new era for Christians, many medieval kingdoms also chose March 25 as the day on which they began their new year (*see also* **Kalends**; **New Year's Day**). In 1582 Pope Gregory XIII called for calendar reforms which included switching New Year's Day to January 1 (*see also* **Old Christmas Day**). Nevertheless, several centuries passed before most European countries had adopted the reformed, Gregorian calendar.

Many Christians still recognize March 25 as a religious holiday, although they have slightly different names for the observance. Roman Catholics currently refer to the feast as the "Annunciation of the Lord," the Orthodox know it as the "Annunciation of the Mother of God," and many Anglicans call it the "Annunciation of Our Lord to the Blessed Virgin Mary." The English also call the festival "Lady Day." The Feast of the Annunciation often occurs during Lent. Those Christians who fast during Lent, for example, Roman Catholics and Orthodox, are allowed to modify the fast on this day.

Over the centuries the Annunciation became a favorite scene for western European painters interested in depicting the life of the Blessed Virgin Mary. The scene also appears frequently in stained glass windows and other church decorations. Many famous artists have bequeathed us their versions of the Annunciation, including Robert Campin (c. 1378-1444), Fra Angelico (c. 1400-1455), Sandro Botticelli (1445-1510), El Greco (1451-1614), Leonardo Da Vinci (1452-1519), and Adolphe-William Bouguereau (1825-1905). In these paintings Mary often appears to be reading or spinning when the angel arrives, activities which represent her piety. A container of water may sit beside her, or the angel may offer her lilies, both of which symbolize her purity. The Holy Spirit commonly takes shape as a descending dove or as a ray of light streaming through the window.

Further Reading

Auld, William Muir. *Christmas Tidings*. 1933. Reprint. Detroit, Mich.: Omni-graphics, 1990.

Cross, F. L., and E. A. Livingstone. *The Oxford Dictionary of the Christian Church*. Second edition, revised. Oxford, England: Oxford University Press, 1984.

The Glory and Pageantry of Christmas. Maplewood, N.J.: Time-Life Books, 1963.

Henderson, Helene, and Sue Ellen Thompson, eds. *Holidays, Festivals, and Celebrations of the World Dictionary*. Second edition. Detroit, Mich.: Omni-graphics, 1997.

Metford, J. C. J. *The Christian Year*. London, England: Thames and Hudson, 1991.

———. *Dictionary of Christian Lore and Legend*. London, England: Thames and Hudson, 1983.

Rouvelas, Marilyn. *A Guide to Greek Traditions and Customs in America*. Bethesda, Md.: Nea Attiki Press, 1993.

Stuhlmueller, C. "Annunciation." In *New Catholic Encyclopedia*. Volume 1. New York: McGraw-Hill, 1967.

Armenia, Christmas in

Most Armenians celebrate *Soorp Dznoont* — Christmas — on January 6. The reasons for this unusual date emerge quite literally from the pages of ancient history. In the fourth century Roman Catholic Church officials established the date of Christmas as **December 25**. Before that time the Armenians and some other Christians celebrated the Nativity of **Jesus** and his baptism on the same day, January 6 (*see also* **Epiphany**). Eventually other Christian communities accepted the Roman date for the Nativity. The Armenians, however, never accepted the new date for Christmas and continued to celebrate it on January 6.

When Pope Gregory XIII instituted the Gregorian calendar in 1582, some Armenians rejected the reforms and stuck instead to the old, Julian calendar (*see* **Old Christmas Day**). Today Armenians living in the Holy Land still use the Julian calendar to determine their feast days. The Julian calendar is now a full thirteen days ahead of the Gregorian calendar. So, when these Armenians celebrate Christmas on January 6 according to the Julian calendar, the Gregorian calendar counts the day as January 19. In **Bethlehem** special services for Armenian Christians take place at the Church of the Nativity on January 19.

New Year's Day and Christmas in Armenia

In Armenia children receive **gifts** on **New Year's Day**. This custom began during the Soviet era (1917-91), when government officials discouraged the celebration of religious holidays such as Christmas. They promoted instead the celebration of New Year's, a secular holiday, and tried to transfer some Christmas customs to this date. For example, they disapproved of Christmas gift bringers such as **Baboushka**, whose story includes biblical themes. Communist officials attempted to replace her with another popular folk figure, **Grandfather Frost**, the spirit of winter, who brings gifts to children on New Year's Day. Armenians still give children sweets and toys on

New Year's, but since the fall of the Communist government some people have begun to recognize the gift bringer as **Father Christmas** rather than Grandfather Frost. Adults also exchange gifts on this day. Popular presents include flowers, alcoholic beverages, and items made from silver.

Armenian families prepare for Christmas by giving their homes a thorough cleaning. Housewives find ways to display their fancy needlework and spend hours in the kitchen cooking and baking. "Princely trout," or *ishkhanatsoog*, is a popular Christmas Eve dish. Christmas church services begin at midnight on Christmas Eve. According to tradition, heralds announce the services, striding through the streets with stout staves, chanting, "Today is a great day of the feast of the birth of Jesus, Good News! O ye good Christians, come to the holy church."

Church services are also held on Christmas Day, January 6. These services feature a ceremony known as the Blessing of the Waters, which commemorates Jesus' baptism. The priest uses a wand made from basil leaves to sprinkle water on the congregation. After church Armenians pay visits to friends and neighbors. A large family meal follows, at which close relatives, distant relatives, friends, and even strangers are welcome. Gifts of money and clothing are distributed after dinner. Then children grab handkerchiefs and band together in small groups that scurry up to the rooftops to sing:

> Rejoice and be glad
> Open your bag
> And fill our handkerchiefs
> Hallelujah, hallelujah.

People who hear their cries offer them coins, nuts, and fruit.

Further Reading

Kasbarian, Lucine. *Armenia*. New York: Dillon Press, 1998.

Terjimanian, Hagop. *Feasts and Holidays of the Armenian People*. Santa Monica, Calif.: Abril Bookstore, 1996.

"Auld Lang Syne"

At many **New Year's** Eve parties, the song "Auld Lang Syne" is played or sung at midnight, as a means of saying farewell to the old year and greeting the new. The phrase "auld lang syne" is Scottish dialect for "old long ago." The song itself is attributed to Robert Burns (1759-1796), Scotland's most famous poet.

Robert Burns's Restoration

Burns scholars recognize that the poet did not write the entire song. They point to a letter that Burns wrote to a friend in which Burns admits as much. Rather, he found a fragment of an old folk ditty, restored it, and added new verses. In the letter, Burns paid high tribute to the anonymous writer of the brief text that he elaborated on:

> Light be the turf on the breast of the heaven-inspired poet who composed this glorious fragment! There is more of the fire of native genius in it that in half a dozen of modern English Bacchanalians [*Robert Burns Encyclopedia* web page].

No one knows exactly how much of the song was written by Burns, but scholars believe that the poet definitely wrote what are now the song's third and fourth verses.

Though Burns paired his lyrics with an already existing Scottish folk tune, his editor decided to publish them with a different old Scottish folk melody, the one we still use today. In Scotland the popularity of "Auld Lang Syne" grew over the years, until it displaced "Good Night and Joy Be Wi' You A'" as the song traditionally sung at the break up of a festive gathering.

Words to the Song

Subsequent generations of singers have made slight changes to Burns's original poetry. The verses to the entire song, as penned by Burns, follow:

	(Standard English Translation)
Should auld acquaintance be forgot	Should old acquaintances be forgotten,
And never brought to mind?	And never brought to mind?
Should auld acquaintance be forgot	Should old acquaintances be forgotten,
And days o auld lang syne?	And days of old long ago?

Chorus (repeated after each verse)	
And for auld lang syne, my jo	And for old long past, my joy,
For auld lang syne,	For old long ago.
We'll tak a cup o kindness yet,	We will take a cup of kindness yet,
For auld lang syne.	For old long ago.

And surely ye'll be your pint-stowp!	And surely you'll pay for your pint-vessel!
And surely I'll be mine!	And surely I'll pay for mine!
And we'll tak a cup o' kindness yet,	And we'll take a cup of kindness yet,
For auld lang syne.	For old long ago.

We twa hae run about the braes	We two have run about the hillsides
And pu'd the gowans fine;	And pulled the wild daisies fine;
But we've wander'd mony a weary foot	But we've wandered many a weary foot
Sin auld lang syne	Since old long ago.

We twa hae paidl'd i' the burn,	We two have paddled in the stream,
Frae mornin' sun till dine;	From morning sun till noon;
But seas between us braid hae roar'd	But seas between us broad have roared
Sin auld lang syne.	Since old long ago.

And there's a hand, my trusty fiere!	And there is a hand, my trusty friend!
And gie's a hand o thine!	And give me a hand of yours!

And we'll tak a right guid	And we will take a right
willie waught,	good-will drink,
For auld lang syne.	For old long ago.

"Auld Lang Syne" Becomes an American New Year's Song

So how did this old Scottish tune become so well known in America? The answer lies in the power of television to publicize and promote. In 1943, the New Year's Eve festivities taking place in **New York City's Times Square** were televised for the first time. As viewers waited for midnight to arrive, they were treated to coverage of Guy Lombardo's dance band, playing live at the Grill Room of the Roosevelt Hotel (in later years the venue changed to the Waldorf-Astoria Hotel). Guy Lombardo decided to close out his New Year's Eve performances with the tune "Auld Lang Syne." Having grown up in western Ontario, a region of Canada with a significant population of Scottish descent, he was familiar with the tune. In fact, when playing locally he frequently ended his performances with the song. Although he doubted that many Americans were familiar with "Auld Lang Syne," he played it anyway as a way of musically tipping his hat to the broadcast's corporate sponsor, Robert Burns's Panatella cigars. Guy Lombardo and his dance band became a fixture on these New Year's Eve broadcasts, and so did the song "Auld Lang Syne." This yearly television exposure encouraged Americans to adopt as their own the custom of singing "Auld Lang Syne" to bid farewell to the old year.

Further Reading

Pool, Daniel. *Christmas in New York*. New York: Seven Stories Press, 1997.

Web Sites

"Burns Country," a web site devoted to the promotion and enjoyment of the works of Robert Burns, includes the "Auld Lang Syne" entry from the *Robert Burns Encyclopedia*: http://www.robertburns.org/encyclopedia/Auld LangSyne.5.shtml

The World Burns Club furnishes a history of the song "Auld Lang Syne" on its web site: http://www.worldburnsclub.com/newsletterauld_lang_syne_ what_about.htm

Australia, Christmas in

Christmas comes to Australia during that continent's summer season. Therefore, Australians celebrate the festival with barbecues, beach parties, parades and other outdoor events. In fact, many Australians take their summer vacations during the Christmas holiday season.

The English brought Christmas to Australia in the late eighteenth century when they established the country as a colony of Great Britain. Australians have preserved much of their country's British Christmas heritage, especially carol singing, **gift** exchanges, **Christmas trees**, and the hearty, oven-roasted English Christmas dinner, though this last custom loses some of its appeal in the sweltering summer heat. Australia has adopted **Santa Claus** as its Christmas gift bringer, and many heavily sweating Santas, garbed in some variation of the traditional red velvet suit, cap, boots and beard, can be found at Christmas-related events throughout the holiday season.

Christmas Decorations

The traditional pine Christmas tree, decorated with tinsel, **ornaments**, and lights, is an important seasonal decoration in Australia. In addition to the tree, Australians have incorporated two local plants, the Christmas bell and the Christmas bush, into their holiday decorations. The Christmas bell produces green, glossy leaves and yellow or red bell-shaped flowers. Several different varieties of the Christmas bush put forth various kinds of flowers in the spring and summer, including one that sports white star-shaped flowers in the spring which drop to reveal brilliant red calyces at Christmas time. Some families decorate these plants with tinsel in honor of the holiday. Finally, homes, schools, shops and other places of business celebrate the season with displays of colored lights.

Christmas Eve and Day

On Christmas Eve many Australians attend carol-singing events known as "Carols by Candlelight." Norman Banks, a radio announcer from the city of Melbourne, started this tradition in 1938. It is said that while walking the streets on Christmas Eve of the previous year, he caught a glimpse of an old woman through a lighted window. She was sitting all alone next to her radio, holding a lighted candle and singing along with the **Christmas carols** that were being broadcast on the radio. The sight warmed his heart and also stirred him to create an event for those who found themselves alone on Christmas Eve. The following year he organized and broadcast "Carols by Candlelight," a sing-along caroling session in which participants held lit candles. The observance became more and more popular and eventually spread from Melbourne to other cities. Each year thousands of Australians attend these events, usually held in outdoor amphitheaters so that people can enjoy the balmy summer evening air as they listen to musical performances and sing the songs of the season amidst a sea of glowing candles. In addition to the traditional European tunes, a number of original Australian Christmas carols may be sung, such as "The Melbourne Carol," "Six White Boomers," and "The Three Drovers."

Australian children have their own version of the Christmas **stocking**, which often makes its first appearance on Christmas Eve. Before going to bed Australian children hang pillowcases from the ends of their beds. Santa leaves small gifts in the pillowcase; he deposits larger gifts under the Christmas tree.

Many Australian families open their presents over breakfast on Christmas morning. Religious people will also attend church. Later that afternoon many people enjoy listening to the Queen of England give her annual Christmas speech on the radio (*see also* **England, Christmas in**).

Christmas Dinner

Over the years Australians have come up with a number of Christmas dishes all their own. Some of these reflect the country's rugged colonial history. For example, a dish called "colonial goose" substitutes a stuffed leg of lamb for the more traditional English roast goose. "Billy can pudding" offers a simplified version of **plum pudding** made in a kind of tin tub used to carry water. Other colonial recipes include "Christmas damper," a quick Christmas bread, and "drover's plum pudding," a kind of rice pudding made with raisins and nuts. "Father Christmas salad," a red, white, and green mixture of cherries, pistachio nuts, and lychees, represents another original Australian Christmas recipe.

Many Australians eat their Christmas dinner out of doors, in order to enjoy the summer sunshine. Some barbecue or take picnics to the beach or other outdoor beauty spots. Others eat a cold meal at home, often combining salads with cold meat dishes. Still others, in spite of the heat, prefer an English Christmas dinner, complete with roasted meat, potatoes and gravy. Many families, no matter what they have for dinner, choose to end the meal with a hot Christmas pudding (*see also* Plum Pudding).

Boxing Day

December 26, **Boxing Day**, is a holiday in Australia. People enjoy sporting matches on this day (*for more on the day's traditional sports, see* **St. Stephen's Day**). It serves as the occasion for a number of important events, including the Sydney-to-Hobart Yacht Race and opening day test match held at the Melbourne Cricket Ground.

Other December Holidays

Australia is a diverse society that hosts many different ethnic and religious groups. Its Jewish citizens often begin their **Hanukkah** celebrations in December, and in some years the Muslim holiday of Ramadan falls in December. Many former citizens of Hong Kong have immigrated to Australia. They and their descendants often celebrate a Taoist festival called Ta Chiu on December 27, in which they thank their ancestors and the deities for their protection and ask these spirits to bless and renew their lives. Australia's original inhabitants, the Aborigines, do not observe a festival of their own at this time of year. In the north of the country, however, many indigenous Australians mark the end of their six-season year in late December.

Christmas in July

Some Australians tire of reinventing Christmas as a hot weather holiday. In recent years many have attended Christmas in July celebrations, where a traditional English Christmas celebration takes place in July. These celebrations fulfill the desires of those who long to celebrate Christmas by snuggling next to an open fire and partaking of a hearty English Christmas dinner on a wintry evening.

Further Reading

Bowler, Gerry. *The World Encyclopedia of Christmas.* Toronto, Ontario, Canada: McClelland and Stewart, 2000.

Griffin, Robert H., and Ann H. Shurgin, eds. *The Folklore of World Holidays.* Second edition. Detroit, Mich.: Gale, 1999.

Hubert, Maria, comp. *Christmas Around the World.* Stroud, Gloucestershire, England: Sutton, 1998.

McGregor, Malcolm, ed. *Christmas in Australia.* Milsons Point, Australia: Hutchinson Australia, 1990.

Tucker, Cathy C. *Christmas Worldwide.* Philadelphia, Pa.: Xlibris, 2000.

Web Sites

The following web site, sponsored by the Australian government's Department of Communications, Information Technology and the Arts, offers information on Christmas celebrations in Australia: http://www.acn.gov.au/articles/1998/11/xmas.htm

The Australian National Botanic Gardens sponsors a page on native plants associated with Christmas. Gives photos as well as text from *Australian Native Plants* by John Wrigley and Murray Fagg (1996): http://www.anbg.gov.au/christmas/christmas.html

Baboushka

Before the Revolution of 1917, Russian children received Christmas **gifts** from Baboushka, an old woman whose story is told in a Russian legend. *Baboushka* means "grandmother" in Russian. After the Revolution the government discouraged tales about folk characters like Baboushka, whose story refers to religious beliefs. Instead they promoted tales about completely secular characters such as **Grandfather Frost**, who currently serves as **Russia**'s gift bringer. With the fall of Russia's Communist regime in 1991, many old beliefs and practices have been returning, and Baboushka may, too. Baboushka closely resembles the traditional Italian gift bringer, La **Befana**.

The Legend of Baboushka

A long time ago an old woman lived alone in a house by the road. She had lived alone so long that her days and her thoughts were filled only with sweeping, dusting, cooking, spinning, and scrubbing. One evening she heard the sound of trumpets and men approaching on horseback. She paused for a moment, wondering who they could be. Suddenly she heard a knock on her door. Upon opening it she discovered three noble men standing before her (*see* **Magi**). "We are journeying to **Bethlehem** to find the child who has been born a King," they told her. They invited Baboushka to join them. "I haven't finished my work," she replied "and the nights are so cold here. Perhaps it would be better if you came in by the fire." But the strangers would not delay their journey and departed into the night. Sitting by the fire, Baboushka began to wonder about the child and regret her decision to stay home. Finally she gathered a few trinkets from among her poor possessions and set off into the night. She walked and walked, inquiring everywhere for the lordly men and the newborn King, but she never found them. Each year on **Epiphany** Eve (or **Twelfth Night**) Baboushka searches Russia for the Christ child. She visits every house, and even if she doesn't find him, she still leaves trinkets for well-behaved children.

Variations

In one version of the tale, the wise men ask Baboushka the way to Bethlehem and she intentionally deceives them. In another, the wise men ask for lodgings for the night and Baboushka refuses them. In yet a third the Holy Family passes by her door on their journey from Bethlehem to **Egypt** (*see* **Flight into Egypt; Holy Innocents' Day**). They beg hospitality from her, but she turns them away with nothing. In spite of their differences, each story concludes in the same way. Baboushka regrets her lack of concern, seeks out the people she has rejected, and eventually becomes a magical figure who travels the world at Christmas time bringing gifts to children.

Further Reading

Del Re, Gerard, and Patricia Del Re. *The Christmas Almanack*. Garden City, N.Y.: Doubleday, 1979.

Henderson, Yorke, et al. *Parents' Magazine Christmas Holiday Book*. New York: Parents' Magazine Press, 1972.

Philip, Neil, ed. *Christmas Fairy Tales*. New York: Viking, 1996.

Robbins, Ruth. *Baboushka and the Three Kings*. Berkeley, Calif.: Parnassus Press, 1960.

Baby

The figure of a baby is a symbol of the new year in general and **New Year's Day** in particular. The New Year's baby often wears a sash draped across one shoulder. The sash bears the number of the new year (for example, "2003"). The New Year's baby shares its seasonal billing with another baby associated with the midwinter holidays, that is, the baby **Jesus**, whose birth is celebrated on Christmas Day.

Americans adopted the New Year's baby from German immigrants. In **Germany**, the history of the baby as a New Year's symbol can be traced back to a fourteenth-century folk song. At least one scholar has identified an even earlier use of the baby as a holiday symbol. Theodor Gaster claims that the ancient Greeks used the baby as a symbol of the wine and vegetation god Dionysus during Lenaia, a January festival honoring his rebirth that was widely celebrated in Athens. (*For a similar symbol, see also* **Russia, Christmas in**.)

Further Reading

Gaster, Theodor. *New Year, Its History, Customs and Superstitions*. New York: Abelard-Schuman, 1955.

James, E. O. *Seasonal Feasts and Festivals*. 1961. Reprint. Detroit, Mich.: Omnigraphics, 1993.

Barring Out the Schoolmaster

American youngsters take their two-week vacation at Christmas time for granted. In past centuries, however, teachers expected pupils to study right through the **Christmas season**. If the students dared, they resorted to an old custom called "barring out the schoolmaster" in order to gain a week's leisure. Arriving early at school, students barricaded themselves in the classroom. This act began a kind of siege that could last for days. It ended when the teacher succeeded in breaking into the classroom, or when he or she gave in to the students' demands. If the students managed to keep the teacher out for a total of three days, they were automatically considered to have won the standoff.

In **England**, Scotland, and **Ireland** students staged barring-outs most frequently around Christmas, but they also occurred around Easter, Shrove Tuesday (the day before Lent begins), and harvest time. Students often chose **St. Nicholas's Day** or **St. Thomas's Day** to begin their wintertime takeovers. In order to mount a successful barring-out, students stockpiled food, drink, and sometimes even weapons. Indeed, violence often erupted during the battle for control of the classroom. If the schoolmaster succeeded in breaking in to the classroom, the students were severely beaten. Therefore, the students defended their territory with such weapons as swords, clubs, and even pistols. Records indicate that shots from excited boys sometimes injured or killed schoolmasters and town officials. Teachers could restore peace and order immediately by giving in to the students' demands. These demands were spelled out in a treaty signed by the students and the teacher. The treaty always included a guarantee that no one taking part in the uprising would be punished.

History

In Britain the custom of barring out the schoolmaster arose sometime in the sixteenth century. The number of schools and students increased greatly during that century. Due to the lack of generally accepted educational standards, schoolmasters ruled their classrooms with complete authority. They flogged their pupils frequently, a practice that was considered an appropriate educational tool and disciplinary measure in that era. The primary goal of most barring-outs was a reduction in the rate and severity of whippings as well as the granting of a few days' vacation. The frequency of these student take-overs declined throughout the eighteenth century as school charters began to limit the authority of teachers and guarantee vacation days. By the nineteenth century, barring-outs had nearly vanished in Britain.

At some point the custom appears to have migrated to the United States, where it survived a bit longer in a somewhat less violent form (*see* **America, Christmas in Colonial; America, Christmas in Nineteenth-Century**). Barring-outs were a common Christmas time occurrence in nineteenth-century Pennsylvania. These mock battles crowned the school year, as far as the gleeful students were concerned. Thomas Mellon (1813-1908), the wealthy financier who later founded the Mellon Bank, fondly remembered taking part in Christmas barring-outs in his youth. Whichever side lost furnished the school with several bushels of apples and gallons of cider, which were consumed by all on the first day of vacation. Like their British counterparts, American students resorted to barring-outs as a way of securing vacation days. The custom faded in the mid-nineteenth century as public schooling, with its standard schedule of vacation days, spread throughout the country. (*For more on Christmas in Pennsylvania, see* America, Christmas in Nineteenth-Century; **Amish Christmas; Bethlehem, Pennsylvania, Christmas in; Knecht Ruprecht**.)

Further Reading

Cathcart, Rex. "Festive Capers? Barring-Out the Schoolmaster." *History Today* 38, 12 (December 1988): 49-53.

Hole, Christina. *British Folk Customs*. London, England: Hutchinson and Company, 1976.

Hutton, Ronald. *The Stations of the Sun*. Oxford, England: Oxford University Press, 1996.

Shoemaker, Alfred L. *Christmas in Pennsylvania*. Kutztown, Pa.: Pennsylvania Folklore Society, 1959.

Bay. *See* Laurel

Befana
La Strega, La Vecchia

On **Epiphany** Eve children in **Italy** go to bed expecting La Befana to visit the house during the night. She leaves **gifts** for children who have been good during the past year and warns those who have misbehaved. The name "Befana" comes from the Italian word for Epiphany, *Epiphania*. La Befana may also be referred to as *La Strega*, meaning "the witch," or *La Vecchia*, meaning "the old woman." Although not much is known about the history of this figure from Italian legend, some authorities believe that La Befana may be related to **Berchta**, another witch-like figure who visits homes in central and northern Europe during the **Twelve Days of Christmas** and, especially, on **Twelfth Night**. La Befana also appears to be related to **Baboushka**, a Russian folk figure about whom a nearly identical tale is told.

The Legend of La Befana

There once was an old woman who lived alone by the side of the road. Her husband and child had died years ago. To forget her loneliness, she busied herself with many household tasks. One day three richly dressed men stopped at her house and asked her the way to **Bethlehem**. They invited the old woman to accompany them on their journey to worship the Christ child who had just been born there. The old woman grumbled, "I'm much too busy with my daily chores to go with you, and besides I've never even heard of Bethlehem." After the Three Kings, or **Magi**, had left, the old woman began to regret her decision. She gathered a few trinkets from among her simple belongings to present to the child as gifts. The she grabbed her broom and hurried after her visitors. The old woman walked and walked, but never caught up with the Three Kings and never found the Christ child. She didn't give up, however. Each year on Epiphany Eve she flies over the world on her broom searching for the Christ child. She checks each house where children live, diving down the chimney. Even when she doesn't find Him she bestows sweets and gifts on well-behaved children. Naughty children may receive ashes, coal, or a birch rod.

Customs

Prior to Epiphany, children write letters to La Befana asking her for the gifts they would like to receive (*see also* **Children's Letters**). In some places, rag dolls representing La Befana are hung in windows as seasonal decorations. On Epiphany Eve children hang a **stocking** or a suit of clothes near the fireplace. During the night La Befana fills the stockings or the pockets of their clothes with sweets and gifts. In some cities it was customary for groups of young people to gather on Epiphany Eve and make a great deal of noise with drums and musical instruments to welcome La Befana. In many parts of Italy today, **Santa Claus,** or *Babbo Natale,* has displaced La Befana as the **Christmas season** gift bringer (*see also* **Italy, Christmas in**).

Further Reading

Hottes, Alfred Carl. *1001 Christmas Facts and Fancies.* 1946. Reprint. Detroit, Mich.: Omnigraphics, 1990.

Leach, Maria, ed. *Funk and Wagnalls Standard Dictionary of Folklore, Mythology, and Legend.* New York: Harper and Row, 1984.

Ross, Corinne. *Christmas in Italy.* Chicago: World Book-Childcraft International, 1979.

Bells

In the United States we tend to associate bells both with emergencies and with such joyous occasions as weddings and Christmas celebrations. This association between bells and Christmas can be traced back to the Middle Ages, when Church officials began to use bells for worship and celebration. Medieval European bell customs, in turn, developed out of a wide array of beliefs and practices associated with bells in ancient times.

Bells in the Ancient World

People rang bells for many reasons in the ancient Mediterranean world, especially religious purposes. Jewish high priests hung tiny golden bells from the hems of their robes. The jingling bells repelled any evil spirits who might be lurking about the threshold of the temple. Some evidence suggests that the ancient Greeks also used bells in a number of religious rituals. The ancient Romans sounded bells on many occasions. They rang during civic ceremonies, chimed alongside other musical instruments during festivals and feasts, announced the beginning of religious rituals, publicized the opening of markets and public baths, and warned the people of fires and other emergencies. Evidence suggests that the Romans associated bells with the dead and believed bells could protect them against evil spirits.

Church Bells

As Christianity spread throughout Europe, Christian leaders slowly began to adapt bell-ringing traditions to Christian worship. Like the Romans, they used bells as a means of making public announcements. Since they wanted these announcements to carry over longer distances, they began casting large bells in addition to the smaller hand-held bells known since ancient times. They mounted these larger bells in high places and sounded them by the pulling of ropes or other devices. In early medieval times monasteries began ringing bells to announce the start of religious services. By the tenth century churches throughout Europe, from cathedrals to tiny rural chapels, were equipped with bells for the same purpose.

Bell Lore

Like their predecessors in the ancient world, these church bells were credited with mysterious powers. For example, folklore hinted that bells possessed something akin to a life force, a personality, and a soul. Many legends throughout Europe told of bells ringing of their own accord to warn the public of some upcoming disaster. Other legends related stories of bells that refused to sound or that expressed their unhappiness with human actions in other ways. Numerous legends spread word of talking bells. According to folk belief, some bells sounded in tones that seemed to repeat a certain phrase, often praising their makers or lamenting an unjust act. Other bells refused to be silenced, continuing to ring on Christmas Eve even though buried underground or sunk in deep waters. People also commonly believed that church bells had the power to protect them from harm. Church bells were rung to ward off thunderstorms, frighten away witches, and halt outbreaks of disease. Folk belief suggested that the dead ascended to heaven on the sound of ringing church bells.

Bell Customs

In addition to these folk beliefs and legends, Roman Catholic custom called for the consecration of bells used for church services. This mark of respect reflected the fact that bells served quite literally as the voice of the church building in which they were installed. Bells were prepared for this ceremony, commonly known as baptizing a bell, by draping them in white cloth and festooning them with flowers. During these services the bells were anointed, incensed, and officially named in the presence of their godparents, usually the donors. Some old legends tell of bells that refused to sound until baptized. People equated the sound of ringing bells with the voice of a person in prayer. Therefore, they frequently inscribed brief prayers on the bells so that the bell might offer the prayer to heaven. Other popular bell inscriptions state the bell's purpose or powers, for example, "I call the living, I bewail the dead, I break up storms."

Church bells were most commonly used for worship and celebration. The big bells adopted by churches during the Middle Ages rang to call parishioners to religious services. They also chimed at certain points during the service so that those standing outside or those at home and at work could join in the prayers. In addition, churches tolled their bells to announce local deaths (*see* **Devil's Knell**). Many churches had four or five bells. The more important the occasion, the more bells rang to honor it. A high mass warranted three bells, for example. On the principal feast days, such as Easter and Christmas, four or five bells pealed together to celebrate the joyous occasion. In medieval **England** Christmas bell ringing began in **Advent**, with a loud clang coming on the first Sunday in Advent to alert parishioners that they had entered the Advent season. Many of these practices were discontinued by Protestant churches after the Reformation, however.

Bells and Christmas

Today fewer churches carry out the old Christmas tradition of bell ringing, and the folklore surrounding bells has been largely forgotten. Nevertheless, the public imagination still links bells with Christmas. A number of well-known Christmas poems and **Christmas carols** depict pealing or jingling bells as joyful emblems of the holiday. In addition, bells appear as symbols of the holiday on many Christmas decorations. Finally, representatives of charitable causes seeking donations at Christmas time often announce their presence on street corners by ringing hand-held bells. (*See also* **Salvation Army Kettles**.)

Further Reading

Auld, William Muir. *Christmas Traditions*. 1931. Reprint. Detroit, Mich.: Omnigraphics, 1992.

Bigelow, A. L. "Bells." In *New Catholic Encyclopedia*. Volume 2. New York: McGraw-Hill, 1967.

Del Re, Gerard, and Patricia Del Re. *The Christmas Almanack*. Garden City, N.Y.: Doubleday, 1979.

Hottes, Alfred Carl. *1001 Christmas Facts and Fancies*. 1946. Reprint. Detroit, Mich.: Omnigraphics, 1990.

Leach, Maria, ed. *Funk and Wagnalls Standard Dictionary of Folklore, Mythology, and Legend*. New York: Harper and Row, 1984.

Metford, J. C. J. *Dictionary of Christian Lore and Legend*. London, England: Thames and Hudson, 1983.

Price, Percival. *Bells and Man*. Oxford, England: Oxford University Press, 1983.

Belsnickel. *See* Knecht Ruprecht

Berchta

Bertha, Frau Gaude, Hertha, Holda, Holde, Holle, Perchta

Several very similar female spirits once visited the peoples of northern Europe during the long midwinter nights. Many authors believe these figures to be the remnants of pagan Germanic goddesses. Associated with the home and hearth, spinning, children, and **gift giving**, these pagan goddesses may have been very early ancestors of **Santa Claus**. The coming of Christianity transformed these goddesses into minor magical figures and concentrated the season of their appearances during the **Twelve Days of Christmas** and, especially, **Twelfth Night**. Throughout this transformation, the German goddess Berchta retained the strongest associations with the **Christmas season**.

The Winter Goddess of Northern Europe

The winter goddesses of northern Europe, known as Berchta (or Perchta) and Holde (or Holda, Holle), shared many characteristics and are sometimes spoken of as variants of the same winter goddess. This sky goddess sailed the winds dressed in a mantle of snow. To the people of Alsace-Lorraine she sometimes appeared wearing a crown of fire, a trait that would later provide a tenuous connection to **St. Lucy**. In attending to the affairs of home and hearth, she acted as the patroness of those who spun thread, rewarding the industrious and punishing the lazy and sloppy. She also spun: not thread, but the fates of human beings. Motherhood and the fertility of the earth also concerned the goddess, who was known as a guardian of children and a protector of fields. Folklore often pictured the goddess flying through the night accompanied by the **ghosts** of children and other supernatural creatures, often phantom dogs, goats, or horses. She appeared most often during the Twelve Days of Christmas. Some believed that she led the **Wild Hunt**, a riotous procession of ghosts who rode across the night skies during **Yule**.

Folklore Associated with Berchta

As Christianity established itself as the dominant religion in Europe, the image of this goddess shrank and changed, although elements of her old concerns and powers remained. In Christian times, people in many German-speaking lands expected the ambivalent figure of Berchta to visit during the winter holidays. Although Berchta herself appeared as ugly and disheveled, she inspected barns and homes for cleanliness. She rewarded the neat and industrious and punished the lazy.

Since Berchta was the patroness of spinners, one custom demanded that women cease their spinning work during the Twelve Days of Christmas out of respect for her (*see also* **St. Distaff's Day**). Another custom advised that each house consume a special food on Twelfth Night and leave the remains for Berchta. If a household did not offer food, Berchta would cut open the stomachs of the inhabitants and remove the contents. Although she would punish lazy or naughty children, Berchta rewarded well-behaved children with gifts or good luck, and enjoyed rocking babies' cradles when no one was looking. Mothers would sometimes threaten their children that if they didn't behave, Berchta would come for them. Her nighttime processions frightened those who witnessed them, but in passing she and her followers bestowed fertility on the fields below. The spirits and souls that followed in her train were called Perchten, and, in some German-speaking areas, the night when she was most likely to appear, Twelfth Night, was called *Perchtennacht*. Although it is difficult to trace the relationship of one mythological figure to another, Berchta may also be related to the Italian **Befana** and to another German spirit, **Frau Gaude**.

Folklore Associated with Holde

Most of the beliefs and practices associated with Berchta are also connected to Holde. Some differ, however. The people of northern **Germany** spoke more often of Holde than of Berchta. They often imagined Holde, whose name means "the kindly one," as a beautiful woman. When Holde shook out her feather bed in the sky, heavy snowfalls showered the lands below. In Christian times Holde acquired associations with witchcraft, and those thought to be witches were said to "ride with Holde."

Another Winter Goddess, Hertha

In pagan times, some Norse and Germanic-speaking peoples called their winter goddess Hertha or Bertha. This goddess shares many characteristics with Berchta and Holde, and may be related to them. Hertha was the patroness of home and hearth who visited her people around the time of the **winter solstice**. Householders decorated their dwellings with evergreens in order to entice her to visit (*see* **Greenery**). They also made flat stone altars for her and set fire to fir branches on top of them. It was believed that Hertha entered the home through the rising smoke, conferring upon the wise the ability to foretell the futures of those around the flames. At least one author suspects that Santa Claus's descent through the chimney at Christmas time echoes the descent of Hertha through the chimney smoke.

Further Reading

Hottes, Alfred Carl. *1001 Christmas Facts and Fancies*. 1946. Reprint. Detroit, Mich.: Omnigraphics, 1990.

Leach, Maria, ed. *Funk and Wagnalls Standard Dictionary of Folklore, Mythology, and Legend*. New York: Harper and Row, 1984.

Miles, Clement A. *Christmas in Ritual and Tradition*. 1912. Reprint. Detroit, Mich.: Omnigraphics, 1990.

Motz, Lotte. "The Winter Goddess: Perchta, Holda, and Related Figures." *Folklore* 95, 2 (1984): 151-61.

Bethlehem

Both **Gospel accounts of Christmas** state that **Jesus** was born in the town of Bethlehem. Bethlehem is located in the Palestinian Authority, within the modern nation of Israel. The city of Jerusalem lies just five miles to the north. The town's name means "house of bread" in Hebrew, reflecting its location in a fertile zone of the Judean desert.

The Birthplace of Jesus

One of the greatest heroes of the Old Testament, King David, was born in Bethlehem. Both gospel accounts of Christmas assert that Jesus was a descendant of David. In fact, in the **Gospel according to Luke** this ancestry indirectly caused Jesus to be born in Bethlehem. In Luke's account, the Romans wanted to conduct a census and ordered everyone to return to their ancestral home in order to be counted. This decree forced **Joseph** and his pregnant wife **Mary** to travel to Bethlehem. Shortly after they arrived, Jesus was born. The **Gospel according to Matthew** does not mention the census and implies instead that Jesus' parents lived in Bethlehem. Matthew's and Luke's claims that Jesus had been born in Bethlehem were especially significant to those who knew Jewish scripture, since the Jewish prophet Micah had declared that the Messiah would be born in that town (Micah 5:2).

The Church of the Nativity

According to early Christian tradition, Jesus had been born in one of the caves that local people used to shelter animals. As early as the second century A.D., pilgrims began to visit the cave where Jesus was said to have been born. The Roman emperor Hadrian (76-138 A.D.) constructed a shrine to the pagan god Adonis over this site. In approximately 325 A.D., after the conversion of the Roman Empire to Christianity, the empress Helena (c. 248-c. 328 A.D.) had the temple

to Adonis destroyed and built the Church of the Nativity over the presumed site of Jesus' birth. Almost nothing of this original church remains. It was severely damaged in a war that took place several centuries after its construction. According to legend, Persian invaders were about to destroy the church completely, when they noticed a mural depicting the Three Kings, or **Magi**, wearing Persian dress. Recognizing that the church in some way honored Persian sages of the past, the invaders spared it from total destruction. The great Byzantine emperor Justinian (483-565 A.D.) rebuilt the Church of the Nativity in the sixth century A.D. It has been repaired many times since then, but its basic design remains the same. The main door to the church, called the Door of Humility, was built so low that people have to bow down to enter. The original purpose of the design was to prevent Muslims from riding into the church on their horses. Because entering through this door requires one to bow one's head, which also serves as a gesture of reverence for this Christian holy site, Jews have traditionally objected to using the Door of Humility.

Today the Church of the Nativity is an Eastern Orthodox shrine. The cave in which Jesus was born lies underneath the church. Known as the "Grotto of the Nativity," this underground chamber is a site of intense religious devotion for Christians of many different denominations. In the nineteenth century friction arose over which denomination would exercise the most control over the Grotto. In the midst of this conflict, the star marking the spot where Jesus' manger had lain mysteriously disappeared. Each faction accused the others of the theft. Some writers claim that tensions caused by the star's disappearance helped to provoke the Crimean War. The Sultan of Turkey eventually assisted in resolving this dispute by placing a new fourteen-pointed star in the Grotto. Pilgrims to Bethlehem today can still see this large silver star covering the spot on the floor where, according to legend, Mary gave birth to Jesus. The star bears an inscription in Latin, *Hic De Virgine Maria, Jesus Christus Natus Est,* which means, "Here Jesus Christ was born of the Virgin Mary."

Eastern Orthodox officials share the Grotto of the Nativity with Roman Catholic and Armenian Orthodox clergy. At Christmas time Roman Catholic clergy oversee the **Nativity scene**, while Orthodox clergy control the altar.

In the spring of 2002, Israeli military forces invaded the West Bank town of Bethlehem as part of Israel's campaign to eliminate Palestinian terrorism. Dozens of people sought refuge in the Church of the Nativity, hoping that such a holy site would not be attacked. Among them were ordinary townspeople, Palestinian gunmen, and clergy members. The Israeli soldiers surrounded the church and prevented people, food, and medical supplies from entering. After a dramatic five-week standoff, the gunmen agreed to go into permanent exile, and the Israelis called off their soldiers. A few windows were damaged during the siege, but no permanent harm was done to the church.

Christmas in Bethlehem

Bethlehem attracts many Christian pilgrims, especially during the **Christmas season**. The biggest crowds gather on December 24 and 25, when most Western Christians celebrate the Nativity. On December 24 Roman Catholic priests celebrate **Midnight Mass** in St. Catherine's Roman Catholic Church, which lies inside the grounds of the Church of the Nativity. The event begins with a motorcade procession from Jerusalem to Bethlehem, led by the Latin Patriarch of Jerusalem, the highest-ranking Roman Catholic official in Israel. Those practicing Roman Catholics who have obtained advance tickets for the Midnight Mass crowd into St. Catherine's church. This service includes a procession to the Grotto of the Nativity, where the figurine representing the baby Jesus is placed in the Nativity scene. The throng that remains outside can watch a televised broadcast of the service on a screen set up in Manger Square.

Other opportunities for Christmas Eve worship include an Anglican service held at the Greek Orthodox monastery attached to the Church of the Nativity and a Protestant carol service, which takes place at a field just outside Bethlehem. The crowd that assembles in the field sings **Christmas carols**, commemorating the evening two thousand years ago when a small band of **shepherds** received a miraculous announcement of Jesus' birth and witnessed a host of **angels** singing praises to God (*see also* Gospel According to Luke). No one knows the exact location of the field mentioned in the Bible. At least three different groups have laid claim to their own shepherds' field. The Christmas Eve carol service takes place at the

Y.M.C.A.'s field. The Orthodox Church, however, maintains its own shepherds' field, as does the Roman Catholic Church.

Bethlehem hosts somewhat smaller celebrations on January 7, when many Orthodox Christians celebrate Christmas, and again on January 19, when Armenian Orthodox Christians observe the holiday (*see also* **Armenia, Christmas in**).

Rachel's Tomb

Jewish and Muslim pilgrims come to Bethlehem to visit another holy site: the Tomb of Rachel. Rachel's death and burial are mentioned in the Bible (Genesis 35:20). Folk tradition declares that Rachel was laid to rest in Bethlehem, although biblical scholars deny that this is the correct site.

Further Reading

Baly, Denis. "Bethlehem." In Paul J. Achtemeier, ed. *The HarperCollins Bible Dictionary*. Revised edition. San Francisco, Calif.: HarperSanFrancisco, 1996.

Brockman, Norbert C. *Encyclopedia of Sacred Places*. New York: Oxford University Press, 1998.

Christmas in the Holy Land. Chicago: World Book, 1987.

Clynes, Tom. *Wild Planet!* Detroit, Mich.: Visible Ink Press, 1995.

Del Re, Gerard, and Patricia Del Re. *The Christmas Almanack*. Garden City, N.Y.: Doubleday, 1979.

Norris, Frederick W. "Bethlehem." In Everett Ferguson, ed. *Encyclopedia of Early Christianity*. Volume 1. New York: Garland, 1997.

Weiser, Francis X. *The Christmas Book*. 1952. Reprint. Detroit, Mich.: Omnigraphics, 1990.

Bethlehem, Pennsylvania, Christmas in

The town of Bethlehem, Pennsylvania, promotes itself as America's "Christmas City." The city's most notable Christmas customs reflect the religious heritage of its founders, who were Moravian Christians from central Europe.

The Moravians

The Moravians are mainstream Protestant Christians whose denomination was established in 1457 in what is now the Czech Republic. Many died during religious persecutions that took place in the seventeenth century. In the eighteenth century a German nobleman, Count Zinzendorf, undertook the protection of the remaining Moravians and allowed them to settle on his land. Seeking religious freedom and the opportunity to spread the teachings of **Jesus** Christ to American natives, settlers, and **slaves**, bands of Moravians began to emigrate from **Germany** to the American colonies in the eighteenth century.

History of Bethlehem, Pennsylvania

In the mid-eighteenth century Moravians founded two towns along the Lehigh River in Pennsylvania. The first they named Nazareth, after the town where Jesus grew up. The second they called **Bethlehem**, after the town in which Jesus was born.

In 1741 Count Zinzendorf visited the settlement of Bethlehem and spent Christmas there. His approval of the colonists' proposal to name the town Bethlehem finalized their decision. On Christmas Eve he led the community in singing a German hymn which, in his eyes, helped to explain why the colonists had made a wise choice in naming the new town. The first verse of the hymn reminds listeners that:

> Not Jerusalem
> Lowly Bethlehem
> 'Twas that gave us Christ to save us,
> Not Jerusalem.

Bethlehem's Moravian congregations still sing this hymn every Christmas Eve.

In the early days, Bethlehem was a closed community, meaning that only Moravians could live there. This policy changed in 1845. In the late nineteenth century iron mines and foundries emerged as important businesses in the Lehigh Valley. In 1899, Bethlehem Steel, a giant of America's steel industry, was founded in the town of Bethlehem. Bethlehem Steel flourished throughout most of the twentieth century, drawing many immigrants from various ethnic groups to the area. Competition from cheaply produced foreign steel began to affect the steel industry in the 1970s. This challenge finally resulted in Bethlehem Steel closing its doors in 1995.

Christmas Candles and Lights

In 1937 the Bethlehem Chamber of Commerce began to promote the town's Christmas celebrations as a tourist attraction, billing Bethlehem as "Christmas City U.S.A." The city's residents quickly adopted the campaign, organizing a city-wide display of Christmas lights. Bethlehem's most distinctive lighting custom consists of placing a single lit candle in the windows of homes, stores, and other businesses. Though it can only be traced back to the late 1920s, some researchers claim that early Moravian immigrants brought this custom with them from a Moravian community in Germany. There the flame from a single candle left burning in the window during **Advent** was understood to signal a welcome for the Christ child. By 1940 this custom had spread far beyond Bethlehem's Moravian community to become a city-wide practice. For reasons of safety many today have replaced real candles with electric lights shaped like candles. Many people in Bethlehem light the candles in their windows on the first Sunday in Advent and keep them lit until **Epiphany**.

The city also hosts an impressive outdoor lighting display. Popular nighttime bus tours led by guides in traditional Moravian dress fill up quickly during the holiday season. On nearby South Mountain a giant, electrically lit star beckons visitors to the Christmas city. First erected in 1935, the "Star of Bethlehem" has been rebuilt several times. This traditional, five-pointed Christmas star with extending rays of light measures 81 feet in height and 53 feet in width. Two hundred forty-six light bulbs keep the display glowing through the night. In past times the city of Bethlehem only lit the star during the **Christmas season**. Since the mid-1990s, the city has kept it illuminated year-round. Indeed, the five-pointed star can be found on the city's official seal. There the five points stand for religion, education, music, industry, and recreation, five important components of the city's identity.

Moravian Stars

The Moravian star constitutes another Moravian-style Christmas decoration that can now be found throughout the town. These three-dimensional stars, made of paper, leaded glass, or plastic, may be illuminated from within by an electric bulb. Although Moravian star-makers shape these ornaments with varying numbers of points, the most common kind of Moravian star has 26 points. Moravian stars are displayed in Bethlehem's homes, shops, and Moravian churches.

Community Putzes

Bethlehem's Moravians have also contributed the Christmas **putz** to the town's repertoire of Christmas customs. A putz is a miniature **Nativity scene**, depicting not only Jesus' birth in a manger, but also scenes of life in the surrounding countryside (*see also* **Christmas Village**). In past times members of the Moravian community vied with one another to see who could build the most imaginative and elaborate putz. Between Christmas and Epiphany they visited one another's homes to compare and enjoy the putzes. The custom of putz visiting also caught on with non-Moravians. Things started to get out of hand in the 1930s, when one particularly successful putz-building family, that of Edward Neisser, received just under 1,000 Christmas season visitors.

Neisser suggested that the town build a community putz for the public to enjoy. The Chamber of Commerce took him up on that suggestion in 1937. The first community putz, set up in the office of the Chamber of Commerce, drew 14,000 visitors and so interrupted the Chamber's duties that they found another location for it the following year. In 1939 the community putz was built in the lobby of Hotel Bethlehem. Two hundred volunteers helped manage the putz by reading the narration for the display and working the lights. The attraction drew 30,000 visitors, overwhelming the hotel. Several more changes of venue followed until three community putzes were established in local Moravian churches.

Since the beginning, members of Bethlehem's Moravian churches have built and managed the community putzes. These days the members of Bethlehem's Central Moravian Church appoint a committee to manage this task. The process begins with an expedition to the Pocono Mountains in November to gather moss. It takes volunteers about a week to construct the putz. Viewing begins at the start of Advent. Several times a day visitors can enter the darkened auditorium to view the putz, while a guide reads a narrative describing the scene. The lights in each section of the putz rise as the guide tells the story of those figures.

Religious Services

Bethlehem's Moravian churches hold a special kind of religious service, called a **lovefeast**, around Christmas time. In addition, Moravians, like many other Christians, also hold special services on Christmas Eve. The Moravian Christmas Eve vigil resounds with instrumental music and hymns. The hymn, "Jesus, Call Thou Me," led by Count Zinzendorf in 1741, is always sung, as is another favorite Moravian Christmas hymn called "Morning Star." Each year a specially selected child soloist wins the honor of leading this hymn. As the last verse of this hymn begins, praising the Lord whose splendor shines in the darkness, the servers enter the darkened church carrying trays of lit beeswax candles, trimmed at the bottom with red paper and ribbon (*see also* **Christingle**). They are distributed to the congregation, and, holding glowing candles, worshipers continue to sing songs about God's light shining in the darkness.

Concerts

Visitors to Bethlehem also have the opportunity to hear many Christmas concerts, some featuring Moravian music. Moravians have long encouraged music making within their communities. The early Moravians composed thousands of musical pieces, safeguarded the biggest collection of music in the American colonies, and harbored amongst them many instrument makers. One unusual feature of the distinguished Moravian musical heritage is the trombone choir, an ensemble made up entirely of tenor, bass, alto, and soprano trombones. Moravians brought the first trombones to this country in the mid-eighteenth century, where they continued to be a novelty outside Moravian communities until well into the nineteenth century.

Historic District

Although today people of many different ethnic and religious groups live in Bethlehem, the town's historic ties with the Moravians give it its most distinctive Christmas customs. In addition to these customs, the town maintains a fine collection of colonial and early American buildings, including the Sun Inn, an establishment that dates back to colonial times and once hosted George and Martha Washington, as well as other famous patriots of the American Revolution. (*For more on Christmas in Pennsylvania, see* **America, Christmas in Nineteenth-Century; Amish Christmas; Barring Out the Schoolmaster; Knecht Ruprecht**.)

Further Reading

Bethlehem's Early History. Bethlehem, Pa.: Historic Bethlehem Partnership Educational Services, 1999.

Butterfield, Lee. "Christmas in the Community of the First Moravian Church, Bethlehem, Pennsylvania, U.S.A." In Maria Hubert, comp. *Christmas Around the World*. Stroud, Gloucestershire, England: Sutton, 1998.

Kainen, Ruth Cole. *America's Christmas Heritage*. New York: Funk and Wagnalls, 1969.

Sawyer, Edwin A. *All About the Moravians*. Bethlehem, Pa.: The Moravian Church in America, 2000.

Sweitzer, Vangie Roby. *Christmas in Bethlehem*. Bethlehem, Pa.: Central Moravian Church, 2000.

Web Sites

"The Putz," a page from the Moravian Church in America's web site at: http://www.moravian.org/faq/putz.html

An explanation of the Moravian Christmas putz offered by the East Hills Moravian Church, located in Bethlehem, Pennsylvania: http://easthillsmc.org/putz.html

An official site of the Moravian Church in America that offers a variety of information about Moravian beliefs and practices: http://www.moravian.org

Birth of the Invincible Sun
Birth of the Unconquered Sun

In the first centuries after the death of **Jesus**, a new religious cult swept across the Roman Empire. Traditional Roman religion included festivals and ceremonies associated with a wide variety of gods. Followers of the new religion focused their devotions on one god. They called this god "Mithras" or "Sol" and observed his birthday on **December 25** with a festival known as the *Natalis Sol Invicti*, or the Birth of the Invincible Sun.

Origins of Mithraism

The god Mithras originated in Persia. Ancient Hindu and Zoroastrian texts mention a minor god, Mithra or Mitra, who was associated with the sun, the light that falls between heaven and earth, mediation, and contracts. Most scholars believe that Roman soldiers encountered this god when stationed in the eastern part of the Empire. As their military assignments moved them from one region to another, they spread the cult of Mithras throughout the Roman world. The image of the god changed as the cult of Mithras developed and grew. To his Roman followers Mithras became the god who created the world, the god who would never age or die, the one who was the first and last cause of all things, who upheld standards of justice and truth, and who would bring about a just, new age that would last forever.

Roman Sun God Worship

Mithraism began to spread throughout the Roman Empire in the late first century. The religion reached the height of its popularity in the second through fourth centuries. The Roman Mithras still retained his association with the sun, an association that grew stronger rather than weaker over time, perhaps due to the rising popularity of the Roman sun god, Sol. Although Sol was only one of the group of gods recognized by traditional Roman religion, the Romans viewed

Sol and Mithras as more or less the same deity. During the second century Sol became increasingly associated with the supremacy of the emperor and of the Roman Empire. One of Sol's new titles, *invictus*, or "the invincible one," may well have been borrowed from those titles customarily applied to the emperor.

In 274 the Roman emperor Aurelian (c. 215-275) endorsed Sol's rising popularity by naming the sun god the sole protector of the Empire. He also instituted a festival celebrating the birthday of the god, called "the Birth of the Invincible Sun" (also translated as "Birth of the Unconquered Sun"). Most scholars believe that people celebrated this festival on December 25. Mithraism and the cult of Sol Invictus began to die out in the late fourth century and early fifth century as Christianity became the official religion of the Empire and began to gather large numbers of adherents.

Ceremonies and Celebrations

Very little is known about Roman Mithraism since it demanded that its followers keep Mithraic beliefs and practices secret from outsiders. Archeological investigations have revealed the basic outlines of the religion, however. These include some striking parallels with the emerging Christian faith. Members gathered together periodically to share a common meal. New members of the religion were brought into the faith through a baptismal ceremony. During this ceremony the officiants "sealed" the new members as devotees of Mithras by branding them on their foreheads. The initiate was expected to progress through seven levels of knowledge, each marked by its own sacrament. Finally, a blissful immortality awaited believers after death.

Mithraism also differed from Christianity in important ways. Only men could join the new cult. In fact, Roman soldiers comprised a large percentage of the membership. The sacrifice of a bull appears to have been a central ritual or mythic image in the worship of the god. Remains of Mithraic churches, built to resemble caves, feature wall paintings depicting the god Mithras slaying a bull. Sacred fires seem to have burned on the altars of these churches. Furthermore, astrology appears to have played an important part in Mithraic beliefs.

Ancient records attest to the fact that horse races were held in the Roman Circus in honor of the sun god's birthday, but little else is known about how the devotees of Mithras celebrated the festival of his birth. According to the ancient Roman calendar, **winter solstice**, the shortest day of the year, fell on December 25. Scholars suggest that worshipers viewed this natural event as symbolic of the birth of the sun god and therefore celebrated the festival on that day.

Mithraism and Early Christianity

Mithraism had enough adherents in the first centuries after Jesus' death to provide some degree of competition for the fledgling Christian faith. Its popularity prompted some early Christian leaders to preach against it. They denounced Mithraic ceremonies as misleading parodies of Christian rituals. In spite of their opposition to the cult, in the middle of the fourth century Christian authorities selected December 25 as the day on which to celebrate the Nativity of Jesus Christ. Scholars believe that they did so largely in order to divert people away from competing, pagan celebrations held on or around that date, such as the Birth of the Invincible Sun, **Saturnalia**, and **Kalends**.

Further Reading

Fears, J. Rufus. "Sol Invictus." In Mircea Eliade, ed. *The Encyclopedia of Religion.* Volume 13. New York: Macmillan, 1987.

Gnoli, Gherardo. "Mithraism." In Mircea Eliade, ed. *The Encyclopedia of Religion.* Volume 9. New York: Macmillan, 1987.

Heinberg, Richard. *Celebrate the Solstice.* Wheaton, Ill.: Quest Books, 1993.

Hutton, Ronald. *The Stations of the Sun.* Oxford, England: Oxford University Press, 1996.

James, E. O. *Seasonal Feasts and Festivals.* 1961. Reprint. Detroit, Mich.: Omnigraphics, 1993.

Salzman, Michele Renee. *On Roman Time.* Berkeley, Calif.: University of California Press, 1990.

Smith, C. "Christmas and Its Cycle." In *New Catholic Encyclopedia.* Volume 3. New York: McGraw-Hill, 1967.

Black Peter
Zwarte Piet

Children in the Netherlands receive presents on **St. Nicholas's Day**, December 6. According to old Dutch folk beliefs, each year **St. Nicholas** and his helper, *Zwarte Piet*, or Black Peter, sail from **Spain** to Holland in a ship loaded with presents for good children. Nowadays, Black Peter not only carries St. Nicholas's sack of presents, but also brandishes a birch rod which he uses to discipline undeserving children. Truly troublesome youngsters face sterner punishment. Black Peter tosses them into his sack and carries them back to Spain with him (*see also* **Cert; Knecht Ruprecht**).

History

During the Middle Ages "Black Peter" was a common nickname for the Devil. One tale of those times proclaimed that each year on his birthday, St. Nicholas kidnapped the Devil and made the evildoer assist him in his good works. On St. Nicholas's Eve the good saint and his reluctant helper flew from house to house dropping presents down the chimney. Somehow these **gifts** landed in the **shoes** that the children placed by the fire before going to bed.

Black Peter traditionally appears as a dark-skinned man dressed in the costume of a sixteenth-century Spaniard. Perhaps this image of Black Peter developed during the sixteenth century, when the Dutch suffered under Spanish rule. The Dutch may have associated Spain with dark-skinned people since a north African ethnic group known as the Moors ruled parts of Spain from the eighth to the fifteenth centuries. An alternative explanation for Peter's darkened skin links it to his duties as St. Nicholas's assistant. Some speculate that Black Peter may have acquired a permanent coating of ashes and soot from scrambling down so many chimneys. Still, the most likely explanation for Peter's dark skin comes from old folk beliefs. Medieval Europeans often imagined the devil as black-skinned.

Contemporary Customs

Each year the arrival of St. Nicholas and Black Peter is reenacted in Amsterdam, the capital of the Netherlands. A great crowd gathers to witness the arrival of the ship bearing the saint and his helper. A white horse, St. Nicholas's traditional mode of transport, stands ready to serve the saint. The music of a brass band adds to the festive atmosphere. As the gift bringers descend from the ship, the crowd easily identifies Nicholas by his red bishop's robe and hat and the white beard that flows from his face to his chest. In addition to his embroidered jacket, puffed, knee-length pants, and feathered cap, Black Peter carries a bulging sack of presents, some birch rods, and a large red book in which he has recorded the good and bad deeds of Holland's children. After greetings have been exchanged with the mayor, the saint and his helper lead a parade to Amsterdam's central plaza. There the royal family officially welcomes Holland's **Christmas season** gift bringers.

On St. Nicholas's Eve children may receive home visits from St. Nicholas and Black Peter, usually played by family members or friends. The pair's detailed knowledge of the children's good and bad deeds during the past year often astonishes the younger children. In recent years the increasing popularity of exchanging presents on Christmas Day has somewhat reduced the importance of St. Nicholas and Black Peter in Holland's Christmas celebrations.

Further Reading

Del Re, Gerard, and Patricia Del Re. *The Christmas Almanack*. Garden City, N.Y.: Doubleday, 1979.

Joy Through the World. New York: Dodd, Mead, and Company, 1985.

MacDonald, Margaret Read, ed. *The Folklore of World Holidays*. Detroit, Mich.: Gale Research, 1992.

Russell, Jeffrey Burton. *Lucifer: The Devil in the Middle Ages*. Ithaca, N.Y.: Cornell University Press, 1984.

Sansom, William. *A Book of Christmas*. New York: McGraw-Hill Book Company, 1968.

Spicer, Dorothy Gladys. *Festivals of Western Europe*. 1958. Reprint. Detroit, Mich.: Omnigraphics, 1994.

Boar's Head

Wild boars are large, fierce, pig-like animals with curled tusks. In the Middle Ages the heads of these fearsome male animals, relatives of the domestic pig, composed the central dish of the Christmas banquet in some parts of **Europe**. Queen's College at England's Oxford University still maintains this traditional feast. The custom has long since died out in most places, however. Some believe that the boar began its association with Christmas in pagan Scandinavia. In Scandinavia today pork dishes continue as Christmas favorites, and Christmas cookies often take the shape of a pig. In Sweden the head of a pig, garnished with pastry, flags, and an apple between its jaws, may still be placed at the center of the Christmas buffet table.

Origins

Some researchers locate the origins of the Christmas boar's head feast as far back as pagan times. They note that both the pagan Scandinavians and Celts not only relished the boar's meat, but also gave the animal a respected place in their mythology. Among the Germanic peoples the boar was associated with the dead. The Scandinavians and Celts cast fearsome images of the boar onto their war helmets. The Scandinavians imagined that the souls of fallen warriors lived on in a heaven where they feasted on wild boar every day. The meat was provided by a magical animal that was slaughtered, eaten, and appeared anew and alive daily. Among the ancient Scandinavians, the boar also served as the companion animal to the god Frey. Frey represented many things, among them sunlight, peace, prosperity, and fertility. The pagan Scandinavians sometimes described the course of the sun across the sky as Frey riding the heavens on his shining, golden boar.

An ancient Scandinavian saga, or poem, describes the sacrifice of a wild boar as an important component of the ancient **Yule** festival. The worshipers dedicated this sacrifice to Frey. So holy was the sacrificial boar that warriors swore oaths over its body. Since Frey was the patron of fertility, some interpret this as a rite designed to increase crop yields and herds in the coming spring.

While some writers believe that a seasonal taste for the pork can be traced back to these pagan practices, others point out that November and December served as the traditional months for the slaughter of pigs in pre-industrial times. At this point in the year pigs were consuming the last of the forest's free pig feed: acorns and beechnuts. Small farmers either had to find more feed, let the pigs go hungry, or slaughter them. According to these authors, this seasonal cycle may provide the true explanation for the boar's place at the Christmas feast.

History

In medieval **England**, the boar's head graced the tables of the prosperous at Christmas time as well as on other feast days. Preparing and serving this robust dish required the combined efforts of many people. The beleaguered cook might spend more than a week skinning, soaking, salting, preserving, and finally cooking this awkward piece of meat. In the final stages the cook garnished the boar's head with **rosemary** and inserted an apple, orange, or lemon in its mouth. In rich and noble houses much ceremony surrounded the presentation of this dish. The steward brought the boar's head into the hall on a special platter, accompanied by minstrels. Other servants, and sometimes even the huntsmen who killed the beast, participated in the procession into the hall, adding to the spectacle. Wild boar were known as formidable prey, which may have bestowed additional glamour on this dish. Sometime in the twelfth century, however, the wild boar became extinct in England. Its demise left the domesticated pig to take over this Christmas duty. While the traditional boar's head feast entertained the wealthy at Christmas time, ordinary folks often made do with beef, goose, or Christmas pies.

In the mid-seventeenth century a new religious sect called the **Puritans** rose to power in England. The Puritans disapproved of many aspects of traditional English Christmas celebrations, including the lusty feasting and drinking. During their reign they succeeded in curtailing and, in some cases, even outlawing many of these practices. After the Puritan campaign against Christmas subsided, the boar's head never again regained its widespread popularity among the wealthy as the main dish for the Christmas feast.

Queen's College

In spite of the disappearance of the boar's head among the general population, this traditional feast was maintained at Oxford University's Queen's College. Each year at Christmas time the boar's head dinner takes place in the college's dining hall. This tradition began in the fourteenth century, shortly after the founding of the college. The process begins in the kitchen, where the chef garnishes the boar's head with bay (*see* **Laurel**) and rosemary, tucks an orange into its mouth, and places it on a silver platter. Four men carry this dish into the dining hall, preceded by a solo singer and followed by the college choir. The soloist and choir sing the "Boar's Head Carol" as they process into the hall, pausing for the soloist to sing each verse. Finally the boar's head is set upon the high table. The provost then removes the orange and offers it to the lead singer, and distributes the rosemary and bay among the choir and guests.

The tune and words to the "Boar's Head Carol" have changed over time. A version popular in the early seventeenth century describes the killing of the boar as a beneficial act that not only prevents him from ruining crops, but also provides tasty meat for the assembled company. The more recent version of the carol, with its Latin refrain, focuses on the feast at hand and gives thanks to God:

Solo: The boar's head in hand bear I
Bedecked with bays and rosemary
I pray you, my masters, be merry
Quot estis in convivio (So many as are in the feast)

Chorus: *Caput apri defero, Reddens laudes domino*
(The boar's head I bring, giving praises to God)

Solo: The boar's head as I understand,
Is the rarest dish in all this land,
Which thus bedecked with a gay garland
Let us *servire cantico* (serve with a song)

Chorus: *Caput apri defero, Reddens laudes domino*

Solo: Our steward hath provided this
In honor of the King of bliss
Which, on this day to be served is
In *reginensi atrio* (the Queen's hall)

Chorus: *Caput apri defero, Reddens laudes domino*
[Duncan, 1992, 186-87]

The denizens of Queen's College invented an amusing story by way of offering an explanation for their traditional Christmas dinner. On a winter's day hundreds of years ago a student named Copcot went walking in the nearby Shotover woods. He carried with him a volume of Aristotle, which he had been striving in vain to comprehend. Suddenly a boar sprang out of the underbrush and charged toward him. Copcot thrust the book down the boar's throat, crying out in Latin, "Graecum est!" (approximately, "it's Greek to me!"). The boar choked to death on this undigestible work. Since Copcot could ill afford to lose a book, he chopped off the boar's head, retrieved his Aristotle, and carried both back to the college. The college feasted on Copcot's trophy, and a tradition was born.

Further Reading

Crippen, Thomas G. *Christmas and Christmas Lore*. 1923. Reprint. Detroit, Mich.: Omnigraphics, 1990.

Del Re, Gerard, and Patricia Del Re. *The Christmas Almanack*. Garden City, N.Y.: Doubleday, 1979.

Duncan, Edmondstoune. *The Story of the Carol*. 1911. Reprint. Detroit, Mich.: Omnigraphics, 1992.

Gelling, Peter, and Hilda Ellis Davidson. *The Chariot of the Sun and Other Rites and Symbols of the Northern Bronze Age*. New York: Frederick A. Praeger, 1969.

Guerber, H. A. *Myths of Northern Lands*. 1895. Reprint. Detroit, Mich.: Singing Tree Press, 1970.

Hadfield, Miles, and John Hadfield. *The Twelve Days of Christmas*. Boston, Mass.: Little, Brown, and Company, 1961.

Henderson, Yorke, et al. *Parent's Magazine's Christmas Holiday Book*. New York: Parents' Magazine Press, 1972.

Hole, Christina. *Christmas and Its Customs*. New York: M. Barrows and Company, 1958.

Muir, Frank. *Christmas Customs and Traditions*. New York: Taplinger, 1977.

Stevens, Patricia Bunning. *Merry Christmas!: A History of the Holiday*. New York: Macmillan, 1979.

Boxing Day

The boxing which takes place on Boxing Day has nothing to do with the prize-fighting ring. Christmas boxing originated in **England**, where the word "boxing" refers to the distribution of small **gifts** of money. Boxing Day, which falls on December 26, is a holiday in England, Canada, **Australia**, New Zealand, the Bahamas (*see* **Jonkonnu**), and other nations with past or present ties to the United Kingdom.

Origins and Development

Some writers believe that boxing can be traced back to the Middle Ages. They note that parish priests of that era customarily opened up the church alms-box on December 26, **St. Stephen's Day**. Then the priests distributed the coins it contained to the needy. Perhaps this custom attached itself to St. Stephen's Day because the saint's role in the Christian community of which he was a member was to ensure the fair distribution of goods. In any case, this practice gave rise to the use of the term "box" to denote a small gift of money or a gratuity. In Scotland these tips were called "handsels" and were given on Handsel Monday, that is, the first Monday of the new year.

By the early seventeenth century, the Church's St. Stephen's Day tradition had inspired working people to adopt the custom of saving whatever tips they had been given throughout the year in clay boxes which they broke open on December 26. By the late seventeenth century they began to solicit tips from all those who had enjoyed their services during the year. They collected the last of these "boxes" on December 26, after which they broke open these containers and used the money to buy Christmas treats. In the nineteenth century many bought tickets to **pantomime** shows, which in those days usually opened on December 26. By the nineteenth century the custom of boxing had so colored the character of the day that many people began refer to December 26 as Boxing Day rather than St. Stephen's Day. Parliament declared Boxing Day a public holiday in 1871.

Resistance

By the eighteenth century middle- and upper-middle-class people were complaining about the increasing numbers of tradesmen who petitioned them for Christmas boxes. By mid-century some families were paying up to thirty pounds in these annual tips. Naturally, one's employees and domestic servants received some extra financial consideration at Christmas time. In addition to one's own workers, however, a small horde of neighborhood service providers might turn up at one's door on the twenty-sixth of December asking for a Christmas box. These included dustmen, lamplighters, postmen, errand-runners, watchmen, **bell** ringers, chimneysweeps, sextons (church custodians), turncocks (men who maintained the water pipes), and others. What's more, shop assistants, tradesmen, and their apprentices often expected a Christmas box from their customers. In 1710, English author Jonathan Swift (1667-1745) wrote, "By the Lord Harry, I shall be undone here with Christmas boxes. The rogues of the coffee-house have raised their tax, every one giving a crown, and I gave mine for shame, besides a great many half-crowns to great men's porters" (Hutton, 1996, 23).

Stephening

At one point, the citizens of Buckinghamshire, England, raised the practice of boxing to new heights. Residents of some villages in the region claimed the right to a free meal at the local rectory on St. Stephen's Day. Since the rectors had to pay for the meal out of their own pockets, they naturally began to resist this custom, know as "Stephening." It is told that one year a rector from the village of Drayton Beauchamp locked himself in the rectory on December 26 and refused to let the housekeeper answer the many knocks at the door. In this manner he thought to escape doling out the free meal of bread, cheese, and ale demanded by the town's residents. When the townspeople realized what was going on, however, they broke into the building and helped themselves to a meal that completely emptied his larders. In 1834 the Charity Commission, finding no legal or traditional entitlement to this yearly looting, put an end to the custom.

Decline

By the late nineteenth century Christmas boxing began to diminish. This decline continued into the twentieth century, and, slowly, the Christmas box disappeared from the ranks of English seasonal customs. The English still give a few tips at Christmas time, but they are no longer specifically associated with Boxing Day. In fact, some people now think of Boxing Day as the day to throw out the boxes their Christmas gifts came in.

Further Reading

Chambers, Robert. "December 26 — Christmas-Boxes." In his *The Book of Days.* Volume 2. 1862-64. Reprint. Detroit, Mich.: Omnigraphics, 1990.

Hadfield, Miles, and John Hadfield. *The Twelve Days of Christmas.* Boston, Mass.: Little, Brown and Company, 1961.

Hole, Christina. *British Folk Customs.* London, England: Hutchinson and Company, 1976.

Hutton, Ronald. *The Stations of the Sun.* Oxford, England: Oxford University Press, 1996.

MacDonald, Margaret Read, ed. *The Folklore of World Holidays.* Detroit, Mich.: Gale Research, 1992.

Muir, Frank. *Christmas Customs and Traditions.* New York: Taplinger, 1977.

Weiser, Francis X. *Handbook of Christian Feasts and Customs.* New York: Harcourt, Brace and World, 1952.

Boy Bishop
Bairn Bishop, St. Nicholas Bishop

In the Middle Ages the **Christmas season** offered a special delight to a few lucky boys. On December 28, **Holy Innocents' Day**, religious communities, cathedrals, colleges, schools, and parish churches throughout **Europe** permitted an ordinary choirboy to take over the role of the local bishop. Known as the boy bishop, these kings-for-a-day were enormously popular with the people, in spite of the reservations of some Church authorities. They wore episcopal robes and rings especially made for boys, led processions, officiated at services, preached sermons, made visitations, and received **gifts**. What's more, the administrators of local cathedrals were sometimes expected to entertain the boy bishop and his entourage in a manner befitting their assumed rank. These festivities came to an end around the sixteenth century, when Church and state officials finally prohibited boy bishops. In some areas, however, the custom lingered on. One French diocese supported a boy bishop until 1721. In recent years some English cathedrals have revived the medieval custom of sponsoring a boy bishop at Christmas time.

Beginnings

During medieval times custom permitted the low-ranking church staff, such as deacons, sub-deacons, and choirboys, to engage in a number of boisterous celebrations and mock religious services during the days that followed Christmas. They included the reign of the boy bishop on Innocents' Day. These frolics were sometimes referred to collectively as the **Feast of Fools**. Some experts believe that these customs may have evolved out of the topsy-turvy festivities that characterized the Roman winter feast of **Saturnalia**. During Saturnalia, things were not always as they seemed. Men masqueraded as women or animals, and mock kings were selected to preside over feasts. Some authors believe that the habit of celebrating midwinter with playful role reversals may have persisted into medieval times, inspiring the creation of the boy bishop. The chosen boy was also known as the "bairn bishop," bairn being an archaic word for child.

Historians are still trying to piece together the origins of this custom. Some believe that the boy bishop was originally associated with **St. Nicholas's Day**, December 6. They suspect that the boy bishop's reign shifted to Holy Innocents' Day over time. These writers point out that **St. Nicholas** was a bishop in his lifetime and became the patron saint of children after his death. Therefore, they reason, it makes sense for the custom of the boy bishop to have developed around the celebrations held in St. Nicholas's honor. Indeed, in some areas of **England** the boy bishop ruled on St. Nicholas's Day and was known as the "St. Nicholas Bishop." Furthermore, even though most cathedrals held the ceremonies associated with the boy bishop on Innocents' Day, many held elections for the boy bishop on St. Nicholas's Day. Some researchers have concluded that the boy bishop held office from St. Nicholas's Day to Holy Innocents' Day. During this time he enjoyed many of the privileges of a real bishop and attended to many of the responsibilities. Other writers point out that Innocents' Day also provided an appropriate occasion on which to elevate a boy to the role of bishop, since it commemorated the martyrdom of **Bethlehem**'s male children.

The earliest known historical record of a boy bishop comes from what is now Switzerland. It tells us that in 911 A.D. King Conrad I and the bishop of Constance visited the monastery of St. Gall and attended a service presided over by the boy bishop and his choirboy attendants. The king entertained himself during the service by rolling apples into the aisles in an attempt to distract the children from their solemn duties. Apparently, the children demonstrated more dignity than did the king, since none stooped to pick up these tempting sweets.

Costumes

Various customs surrounding the boy bishop reveal that this role reversal not only enjoyed popular support, but also received some degree of support from the Church. The institutions that sponsored boy bishops kept vestments specially made for them. These vestments were as luxurious and expensive as those made for real bishops. One old document describes a boy bishop's miter as being made of white silk, covered with flowers embroidered in silver and **gold** threads and ornamented with precious stones.

Ceremonies

The reign of the boy bishop began on the eve of Holy Innocents' Day in most places. At England's Salisbury Cathedral the choirboys, dressed in the silk robes of archdeacons and canons (clerical staff) and led by the regally clad boy bishop, began their procession towards the altar near the end of vespers, the evening prayer service, on December 27. The boy bishop censed the altar, after which the canons rose from their chairs and went to the places vacated by the choir. The choirboys then assumed the seats normally occupied by the clergy. This seating arrangement persisted until vespers on the following day. Moreover, during that time the canons took over the choirboys' duties at services, such as carrying the book, candles, and incense. The boy bishop presided over all services until vespers on Holy Innocents' Day. Most researchers believe he was not permitted to say mass, although at York and Winchester cathedrals it appears that he may have done so. On Innocents' Day the boy bishop led a procession through the streets, blessing the people as he went. The procession, along with his Innocents' Day sermon, formed the highlights of his brief career. Only a few of these sermons have survived to the present time, and all show clear signs of having been written by adults. In their tone and choice of topic, they range from humorous to tedious. In one sermon the boy bishop, referring to the choirboys and other children present, quipped, "It is not so long since I was one of them myself" (Miles, 1990, 307).

Customs

In addition to his clerical duties, the boy bishop was expected to pay visits to churches, monasteries, and dignitaries throughout his diocese. The boy bishop and his entourage carried out this duty with zest, riding out in full regalia to receive the kind of respect, courtesies, gifts, feasts, and entertainments that would normally be offered to a real bishop. Many boys found that it took several days to execute this responsibility properly. Indeed, in 1396 the boy bishop of England's York Cathedral finally concluded his round of visitations on **Candlemas**. He collected more than eight pounds over the course of these visits. Of course, he did pay out a large portion of that sum in meeting the expenses of his entourage, which included a preacher, a steward, two singers, two attendants, and all their horses.

In general, people seem to have been amused by the boy bishop and welcomed his visits. In wealthy households the **Lord of Misrule** arranged food, drink, and gifts for the boy bishop and his entourage. It appears that, in return, the boys often entertained the household with songs or speeches. England's Queen Mary (1516-1558) is said to have received the boy bishop of St. Paul's Cathedral, who entertained her with a song. Since many churches, schools, and religious communities sponsored boy bishops, however, any one diocese might contain a small but highly active squad of miniature Christmas bishops, whose trails were sure to overlap. Thus, especially wealthy and high-ranking households and institutions sometimes received visits by more than one boy bishop during the Christmas season.

Controversy

In spite of the costs and potential inconvenience this custom presented to ordinary people, most did not complain. Church authorities, though, led periodic campaigns to curtail the activities of the boy bishop and his court of choristers. These sporadic crusades appear to have been triggered either by the boys' unruly behavior or by disruptions caused by onlookers. In England the dean of St. Paul's Cathedral limited the rights of the boy bishop to demand either service by or entertainment from the canons in 1263. Similar limitations were enacted at Salisbury in 1319. In addition, however, Salisbury officials warned that anyone who shoved the boys or blocked their rightful activities risked excommunication. In 1443 authorities from Salisbury Cathedral penned a decree restricting the choristers from disrespectful behavior.

Tradition gave the choirboys the right to elect the boy bishop without interference from adults. Perhaps fearing that things could get out of hand, authorities at various English cathedrals slowly chipped away at this tradition. In 1263 officials at St. Paul's Cathedral eliminated this privilege entirely, claiming it for themselves. Authorities at

York Cathedral proceeded more slowly, announcing qualifications for the post of boy bishop in 1367. They stipulated that the choir must choose a boy from among those with the longest and most exemplary records of service to the Cathedral. The boy also must possess both good looks and an acceptable singing voice. At Salisbury Cathedral the takeover attempt backfired. The choirboys revolted when the precentor (choral minister) attempted to curtail their free election of the boy bishop in 1449. The dean quickly convened a meeting of the canons, who upheld the choristers' right to choose the boy bishop without outside interference.

Decline

After its introduction in the tenth century, the custom of sponsoring boy bishops at Christmas time spread throughout Europe, becoming a common practice by the thirteenth century. Although known in many lands, boy bishops were especially popular in England, **France**, and **Germany**. The custom fell out of favor in the fifteenth century, an era of religious turmoil in which many old practices were questioned or eliminated (*see also* **Puritans**). In England King Henry VIII issued a proclamation forbidding the boy bishop in 1541. His lengthy edict demonstrates the changing attitudes of the time:

> Whereas heretofore dyvers and many superstitions and chyldysh observances have been used, and yet to this day are observed and kept, and in many and sundry parts of this realm, as upon Saint Nicholas, Saint Catherine, Saint Clement, the Holy Innocents, and such like, children be stranglie decked and apparayled to counterfeit priestes, bishoppes, and women, and so be ledde with songes and daunces from house to house, blessing the people and gatheryng of money; and boyes do singe masse and preache in the pulpitt, with suche other unfittinge and inconvenient usages, rather to the deryson than any true glory of God, or honor of his sayntes: The Kynges Maiestie therefore, myndinge nothinge so moche as to advance the true glory of God without vaine superstition, wylleth and commanded that from henceforth all such superstitious observations be left and clerely extinguished throwout his realmes and dominions, for asmuch as the

same doth resemble rather the unlawfull superstition of gentilitie, than the pure and sincere religion of Christe [Mackenzie, 1987, 15].

Revival

In recent years the boy bishop has sprung back to life in England. A few churches, among them Hereford Cathedral, have reinstituted some of the ceremonies and customs surrounding the boy bishop. On December sixth the boy bishop presides over an elaborate service at Hereford Cathedral. Dressed as a real bishop, the chosen boy walks at the head of a formal procession, gives the sermon, and leads the prayers and blessings. At one point in the service the real bishop of Hereford rises and offers the boy bishop his seat. Contemporary boy bishop ceremonies are observed on St. Nicholas's Day. In this way, they neither conflict with nor find themselves overshadowed by the celebrations and ceremonies already clustered around Christmas Day.

Further Reading

Chambers, Robert. "December 6—The Boy Bishop: Eton Montem." In his *The Book of Days*. Volume 2. 1862-64. Reprint. Detroit, Mich.: Omnigraphics, 1990.

Henisch, Bridget Ann. *Cakes and Characters: An English Christmas Tradition*. London, England: Prospect Books, 1984.

Hole, Christina. *British Folk Customs*. London, England: Hutchinson and Company, 1976.

Howard, Alexander. *Endless Cavalcade*. London, England: Arthur Baker, 1964.

Hutton, Ronald. *The Rise and Fall of Merry England*. Oxford, England: Oxford University Press, 1994.

———. *The Stations of the Sun*. Oxford, England: Oxford University Press, 1996.

Mackenzie, Neil. "Boy into Bishop." *History Today* 37, 12 (December 1987): 10-16.

Miles, Clement A. *Christmas in Ritual and Tradition*. 1912. Reprint. Detroit, Mich.: Omnigraphics, 1990.

Pimlott, J. A. R. *The Englishman's Christmas*. Atlantic Highlands, N.J.: Humanities Press, 1978.

Brazil, Christmas in

Due to Brazil's location in the Southern Hemisphere, its people cele-brate a summertime, rather than a wintertime, Christmas (*see also* **Winter Solstice**). The Brazilian **Christmas season** lasts from mid-December to January 6. Contemporary Brazilian Christmas customs reflect the influence of European and North American Christmas traditions.

Papai Noel, the Three Kings, and Gifts

Brazilians inherited the Latin Christmas tradition of distributing pre-sents to children on Three Kings Day, or **Epiphany**. During the sec-ond half of the twentieth century, however, **Santa Claus** became increasingly popular in Brazil. Nowadays, children may receive pre-sents from Santa Claus on Christmas Eve, as well as additional treats from the Three Kings, or **Magi**, on Epiphany. Children from poor families may receive clothes and shoes as Christmas presents, where-as children from richer families may receive toys and other less essential items. Adult family members and friends also exchange Christmas **gifts**. On the eve of Epiphany children leave their **shoes** beside the window or outside the front door. In the morning they find them filled with candy.

In spite of the summer heat Santa Claus, or *Papai Noel* as he called in Brazilian Portuguese, visits Brazil in his red and white fur-trimmed suit and hat, black boots, and long, white beard. The Brazilians have improvised somewhat on the Santa Claus myth. For example, Santa enters and leaves homes by the front door rather than the chimney. This makes sense to Brazilians since few homes in that tropical coun-try have fireplaces and chimneys. Moreover, Papai Noel travels to Brazil in a helicopter rather than a sled drawn by flying **reindeer**. His official arrival in Brazil takes place in mid-December when he touch-es down in Rio de Janeiro's Maracanã stadium amidst a roaring crowd. These "Santa Claus arrival" events may be staged in other large cities as well. Brazilian children, like their American counterparts, hope to spot Papai Noel at one of their town's busy shopping centers in the days before Christmas.

Visits and Christmas Dinner

Christmas dinner provides a very special occasion for families and friends to visit. Brazilians eat Christmas dinner late in the evening on Christmas Eve. The meal often features roast turkey with *farofa* stuffing, which is made out of toasted manioc flour, onions, garlic, turkey livers and gizzards, olives, hard-boiled eggs, and bacon. Other popular Christmas dishes include dried cod, an assortment of fruit, and a dessert called *rabanada*, which resembles French toast. Champagne, wine, and fruit punch often accompany the meal. Most families dine around 10 or 11 p.m. Afterwards many attend the *Missa do Galo,* or **Midnight Mass** (*see also* **Misa de Gallo**). These services may be held in Roman Catholic churches or on outdoor stages set up for the occasion. In recent years some people have begun to stay home to watch the television broadcast of the pope's celebration of Midnight Mass in Rome.

Christmas Trees and Nativity Scenes

Many Brazilians decorate their homes with a **Christmas tree.** In southern Brazil parents often take on the job of decorating the tree themselves. On Christmas Eve they lock themselves in the parlor until the tree has been studded with glowing candles and garlanded with **ornaments**, such as metallic balls, figurines, and **poinsettia** blossoms. The magical sight of the decorated tree delights the children when they are finally allowed to enter the room. In spite of the popularity of the Christmas tree, the **Nativity scene** remains the focus of home decoration and celebration in most of Brazil. Nativity scenes, or *presépios,* also appear in churches and town squares. Children usually participate in setting up the Nativity scene, adding toys, fruit, or foliage to the family's collection of figurines. In the south families may wait until the day before Christmas to set up the Nativity scene. In other areas they may begin constructing the presépio in mid-December.

Cards, Charity, Plays

Brazilians have adopted the custom of sending Christmas greetings in the form of **Christmas cards**. Until recently, many of these cards reproduced the winter scenes commonly found on European and North American Christmas cards. Now Brazilians may opt for cards depicting the sunny scenes more typical of December weather in Brazil. In Brazil Christmas is also a time for charitable giving. Churches hold many fund-raising events during the **Christmas season**. They usually donate the proceeds to poor families who need financial assistance in order to celebrate Christmas. Another Brazilian custom calls for the presentation of **Nativity plays** during the season. Most of these plays treat religious themes. Folk plays treating rural life and lore may also be presented during this time. These folk plays often include songs and dances. The most popular of these is called *Bumba-meu-Boi*, or "Beating My Ox." The story revolves around a bull that is killed and then brought back to life.

Further Reading

Brazil. Danbury, Conn.: Grolier Educational, 1997.

Christmas in Brazil. Chicago: World Book, 1991.

Milne, Jean. *Fiesta Time in Latin America*. Los Angeles: Ward Ritchie Press, 1965.

Wakefield, Charito Calvachi. *Navidad Latinoamericana, Latin American Christmas*. Lancaster, Pa.: Latin American Creations Publishing, 1997.

Bulgaria, Christmas in

Christianity is the predominant faith in the eastern European nation of Bulgaria, though the country also hosts a sizeable Muslim minority (13 percent). Most Bulgarians who profess the Christian faith are Orthodox. Like other Orthodox Christians around the world, they fast during **Advent**, the period of spiritual preparation that precedes the Christmas festival. For the strictly observant, this means avoiding wine, meat, and dairy products for the duration of the fast, which ends on **December 25**.

Christmas Season

Bulgarians consider that the **Christmas season** begins on December 20, a day they call *Ignazhden*. A Bulgarian folk belief teaches that **Mary, Jesus'** mother, experienced her first contractions on this day. Christmas Day festivities begin on December 24 and extend through December 26. These festivities include special religious observances and frolics that resemble those of Carnival. In addition, bands of boys or young men, known as *koledari*, wander through the streets, stopping at homes to sing **Christmas carols**, dance, and offer blessings. People give them fruit, bread, and other treats as a means of thanking them for their efforts. Traditional koledari wear colorful folk costumes and carry beautifully carved oaken staves.

Christmas Dinner

Many Bulgarian Christmas customs pertain to the Christmas dinner. This should be a sumptuous meal, so as to attract abundance in the new year. The woman of the house bakes a special loaf of bread, which the head of the household breaks into pieces, giving one to each family member and saving some for the family's animals. In some areas people observe the tradition of burning incense over the dinner table and over the farm animals. One Bulgarian Christmas tradition requires whoever serves the Christmas pie to set aside the first piece for "Grandpa Vassil." This fictional character stands for any wayfarer, while the custom itself reminds diners that this night above all others is one on which to welcome strangers to share their feast.

New Year's Eve and Day

Bulgarian folk tradition assigns the burning of the **Yule log** to New Year's Eve. An old folk custom dictated that the hearth first be cleaned with a broom made from juniper. At sunset on New Year's Eve the oldest male in the household lights the Yule log. If it burns through the night, the family can hope for wealth and fertility in the year to come.

Bands of male carolers roam the streets on New Year's Eve as well as at Christmas time. These carolers, called *sourvakari*, carry wands made of dogwood branches. They lightly slap people on the back with these wands, wishing them long life, good health, and abundance. Groups of boys may repeat this custom on **New Year's Day**. In exchange for this blessing people offer the boys coins, fruit, or candy.

New Year's Day is celebrated with a large meal, which acts as a charm to ensure a prosperous new year. The bread traditionally served with this meal is decorated with emblems representing vines and bee hives. *Banitza*, a kind of cheese pastry, is a popular New Year's dish. On this occasion bakers place cornel (dogwood) buds inside the pastry. These buds symbolize good luck and good health for family members and livestock.

Grandfather Frost, the Russian gift bringer, visits Bulgaria on New Year's Day. This custom may have been imported during the recent period in which Bulgaria was ruled by the Russian-led Union of Soviet Socialist Republics (U.S.S.R.)

Further Reading

Griffin, Robert H., and Ann H. Shurgin, eds. *The Folklore of World Holidays.* Second edition. Detroit, Mich.: Gale, 1999.

Resnick, Abraham. *Bulgaria. Enchantment of the World.* Chicago: Children's Press, 1995.

Stavreva, Kirilka. *Bulgaria. Cultures of the World.* Tarrytown, N.Y.: Marshall Cavendish, 1997.

Web Site

"Wonderland Bulgaria," a web site maintained by Iliana Rakilovska, Irina Simeonova, Maria Nankova, and Kamen Minchev, furnishes information on the history, population, folklore, and geography of Bulgaria. For information on Bulgarian folk festivals, see: http://www.omda.bg/engl/ethno graphy/festivals.html

Candlemas

Feast of the Presentation of Christ in the Temple,
Feast of the Purification of the Blessed Virgin,
The Meeting of the Lord

The **Gospel according to Luke** tells us that **Joseph** and **Mary** brought the baby **Jesus** to the temple six weeks after his birth (Luke 2:22-24). Once there they observed the Jewish ceremony by which firstborn sons were presented to God. Furthermore, Mary fulfilled the purification rites, which Jewish law required women to undergo forty days after the birth of a son. Another very significant event occurred while the Holy Family was at the temple. Simeon and Anna, a holy man and a prophetess, recognized the infant as the Messiah. Simeon declared that the child would be "a light that will bring revelation to the Gentiles" (Luke 2:32). The Christian feast of Candlemas commemorates all these events. It is celebrated on February 2, forty days after Christmas. Candlemas gets its name from a number of candle-related customs connected with the feast. By the

95

Middle Ages the blessing of candles, the distribution of blessed candles among parishioners, and candlelit processions had all established themselves as common elements in western European Candlemas services.

History

The earliest known description of the feast comes from late fourth-century Jerusalem. This early celebration consisted of a solemn procession followed by a sermon and mass. The description named the feast simply "the fortieth day after **Epiphany**." Since at that time Jerusalem Christians were celebrating both Epiphany and the Nativity on January 6, the festival fell on the fourteenth of February (*see also* **December 25**). From Jerusalem the new festival spread throughout the East. The Greeks called it *Hypapante Kyriou*, or "The Meeting of the Lord," a name that reflected their emphasis on the meeting between Simeon, Anna, and the infant Jesus. The feast began to appear in the West in the seventh and eighth centuries. Westerners celebrated it on February 2, since by that time Rome had assigned the celebration of the Nativity to December 25. Roman officials called the feast the "Purification of Mary," reflecting their emphasis on Mary's fulfillment of Jewish law.

Several centuries passed before western European Candlemas observances consolidated around a distinctive set of traditions. Candles were used in the services as early as the mid-fifth century in Jerusalem. Nevertheless, Pope Sergius I (687-701 A.D.) is generally credited with ordering the first candlelit processions to accompany church services in Rome. In what is now **France**, the blessing of candles developed during the Carolingian Empire, near the close of the eighth century. By the eleventh century the blessing of candles, the distribution of blessed candles, and candlelit processions had become widespread elements in the western European observance of Candlemas. The feast got its English name, Candlemas, meaning quite literally "candle mass," from these customs. Since the eighteenth century the representatives of various religious communities have offered the pope large, decorated candles on Candlemas.

Contemporary Candlemas services generally emphasize Christ as the Light of the World. In addition, the officiant often blesses and distributes beeswax candles. In some traditions parishioners bring candles from home to be blessed during the service. In past times Candlemas processions filed out into the churchyard and past the graves of the departed. Contemporary Candlemas processions, however, usually remain within the church.

Some researchers suggest that Christians simply adopted Candlemas and its customs from pagan celebrations held at the same time of year. On February 1 the pagan Celts celebrated Imbolc, a festival associated with the return of the spring goddess Bride (later, St. Bridget). In some areas sacred fires and candles burned through the night in honor of Bride's return. In ancient Rome people observed purification rites throughout the month of February, which included a procession through the city with lit candles. In addition, they celebrated the return of their spring goddess, Ceres, on February first. Pagans in other Mediterranean cultures also welcomed the return of a spring deity. Many of these observances featured fire rituals and torchlit processions.

While some writers believe that these pagan practices gave rise to the observance of Candlemas and its customs, most contemporary scholars doubt that these pagan rituals exerted strong influence on medieval Christians. The doubters point out that these pagan fire ceremonies had died out by the time candles became part of the Christian festival. They also claim a specifically Christian symbolism for the Candlemas tapers. The candles recall the words of Simeon who proclaimed that Jesus would become "a light" unto the Gentiles.

Christmas Customs

Jesus' presentation in the temple and Mary's fulfillment of the rites of purification mark the end of the series of events associated with Jesus' birth in the Gospels. In a similar vein, many old European Christmas customs were practiced until Candlemas. For example, in some areas **Nativity scenes** were taken apart and put away on Candlemas. In other areas Christmas **greenery**—such as **rosemary, laurel, mistletoe, holly**, and **ivy**—and other seasonal decorations were finally removed on Candlemas. The English poet Robert Herrick (1591-1674) summarized Devonshire folk customs and beliefs concerning the removal of such decorations in the following poem:

> Candlemas Eve Carol
>
> Down with rosemary, and so
> Down with bays and mistletoe;
> Down with the holly, ivy, all
> Wherewith ye dressed the Christmas hall,
> That so the superstitious find
> No one least branch there left behind;
> For look, how many leaves there be
> Neglected there, maids, trust to me,
> So many goblins you shall see [Urlin, 1992, 30].

In another verse Herrick informs us that the **Yule log** was kindled one last time on Candlemas and then stored till the following year. Herrick implies that Candlemas concludes the **Christmas season** with the following lines:

> End now the White Loafe and the Pye
> And let all sports with Christmas dye [Miles, 1990, 353].

Herrick's sentiments echo the lyrics of a fifteenth-century English **Christmas carol**, which exclaims, "Syng we Yole tyl Candlemas" (Sing we Yule till Candlemas).

Further Reading

Chambers, Robert. "February 2 — Candlemass." In his *The Book of Days*. Volume 1. 1862-64. Reprint. Detroit, Mich.: Omnigraphics, 1990.

Cowie, L. W., and John Selwyn Gummer. *The Christian Calendar*. Springfield, Mass.: C. and G. Merriam Company, 1974.

Henderson, Helene, and Sue Ellen Thompson, eds. *Holidays, Festivals, and Celebrations of the World Dictionary*. Second edition. Detroit, Mich.: Omnigraphics, 1997.

Hutton, Ronald. *The Pagan Religions of the Ancient British Isles*. Oxford, England: Basil Blackwell, 1991.

James, E. O. *Seasonal Feasts and Festivals*. 1961. Reprint. Detroit, Mich.: Omnigraphics, 1993.

MacDonald, Margaret Read, ed. *The Folklore of World Holidays*. Detroit, Mich.: Gale Research, 1992.

Metford, J. C. J. *The Christian Year*. London, England: Thames and Hudson, 1991.

Miles, Clement A. *Christmas in Ritual and Tradition*. 1912. Reprint. Detroit, Mich.: Omnigraphics, 1990.

Slim, Hugo. *A Feast of Festivals*. London, England: Marshall Pickering, 1996.

Smith, C. "Candlemas." In *New Catholic Encyclopedia*. Volume 3. New York: McGraw-Hill, 1967.

Thompson, Sue Ellen, ed. *Holiday Symbols*. Detroit, Mich.: Omnigraphics, 1998.

Toon, Peter. "Candle; Candlemas." In J. D. Douglas, ed. *The New International Dictionary of the Christian Church*. Revised edition. Grand Rapids, Mich.: Zondervan Publishing House, 1978.

Urlin, Ethel. *Festivals, Holy Days, and Saints' Days*. 1915. Reprint. Detroit, Mich.: Omnigraphics, 1992.

Weiser, Francis X. *The Handbook of Christian Feasts and Customs*. New York: Harcourt, Brace and World, 1952.

Candles

For candle customs associated with the celebration of Christmas, *see* **Advent Candle; Advent Wreath; Candlemas; Christingle; Christmas Candles; Christmas Symbols; Denmark, Christmas in; Farolitos; Ireland, Christmas in; Plygain; Pyramid; St. Lucy's Day; Saturnalia**

Candy Cane. *See* **Urban Legends**

99

Ceremony of Lessons and Carols

On the afternoon of December 24 a special Christmas service takes place at Cambridge University's King's College Chapel. Known as the "Ceremony of Lessons and Carols," this service features nine Bible readings accompanied by nine **Christmas carols** or other appropriate musical works. The King's College service, first broadcast in 1928, helped to popularize this special Christmas observance. Today many churches in **England**, the United States, and around the world hold their own versions of this ceremony.

An Anglican bishop, Edward W. Benson, who later was archbishop of Canterbury, devised the first Ceremony of Nine Lessons and Carols. Benson is said to have modeled the new carol service on medieval vigil services. Benson presented the first Ceremony of Lessons and Carols on Christmas Eve in 1880. The service took place in the wooden shed that served as the cathedral in Truro, England. The Bible lessons were read by a wide spectrum of church officers, beginning with a chorister and ending with the bishop.

The service quickly began to spread to other congregations. Eric Milner-White, dean of King's College Chapel, introduced the service there in 1918. The Order of Service was revised in 1919, and the song "Once in Royal David's City" established as the opening hymn. The King's College service is still broadcast every year on the radio (except in the year 1930), and in recent years it has also been aired on television.

The Ceremony of Lessons and Carols has spread far beyond its native land. Churches all over the world now offer their version of the service during **Advent**. The standard format calls for a series of alternating Bible readings and carols, bracketed by opening and closing prayers. Although the choice of lessons and carols may vary, the heart of the service remains the same. The series of readings describes the unfolding of God's love for humanity from a biblical perspective. The carols enhance the beauty of the service by treating the same subject in music.

Further Reading

Howard, Alexander. *Endless Cavalcade*. London, England: Arthur Baker, 1964.

Web Site

A site sponsored by Cambridge University's King College Chapel offers information on their famous Ceremony of Lessons and Carols service: http://www.kings.cam.ac.uk/chapel/ninelessons/

Cert

Folk beliefs assign **St. Nicholas** the role of Christmas **gift** bringer in Czechoslovakia. According to Czechoslovakian folklore, two oddly matched companions aid the good saint in his labors. On December sixth, **St. Nicholas's Day**, Nicholas descends from heaven on a golden rope accompanied by an **angel** dressed in white and a demon known as a cert. The cert wears black clothing and carries a whip and chain. He frightens naughty children, reminding them of the punishment in store for them if they don't mend their ways. (*See also* **Black Peter**.)

Further Reading

Del Re, Gerard, and Patricia Del Re. *The Christmas Almanack*. Garden City, N.Y.: Doubleday, 1979.

Foley, Daniel J. *Christmas the World Over*. Philadelphia, Pa.: Chilton Books, 1963.

Stevens, Patricia Bunning. *Merry Christmas!: A History of the Holiday*. New York: Macmillan, 1979.

"A Charlie Brown Christmas"

"A Charlie Brown Christmas" charmed millions of Americans when it made its debut in 1965. This animated television special weaves a story around the Christmas-time antics of the characters from Charles Schulz's (1922-2000) popular cartoon-strip "Peanuts." While the other kids look forward to Christmas and enjoy winter-time activities, like skating, Charlie Brown alone feels anxious and depressed (*see* **Depression**). He consults Lucy, who fancies herself an amateur psychiatrist. She advises him to "get involved" with something and makes him the director of the school Christmas play. His involvement ends when the other kids laugh at the straggly **Christmas tree** he brings back to adorn the stage. Then Linus, quoting from the Bible, reminds the kids what Christmas is all about (*see* **Gospel Accounts of Christmas**). Afterwards Charlie Brown takes his Christmas tree home. The other kids change their minds about the tree and help Charlie Brown decorate it.

Charles Schulz's "Peanuts"

Charles Schulz's "Peanuts" was one of the most successful comic strips of all time. More than 300 million people worldwide followed the strip, which was translated into 20 different languages. Schulz's pint-sized characters approach life with a unique combination of wisdom, innocence, anxiety, and hip self-assurance that attracts both adult and juvenile readers. People who knew Charles Schulz find many similarities between the cartoonist and his main character, the worried and hapless Charlie Brown. Yet Schulz was able to translate his nervousness into an appealing art form, which in turn brought him millions of fans and millions of dollars. Among the many honors given to the cartoonist include his mention in the 1984 *Guinness Book of World Records* when the 2,000th newspaper subscribed to his strip, and his induction into the Cartoonist Hall of Fame in 1986. In 1990 the French government named him a "Commander of Arts and Letters."

On December 14, 1999, Schulz, who was battling cancer, reluctantly announced his retirement to the world. One of the last honors received by this long-time resident of Santa Rosa, California, was given to him by the California state legislature, which declared February 13, 2000 "Charles Schulz Day." On this day the last "Peanuts" strip was scheduled to run in newspapers across the country and around the world. Schulz died in his sleep on February 12, just hours before a saddened public enjoyed his final strip. In May of 2000 the Congress of the United States posthumously awarded him the Medal of Honor.

The Making of "A Charlie Brown Christmas"

"A Charlie Brown Christmas" began life as a twinkle in the eye of producer Lee Mendelson. He, Schulz, and animator Bill Melendez had worked together a couple of years earlier on a documentary of Schulz and his cartoon characters. When Mendelson discovered that Coca Cola was looking for a Christmas special and was interested in the Peanuts characters, he assured them of both his and Schulz's interest in the project. Then Mendelson rushed to Schulz's house to inform him of the idea and convince him that it was a good one. Luckily, Schulz readily agreed to work on the project, and together the two of them came up with an outline for the show. The outline specified that the story would contain a school play, winter-time fun and games, a reading from the Bible, and a combination of jazz and traditional Christmas music. Coca Cola liked the outline, and production immediately began on the show.

Mendelson right away invited Bill Melendez to take charge of the animation. The three men met to develop the story. Mendelson contributed the idea of structuring some of the action around a Christmas tree, an inspiration he took from Hans Christian Andersen's short story "The Fir Tree." Schulz qualified the concept, by insisting that the tree be a "Charlie Brown" type of tree. The work progressed with Schulz masterminding the dialogue and situations, while Melendez translated them into an animated cartoon.

The three men were eager to hire jazz pianist Vince Guaraldi, whom they had worked with before on the Schulz documentary. They wanted to reuse the "Linus and Lucy" theme developed by Guaraldi several years ago as well as give him an opportunity to create new music. Guaraldi signed on and production went into full swing. The animators produced 10,000 drawings for the half-hour show. Passing them by the camera at the rate of 12 per second made the cartoon characters appear to move.

"A Charlie Brown Christmas" broke new ground in several ways. By having one of the characters recite the biblical narrative of **Jesus'** birth, it introduced a moment of serious religious contemplation into a cartoon aimed at children. Although Mendelson was doubtful, Schulz, a quietly religious man, insisted that his Christmas show contain a religious theme. In addition, the three men decided to hire child actors to dub in the cartoon characters' voices. Up till that time, adult actors had typically filled in all the voices in animated cartoons, even those of child characters. Finally, the jazz piano music provided by Vince Guaraldi delighted both adults and children, who previously had been accustomed to cartoons accompanied by simple jingles rather than serious music.

Reactions to "A Charlie Brown Christmas"

The crew finished work on the show one week before it was scheduled to air on television. Top CBS executives screened the special shortly before it was televised. Disappointed by what they considered its slow pace, they assured Mendelson that although they would air the program, they wouldn't be interested in any further Charlie Brown shows.

This assessment crushed Mendelson, Schulz, and Melendez. Hope revived when the special received a good pre-broadcast review in *Time* magazine. On December 9, 1965, the show was broadcast nationwide. Ratings proved it to be a hit with the American public, and ranked it as the second-most popular show on television during its time-slot. Several months later the three men received an Emmy Award for Best Network Animated Special. "A Charlie Brown Christmas" also received a Peabody Award for excellence in family programming. Rerun in the years that followed, the show continued to receive high ratings.

Charles Schulz went on to create 45 animated television specials based on his famous cartoon-strip characters. "A Charlie Brown Christmas," his first, remained his favorite. Vince Guaraldi's album of music from the show, entitled "A Charlie Brown Christmas," went platinum (sold over 1,000,000 copies). Later released as a CD, it continues to be a best-selling Christmas album.

Further Reading

Johnson, Rheta Grimsley. *Good Grief: The Story of Charles M. Schulz*. Kansas City, Mo.: Andrews and McMeel, 1995.

Mendelson, Lee. *A Charlie Brown Christmas: The Making of a Tradition*. New York: HarperCollins, 2000.

Web Site

The Charles M. Schulz Museum, located in Santa Rosa, California, offers a web site with information on Schulz and his achievements: http://www.charlesmschulzmuseum.org

Cherry Tree

Legend, song, and custom link the cherry tree to the **Christmas season**. In all three the cherry tree performs unusual feats in response to the power of God or the magic of the season.

Legends

An old Christian legend, first recorded in the apocryphal Gospel of Pseudo-Matthew, makes the cherry tree the subject of one of the infant **Jesus'** first miracles. The original Latin text containing the tale dates back to the eighth or ninth century. This version of the story tells of an event that occurred shortly after Jesus' birth. **Joseph, Mary,** and the infant Jesus were traveling in the desert. The couple spied a palm tree and went to rest under its shadow. Joseph worried about how they were going to find water. Mary expressed a wish for the dates she saw hanging high above them. Joseph scolded his wife for asking for something so far out of his reach. Then the baby Jesus spoke to the tree, ordering it to bend down so his mother could gather the fruit. The tree obeyed. Jesus also commanded an underground spring to surface so they could drink and fill their water bags.

As the tale passed from one teller to another, many variations occurred. In later versions of the story the incident takes place before Jesus is born. Moreover, as the tale became popular in **Europe**, the tree which Jesus commands to bow down changes to species more familiar to Europeans. In Britain, the newer versions of the story featured a cherry tree. In these later interpretations of the tale, Joseph and his pregnant wife are walking by some cherry trees laden with ripe fruit. Mary asks Joseph to pick some cherries for her. He refuses in a rude manner, with the implication that he still questions the origins of her mysterious pregnancy. Jesus, from inside the womb, then commands the cherry tree to bow down so his mother can pick fruit. Joseph stands by sheepishly and observes this miracle. The earliest recorded version of this story in the English language appeared in a fifteenth-century miracle play. Eventually this popular tale was set to music in the Christmas song known as "The Cherry Tree Carol" (*see also* **Christmas Carol**).

Customs

In medieval Europe a miracle play concerning the expulsion of **Adam and Eve** from the Garden of Eden was often performed around Christmas time. The play featured one central prop, the **paradise tree**. Apples hung from its branches as a symbol of Eve's act of disobedience, but some also added cherries as a symbol of Mary.

According to an old custom, Germans, Czechs, Austrians, Poles, and other central and eastern Europeans begin Barbara branches on December 4, **St. Barbara's Day**. A branch is broken off a cherry tree and kept in a pot of water near the stove. This premature warmth encourages the branch to blossom. Old folklore suggests that if the buds blossom on Christmas Eve, the girl who tended the branch will find a good husband within the year. Others interpret the Christmas flowers as signs that good fortune will visit the household in the coming year. This old custom has regained some popularity among Western Christians. Instead of cherry branches, some people use apple, plum, almond, forsythia, jasmine, or horse chestnut branches.

Further Reading

Coffin, Tristram P. *The Book of Christmas Folklore*. New York: Seabury Press, 1973.

Crippen, Thomas G. *Christmas and Christmas Lore*. 1923. Reprint. Detroit, Mich.: Omnigraphics, 1990.

Leach, Maria, ed. *Funk and Wagnalls Standard Dictionary of Folklore, Mythology, and Legend*. New York: Harper and Row, 1984.

MacDonald, Margaret Read, ed. *The Folklore of World Holidays*. Detroit, Mich.: Gale Research, 1992.

Thompson, Sue Ellen, ed. *Holiday Symbols*. Detroit, Mich.: Omnigraphics, 1998.

Weiser, Francis X. *The Christmas Book*. 1952. Reprint. Detroit, Mich.: Omnigraphics, 1990.

Children's Letters

The urge to send greetings at Christmas time seizes people of all ages. Businesses prepare hundreds of thank-you notes for their customers. Adults salute family and friends with **Christmas cards**. Even children get in on the act by sending letters to the child **Jesus** and to **Santa Claus**.

Letters to the Child Jesus

An old Austrian custom encouraged children to write letters to the child Jesus on the night before **St. Nicholas's Day**. These letters contained lists of things the children wanted for Christmas. The youngsters placed the letters on the windowsill before going to bed. When the children discovered that the letters had disappeared overnight, their parents assured them that **St. Nicholas** had taken the letters back to heaven to deliver to the child Jesus. In that way the Christ child knew what to bring the children on Christmas Eve (*see also* **Christkindel**). In some South American countries old customs suggested that children leave their letters for the child Jesus in front of the crib contained in the family **Nativity scene**. They did so between December 16 and 24, the days on which the Hispanic folk play called Las **Posadas** was being enacted. Older family members explained the disappearance of the letters by hinting that **angels** delivered them to heaven.

Letters to Santa Claus

In the nineteenth and twentieth centuries children in many lands adopted Santa Claus as the Christmas **gift** bringer. In the 1880s American cartoonist Thomas Nast (1840-1902) gave Santa Claus an address, the **North Pole**. Soon afterwards American children began writing letters to Santa Claus, hoping to guide him in his choice of gifts for them. Since 1929 the United States Postal Service has been trying to answer these letters. Each year postal employees and community volunteers read and respond to the letters. Some volunteers, touched by the earnest requests of underprivileged tots, find ways of sending the children some of the requested gifts.

In 1997 postal workers all over the country reported the first decline ever in the numbers of letters sent to Santa Claus at Christmas time. Some postal divisions noticed a steep seventy-percent drop in these letters. No one knows why so many kids all at once lost interest in writing letters to Santa. Perhaps they suddenly discovered e-mail. In any case, the Postal Service hired actress Maureen O'Hara, who starred in the 1947 Hollywood Christmas film, *Miracle on 34th Street*, to head a campaign publicizing the volunteer program dedicated to answering these letters and encouraging children to continue sending letters to Santa.

While American children believe that Santa dwells at the North Pole, Finnish children know that he lives in Korvatunturi, in the far north of Finland. Korvatunturi means "Ear Mountain," so it is the perfect abode for a man whose primary job is listening to and fulfilling children's wishes. Since the 1950s the post office in the small northern town of Rovaniemi has been handling Santa's mail. Apparently, the Finnish belief that Santa resides at Korvatunturi has spread. These days Rovaniemi receives about 500,000 letters to Santa each year from children in 160 countries. The Finns also make an attempt to answer these letters. To reach Santa Claus via the Finnish postal service, write him at Santa Claus' Main Post Office, 96930 Arctic Circle, Finland. In 1997 even children who didn't initiate contact with Santa could receive an unsolicited letter from him. To make this happen, an adult needs to send the child's name and address in block letters, along with four international reply coupons (available at your local post office) to the address above. Please note that the Finnish Santa is fluent in twelve languages and needs to know which of these to respond in.

Some Icelanders wish to popularize the idea that Santa Claus lives in **Iceland**. At one point the government-run Iceland Board of Tourism answered the thousands of children's letters to Santa that arrived in Iceland. After funding cuts decimated this program a private foundation stepped in to answer these letters. For a fee of $4.95 (U.S. dollars), an organization called North Pole, Inc.—whose mailing address is P.O. Box 358-121, Reykjavik, Iceland—will send your child a return letter from Santa, along with a little story, photos of Santa Claus at home, and a diploma with the child's name on it.

Other far northern nations, such as Sweden, Greenland, and Canada also claim to be the home of Santa Claus. Sweden receives tens of thousands of children's letters to Santa Claus each year. The Swedish post office makes every effort to answer these letters.

Letters to Other Gift Bringers

In **England** children send letters to **Father Christmas** listing the gifts they would like to receive for Christmas. English children developed a clever way of delivering these letters. They toss the letters into the fireplace, relying on the flames to transform them into a kind of magical smoke that wafts up the chimney and across England to Father Christmas. In **Italy** children write letters to La **Befana** requesting that she bring them certain toys and treats when she visits their home on **Epiphany** eve. Spanish children write similar letters to the Wise Men, or **Magi**, in the weeks before Epiphany. French children send letters to Père Noël, hoping to influence the gifts he brings them on Christmas Eve.

Seals and Stamps

At the turn of the twentieth century a number of charitable organizations hit on a way to use the flood of Christmas mail to raise some badly needed revenue. They began to sell **Christmas seals** which could be used to decorate envelopes and packages. In the 1960s the U.S. Postal Service chimed in by producing special Christmas stamps during the holiday season. Unlike the seals, the stamps function as valid postage. They add a further decorative note to holiday season mail.

Further Reading

Del Re, Gerard, and Patricia Del Re. *The Christmas Almanack*. Garden City, N.Y.: Doubleday, 1979.

Schmelz, Abigail. "Xmas Dreams Dashed as Santa Letters Go Unopened." *Reuters* (December 19, 1996).

Weiser, Francis X. *The Christmas Book*. 1952. Reprint. Detroit, Mich.: Omnigraphics, 1990.

Web Site

For more information on North Pole, Inc., the Icelandic organization that sends out return letters to children who write to Santa Claus in Iceland, visit their web site at: http://www.santa.is

Chrismon Tree

The Chrismon tree adapts the traditional **Christmas tree** to more strictly Christian uses. It consists of an evergreen tree decorated with traditional Christian symbols of **Jesus**. In fact, the word "Chrismon" resulted from the combination of two words, "Christ" and "monogram." Originally, only monograms of Christ decorated the tree. As churches and families adopted the custom, however, they began to create new symbols of Christ to adorn their trees. Only the colors white and **gold** appear on these **ornaments**. These are the liturgical colors for Christmas Day. White represents Jesus' purity and perfection, while gold stands for his majesty and glory. White lights may further embellish the tree, reminding viewers that Jesus is "the light of the world" (John 8:12).

Further Reading

Augustine, Peg, comp. *Come to Christmas*. Nashville, Tenn.: Abingdon Press, 1993.

Christingle

Christingle is the name of a special Protestant Christmas Eve service popular in **England**. The word also refers to the decorated candles distributed to children at this service. Christingle candles can be traced back to the Moravians, a group of Protestant Christians whose denomination was founded in the fifteenth century in what is now the Czech Republic (*for more on the Moravians, see* **Bethlehem, Pennsylvania, Christmas in; Lovefeast**).

Moravians have long distributed beeswax candles, trimmed with red paper or ribbon, to worshipers at their Christmas Eve services. As the congregation sings hymns they hold up their flickering candles, symbolizing the Christ child or the Christ light. Moravians brought this custom with them to England, where the German *Christkindel* (Christ child) became "Christingle."

As the years went by, the design of the candle changed and acquired new symbolism. Children attending today's Christingle services receive an orange into which a candle, festooned with red and white ribbons and paper, has been inserted. Raisins, nuts, candies, and other sweets, skewered onto toothpicks, surround the candle. While the candle still stands for Christ, the orange is said to represent the world. The sweets may symbolize the sweetness that comes from following Christ or the bounty of the earth, and the red and white paper represents the blood of Christ and its power to purify. (*For a similar custom, see* **Wales, Christmas in.**)

Christingle services and candles can also be found in Labrador, Canada, and other places where English Moravians sent missionaries. Instead of an orange, the people of Labrador insert their Christingle candles into an apple. In England the Christingle service and candles have spread beyond Moravian churches, becoming popular with other Protestants as well.

Web Sites

The Moravian Church in America offers a page on the Christingle at: http://www.moravian.org/faq/christingle.html

The Royal School of Church Music, a non-profit organization dedicated to promoting all styles of church music in all denominations, offers information on Christingle services at: http://www.rscm.com/sundaybysunday/christingle_services.htm

Christkindel

Christ Child, Christkind, Kriss Kringle

In parts of **Germany**, Switzerland, and Austria the *Christkindel* or *Christkind* brings children their Christmas **gifts**. Christkindel means "Christ child" in German. Some people understand the Christ Child to be the child Jesus; others view the Christ Child as an **angel**, who appears as a young girl with golden wings, long blond hair, and flowing robes.

In past times a rather threatening spirit known as Hans Trapp accompanied the Christ Child in some German-speaking regions. Hans Trapp dressed in furs and carried a rod, making it his duty to punish children who had behaved badly (*see also* **Knecht Ruprecht**). The Christ Child generally intervened on the naughty child's behalf, however.

The Christ Child became a German gift bringer around the seventeenth century. During the Reformation, Protestant reformers wanted to teach children that all blessings come directly from God. Rather than let children continue to believe that **St. Nicholas** brought their gifts, they introduced the concept of the Christkindel. Nuremberg, Germany's famous **Christmas market**, which displays hundreds of gift items each year, adopted the name "Christ Child Market" in the seventeenth century.

German immigrants brought the notion of the Christkindel with them to the United States. Over time the customs and lore connected with Christkindel faded and the word itself changed to "Kriss Kringle." The growing popularity of **Santa Claus** in the United States eventually eclipsed any remaining notion of the Christ Child, and Kriss Kringle became simply another name for Santa.

Further Reading

Del Re, Gerard, and Patricia Del Re. *The Christmas Almanack*. Garden City, N.Y.: Doubleday, 1979.

Miles, Clement A. *Christmas in Ritual and Tradition*. 1912. Reprint. Detroit, Mich.: Omnigraphics, 1990.

Stevens, Patricia Bunning. *Merry Christmas!: A History of the Holiday*. New York: Macmillan, 1979.

Christmas Ale
Christmas Beer, Yule Ale

In recent years a growing number of small American breweries have marketed special Christmas ales during the holiday season. These companies have revived the ancient northern European tradition of celebrating the midwinter holidays with specially brewed beers.

Yule Ale

A number of experts believe that the pagan Scandinavians celebrated their midwinter **Yule** festival by brewing and drinking special beers. Norse mythology taught that the god Odin instructed humans in the brewing of alcoholic beverages. The people drank to Odin during Yule. They may have been invoking him either as the patron of ale or as the lord of the dead, since they honored the spirits of the deceased during Yule. Some researchers believe that the ancient Scandinavians also raised their glasses to other gods during the festival, including Frey, the fertility god.

The connection between the Yule season and drinking remained strong as Scandinavia adopted Christianity in the Middle Ages. "Drinking Yule" became a standard phrase referring to the celebration of the holiday (*see also* **Wassail**). In **Norway** medieval law modified the ancient practice of toasting the gods when drinking Yule ale. It stipulated that Christmas beer should be blessed in the name of Christ and **Mary** for peace and a good harvest. What's more, medieval law required every household to bless and drink Yule beer. Norwegians usually drank their Christmas ale out of special cups, sometimes reserving ancient drinking horns for this purpose.

Seasonal Ales

In Norway the tradition of brewing and blessing special beers for Christmas flourished until the nineteenth century. Tradition dictated that all Christmas baking, slaughtering, and brewing be finished by **St. Thomas's Day**, December 21. For this reason Norwegian folk tradition dubbed him "St. Thomas the Brewer." In past times Norwegians visited each other on St. Thomas's Day in order to sample one another's Christmas ale.

In Germany beer-makers developed and maintained a tradition of brewing special seasonal ales. Perhaps the most well known were those served for the fall harvest festivals. German beer drinkers still anticipate the arrival of these slightly stronger and darker beers, named Oktoberfest or Märzenbiers, each autumn. German brewers also craft distinctive beers for the **Christmas season**, as well as for spring and summer.

Church Ales

In the Middle Ages northern Europeans drank quite a lot of beer. Beer's popularity may have sprung in part from the fact that, due to poor sanitary conditions, fermented alcoholic beverages were less likely than water to transmit diseases. The climate in much of northern **Europe** will not support wine grapes very well, so the people of the north specialized in beer-making.

In medieval times most monasteries brewed their own beer. In fact, monastic brews were considered among the best in medieval Europe. In the late Middle Ages parish churches in **England** began to ferment beers to be sold to the public on feast days. These events, called church ales, raised money for church supplies, repairs, and improvements. The most important church ale of the year occurred at Whitsuntide (Pentecost and the week that follows). Other important church ales took place at Easter, May Day, Christmas, and various patron saints' days. These party-like events featured the consumption of ample quantities of food and drink, along with dancing, **game** playing, and other forms of revelry. They died out in most places by the eighteenth century, succumbing to long-standing opposition by those who objected to the boisterous behavior that occurred at these church events.

Christmas Ale

The northern European preference for celebrating the Christmas season with specially brewed ales emerged from all of the above traditions. Midwinter brews tended to be darker, spicier, and slightly more alcoholic than other beers, which made them a special treat. With the rise of industrial breweries, however, handcrafted seasonal beers all but vanished. In the United States seasonal beers disappeared after World War II. In 1975 a tiny San Francisco firm, the Anchor Brewing Company, reintroduced American beer drinkers to Christmas ale. Their success inspired many other small breweries to follow suit.

Further Reading

Henriksen, Vera. *Christmas in Norway*. Oslo, Norway: Johan Grundt Tanum Forlag, 1970.

Hole, Christina. *British Folk Customs*. London, England: Hutchinson and Company, 1976.

Hutton, Ronald. *The Rise and Fall of Merry England*. Oxford, England: Oxford University Press, 1994.

Rhodes, Christine, ed. *Encyclopedia of Beer*. New York: Henry Holt and Company, 1995.

Christmas Bonus

As Christmas approaches, many American workers look forward to receiving a Christmas bonus, usually a lump sum of money added to their December paycheck. This Christmas **gift** from employer to employee may have been inspired by English **Boxing Day** customs. Although the Christmas bonus began as a voluntary gift, it evolved into an expected increase in one's December salary.

By the late nineteenth century many American employers had adopted the custom of distributing Christmas bonuses among their workers. These personalized exchanges often took place at office Christmas parties, another new, late nineteenth-century custom. The boss himself usually presented each worker with their presents or money. Often the employer tied the gift to the employee's performance during the year.

Christmas bonuses became increasingly common throughout the last decades of the nineteenth century, but between 1900 and 1920, these kinds of personalized exchanges all but disappeared. Labor unions, which grew in numbers and in influence during this period, began to bring the issue of the Christmas bonus to the bargaining table. Unionists argued that workers depended on these bonuses and needed to know in advance approximately how much they would receive. They objected to the nineteenth-century practice whereby the bonuses were distributed according to the whims of managers and bosses. As the twentieth century rolled on, their arguments prevailed. Christmas bonuses were increasingly calculated according to agreed-upon formulas. These formulas often took into account such things as salary level and years of service.

In recent years the number of companies giving Christmas bonuses has declined. Some firms have switched to year-round incentive programs that reward effective employees. Others provide employees with a lavish Christmas party or a day off in lieu of a bonus. According to the Bureau of National Affairs in Washington, D.C., about nine percent of companies with 1,000 or more workers distributed Christmas bonuses in 1999. Workers in small companies were luckier, with about 25 percent of their employers offering modest cash bonuses at Christmas time.

Further Reading

Del Re, Gerard, and Patricia Del Re. *The Christmas Almanack*. Garden City, N.Y.: Doubleday, 1979.

Ostrowski, Jeff. "Companies Moving Away From Christmas Bonuses, Study Finds." *The Palm Beach Post* (December 24, 1999): 1D.

Waits, William. *The Modern Christmas in America*. New York: New York University Press, 1993.

Christmas Cakes

Christmas Breads, Yule Bread, Yule Cakes

Bread is a staple food in European cuisine. Since medieval times European cooks have enriched this everyday food for the Christmas table. These early cooks began a tradition that continues to this day. People from many different nations still celebrate Christmas with a variety of rich breads and cakes.

European Christmas Breads and Cakes

The cuisine of medieval **Europe** did not feature a strong distinction between breads and cakes. For festive occasions bakers produced special breads we might consider akin to cake. As medieval cooks sharpened their understanding of various leavening agents, a distinction between bread and cake slowly began to emerge. Early Christmas cakes reflect this blurring of culinary categories. One early recipe for ginger cake mixed dry bread crumbs with spices and honey. The pasty dough resulting from this process was molded into various decorative shapes. Cakes featuring spices and honey were among the earliest European Christmas baked goods. Their descendants, often having evolved into cookies, populate contemporary Christmas celebrations. They include our own familiar **gingerbread**, northern Europe's peppernuts (*Pfeffernüsse*), **Germany**'s *Lebkuchen* and *Springerle*, and Holland's *speculaas*. Cooks of past eras also enriched breads and cakes by adding extra fats, dried and candied fruits, and nuts. The traditional holiday fare of many European nations still include breads of this sort. Examples include Italian *panettone*, German *Stollen*, Swedish *saffransbrod*, Norwegian *Julekake*, and Greek *Christopsomo*.

Yule Doughs

In the Middle Ages people celebrated Christmas with *Yule dows*, or "Yule doughs." These pastries, shaped like animals or people, frequently the baby **Jesus**, constituted a special holiday treat. Nineteenth-century English and American bakers revived this old custom, calling their creations "Yule dollies." They often shaped them like young girls or dolls, and decorated them with icing, colored illustrations (glued onto the cookies with eggwhite), feathers, or other adornments. Typically, these decorated cookies served as **ornaments** for the newly popular **Christmas tree**. Today's Christmas bakers still shape and decorate gingerbread "men" in similar ways.

Scandinavian Cakes and Customs

A number of European Christmas customs grew up around the special cakes and breads of the season. A Swedish document dating from the middle of the sixteenth century notes that at Christmas time bakers concocted a special Christmas loaf about the length, width, and height of a five-year-old child. The writer continues by noting that people gave this kind of bread away to friends and even to strangers as an act of Christmas charity. The Scandinavians rolled other Christmas loaves, of smaller dimensions, into symbolic shapes such as a cross, a boar, or a goat (*see also* **Boar's Head**; **Yule Goat**; **St. Lucy's Day**). Certain superstitions attached themselves to these special Christmas loaves. According to one belief, a family should not finish their Christmas cake until **Epiphany**. Another decreed that the family guard the cake untouched until **Candlemas**. One Norwegian custom suggested that the Christmas loaves be prepared from grain gleaned from the straw left over in the fields after harvest.

Twelfth Night and Christmas Cakes

For many centuries the English, French, Dutch, and German peoples celebrated **Twelfth Night** by eating cakes. In **France** the custom can be traced as far back as the thirteenth century. The cakes provided more than a fitting end for a holiday meal, however. A bean, pea, or tiny china doll was baked inside the cake. The diner whose slice of cake contained the object was hailed as **King of the Bean**. This "king" ruled over the remainder of the feast. Sometimes the baker also dropped a pea inside the cake batter. The woman who found the pea in her slice of cake reigned as queen alongside the king. A French custom suggested that the hosts of the Twelfth Night feast reserve the first piece of the cake for God and the second for the Virgin **Mary**. These slices were offered to the first poor person who came to the house.

By the eighteenth century English bakers had elevated Twelfth Night cakes into virtual pieces of art. They molded these enormous cakes into a variety of elaborate shapes and covered them with fanciful decorations made out of icing. For example, a baker might construct a cake that resembled a fortress, complete with flying flags and posted sentinels. Some were so heavy, they required two men to carry them. Bakeries displayed these examples of the confectioner's art in shop windows.

The celebration of Twelfth Night declined in the mid-nineteenth century. As a result of fading interest in the holiday, the Twelfth Night cake was drawn into the orbit of the more powerful midwinter holiday, Christmas. During this transition the cake shrank in size. Oddly enough, the custom of secreting charms within the Twelfth Night cake transferred itself to another Christmas dessert, **plum pudding**. Thereafter, the Christmas cake functioned solely as a homemade dessert.

Greek New Year Bread

In **Greece** the custom of inserting a special charm into holiday bread or cake attached itself to **New Year's** Eve celebrations instead of to Christmas or Epiphany. In Greece a special cake or bread known as *vasilopita*, or **St. Basil's** bread, appears on the table on New Year's Eve. The bread and cake are named after St. Basil the Great (c. 329-379), whose feast day Orthodox Christians observe on January 1. Housewives bake a coin into the vasilopita. Whoever finds the coin in their serving will attract good luck in the coming year. Some families observe a special ceremony when cutting and distributing the holiday bread. The head of the family blesses the bread and makes the sign of the cross over it. The bread is sliced and the first piece offered to Christ, the second to the Virgin Mary, the third to St. Basil, and the fourth to the poor. The next piece goes to the head of the family. The rest of the family receive their pieces according to age, the eldest first.

Further Reading

Henisch, Bridget Ann. *Cakes and Characters: An English Christmas Tradition.* London, England: Prospect Books, 1984.

Henriksen, Vera. *Christmas in Norway.* Oslo, Norway: Johan Grundt Tanum Forlag, 1970.

Hole, Christina. *British Folk Customs.* London, England: Hutchinson and Company, 1976.

Miles, Clement A. *Christmas in Ritual and Tradition.* 1912. Reprint. Detroit, Mich.: Omnigraphics, 1990.

Poole, Shona Crawford. *The Christmas Cookbook.* New York: Atheneum, 1979.

Rouvelas, Marilyn. *A Guide to Greek Traditions and Customs in America.* Bethesda, Md.: Attica Press, 1993.

Weaver, William Woys. *The Christmas Cook.* New York: HarperPerennial, 1990.

Christmas Candles
Yule Candle

In past centuries families throughout the British Isles, **Ireland**, **France**, **Denmark**, and Scandinavia observed Christmas by lighting especially large candles. Home Christmas celebrations took place in the glow of these enormous tapers. Some families lit the candles on Christmas Eve, in which case custom called for the candle to burn until morning. Others lit their candles on Christmas morning and kept them burning throughout the day. Large candles of this sort were also used in Christmas church services (*see also* **Christingle**).

People interpreted the meaning of these Christmas candles in several different ways. Many believed the large candle served as a natural symbol for the coming of **Jesus** Christ, "the light of the world." Others said it represented the **Star of Bethlehem**. Many folk beliefs suggest that people commonly viewed the home Christmas candle as representing the family's future in some way. In some parts of **England** people varied this custom by using many regular-sized candles instead of one extra-large one. In nineteenth-century England many grocers and chandlers (candlemakers) presented their regular customers with the **gift** of a large candle at Christmas. In parts of

Denmark people lit two candles, one representing the male head of the household, the other the female household head. Whichever burned out first was said to foretell which of them would die first. Scottish folklore claimed that if the Christmas candle burned out before midnight the family would soon experience some kind of calamity. Scandinavian tradition agreed that bad luck would surely visit any family whose **Yule** candle burned out during the holy night, possibly the death of a family member. While the flame burned, however, many Scandinavians believed that the light of the Yule candle conferred a blessing on all it touched. Families brought good things to eat and drink, money, clothing, and other desirable goods within the circle of candlelight in the hopes that they would be blessed with more of these things in the coming year.

Some peoples believed that the remains of the candle retained their power to bless and protect even after Christmas had passed. In Sweden people rubbed the stub of their Yule candle against their plows or used it to make the sign of the cross over their animals. In other parts of Scandinavia people fed the candle stub to their barnyard fowl or saved it as a charm against thunder and lightning. (*See also* **Advent Candle**.)

In **Estonia, Germany,** and **Lithuania** people light candles at family gravesites on Christmas Eve. This practice may be linked to old folk beliefs concerning the return of the dead at Christmas time (*see also* **Ghosts**; *for another Christmas Eve candle custom, see* **Australia, Christmas in**).

Further Reading

Crippen, Thomas G. *Christmas and Christmas Lore.* 1923. Reprint. Detroit, Mich.: Omnigraphics, 1990.

Henriksen, Vera. *Christmas in Norway.* Oslo, Norway: Johan Grundt Tanum Forlag, 1970.

Miles, Clement A. *Christmas in Ritual and Tradition.* 1912. Reprint. Detroit, Mich.: Omnigraphics, 1990.

Muir, Frank. *Christmas Customs and Traditions.* New York: Taplinger, 1977.

Pimlott, J. A. R. *The Englishman's Christmas.* Atlantic Highlands, N.J.: Humanities Press, 1978.

Weiser, Francis X. *The Christmas Book.* 1952. Reprint. Detroit, Mich.: Omnigraphics, 1990.

Christmas Card

Historians credit the English with the invention and popularization of the Christmas card during the early years of the Victorian era (*see also* **Victorian England, Christmas in**). By the 1860s an entire industry had grown up around the design and production of Christmas cards in **England**. This industry soon spread to other countries. Throughout the twentieth century ever-increasing numbers of people embraced the Christmas card, making the practice of sending greeting cards one of the **Christmas season**'s most popular customs.

Possible Origins

Researchers speculate that a number of pre-existing customs inspired the creation of the first Christmas card. **New Year's** cards, for example, date back to the early years of European printing. The oldest surviving New Year's card was printed in 1466. Apparently, these cards never became very popular. Many surviving examples depict the boy **Jesus** in the company of flowers and birds. These cards began to disappear in the sixteenth and seventeenth centuries, perhaps due to religious ideas popularized during the Reformation (*see also* **Puritans**). In the late eighteenth century the development of a new printing process called lithography corresponded with an increase in the production of New Year's cards.

Valentine cards probably exercised more influence on the look of the new Christmas cards than did New Year's cards. Valentine cards were already popular in the early nineteenth century when the very first Christmas cards were printed. Some early producers of Christmas cards used designs very similar to those they printed on Valentine cards. Nowadays, these romantic Christmas card designs, brimming with leaves, flowers, and lace, seem unsuited to the Christmas season.

Even before the advent of the Christmas card, some people sent Christmas or New Year's letters (*see also* **Children's Letters**). As early as the 1730s English writer Alexander Pope (1688-1744) remarked upon the frequency with which the English sent seasonal greetings and good wishes to friends around Christmas time. Eventually the Christmas card replaced the Christmas or New Year's letter. This change dismayed those who preferred a more substantial greeting than could be conveyed in the brief sentiment printed on the cards.

The First Christmas Card

The first Christmas card was designed by Englishman J. C. Horsley (1817-1903) in 1843. Three separate images adorn the front of the card. A large center drawing depicts a family gathered around a table, wine glasses in hand. One woman gives a small child a sip of wine, a detail which caused temperance advocates to object. A smaller side panel depicts a well-dressed woman draping a cloak around a poor woman and child. The other side panel depicts the distribution of food among the poor. The producer of this card printed about 1,000 copies and sold them for one shilling each.

Early English Christmas Cards

The new custom did not catch on right away. It took two decades for the Christmas card to establish itself as an annual institution in England. The advent of the penny post, begun in 1840, provided an inexpensive means of posting the cards, which undoubtedly permitted the custom of sending Christmas cards to spread. Before that time, not only had postal rates been higher, but also the post office charged the postage to the addressee rather than to the sender. The public responded enthusiastically to the new postal system. Between 1840 and 1845 the number of letters sent in Great Britain nearly doubled.

The first Christmas cards were modeled after Victorian visiting cards and so did not fold in any way. These small rectangles of pasteboard, about the size of an index card, were printed on one side only. The decorated side bore a lithographed or etched drawing, a greeting, and blank space for the names of both the sender and the addressee. By the 1870s manufacturers had started producing larger cards and folded cards. Some of the early folded cards were designed to open out like cupboard doors; others fell into accordion folds.

Trick cards also originated in the 1870s. Their clever designs delighted Victorians. Pulling a paper lever on the face of a card, for example, might add to or subtract something from the design or change it completely. Pop-up cards also tickled Victorian fancies. Some cleverly designed cards contained hidden images that appeared only if viewed from a certain angle or in a certain light.

Victorian Christmas Cards in Their Heyday

By the 1880s Victorian Christmas cards reflected the ornate taste of the age. Designers embellished the images printed on the cards with a variety of materials, including paper lace, real lace, shells, seaweed, dried grass, flowers, silk, velvet, chenille, tinsel, celluloid, crewel work, metal plates, and small sachets of scented powders. They frosted surfaces with powdered glass or aluminum. For a finishing touch they embossed or scalloped the edges of their cards, or even finished them with lace, cords, ribbons, or silk.

Some of the most common images found on Victorian Christmas cards are still familiar symbols of the holiday to us today. These include **holly, ivy, mistletoe,** and, to a lesser extent, **robins, wrens,** winter landscapes, and Christmas feasts and parties. Other images that adorned their cards seem less central to the festival. For example, flowers, shrubs, and trees, often in great profusion, served as perhaps the most popular subjects portrayed on the Victorian Christmas card. Due to the abundance of flowers and leaves, these cards often appear to depict a summer, rather than a winter, scene. Many other cards carried images of children, often at play. Some of these children seem to be unnaturally angelic lads and lasses, others clearly pranksters. Animals, often portrayed carrying out human activities and sometimes wearing human clothing as well, provided another popular subject for the Victorian Christmas card.

Victorians also enjoyed Christmas cards that featured new inventions, such as the bicycle, the steamship, and the motorcar. Other Victorian Christmas card subjects strike modern viewers as somewhat inappropriate images with which to represent Christmas. For example, portraits of beautiful girls and women appeared frequently on Victorian Christmas cards. Some of these women and girls appear partially nude or clad only in gauzy robes, startling modern sensibilities conditioned to approach the Christmas card as something devoid of sensuality.

The dead robin constitutes another curious Victorian preference in Christmas card decoration. During the 1880s many of the cards featuring robins depicted a dead bird lying in the snow. Perhaps the Victorian fondness for images and stories that evoked pity and other tender emotions can explain this rather bizarre motif.

Early American Christmas Cards

Although the first American Christmas card dates back to the 1850s, the American Christmas card industry did not take off until the 1870s. Historians credit a German immigrant named Louis Prang with bringing this industry to full flower. In 1875 his print shop introduced a line of visiting cards that included a Christmas greeting. An appreciative public snapped up his entire stock. Prang expanded his line of Christmas cards in the years that followed. At first his designs resembled those of the early Victorian cards from England. Embellished with flowers, leaves, butterflies and birds, the printed images evoked springtime rather than illustrating the Christmas sentiments that accompanied them. Soon, however, Prang's workshop began to turn out cards decorated with recognizable **Christmas symbols**, such as holly, ivy, and **poinsettias**. As these designs became more complex, the cards grew in size, eventually measuring about seven by ten inches. The American public loved Prang's novelties. Many foreign buyers also admired and collected Prang's cards.

Several factors contributed to Prang's extraordinary success. A printer by trade, Prang combined expert printing skills, innovative lithography techniques, and clever marketing ploys to catch the public's attention. But Prang was more than a savvy salesman. He passionately believed that mass-produced images could introduce fine art to those who would never otherwise be exposed to it. Prang's studio developed a reputation for high artistic standards.

In 1880 he instituted a yearly competition for the best Christmas card design. Prang put his money where his mouth was. He awarded $1,000 to the first-place winner and $500 to the second-place winner. He also gave $300 and $200 prizes. Prang called on well-known figures in the American art world to serve as judges, including stained-glass artist Louis C. Tiffany (1848-1933), painter Samuel Colman (1832-1920), and architect Richard M. Hunt (1827-1895). Prang also let the public vote on which designs they preferred, and winners of the "Public Prizes" received the same hefty cash awards as those contestants whose work was selected by the panel of artists. Although Prang's competition lasted only a few years, during its day it was considered one of the highlights of the New York art season. Prang's dissatisfaction with the quality of the works presented at his competitions caused him to switch tactics after a few years and commission well-known artists to submit designs.

Unlike his competitors in Victorian England, Prang rejected trick cards and scorned fancy embellishments of lace and other materials as vulgar. During the 1870s and 1880s Christmas cards printed in continental Europe began to infiltrate British and American markets. Prang left the Christmas card business in the 1890s, when his sales figures began to falter.

Increasing Popularity

In spite of his enthusiasm for popularizing refined art, Prang's expensive Christmas cards circulated primarily among the well-to-do. During the 1890s and 1900s the majority of American Christmas **gift** givers exchanged flimsy knickknacks with their friends. By the second decade of the twentieth century, though, Americans turned towards cards as a tasteful and inexpensive alternative for the useless trinkets everyone gave and, apparently, no one wanted. The new, inexpensive Christmas cards quickly grew in popularity, especially during World War I.

Today, American greeting card manufacturers sell more cards for Christmas than any other holiday. In 2001 the nation's Greeting Card

Association projected sales of 2 billion Christmas cards. These cards account for just over 60 percent of the industry's total sales. Indeed, it has been estimated that over 75 percent of all Americans send greeting cards at Christmas time.

Further Reading

Buday, George. *The History of the Christmas Card*. 1954. Reprint. Detroit, Mich.: Omnigraphics, 1992.

Comfort, David. *Just Say Noel!* New York: Fireside Books, 1995.

Muir, Frank. *Christmas Customs and Traditions*. New York: Taplinger, 1977.

Restad, Penne. *Christmas in America*. New York: Oxford University Press, 1995.

The Time-Life Book of Christmas. New York: Prentice Hall, 1987.

Waits, William. *The Modern Christmas in America*. New York: New York University Press, 1993.

Web Sites

A site sponsored by the Greeting Card Association:
http://www.greetingcard.org

A site sponsored by Victoriana.com contains pages that offer images and text descriptions of Victorian Christmas cards:
http://www.victoriana.com/christmas/default.htm

A Christmas Carol

A Christmas Carol, by Charles Dickens (1812-1870), is perhaps the best-known and best-loved Christmas story of all time. Some writers even credit the tale with changing the way nineteenth-century Britons and Americans celebrated Christmas. *A Christmas Carol* tells the story of a greedy, rich, Christmas-hating old man named Ebenezer Scrooge. One Christmas Eve Scrooge receives a visit from three spirits. These spirits — the Ghost of Christmas Past, the Ghost of Christmas Present, and the Ghost of Christmas Yet To Come — show him scenes from his past, present, and future. This supernatural experience transforms him into a joyous, generous soul who cherishes Christmas above all other times of year.

Life and Times of Charles Dickens

Charles Dickens was born on February 7, 1812, just outside Portsmouth, **England**. The second of seven children, Charles was brought up in a lower-middle-class household plagued by his father's tendency to fall into debt. In 1821 the Dickens family moved to London where the young Charles witnessed firsthand the poverty and despair of the city's slums. In 1824, Charles's father was sent to Marshalsea Prison for failure to pay off a debt. The entire family moved into the prison, except Charles who, at the age of twelve, went to work in a blacking (shoe polish) factory. Although he was not treated cruelly, the young Charles worked twelve hours a day and felt deeply shamed by his family's situation. Several months later Charles's father inherited a small sum of money, which permitted him to pay the debt and leave prison. Although Charles's mother wanted her son to continue working at the blacking factory, Charles's father insisted that he receive some kind of education. Even after he became a successful novelist, Dickens's resented his mother for her willingness to send him back to a life of drudgery.

In 1827 Charles began his adult career as a solicitor's clerk. Shortly thereafter, he mastered shorthand and became a reporter. In 1833 he began to submit sketches and stories to newspapers and magazines under his pen name, "Boz." In a few years he acquired a wide readership. By 1837 *Sketches by Boz* and *The Pickwick Papers*, both published serially, had brought him fame and financial security. He went on to become one of Victorian England's most prolific and best-loved authors. Dickens never forgot his early brushes with poverty, however, and throughout his life he wielded both his voice and his pen against his society's harsh treatment of the poor. His works of fiction offered middle-class readers disturbing glimpses inside nineteenth-century workhouses (prison-like institutions meting out hard labor to the destitute), painted moving portraits of those confined to debtors' prisons, and sketched the often-desperate plight of the working poor.

The Writing of A Christmas Carol

In an indirect way Dickens's concern for the poor brought him the inspiration needed to write *A Christmas Carol.* In September of 1843, at the invitation of Miss Angela Burdett Coutts, a wealthy philanthropist and a friend of Dickens, he toured one of London's Ragged Schools. Funded by private charity, these schools sought to educate some of the city's poorest children. The visit moved him deeply. Several weeks later he traveled to Manchester to speak at a fundraising event for the Athenaeum, an organization dedicated to educating workers, where he addressed the link between poverty and ignorance. While in Manchester, the idea of transforming his impressions of the Ragged School into a work of fiction planted itself in his imagination. In October he plunged into a new story called *A Christmas Carol.* To be sure, financial as well as social concerns motivated Dickens to undertake this new project. Sales of his latest novel, *Martin Chuzzlewit*, were floundering. Dickens felt sure that a story like the *Carol* would appeal to readers at Christmas time and thus generate needed cash.

Dickens blazed through the writing of the *Carol*, completing the manuscript in only six weeks. The project seized hold of him, inspiring him to work from morning until late at night. He passed some of these nights striding as many as fifteen or twenty miles through the shadowy, still London streets, meditating on the story. In a letter to a friend he confessed that the work so charged his emotions, he found himself alternately laughing and weeping.

Dickens financed the publication of the slim little book himself, insisting on illustrations and a quality binding. It arrived in bookstores on December 19, 1843. Dickens complained that booksellers seemed uninterested in promoting the story. Nevertheless, the entire first printing, 6,000 copies, sold out in five days. After subtracting what it had cost him to produce the book, though, Dickens earned very little from its first printing. Still, Dickens celebrated Christmas merrily that year, exclaiming in a letter to a friend that he had rarely experienced a **Christmas season** so full of dining, dancing, theatergoing, party **games**, and good cheer. He even attended a children's party where he entertained the assembled company with magic tricks, to all appearances dumping the raw ingredients of a **plum pudding** into a friend's hat and pulling out the finished product.

Public Readings

By March of 1844, three months after its first printing, *A Christmas Carol* was in its sixth edition. Enthusiastic letters poured in from an appreciative public. Some readers told Dickens that they kept the book on a little shelf all by itself, others that they read it aloud to their families. In 1853 Dickens himself began a series of public readings of the work that would last the rest of his life.

As the public readings became more frequent, Dickens developed them into polished performances. It took him three hours to read through *A Christmas Carol* as printed, so he began to edit his own little copy of the book, eliminating dialogue and description that he felt could be cut without damaging the tale. He reduced the story to two hours, added some stage directions, and memorized the entire text. The public readings thus became recitations. Just in case his memory failed him, he kept a copy of the book with him on stage.

Dickens performed his first public reading of the *Carol* in December of 1853 as a benefit for the Birmingham and Midland Institute. More than two thousand people attended. Charities soon besieged the author with requests that he perform a reading on their behalf. Dickens complied with some of these requests, but also began a series of public readings for which he sold tickets. These readings generated a tidy second income for the author. Dickens incorporated parts of his other works in these public readings as well. *A Christmas Carol*, however, remained one of the most popular and most often requested works in his repertoire.

In 1865 Dickens performed a series of public readings in the United States. He opened in Boston with a reading of *A Christmas Carol*. The ticket line stretched half a mile in length on the night before the box office opened. Although the tickets sold for $2 apiece, scalpers priced tickets to the sold-out performance as high as $26 each. Many prominent American literary figures attended this reading. Dickens continued on to Philadelphia, New York, Baltimore, and Washington, D.C. In New York five thousand people stood in line on a bitterly cold night waiting for the chance to buy a ticket in the morning. In Washington Dickens received an invitation to meet President Andrew Johnson.

In the spring of 1870 Dickens struggled to complete a series of scheduled readings. During intermissions he staggered backstage to lie on a sofa while concerned doctors checked his vital signs. After completing the March 15 reading of *A Christmas Carol*, he returned to the stage for a final round of applause and announced, with tears on his face, that the audience had just witnessed his last public performance. He died three months later, on June 9, 1870, and was buried in Westminster Abbey alongside the composer George Frideric Handel, another great contributor to the artistic legacy of Christmas (*see also* **Messiah**).

The **Carol** *as a Ghost Story*

Contemporary readers tend to approach *A Christmas Carol* as a tale about the holiday, thus overlooking the fact that it is also a **ghost** story. In Dickens's day, English tradition called for the telling of ghost stories at Christmas time. Dickens conceived *A Christmas Carol* as an exemplary addition to this genre. He draws our attention to the ghostly aspect of the tale in its full title, which reads *A Christmas Carol in Prose, Being a Ghost Story of Christmas*. The preface continues the ghost theme in a humorous vein: "I have endeavoured in this Ghostly little book to raise the Ghost of an Idea which shall not put my readers out of humour with themselves, with each other, with the season, or with me. May it haunt their houses pleasantly, and no one wish to lay it." Dickens urged his readers to approach the tale as a classic English ghost story. In fact, he advised the public to read the *Carol* out loud, in a cold room by candlelight.

The **Carol** *as Personal History*

Dickens's *Carol* is more than a simple ghost story, however. It contains a clear moral message about the perils of selfishness, both for the individual and for society. Readers familiar with Dickens's consistent admiration of humility, simplicity, and familial warmth, as expressed in his many works of fiction, may be surprised to learn that in a letter to a friend Dickens admitted that he based the character of Scrooge on the worst aspects of his own personality. Perhaps because of his own childhood hardships, Dickens sometimes obsessed about the benefits of wealth and the need to make money. In addition, unlike Scrooge's clerk, the poor but noble Bob Cratchit, Dickens was neither affectionate nor attentive as a husband and father.

Dickens plucked several other elements of the *Carol* story out of his own life experience. The Cratchit home resembled the house that Dickens lived in when his family first moved to London. Like Scrooge, Dickens had an elder sister named Frances, whom he called Fanny. Dickens's own younger brother, known to the family as "Tiny Fred," and his nephew, a sickly, disabled boy, inspired the creation of Tiny Tim. Dickens's experience at the Ragged Schools and the Manchester Athenaeum materialized as Ignorance and Want, the two starving children who cling to the legs of the Ghost of Christmas Present. The Spirit cautions Scrooge, and by extension his Victorian audience, to "Beware them both, and all of their degree, but most of all beware this boy [Ignorance], for on his brow I see that written which is Doom, unless the writing be erased."

The **Carol** *as Christmas Philosophy*

In *A Christmas Carol* Dickens insists that the Christmas holiday offers a solution to the problems of selfishness and greed. As the story closes, the narrator assures us that Scrooge became a kind, humble, and generous person as a result of his experience with the Spirits. *A Christmas Carol* suggests that Christmas has the potential to awaken all our hearts and thus to transform society. Scrooge's young nephew understands the power of Christmas to renew and transform, and early in the story explains that Christmas time is

> a good time; a kind, forgiving, charitable, pleasant time; the only I know of, in the long calendar of the year, when men and women seem by one consent to open their shut-up hearts freely, and to think of people below them as if they really were fellow-passengers to the grave, and not another race of creatures bound on other journeys. And therefore, . . . though it has never put a scrap of gold or silver in my pocket, I believe that is *has* done me good, and *will* do me good; and I say, God bless it!

Dickens himself was not an overtly religious man. Nevertheless, the Christmas philosophy outlined in *A Christmas Carol* promotes a secular observance of the festival in keeping with the religious spirit of the holiday. Given Dickens's indifference towards religion, it is somewhat ironic that this approach to the holiday helped to heal the centuries-old breach between those religious sects that celebrated Christmas and those that condemned it (*see* **America, Christmas in Colonial; Puritans**). In its day, however, some critics condemned the *Carol* for purporting to discuss the subject of Christmas with few references to the birth of **Jesus**. This omission may well reflect Dickens's dislike of the Church, which he found sadly out of touch with the social problems of his day.

Other Christmas Works

Although *A Christmas Carol* became Dickens's best-known treatise on the subject of Christmas, the holiday figures prominently in other writings as well. He wrote a number of short stories concerning Christmas, including "The Chimes," "The Cricket on the Hearth," "The Battle of Life," "The Haunted Man," "The Holly Tree," "The Seven Poor Travellers," "The Poor Relation's Story," and "The Haunted House." In addition, *The Pickwick Papers* contains a delightful depiction of Christmas festivities at a large house in the country. American author Washington Irving's (1783-1859) earlier depiction of Christmas celebrations in an English manor house may well have inspired this passage. Indeed, regarding his love of Irving's books, Dickens once confessed, "I don't go upstairs two nights out of seven without taking Washington Irving under my arm." The *Pickwick Papers* also contains the story of a grumpy, old sexton (church custodian) visited by ghosts on Christmas Eve. Dickens expanded and improved upon this plot idea in *A Christmas Carol*.

Dickens's portrayal of Christmas as a season of good cheer among family and friends and good will towards the less fortunate came to represent the ideal version of the holiday for many nineteenth-century Britons and Americans (*see also* **America, Christmas in Nineteenth-Century; Victorian England, Christmas in**). These ideals still color contemporary Christmas celebrations, perhaps explaining the *Carol*'s enduring popularity. Indeed, public readings, stage adaptations, and screen versions of this classic Christmas tale continue to delight audiences each year at Christmas time.

Further Reading

Davis, Paul. *Charles Dickens, A to Z.* New York: Facts on File, 1998.

Dickens, Charles. *The Christmas Books.* Oxford, England: Oxford University Press, 1960.

Hallinan, Tim. *A Christmas Carol Christmas Book.* New York: International Business Machines Corporation, 1984.

MacKenzie, Norman, and Jeanne MacKenzie. *Dickens, A Life.* Oxford, England: Oxford University Press, 1979.

Pimlott, J. A. R. *The Englishman's Christmas.* Atlantic Highlands, N.J.: Humanities Press, 1978.

Priestly, J. B. *Charles Dickens and His World.* New York: Charles Scribner's Sons, 1961.

Sammon, Paul. *The Christmas Carol Trivia Book.* New York: Citadel Press, 1994.

Stapleton, Michael, comp. *The Cambridge Guide to English Literature.* Cambridge, England: Cambridge University Press, 1983.

Web Site

A site sponsored by the Dickens Project at the University of California contains information about *A Christmas Carol*: http://humwww.ucsc.edu/ dickens/dea/ACC/ACC.index.html

Christmas Carol
Noël, Villancico

Over the centuries Christmas has inspired countless songs. Which of the many pieces of vocal music written for Christmas qualify as true Christmas carols? Most writers assume Christmas carols to be those songs about Christmas whose tune and lyrics are widely known and whose popularity is maintained primarily through folk traditions rather than **commercial** promotions. By this definition, the fine Christmas works written by classical composers are not true Christmas carols, since they are musically quite complex and known to relatively small numbers of people. The fact that people sing carols for enjoyment and entertainment also figures in their definition. This criterion might exclude a number of lesser-known church hymns, since people usually sing them only during church services. In addition, most carols take as their subject matter the legends, customs, or religious celebration of Christmas. Therefore, some people would not include popular songs such as "I Saw Mommy Kissing Santa Claus," or even the hit song **"White Christmas"** in a collection of carols, since these songs achieved popularity through commercial mechanisms and do not address traditional Christmas themes or religious celebration. Others might quarrel with these criteria, arguing that the subject matter of these songs and the manner in which they achieved popularity simply reflect the commercial interests and cultural outlook of the twentieth century.

Why are these traditional Christmas songs called "carols," anyway? Some scholars trace the English word "carol" all the way back to the ancient Greek word *coros*. In ancient Greek drama the coros, or "chorus," appeared from time to time during the play singing commentaries on the plot and often dancing as well. By the late Middle Ages, the word "carol" had come to mean singing and dancing in a circle, as children do when singing "Ring Around the Rosy." In the Middle Ages people caroled on many different occasions. By the sixteenth century, however, this musical genre had acquired a special association with the **Christmas season**, while its earlier association with dance was fading away. Already a large number of Christmas carols circulated throughout Europe. A number of these, such as the English "I Saw Three Ships" and the German "Lo, How a Rose E'er Blooming," are still sung today.

Earliest Christmas Songs

The earliest recorded Christmas carol was the one that the **angels** sang to the **shepherds** when announcing **Jesus'** birth (*see* **Gospel According to Luke**):

> Glory to God in the highest,
> And on earth peace among men with whom he is pleased!
> (Luke 2:14).

Latin hymn writers provided the first Christmas songs sung by the early Christians. "Veni, redemptor gentium" (Redeemer of the Nations Come), written by St. Ambrose, archbishop of Milan (339-397), is the earliest surviving example of these works. Others include "A Solis Ortus Cardine" (From East to West, From Shore to Shore) by Sedulius (fifth century) and works by the Spanish poet Prudentius (348-after 405). These early Christmas hymns were written by monks or other religious scholars for use in worship. They tend to approach Christmas from a theological perspective and emphasize the role of the Nativity in humankind's salvation.

Medieval Christmas Carols

In the late Middle Ages a new spirit slowly infused the poetry and songs written about Christmas. Artists began to describe the people and events of the Nativity and react to them in emotional terms. Some credit St. Francis of Assisi (1181 or 1182-1226) with instilling a new spirit of simplicity and joy in worship, thereby indirectly bringing about these changes (*see also* **Nativity Scene**). Some even believe that he wrote Christmas carols. If he did, none have survived. The work of one of his followers, the Franciscan mystic Jacapone da Todi (1228-1306), exemplifies the impact of these new attitudes towards the Nativity. His songs depict the Christmas miracle in homely images, such as that of the Virgin cradling and nursing her child. Whereas earlier church hymns had been written in Latin, a language known only by scholars, da Todi composed joyful songs in Italian so that ordinary people could sing them. These innovations gave birth to the Christmas carol as we know it.

The Golden Age

The creativity unleashed in the late Middle Ages revealed itself in an outpouring of Christmas songs over the next several centuries. By the fourteenth century Christmas carols in vernacular languages were sprouting up all over **Europe**. In **Germany** carol writers blossomed under the liberating influence of mystics like Meister Eckehart (1260?-1327). Fourteenth- and fifteenth-century German carol writers bequeathed us such treasures as "Lo, How a Rose E'er Blooming," "In Dulci Jubilo" (Good Christian Men Rejoice), and "Joseph, Lieber Joseph Mein."

In late medieval **England** the mystery or miracle plays performed around Christmas time inspired the composition of a number of carols (*see also* **Nativity Play**). "The Coventry Carol," for example, accompanied the Pageant of the Shearmen and Tailors, a Christmas play produced annually by that guild. In the fifteenth and sixteenth centuries Christmas carols and verses flowed from the pens of English writers. This epoch gave birth to such well-loved songs as "The First Nowell" (*see also* **Noel**) and "God Rest You Merry, Gentlemen." In fact, the earliest surviving collection of English Christmas carols dates from this period and bears the following inscription:

> I pray you, sirrus, boothe moore and lase,
> Sing these caroles in Cristëmas [Miles, 1992, 27].

These English carols played a central role in another English Christmas custom, wassailing (*see* **Wassail**). Indeed, a number of traditional English and Welsh carols treat secular Christmas customs, such as feasting, drinking, and seasonal decorations. Examples include "The Boar's Head Carol," first printed in 1521, and others more difficult to assign dates to, such as "The Holly and the Ivy," "Deck the Halls," and various wassailing songs (*see also* **Boar's Head**). In medieval and Renaissance England people viewed merrymaking as an integral part of the celebration of the Nativity. As one English carol writer put it:

> Make we myrth
> For Christes byrth [Pimlott, 1978, 16].

Further south in **France**, carol writing blossomed in the sixteenth and seventeenth centuries. Although a number of French Christmas carols, or *noëls*, appeared in the fifteenth century, the real surge in the composition and spread of these songs occurred in the following century. Many songwriters of this era placed the singer in the position of one of the original pilgrims to **Bethlehem**. The songs describe the singer's journey and the people met along the way, who typically turn out to be from neighboring villages. The singer identifies the other pilgrims by their behavior and appearance, which usually exemplifies the negative reputation that their town has acquired in the eyes of its neighbors. By contrast, the seventeenth-century Provençal carol, "Bring a Torch, Jeannette, Isabella," sweetly urges villagers to pay reverence to the sleeping Christ child. Perhaps its gentler tone contributes to the song's continuing appeal.

In **Spain** carol writing flourished in the sixteenth and early seventeenth centuries. Unlike the satirical carols popular in France, these Spanish carols, or *villancicos*, convey both tenderness and reverence. The following verses from an old Spanish carol exemplify these sentiments:

> In a porch, full of cobwebs
> Between the mule and the ox
> The Savior of souls is born. . . .

In the porch at Bethlehem
Are star, sun, and moon
The Virgin and St. Joseph
And the Child who lies in the cradle.

In Bethlehem they touch fire
From the porch the flame issues
It is a star of heaven
Which has fallen into the straw. . . .

To the new-born child all bring a gift
I am little and have nothing
I bring him my heart [Miles, 1992, 66-67].

The Reformation and Beyond

The change in religious beliefs and attitudes associated with the Reformation checked the creation of carols in many areas of northern Europe, especially Britain. In England the **Puritans'** rise to power in the mid-seventeenth century corresponded with a drop-off in the writing of carols. Nevertheless, the common people continued to sing the old carols and so kept many of them alive. Sterner religious authorities gained control in Scotland. In the late sixteenth century these authorities forbade many old Christmas pastimes altogether, including carol singing. In Germany the Reformation also inhibited carol writers, although at the same time it inspired the creation of some fine Christmas hymns. In France the Reformation had little effect on Christmas music. Instead, the change of attitudes that accompanied the revolution of 1789 hushed the singing of noëls and discouraged their composition.

The spirit of the Reformation infused many of the Christmas songs written in the centuries that followed with the flavor of church hymns. Indeed, many of the seventeenth-, eighteenth-, and nineteenth-century carols familiar to us today were written expressly for church use or by members of the clergy. Examples include "Joy to the World," written by the famous English hymn writer Isaac Watts in 1692, and "O Come All Ye Faithful" penned by another religious Englishman, John Francis Wade, in 1742. An anonymous French composer gave us "Angels We Have Heard on High" in the mid-eighteenth century. Fellow Frenchman Adolphe Charles Adam of-fered "O Holy Night" in the following century. English hymn writer James Montgomery wrote the words to "Angels from the Realms of Glory" in 1816, which were later paired with a tune composed by Henry Smart.

In the early 1800s an Austrian priest and his organist composed "Silent Night." Its enduring popularity notwithstanding, "Silent Night" came into the world as the slap-dash creation of a single evening: Christmas Eve, 1818. Finding himself without a functioning organ for the Christmas Eve service, Father Josef Mohr scribbled down some verse and asked his organist Franz Gruber to quickly score it for voices so that the choir could sing it for that evening's **Midnight Mass**. The song circulated for many years among Austrian folk singers and eventually acquired international popularity before its authorship was traced back to Mohr and Gruber.

The Nineteenth-Century Revival

The Christmas carol appeared to be dying out in early nineteenth-century England. Observers of English folk customs lamented that only a scattered handful of old people knew and sang the traditional songs. By mid-century the institution of the **waits** (bands of night-time carolers) was collapsing. English folklorists predicted the imminent demise of the Christmas carol. These alarm bells inspired the collection and publication of several volumes of English Christmas carols in the early to mid-nineteenth century. The publication of these collections coincided with the budding Victorian interest in the celebration of Christmas (*see* **Victorian England, Christmas in**). Soon the flagging tradition of the Christmas carol gained new momentum among the middle classes. By the 1870s churches began to incorporate these almost forgotten Christmas songs into their holiday services. In 1880 an Anglican bishop first devised the Ceremony of Nine Lessons and Carols, a special Christmas service blending Bible readings with carol singing.

The nineteenth century not only hosted a revival of the Christmas carol in Europe, but also witnessed a burst of new interest in the genre in the United States. Americans were just beginning to accept Christmas as a public and religious holiday in the mid-nineteenth

century after centuries of opposition by Puritans and other religious denominations (*see* **America, Christmas in Nineteenth-Century**). As if making up for lost time, a number of American clergymen made significant contributions to our Christmas carol heritage in this era. A Unitarian minister named Edmund Sears composed "It Came Upon a Midnight Clear" in 1849. Two Episcopalian clergymen soon added their contributions to the American repertoire. The Reverend John Henry Hopkins, Jr., authored "We Three Kings of Orient Are" in 1857, and the Reverend Phillips Brooks presented "O Little Town of Bethlehem" in 1865.

Carol Services and Ceremonies

A number of carol services and ceremonies predate the nineteenth-century English **Ceremony of Lessons and Carols**. Historical evidence suggests that the Welsh attended yearly **Plygain** services at least as far back as the seventeenth century. Las **Posadas**, an Hispanic folk play commemorating **Mary** and **Joseph**'s search for shelter in Bethlehem, also dates back hundreds of years. Other Christmas carol ceremonies include the Scandinavian *Julotta* service and the contemporary American Christmas pageant. Julotta, a church service consisting mostly of carol singing, takes place early on Christmas morning in churches glowing with the light of hundreds of candles. The Australian "Carols by Candlelight" represents a twentieth-century addition to the world's carol ceremonies. Radio announcer Norman Banks organized and broadcast the first community carol-sing in Melbourne in the late 1930s. An appreciative public turned the event into a yearly tradition. Decades later the event flourishes, drawing tens of thousands of people together to sing the traditional songs of the season by candlelight (*see also* **Australia, Christmas in**).

Twentieth-Century America

Throughout the month of December contemporary Americans absorb Christmas carols in a variety of formats, from Christmas concerts to church services to radio and television specials to mall Muzak. The diversity of songs included in these programs reflects our rich historical and ethnic heritage. In addition to a variety of old

European carols and the nineteenth-century Anglo-American additions mentioned above, the American carol repertoire includes a number of African-American folk songs. These include the beloved nineteenth-century spirituals "Go Tell It on the Mountain," "Mary Had a Baby," and "Rise Up, Shepherd, and Follow."

Twentieth-century composers have unleashed legions of new Christmas songs. Unlike their nineteenth-century counterparts, however, relatively few of these new songs are religious in subject matter. Exceptions include the haunting ballad "I Wonder as I Wander" and the simple, reverent "Do You Hear What I Hear?" Many of the more familiar tunes, however, adopt a more secular approach to the celebration of Christmas. Some of these songs include "Rudolf the Red-Nosed Reindeer," "Let It Snow, Let It Snow, Let It Snow," "Frosty the Snowman," "Silver Bells," "Santa Claus Is Coming to Town," "Winter Wonderland," and "White Christmas." These songs reflect twentieth-century Americans' renewed interest in the secular joys of the season and the delights it brings to children.

Further Reading

Crippen, Thomas G. *Christmas and Christmas Lore*. 1923. Reprint. Detroit, Mich.: Omnigraphics, 1990.

Dearmer, Percy, R. Vaughan Williams, and Martin Shaw. *The Oxford Book of Carols*. London, England: Oxford University Press, 1965.

Del Re, Gerard, and Patricia Del Re. *The Christmas Almanack*. Garden City, N.Y.: Doubleday, 1979.

Duncan, Edmondstoune. *The Story of the Carol*. 1911. Reprint. Detroit, Mich.: Omnigraphics, 1992.

Emurian, Ernest K. *Stories of Christmas Carols*. Revised edition. Boston, Mass.: W. A. Wilde Company, 1967.

Hadfield, Miles, and John Hadfield. *The Twelve Days of Christmas*. Boston, Mass.: Little, Brown and Company, 1961.

Hutton, Ronald. *The Stations of the Sun*. Oxford, England: Oxford University Press, 1996.

Leach, Maria, ed. *Funk and Wagnalls Standard Dictionary of Folklore, Mythology, and Legend*. New York: Harper and Row, 1984.

Miles, Clement A. *Christmas in Ritual and Tradition*. 1912. Reprint. Detroit, Mich.: Omnigraphics, 1992.

Palmer, Geoffrey, and Noel Lloyd. *A Year of Festivals*. London, England: Frederick Warne, 1972.

Pimlott, J. A. R. *The Englishman's Christmas*. Atlantic Highlands, N.J.: Humanities Press, 1978.

Studwell, William E. *The Christmas Carol Reader*. Binghamton, N.Y.: Haworth Press, 1995.

———. *Christmas Carols: A Reference Guide*. New York: Garland Publishing, 1985.

Christmas Club

In the United States many banks and credit unions offer their customers the opportunity to save money for Christmas by opening a special "Christmas club" savings account. Account holders make small but regular deposits throughout the year. In early November the bank sends the customer a check for the total amount saved. These savings then finance the purchase of Christmas **gifts** and other seasonal expenditures.

A shoe factory owner from Carlisle, Pennsylvania, devised the first Christmas club for his workers in the year 1905. In 1910 a salesman named Herbert F. Rawll got wind of the idea and began to promote the clubs to banks. The opportunity for personal profit fired Rawll's enthusiasm for the project. As a ledger salesman, Rawll not only sold banks on the idea of sponsoring Christmas club accounts, but also provided them with the special forms needed to keep track of the transactions. Both banks and bank customers eagerly embraced the new accounts. In two years the dynamic Rawll had convinced more than 800 banks to offer the special accounts. By the mid-1920s, about 8,000 banks offered Christmas club accounts to their patrons.

The new Christmas clubs flourished because they fulfilled the needs of financial institutions and consumers. In the early twentieth century manufactured items all but replaced the homemade gifts that had characterized American Christmas giving in the nineteenth century (*see also* **Commercialism**). The clubs provided consumers a mechanism through which they could accumulate enough money to buy and to give ready-made Christmas gifts. In the meantime banks were searching for ways to attract new customers, especially lower- and middle-income people who had previously avoided putting their money in banks. The new accounts succeeded in bringing in these new customers. Moreover, they helped overcome the popularly held image of banks as snobby, coldhearted institutions that served only the well-to-do.

Today many Americans still rely on Christmas clubs to fund their Christmas purchases. The conditions placed on these accounts vary from bank to bank. Consumers interested in opening a Christmas club account should compare interest rates, penalties for early withdrawal, minimum payments, fees, and balance requirements.

Further Reading

Del Re, Gerard, and Patricia Del Re. *The Christmas Almanack*. Garden City, N.Y.: Doubleday, 1979.

Waits, William B. *The Modern Christmas in America*. New York: New York University Press, 1993.

Christmas Crackers

In Great Britain Christmas crackers are a common holiday party favor. Wrapped in colored paper, these cardboard tubes contain a fortune (or motto) and a small toy. When pulled from both ends, they burst open with a popping noise.

Christmas crackers present us with one of the few Christmas customs whose origins are definitely known. They were invented in the mid-nineteenth century by an English confectioner named Thomas Smith. Smith visited Paris in 1844. He brought home with him the idea of marketing a bonbon wrapped in a bit of tissue paper, similar to those he had seen in Paris shop windows. Sales were slow, especially after Christmas, so Smith came up with the idea of adding a motto. This helped, but more was needed. Soon he hit upon a way of getting the crackers to open with a small bang. Smith marketed his novelty as a Christmas amusement in 1846, hoping to cash in on the growing Christmas market (*see also* **Victorian England, Christmas in**). Smith's Christmas cracker caught on with the public, eventually giving rise to a new British Christmas tradition.

The name as well as the contents of Smith's invention have changed over time. In the early days Smith called his novelty a "cosaque" rather than a cracker. This name probably refers to the Cossacks, a people from southern Russia who were feared soldiers and famed horseback riders. According to nineteenth-century advertisements, Smith's crackers contained such things as paper hats, night-caps, masks, puzzles, games, toys, hair dye, flowers, perfume, Japanese trinkets, tiny harps, and toys of a scientific bent. Today's crackers typically hold paper hats, whistles, and a variety of inexpensive plastic toys. Nineteenth-century cracker mottoes hoped to amuse or inspire the recipient with a few lines of light verse. Since those times mottoes have shifted towards jokes, riddles, and puns.

Tom Smith's cracker company has survived till this day, although it now faces competition from several other firms. In spite of this competition, Smith's company turns out about 38 million crackers each year. The firm sells most of these in the United Kingdom, but ships about fifteen percent abroad. In an effort to boost off-season sales, the company has introduced new designs suitable for other holidays, including Halloween and the Fourth of July, and such special occasions as weddings and children's birthday parties.

Further Reading

Muir, Frank. *Christmas Customs and Traditions.* New York: Taplinger, 1977.

Pimlott, J. A. R. *The Englishman's Christmas.* Atlantic Highlands, N.J.: Humanities Press, 1978.

Sansom, William. *A Book of Christmas.* New York: McGraw-Hill Book Company, 1968.

Street, Ed. "Tom Smith's Novelty—The English Christmas Cracker." *The World and I* 11, 12 (December 1, 1996): 190-95.

Christmas Drama

For Christmas customs that include an element of playacting, *see* Black Peter; "A Charlie Brown Christmas"; *Christmas Carol, A*; Feast of the Ass; *How the Grinch Stole Christmas*; Jonkonnu; Knecht Ruprecht; Masque; *Miracle on 34th Street*; Mumming; Nativity Play; Nativity Scene; *The Nutcracker*; Pantomime; Paradise Tree; Pastores; Plough Monday; Poland, Christmas in; Posadas; Star Boys; "White Christmas"; Yule Goat

Christmas Lads

Christmas Boys, Jola-Sveinar, Yuletide Lads

In **Iceland** thirteen leprechaun-like creatures known as the *Jola-Sveinar*, or Christmas Lads, visit homes during the **Christmas season**. An old Icelandic legend tells us that they are the sons of a giant female troll named Gryla. The first lad arrives on the thirteenth day before Christmas. Another comes on the following day. This continues until the household hosts all thirteen boys on Christmas Eve. One boy departs on Christmas day and another on the following day, until the last withdraws on the twelfth day after Christmas, or **Epiphany**. In some older versions of this folklore, there are only nine Christmas Lads.

The early tales of the Christmas Lads painted them as fearsome creatures. Their mother, Gryla, was reputed to eat misbehaving children; her offspring inherited the same appetite for troublemakers. Adults used to remind children that the Christmas Lads waited for them in the winter time darkness in order to frighten the youngsters into good behavior. This custom inspired so much trauma that in 1746 the government denounced it.

Both the character and the appearance of the Christmas Lads changed over the years. The first record of the Lads dates back to the seventeenth century, when a man named Stephan Olafsson wrote a poem about the ogre Gryla, her husband Leppaludi, and her sons, the malicious **Yule** Boys. At this time Icelanders pictured the Lads as gigantic, lumbering trolls. By the nineteenth century, however, they looked more like peasant farmers. Instead of eating children, these oafish Lads vexed householders during their visits. They stole sausages, candles, and the family's best grain. One might leave a room neat and clean only to find it askew upon returning. After Christmas they attempted to steal away with the household's naughty children. In the twentieth century they shrank even further in size and began to resemble miniature Santas. Like **Santa Claus**, they now leave **gifts** of candy for good children, who leave their **shoes** on the windowsills in the days before Christmas to receive this reward.

The names and numbers of Christmas Lads varied over the years. Earlier records account for only nine Lads. In 1864, however, a writer named Jon Arnason named and described thirteen Christmas Lads. He called them Candle-Beggar (or Candle-Scrounger), Gully-Gawk, Hem-Blower, Shorty (also known as Stump), Meat Hook, Spoon-Licker (or Ladle-Licker), Sheep-Cot Clod (also known as Fence-post), Skyr-Gobbler (Skyr is a kind of Icelandic yogurt), Pot-Scraper (or Pot-Licker), Sausage-Swiper, Bowl-Licker, Window-Peeper, and Door-Sniffer (or Keyhole Sniffer). The fact that there were thirteen of them meant that the first would arrive on the eve of **St. Lucy's Day**, December 13, and last would come on Christmas Eve. It also meant that the house would host these elf-like creatures throughout the **Twelve Days of Christmas**, since the last Lad would depart on Epiphany. The names given these creatures by Arnason describe their favorite activities and gives an idea of the kind of mischief that nineteenth-century Icelanders attributed to them. Arnason's flight of imagination took root with the Icelandic people, who today generally recognize the same thirteen Christmas Lads.

Further Reading

Lehane, Brendan. *The Book of Christmas*. Chicago: Time-Life Books, 1986.

MacDonald, Margaret Read, ed. *The Folklore of World Holidays*. Detroit, Mich.: Gale Research, 1992.

Osmond, Stephen. "Long Night of Dreams: Midwinter Celebrations in Iceland." *The World and I* 11, 1 (January 1996): 206 (12).

Ross, Corinne. *Christmas in Scandinavia*. Chicago: World Book, 1977.

Simpson, Jacqueline. *Icelandic Folktales and Legends*. Berkeley, Calif.: University of California Press, 1972.

Christmas Markets

In such European countries as **Germany**, Belgium, Austria, Holland, **Spain**, Sweden, and **Italy**, special outdoor Christmas markets flourish during the **Christmas season**. Local merchants construct stalls in an open square or plaza and decorate them with **Christmas symbols** and themes. Goods for sale typically include handmade Christmas crafts and specialty foods. Christmas music, dramas, and other entertainments add to the holiday atmosphere. Christmas markets allow shoppers to buy unique **gifts** while enjoying this special seasonal environment.

Christmas Markets in Germany

Germany's markets are especially famous. While strolling through the market German shoppers may sample a wide range of foodstuffs, such as smoked sausages, roasted chestnuts, roast chicken, candy, waffles, Viennese almonds, toffee apples and chocolate-dipped fruit, as well as various regional specialties. Many shoppers sip hot mulled wine as they saunter from booth to booth. Christmas music, holiday plays, and visits from **St. Nicholas** offer additional distractions from the cold. Gifts and decorations typically available at German markets include **Christmas trees**, straw stars, gold foil **ornaments**, wooden figurines, nutcrackers, **gingerbread** houses, a variety of simple toys, candles, candleholders, nuts, cookies, postcards, chocolates, and *Stollen*, a special Christmas bread enriched with dried fruit (*see also* **Christmas Cake**).

Major Christmas markets entertain the public each year in Berlin, Cologne, Dresden, Frankfurt, Hamburg, Hanover, Magdeburg, Munich, and Nuremberg. Some of these markets began as specialty markets and have since expanded into general fairs. The Munich market originally sold only **Nativity scenes**, while in its early days the Dresden market specialized in Stollen. Germany's markets run throughout the **Advent** season.

Germany's two oldest markets are held in Munich and Nuremberg. Nuremberg's "Christ Child Market" started in the seventeenth century in order to fill the new demand for Christmas presents. In the sixteenth century Germany's Protestant reformer Martin Luther began the custom of giving gifts to children at Christmas, attributing them to the Christ child (*see also* **Christkindel**). Not only did the Nuremberg market adopt "Christ Child" as its name, but it also selected a youngster to dress as the Christ child and distribute gifts to children attending the market. This custom continues today. Each year the market opens on the Friday closest to **St. Barbara's Day**, December 4, and runs until Christmas Eve. Regional specialties from the Nuremberg market include gold foil **angels**, wooden toys, honey cakes (*Lebkuchen*), and prune people (*Zwetschgenmännla*), figurines made out of dried prunes.

Christmas Markets in Sweden

In December visitors to Stockholm, Sweden, will find a Christmas market located in Gamla Stan, or Old Town. Another market, set up in Skansen Park, specializes in traditional Swedish handicrafts and food products. People interested in art and design often stop off at Konstfack, where the Art School of Stockholm hosts a Christmas market featuring the work of its students.

Liseburg Park, in the city of Gothenburg, holds a fabulous Christmas market each year. Decorated Christmas trees and millions of twinkling Christmas lights ornament the park for the holiday season. Singing choirs, booths selling traditional Swedish Christmas foods, and an ice skating rink provide additional holiday atmosphere. The park also serves as the site of the crowning of Gothenburg's Lucia (*see also* **St. Lucy's Day**).

Christmas Markets in Italy

In Italy Christmas markets bring a carnival atmosphere to many main plazas during the weeks before Christmas. Italian markets feature Nativity scene figurines, ornaments, decorations, toys, clothing, gift items, flowers, candy, balloons, fresh fish, snacks, specialty foods, and musical entertainment. The cities of Milan, Venice, Florence, Palermo, and Rome hold yearly Christmas markets, as do many smaller towns and cities throughout Italy.

Christmas Markets in Belgium

Christmas markets also enrich the holiday season in towns and cities throughout Belgium. Many Belgians favor the "European Christmas Market," held for several days around December 8 in Brussels. The stalls at this market display goods from every member state of the European Union, and from many others besides. The Christmas market at Liege lasts longer, however: it continues until **New Year's** Eve.

Further Reading

Christmas in Germany. Lincolnwood, Ill.: Passport Books, 1995.

Christmas in Italy. Chicago: World Book-Childcraft International, 1979.

Henderson, Helene, and Sue Ellen Thompson, eds. *Holidays, Festivals, and Celebrations of the World Dictionary*. Second edition. Detroit, Mich.: Omnigraphics, 1997.

Russ, Jennifer M. *German Festivals and Customs*. London, England: Oswald Wolff, 1982.

Web Sites

A site sponsored by the German Information Center in New York and the German Embassy in Washington, D.C., contains a page on the Christ Child Market: http://Germany-info.org/ (Search "Christmas market")

The November/December 2001 Newsletter of the Scandinavia Tourism Board of North America offers information on holiday celebrations in Denmark, Finland, Iceland, Norway, and Sweden at: http://www.goscandinavia.com/frnewsletter.html

Christmas Rose

Black Hellebore, Snow Rose, Winter Rose

This five-petalled rose blooms around Christmas time and so acquired the popular names "Christmas rose," "winter rose," and "snow rose." Although at first glance the flowers appear to be white, the petals also carry a faint hint of pink. Botanists have identified the plant as a member of the buttercup family and have named it *Helleborus niger*. This Latin designation translates to "Black Hellebore," a name which refers to the plant's distinctive black roots. In the nineteenth century the Christmas rose was widely cultivated in **England** for sale during the **Christmas season**. This practice faded in the twentieth century. The French, however, still enjoy decorating their holiday tables with bouquets of Christmas roses. In **Germany** the rose continues to serve as a **Christmas symbol**.

The Legend of Madelon

The following folktale explains not only the origins of the Christmas rose, but also its association with the season. On a winter's night long ago a poor **shepherd** girl named Madelon beheld a strange procession approaching the field where she kept watch over her sheep. It was the **Magi** on their way to **Bethlehem**. Madelon gazed in awe at the rich **gifts** the Wise Men brought with them for the Christ child and began to cry with shame. "I cannot give even a single flower," she thought, "since the fields are covered with snow." Suddenly an **angel** appeared and asked the girl the reason for her tears. When Madelon explained, the angel gestured towards the road to Bethlehem. Beautiful white roses spilled across the path. Madelon gathered an armful of the gleaming flowers and joyfully followed the Magi. When she arrived at the manger **Mary** kindly bade her enter and offer her gift. As the fingers of the infant **Jesus** brushed against the petals, they took on the pink glow we still see today in the Christmas rose.

A Swedish Tale

A Swedish legend explains the origins of the Christmas rose in a different way. Once upon a time a beautiful garden flourished in the middle of the Göinge forest each Christmas Eve. Flowers sprang up from the ground, trees bore leaves and fruit, birds sang, and butterflies rippled through the air. One year a kindly abbot and a suspicious monk who had heard rumors about the Christmas paradise set out to find the place. After roaming through the cold, dark, barren forest they finally stumbled across the garden. Even after seeing it with his own eyes, the doubting monk still refused to believe in the miracle. Instead, he decided that it was an illusion created by the Devil. At that moment the magic garden vanished and never came back. Only the Christmas rose remained, to remind us of the miracle garden.

In another version of the story a poor family forced to live out in the middle of the woods discovered the Christmas garden. They enjoyed the miracle for many years before telling the abbot of its existence. When they led the abbot and his monk to the place, the monk's disbelief caused the garden to disappear forever. As it faded away the abbot clutched the flowers at his feet and managed to save a single bulb. The plant which grew from the bulb produced beautiful white flowers the following year at Christmas time. They called this reminder of the miracle garden the Christmas rose.

A French Legend

The French offer yet another tale explaining the origin of the Christmas rose. A long time ago a slow-witted young man named Nicaise lived in a village near the French town of Rouen. The parish priest, his guardian, assigned him the task of ringing the church **bells**. One Christmas Eve, after receiving a scolding from the priest for his foolishness, Nicaise climbed the bell tower to ring the bells for **Midnight Mass**. After completing his task, he fell asleep there. In his dream one of the gargoyles that decorated the rainspouts of the old stone church came to life. The gargoyle boasted that he was the Devil in disguise and began to flatter the lonely and rejected boy. The gargoyle told Nicaise that he liked him very much and offered to grant him three wishes. Nicaise happily accepted the Devil's offer, wishing for intelligence, wealth, and a beautiful wife. As an afterthought, he also asked for some flowers to decorate the church for Christmas, but the Devil angrily refused this last request. Then the Devil informed Nicaise that he must pay a price for the granting of the three wishes. "Exactly one year from now," the gargoyle leered, "I will return and take away your soul as payment. Your only hope of escaping this fate is to make flowers bloom in the winter snow."

In the year that followed Nicaise enjoyed being wealthy, smart, and married to a beautiful woman. But as Christmas drew near, he began to fear the return of the Devil. On Christmas Eve he confessed his fears to the priest, who was horrified at what Nicaise had done. The two knelt before the altar, fervently praying for divine help. As midnight approached, Nicaise prepared himself to climb the bell tower and ring the Midnight Mass bells one more time before being carried off by the gargoyle devil. At that moment a group of children burst through the church doors excited by what they had found outside — flowers growing in the snow. The Christ child had answered their prayers by sending the Christmas rose. (*See also* **France, Christmas in**.)

Further Reading

Hadfield, Miles, and John Hadfield. *The Twelve Days of Christmas*. Boston, Mass.: Little, Brown and Company, 1961.

Hottes, Alfred Carl. *1001 Christmas Facts and Fancies*. 1946. Reprint. Detroit, Mich.: Omnigraphics, 1990.

Lagerlöf, Selma. *The Legend of the Christmas Rose*. New York: Holiday House, 1990.

Ross, Corinne Madden. *Christmas in France*. Chicago: World Book, 1988.

Christmas Seals

Many people embellish the **Christmas cards**, letters, and packages they send during the holiday season with special, decorative stamps called Christmas seals. Although the seals have no value as postage, the money collected in return for them supports various charitable causes. A Danish postmaster came up with the idea for Christmas seals around the turn of the twentieth century. Since then, they have spread to dozens of countries around the world, including the United States.

Danish postmaster Einar Holbøll designed the first mass-produced Christmas seals in 1904. The post office sold four million of the decorative stamps that year, giving birth to a new Danish Christmas tradition. Jacob Riis, an emigrant to the United States, publicized the success of Denmark's Christmas seals in an American magazine article. In 1907 Emily Bissel, a Red Cross worker, adopted the idea of selling Christmas seals as a way of raising money for the Red Cross in Wilmington, Delaware. Her success led other organizations to issue Christmas seals the following year, and soon the idea spread across the country. In 1919 the National Tuberculosis Association, which later became the American Lung Association, cornered the market on Christmas seals, becoming the sole issuer of the decorative Christmas stamps in the United States. Today the seals earn millions of dollars a year for the American Lung Association.

Further Reading

Del Re, Gerard, and Patricia Del Re. *The Christmas Almanack*. Garden City, N.Y.: Doubleday, 1979.

Ross, Corinne. *Christmas in Scandinavia*. Chicago: World Book, 1977.

Christmas Season

How long is the Christmas season? The answer varies from place to place and from age to age. In the United States today, the Christmas season is often equated with the shopping and **gift**-return season. In other times and places, calendar customs or related observances opened and closed the Christmas season.

In past eras Europeans began their Christmas season on a variety of dates on which Christmas-related events and observances took place. In medieval and Renaissance times the English sometimes selected a local **Lord of Misrule**, a kind of clown who presided over Christmas festivities, as early as Halloween or All Saints' Day (November 1). The first day of **Advent**, which occurs on the Sunday closest to November 30, also served as an important date with regard to the European Christmas season. In some parts of Europe the Christmas season began on December 6, **St. Nicholas's Day**. In Sweden the season still begins with **St. Lucy's Day** on December 13.

For many centuries the **Twelve Days of Christmas** stood at the heart of the European Christmas season. The Twelve Days begin on **December 25** and last until **Twelfth Night**. This period includes a number of other observances such as **St. Stephen's Day**, **St. John's Day**, **Holy Innocents' Day**, the **Feast of the Circumcision**, and **New Year's Day**.

Virtually no one ended their seasonal celebration on December 26, the day after Christmas. Even today, Americans extend the Christmas season through New Year's Day. In the past, however, many Europeans assumed that Christmas ended on **Epiphany**, January 6. An old English folk custom sent farm laborers back to work on **Plough Monday**, the Monday after the Twelfth Day of Christmas. Women resumed their labors on **St. Distaff's Day**, January 7. Scandinavian folk beliefs taught that the Christmas season ended on January 12, the twentieth day of Christmas, which the Swedes and Norwegians celebrate as **St. Knut's Day**. In Scotland's Shetland Islands, however,

Christmas lasted until Old Twenty-Fourth night, which was marked by a festival called **Up Helly Aa** (*see also* **Old Christmas Day**). In past centuries some English Christmas customs, such as decorating homes with **greenery**, extended as late as **Candlemas**, February 2. In other areas of **Europe** people finally dismantled their **Nativity scenes** on Candlemas.

In Latin America, eastern Europe, and the Middle East different dates and observances may mark the beginning and the end of the Christmas season. In **Syria** the Christmas season opens with **St. Barbara's Day** on December 4. In a few Latin American countries the Christmas season begins on December 8 with the Feast of the Immaculate Conception. In the **Philippines** and some parts of Latin America, the holiday season begins on December 16 with a Christmas novena (a series of special religious services or private devotions offered on nine consecutive days; *see also* **Misa de Gallo; Posadas, Las**). In **Russia** Orthodox Christians still schedule their feast days according to the old, Julian calendar (*see* Old Christmas Day). Therefore, they celebrate Christmas on January 7, as do Orthodox Ethiopians (*see also* **Ethiopia, Christmas in**). Orthodox Armenians living in the Holy Land who follow the Julian calendar celebrate Epiphany and Christmas together on January 19 (*see also* **Armenia, Christmas in**).

In recent years **commercial** interests have defined the Christmas season for many Americans. In the early twentieth century retailers promoted the idea that the Christmas shopping season begins on the day after Thanksgiving. These days, however, retailers may bombard consumers with Christmas merchandise and promotions as early as October.

Further Reading

MacDonald, Margaret Read, ed. *The Folklore of World Holidays*. Detroit, Mich.: Gale Research, 1992.

Christmas Sheaf

One old Scandinavian Christmas custom is for the birds . . . literally. Many Nordic families offer food to the birds at Christmas time. The traditional offering consists of a sheaf of grain placed on a pole, fence, or rooftop. Those who do not have access to cereal stalks may substitute a plate of grain, bread, or seeds. Scandinavians call the bundle of grain stalks a "Christmas sheaf." They place it outside on Christmas Eve or Christmas morning in order to include the birds in the feasting that is taking place inside the home.

Several other Scandinavian customs encourage the kind treatment of animals at Christmas time. Tradition dictates that farmers give horses and cows extra helpings of food. In **Norway** hunters withdraw snares and traps during the **Christmas season**. Some believe that these customs, including the feeding of birds at Christmas time, arose as a way of spreading the spirit of kindness and plenty that infuses human celebrations of Christmas throughout the animal kingdom. Others argue that the Christmas sheaf originally worked as a kind of magic rite. They believe the sheaf may have served as a sacrifice to pre-Christian fertility spirits or as a charm to keep the birds from harming the coming year's crops. In any case, contemporary Scandinavians delight in the eager pecking and joyous chatter of the birds who find the sheaf on Christmas morning.

Further Reading

Del Re, Gerard, and Patricia Del Re. *The Christmas Almanack*. Garden City, N.Y.: Doubleday, 1979.

Foley, Daniel J. *The Christmas Tree*. Philadelphia, Pa.: Chilton Company, 1960.

Henriksen, Vera. *Christmas in Norway*. Oslo, Norway: Johan Grundt Tanum Forlag, 1970.

Ross, Corinne. *Christmas in Scandinavia*. Chicago: World Book, 1977.

Christmas Symbols

Over the centuries many Christmas symbols have emerged from the lore, legends, and customs surrounding Christmas. The more familiar of these symbols include **Christmas trees**, stars (*see* **Star of Bethlehem**), **Nativity scenes**, **Advent calendars**, candy canes (*see* **Urban Legends**), **angels**, **bells**, **cherry trees**, **Christmas cards**, **farolitos**, **holly**, **ivy**, **gifts**, **mistletoe**, **poinsettias**, **plum pudding**, **reindeer**, **robins**, and **wreaths**. Folk figures such as **Santa Claus**, La **Befana**, **Father Christmas**, **Grandfather Frost**, the **Jultomten**, the **Snow Maiden**, the **Weihnachtsmann**, and the **Yule goat** also serve as symbols of the holiday.

Lost and Lesser-Known Christmas Symbols

In addition to the well-known Christmas symbols listed above, a number of archaic and lesser-known images have also emerged out of Christmas folklore. An ox and an ass, often pictured standing alongside the infant **Jesus**, also appear occasionally as symbols of the holiday. Although neither of the **Gospel accounts of Christmas** mentions these animals, Christmas folklore assigned them a place at Jesus'birth as early as the Middle Ages (*see* **Nativity Legends**). Their connection to the Nativity can be traced back to a verse from the Book of Isaiah, which states, "An ox knows its owner and a donkey its master's stall" (Isaiah 1:3). Many Christians took this verse as a reference to the birth of Jesus in a stable (*see* **Gospel According to Luke**). Hence, they imagined that an ox and an ass witnessed and recognized the holy birth.

Before the advent of gas and electric lighting, candles and fires of all sorts illuminated the long, dark nights of the **Christmas season** and gave rise to many Christmas customs (*see* **Advent Candle; Advent Wreath; Christmas Candles; Luminarias; Martinmas; St. Lucy's Day; Up Helly Aa;** and **Yule Log**). The Yule log and the Christmas candle may at one time have served as familiar Christmas symbols, although these customs have since declined. Today we still associate the Christmas season with fires and lights, usually Christmas tree lights, holiday display lights, and the small blazes that warm our home fireplaces (*see also* **Ornaments**).

The Christmas ship represents an archaic Christmas symbol which has fallen out of general usage and understanding. Several medieval **Christmas carols** describe Christmas as a ship bearing spiritual aid to us from afar. One sixteenth-century carol describes the Christmas ship in the following fashion:

> There came a ship far sailing then,
> St. Michael was the steersman
> St. John sat in the horn;
> Our Lord harped, our Lady sang,
> And all the bells of heaven rang
> On Christmas in the morn [Crippen, 1990, 156].

The words of another song depict Jesus on a ship sailing towards earth to be born into human flesh. Thus "anchored" into our existence, he sacrifices himself for our salvation. Another old song, "I Saw Three Ships," still circulates among carol singers today. This fifteenth-century song also depicts Christ and **Mary** on board the Christmas ship as it sails into **Bethlehem** on Christmas morning.

165

Some scholars think that another early version of this carol placed the Three Kings, or **Magi**, on board the ships that sail towards Bethlehem. Although the inland town of Bethlehem does not have a harbor, this detail did not seem to bother the lyricists of the medieval era.

An old carol of German origin still sung today, "Lo, How a Rose E'er Blooming," presents the rose as a symbol of the birth of Jesus. The lyrics of the song refer back to the Old Testament prophecy that declares, "there shall come forth a rod out of the stem of Jesse, and a branch shall grow out of his roots" (Isaiah 11:1). Many Christians take this phrase as a reference to the coming of Jesus. The song extends this horticultural imagery by declaring of Jesus' birth, "Lo, how a rose e'er blooming from Jesse's lineage hath sprung." During the Middle Ages the rose also represented the Virgin Mary, an image to which the song also makes reference. Although it is not a familiar holiday image to many Americans, the Germans still use the rose as a Christmas symbol (*see also* **Christmas Rose**).

Further Reading

Crippen, Thomas G. *Christmas and Christmas Lore.* 1923. Reprint. Detroit, Mich.: Omnigraphics, 1990.

Del Re, Gerard, and Patricia Del Re. *The Christmas Almanack.* Garden City, N.Y.: Doubleday, 1979.

Studwell, William E. *The Christmas Carol Reader.* Binghamton, N.Y.: Haworth Press, 1995.

Christmas Tree

The Christmas tree originally hails from **Germany**. Today, it is a recognized symbol of the holiday in many parts of the globe. The earliest historical reference to decorated Christmas trees in German homes dates back to the sixteenth century (*see also* **Christmas Village; Ornaments**). Several theories concerning the beginning of the Christmas tree custom, however, suggest that its origins lie much further in the past.

Legends

A number of legends offer fanciful explanations for the origins of the Christmas tree. According to one, St. Boniface (c. 675-754) began the custom in the eighth century. One Christmas Eve this English missionary to the German-speaking peoples came across some pagans preparing a human sacrifice before an oak tree. He struck the oak tree a single blow with his axe, which felled the tree. Duly impressed by this miraculous feat, the people abandoned their old ways and embraced Christianity. The saint pointed to a small fir tree laying among the ruins of the oak and told them to take that as the symbol of their new faith and of the birth of the Christ child.

Legends dating back to tenth-century **Europe** tell of trees that mysteriously burst into bloom on Christmas Eve (*see also* **Glastonbury Thorn**). Some writers suggest that this myth inspired people to bring decorated trees into their homes at Christmas time. A German legend elaborates on this theme. According to this tale, a humble woodcutter heard a knock on his door one freezing winter night. Upon opening it he discovered a shivering, poor child. The woodcutter and his wife offered the child hospitality for the night, feeding him and offering him their own warm bed close to the fire. The next morning the grateful child appeared before them, radiant and beautiful. Awareness dawned in them that their guest was in fact the Christ child (*see also* **Christkindel**). Before departing the Christ child gave them a twig from a fir tree, declaring that it would blossom for them year after year. Unable to imagine how this could occur, they tossed the twig away. Nevertheless, it grew into a beautiful fir tree, which suddenly blossomed with golden apples and silver nuts. The miraculous blooms appeared each year at Christmas time.

Another Christian legend attributes the Christmas tree to Martin Luther (1483-1546). One Christmas Eve the great religious reformer found himself walking through the woods. The beauty of the stars shining through the branches of the fir trees deeply moved him. He cut down a small tree, brought it home with him, and covered it with lit candles, explaining to his family that its light and beauty represented Christ, the light of the world. Although this legend helped to increase the popularity of the Christmas tree it should be pointed out that the earliest known document describing a Christmas tree lit with candles was written about a century after Luther's death.

Origins

No one can confirm the exact origin of the Christmas tree. Some writers base their explanation of the Christmas tree on the theory that in ancient times the pagan peoples of northern Europe revered trees. They propose that the venerable pagan symbol of the tree survived the transition to Christianity by attaching itself to the Christian midwinter holiday, Christmas. Little solid historical evidence exists to support this viewpoint, however. Others believe that the ancient Roman custom of decorating homes and temples with **greenery** during **Kalends** survived for centuries, eventually inspiring the people of the north to decorate their homes with small evergreen trees at that time of year. Still others view the Christmas **pyramid** as the ancestor of the Christmas tree.

Finally, a number of researchers disagree with all of these arguments. They point out that the earliest historical records of decorated trees being used to celebrate Christmas come from the Middle Ages. Fir trees decorated with apples served as the central prop for the paradise play, a kind of folk religious drama often performed on December 24 (*see also* **Nativity Play**). These props were called **paradise trees**, and some researchers believe they were the forerunners of the Christmas tree. The plays eventually fell out of favor with Church officials and the populace. Nevertheless, some writers be-

lieve that people from parts of France and Germany retained the custom of celebrating Christmas with a decorated tree, which eventually became known as a Christmas tree.

Early History

The earliest historical reference to Christmas trees as such dates back to sixteenth-century Germany. In 1561 an ordinance posted in Alsace declared that each burgher was allowed only one Christmas tree and that his tree could be no more than "eight shoes" in height. Apparently the custom of bringing a living tree into the home at Christmas time was so popular that deforestation was already become something of a problem. In 1605 a traveler to the city of Strasbourg described the German custom of bringing a fir tree into the drawing room at Christmas time and decorating it with apples, wafers, paper roses, gilt, and sugar ornaments. Documents from the same century also record objections to the Christmas tree custom on the part of religious reformers, who argued that it detracted from the spiritual significance of the holiday. On the whole, however, the Christmas-tree-loving Germans appear to have ignored these objections.

The Christmas pyramid found favor with many German families during the seventeenth and eighteenth centuries. Some German families preferred to decorate a pyramid rather than a Christmas tree. Other families had both in their parlors. Still other families preferred to center home celebrations around a **Nativity scene**. For the most part, the Nativity scene held sway in southern Germany, where Catholics were more numerous. The tree dominated in northern Germany, where more Protestants lived. By the nineteenth century the increasing appeal of the Christmas tree contributed to the decline of the Christmas pyramid.

During the nineteenth century the Christmas tree became increasingly popular in all parts of Germany, but also spread to other countries. Around 1840 the English monarch Queen Victoria and her German-born consort Prince Albert celebrated Christmas with a decorated tree. Although the Christmas tree was known in **England** before that time, this stamp of royal approval transformed the tree into a fashionable, new addition to the English Christmas. In like manner, the German-born Princess Helene of Mecklenberg started a Christmas tree trend in **France** in 1837 by celebrating her first Christmas in that country with a decorated tree. Many Scandinavians adopted the Christmas tree in the mid-nineteenth century, as did many Americans, Russians, and other northern Europeans. Southern Europeans, for the most part, stuck with their traditional Nativity scenes. Indeed, the Nativity scene remains the focus of home Christmas celebrations in much of southern Europe.

The Christmas Tree Comes to America

Some writers claim that Hessian soldiers who fought on behalf of the British in the American Revolution erected the first Christmas trees on American soil. No solid historical evidence exists to back up this claim, however. Several contemporary folklorists instead claim that German immigrants, such as those of the Pennsylvania Dutch country, brought the custom with them to the United States. Occasional references to the novelty of a decorated Christmas tree are scattered throughout newspapers on the East Coast from the early 1800s. In fact, the trees were considered so exotic that some organizations set them up and then charged people money in order to view them.

By the 1840s the Christmas tree was widely known in the United States. Publication of *Kriss Kringle's Christmas Tree* in 1845, a children's book about the custom, helped to popularize the holiday tree. The first American Christmas trees were only a few feet tall and were displayed on tables, following the German fashion. As the size of the tree grew to accommodate an ever-increasing load of ornaments, Americans moved the tree to a stand on the floor. Many of these early American ornaments were in fact Christmas **gifts** and treats. These might include **gingerbread** and other cookies, pretzels, apples, lemons, oranges, raisins, nuts, figs, **sugarplums**, strings of cranberries or popcorn, candy, dolls, books, thimbles, scissors, mittens, **stockings**, shoes, paper roses, glass balls, and ornaments made of egg shells or cotton.

Families gradually began to exchange heavier, more substantial gifts. Before 1880 people usually hung their unwrapped gifts from the tree with thread or string. After that time, **wrapping paper** and fancy decorated boxes started to become fashionable. As Christmas presents grew too large or heavy to hang on the tree, people began to place them beneath the tree.

The Christmas Tree Becomes an American Institution

During the second half of the nineteenth century the Christmas tree cast its roots deep into American Christmas celebrations. Its presence undermined the role of the Christmas stocking as a receptacle for gifts in many homes. Christmas trees began to sprout up in school holiday celebrations. They even worked their way into churches, in spite of some initial opposition to what was perceived as a suspiciously heathen custom. Mark Carr, a logger from New York's Catskill Mountains, created the first Christmas tree lot in 1851. For the price of one dollar he rented a sidewalk in **New York City** and sold cut trees to city dwellers. His business appeared to be so profitable that the owner of the sidewalk increased his rent to $100 the following year. In 1856 Franklin Pierce became the first American president to celebrate Christmas in the **White House** with a decorated tree. As the tree became a familiar and cherished part of American Christmas celebrations, people began to make fancy ribbon and lace ornaments as well as to collect store-bought ornaments for their trees. Unlike the gifts and treats which had covered their trees in past years, these ornaments could be saved and reused the following year.

One writer estimates that by the turn of the twentieth century, about one in five American homes displayed a decorated tree at Christmas time. Many of those who could not afford to set up a tree in their homes still enjoyed community or church trees. President Theodore Roosevelt expressed early ecological concerns about the national consumption of evergreen trees at Christmas time. Around the year 1900 he discontinued the use of Christmas trees in the White House. His sons, however, unable to resist the lure of a decorated Christmas tree, smuggled an evergreen into one of their bedrooms. Roosevelt eventually changed his position on Christmas trees after one of his advisors assured him that America's forests could survive the yearly harvest.

In the following decades Christmas trees appeared in more and more American homes. In the year 2000, 79 percent of U.S. homes displayed a Christmas tree during the holiday season. About 31 percent of American homeowners bought real Christmas trees, while 49 percent of homeowners relied instead upon artificial trees (and two percent of homes contained both a real and an artificial tree). Christmas tree growers harvest and sell about 33 million real trees annually.

Symbolic Trees

The Christmas tree has become a potent symbol of peace and goodwill. This symbolism underlies the ceremonies surrounding many public Christmas trees. President Woodrow Wilson presided over the first **National Christmas Tree** ceremony on Christmas Eve in 1913. Although Wilson established the ceremony near the Capitol Building, President Calvin Coolidge moved the national Christmas tree to the vicinity of the White House. In 1923 he led the first ceremonial lighting of the national Christmas tree. This yearly ceremony has continued ever since, with the exception of the years between 1942 and 1945, when wartime blackouts prohibited the festive, outdoor lights. After the Korean War, a Christmas "pageant of peace" was attached to the lighting of the national Christmas tree, which entailed rescheduling the lighting ceremony to a date before Christmas Eve (*see also* **Nation's Christmas Tree**).

The English, too, have a kind of national tree. Each year since 1947 the citizens of **Norway** have donated an immense evergreen tree to the people of the United Kingdom in gratitude for British aid during World War II. This tree towers over London's Trafalgar Square during the **Christmas season**.

Further Reading

Comfort, David. *Just Say Noel!* New York: Fireside Books, 1995.

Del Re, Gerard, and Patricia Del Re. *The Christmas Almanack*. Garden City, N.Y.: Doubleday, 1979.

Foley, Daniel J. *The Christmas Tree*. Philadelphia, Pa.: Chilton Books, 1960.

Miles, Clement A. *Christmas in Ritual and Tradition*. 1912. Reprint. Detroit, Mich.: Omnigraphics, 1990.

Russ, Jennifer. *German Festivals and Customs*. London, England: Oswald Wolff, 1982.

Snyder, Phillip V. *The Christmas Tree Book*. New York: Viking Press, 1976.

Stevens, Patricia Bunning. *Merry Christmas!: A History of the Holiday*. New York: Macmillan, 1979.

Web Sites

A site sponsored by the National Park Service on the National Christmas Tree: http://www.nps.gov/ncro/PublicAffairs/NationalChristmasTree.htm

The National Christmas Tree Association, a group that represents growers, offers facts and figures concerning real Christmas trees at their web site: http://www.realchristmastrees.org

Christmas Village

Christmas garden, Christmas yard

For many centuries people have delighted in constructing miniature landscapes for Christmas. The **Nativity scene**, a life-sized or miniature depiction of the scene of **Jesus'** birth, dates back to the thirteenth century. In the eighteenth century some central Europeans enjoyed creating miniature village scenes—called Christmas gardens—which they set up under their **Christmas trees**. The Moravians brought this tradition with them to America, and from it developed their own custom of Christmas **putz** building. The putz included a Nativity scene within a complicated town and country landscape. The idea of creating a miniature world underneath the Christmas tree soon spread beyond the German-American communities that imported it to this country. It survives to this day, though nowadays most people buy the figurines and buildings from **gift** shops rather than make them at home.

Christmas Gardens and Yards

In the nineteenth century many Americans placed a miniature fence around their Christmas trees (*see also* **America, Christmas in Nineteenth-Century**). This fence enclosed an area sometimes referred to as a Christmas garden or Christmas yard. Inside the fenced area families arranged small figurines of people or animals, along with various toys. Magazine articles taught children how to make miniature houses out of cardboard to complement these scenes. Adults also worked on the little settlements. Home crafters created a wide variety of scenes, including vignettes of circus life, Indian villages, clusters of young people skating on frozen lakes, charming gardens, prosperous farms, and snug log cabins.

By the 1890s manufacturers supplied the public with a steady stream of ready-made miniature cardboard buildings and figures, as well as fences to mark off the magical territory of the Christmas garden. In the 1920s Germany exported large numbers of Christmas village sets to the U.S. and Canada. In the 1930s Japan added to the supply. During the 1920s and 1930s the buildings came with cellophane windows, designed to permit the consumer to illuminate them from within with an electric light bulb. While some people placed the little homes and shops below their tree, others hung them from the tree as Christmas **ornaments**, or filled them with candy. In the 1940s and 1950s, toy train sets became extremely popular Christmas gifts for boys. The train sets, too — with all their accessories — furthered the tradition of setting up a world in miniature beneath the tree.

In 1976 a company called Department 56 introduced a series of miniature ceramic figures and buildings that formed a set called "Snow Village." Snow Village depicts a small Midwestern town during the **Christmas season**. These products became very popular in just a few years. Soon the company began to branch out, offering buyers a Dickens Village (modeled on Charles Dickens's classic tale *A Christmas Carol*), Christmas in the City (based on **New York City** Christmas scenes), a New England Village, an Alpine Village, a **Bethlehem** Village, and a **North Pole** Village featuring **Santa Claus**. By 1996 Department 56 was earning $126 million a year in profits. Naturally, other companies tried to cash in on the lucrative trade in Christmas villages. Target Stores developed a Christmas Village based on the 1946 film *It's a Wonderful Life*. Kmart came up with its own Christmas town and Mervyns of California starting selling replicas of the California missions — historic California church com-

175

pounds dating back to the time when California was part of **Spain** and **Mexico**. Collecting and displaying miniature villages of this kind at Christmas time has become a popular American Christmas custom in recent decades.

Further Reading

Marling, Karal Ann. *Merry Christmas!* Cambridge, Mass.: Harvard University Press, 2000.

Web Sites

Department 56's web site offers a brief history of the company and its products: http://www.dept56.com/history.asp

"Christmas Villages," a page from the Christmas Traditions in France and Canada exhibit sponsored by the Virtual Museum of Canada: http://www.virtualmuseum.ca/Exhibitions/Noel/angl/village.htm

Commercialism

Over the past century Americans have turned Christmas into a very expensive holiday. Richard Feinberg, professor of consumer sciences and retailing at Purdue University, estimated that Christmas-related expenses would cost Americans $800 billion in the year 2002. In fact, these Christmas purchases account for just under twenty percent of all retail goods sold in the United States each year and up to fifty percent of retailers' yearly profits.

Americans spend time as well as money on maintaining their Christmas shopping habits. According to one survey, 97 percent of Americans buy Christmas presents. Nevertheless, only 28 percent of those who bought presents said that they enjoyed Christmas shopping very much. In spite of widespread ambivalence about the task, the average American household buys and wraps thirty Christmas **gifts** each year. About 62 percent of all American women begin this time-consuming enterprise before Thanksgiving. Men outnumber women in the ranks of those who dislike Christmas shopping, so it is not surprising that they are much more likely to dawdle over this task.

Although retailers may relish this yearly orgy of consumption, other groups denounce it. Some women complain that the pressure of shopping for and wrapping a heap of Christmas gifts exhausts them, especially when added to the extra cooking, entertaining, and decorating that takes place around Christmas time (*see also* **Depression**). Others protest that the yearly tidal wave of spending has all but drowned the religious or spiritual meaning of the holiday. Still others worry about the waste of environmental resources. They point out that our current Christmas consumption habits produce five million extra tons of garbage between Thanksgiving, the kick-off of the Christmas shopping season, and Christmas Day. Indeed, in 1994 the American Greetings Company sold 1.7 billion linear feet of Christmas **wrapping paper**, enough to circle the globe 12 times. Finally, many Americans may simply be spending more they can afford to on maintaining their material Christmas celebrations. For example, one survey has shown that it takes the average American four months to pay off all their holiday purchases. How did Americans come to celebrate Christmas with such a greedy grab for worldly goods?

Christmas in Nineteenth-Century America

At the beginning of the nineteenth century, Christmas was not a very important holiday in this country. In fact, in many states it was not even a legal holiday (*see also* **Colonial America, Christmas in**). In the early part of the nineteenth century Americans who celebrated Christmas sometimes gave gifts to the poor and to servants, following old European Christmas customs (*see* **Boxing Day; Twelve Days of Christmas**). Christmas gifts were not all that common, and most Christmas expenditures went instead towards food and drink. Presents to friends and family, often distributed on **New Year's Day** instead of Christmas, usually consisted of inexpensive, homemade items, such as wooden toys, handmade articles of clothing, or homemade foods. The well-to-do might buy fancier New Year gifts for friends and family members, such as jewelry, watches, pens, pin cushions, gloves, and snuff boxes.

177

American Christmas celebrations changed significantly during the second half of the nineteenth century, however. The holiday became more popular as **Puritan** objections to Christmas faded, and the customs of Christmas-celebrating emigrant groups, such as the Germans and Irish, blended with those of more liberal Anglo-Americans. Americans adopted the **Christmas tree**, and **Santa Claus** emerged as a uniquely American Christmas gift bringer. Christmas gifts became increasingly common, although many still preferred to give homemade rather than store-bought items (*see also* **Ornaments**).

Commercial Influence on Christmas

In the decade following the Civil War, American retailers began to cash in on the increasing popularity of Christmas. After 1870, newspaper advertisements promoting products as potential Christmas gifts appeared in New York and Philadelphia papers with increasing frequency. In 1874 **Macy's** department store in New York promoted the purchase of Christmas gifts to passersby with a magnificent **store window display** featuring $10,000 worth of imported dolls. Other department stores soon followed suit with lavish Christmas displays.

Some Americans still felt that store-bought goods seemed too impersonal and too commercial to give as Christmas gifts. Retailers, manufacturers, and advertisers employed several devices to break down this resistance to manufactured goods. Retailers began to package Christmas purchases in special Christmas wrapping paper as a way of increasing the festivity of store-bought items. The special wrapping paper lifted the item out the realm of ordinary purchases and identified it specifically as a Christmas gift. Manufacturers chimed in by shipping all sorts of ordinary goods in special Christmas packaging. Advertisers ran campaigns suggesting that mass-produced items, such as handkerchiefs, umbrellas, and socks made "ideal" Christmas presents.

In the early twentieth century retailers and advertisers sent Santa Claus to work for them. He appeared in many an advertisement, endorsing all manner of ordinary household items as perfect Christmas gifts. Moreover, around 1900 he began to appear at department stores and on street corners in business districts throughout the country. These hired Santas attracted customers to stores and collected donations for charitable causes.

As Christmas sales increased, retailers began to rely upon them for a high percentage of their yearly revenues. In order to lengthen this very profitable time of year, some stores began to promote the idea that the Christmas shopping season began on the day after Thanksgiving. In 1920 Gimbel's department store of Philadelphia sponsored the first Thanksgiving parade. The parade alerted Philadelphians to the start of the Christmas shopping season and quite naturally featured the American Christmas gift bringer, Santa Claus. Hudson's department store in Detroit and Macy's in New York soon adopted this festive advertising gimmick, planning their first Thanksgiving parades in 1924. So profitable was the Christmas shopping season that retailers lobbied President Franklin Roosevelt to prolong it from three weeks to four weeks. In 1939, after a decade of slow sales caused by the Depression, the head of Ohio's Federated Department Stores caught Roosevelt's ear with the argument that a longer Christmas shopping season would boost Christmas sales. Roosevelt acted on this advice, shifting the date of Thanksgiving from November 30 to November 23. In 1941 Congress changed the date of Thanksgiving again, decreeing that it fall on the fourth Thursday in November. A four-week Christmas shopping season was thus firmly established.

Changing Consumer Preferences

Shifts in the American economy also aided retailers in the quest for Christmas customers. As America shifted from an agricultural to an industrial economy in the late nineteenth century, many people lost both the leisure and the necessary raw materials to make homemade gifts. They turned instead to the marketplace for their Christmas presents. Furthermore, most Americans seemed to find the new industrially manufactured items highly desirable, and many now had the cash to buy them. The great shift from homemade to manufactured Christmas gifts took place between 1880 and 1920. After 1920 Americans relied almost exclusively on store-bought Christmas gifts.

Before 1910 people who purchased Christmas gifts often gave cheap, decorative items, such as ceramic knickknacks, to friends and family. These frivolous novelty gifts fell out of favor in the early twentieth century. People began to send **Christmas cards** to their friends, distant relatives, and business associates in lieu of these gimmick gifts. Family members and close friends received gifts that were more useful, though more expensive, than the old gimcracks had been. These included such items as tools and household appliances.

By the late 1920s buyers' preferences began to shift again, this time towards luxury items such as jewelry and fine clothing. The homemade Christmas gifts of the mid-nineteenth century had satisfied people's basic needs. Now, consumers were expected to familiarize themselves with the tastes, and discover the secret desires, of each person for whom they bought gifts. In order to aid shoppers in this stressful mental exercise, retailers came up with a new idea: gift certificates.

Financing Christmas

The increasing commercialization of Christmas affected American saving and spending habits. By the early twentieth century many employers offered their workers a special **Christmas bonus**. This token addition to their regular wages helped workers to participate in the new, materialist Christmas. As this participation still strained the budgets of many working people, **Christmas clubs** sprang up to help them save money throughout the year in order to finance a December spending spree.

Conclusion

America's Christmas spending habits were established during the early twentieth century. As the United States became an affluent nation, Americans began to celebrate Christmas by spending large sums of money. Some point out, however, that America's Christmas consumption habits merely reflect her year-round consumption habits, which are extravagant by world standards. The average citizen of Vietnam earned $360 in 2000. Compare that with the $1,161 the average American family planned to spend on Christmas gifts alone in the same year. Other affluent nations also celebrate materially extravagant Christmases. For most Japanese, Christmas is neither a traditional folk holiday nor a religious holiday, yet they spent $7.5 billion for Christmas presents in 1993.

Many people have grown dissatisfied with the materialistic customs that characterize contemporary Christmas celebrations. In a 2002 survey, over seventy percent of Americans questioned said that they would like to reduce their Christmas spending and gift giving. Religious organizations, consumer advocates, and groups within the voluntary simplicity movement are supporting their followers in this endeavor.

Further Reading

Barnett, James H. *The American Christmas*. New York: Macmillan, 1954.

Belk, Russell. "Materialism and the Making of the Modern American Christmas." In Daniel Miller, ed. *Unwrapping Christmas*. Oxford, England: Clarendon Press, 1993.

Comfort, David. *Just Say Noel!* New York: Fireside Books, 1995.

Evergreen Alliance. *The First Green Christmas*. San Francisco, Calif.: Halo Books, 1990.

McKibben, Bill. *Hundred Dollar Holiday*. New York: Simon and Schuster, 1998.

Robinson, Jo, and Jean Coppock Staeheli. *Unplug the Christmas Machine*. New York: William Morrow and Company, 1982.

St. James, Elaine. *Simplify Your Christmas*. Kansas City, Mo.: Andrews McMeel Publishing, 1998.

Schmidt, Leigh Eric. *Consumer Rites: The Buying and Selling of American Holidays*. Princeton, N.J.: Princeton University Press, 1995.

Tyson, Ann Scott. "Christmas Without Shopping." *Christian Science Monitor* (Thursday, December 11, 1997): 1.

Waits, William. *The Modern Christmas in America*. New York: New York University Press, 1993.

Web Sites

A site sponsored by Alternatives, a Christian non-profit group advocating simpler living and less wasteful holiday celebrations: http://www.simple living.org

A site sponsored by the Center for a New American Dream, a non-profit organization in Takoma Park, Md., dedicated to reducing consumption, enhancing quality of life, and protecting the environment, contains the pamphlet "Simplify the Holidays": http://www.newdream.org/publications

December 25

The earliest Christians did not celebrate Christmas. In fact, the first Christian calendar listing December 25 as the Feast of the Nativity was compiled in 336 A.D. Since neither of the two biblical accounts of the Nativity—found in the **Gospel according to Luke** and the **Gospel according to Matthew**—gives the date of **Jesus'** birth, how did December 25 come to be the date on which Christians celebrate Christmas? (*See also* **Gospel Accounts of Christmas; Jesus, Year of Birth.**)

Birthdays in the Ancient World

In the ancient world various pagan peoples celebrated the birthdays of gods and important individuals. In fact, many pagan myths explained the miraculous births of the gods. This association with paganism caused some early Christian thinkers to oppose the celebration of birthdays on principle. For example, in his commentary on the Gospel of Matthew, the Christian teacher and writer Origen

(c. 185-c. 254) argued that Christians should not observe birthdays since scripture depicts only wrongdoers like the pharaohs and **Herod** celebrating their birthdays.

Selection of December 25

By the fourth century, however, Christian leaders had overcome their reluctance to honor the birthday of Jesus Christ. Now they had to decide upon a date for the new feast. The first mention of Christmas observances taking place on December 25 occurs in the Philocalian calendar, a Church document written in 336 A.D. Some scholars believe that Christian authorities scheduled the Feast of the Nativity for December 25 in order to draw people away from the pagan festivals celebrated on or around that date. The madcap revels associated with the Roman holiday of **Saturnalia** ended on December 23, just two days earlier. On January first the Romans observed **Kalends**, their new year festival. Finally, on December 25 devotees of Mithras and Sol celebrated the **Birth of the Invincible Sun**.

According to the calendar used by the ancient Romans, the **winter solstice** fell on December 25, making it a perfect day on which to commemorate the rebirth of the sun. The cult of the sun god was especially popular with the Romans between the second and the fourth centuries, a time when Christianity was struggling to establish itself as a legitimate faith. By selecting December 25 as the date for the new Feast of the Nativity, Christian leaders probably hoped to convince sun god worshipers to celebrate the birth of Jesus rather than the birth of the sun.

Some early Christian thinkers offered other, more convoluted explanations for the choice of December 25. They based these explanations not only on their interpretations of scripture, but also on Christian lore and then-popular beliefs concerning the significance of round numbers. According to one scholar, Church leaders tried to figure out the date of Jesus' birth from the date traditionally given for his death, March 25. Since they wanted to come up with a round number for Jesus' age at death, they assumed he was also conceived on March 25. Therefore, he must have been born nine months later on December 25.

Other Christian thinkers drew parallels between Christ and the sun based on Bible passages that describe the Messiah as "the sun of righteousness" (Malachi 4:2) and "the light of the world" (John 8:12). According to this line of thought, Jesus' incarnation represented a new creation, as when God created the world. According to the Book of Genesis, God's first act was to create light, an act that separated light from darkness. Therefore, they reasoned, God must have created the world at the time of the spring equinox, when the world is separated into two equal halves of light and darkness. Since Jesus himself stood for the new creation, Jesus must also have been conceived at the time of the spring equinox (*see also* **Annunciation**). According to the Julian calendar then in use, spring equinox fell on March 25. Allowing for a nine-month gestation period, Jesus would then have been born on December 25.

The solar symbolism attached to Jesus in this explanation concluded with his birth on the winter solstice, the date when the sun "returns" and the days begin to lengthen. By equating Jesus with the sun, Christian leaders adopted and yet subtly undermined the logic of sun god worshipers. For example, one early Christian writer thundered, "They [the pagans] call December twenty-fifth the Birthday of the Unconquered: Who is indeed so unconquered as our Lord? . . . or, if they say that it is the birthday of the sun: *He* is the Sun of Justice."

Division of Christmas and Epiphany

The introduction of Christmas as a separate feast clashed with the way in which many churches had been celebrating **Epiphany**. The first Epiphany celebrations occurred in second-century **Egypt**. The feast spread to other Christian communities during the next two hundred years, although considerable variation existed between these scattered celebrations. This holiday might commemorate any of the four, recognized occasions on which Jesus' divinity revealed itself to those around him: his birth, the adoration of the **Magi**, his baptism, and the miracle at the wedding in Cana. After creating a separate holiday to honor Jesus' birth, the Roman Church shifted the focus of its Epiphany celebrations to the adoration of the Magi. When the Eastern Churches finally accepted Christmas, they used the holiday to honor both Jesus' birth and the adoration of the Magi. Afterwards, their Epiphany celebrations focused on Jesus' baptism.

187

Spread of the New Feast

Sometime around the year 350 Pope Julius (d. 352) or Pope Liberius (d. 366) officially adopted December 25 as the Feast of the Nativity. After Church leaders established the holiday in Rome, they attempted to convince the churches in the eastern part of the empire to accept this feast. St. Gregory of Nazianzus (c. 330-c. 398) introduced the festival in Constantinople in 379. In 386 St. John Chrysostom preached to Christians in Antioch, advising them to accept the festival on this date, in spite of the fact that some still preferred to celebrate the Nativity on January 6. Most of the Eastern Churches accepted the new feast in the years between 380 and 430 A.D. Jerusalem Christians did not accept the new festival until the middle of the sixth century. The Armenians never accepted the new festival. Today, the Armenian Orthodox Church still celebrates the Nativity of Christ on January 6, Epiphany. Those Armenian Orthodox congregations in the Holy Land that still use the Julian calendar celebrate the festival on January 19 (*see* **Armenia, Christmas in; Old Christmas Day**).

Origins of the Word "Christmas"

Since Latin was the official language of the Roman Church, its leaders called the new festival commemorating Jesus' birth *Dies Natalis Domini,* or the "Birthday of the Lord." The more formal name for the holiday was *Festum Nativitatis Domini Nostri Jesu Christi,* or the "Feast of the Nativity of Our Lord Jesus Christ." Our English word for the festival, "Christmas," didn't evolve until centuries later. The term appears in documents from the eleventh and twelfth centuries, written in Old English as *Christes maesse,* which means "Christ's Mass." English speakers soon formed a contraction out of the two words. The name of the festival passed through many forms in the centuries that followed, including *kryst-masse, cristmasse, crystmasse, Chrysmas,* and *Cristmas.* The term "Christmas" came into the English language sometime between the late sixteenth and late seventeenth centuries.

In casual writing, the word Christmas sometimes appears as "Xmas." Some people dislike the informality of this abbreviation and the fact that it removes the word "Christ" from the word Christmas. Others find it less objectionable. They point out that the "x" may be said to stand for the Greek letter "X" (chi), which is the first letter in the Greek word for Christ.

Further Reading

Baldovin, John F. "Christmas." In Mircea Eliade, ed. *The Encyclopedia of Religion.* Volume 3. New York: Macmillan, 1987.

Cross, F. L., and E. A. Livingstone, eds. *The Oxford Dictionary of the Christian Church.* Second edition, revised. Oxford, England: Oxford University Press, 1983.

Del Re, Gerard, and Patricia Del Re. *The Christmas Almanack.* Garden City, N.Y.: Doubleday, 1979.

James, E. O. *Seasonal Feasts and Festivals.* 1961. Reprint. Detroit, Mich.: Omnigraphics, 1993.

Metford, J. C. J. *The Christian Year.* London, England: Thames and Hudson, 1991.

Smith, C. "Christmas and Its Cycle." In *New Catholic Encyclopedia.* Volume 3. New York: McGraw-Hill, 1967.

Stander, Hendrik F. "Christmas." In Everett Ferguson, ed. *Encyclopedia of Early Christianity.* Volume 1. New York: Garland, 1997.

Weiser, Francis X. *The Christmas Book.* 1952. Reprint. Detroit, Mich.: Omnigraphics, 1990.

Denmark, Christmas in

The people of Denmark enjoy a **Christmas season** full of good food and good cheer. At least one Danish Christmas custom, **Christmas seals**, has become popular in the United States and other countries.

Christmas Countdown

Danes use **Advent calendars** and calendar candles to help them count the days until Christmas. Danish calendar candles display a series of numbers down one side. These numbers represent the dates between the beginning of **Advent** and Christmas Day. The candle is lit each day until the number representing that day melts away. **Advent wreaths** are also popular in Denmark.

Christmas Symbols and Decorations

As Christmas draws near, Danish people adorn both their homes and the city streets with a variety of **Christmas symbols** and decorations. The most popular Christmas symbol in Denmark is the red heart. It represents the love that infuses Danish Christmas celebrations. The Danish flag is another popular Christmas image. The flag displays a white cross on a red background. Red and white serve as Denmark's Christmas colors. One often sees the popular Christmas heart woven out of strips of red and white paper. Moreover, many Danes light up the dark December afternoons and evenings with flickering red and white **Christmas candles**. Danes also fashion many Christmas decorations from **greenery**, especially **mistletoe** and **holly**, which is called *Kristdorn*, or "Christ thorn."

The *nisse* or *Julnisse* is another popular Christmas image (*see also* **Christmas Lads; Jultomten**). According to Danish folklore, the nisser are small, **elf**-like creatures who live in dark, quiet corners of homes and barns. They possess certain magical powers, which they can use to create annoying household mishaps. Around Christmas time the Julnisser, or "Christmas" nisser, become active. Householders must appease them with a bowl of porridge on Christmas Eve or they will pull pranks on family members.

Preparations

In the weeks before Christmas Danish families give their homes a thorough cleaning. The cleaning prepares them to receive the many visitors who are likely to be entertained during the Christmas season. Christmas baking also begins early. Not only must there be enough holiday treats to satisfy family members, but also guests must be entertained with the special holiday dainties. Favorite Danish Christmas cookies include spicy, brown sugar, almond cookies called *brune kager*, deep-fried butter cookies called *kleiner*, and hard spice cookies called *pebbernødder*. *Julekage*, Christmas coffee cake, is another popular treat, along with *vanillekranse*, vanilla butter cookies shaped like wreaths.

In past times well-to-do Danish families often gifted their servants with a plate of Christmas cookies. The servants not only enjoyed the cookies but treasured the plates, which were nicer than their own. In the nineteenth century Danish plate makers began to issue special blue-and-white plates painted with holiday designs and numbered by year. Today people collect these plates. Another Danish Christmas custom achieved worldwide popularity. Around the turn of the twentieth century a Danish postmaster invented the Christmas seal as a way of raising money for charity. Today people in many countries decorate their **Christmas cards**, packages, and letters with Christmas seals.

The Danish people adopted the German custom of decorating their homes with a **Christmas tree** in the nineteenth century. Many Danish families sit down together and make their own Christmas **ornaments** out of colored paper and paste. Typical designs include garlands of Danish flags, hearts, nisser, stars, drums, **bells**, and cones, which are filled with sweets and nuts. **Christmas crackers** may also be hung on the tree.

Christmas Parties

Many companies, unions, and other organizations give Christmas parties during the month of December. Office parties often take the form of sumptuous Friday lunches that last all afternoon. Family members also attend these events. Some researchers believe these parties are the modern-day equivalent of community Christmas parties, called *Jultraefests*, or "Christmas tree parties," that used to take place in Danish villages and towns.

Christmas Eve

The Danes enjoy *Juleaften*, or "Christmas Eve," so much that they begin preparing for it the day before, on *lille Juleaften*, or "Little Christmas Eve." On Little Christmas Eve they take care of last-minute chores and errands and begin cooking Christmas dinner, which is served on Christmas Eve. On December 24 many Danes leave a **Christmas sheaf** outside so that the birds may also enjoy a special Christmas meal. All over Denmark church bells chime at 4:00 p.m. on Christmas Eve. Shops and offices close, and people scurry home.

For many families, Christmas Eve festivities begin with candlelight church services. Afterwards people return home to an elaborate Christmas dinner. Before sitting down to eat, many families set a flickering candle in the window. The candle signals an offer of hospitality to any lonely or hungry person who passes by (*see also* **Advent Candle**). Popular main dishes include roast goose and roast pork. Roasted potatoes, cabbage, and cucumber salad often appear as side dishes. In the old days, many housewives presented a kind of rice pudding as a first course. Nowadays, the rice pudding serves as a dessert. The cook hides an almond in each batch of pudding. Whoever finds the almond in their serving gets a special little **gift**, usually some chocolate or marzipan.

After dinner the family gathers around the Christmas tree. According to one old tradition, the parents shut themselves in the parlor alone on Christmas Eve to decorate the tree and light the candles that cover it. Thus, the youngsters got their first view of the lit and decorated tree on Christmas Eve. While fewer families observe this old tradition today, many Danes still light their trees with candles rather than electric lights. Usually an older family member slips into the parlor alone to light the candles. When everything is ready, the rest of the family enters. They join hands around the tree and sing **Christmas carols**. Afterwards the family opens their gifts. In families with small children, the father may leave the room briefly and the Danish gift bringer, *Julemand*, may put in a brief appearance. Julemand is supposed to look and act much like **Santa Claus**, although few children miss his resemblance to their father during these home visits. Danish families open their presents one by one and everyone admires each gift. They also save the Christmas cards they receive in the days before Christmas and open them after the gifts on Christmas Eve.

Christmas Day and Second Christmas Day

On Christmas Day people visit with friends and family members. Around midday most households serve a *kolde bord*, or "cold table." Everyone makes open-face sandwiches from this buffet of cold meats, bread, spreads, cheese, and appetizers. Hosts and guest toast one another with small glasses of *aquavit*, a Scandinavian liquor. December 26 is also a holiday in Denmark. The Danes call it "Second Christmas Day" and often spend it visiting relatives whom they missed on Christmas Day. Theatergoing is another popular activity, and many theaters begin showing a new play on this date.

New Year's Eve and Epiphany

Holiday merrymaking continues on **New Year's** Eve. Many Danes go to parties on New Year's Eve or entertain guests at home. In the early part of the evening the Queen makes her annual New Year's speech to the nation. Many Danes tune in for this annual event. The Danes play practical jokes on one another for New Year's Eve. Wise people pull their belongings into the house. If not, the next morning they might find their bicycle on someone's rooftop or their garden tools gone missing. Noisemaking is another old New Year's Eve custom. In the old days farmers shot off guns to usher in the new year (*see also* **Shooting in Christmas**).

Nowadays, most Danes have found safer ways to raise a din on the last evening of the year. In Copenhagen, people gather together at the town square on New Year's Eve to sing and to listen to the city hall clock ring in the new year. Danes also celebrate the new year with fireworks.

The Christmas season ends on **Twelfth Night**, or **Epiphany** Eve. Remaining Christmas trees are taken down on this day and ornaments stored for the next year. Some families light three candles on Epiphany Eve, which stand for the three Wise Men, or **Magi**, who visited the baby **Jesus**.

Further Reading

Fertig, Terry. *Christmas in Denmark*. Chicago: World Book, 1986.
Spicer, Dorothy Gladys. *The Book of Festivals*. 1937. Reprint. Detroit, Mich.: Omnigraphics, 1990.

Depression

For many people the Christmas blues lurk right below the festive reds and greens of the holiday season. According to one national poll, about twenty-five percent of all Americans confessed to feeling sad around Christmas time.

Unrealistic Expectations

Our culture bombards us with the message that the **Christmas season** is the happiest time of year, a time for festive parties, loving family get-togethers, lavish gift giving, and constant good cheer. These high emotional, social, and material expectations set us up to be disappointed. Many people find it difficult to fulfill the cultural ideal of non-stop Christmas conviviality. This ideal may easily defeat people with difficult family situations, those who lost a loved one during a previous holiday season, the socially isolated, and those estranged or far away from their families. This failure to meet cultural expectations, along with the belief that "everyone else is having a good time," can result in depression.

High material expectations for the holiday may pose similar problems, especially for those on limited budgets (*see also* **Commercialism**). So great are the pressures to buy that some people bring financial hardship on themselves by spending more then they can really afford on holiday preparations and **gifts**. The resulting stress may open the door to depression.

Even those who can afford to participate fully in the gift giving, decorating, cooking, eating, drinking, and partygoing may sink into holiday season sadness, however. Stress and exhaustion brought on by an endless whirl of activities as well as overindulgence in food and drink also contribute to feelings of depression. Women may be particularly prone to this syndrome, as our culture assigns them the primary responsibility for shopping, cooking, decorating, and creating "special" family celebrations.

Advice

Therapists advise those with a tendency to suffer from this form of Christmas season sadness to discard their unrealistic expectations of the holidays. Often these spring from childhood nostalgia and romantic images promoted in the media rather than from a realistic assessment of one's own wishes, needs, limitations, and personal circumstances. In spite of our dreams of instant holiday happiness, these limitations and circumstances seldom vanish underneath the tinsel and colored lights of the Christmas season. Moreover, the stress of holiday preparations, travel, and family visits may aggravate whatever tensions exist in any of these areas. To avoid resentments bred by overwork, psychologists suggest that those saddled with organizing and hosting holiday celebrations delegate responsibilities to others.

Psychologists point out that family tensions that simmer below the surface during the rest of the year very often boil over when the family gathers together for the holidays. Although many people feel that family fights "ruin" holiday get-togethers, it may be more realistic to assume that if family members quarrel during the rest of the year, they will quarrel on Christmas.

Psychologists also recommend giving oneself, others, and the occasion permission to be less than perfect. They remind us that although the dynamic of family get-togethers often encourages everyone to assume old family roles, we may choose otherwise. Although we may make these choices for ourselves, psychologists counsel us to avoid using Christmas celebrations as a forum for changing family relationships. They point out, for example, that challenging Auntie May about her drinking is likely to lead to a confrontation, and that attempting to squeeze a year's worth of "quality time" with family members into a single holiday is doomed to failure.

Those who have experienced the loss of a loved one in the past year need to accept their current mental, emotional, and physical limits and openly acknowledge that this year's celebrations will be different. Counselors also recommend that those who grieve take time to evaluate which social obligations, family traditions, and religious observances will comfort and strengthen them, and which could overwhelm them. They also suggest that mourners seek the company of comforting people and make occasions to talk about their loved one. It may be best to plan provisionally and be prepared to alter arrangements as necessary to suit one's needs.

Christmas Suicides

It is widely believed that the rate of suicides increases during the holiday period. Although many Americans admit to feeling sad during the holiday season, studies reveal that the suicide rate does not increase around Christmas time.

Winter Weather

The winter weather itself plunges some people into depression. S.A.D., seasonal affective disorder, causes its sufferers to become depressed during the dark days of winter that coincide with the holiday season in the Northern Hemisphere. Christmas, New Year's Day, **Hanukkah**, Thanksgiving, and **Kwanzaa** all cluster around the time of the **winter solstice**. At this time of year, the days are short, the sunlight weak, the skies often overcast, and the nights long. People suffering from S.A.D. react strongly to the lack of light, falling into states of lethargy and depression that last for months. Other symptoms may include increased appetite, an excessive desire for sleep, irritability, anxiety, decreasing self-esteem, and difficulty concentrating.

Experts estimate that about six percent of all Americans exhibit symptoms of full-blown S.A.D. About fourteen percent suffer from a milder version of these symptoms known informally as the "winter blues." Some psychologists claim that among S.A.D. patients, women outnumber men by a four-to-one ratio. Others point out, however, that these figures may be somewhat skewed since men have more difficulty than do women in admitting to mood-related problems.

In the Northern Hemisphere the incidence of S.A.D. increases as one travels northward because the northern latitudes enjoy fewer winter daylight hours. Researchers have discovered that about 28 percent of the population of Fairbanks, Alaska, suffers to some degree from S.A.D. The city of Tromsø, **Norway**, lies 200 miles south of the Arctic Circle. There the sun sets in November and inhabitants endure midwinter darkness until day breaks again in late January. The people of Tromsø refer to this period as the *mørketiden*, or "murky time." Each year the mørketiden ushers in an increase in the incidence of physical and mental illness, domestic violence, alcoholism and other forms of drug abuse, arrests, suicides, and poor school performance. Like the inhabitants of many other towns in northern Norway, the people of Tromsø observe a joyous yearly festival, "Sun Day," on the day the sun returns.

If you suspect you may be suffering from S.A.D., seek professional diagnosis and treatment. Many people affected by S.A.D. have found relief in light therapy treatments, medication, changes in diet, or other lifestyle alterations.

Further Reading

Marano, Hara Estroff. "Surviving Holiday Hell." *Psychology Today* 31, 6 (November-December 1998): 32-36.

Peters, Celeste A. *Don't Be SAD*. Calgary, Canada: Script Publishing, 1994.

Robinson, Jo, and Jean Coppock Staeheli. *Unplug the Christmas Machine*. New York: William Morrow and Company, 1982.

Rosenthal, Norman E. *Winter Blues*. New York: Guilford Press, 1993.

Smith, Harold Ivan. *A Decembered Grief: Living with Loss While Others Are Celebrating*. Kansas City, Mo.: Beacon Hill Press of Kansas City, 1999.

Whybrow, Peter, and Robert Bahr. *The Hibernation Response*. New York: Arbor House, William Morrow, 1988.

Devil's Knell
Devil's Funeral, Old Lad's Passing Bell

According to an old European custom, local deaths were announced by the ringing of church **bells**. In England this sound was known as a "death knell." Since old English and Irish folk beliefs asserted that the Devil died when **Jesus** was born, some towns developed a tradition of ringing the church bells near midnight on Christmas Eve to announce the Devil's demise. In **England** the custom was called tolling or ringing "the Devil's knell" or "the Old Lad's Passing Bell." In **Ireland** the Christmas Eve bell ringing became known as the "Devil's Funeral."

Although religious officials forbade this custom after the Reformation, the practice survived in the English town of Dewsbury in Yorkshire. The Dewsbury tradition dates back to the mid-thirteenth century. It was briefly discontinued in the early 1800s and then reinstated. Local officials interrupted the practice again in 1940, since during World War II bell ringing was forbidden except as an announcement of invasion. The inhabitants of Dewsbury revived their bell-ringing tradition in 1948. According to custom, a team of local residents rings a certain bell in the Dewsbury parish church once for every year that has passed since Christ's birth. The bell ringing begins at eleven p.m. on Christmas Eve and is timed to end at midnight. The custom prevents the Devil from infiltrating the parish during the coming year, according to folk beliefs.

An old legend explains the history of the Devil's knell bell and hints at another origin for the Christmas Eve bell-ringing custom. Long ago a local man of means, named Thomas de Soothill, murdered a young man in his service. As penance for his crime he donated a large bell to the Dewsbury church. He requested that the bell toll every year on Christmas Eve as a reminder of his sin. Until recently, the Dewsbury bell was called "Black Tom of Soothill" in reference to this legend.

Further Reading

Foley, Daniel J. *Christmas the World Over*. Philadelphia, Pa.: Chilton Books, 1963.

Hole, Christina. *British Calendar Customs*. London, England: Hutchinson and Company, 1976.

Howard, Alexander. *Endless Cavalcade*. London, England: Arthur Baker, 1964.

Spicer, Dorothy Gladys. *Yearbook of English Festivals*. 1954. Reprint. Detroit, Mich.: Omnigraphics, 1993.

Ecuador, Christmas in

In Ecuador Christmas begins with **Advent**, a season rich in customs and celebrations. As Christmas draws near, town officials close off certain streets in order to make space for street vendors selling Christmas sweets and trinkets. Many people begin collecting toys, used clothes, and candy to give to poorer families so that their children will also have Christmas presents to open.

Parties

Employees eagerly await the customary Christmas party, as well as the **Christmas bonus**, or *aguinaldo*, which employers are legally required to give to workers. Parades of people dressed as **Mary**, **Joseph**, the **shepherds**, and the Three Kings (*see also* **Magi**) file through workplaces, schools, and neighborhoods. People without costumes follow, carrying candles and singing **Christmas carols**.

Religious Observances

A nine-day Christmas novena (a series of special prayer services offered on nine consecutive days) begins on December 16 and lasts until December 24. These sessions of prayer and song offer occasions for family and friends to spend the evening at one another's homes. In addition, **Nativity scenes** appear in churches, homes, schools, and workplaces at this time. Some of these locations sponsor competitions for the best Nativity scene. Many families also add a **Christmas tree** to their home decorations.

Christmas Eve

Churches hold **Midnight Mass** on Christmas Eve, but many people prefer to spend the evening at home with loved ones. Ecuadorian folklore asserts that **Jesus** was born at the stroke of midnight, and many people choose to spend this special hour at home with family (*see also* **Misa de Gallo**). Those assembled at home count down the last moments before midnight, and, on the stroke of twelve, exchange hugs with all present. In the past families sat down to a large meal just after midnight (*see also* **Réveillon**). Nowadays, however, many dine some time before midnight. A traditional Christmas dinner might offer roast chicken, stuffed turkey, or roast pork. *Pristiños*, or molasses pastries, usually complete the meal. Many also serve *canelazo*, a sweet hot beverage made by heating water, sugar, cinnamon, cloves, and liquor together. Traditionally, Ecuadorians open their Christmas **gifts** after dinner on Christmas Eve.

Ecuador's most spectacular parade, the *Pase del Niño Viajero*, takes place in the city of Cuenca on the morning of December 24. Participants ride in cars, trucks, or on donkeys, each decorated with emblems of abundance. These emblems range from paper money to bunches of fruit to bottles of liquor and roasted meats. Bands of folk musicians as well as biblically costumed children round out the procession.

Holy Innocents' Day and Epiphany

The festivities continue on December 28, **Holy Innocents' Day**. People celebrate with costume parties and practical jokes. These jokes, called *inocentadas*, usually revolve around prank phone calls or fake candies. Costumed pranksters may parade openly down the main streets of towns and cities. The **Christmas season** ends with **Epiphany** on January 6.

Further Reading

Clynes, Tom. *Wild Planet!* Detroit, Mich.: Visible Ink Press, 1995.
Wakefield, Charito Calvachi. *Navidad Latinoamericana, Latin American Christmas.* Lancaster, Pa.: Latin American Creations Publishing, 1997.

Eggnog

Many Americans celebrate the **Christmas season** by imbibing a curious mixture of beaten eggs, spirits, and spices known as eggnog. This drink dates back to the colonial era. In those days, people sometimes called rum "grog." This fact leads some to believe that eggnog's original name was "egg and grog," which was later shortened into "eggnog." In spite of its American credentials, eggnog resembles a number of traditional northern European Christmas specialties, including the English **lamb's wool** and syllabub, the Dutch *advocaat*, and the Norwegian *eggedosis*. All of these recipes blend beaten eggs with wine, ale, or spirits. Lamb's wool may also contain cream or milk. American eggnog recipes usually call for some combination of beaten eggs, brandy, cream, sugar, and nutmeg.

Eggnog has been enlivening American Christmas festivities for several centuries. George Washington's Christmas guests might well have staggered home after one cup too many of his favorite eggnog preparation. His recipe requires one quart of cream, one quart of milk, one dozen eggs, one pint of brandy, one-half pint of rye, one-quarter pint of rum, and one-quarter pint of sherry (*see also* **America, Christmas in Colonial**). First Lady Dolley Madison entertained her guests with cinnamon eggnog, one of her Christmas specialties (*for more on American presidents, see* **White House, Christmas in**).

In 1826 cadets at the prestigious West Point Military Academy risked their careers for a taste of the traditional midwinter cheer. They staged a secretive eggnog party in direct disobedience of Superintendent Thayer's order that the academy observe a dry Christmas season. Designated cadets snuck the contraband ingredients past the sentries. On Christmas Eve they blackened the windows in their barracks, posted guards to warn of the approach of officers, and began the festivities. Officials somehow stumbled upon the scene at 4:30 a.m. The encounter between the drunken students and the outraged officers resulted in a bloody melee that left one cadet charged with attempted murder. The so-called "Eggnog Riot" eventually led to the voluntary resignation of six cadets and the court martial of nineteen of their fellows. Eleven of these were dismissed from the academy. Since seventy young men took part in the escapade, one might conclude that most got off easy. Many of these cadets hailed from prominent American families. Jefferson Davis, future president of the Confederate States of America, was one of them. As punishment for his participation in the eggnog conspiracy, school authorities arrested him and confined him to his quarters until February of the following year (*see also* **America, Christmas in Nineteenth-Century**).

In the late twentieth century fewer and fewer Americans seem willing to abandon themselves to the full-fledged eggnog experience. New low-fat and non-alcoholic versions of the old Christmas favorite sprout up every year, reflecting contemporary health concerns. The following old-fashioned eggnog recipe offers us a glimpse of the uninhibited pleasures of past eras:

> Whisk together six eggs and two cups of sugar until fluffy and light. Continue stirring while slowly adding one quart of bourbon whiskey and one cup of rum. Slowly add four cups of milk, four cups half-and-half, and one cup heavy cream stirring all the while. Add grated nutmeg as desired. Chill and serve.

Further Reading

Sansom, William. *The Book of Christmas*. New York: McGraw-Hill Book Company, 1968.

Snyder, Phillip. *December 25th*. New York: Dodd, Mead, and Company, 1985.

Stevens, Patricia Bunning. *Merry Christmas!: A History of the Holiday*. New York: Macmillan, 1979.

Egypt, Christmas in

Members of the ancient Coptic Orthodox branch of the Christian faith make up about seven percent of Egypt's population. They celebrate Christmas on January 7 (*see also* **Old Christmas Day**). The Coptic Orthodox Church encourages believers to fast for some or all of **Advent** as a means of preparing themselves for the celebration of the Nativity. In Egypt Coptic Christians fast by refraining from eating during the daylight hours and by abstaining from meat, eggs, and dairy products during the fasting period. On Christmas Eve the faithful attend midnight services held in Coptic churches. The most famous of these services takes place in St. Mark's Cathedral in Cairo and is presided over by the head of the Coptic Orthodox Church. The families return home afterwards to break their fast and distribute **gifts** and new clothes to their children. Egypt's Coptic Christians also bake a special cookie, called *kahk*, in the shape of a cross as a Christmas treat. Egyptian Muslims use the same recipe for the cookies they bake for Id-al-Fitr, an important Muslim feast that breaks the month-long fast of Ramadan.

In January of 2003, Christmas (January 7) was observed as a national holiday in Egypt. This was the first time in the history of modern Egypt that a Christian holy day was formally recognized by the government. Egyptian President Hosni Mubarak issued a presidential decree authorizing the observance, making it the nation's eighteenth legal holiday.

Further Reading

Abbas, Jailan. *Festivals of Egypt*. Cairo, Egypt: Hoopoe Books, 1995.
Associated Press. "Egypt Makes Christmas a National Holiday." *New York Times* (January 6, 2003).

Elves

Contemporary Christmas lore suggests that **Santa Claus** lives at the **North Pole**, accompanied by a band of elves. These elves staff Santa's workshop, manufacturing the millions of toys Santa brings to children at Christmas time. What exactly are elves and how did they become associated with Santa Claus and the celebration of Christmas?

Elves and Fairies

Folk descriptions of a magical and mostly invisible race of beings can be found in the lore of peoples from all parts of the globe. This belief was particularly common among the peoples of **Europe** and Asia. In Europe these beings were known by many names. Folklorists often refer to them as "fairies," a common English term for these creatures. Some trace belief in fairies back to the ancient Romans and their legends about the deities known as the "Three Fates." Indeed, some folklorists locate the origins of the English word "fairy" in the Latin word for "fate," *fatum.* Eventually, the Three Fates evolved into spirits known as *fata* in Italian and *fada* in Spanish. These beings hovered about babies at the time of their births, bestowing upon them strengths, weaknesses, and destinies. In French-speaking areas, however, these magical creatures were called *fée*, a word some experts link to the Old French verb for "enchant," *féer*. The English adopted the French term for these creatures, translating it as "fay," or later, "fairy."

Ireland and the British Isles were particularly rich in fairy folklore. A multitude of names arose for these magical beings. The Irish knew them as the Síde, or "people of the hills"; the Welsh called them Tylwyth Teg, the "fair family"; and the Scottish talked of two distinct groups — the Seelie (blessed) Court and the Unseelie (unblessed) Court. Other names for them included the Little People, the Good Folk, the Gentry, Puck, Robin Goodfellow, pixies, and brownies. English speakers might also have referred to these beings as elves. The word "elf" came into English from the Nordic and Teutonic languages, apparently arriving in **England** when Scandinavian peoples invaded in the Middle Ages. The beings known to the English as fairies were called *alfar* in Scandinavia, a word that evokes mountains and water. The English incorporated this word into their own language as "elf."

Fairy folklore taught that, although these magical creatures inhabited the natural world all around us, they often chose to remain invisible. When visible, they frequently appeared in human form. They could, however, take the shape of a flower, a flame, a bird, a jewel, a woodland animal, or any other element of the natural world. Folk beliefs advised people to tread warily if they sensed that these magical and unpredictable creatures were about. On the one hand, elves and fairies often used their powers to aid humans, for example, by providing **gifts** of food or toys for children, or by breaking evil enchantments. On the other hand, if provoked they could just as easily harm humans. They sometimes stole human children, ruined crops, and caused household accidents.

European Christmas Elves

The folklore of many European countries warned that spirits of all kinds were particularly active during the **Twelve Days of Christmas**. British folklore cautioned that fairies and the Will O' the Wisp haunted these long, dark nights. The famous English playwright William Shakespeare (1564-1616) disagreed, however. The following lines from the play *Hamlet* voice his dissenting opinion:

> Some say, that ever 'gainst that season comes
> Wherein our Saviour's birth is celebrated,
> The bird of dawning singeth all night long:
> And then, they say, no spirit can walk abroad;
> The nights are wholesome; then no planets strike,
> Nor fairy takes, nor witch hath power to charm;
> So hallow'd and so gracious is the time.

The Scandinavians did not share Shakespeare's sentiments. Their lore reminded them that the arrival of the Christmas season awakened the **Jultomten** (also known as the *Julnissen, Julenissen,* or *Joulutonttuja*). Every homestead hosted at least one of these elf-like creatures. They slept and hid in dark corners for most of the year, but became bold and **merry** around Christmas time. In fact, they expected householders to provide them with good cheer on Christmas Eve. If the family neglected to leave out an offering of food before going to bed, the Jultomten might curdle the milk or cause other household mishaps. In Sweden, **Norway**, and Finland these elves eventually evolved into Christmas gift bringers, a role they still carry out today. In **Iceland** prankster elves known as the **Christmas Lads** vex householders at Christmas time.

American Christmas Elves

These European traditions may have influenced the creation of the American Santa Claus, his workshop, and his elven helpers. This vision of Santa's world was constructed in large part by two men over a century ago: classics professor Clement C. Moore (1779-1863) and illustrator Thomas Nast (1840-1902). In the early nineteenth century Moore, a professor at General Theological Seminary, scribbled down a little Christmas poem for children. Titled "A Visit From St. Nicholas," it described the nocturnal activities of the Christmas gift bringer who would later be known as Santa Claus. This description depicted Santa Claus as a "jolly old elf" who arrives in a "miniature sleigh." Moore's vision of Santa Claus, which had already begun to shape the American public's image of Santa Claus, was further refined by those who followed. Although Thomas Nast was not the first writer or illustrator to place Santa in the company of a band of elves, he was the most influential. In the late nineteenth century Nast published a series of cartoons that elaborated on the image of Santa Claus established by Moore. Nast enlarged Santa to human size and gave him a home, the North Pole. He retained the connection between Santa Claus and elves, however, by depicting them as Santa's labor force.

Whereas the elves of traditional European folklore whiled away the hours dancing in moonlit meadows and sleeping under the stairs, Santa's elves busied themselves in his workshop all year round. Clearly Nast's elves emerged from the imagination of an industrial age, unlike their older, European counterparts. Nevertheless, the fact that both Nast and Moore included references to elves in their creations may well reflect the influence of northern European folklore associating Christmas time with the activities of elves. The American people may have embraced yet another element of European elf lore in their Christmas celebrations. The American custom of leaving a snack of cookies and milk for Santa Claus on Christmas Eve closely resembles the Scandinavian practice of placating the Jultomten. In any case, Nast's vision of Santa and his North Pole workshop gained widespread acceptance in the United States. As Santa Claus became an international folk figure, so, too, did Santa's helpers and year-long companions, the North Pole elves.

Further Reading

Briggs, Katharine. *An Encyclopedia of Fairies*. New York: Pantheon Books, 1976.

Hole, Christina. *British Folk Customs*. London, England: Hutchinson and Company, 1976.

Leach, Maria, ed. *Funk and Wagnalls Standard Dictionary of Folklore, Mythology, and Legend*. New York: Harper and Row, 1984.

Restad, Penne. *Christmas in America*. New York: Oxford University Press, 1995.

Emancipation Day

Christmas was a mixed blessing for many African Americans during slavery times. On the one hand, many plantation slaves received **gifts**, time off, extra food rations, and visiting privileges (*see* **Slaves' Christmas**). On the other hand, they dreaded the coming of the new year, when the holidays ended and some slave masters announced which slaves would be sold off or sent to work on neighboring plantations that year, thereby breaking up families and friends.

First Celebrations

On January 1, 1863, President Abraham Lincoln (1809-1865) signed the Emancipation Proclamation into law, turning the day from one of sorrow into one of great joy. The proclamation granted immediate freedom to most slaves in the American South. Lincoln, occupied with the **New Year's Day** reception (or levee) that nineteenth-century presidents hosted on January 1, did not sign the document until that afternoon (*see also* **White House, Christmas in**). African Americans in Washington, D.C., snatched up copies of the evening newspapers containing the full text of the proclamation as soon as they were printed. Shouts of joy went up as the proclamation was read aloud to the congregation gathered at Washington, D.C.'s Israel Bethel Church. Spontaneous celebrations soon broke out all over the city and lasted until the small hours of the morning, punctuated for some time by the booming of the Navy Yard cannons.

In Boston, a city known for its abolitionist sympathies, a program of celebration had been prepared some time in advance (Lincoln having announced his intention to sign the Emancipation Proclamation 100 days earlier). The city's music hall hosted a gala event that afternoon, at which the orchestra played Beethoven's Fifth Symphony. In addition, well-known poet Ralph Waldo Emerson (1803-1882) recited his "Boston Hymn," written specially for this event. Other noted literary and political figures also attended the celebration, including Henry Wadsworth Longfellow (1807-1882), Oliver Wendell Holmes

(1841-1935), John Greenleaf Whittier (1807-1892), Edward Everett Hale (1822-1909), Charles Eliot Norton (1827-1908), Harriet Beecher Stowe (1811-1896), and Josiah Quincy (1772-1864). Another gathering took place that evening at Tremont Temple. The crowd cheered wildly when it was announced that the text of the Emancipation Proclamation was coming in over the telegraph wires. African-American author William Wells Brown (1815-1880) and orator Frederick Douglass (1817-1895) were in attendance there.

Annual Celebrations

Not everyone received the news of emancipation on January 1. African Americans in Texas had to wait till June 19, 1865, when United States General Gordon Granger arrived in Galveston. There he issued General Order number three, announcing the news of the Emancipation Proclamation and freeing the slaves in accordance with the now two-and-a-half-year-old law.

African Americans in east Texas, western Louisiana, southwestern Arkansas, and southern Oklahoma memorialized June 19, the joyous day of their liberation, by turning it into an annual holiday called Juneteenth. African Americans in Georgia, Alabama, North Carolina, South Carolina, Virginia, **New York City**, and Boston continued to celebrate the anniversary of their independence on January 1, Emancipation Day.

Early observances of Emancipation Day were modeled after **Watch Night** celebrations. Some African-American communities continue to commemorate January 1 as Emancipation Day. Typical proceedings revolve around church services that include a reading of the Emancipation Proclamation, sermons, prayers, and the singing of spirituals as well the song "Lift Every Voice and Sing," known informally as the African-American national anthem.

Further Reading

Franklin, John Hope. *The Emancipation Proclamation*. Garden City, N.Y.: Doubleday, 1963.

Taylor, Charles A. *Juneteenth*. Madison, Wis.: Praxis, 1995.

Wiggins, Williams H. *O Freedom! African-American Emancipation Celebrations*. Knoxville, Tenn.: University of Tennessee Press, 1987.

England, Christmas in

The English Christmas has gone through a number of striking transformations in its nearly two-thousand-year history (*see also* **Europe, Christmas in Medieval; Myrrh; Puritans; Twelve Days of Christmas; Victorian England, Christmas in**). Current English Christmas celebrations bear some resemblance to American celebrations. This resemblance is partly due to the fact that English settlers brought many of their Christmas customs to America during colonial times (*see also* **America, Christmas in Colonial**). The fact that the British and American peoples have adopted similar Christmas customs since that time may be even more significant in explaining the resemblance.

Like many Americans, the English celebrate the holiday with a **Christmas tree, gifts,** and **Christmas carols**. Over the centuries the English developed a large stock of Christmas carols. Many of these songs, such as "O Come All Ye Faithful," "Joy to the World," and "God Rest You Merry, Gentlemen," have also established themselves in the American carol repertoire. Caroling, a popular Christmas custom in England, keeps these songs in circulation. Another popular custom in both countries, sending **Christmas cards**, began in England in the nineteenth century. The English decorate their homes with **greenery** for the **Christmas season**. Old traditions promote **holly, ivy,** and **mistletoe** as the most appropriate plants for this purpose, but other green branches may also be used. After nightfall brilliant light displays illuminate the main avenues of many towns and cities (*see also* **Ornaments**).

Father Christmas

In England children expect **Father Christmas** to bring them their gifts. Children write letters to Father Christmas explaining what kind of Christmas gifts they would like to receive (*see also* **Children's Letters**). Instead of mailing them, they burn them in the fireplace, relying on magic to float their words up the chimney and across England to the ears of Father Christmas.

Christmas Eve

Christmas carols ring out all across England on December 24. For those who prefer to stay at home, British television and radio stations broadcast many musical performances. At King's College Chapel in Cambridge, lines form early for seats at the famous **Ceremony of Lessons and Carols** service.

Christmas Day

Children dash to the fireplace on Christmas morning to retrieve their now-full Christmas **stockings**. Many homes also keep a Christmas tree, underneath which family members will find another heap of gifts. Unwrapping these gifts is one of the highlights of Christmas Day. Other highlights include sitting down to a large, festive meal and listening to the Queen's speech. Each year British television broadcasts the Queen's Christmas greeting to her subjects. King George V began this Christmas tradition in 1932. Other popular Christmas Day activities include attending Christmas morning church services and playing parlor **games**. Indeed, Christmas game playing is a very old tradition in England.

Christmas dinner in England may feature roast goose, roast turkey, or roast beef. Potatoes, gravy, and vegetables usually accompany the main dish. **Plum pudding**, the traditional Christmas dessert, crowns the meal in many English households. Since the pudding contains a coin, and perhaps other good-luck tokens as well, diners must bite gently in order to avoid breaking their teeth. A kind of party favor known as a **Christmas cracker** adds a playful note to the holiday meal. **Wassail**, a traditional holiday punch, may follow the repast.

Boxing Day

The day after Christmas is also a holiday in England. It is called **Boxing Day**, although in the past it was known as **St. Stephen's Day**. Many families go to the theater to see a **pantomime** on this day. Fox hunting is another traditional Boxing Day activity. The English also enjoy other sporting events, such as soccer matches and car races, on this day. The **wren hunt**, a custom once practiced in England on St. Stephen's Day, still survives in **Ireland**.

Regional Customs

In past times people in some regions of England saluted their fruit trees with song and ale in honor of Christmas. This custom, known as wassailing the apple trees, still continues in a few places (*see* **Wassailing the Fruit Trees**). In the medieval era the well-to-do feasted on wild boar for Christmas. Today, an elaborate **boar's head** dinner survives at Oxford's Queen's College. An old Christmas Eve custom called ringing the **Devil's knell**, persists in the town of Dewsbury in Yorkshire. This practice sprang up around the folk belief that the Devil dies each year at the moment when Christ is born. The church **bells** still toll on Christmas Eve in Dewsbury, announcing the Devil's demise. On New Year's Eve many people in northern England welcome **firstfooters**. A firstfooter, the first person to cross one's threshold after the start of the new year, sets the household's luck for the coming year.

Lesser-Known Days and Customs

In pre-industrial England, numerous minor days of observance studded the Christmas season calendar. These included **Stir-Up Sunday**, **St. Thomas's Day**, St. Stephen's Day, **Holy Innocents' Day**, **St. Distaff's Day**, **Twelfth Night**, and **Plough Monday**. More important holidays, like **Epiphany** and **Candlemas**, were also celebrated. What's more, after 1752, when England adopted the Gregorian calendar reform, some people continued to honor the previous date for Christmas, giving rise to the observance of **Old Christmas Day**. Most of these minor holy days and holidays faded away during the nineteenth century, as the English calendar was reorganized around the industrial work week.

Though many of the customs associated with these days have faded as well, some weathered the transition. For instance, the town of Glastonbury still awaits the blooming of the **Glastonbury thorn** on or near Old Christmas Day.

Extinct Customs

Throughout their long history the English have adopted and invented many distinctive Christmas customs. They have also discarded a number of customs over the years. One such discarded custom, electing a **Lord of Misrule** to preside over Christmas festivities, fell out of favor in the seventeenth century. While the Lord of Misrule ruled over towns, schools, courts, and noble households, the **boy bishop** supervised the revelry taking place in church circles. The boy bishop did not outlast the Middle Ages, although this custom has been revived in a few churches. The boys who lived in the centuries that followed found another Christmas time sport: **barring out the schoolmaster**. If successful in keeping their teacher from entering the classroom in the days before Christmas, they won themselves a couple days of vacation from school.

Another old English Christmas custom, **mumming**, gave ordinary people license to disguise themselves in old clothes, mask their faces with burnt cork, and roam about the town engaging in horseplay. Around the time of the Renaissance, the wealthy developed their own version of this custom. They began to celebrate the Christmas season with **masques**, elaborate costumed balls that included dancing and perhaps a bit of playacting as well.

Although masques themselves began to die out as a form of Christmas entertainment in the late seventeenth century, the English continued to celebrate Twelfth Night with costume balls and playacting until the nineteenth century. During the nineteenth century many English families decorated their homes with a **kissing bough** for the Christmas season. Anyone passing beneath this spherical bunch of greenery could be claimed for a kiss. The kissing bough did not survive the transition to the twentieth century. Neither did the **waits**. These semi-official bands of musicians used to wander the streets during the Christmas season, singing for food, drink, and tips. They disbanded during the nineteenth century, when people began to view their activities less as a seasonal entertainment and more as an annoyance. (*For more on extinct Christmas season entertainments, see* **Games; Ghosts.**)

Further Reading

Crippen, Thomas G. *Christmas and Christmas Lore*. 1923. Reprint. Detroit, Mich.: Omnigraphics, 1990.

Hutton, Ronald. *The Stations of the Sun*. Oxford, England: Oxford University Press, 1996.

McInnes, Celia. *An English Christmas*. New York: Henry Holt and Company, 1986.

Miles, Clement A. *Christmas in Ritual and Tradition*. 1912. Reprint. Detroit, Mich.: Omnigraphics, 1990.

Patterson, Lillie. *Christmas in Britain and Scandinavia*. Champaign, Ill.: Garrard Publishing Company, 1970.

Pimlott, J. A. R. *The Englishman's Christmas*. Atlantic Highlands, N.J.: Humanities Press, 1978.

Ross, Corinne. *Christmas in Britain*. Chicago: World Book, 1978.

Epiphany

Blessing of the Waters Day,
Día de los Tres Reyes (Three Kings Day),
Feast of Baptism, Feast of Jordan, Feast of Lights,
Feast of the Three Kings, Fête des Rois,
Le Jour de Rois (Kings' Day), Night of Destiny,
Old Christmas Day, Perchtennacht, Theophania,
Timkat, Twelfth Day, Twelfth Night

Epiphany is a Christian feast day celebrated on January 6. The holiday commemorates the revelation of **Jesus'** divinity to those around him. In Western Christianity, the observance of Epiphany focuses on the adoration of the **Magi**. In Eastern Christianity the holiday emphasizes Jesus' baptism. Over the centuries European folklore has assigned numerous legends and customs to Epiphany, some of which bear little direct relationship to the life of Jesus. In many countries Epiphany marks the end of the **Christmas season**.

The Meaning of Epiphany

The word "epiphany" comes from the Greek term *epiphaneia*, meaning "manifestation," "appearance," or "showing forth." In the ancient world, the term designated occasions on which visiting kings or emperors appeared before the people. The writers of the Gospels used this term to describe occasions on which Jesus' divinity revealed itself to those around him. Ancient writers applied another Greek word, *theophaneia*, or "theophany," to the appearance of a god before human beings. Early Christians also used the word theophany in reference to their Epiphany celebrations. This usage continued in the Greek world, where today the Greek Orthodox Church refers to Epiphany as *Theophania*. Moreover, Eastern Orthodox Christians sometimes call Epiphany the "Feast of Lights." This name reflects their belief that baptism confers spiritual illumination.

The History of Epiphany

Early Christians were celebrating Epiphany before they began to observe Christmas. The first celebrations of Epiphany occurred in second-century **Egypt**. Like Christmas, the date chosen for Epiphany has no firm historical or scriptural grounding. Some scholars believe that January 6 was selected by the earliest celebrants in order to upstage a **winter solstice** festival held in honor of an Egyptian sun god on that date. Indeed, according to one ancient Egyptian calendar, winter solstice fell on January 6. Some ancient Egyptians recognized that day as the birthday of the Egyptian god Osiris. Other sacred events held on that day include a festival commemorating the birth of the god Aeon from his virgin mother, Kore.

From the second century onward, scattered celebrations of Epiphany occurred among various groups of Christians, although no consensus emerged as to what events the holiday commemorated. Christian liturgy identifies four instances in which Jesus' divine nature manifested itself on earth: at his birth, at the adoration of the Magi, at his baptism, and when he changed water into wine at the wedding in Cana. Early Epiphany celebrations honored any one or more of these events. By the third century most Eastern Christians were celebrating Epiphany. By the late fourth century most Western Christians had also adopted the feast. Eastern and Western celebrations evolved around different themes, however. When the Western Church designated **December 25** as the Feast of the Nativity in the mid-fourth century, Western Epiphany celebrations consolidated around the revelation of Jesus' divinity to the Magi. When the Eastern Church embraced Christmas, between 380 and 430 A.D., Christmas absorbed

the celebration of both the Nativity and the adoration of the Magi. Thus, Eastern Epiphany observances remained dedicated to the commemoration of Jesus'baptism.

In the Middle Ages, popular western European Epiphany celebrations focused on the Magi's journey. People began to refer to the Magi as kings and saints and to Epiphany as the "Feast of the Three Kings." Festivities of the day included **Nativity plays**, many of which featured the story of the Three Kings. Another boisterous medieval ceremony, the **Feast of Fools**, was also sometimes performed in churches on Epiphany.

In 1336 the city of Milan, **Italy**, hosted a splendid procession and play to commemorate the Feast of the Three Kings. Three men, sumptuously dressed as kings and surrounded by an entire retinue of costumed pages, body guards, and attendants, paraded through the city streets following a gold star which hung before them (*see also* **Star of Bethlehem**). At one juncture, they encountered King **Herod** and his scribes. The Wise Men asked where Jesus was to be born, and King Herod, after consulting the scribes, answered "**Bethlehem**." The kings and their followers continued on to St. Eustorgius Church, bearing their gifts of **gold, frankincense**, and **myrrh** ceremoniously before them. The crowd spilled into the church, preceded by trumpeters, horn players, donkeys, apes, and other animals. To one side of the high altar awaited **Mary** and the Christ child, in a manger complete with ox and ass. Although we might consider this noisy and colorful Epiphany celebration unseemly, medieval Europeans enjoyed this mixture of ceremony, carnival, and religion.

In Spanish-speaking countries today, Epiphany retains this strong association with the Magi and is called *Día de los Tres Reyes*, or Three Kings Day. The French call the holiday *Le Jour de Rois* or *Fête des Rois*: Kings' Day or the Feast of the Kings (*see also* **France, Christmas in**). The British sometimes refer to the holiday as Twelfth Day, and the evening before as **Twelfth Night**, since it occurs twelve days after Christmas. Twelfth Day marks the end of the Christmas season, also known as Twelfthtide or the **Twelve Days of Christmas**. Since late medieval times the British had enjoyed feasts and masquerades on Twelfth Night, but these celebrations have declined since the nineteenth century.

Folklore and Customs

In Italy and Spanish-speaking countries, children receive **gifts** on Epiphany rather than on Christmas. Furthermore, in Spanish-speaking countries, the Three Kings, *Los Reyes Magos*, deliver the presents rather than **Santa Claus**. On Epiphany Eve children leave a **shoe** on their doorstep or balcony, along with some straw for the Magi's camels. In the morning they find that the grateful Wise Men have filled their shoes with treats. In Italy La **Befana**, an old woman from an Italian legend, distributes presents on Epiphany. La Befana was too busy to aid the Magi on their journey to worship the newborn Jesus. As a punishment for her lack of piety, she now wanders the world during the Christmas season bringing gifts to children. In Russian folklore, a woman named **Baboushka** plays a similar role. **Berchta** (or Perchta), a more fearsome female figure, appears on Epiphany Eve in **Germany** and Austria. She punishes wrongdoers and rewards well-behaved children. In these countries Epiphany is also known as *Perchtennacht*. In **Syria** and **Lebanon** Epiphany may be called "The Night of Destiny" (*Lailat al-Qadr*), a name it shares with a Muslim holiday. In these lands the Christmas gift bringer is a mule or a camel.

In Sweden, **Norway**, Germany, Switzerland, and **Poland**, groups of costumed children known as the **star boys** parade through the streets of town singing songs or performing plays about the Three Kings on Epiphany Eve.

An old German tradition encourages people to bring salt, water, chalk and incense to church on Epiphany Eve to be blessed. Upon returning home, they sprinkle the blessed water over their fields, animals, and homes, and cook with the salt. They burn the incense and waft the smoke throughout their homes as a defense against evil spirits. In both Germany and Austria, the initials CMB—which stand for the names attributed to the Three Kings in legend, Caspar, Melchior, and Balthasar—may be written over doorways with blessed chalk in order to protect the house.

In many European countries, such as France, Austria, Germany, and **England**, festive meals were once planned for Epiphany featuring a special cake. A coin, pea, bean, or tiny china doll was baked inside the cake, and the person who found the object in their slice was considered "king" or "queen" of the feast (*see also* **King of the Bean**; Twelfth Night). In England, tradition reserves the unwelcome chore of removing and storing Christmas decorations for Twelfth Day.

Religious Customs

In both Roman Catholic and Orthodox churches, water is blessed on Epiphany and distributed to the faithful for use in home religious observances. Among Orthodox Christians, Epiphany is also known as Blessing of the Waters Day. In past centuries priests blessed Egypt's Nile River. Both Christians and Muslims would then immerse themselves in the now holy waters, often driving their animals into the river as well to share in the blessing. In Palestine, the River Jordan was blessed. Thousands of worshipers then submerged themselves up to three times in the holy currents. Many Orthodox parishes observe similar Epiphany rites today. For example, the congregation may walk to a nearby river or other body of water which the priest then blesses. In some parts of the world, congregants joyfully immerse themselves in the blessed water. Another popular Orthodox observance involves tossing a crucifix into the water. The first to retrieve the cross is often thought to acquire good luck for the coming year.

The blessing of homes is a Roman Catholic ritual connected with Epiphany. The pastor blesses each room of the house using holy water and incense, and recites special prayers. Then he writes the year and the initials CMB inside the door with blessed chalk. In the year 1999, for example, he would write 19 CMB 99. Orthodox priests also bless homes on Epiphany.

Epiphany is not only a Christian feast day, but may also be considered a season of the Christian year encompassing the period between January 6 and the beginning of Lent. The length of this period varies in accordance with the day on which Easter falls each year.

Further Reading

Bassett, Paul M. "Epiphany." In Everett Ferguson, ed. *Encyclopedia of Early Christianity.* Volume 1. New York: Garland, 1997.

Bellenir, Karen, ed. *Religious Holidays and Calendars: An Encyclopedic Handbook.* Second edition. Detroit, Mich.: Omnigraphics, 1998.

Chambers, Robert. "January 6—Twelfth-Day." In his *The Book of Days*. Volume 1. 1862-64. Reprint. Detroit, Mich.: Omnigraphics, 1990.

Crippen, Thomas G. *Christmas and Christmas Lore*. 1923. Reprint. Detroit, Mich.: Omnigraphics, 1990.

Gwynne, Walker. *The Christian Year: Its Purpose and History*. 1917. Reprint. Detroit, Mich.: Omnigraphics, 1990.

Henderson, Helene, and Sue Ellen Thompson, eds. *Holidays, Festivals, and Celebrations of the World Dictionary*. Second edition. Detroit, Mich.: Omnigraphics, 1997.

James, E. O. *Seasonal Feasts and Festivals*. 1961. Reprint. Detroit, Mich.: Omnigraphics, 1993.

McArthur, A. Allan. *The Evolution of the Christian Year*. Greenwich, Conn.: Seabury Press, 1953.

Miles, Clement A. *Christmas in Ritual and Tradition*. 1912. Reprint. Detroit, Mich.: Omnigraphics, 1990.

Muir, Frank. *Christmas Customs and Traditions*. New York: Taplinger, 1977.

Rouvelas, Marilyn. *A Guide to Greek Traditions and Customs in America*. Bethesda, Md.: Nea Attiki Press, 1993.

Spicer, Dorothy Gladys. *46 Days of Christmas*. New York: Coward-McCann, 1960.

Thompson, Sue Ellen, ed. *Holiday Symbols*. Detroit, Mich.: Omnigraphics, 1998.

Urlin, Ethel L. *Festivals, Holy Days, and Saints' Days*. 1915. Reprint. Detroit, Mich.: Omnigraphics, 1992.

Weiser, Francis X. *Handbook of Christian Feasts and Customs*. New York: Harcourt, Brace and World, 1952.

Web Site

A site sponsored by the Greek Orthodox Archdiocese of America, contains an article by the Rev. Thomas Fitzgerald: http://www.goarch.org/en/ourfaith/articles/article7113.asp

Estonia, Christmas in

Estonians trace some of their Christmas customs back to a pre-Christian midwinter festival called **Yule**. The Estonian word for Christmas, *Jõulud*, comes from the Scandinavian word *Jul*, which in turn is related to the English word Yule. Estonian folklorists believe that before Christianity came to Estonia, people celebrated this midwinter festival at the time of the **winter solstice**. Early Christmas celebrations lasted about seventeen days, from **St. Thomas's Day**, December 21, to **Epiphany**, January 6. In coastal areas people ended their celebrations on January 7, which they observed as **St. Knut's Day**. During this festive period people feasted on special foods and refrained from certain kinds of work. Today most ethnic Estonians are Protestant Christians (Lutherans), but the country also hosts a sizeable minority of Orthodox and other Christians.

Preparations

Like their counterparts in **Germany** and the Nordic countries, most Estonians observe **Advent** — a four-week period of spiritual preparation that precedes Christmas — with **Advent calendars** and **Advent candles**. The weeks before Christmas may also be filled with house-cleaning, cooking, decorating, and shopping.

Christmas straw is an important seasonal decoration in Estonia (*see also* **Yule Straw**). In past times families strewed their floors with straw, which became a playground for the children. The straw reminded family members of **Jesus'** birth in a stable. In some places people twisted the straw into crowns. Folklorists believe that this custom came to Estonia from Finland. The custom of fashioning Christmas crowns from straw nearly died out in the twentieth century, but was revived in the 1970s.

The **Christmas tree** is another prominent Christmas decoration in Estonia. Estonians prefer fir trees, but when fir is not available they will also use pine. Christmas trees became popular in the nineteenth century, when Estonians adopted the custom from Germans living in the Baltic Sea area. Some writers claim, however, that Estonian Christmas trees can be traced back to the year 1441, when one stood in front of the town hall in Tallinn, Estonia's capital.

St. Thomas's Day

St. Thomas's Day, December 21, is considered the real start of the **Christmas season**. Old traditions dictate that householders complete the brewing of their **Christmas ale** on this day. The men of the household usually took charge of this chore. Folklore recommended that they attend to the brewing in the dead of night, in order to avoid the possible ruin that a neighbor's evil eye could wreak on the brew. People drank so much beer at Christmas time that Estonians nicknamed the season "the beer holidays." Householders readied large quantities of beer by St. Thomas's Day, because tradition required that no further beer be brewed until Epiphany. Certain forms of work were prohibited from St. Thomas's Day until the end of Christmas season. Some say that noisy forms of work, such as driving horses, spinning, and grinding, disturbed the spirits, who were particularly active during this time (*see also* **Ghosts**).

Christmas Eve

The president of Estonia maintains a centuries-old ceremony by declaring the **Peace of Christmas** each year on the afternoon of December 24. In the seventeenth century Queen Kristina of Sweden introduced this custom to Estonia.

Christmas Eve is the high point of the Christmas season. Estonians begin their celebrations by taking a sauna. Then they attend a Christmas Eve service. Sometimes parents give children new shoes and clothing to wear to this service as a kind of early Christmas **gift**. The traditional Christmas Eve meal consists of a large number of dishes, anywhere between seven and twelve. Sausage, brawn (boiled pork leg), pig's head, or some other form of pork is usually served (*see also* **Boar's Head**). Other popular dishes include sauerkraut, pâté, potato and beet salad, a special bread called "Christmas Barrow," **gingerbread**, and beer.

Folk tradition insisted that many powerful supernatural forces are active on this evening, which made it a potent time for fortune-telling, a traditional Christmas Eve activity. An abundance of food on Christmas Eve signified that the house would enjoy plenty of food in the year to come. Another superstition advised that, having eaten seven different dishes on Christmas Eve, the men of the household would gain the strength of seven men. The dead were thought to return to their old homes on Christmas Eve (*see also* Ghosts). Estonians left the remains of the Christmas Eve dinner on the table all night, in case the spirits wanted to refresh themselves. Estonian folklore also recommended that the fire be kept going all night.

From Christmas Day to New Year's Eve

Estonian tradition calls for families to spend a quiet Christmas Day at home. In past times people spent the day enjoying the company of family members, singing religious music, and reading the Bible. Parties and visits were left until the following day. The first visitor to the house, both at Christmas and on New Year's Eve, determined the household's luck (*see also* **Firstfooting**). If the first visitor was a woman, the household could expect a run of bad luck. Estonians traditionally celebrated Christmas through December 27, **St. John's Day**. The remaining days in the year were viewed as "half-holidays," in which people did some work, but also spent time celebrating with friends and neighbors.

Christmas under Soviet Rule

The Russian-led U.S.S.R. (United Soviet Socialist Republics) occupied and ruled Estonia from 1940 to 1991. The Soviet government forbade religious holidays and tried to persuade the Estonian people to transfer their Christmas festivities to **New Year's Day**, a secular holiday. Although most people had to go to work on Christmas Day, many continued to attend Christmas Eve religious services. As a means of protesting the government's political ideology and its repressive stance towards religion, people also began to observe the day by visiting their relatives' graves and leaving lit candles there after the Christmas Eve service.

Christmas since Independence

After the fall of the Soviet government, the newly independent Estonian people reinstated Christmas as a national holiday. In recent years Estonian Christmas celebrations have been influenced by those of the Scandinavian countries. The most popular of the recently imported customs seems to be that of the office party, often called "little Christmas" or "pre-Christmas" in Estonia. These festive gatherings take place in the first part of December, and usually feature mulled wine, along with a tasty array of food and drinks. Some young people now leave their **shoes** out on a windowsill in the weeks before Christmas and wait for the **elves** to come fill them with treats, a task usually undertaken instead by their parents.

Further Reading

Bowler, Gerry. *The World Encyclopedia of Christmas.* Toronto, Ontario, Canada: McClelland and Stewart, 2000.

Web Site

"Christmas Customs in Estonia," an article posted on the web by Estonia's Ministry of Foreign Affairs at: http://www.mfa.ee/estonia/kat_174/1191.html

Ethiopia, Christmas in
Ganna, Genna, Leddat

In spite of Ethiopia's ancient Christian heritage, Christmas, or *Leddat*, is not a very important holiday there. In fact, most people call the holiday *Ganna* or *Genna* after a ball **game** by the same name which by custom is played only once a year, on Christmas afternoon. About forty percent of Ethiopians are Christians, forty-five percent are Muslim, and the remaining fifteen percent are split among several different religions. Most Ethiopian Christians belong to the Ethiopian Orthodox Church, which adheres to a different church calendar than that commonly found in the West (*see also* **Old Christmas Day**). Therefore, Ethiopians celebrate Genna Day on January 7. More elaborate celebrations take place twelve days later, on **Timkat**, or **Epiphany**.

Ethiopia embraced Christianity in the early fourth century, long before Christianity had taken root throughout **Europe**. During the thirteenth century King Lalibela ordered the construction of magnificent churches carved out of solid rock in a town that now bears his name. Contemporary Ethiopian Christmas observances include pilgrimages to these churches. Thousands make the journey to Lalibela each year, though it may mean walking for days, weeks, or even months. Those gathered there on Christmas morning share a meal. Then, church services are held at *Beta Mariam*, one of the underground churches, whose name means "House of Mary" (*see also* **Mary**). During the lengthy service a cross is passed through the crowd for worshipers to kiss.

Ethiopian Christmas celebrations also include processions in which revered icons (religious images used in prayer and worship) are removed from churches and carried through the streets. In addition, many participate in an all-night vigil on Christmas Eve. A meal of beans and bread sustains worshipers through a night of singing, dancing, and praying. Christmas Day services include religious dances. Percussionists playing drums, prayer sticks, and an instrument known as the *tsenatsel,* or sistrum, create a rhythm for the dancers.

As a rule, Ethiopians do not exchange **gifts** at Christmas. Young children may receive simple presents from their parents, however. Boys and young men look forward to Christmas because of the opportunity to participate in the yearly genna match. These popular events crown many peoples' Christmas celebrations. Genna, played with bent wooden bats and wooden or leather balls, resembles hockey. The opposing teams compete fiercely, and serious injuries sometimes result. In spite of the verbal and physical aggression that takes place, the players enjoy the game enough to continue playing until dusk.

Further Reading

Henderson, Helene, and Sue Ellen Thompson, eds. *Holidays, Festivals, and Celebrations of the World Dictionary.* Second edition. Detroit, Mich.: Omnigraphics, 1997.

Levine, Donald N. *Wax and Gold.* Chicago: University of Chicago Press, 1965.

MacDonald, Margaret Read, ed. *The Folklore of World Holidays.* Detroit, Mich.: Gale Research, 1992.

Naythons, Matthew. *Christmas Around the World.* San Francisco, Calif.: Collins San Francisco, 1996.

Web Site

A site sponsored by the Ethiopia Tourism Commission:
http://www.visitethiopia.org/cultatt.htm

Europe, Christmas in Medieval

Medieval Europeans celebrated Christmas without **Santa Claus**, **Christmas trees**, and Christmas morning **gift** exchanges. Not only would we fail to spot these familiar elements of contemporary Christmas celebrations if transported back in time to medieval Europe, but we would also witness a number of extinct Christmas customs now strange to us. Nevertheless, the **Christmas season** and a few of its enduring customs first took shape during this era.

Christmas Season

In the fourth century Church authorities chose **December 25** as the date on which Christians would celebrate the Nativity. They placed Christmas near two important Roman feasts, **Saturnalia** (December 17 to 23) and **Kalends** (January 1 to 5). Moreover, they scheduled it on the same day as the **Birth of the Invincible Sun**, a festival dedicated to the sun god. This meant that the major Christian feasts of Christmas and **Epiphany** (January 6) opened and closed a thirteen-day period during which many recent converts were already accustomed to celebrate.

Eventually, the Church decided to accept this inclination to celebrate a midwinter festival rather than fight it. In 567 the Council of Tours declared the days that fall between Christmas and Epiphany to be a festal tide. This decision expanded Christmas into a Church season stretching from December 25 to January 5. This Church season became known as "Christmastide," but ordinary folk called it the **Twelve Days of Christmas**.

As Christianity became more firmly rooted in Europe, political leaders declared the Twelve Days to be legal holidays. Near the end of the ninth century King Alfred the Great of **England** (849-899) mandated that his subjects observe the Twelve Days of Christmas, outlawing all legal proceedings, work, and fighting during that time. The Norwegian King Haakon the Good (d. c. 961) established the

Christian observance of the festival in **Norway** in the middle of the tenth century.

Entertainments

Medieval Europeans celebrated throughout the Twelve Days of Christmas. They might attend religious services or watch mystery plays that retold biblical stories pertinent to the season (*see* **Feast of the Ass; Nativity Plays**). In addition, the well-to-do made music, played **games**, danced, told stories, hunted, jousted, and feasted. In late medieval times the elite of some European countries began to celebrate the season with roving, costumed events known as **masques**. In a more homemade version of this custom, ordinary folk dressed as **mummers** or received a band of mummers into their home or tavern. In England peasants who worked on large estates rested from their customary chores during the Twelve Days. Moreover, they partook of a communal feast provided to them by the lord of the estate, offering him in return a gift of farm produce. In England Christmas festivities ended on **Plough Monday**, when farm laborers went back to work.

Christmas Feasts in Medieval Europe

In the late Middle Ages, the typical English Christmas dinner probably included roast meat, chicken, or wild fowl, white bread (a medieval luxury), and ale or cider. The rich, of course, fared somewhat better. When the Bishop of Hereford hosted a Christmas feast for his household and 41 guests in the year 1289, his kitchens sizzled with a wide variety of roasted meats. The bishop's hard-working chefs butchered and cooked two oxen, four pigs, four deer, two calves, sixty fowls, eight partridges, and two geese. In addition, they brewed beer, baked bread, and prepared cheese for all. The assembled company washed down their meal with forty gallons of red wine and four gallons of white wine, as well as an "unscored" amount of beer.

A wide variety of what we might consider unusual fowl could appear on a medieval Christmas menu, such as swans and peacocks. The chefs of the well-to-do strove to present these beautiful birds in artful ways. For example, they might decorate the roasted carcass, often enclosed in pastry, with the bird's plucked feathers and place a lighted wick in the bird's beak. In addition to peacock and swan, medieval diners also relished heron, crane, bittern, plover, snipe, and woodcock. Chefs searching for a make-ahead dish that would resist spoilage often created large fruit, meat, and butter pies for the Christmas table. These pies later evolved into the dish we know as **mincemeat pie**.

The wealthy and noble often served wild boar for Christmas, commanding their pages to bring the roasted **boar's head** to the table with great ceremony. Indeed, boar's flesh (known as "brawn"), as well as pork were favorite Christmas meats. The English often accompanied these roasted meats with **Christmas ale** and **wassail**. Lastly, like their counterparts in the rest of Europe, medieval Britons celebrated throughout the Twelve Days of Christmas. The largest and most festive meal was often served on **Twelfth Night**, or on Epiphany.

The French also celebrated the Christmas season with lavish feasts and openhanded hospitality. Castle doors were thrown open and wayfarers welcomed to feast at the lord and lady's table. When poor folk appeared at the door they were given food and, sometimes, clothing as well. Like their English counterparts, cooks in French castles served swan, peacock, and, occasionally, even stork to their guests. These guests might number into the hundreds. After they had sated their appetites, the guests could relax and enjoy entertainments provided by storytellers, jugglers, dancers, magicians, or traveling musicians. (*See also* **France, Christmas in**.)

Famous English Christmas Feasts

In the Middle Ages English monarchs sometimes threw Christmas feasts of legendary proportions. Often these feasts doubled as affairs of state, with the king hosting foreign dignitaries, local nobility, visiting knights, and other important guests. The assembled company might easily number well into the hundreds; some records declare the thousands. Moreover, this legion of hungry guests might stay for some or all of the Twelve Days of Christmas.

Knowing the scale of these dinner parties helps to put some of the royal menus in perspective. For example, in 1213 King John of England (1167-1216) provided his guests with one of the largest and most sumptuous Christmas banquets on record. The shopping list for this gargantuan feast included 200 pigs, 1,000 hens, 15,000 herrings, 10,000 salt eels, scores of pheasants, partridges and other birds, 27 hogsheads of wine, 100 pounds of almonds, 50 pounds of pepper, and 2 pounds of saffron, as well as other spices. At some point in the preparations the cooks feared they were running short and sent for an additional 2,000 hens and 200 head of pork. King Henry III (1207-1272) is reported to have entertained 1,000 noblemen and knights at York one Christmas. His cooks slaughtered 600 oxen for the feasts, and accompanied the resulting roast beef with salmon pie, roast peacock, and wine.

Needless to say, with such long guest lists, royal cooks could prepare quite a wide variety of dishes for the Christmas feast. Although most of the surviving menus seem to focus on roast meat and fowl, King Henry V (1387-1422) treated his court one year to a diverse Christmas banquet featuring a wide variety of seafood in addition to the traditional brawn and mustard. The assembled company sampled herbed pike, powdered lamprey, jelly colored with flowers, salmon, bream, roach, conger, halibut, crayfish, sturgeon, lobster, whelks, porpoise, carp, tench, perch, turbot, and more. Altogether the king's cooks prepared over forty species of freshwater fish. Afterwards the royal chefs presented the king's guests with a dessert of marchpane (a forerunner of marzipan).

Adapting Pagan Customs

Many researchers believe that medieval Christmas celebrations absorbed a number of pre-existing pagan customs. Church policy itself may have had something to do with this. In the early Middle Ages missionaries found many recent converts unwilling to give up elements of their former celebrations. In the year 601 Pope Gregory the Great wrote a letter to St. Augustine, missionary to Britain, advising him on how to deal with this problem. The letter reveals that missionaries were often encouraged to suggest a Christian significance to old pagan customs, rather than try to abolish them. Pope Gregory reasoned that:

. . . because they [the Anglo-Saxons] are wont to slay many oxen in sacrifices to demons, some solemnity should be put in the place of this, so that on the day of the dedication of the churches, or the nativities of the holy martyrs whose relics are placed there, they may make for themselves tabernacles of branches of trees around those churches which have been changed from heathen temples, and may celebrate the solemnity with religious feasting. Nor let them now sacrifice animals to the Devil, but to the praise of God kill animals for their own eating, and render thanks to the Giver of all for their abundance; so that while some outward joys are retained for them, they may more readily respond to inward joys. For from obdurate minds it is undoubtedly impossible to cut off everything at once, because he who strives to ascend to the highest place rises by degrees or steps and not by leaps [Miles, 1990, 179].

Indeed, the ancient custom of decking homes with **greenery** may have infiltrated medieval Christmas celebrations in just this manner. According to some writers, the roots of this custom lie in the Roman practice of celebrating their midwinter festivals by decorating homes and temples with greenery. Moreover, the Romans celebrated Saturnalia by electing a mock king to preside over the customary feasts. Many mock kings sprouted up during the medieval Christmas season, perhaps as echoes of this ancient custom. They included the Bishop of Fools, who presided over the **Feast of Fools**, the **King of the Bean**, the **Lord of Misrule**, and the **boy bishop**. The old pagan beliefs of the north may also have contributed a few items to medieval Christmas lore. Some writers suspect that **Berchta**, the female spirit that haunted the Twelve Days of Christmas in German-speaking lands, may have evolved from an old Germanic goddess. They attribute the same origin to the band of spirits known as the **Wild Hunt**. Finally, medieval Germans honored Christmas by burning a **Yule log**, another custom that may date back to ancient times.

Creating Christian Customs

On the other hand, a good number of medieval Christmas customs grew out of Church practices or Christian folklore and legends. For example, the customs and festivities associated with the many saints' days scattered throughout the Christmas season blossomed during the Middle Ages. So did the observance of **Advent**, Epiphany, the **Feast of the Circumcision**, and **Midnight Mass**. Nativity plays, the **Nativity scene**, and **Christmas carols** also became popular during this era. The **paradise tree**, a possible forerunner of the Christmas tree, accompanied one of these medieval Nativity plays.

Surviving Medieval Customs

Many of these medieval customs and observances have now faded away. Nevertheless, we still celebrate Christmas by feasting, resting, decking our homes and churches with greenery, and partaking in popular forms of entertainment. Christmas carols remain with us, as do Nativity plays, although we know them today as Christmas pageants or as the Hispanic folk dramas of Las **Posadas** and Los **Pastores**.

Further Reading

Chambers, E. K. *The Medieval Stage*. Volumes 1 and 2. Oxford, England: Clarendon Press, 1903.

The Glory and Pageantry of Christmas. Maplewood, N.J.: Time-Life Books, 1963.

Hutton, Ronald. *The Stations of the Sun*. Oxford, England: Oxford University Press, 1996.

Miles, Clement A. *Christmas in Ritual and Tradition*. 1912. Reprint. Detroit, Mich.: Omnigraphics, 1990.

Muir, Frank. *Christmas Customs and Traditions*. New York: Taplinger, 1977.

Murray, Alexander. "Medieval Christmas." *History Today* 36, 12 (December 1986): 31-39.

Pimlott, J. A. R. *The Englishman's Christmas*. Atlantic Highlands, N.J.: Humanities Press, 1978.

Farolitos

In the American Southwest glowing paper sacks decorate the outlines of buildings, patios, walkways, and plazas at night during the **Christmas season**. These ornamental lights are called farolitos (pronounced fah-roh-LEE-tohs), meaning "little lanterns" in Spanish.

Farolitos are made with brown paper lunch bags, votive candles, and sand. To make one for yourself, turn over the rim of a brown paper bag to form a cuff. This helps to keep the bag open. Next pour several inches of sand into the bag. The sand weighs the bag down and anchors the candle. Place the bag outdoors at night, push a votive candle into the sand, and light the wick. The candlelight shining through the brown paper gives off a mellow, golden glow in the darkness.

Although farolitos came to the Southwest from Mexico, their historical roots can be traced all the way back to China. Spanish merchants made this link possible. From the early sixteenth to the early nineteenth centuries **Spain** held both **Mexico** and the **Philippines** as colonies. Trade relations linked the Philippines with China. These links gave Spanish merchants access to Chinese goods, which they began to export to other places. Chinese paper lanterns, imported from the Philippines to Mexico by Spanish traders, proved popular in the New World. The Mexicans used them for many kinds of celebrations, including Christmas.

By the early nineteenth century the lanterns had spread north to territories now considered part of the United States. Unfortunately, the delicate paper that surrounded the lantern frame quickly perished in the rough conditions to which they were exposed. Frontier settlers soon hit upon a cheaper and sturdier alternative. They began to make lanterns with plain brown wrapping paper made available to them by recently increased trade along the Santa Fe Trail. The new farolitos not only proved hardier but also cast an amber glow that favored the warm colors characteristic of southwestern architecture and landscapes. Today these beautiful lights constitute an important **Christmas symbol** in the American Southwest.

In some areas of the Southwest farolitos are known as **Luminarias**. In other areas the two customs remain distinct. In northern New Mexico, for example, the word "luminarias" refers to small Christmas season bonfires while the decorative brown paper lanterns are known as farolitos.

Further Reading

Christmas in the American Southwest. Chicago: World Book, 1996.

Ribera Ortega, Pedro. *Christmas in Old Santa Fe.* Second edition. Santa Fe, N.M.: Sunstone Press, 1973.

Father Christmas
Christmas, King Christmas, Sir Christmas

Father Christmas is an English folk figure who personified the **Christmas season** for centuries. Unlike **Santa Claus**, Father Christmas originally did not distribute **gifts**. Instead, he represented the mirth, generosity, and abundance associated with the celebration of Christmas. Father Christmas has also been called King Christmas, Sir Christmas, or simply "Christmas."

Early History

Some English folklorists trace Father Christmas back to the late Middle Ages; others believe he originated at a later date. Renaissance **masquers** (maskers) sometimes enjoyed impersonating this symbol of the season. The famous English writer Ben Jonson (1572-1637) chose Father Christmas as the main character in his masque, *Christmas His Masque* (1616). Moreover, Father Christmas often served as the narrator in English **mummers'** plays. He typically entered with a speech like the following:

> In comes I, Father Christmas
> Welcome or welcome not.
> I hope old Father Christmas
> Will never be forgot.

Appearance

Father Christmas always took on the form of an adult male. Some portrayed him as hale and hearty, while others depicted him as gray and wizened. These contrasting images may reflect the influence that other important folk figures, namely, **Father Time** and the Roman god Saturn, had upon the invention of Father Christmas. According to the ancient Romans, abundance, equality, and conviviality marked the lives of Saturn's subjects while the god reigned on earth. The Romans revived these ideals during **Saturnalia**, the midwinter festival held in his honor. In later times these qualities became synonymous with the Christmas season. Eventually they took shape in the image of a large, robust man nicknamed Father Christmas. Popular images of Father Christmas usually showed him wearing a red or green robe with fur trimming and a crown of **holly**, **ivy**, or **mistletoe**.

In his famous story *A Christmas Carol*, the English writer Charles Dickens (1812-1870) presented his readers with a spirit who calls himself "the Ghost of Christmas Present." This **ghost**, however, strongly resembles Father Christmas. Dickens made the association more obvious by surrounding the ghost with emblems of Christmas plenty:

> The walls and ceiling were so hung with living green, that it looked a perfect grove, from every part of which, bright gleaming berries glistened. The crisp leaves of holly, mistletoe, and ivy reflected back the light, as if so many little mirrors had been scattered there; and such a mighty blaze went roaring up the chimney. . . . Heaped up upon the floor, to form a kind of throne, were turkeys, geese, game, poultry, brawn, great joints of meat, sucking-pigs, long wreaths of sausages, mince-pies, plum-puddings, barrels of oysters, red-hot chestnuts, cherry-cheeked apples, juicy oranges, luscious pears, immense twelfth-cakes, and seething bowls of punch, that made the chamber dim with their delicious steam. In easy state upon this couch, there sat a jolly Giant, glorious to see; who bore a glowing torch, in shape not unlike Plenty's horn. . . . It was clothed in one simple deep green robe or mantle, bordered with white fur. This garment hung so loosely on the figure, that its capacious breast was bare, as if disdaining to be warded or concealed by any artifice. Its feet, observable beneath the ample folds of the garment, were also bare; and on its head it wore no other covering than a holly wreath set here and there with shining icicles. Its dark brown curls were long and free: free as its genial face, its sparkling eye, its open hand, its cheery voice, its unconstrained demeanour, and its joyful air.

While Dickens favored the robust version of Father Christmas, others preferred to imagine him as a venerable old man. The elderly Father Christmas peered out at the world from behind a thick grey or white beard. Except for the fact that he did not carry a scythe, this robed and hooded figure closely resembled conventional images of Father Time. This association between Father Christmas and Father Time may well have sprung up because of Christmas' place on the calendar. Scheduled just before the close of the old year and the beginning of the new, the arrival of the holiday tends to call attention to the passing of time.

Recent History

During the nineteenth century the imported American Santa Claus began to appear in **England**. Unlike Father Christmas, Santa Claus brought gifts to children rather than personifying the Christmas season. Moreover, he was vaguely related to the old, European **St. Nicholas** (*see also* **St. Nicholas's Day**). As Santa Claus became popular in England, his identity began to merge with that of Father Christmas. Eventually, Santa Claus all but erased the identity of Father Christmas as a separate and distinct folk figure. Father Christmas retained only his name, while his image and activities all but mirrored those of Santa Claus.

Further Reading

Del Re, Gerard, and Patricia Del Re. *The Christmas Almanack*. Garden City, N.Y.: Doubleday, 1979.

Hutton, Ronald. *The Stations of the Sun*. Oxford, England: Oxford University Press, 1996.

Pimlott, J. A. R. *The Englishman's Christmas*. Atlantic Highlands, N.J.: Humanities Press, 1978.

Siefker, Phyllis. *Santa Claus, Last of the Wild Men*. Jefferson, N.C.: McFarland and Company, 1997.

Father Time

Two old men with white beards have come to symbolize the holiday season. The first, **Santa Claus**, visits homes on Christmas Eve (*see also* **Father Christmas; Weihnachtsmann**). The second, Father Time, appears on **New Year's** Eve. Father Time, a folk figure that personifies time, represents the passing of the old year. He is usually depicted as an old man with a long white beard. Frequently he carries an hourglass, representing the passage of time, and a scythe (an old farm tool used to cut down ripe wheat), reminding us that all living creatures must die and all things come to an end. On occasion he will be depicted with wings, which stand for the idea that time passes very quickly. As the saying goes, "time flies."

Folklorists believe that Father Time may have evolved from an ancient Greek god called Kronos (also spelled Cronos or Chronos). Indeed, *chronos* is the Greek word for "time." The association between Kronos and time, however, does not seem to have existed in the ancient world but rather seems to have sprung up in later ages, due to the similarity between the god's name and the word for time. Kronos was sometimes depicted in Greek art with a curved implement in his hand, resembling a sickle.

At one time the god Kronos ruled the heavens and earth. He gained this position by displacing his father, Uranus, whom he castrated with an instrument similar to a sickle. After defeating his father Kronos married his sister, Rhea, and began to have children by her. He learned, however, that in the future one of his own children would displace him. In an attempt to avoid this fate he swallowed his children as soon as they were born. His wife managed to hide the last of her children, Zeus, from her husband and thus Zeus lived to adulthood. As predicted, Zeus eventually challenged his father's rule and overcame his father in battle. Zeus forced Kronos to cough up the children he had swallowed and so Zeus regained his brothers and sisters: Hestia, Demeter, Hades, Hera, and Poseidon.

When the Romans heard these tales they decided that Zeus was the god they knew as Jupiter, while Kronos was another name for their deity Saturn. According to Roman legend, when Jupiter defeated Saturn in battle, Saturn left Rome and retreated to **Italy**. There he brought about an era of peace, plenty and equality that lived on in legend long after it had ended on earth. The Romans celebrated the joys of this golden age in the midwinter festival called **Saturnalia**.

Further Reading

Barnett, Mary. *Gods and Myths of Ancient Greece*. New York: Smithmark, 1996.

Hamilton, Edith. *Mythology*. Boston, Mass.: Little Brown and Company, 1942.

Leach, Maria, ed. *Funk and Wagnalls Standard Dictionary of Folklore, Mythology, and Legend*. San Francisco, Calif.: Harper and Row, 1984.

Feast of Fools

In the Middle Ages lower clerics in **France**, **Germany**, Bohemia, and **England** celebrated the **Christmas season** by holding mock religious ceremonies that made fun of their usual solemn duties. These lower clerics held low-ranking positions at local churches that involved assisting the priest in his duties or playing a minor role in religious services. Their burlesque rites were known as "The Feast of Fools" and were observed on a variety of days throughout the season. The deacons led the revelry on December 26, **St. Stephen's Day**, the sub-priests (or vicars) on December 27, **St. John's Day**, the choirboys on December 28, **Holy Innocents' Day**, and the sub-deacons on January 1, the **Feast of the Circumcision**. The name "Feast of Fools" was most often given to the rites led by the sub-deacons on January 1. Indeed, these were accounted by some to be the most riotous of all these mock ceremonies.

History

Some scholars trace the roots of the Feast of Fools back to **Kalends**, the Roman new year celebration that lived on for centuries after the fall of the Empire. Other writers point to similarities between the Feast of Fools and some of the customs surrounding **Saturnalia**. By the twelfth century the Feast of Fools had emerged in full force. It first established itself as an observance of the sub-deacons, but soon expanded to encompass other lower clerics. It appears to have been more popular in France than in any other European country. By the end of the twelfth century Parisians were treated to the spectacle several times over during the Christmas season, as the deacons (St. Stephen's Day) sub-priests (St. John's Day), choirboys (Holy Innocents'Day), and sub-deacons (Feast of the Circumcision, Epiphany, or the Octave of Epiphany) all had a go at leading the mock rites.

Historical documents record several centuries of complaints registered by priests, bishops, and other high-ranking Church officials who, in spite of their authority, seemed unable to stop the raucous revelry. Not only did lower clerics relish their festival, but townsfolk also enjoyed the outrageous spectacle. In 1435 the Council of Basle forbade the Feast of Fools. Nevertheless, the lower clergy clung to their yearly spree for another 150 years. Clerics from the cathedral of Amiens, France, continued to celebrate the Feast of Fools until 1721.

Customs

Participants in the Feast of Fools reversed all customary rules of proper church behavior. Instead of presiding over religious services with dignity, seriousness, and reverence, they brought the coarse, lusty, irreverent behavior of the carnival to church. After their wild mass, they often roamed the streets in an equally wild, mock religious procession. In some places merrymakers chose a bishop or archbishop of fools to preside over the celebration. As insignia of his newfound rank he wore a bishop's miter and carried a bishop's staff. Clerical participants in the follies often dressed in street clothing, including women's clothing, masks, garlands of **greenery**, or even in fools' costumes.

Our knowledge of these mock ceremonies comes mostly from the writings of higher clergy who disapproved of the revels. According to one irate cleric who observed the proceedings in mid-fifteenth-century France:

> Priests and clerks may be seen wearing masks and monstrous visages at the hours of the office. They dance in the choir dressed as women, panders or minstrels. They sing wanton songs. They eat black puddings at the horn of the altar while the celebrant is saying Mass. They play at dice there. They cense with stinking smoke from the soles of old shoes. They run and leap through the church, without a blush at their own shame. Finally they drive about the town and its theatres in shabby traps and carts, and rouse the laughter of their fellows and the bystanders in infamous performances, with indecent gesture and verses scurrilous and unchaste [Miles, 1990, 304].

In a similar observance called the **Feast of the Ass**, a donkey carrying a young woman was led into church and made to stand near the altar. This act may have been meant to represent the flight of **Mary**, **Joseph**, and the baby **Jesus** into **Egypt** shortly after Jesus' birth (*see also* **Flight into Egypt**). Nevertheless, the revelers took the opportunity to sing the praises of the ass in Latin and to require the officiant to end the mass by braying three times like a donkey. The congregation responded in kind.

In enacting these rites, those of lesser status in the Church temporarily usurped the roles of higher-ups, performing unflattering impersonations of priests, bishops, and archbishops. In this respect the Feast of Fools resembled other Christmas season rites that authorized similar, temporary inversions of power and status. These include the festivities surrounding the **boy bishop,** the **Lord of Misrule, barring out the schoolmaster**, Holy Innocents' Day, Saturnalia, and **Twelfth Night**.

Further Reading

Chambers, E. K. *The Mediaeval Stage.* Volume 1. Oxford England: Clarendon Press, 1903.

Hutton, Ronald. *The Stations of the Sun.* Oxford, England: Oxford University Press, 1996.

Leach, Maria, ed. *Funk and Wagnalls Standard Dictionary of Folklore, Mythology, and Legend.* New York: Harper and Row, 1984.

Miles, Clement A. *Christmas in Ritual and Tradition.* 1912. Reprint. Detroit, Mich.: Omnigraphics, 1990.

Pimlott, J. A. R. *The Englishman's Christmas.* Atlantic Highlands, N.J.: Humanities Press, 1978.

Stevens, Patricia Bunning. *Merry Christmas!: A History of the Holiday.* New York: Macmillan, 1979.

Feast of the Ass

In the Middle Ages, people in some parts of **France** commemorated the Holy Family's **Flight into Egypt** with a celebration called the Feast of the Ass. Not only did Christian legends place an ass in the stable where **Jesus** was born, but also medieval people imagined **Mary** and the baby Jesus riding on an ass led by **Joseph** as they plodded towards their Egyptian exile. Later, a donkey would carry the adult Jesus into the city of Jerusalem on the week before his death, an event celebrated on Palm Sunday, the Sunday before Easter (John 12:14-15). The ceremonies associated with the Feast of the Ass honored all the donkeys who played roles in these and other well-known Christian stories. They took place on January 14.

The festivities featured a procession in which a young girl with a baby rode through the city streets on an ass while people sang a silly song honoring the creature:

> Orientis partibus
> Adventavit asinus,
> Pucher et fortissimos,
> Sarcinis aptissimus.
> Hez, Sir asne, hez!
>
> From Oriental country came
> A lordly ass of highest fame,
> So beautiful, so strong and trim,
> No burden was too great for him.
> Hail, Sir Donkey, hail (Weiser, 1952, 127).

The ass was then led into a church where religious services took place. Like the **Feast of Fools**, these ceremonies tended to get out of hand. The topsy-turvy ambience of medieval Christmas celebrations encouraged high-spirited excesses that gradually turned the event into a burlesque (*see also* **Europe, Christmas in Medieval**). Particularly raucous celebrations took place in the town of Beauvais. After the procession, the ass entered the church, where it was lavished with food and drink. At the same time, the clergy conducted a kind of parody of the evening prayer service, which ended with everyone braying like an ass as they danced around the befuddled creature. Afterwards actors presented humorous folk plays outside the church doors. The last event of the day was a **Midnight Mass**, which the priest brought to a close by braying three times.

These hijinks caused the Roman Catholic Church to officially suppress the Feast of the Ass in the fifteenth century. It lingered for many years after that in some places, however.

Further Reading

Goldwasser, Maria Julia. "Carnival." In Mircea Eliade, ed. *Encyclopedia of Religion.* Volume 3. New York: Macmillan, 1987.

Leach, Maria, ed. *Funk and Wagnalls Standard Dictionary of Folklore, Mythology, and Legend.* San Francisco, Calif.: Harper and Row, 1984.

Weiser, Francis X. *Handbook of Christian Feasts and Customs.* New York: Harcourt, Brace and World, 1952.

Feast of the Circumcision

Circumcision of Jesus, Feast of the Circumcision and the Name of Jesus, Feast of the Circumcision of Our Lord, Feast of the Holy Name of Our Lord Jesus Christ, Octave of the Birth of Our Lord, Solemnity of Mary

The **Gospel according to Luke** (2:21) reports that eight days after **Jesus** was born, **Joseph** and **Mary** named him and had him circumcised. In doing so, they conformed to an old Jewish custom whereby all male infants are circumcised as a sign of the eternal covenant between God and the Jewish people. The Feast of the Circumcision, observed on January 1, commemorates the Holy Family's compliance with this custom. It also celebrates the naming of Jesus and, in the Roman Catholic Church, Mary's role as the Mother of God.

History

The Feast of the Circumcision received official recognition rather late. Luke's account clearly states that Jesus was circumcised eight days after his birth. After Church authorities established the celebration of Christmas on **December 25**, the obvious date for the remembrance of the Circumcision would be January 1, which falls eight days after the celebration of the Nativity.

In the first few centuries after Christ's birth, however, the vast pagan population of the Roman world was still celebrating **Kalends**, their new year festival, on that date. Numerous early Christian leaders disapproved of the riotous pagan new year celebrations and urged their Christian followers to observe the day with thoughtfulness, fasting, and sobriety instead. In the fourth century A.D., one such leader, a monk named Almacius (or Telemachus) stormed into a crowded Roman stadium on January 1 crying, "Cease from the superstition of idols and polluted sacrifices. Today is the octave of the Lord!" Some report that the enraged crowd stoned the earnest monk to death; others state that the assembled gladiators dispatched him.

This attitude of vehement opposition to the celebrations already taking place on January 1 may explain the reluctance of Church officials to establish a Christian celebration on that day. In an effort to counteract the still-popular festivities surrounding Kalends, the second provincial Council of Tours (567 A.D.) ordered Christians to fast and do penance during the first few days of the new year.

Nevertheless, over the course of the next several centuries, January 1 became a feast day throughout the Christian world. Around the seventh century the Roman Catholic Church introduced a new observance called the "Octave of the Birth of Our Lord" on January 1. In the language of the Church, an "octave" is an eight-day period that includes any great Church festival and the seven days that follow it. Thus, this name signaled that the new observance was to serve as a completion of the Christmas feast. Before that time, however, Christians from Gaul had observed the day as the "Circumcision of Jesus," a name reflecting their emphasis on Jesus' compliance with the Jewish tradition of circumcision. This idea spread from Gaul to **Spain**, and, eventually, to Rome.

The Eastern Churches began to observe January 1 as a commemoration of the circumcision in the eighth century. In the ninth century the Roman Church began to blend its original emphasis on the completion of the octave of Christmas with a commemoration of the Circumcision. Before long the Roman Church incorporated yet another theme into its celebrations. Many observed the feast primarily by expressing gratitude and devotion to Mary, the mother of God. Indeed, some historians recognize the festival as the earliest Catholic feast dedicated to Mary. Eventually, it became the most important Marian feast in the Roman Church.

The Feast of the Circumcision falls in the middle of the **Twelve Days of Christmas**. During the Middle Ages bursts of revelry punctuated this twelve-day period. In spite of the efforts of the early Church to diminish the customary carousing associated with the Roman new year, a new form of riotous display developed around Church celebrations on January 1. From the twelfth to the sixteenth centuries, lower clergy in many parts of **Europe** took part in the **Feast of Fools** on that date. Scandalized authorities managed to eradicate this observance in most areas by the sixteenth century, although it lingered in **France** until the eighteenth century.

Contemporary Observance

The various Christian denominations that observe the feast emphasize different aspects of the events surrounding Jesus' circumcision. In 1969 the Roman Catholic Church changed the name of the observance to the "Solemnity of Mary," a name that reflects their emphasis on Mary's role as mother of the Savior. Orthodox Christians continue to observe the day as the "Feast of the Circumcision of Our Lord." Episcopalians call the festival the "Feast of the Holy Name of Our Lord Jesus Christ." They emphasize the significance of Jesus' name, given to Mary by **Gabriel**—the **angel** of the **Annunciation**—which means literally "God saves" or "God helps." Lutherans compromise by calling the festival the "Feast of the Circumcision and the Name of Jesus." (*See also* **New Year's Day**).

Further Reading

Bellenir, Karen, ed. *Religious Holidays and Calendars*. Second edition. Detroit, Mich.: Omnigraphics, 1998.

Cross, F. L., and E. A. Livingstone, eds. *The Oxford Dictionary of the Christian Church*. Second edition, revised. Oxford, England: Oxford University Press, 1983.

Foley, R. L. "Circumcision of Our Lord." In *New Catholic Encyclopedia*. Volume 3. New York: McGraw-Hill, 1967.

Harper, Howard. *Days and Customs of All Faiths*. 1957. Reprint. Detroit, Mich.: Omnigraphics, 1990.

Holy Days in the United States. Washington, D.C.: United States Catholic Conference, 1984.

Metford, J. C. J. *The Christian Year*. London, England: Thames and Hudson, 1991.

Urlin, Ethel. *Festivals, Holy Days, and Saints' Days*. 1915. Reprint. Detroit, Mich.: Omnigraphics, 1992.

Weiser, Francis X. *Handbook of Christian Feasts and Customs*. New York: Harcourt, Brace and World, 1952.

Fires

For Christmas customs involving the use of fire and bonfires, *see* **Estonia, Christmas in; Guatemala, Christmas in; Hogmanay; Iceland, Christmas in; Luminarias; Martinmas; Up Helly Aa; Williamsburg, Virginia, Christmas in Colonial; Yule; Yule Log; Zagmuk**

Firstfooting

In many parts of **Europe** old superstitions held that the first person to cross one's threshold after the start of the new year determined the household's luck for the coming year (*see also* **Estonia, Christmas in; Germany, Christmas in; Greece, Christmas in; Ireland, Christmas in; Italy, Christmas in; New Year's Day**). That person was called the "firstfooter." People with certain physical characteristics were deemed lucky firstfooters. In most places people welcomed dark-haired men as desirable firstfooters whose visit would confer luck on the entire household. By contrast, women and fair-haired or red-headed men were often deemed unlucky firstfooters whose visit hastened the coming of unfortunate events.

Scotland and England

The folklore of Scotland and **England** contains many references to firstfooters. The earliest historical records of firstfooting in Britain date back to the eighteenth century. Although found in many places throughout Britain, the custom appears to have been most strongly upheld in lowlands Scotland and northern England. There people awaited firstfooters in the early morning hours of January first. In many places custom dictated that firstfooters offer householders small **gifts** of food, spirits, fuel, and money as symbols of prosperity in the coming year. In some places the firstfooter delivered a sprig of **greenery**; in others salt was included in the lucky offerings. Usually the firstfooter exchanged warm greetings with family members upon entering the house, but in some locales he or she said nothing until stirring the fire or adding more fuel to it. Householders in return treated the firstfooter to food and drink and sometimes money, too. Some found this hospitality quite tempting. In Edinburgh, youth with the required physical characteristics sometimes fought one another for the opportunity to go firstfooting in the wealthier neighborhoods, where the rewards given to desirable firstfooters were greatest.

Although many communities favored dark-haired men as firstfooters, other communities preferred women, children, fair-headed men,
or even red-headed men. If the required characteristics occurred in-
frequently within the community, some locales actually searched out
and hired a firstfooter to make these midnight calls. In addition to
gender and hair color, several other physical characteristics disposed
people favorably or unfavorably to a firstfooter. In many places people preferred a young, healthy, and good-looking firstfooter. According to popular beliefs, the flat-footed, lame, sickly, or cross-eyed
brought bad luck with them. In some places, people whose eye-
brows met were considered unlucky. If one's household happened to
be jinxed by the untimely arrival of an unlucky firstfooter, folklore
provided a number of remedies. In areas where people placed a lot
of store in firstfooting, however, women and other people who
would be unwelcome as firstfooters were careful to delay any new
year visits until after their neighbors had all received a firstfooter.

Similar superstitions applied to first encounters on the road after the
start of the new year. Some deemed it lucky if the first person one
met was a child, or if one's first encounter was with an oxcart.
Meeting a beggar, sexton (church custodian), or gravedigger fore-
shadowed unpleasantness to come. Many thought it especially lucky
to meet someone whose arms were full, and unlucky to come across
someone who wasn't carrying anything.

Further Reading

Gaster, Theodor. *New Year, Its History, Customs, and Superstitions*. New York:
Abelard-Schuman, 1955.

Hole, Christina. *British Folk Customs*. London, England: Hutchinson and
Company, 1976.

Hutton, Ronald. *The Stations of the Sun*. Oxford, England: Oxford University
Press, 1996.

Miles, Clement A. *Christmas in Ritual and Tradition*. 1912. Reprint. Detroit,
Mich.: Omnigraphics, 1990.

First Night

First Night is the name of an alternative **New Year's** Eve celebration begun in Boston in the year 1976. The organizers of this event promoted the festivities as an alcohol-free, family-oriented New Year's celebration. Its success prompted an organization called "First Night International" to trademark the phrase "First Night," so that all cities that wish to organize a festival by that name must first join the organization and pay a fee. The First Night idea has caught on, and now over 150 American cities host these festivities on December 31. First Night celebrations have also spread to a number of locations in Canada, New Zealand, and the United Kingdom.

First Night festivals feature a variety of acts, events, and demonstrations showcasing the visual and performing arts. Festival organizers draw primarily on local artists and entertainers. Cities generally stage First Night festivals in a central location and the atmosphere may resemble that of a street fair. Although some open-air entertainment is available to everyone, people who wish to attend events scheduled for indoor venues generally have to buy a pass (usually in the form of a button they wear on their clothing) which entitles them to attend all the events.

One of the stated goals of First Night International is to wean people away from more boisterous, alcohol-laden New Year's Eve celebrations. Their efforts may be viewed as the latest twist on a campaign to reform the midwinter holidays that dates back to the time of the sixteenth-century Protestant Reformation (*see* **Puritans**). Over the centuries various Protestant religious groups have criticized the rowdy and often drunken celebrations that characterize many traditional New Year's Eve celebrations. They tried instead to promote the idea that New Year's Eve is an occasion for serious reflection on one's past, prayer for the future, renewal of one's commitment to serve God, and the setting of personal goals for the coming year (*see* **Resolutions; Watch Night**). The objectives of First Night International are somewhat less lofty. Beyond decreasing alcohol consumption on New Year's Eve, they aim to promote a sense of community, provide family-oriented entertainment, deepen public appreciation for the arts, and bring new life to downtown areas.

Further Reading

Henderson, Helene, and Sue Ellen Thompson, eds. *Holidays, Festivals, and Celebrations of the World Dictionary*. Second edition. Detroit, Mich.: Omnigraphics, 1997.

Web Site

First Night™ International posts a web site at the following address: http://www.firstnight.com

Flight into Egypt

The **Gospel according to Matthew** tells that soon after **Jesus** was born, King **Herod** sent soldiers to **Bethlehem** to kill all the town's male infants (*see* **Holy Innocents' Day**). An **angel** warned **Joseph** of Herod's evil plot and told him to escape with his family to **Egypt**. The Holy Family obeyed the angel's command and departed. This event, called the Flight into Egypt, has been depicted by many artists over the centuries, including Giotto (c. 1267-1337), Titian (1488 or 1490-1576), Albrecht Dürer (1471-1528), and Nicolas Poussin (1594-1665). It is commemorated in Orthodox churches on December 26 —or January 8 in churches that still use the Julian calendar—in a service referred to as the Synaxis of the Theotokos (*for more on the Julian calendar, see* **Old Christmas Day**). *Synaxis* means "meeting" and *Theotokos*, a title given to the Blessed Virgin **Mary**, means "God bearer." In the Middle Ages, some western Europeans, particularly the French, remembered the Flight into Egypt with a festival called the **Feast of the Ass**.

When King Herod died, the angel returned again, notifying Joseph that it was safe for him to return with his family to Judea. When

Joseph learned that Herod's brutal son, Archelaus, had inherited his father's throne, he decided not to return to Bethlehem, and instead moved his family to Nazareth.

Legends

What happened to the Holy Family on this perilous journey into Egypt? The Bible doesn't say. Perhaps because of this omission, legends and lore soon sprouted up around the event. According to one tale, Herod's soldiers knew the Holy Family had escaped and so pursued them. As Mary, Joseph, and Jesus passed some peasants sowing wheat, Mary said to them, "If anyone should ask if we have been here, tell them that we indeed passed by while you were sowing this field of wheat." Miraculously, the wheat sprouted and grew tall overnight. When Herod's soldiers inquired of the peasants and learned that their prey had passed through the region at the time the wheat was planted, they figured that the Holy Family was many days ahead of them and so lost heart and returned to Judea.

An ancient document known as the Arabic Infancy Gospel records another near escape. In this story, the Holy Family is held up by bandits on their way to Egypt. One of the highwaymen, however, feels a special sympathy for the fugitives and refuses to rob them. In fact, he tries to convince the other robber to let them go. The other refuses until the first robber agrees to pay him a girdle and forty coins. The kind-hearted thief does so and the other reluctantly allows the prisoners to depart. The baby Jesus predicts that he and the bandits will die on the same day in the same place. Sure enough, according to the Arabic Infancy Gospel, these men turn out to be the two thieves, the one remorseful and the other not, who were crucified alongside Jesus about thirty years later (Luke 23:93-43).

Another tale, this one from a document called the Apocryphal Gospel of Pseudo-Matthew, finds Joseph losing faith as the family trudges through the desert. They stop underneath a date palm tree where Joseph frets about how to find water. Mary asks her husband to pick her some dates. Joseph scolds her for requesting something so far out of his reach. The infant Jesus, however, speaks to the tree, commanding it to bow down so Mary can gather fruit. The tree responds. Then Jesus orders an underground spring to break through to the surface so that they can drink and fill their water bags. As this tale spread through **Europe**, people changed the date tree to a **cherry tree** and changed the timing of the event so that it takes place before Jesus was born.

Another legend concerning trees reports that the Holy Family passed through a forest on their long journey to Egypt. Every tree except the aspen bowed in reverence as they passed. Irritated by this lack of respect the baby Jesus then cursed the tree, which is why its leaves tremble in the wind till this day.

Another plant that paid respect to the Holy Family on the Flight into Egypt is the Rose of Jericho. It sprang up wherever they passed. It is sometimes called Mary's Rose.

One final tale popular in the Middle Ages proclaims that the Holy Family encountered a gypsy woman on the road to Egypt. She extended her well-wishes to the Holy Family and, noticing Mary's fatigue especially, she took them to a place where they could rest and offered straw for their donkey. She then proceeded to recount Mary's past history. Afterwards she read Jesus' palm and accurately foretold the major events of his life, including the crucifixion. Then she begged for alms, but not in the usual manner. Knowing the true identity of the child, the gypsy woman asked for the gift of genuine repentance and life everlasting.

Further Reading

Gulevich, Tanya. *Encyclopedia of Easter, Carnival, and Lent*. Detroit, Mich.: Omnigraphics, 2002.

Hackwood, Frederick W. *Christ Lore*. 1902. Reprint. Detroit, Mich.: Gale Research, 1969.

Jameson, Anna. *Legends of the Madonna*. 1890. Reprint. Detroit, Mich.: Omnigraphics, 1990.

Leach, Maria, ed. *Funk and Wagnalls Standard Dictionary of Folklore, Mythology, and Legend*. San Francisco, Calif.: Harper and Row, 1984.

Football Bowl Games

Many Americans enjoy watching college football **games** on **New Year's Day**. This tradition dates back to the early years of the twentieth century, when the first of these "bowl" games, the Rose Bowl, got its start.

The Rose Bowl Game and the Tournament of Roses

The Rose Bowl, which takes place in Pasadena, California, began as one component of a yearly festival called the Tournament of Roses. Members of the local Valley Hunt Club started this festival in 1890 as a means of celebrating and publicizing Pasadena's wonderful winter climate and its abundance of winter-time fruit and flowers. The day's entertainments included a parade of flower-bedecked carriages, tug-of-war contests, foot races, and polo matches. The festival quickly became a hit—so much so that in 1895 the Valley Hunt Club turned the event's organization and management over to a new, volunteer group, the Tournament of Roses Association.

In 1902 Tournament officials decided that a collegiate sporting event might attract even more people to their festival. Festival organizers set up an "east versus west" football match, pitting the University of Michigan against California's Stanford University. The game took place in Tournament Park, which sat about 1,000 people. To the amazement of festival organizers, 8,500 spectators came and jostled one another for those seats. The fans expressed more enthusiasm for the game than did the players. By the third quarter Michigan led 49 to 0. R. S. Fisher, captain of the thoroughly pummeled Stanford players, approached Hugh White, the captain of the Michigan team, and tendered Stanford's surrender, reportedly saying, "If you are willing, we are ready to quit." Michigan accepted this admission of defeat and the game ended.

After this poor showing, festival organizers agreed to cancel the football game as part of the Tournament of Roses. Chariot races instead amused the sports-loving public. Eventually these were deemed too dangerous, and football returned to the Tournament of Roses in 1916. Once again, huge crowds overwhelmed the venue. In 1920 festival organizers decided to build a new football stadium in order to better accommodate fans. Modeled after Yale University's then state-of-the-art football stadium, the Yale Bowl, Pasadena's new stadium was dubbed the "Rose Bowl." The first game in the new Rose Bowl Stadium took place on January 1, 1923.

The popularity of this contest grew with each passing decade. In 1927, the Rose Bowl Game became the first sports match to be broadcast on transcontinental radio. In 1952 NBC covered the Rose Bowl, making it the first college football game ever to be shown on national television. In addition, since 1947 sell-out crowds have jammed the Rose Bowl's bleachers to watch the game. In that year Tournament organizers signed an agreement with the Big Ten and Pacific Coast football conferences (the latter would eventually become the Pacific Ten Conference). The Rose Bowl henceforth pitted the top team in each of these conferences against each other.

The Tournament of Roses parade has also grown over the years. Today it includes marching bands, equestrians, motorized floats, a celebrity grand marshal, and a local beauty queen dubbed the Rose Queen, who presides over the parade and game. Each year the Tournament of Roses Association selects a theme for the parade. Flower-covered floats express this theme. Parade rules dictate that the entire surface of the float's exterior be covered with flowers or other plant parts, such as leaves, seeds, or bark. Work begins on the construction of the floats shortly after the previous year's festival comes to a close.

Other New Year's Day Bowl Games

The success of the Rose Bowl Game prompted the creation of additional bowl games in other parts of the country. In 1933 two prominent Miami citizens organized a New Year's Day football game as one element of a new civic event called the Palm Festival. In 1935 this game became the Orange Bowl and was played in the newly constructed Orange Bowl Stadium. In 1996 the contest shifted to the Pro Player Stadium in Ft. Lauderdale.

In 1990 the Orange Bowl's official name changed to the FedEx Orange Bowl, thus providing additional advertising for its major corporate sponsor, Federal Express. In recent years, as the importance of corporate funding has grown, many bowl games have added the names of their primary corporate sponsors in their official titles (*see also* **Commercialism**).

Other New Year's Day Bowl Games include the Southwest Bell Cotton Bowl, played in Dallas, Texas. Played in Cotton Bowl Stadium, the match currently pits a team from the Big 12 against a team from the Southeastern Conference.

The Nokia Sugar Bowl makes its home in New Orleans, Louisiana. Begun in 1935, the game took place in Tulane University's football stadium. In 1975, the Sugar Bowl moved to the Superdome.

A relative late-comer, the Tostitos Fiesta Bowl started in 1971. Played in Sun Devil Stadium on the grounds of Arizona State University, the Fiesta Bowl was originally scheduled for late December, but moved to January 1, or sometimes a neighboring date, in 1981.

Bowl Championship Series

In 1998 the Bowl Championship Series was established to determine the top-ranking team in college football by pitting the number one and number two ranked teams in the nation against each other. This event does not have a permanent home but rather rotates between the Rose Bowl, Orange Bowl, Sugar Bowl, and Fiesta Bowl.

Further Reading

Crump, William D. *The Christmas Encyclopedia*. Jefferson, N.C.: McFarland, 2001.
Michaelson, Herb, and Dave Newhouse. *Rose Bowl Football Since 1902*. New York: Stein and Day, 1977.
Whittingham, Richard. *Rites of Autumn*. New York: Free Press, 2001.

Web Site

The Tournament of Roses Association maintains its own web site with detailed information on the parade and football game:
http://www.tournamentofroses.com

France, Christmas in

The story of the Christ child's birth, as represented in **Nativity scenes**, retold in folk plays, and commemorated in religious services plays a large role in French Christmas celebrations. As one might expect, so, too, does fine food.

St. Nicholas's Day

French children eagerly await **St. Nicholas's Day**, December 6. In honor of the generous saint, adults often give children **gifts** of candy and other treats. Since **St. Nicholas** is the patron saint of Lorraine, the people of that province celebrate his feast day with processions. These processions include men dressed as the saint in long robes, bishop's hats, and crosses. *Père Fouttard*, or "Father Whipper," usually follows behind Nicholas. The children recognize Père Fouttard by his dirty, dark robe, greasy, grey beard, and whip. While St. Nicholas rewards children who have been good, Père Fouttard punishes children who have misbehaved (*see also* **Black Peter; Knecht Ruprecht**).

Père Noël

In France children receive their Christmas gifts from *Père Noël*, or "Father Christmas." French folklore depicts Père Noël as a solemn old man with a white beard. He wears a long, hooded, red robe trimmed with white fur. He resembles **England's Father Christmas** and **Germany's Weihnachtsmann**. In the weeks before Christmas many French children write letters to Père Noël describing the gifts they would like to receive (*see also* **Children's Letters**). They mail these letters to the **North Pole**.

Preparations

As Christmas day draws near, many people give their homes a thorough cleaning. Silver may be polished and fine china brought out of storage for the sumptuous Christmas Eve feast called *réveillon*. Families shop for **Christmas trees** and flowers to decorate the table. The French put all kinds of flowers to this purpose, including **poinsettias**, but a special favorite is the **Christmas rose**. The French also enjoy decorating their homes with **mistletoe**. Another shopping trip may be made to pick up a new figurine for their Nativity scene, which the French call a *crèche*, meaning "crib." Shops and markets throughout France display a wide variety of these engaging, lifelike figures in the weeks preceding Christmas. As a special Christmas treat the family may go to see a **Nativity play**. All over France local theatrical groups present these plays, which retell French Nativity legends. The French call these pastoral tales *pastorales* (*see also* **Pastores, Los**).

Most French families decorate their Christmas trees a few days before Christmas. French Christmas **ornaments** come in a wide variety of shapes and sizes. The fish, once a new year's symbol signifying long life, has become a popular shape for tree ornaments. Although Christmas trees have become popular, the Nativity scene remains the most important Christmas decoration in France. Churches throughout France display Nativity scenes in the weeks before Christmas. French families begin to assemble their Nativity scenes a few days before Christmas. Children especially enjoy this task and may bring home twigs, moss, and rocks to make the setting look more lifelike. Each day the figurines representing the Three Kings move closer to the stable where the Holy Family has taken shelter (*see* **Magi**). In past times **Yule logs** were popular throughout France. Nowadays the Yule log survives in the form of a popular Christmas dessert called a *bûche de Noël*, or "Christmas log." Bakers mold this creme-filled cake into the shape of log.

Christmas Eve

Many French families serve a light snack at dinner time on Christmas Eve. This tides the family over until the more formal meal, which they call *réveillon*, meaning "awakening." This meal will not take place until the middle of the night. Family members pass the evening together singing **Christmas carols** and telling Christmas stories. In addition, the women of the household may spend many hours in the kitchen preparing the Christmas Eve feast. Children place their **shoes** near the fireplace, underneath the Christmas tree,

or near the Nativity scene. In the middle of the night the magical Père Noël will come and fill them with sweets and toys. Late in the evening someone, often the youngest child, completes the Nativity scene by placing the baby **Jesus** figurine into the manger. As midnight approaches small children are tucked into bed and the rest of the family prepares to go to **Midnight Mass**.

After returning from church French families finally sit down to their Christmas Eve banquet. This meal may consist of up to fifteen courses. After passing several hours dining together the family settles down to watch the children open Christmas presents. Families with small children may wait until Christmas morning to open presents, however. As a rule, only children receive presents on Christmas. Adults exchange gifts with one another on **New Year's Day**.

Regional Customs

Located in southern France, the region of Provence boasts a number of distinctive Christmas customs. The region is well known for its *santons*, Nativity scene figurines. In Provence santon makers have sold their wares at Christmas fairs since the early nineteenth century. For generations these artisans have trained their children in the traditional techniques for making the clay figurines. A number of Provençal villages sponsor living Nativity scenes and costumed processions of **shepherds**, **angels**, kings, and pilgrims on Christmas Eve. These candlelight processions begin about an hour before midnight and wend their way to the local church, where participants pay their respects to the Holy Family and attend Midnight Mass.

Christmas cuisine also varies across France. Families in Provence often serve lobster as a first course for réveillon. Roast pheasant or roast lamb often follow. Bread, cheese, green salad, pâté, and wine round out the meal. Provençal custom suggests that hostesses serve thirteen desserts for réveillon, one for Jesus and each of the twelve apostles. Some combination of fresh, glazed, and dried fruit, marzipan, candies, and cakes are usually served. In the snowy French Alps a simpler réveillon meal may be offered, featuring such sturdy dishes as hot broth with noodles and boiled beef. In Brittany, on France's northern coast, buckwheat crepes are served with heavy cream.

New Year and Epiphany

Adults exchange gifts on New Year's Day. The French word for new year's gift, *étrenne*, comes from the Latin word *strenae*, which also means "new year's gift." The ancient Romans offered these gifts to one another at their new year festival, **Kalends**. The **Christmas season** in France closes on January 6 with *Fête des Rois*, Three King's Day, or **Epiphany**.

Further Reading

Del Re, Gerard, and Patricia Del Re. *The Christmas Almanack*. Garden City, N.Y.: Doubleday, 1979.
Ross, Corinne. *Christmas in France*. Chicago: World Book, 1988.

Web Site

A site sponsored by the French Ministry of Culture and Canadian Heritage: http://www.culture.fr:80/culture/noel/angl/noel.htm

Frankincense

The sap of the frankincense tree (*Boswellia carteri* or *Boswellia thurifera*) dries into hard, yellowish brown lumps of gum resin known as frankincense. In biblical times frankincense was prized as the very best kind of incense. It was one of the **gifts** that the **Magi** presented to the baby **Jesus**.

The English word "frankincense" comes from the Old French words *franc encens*, meaning pure or high-quality incense. Although it was most commonly used as incense in ancient times, frankincense was also prescribed as a medicine to treat a wide variety of ailments. Many ancient peoples, such as the Egyptians, Greeks, Romans, Persians, Jews, and Babylonians, burned incense in home and temple worship. The rising fumes from burning incense may have offered worshipers a visual image of prayers ascending to heaven. Scholars speculate that this imagery explains the widespread use of incense in worship. Frankincense is mentioned numerous times in the Old Testament and was one of the four components of the sacred incense burned by the Jewish priests in the Sanctuary. Because of its close relationship with worship, the Magi's gift of frankincense has traditionally been interpreted as a recognition of Jesus' divinity. Another interpretation suggests that it predicts Jesus' future role as a high priest.

In ancient times, Arabia supplied the Mediterranean and Asia with most of their **myrrh** and frankincense. These products were so highly valued and so difficult to obtain outside of Arabia that they became a luxury affordable only by the rich. Thus, the Magi's valuable gift of frankincense may also have signified their recognition of Jesus' great worth.

Until the mid-1700s tradition dictated that the British monarch offer a gift of frankincense, **gold**, and myrrh at the Chapel Royal on **Epiphany**. Heralds and knights of the Garter, Thistle, and Bath accompanied the King on this reenactment of the Magi's pilgrimage. Under the unstable King George III (1760-1820) the procession was abandoned, although the monarch's gift of gold, frankincense, and myrrh is still sent to the Chapel Royal by proxy. A similar royal offering was at one time customary in **Spain**.

Today frankincense trees can be found in Arabia, **Ethiopia**, Somalia, and **India**. Frankincense is still primarily used as incense. Frankincense is a component of the incense burned in Roman Catholic and Orthodox church services. It may also be found in other scented products, such as soap.

Further Reading

Crippen, Thomas G. *Christmas and Christmas Lore*. 1923. Reprint. Detroit, Mich.: Omnigraphics, 1990.

De Hoghton, Charles. "Incense." In Richard Cavendish, ed. *Man, Myth and Magic: An Illustrated Encyclopedia of the Supernatural*. Volume 8. New York: Marshall Cavendish, 1970.

Groom, Nigel. *Frankincense and Myrrh: A Study of the Arabian Incense Trade*. London, England: Longman, 1981.

Peattie, Donald Culross. "Gold, Frankincense, and Myrrh." *Saturday Evening Post* 264, 6 (November 1992): 56.

Frau Gaude

Gaue, Gode, Wode

According to old folk beliefs, Frau Gaude, followed by her pack of phantom dogs, once haunted the streets of German-speaking **Europe** during the **Twelve Days of Christmas**. If she found a house with an open door, she would send in one of her dogs, which the householders would find impossible to drive away. If they killed the dog, it would turn into a stone. Regardless of where the family left the stone, it would always return to their house at night as a whimpering dog, bringing them bad luck throughout the year.

In some regions, Frau Gaude led the **Wild Hunt**, a riotous procession of **ghosts** and spirits who rode across the stormy night skies during **Yule**. Frau Gaude may be a variant of **Berchta**, a pagan winter goddess who faded into a kind of minor bogey in later times. Other names for Frau Gaude include Gaue, Gode, and Wode.

Further Reading

Miles, Clement A. *Christmas in Ritual and Tradition.* 1912. Reprint. Detroit, Mich.: Omnigraphics, 1990.

Gabriel

The Bible names only one of the **angels** who appear in connection with **Jesus'** birth. The **Gospel according to Luke** states that the angel Gabriel appeared to the Blessed Virgin **Mary** to tell her that she would bear a son whom she should name Jesus (Luke 1:26-35). Christians call this event the **Annunciation**.

Gabriel in the Bible

Who is Gabriel and why was he sent to bear such important news? Religious scholars often begin a discussion of the angel by analyzing the meaning of his name. Some say it means "God is my warrior"; others translate it as "man of God." Still others believe it should be translated as "power of God" or "hero of God." Gabriel is one of only two angels mentioned by name in the Hebrew scriptures, or Old Testament (the other is Michael). In the Book of Daniel, Gabriel helps Daniel interpret his visions and informs him of God's plan for the end of time (Daniel 8-12). Gabriel returns again in the New

Testament, or Christian scriptures. In the Gospel according to Luke he appears to Zechariah to tell him that he and his wife will conceive a child, John, who will serve as the forerunner to Jesus Christ (Luke 1:11-20). Shortly afterwards Gabriel visits the Virgin Mary to announce her forthcoming pregnancy (Luke 1:26-38). Thus the Bible tends to cast Gabriel as God's herald. Because he frequently brings news of God's doings to human beings, he is sometimes referred to as the Angel of Revelation.

Gabriel in Christian Art

In the Gospel according to Luke Gabriel identifies himself as someone who "stand[s] in the presence of God" (Luke 1:19). This has led many Christians to conclude that he is one of the few high-ranking angels known as archangels. Over the centuries Christian artists have portrayed Gabriel as a solemn, male figure wearing beautiful robes. In earlier works of art Gabriel often carries a scepter. In more recent works he holds a lily, a symbol of the purity and goodness of the Virgin Mary.

Jewish and Muslim Beliefs

Jewish lore assigns Gabriel many different jobs. The Book of Enoch portrays him as an overseer of the Garden of Eden (*see also* **Adam and Eve Day**). Other apocryphal texts and legends have shown him as one of the four angels who stand round the throne of God, a participant in the destruction of Sodom and the army of Sennacherib, and one of those who prayed for the world at the time of the Great Flood. Muslims, too, honor the angel Gabriel, whom they know as Jibril. They believe him to be the angel who dictated the Qur'an — the holy book of Islam — to the prophet Muhammad.

Christian Lore

Christian lore not only places Gabriel at the scene of Jesus' birth but also at the scene leading up to Jesus' death. Perhaps because of his biblical role as a herald, Christian legends have suggested that Gabriel was the unnamed angel that brought the good news of Jesus' birth to the **shepherds** (Luke 2:8-12). Another folk belief places

Gabriel in the Garden of Gethsemane as Jesus prayed and waited for the men who would come to arrest him and condemn him to death. Both of these tales emphasize Gabriel's role as the angel of mercy. Michael, by contrast, functions as the angel of judgment. (In Jewish lore these roles are reversed, with Michael serving as the angel of mercy while Gabriel acts as the angel of judgment.)

Patronage

In 1951 Pope Pius XII gave Gabriel a new role to play, modernizing his ancient task as a transmitter of messages. He declared Gabriel to be the patron saint of all those who work in the field of telecommunications. Gabriel also serves as the traditional patron of messengers, diplomats, clergy members, postal workers, and stamp collectors.

Further Reading

Davidson, Gustav. *A Dictionary of Angels*. New York: Free Press, 1967.

Fallon, T. L. "Gabriel, Archangel." In *New Catholic Encyclopedia*. Volume 6. New York: McGraw-Hill, 1967.

Godwin, Malcom. *Angels: An Endangered Species*. New York: Simon and Schuster, 1990.

Pope, Hugh. "St. Gabriel the Archangel." In Charles B. Hervermann, ed. *Catholic Encyclopedia*. Nashville, Tenn.: T. Nelson, 1913. Available on the World Wide Web at: http://www.newadvent.org/cathen/06330a.htm

Strauss, Mark L. "Gabriel." In David Noel Freedman, ed. *Eerdmans Dictionary of the Bible*. Grand Rapids, Mich.: William B. Eerdmans Publishing Company, 2000.

Web Site

"Gabriel the Archangel," a page available through Catholic Forum, a web site affiliated with Liturgical Publications of St. Louis, at: http://www.catholic-forum.com/saints/saintg03.htm

Games

In the days before radio, television, video machines, and computers, people entertained one another during the long winter evenings of the **Christmas season**. They told stories, danced, sang songs, or played games. In the twentieth century, as people began to rely on ready-made forms of entertainment provided by the mass media, many of these games died out or became children's pastimes.

Late Medieval and Renaissance England

In late medieval and Renaissance **England** people played a wide variety of games at Christmas time. Outdoor amusements included group games and athletic matches in such sports as archery and tilting. One group game, Prisoner's Base, proved so popular in the time of King Edward III (1312-1377) that players clogged the street leading to Westminster Palace. This congestion caused the king to prohibit the playing of Prisoner's Base near the palace.

During this era the English also enjoyed a variety of parlor games at Christmas time, including Blind Man's Bluff, Leap Frog, Loggats (similar to Nine Pins) and Hot Cockles. In Hot Cockles each player in turn is blindfolded. The blindfolded player puts his hands behind his back, palms up. One of the other players hits the hands of the blindfolded player. The blindfolded player must guess which of the other players has hit him. If he does so correctly, he may penalize the player whom he "caught." Those who preferred a greater mental test might retire to a game of chess, while the physically agile might challenge each other to tennis or skittles.

The English also enjoyed playing cards and gambling at Christmas time, especially with dice. During the reign of the Tudor kings, working people may have found greater pleasure in these games than the well-to-do, since they were prohibited by law from playing games except at Christmas time. In the sixteenth and seventeenth centuries the **Puritans** condemned those who celebrated Christmas by playing games and gambling.

Victorian England

Parlor games remained popular Christmas entertainments through-out the nineteenth century. Victorians favored such games as Snapdragon, Forfeits, Hoop and Hide (Hide and Seek), Charades, Blind Man's Bluff, Queen of Sheba (a variation on Blind Man's Bluff), and Hunt the Slipper (*see also* **Victorian England, Christmas in**).

In Snapdragon players gathered around a bowl of currants (a raisin-like dried fruit) covered with spirits. A lighted match was dropped into the bowl, setting fire to the alcohol. Players challenged one another to grab a flaming currant out of the bowl and pop it into their mouths, thus extinguishing the flames. A bit of light verse describes the fearful delights of this game:

> Here he comes with flaming bowl,
> Don't he mean to take his toll,
>   Snip! Snap! Dragon!
> Take care you don't take too much,
> Be not greedy in your clutch,
>   Snip! Snap! Dragon!
> With his blue and lapping tongue
> Many of you will be stung,
>   Snip! Snap! Dragon!
> For he snaps at all that comes
> Snatching at his feast of plums,
>   Snip! Snap! Dragon!
> But Old Christmas makes him come,
> Though he looks so fee! fa! fum!
>   Snip! Snap! Dragon!
> Don't 'ee fear him, be but bold—
> Out he goes, his flames are cold,
>   Snip! Snap! Dragon! [Chambers, 1990, 2: 738]

Players heightened the effect of the glowing, blue flames by extinguishing all other lights in the room except that cast by the burning bowl.

In Hunt the Slipper players formed a circle around one person. They held their hands behind their backs and passed a slipper around the outside of the circle. The person in the center of the circle had to guess who was in possession of the slipper at any given moment.

A number of other English Christmas games have now disappeared so completely that only their picturesque names remain behind. Folklorists cannot now say how they were played. These forgotten games include Shoeing the Wild Mare, Steal the White Loaf, Post and Pair, Feed the Dove, Puss-in-the-Corner, and The Parson Has Lost His Cloak. Before a Christmas party broke up for the evening, the sleepy guests might play one last, quaintly named game called Yawning for a Cheshire Cheese. The players sat in a circle and yawned at one another. Whoever produced the longest, most open-mouthed, and loudest yawn won a Cheshire cheese.

Other Countries

Some traditional Christmas games are for children. In many nations **Advent calendars** amuse children with a kind of counting game in the weeks before Christmas. Children in **Mexico** often play games with piñatas at holiday season parties. In **Iran** youngsters play egg-tapping games at Christmas time.

Most Christmas games, however, involve adults and younger people. In a number of different countries sporting matches, games of chance, or fortune-telling games are associated with one or more days of the Christmas season. In past times Swedes used to play games with Christmas **gifts**, which they call **Julklapp**, on December 24. On **St. Stephen's Day** both Swedes and Norwegians used to race horses (*see* **Norway, Christmas in**). Ethiopians celebrate Christmas Day by playing ganna, a sport that resembles hockey (*see* **Ethiopia, Christmas in**). In the United States, many people enjoy watching **football bowl games** on **New Year's Day**. In **Lithuania** people entertain themselves on Christmas Eve with fortune-telling games. People in many countries celebrate New Year's Eve by playing games of chance, especially card games. Colonial Americans and Europeans of past centuries enjoyed card games and a kind of charade involving the **King of the Bean** on **Twelfth Night**.

Further Reading

Chambers, Robert. "December 24 — Christmas Games: Snapdragon." In his *The Book of Days*. Volume 2. 1862-64. Reprint. Detroit, Mich.: Omnigraphics, 1990.

Miall, Antony, and Peter Miall. *The Victorian Christmas Book*. New York: Pantheon Books, 1978.

Muir, Frank. *Christmas Customs and Traditions*. New York: Taplinger, 1977.

Pimlott, J. A. R. *The Englishman's Christmas*. Atlantic Heights, N.J.: Humanities Press, 1978.

Gaudete Sunday

In the Roman Catholic Church and the Anglican Communion the third Sunday in **Advent** is sometimes called Gaudete Sunday. *Gaudete* means "rejoice" in Latin. This name comes from the first line of the introit (opening prayer) for the third Sunday in Advent, which encourages parishioners to "rejoice in the Lord always." Although Advent ushers in a period of penance and spiritual preparation, Gaudete Sunday introduces the theme of joy. The lighter mood is reflected in the change in liturgical colors, from the purple of the Advent season to the rose color adopted for Gaudete Sunday. In addition, on Gaudete Sunday parishioners may decorate the church with flowers, and the organ, usually silent during Advent, may be played.

Further Reading

Metford, J. C. J. *The Christian Year*. London, England: Thames and Hudson, 1991.

Germany, Christmas in

German Christmas celebrations braid together a rich heritage of folk, food, and religious customs. Many of these customs have spread to other parts of the globe. Indeed, the **Christmas tree**, which emerged in Germany several centuries ago, has become a nearly universal symbol of the holiday. German Christmas customs and traditions have probably exerted more influence on mainstream American Christmas celebrations than those of any other ethnic group.

Advent

In Germany **Advent** is called *Lichtwochen*, which means "light weeks." The Germans observe Advent with **Advent wreaths** and **Advent calendars**. These two customs, German in origin, have spread far beyond Germany. Carol singing is another popular Advent and Christmas custom. One of the world's most popular **Christmas carols**, "Silent Night," was originally composed in German by an Austrian priest and his organist. Other internationally known carols of German origin include "In Dulci Jubilo" (also known as "Good Christian Men Rejoice"), "Lo, How a Rose e'er Blooming," and "O Christmas Tree, O Christmas Tree." Germany's famous **Christmas markets** offer another way to prepare for Christmas. Traditional German Christmas foods, crafts, and **gifts** can be found at their many, busy stalls. The famous Nuremberg market opens on the Friday closest to **St. Barbara's Day**, December 4, although most Christmas markets are open throughout Advent.

Frauentragen, or "woman carrying," an old German Advent custom still practiced in some areas, closely resembles the Hispanic folk play Las **Posadas**. Children carry a picture or figurine representing the Virgin **Mary** to a neighborhood home. Once there they sing or enact a brief scene from the Nativity story, say a prayer, and place the picture or figurine near the family crucifix. The children return for the image the following evening and carry it to a new home. In this way they act out Mary and **Joseph's** search for lodging in **Bethlehem**.

On Christmas Eve the children carry Mary back to the church, where she takes her place in the **Nativity scene**.

Special Days Within Advent

In past eras various customs and superstitions attached themselves to the saints' days and other special days that fell during Advent. St. Andrew's night, November 30, presented young girls with the opportunity to use folk magic to foresee their marital futures. One old superstition advised girls to wait up until midnight and throw a slipper at the door. If the slipper landed with the toe pointing out the door, they would be leaving their parents' home for their husband's home in the next year. **St. Thomas's Day**, December 21, provided another opportunity for young women to exercise various fortune-telling charms. In past years St. Thomas's night was also known as spinning night. Young women stayed up late into the night spinning thread that might be sold to help pay for Christmas expenses.

On St. Barbara's Day, an old folk tradition recommended cutting branches from **cherry trees** and placing them in vases of water near the fire. If timed correctly these branches, known as "Barbara branches," would bloom on Christmas or Christmas Eve.

St. Nicholas's Day, December 6, offers children a preview of Christmas pleasures to come. On St. Nicholas's Eve youngsters leave a **shoe** or a boot by the fireplace, window, or bedroom door. The next morning they find it filled with sweet treats. Although **St. Nicholas** usually disburses presents, German folklore warns that he will sometimes leave poorly behaved children a stick as a warning of punishment to come. St. Nicholas's assistant, **Knecht Ruprecht**, usually performs the unpleasant task of disciplining naughty children.

The **Knocking Nights** — the last three Thursday nights in Advent — constitute a different sort of **Christmas season** observance. In some regions of Germany folk tradition encourages people to take to the streets making loud noises and wearing frightening masks on these nights. Folk rites designed to ward away evil spirits and influences were also practiced on these days.

Christmas Decorations

Besides Advent calendars and wreaths, home decorations in Germany include red candles, pine twigs, and candlesticks. One regional folk custom encourages families to display candlesticks shaped like miners and **angels** in their windows at Christmas time. Families display one miner for each boy child in the house and one angel for each girl child. The Christmas **pyramid** is another traditional German Christmas decoration. Some researchers believe that this pyramidal arrangement of shelves served as the forerunner to the Christmas tree. Many German families display a Nativity scene in their homes. This is especially popular in Roman Catholic areas. Bavarian craftsman have a reputation for producing marvelous Nativity scenes out of carved wood. Many fine Christmas cribs are produced by German artisans and sold at Christmas markets. The most famous German Christmas decoration, however, is the Christmas tree. In the last several hundred years the Christmas tree has spread throughout the world, and today is recognized as a nearly universal symbol of the holiday.

Christmas Baking

The Germans are famous for their Christmas baking, and, indeed, a German Christmas is filled with many delectable treats. *Christstollen*, also called *Chrisbrot, Stutenbrot*, or *Striezl*, constitutes Germany's most famous **Christmas cake** or bread. To make it bakers enhance a sweet yeast dough with dried fruits, various fruit peels, almonds, and spices. After baking they apply a coating of sugar icing. *Baumkuchen*, or "tree cake," serves as another special Christmas or Advent treat. The log-shaped cake is prepared in such a way that each slice is imprinted with concentric circles resembling tree rings. **Gingerbread** is another German Christmas favorite. The Germans not only shape it into cookies, but also into gingerbread houses. Other well-known German Christmas cookies include *Lebkuchen, Pfeffernüsse*, and *Springerle*. The German baker may also produce other Christmas treats from Germany's storehouse of cookie recipes, including vanilla rings, cinnamon stars, various kinds of nut cookies, spice cookies, macaroons, marzipan, and more.

Gift Bringers

In addition to St. Nicholas, a number of other Christmas gift bringers visit Germany each year. The **Christkindel**, or "Christ Child" usually brings gifts to children in southern Germany. In the north the **Weihnachtsmann**, or "Christmas man" typically delivers the gifts.

Christmas Eve and Day

In Germany Christmas Eve is known as *Heilige Abend*, or "holy night." Throughout Germany many offices and stores close by noon and people scurry home to make last-minute preparations. Lutherans often attend church services on the afternoon of the twenty-fourth, while German Roman Catholics wait until **Midnight Mass**. Many people visit family gravesites on Christmas Eve. In some areas they leave lighted candles on the graves. In rural areas farmers pay their respects to the family farm animals by making sure they are fed before the Christmas tree is lit. This custom honors the folk belief that farm animals were among the first to welcome the baby **Jesus** into the world, since he was born in a stable.

Some German families decorate their Christmas trees on the afternoon of December 24. Mother and father may do so behind closed doors, allowing the children their first view of the illuminated tree after sunset. Some German families still light their trees with candles, although others now prefer electric lights as a safer option. In addition to store-bought **ornaments** German families festoon their Christmas trees with cookies and candies. Families often read the Christmas story aloud by the light of the Christmas tree candles and sing their favorite carols before settling down to open gifts. In some families parents give children sparklers to hold while they stand around the tree and sing.

Today Germans display their Christmas presents under the tree or near the Nativity scene. In the past, however, some gifts were tossed through an open window or door and were known as **Julklapp**, or "Christmas knocks." Gift givers wrapped these boxes in many different layers, with a different name attached to each layer. Part of the fun lay in finding out who the gift was really for.

Many different dishes appear on Christmas Eve menus in Germany. In past times, carp was standard fare on Christmas Eve, in keeping with the Roman Catholic tradition of fasting on December 24. In Roman Catholic areas of Germany people may still prepare a meatless meal for Christmas Eve. Sweetened rice pudding, a dish which still finds favor with some Scandinavians, once served as another traditional Christmas dish in Germany (*see also* **Denmark, Christmas in; Norway, Christmas in**).

In Germany Christmas Day is sometimes referred as the "First Day of Christmas," *der erste Weihnachtstag*. Germans typically spend the day at home with their families or visit relatives. The main meal of the day usually features roast goose.

The Twelve Days of Christmas

The rest of the **Twelve Days of Christmas** fall between Christmas and **Epiphany**. In past times many superstitions attached themselves to this time of year. Many people believed that the **Wild Hunt**, a band of fierce spirits, rode abroad on these nights. **Berchta**, a witch-like figure, was also said to wander through German-speaking lands at this time of year. Many of the old folk customs associated with the Twelve Days offered protection from these roaming phantoms. For example, Germans often burned incense as a means of frightening off evil spirits. The Twelve Days were sometimes called the "Smoke Nights" in reference to this custom. Loud noises were believed to ward off evil creatures as well, and many noisemaking customs attached themselves to this season. According to folk tradition, wearing frightening masks and costumes also put evil influences to flight, and in some areas people went from house to house in such garb. In Bavaria women refrained from spinning, baking, washing, and cleaning during the Twelve Days of Christmas, believing it unlucky. For this reason the period became known as the "Twelve Quiet Days."

The magic of the Twelve Days also extended to fortune-telling. One folk belief cautioned that events that occurred during these twelve days set the pattern for the twelve months to come. For example, rain on the second day of Christmas meant that much rain would fall during February, the second month of the year. Folklore advised young girls to harness the magical properties of the twelve days to see their own futures. They could choose from a number of spells and charms designed to foretell whether or not they would marry in the coming year, and to reveal the identity of their future husbands. For example, the sparks of a fire lit on **New Year's** Eve might spell out their future husband's name, or the entire peel from an apple, tossed over one shoulder might fall in such a pattern as to give a clue to the boy's identity. These charms were especially popular on New Year's Eve.

St. Stephen's Day

Germans celebrate **St. Stephen's Day**, December 26, in much the same way they celebrate Christmas, with family visits. In the evening many Germans enjoy dining out and attending the theater. Since St. Stephen is the patron saint of horses, many old St. Stephen's Day customs involve these animals. In rural areas, farmers still ride their horses in processions to be blessed. Moreover, horse trainers and breeders often sponsor equestrian processions on this day.

New Year's Eve

New Year's Eve is also known as *Silvester Abend,* or Sylvester's Eve, in recognition of the fact that December 31 is **St. Sylvester's Day**. Germans celebrate New Year's Eve with parties, fortune-telling, and practical jokes. Traditional party foods include carp, herring salad, hot wine punch, and champagne. *Bleigiessen,* or molten lead pouring, is a traditional method of fortune-telling on New Year's Eve. A partygoer drops a spoonful of molten lead into water and lets it harden. The shape it takes will foretell something about what that person will be doing in the coming year. Many luck charms and superstitions have also attached themselves to New Year's Eve. One folk belief warns that spilling salt on New Year's Eve brings bad luck. By contrast, coming into contact with a pig, chimney soot, or a chimneysweep on New Year's Eve brings good luck. Sometimes a thoughtful party host will bring both a live pig and a chimneysweep to his New Year's party as a way of offering good luck to his guests. Another superstition advises that the sight of a young, dark-haired man soon after the start of the new year brings good luck (*see also* **Firstfooting**).

In the days following Christmas many shops sell joke goods. These include things like sugar cubes that have a spider inside them, or chocolates filled with mustard instead of candy. The Germans celebrate the new year by playing these kinds of jokes on one another. Noisemaking is another important New Year's custom. Fireworks explode at midnight, and in some villages, horn players "blow in" the new year from the local church tower. In other regions people shoot off guns or even small cannons in honor of the new year (*see* **Shooting in Christmas**).

Epiphany

Epiphany, January 6, is called *Dreikönigstag,* or "Three Kings' Day" in Germany. In past times many people celebrated **Twelfth Night**, or Epiphany Eve, as the end of the Christmas season. Some Germans still follow this old custom, electing a **King of the Bean** and Queen of the Bean to preside over Twelfth Night or Epiphany parties. Another old Epiphany custom, the caroling of the **star boys**, or star singers, also survives in contemporary Germany. Nowadays these costumed lads, dressed as the Three Kings, or **Magi**, may collect coins for charitable causes rather than treats for themselves.

The blessing of homes with incense, holy water, and the initials of the Three Kings is a religious custom connected with Epiphany. The Germans use the initials CMB to represent the Three Kings, which come from the names most associated with the Magi in folklore: Caspar, Melchior, and Balthasar. These initials are printed over the front door in chalk, surrounded by the numbers representing the year. Thus, in 1999 the inscription would read 19 CMB 99.

Two final Christmas customs take place in German homes on Epiphany. Many German families add the figures representing the Three Kings to their Nativity scenes on this day. In addition, Christmas trees are taken down, and children are permitted to eat the treats that have been used as decorations.

Further Reading

Christmas in Germany. Second edition. Lincolnwood, Ill.: Passport Books, 1996.

MacDonald, Margaret Read, ed. *The Folklore of World Holidays*. Detroit, Mich.: Gale Research, 1992.

Russ, Jennifer M. *German Festivals and Customs*. London, England: Oswald Wolff, 1982.

Web Sites

The German Embassy in Washington, D.C., maintains a number of pages describing German Christmas foods and customs on its web site. Go to the site listed below, click on "search," and enter the word "Christmas": http://www.germany-info.org

A site sponsored by German instructor Robert J. Shea, Missouri: http://www.serve.com/shea/germusa/customs.htm

Ghana, Christmas in

In Ghana traditional Christmas observances revolve around large family gatherings, feasts, singing, and church services. About forty percent of Ghanaians are Christians. The rest are followers of traditional African religions or Muslims. In recent years Christmas **commercialism** has crept into west African countries such as Ghana. In richer, urban areas people have begun to celebrate the holiday with decorated **Christmas trees**, electric Christmas lights, **Santa Claus**, **Christmas cards**, and **gift** exchanges. Even some non-Christians take part in this commercial Christmas. Yet most Ghanaian Christians, especially outside the cities, still celebrate the holiday in the traditional fashion.

Before Christmas

Many churches blossom with flowers and palm branches during **Advent**. As Christmas approaches, some congregations decorate a tree on the church grounds in honor of the coming holiday. In the last few days before Christmas jam-packed buses, trucks, cars, and boats criss-cross the country, ferrying people back to their ancestral towns and villages. **Christmas carols** blare from radios, loudspeakers, and televisions all over Ghana during this season.

Christmas Eve

On Christmas Eve families gather for a special dinner, often consisting of chicken stew or dishes made from rice and goat meat. Then they head off to church services that usually include a **Nativity play** or Christmas pageant performed by the congregation's youth. After church, people greet one another and exchange good wishes for the holiday. Processions form and ramble joyfully through the streets, led by bands of musicians. Children dash about shouting, *"Egbona hee, egogo vo!"*, "Christ is coming, he is near!" Fireworks may also take place on Christmas Eve.

Christmas Day

On Christmas Day festivities begin quite early, sometime before dawn, as groups of carolers go door to door singing songs. House-holders typically offer small presents to the singers, who stand for the band of **angels** that brought the good news of **Jesus'** birth to the **shepherds**. Caroling of the same sort may also take place on Christmas Eve. Christmas Day church services are scheduled for mid-morning. They feature the retelling of the Nativity story and the singing of many hymns and carols in local languages. After the service is over, children collect candies and other sweet treats said to have come from **Father Christmas**. Some also receive a book, new clothes, or shoes as Christmas presents. People greet each other, saying *"Afishapa,"* which means **"Merry Christmas and Happy New Year."**

Christmas celebrations continue through the day as families, friends, and neighbors gather for feasts and dances. Typical foods eaten at Christmas time include peanut soup, *fufu* (a paste made from mashed yams), okra soup, and some kind of meat, such as chicken, goat, sheep, beef, or pork. Brightly colored paper **ornaments** pinned up throughout the house set a cheery mood for the festivities. Many Ghanaian families also festoon a tree growing in their courtyard with paper ornaments. Often mango, guava, or cashew trees serve this purpose. Other families will bring a single tree branch into the house and decorate it with lights and ornaments.

In Ghana many people observe the libation ceremony, a traditional folk ritual, at Christmas time. In this ritual people drink from a cup and then pour some of its contents on the ground as a symbolic offering to their ancestors.

After Christmas

Ghanaian Christmas celebrations traditionally last for eight days. Caroling children visit homes during this time, hoping that house-holders will reward their musical efforts with small gifts. The children often sing original songs or play homemade instruments.

Further Reading

Gonza, Sam. "Reclaiming the True Meaning of Christmas." All Africa News Service, Nairobi, Kenya (December 21, 1998).

Griffin, Robert H., and Ann H. Shurgin, eds. *The Folklore of World Holidays*. Second edition. Detroit, Mich.: Gale Research, 1999.

Sullivan, Tim. "The Modern, Material Christmas Makes Headway in West Africa." Associated Press Online (December 21, 1998).

Tucker, Cathy C. *Christmas Worldwide*. Philadelphia, Pa.: Xlibris, 2000.

Web Sites

The following page, posted by the Rev. Peter E. Adotey Addo, a writer and United Methodist minister born in Ghana, describes Christmas celebrations in his native country: http://www.addo.ws/afishapa.htm

For a short story by the Rev. Peter Addo describing a boy's Christmas in Ghana, see: http://www.southerncrossreview.org/3/fireedit.html

Ghosts

Spirits of many kinds haunt the Christmas folklore of northern **Europe**. Some folklorists believe that in ancient times the Germanic and Scandinavian peoples associated the midwinter **Yule** festival with the return of the dead. Old tales tell of a band of ghosts called the **Wild Hunt** that charged through the nighttime sky during the **Twelve Days of Christmas**. In **Norway**, **Estonia**, **Latvia**, and **Lithuania** old folk beliefs concerning the Christmas time visits of the dead linger on. In the German region of Bavaria, some people believe that restless spirits walk abroad during the **Knocking Nights**, the Thursday nights in **Advent**. In Estonia, **Germany**, and Lithuania some people visit family graves on Christmas Eve, leaving behind lit candles (*see also* **Christmas Candles**).

In the German-speaking lands **Berchta**, too, wandered through the long, dark evenings. **Elves** peeked out from behind trees and beneath footstools in many countries. In others, trolls lumbered and witches flitted through the darkness. In Scandinavia the **Jultomten** appeared each year at Christmas time. In **Iceland** the closely related **Christmas Lads** played pranks on householders. Far to the south the **kallikantzari** vexed Greek families.

In **England** as well, certain folk beliefs warned that ghosts and other supernatural creatures lurked in the long shadows of the Twelve Days.

England

One old English tradition called for the telling of ghost stories at Christmas time. Perhaps this custom developed out of ancient beliefs concerning the return of the dead during the Yule festival. Indeed, in the eighth century St. Bede (c. 672-735), a scholarly English monk, wrote that the Anglo-Saxon people left food on their tables overnight during the **Christmas season** so that visiting spirits could partake of the feast. In spite of these yearly visits, it took the English Christmas ghost another millennia to achieve notoriety. One man, English author Charles Dickens, brought this to pass. His Christmas ghost story, *A Christmas Carol*, became perhaps the most well known and best-loved Christmas tale of the nineteenth and twentieth centuries.

Contemporary readers tend to experience *A Christmas Carol* as a story about the meaning of Christmas. Nevertheless, Dickens also intended his readers to approach *A Christmas Carol* as a ghost story. He draws our attention to the ghostly aspect of the tale in its full title, which reads *A Christmas Carol in Prose, Being a Ghost Story of Christmas*. The preface continues the ghost theme in a humorous vein: "I have endeavoured in this Ghostly little book to raise the Ghost of an Idea which shall not put my readers out of humour with themselves, with each other, with the season, or with me. May it haunt their houses pleasantly, and no one wish to lay it." Finally, Dickens urged his audience to read the *Carol* out loud, in a cold room by candlelight. Dickens so enjoyed ghost stories that he wrote a number of them over the years, including several more Christmas ghost stories, such as "The Story of the Goblins Who Stole a Sexton," "The Haunted Man," "The Haunted House," and "A Christmas Tree."

Further Reading

Cramer, Kathryn, and David G. Hartwell. *Christmas Ghosts*. New York: Arbor House, 1987.

Crippen, Thomas G. *Christmas and Christmas Lore*. 1923. Reprint. Detroit, Mich.: Omnigraphics, 1990.

Dickens, Charles. *The Complete Ghost Stories of Charles Dickens*. Peter Haining, ed. New York: Franklin Watts, 1983.

Miles, Clement A. *Christmas in Ritual and Tradition*. 1912. Reprint. Detroit, Mich.: Omnigraphics, 1990.

Gift Bringers

For descriptions of Christmas gift bringers from around the world, *see* **Baboushka**; **Befana**; **Berchta**; **Black Peter**; Camel (*see* **Lebanon, Christmas in**; **Syria, Christmas in**); **Cert**; **Christkindel**; **Christmas Lads**; **Father Christmas**; **Grandfather Frost**; Julemand (*see* **Denmark, Christmas in**); **Jultomten**; **Knecht Ruprecht**; **Magi**; Père Noël (*see* **France, Christmas in**); **St. Basil's Day**; **St. Nicholas**; **Santa Claus**; **Snow Maiden**; Star Man (*see* **Poland, Christmas in**); **Weihnachtsmann**; **Yule Goat**

Gifts

Europeans have exchanged midwinter gifts with one another since ancient times. Until relatively recently, however, most of these gifts traded hands around **New Year's Day** rather than on Christmas Day. As Christmas became an increasingly important holiday, people began to exchange gifts on Christmas rather than on New Year's Day (*see also* **America, Christmas in Nineteenth-Century; Victorian England, Christmas in**).

Roman Gifts

Historians trace midwinter gift giving back to the ancient Romans. The Romans bestowed gifts and good wishes on friends and family during **Kalends**, their new year festival. The oldest and, thus, perhaps the most "traditional" of these gifts were small twigs from the groves of the goddess Strenia. Later, the Romans added cakes and honey (symbolizing a "sweet" new year), and coins (symbolizing wealth) to the roster of traditional new year gifts. The Romans called these gifts *strenae* after Strenia. The modern French word for new year's gift, *étrenne*, echoes this old Latin name. In addition to exchanging gifts with friends and family, many Romans offered gifts and *vota*, wishes for prosperity, to the emperor. The Romans also gave one another gifts for **Saturnalia**, a winter festival occurring about a week before Kalends. Traditional Saturnalia gifts included wax candles called *cerei*, wax fruit, and clay dolls called *signillaria*. These gifts, too, expressed the good will of the sender.

Medieval Gifts

The Roman custom of exchanging midwinter gifts appears to have spread throughout **Europe** and to have survived well into the Middle Ages. In medieval **England**, however, people gave these New Year's gifts to those immediately above and below them in the social hierarchy. For example, peasants who worked on landed estates brought gifts of farm produce to the local lord during the **Twelve Days of Christmas**. Custom dictated that the lord respond by inviting them to a Christmas feast. The nobility brought gifts to the king or queen. The monarch in turn gave gifts to the members of his or her court. These gifts did not necessarily express affection but rather acknowledged one's place in a system of social rank. Perhaps more personal kinds of gift exchanges also took place. If so, historical records fail to mention them.

In England the New Year's gift flourished during the fifteenth and sixteenth centuries. Some abuses did occur, however. In 1419 the City of London restricted its law officers from demanding New Year's gifts from the public. Apparently, sergeants and other officers had been promising cooks, brewers, and bakers that they would overlook past or future offenses in exchange for a gift of their wares.

Royal Gifts

Queen Elizabeth I (1533-1603) relished her New Year's gifts. Court records indicate that the queen received silk and satin garments (once, a sea-green silk petticoat), jewelry and personal items made from precious metals (for example, a jeweled toothpick), perfume, cakes, pies, and preserved fruits. Her gentlewomen offered her embroidered cushions, handkerchiefs, pillows, and articles of clothing. In return Elizabeth bestowed gifts of silver and gold on her courtiers. The custom of presenting gifts to the monarch faded away in the eighteenth century.

Seventeenth- and Eighteenth-Century Gifts

During the seventeenth and eighteenth centuries the English began to give New Year's gifts to family and friends. Popular gifts included oranges, **gingerbread**, **rosemary**, wine, marzipan, gloves, **stockings**, and other articles of clothing, jewelry, and objects made of metals, such as snuff boxes, tea urns, pens, and watches. Children sometimes received little bound books, often texts of religious instruction. By the early nineteenth century, for reasons which remain unclear, the New Year's gift finally appeared to be dying out. Instead of disappearing completely, however, the expanding Christmas holiday revived and absorbed the ancient custom of midwinter gift giving.

Saint Nicholas's Day Gifts

In addition to New Year's Day, some medieval Europeans also gave gifts on **St. Nicholas's Day**. The St. Nicholas's Day gift differed slightly from the New Year's gift. On the saint's day adults gave gifts to youngsters as a way of honoring the patron saint of children (*see also* **St. Nicholas**). Some researchers think that the custom of giving gifts to children on St. Nicholas's Day started as early as the twelfth century. At that time nuns from central **France** started to leave gifts on the doorsteps of poor families with children on St. Nicholas's Eve. These packages contained nuts and oranges and other good things to eat. Some researchers believe that ordinary people adopted the custom, spreading it from France to other parts of northern Europe. Other writers suppose that the folklore surrounding St. Martin may have inspired the traditions that turned St. Nicholas into a gift giver. In past centuries St. Martin, another bishop saint, was said to ride through the countryside delivering treats to children on the eve of his feast day (*see also* **Martinmas**).

Boxing Day Gifts

Boxing Day, or **St. Stephen's Day**, provided another occasion for midwinter gift giving in England. Many writers believe that the English custom called "boxing" can be traced back to the Middle Ages. In that era parish priests customarily opened up the church alms-box on December 26, St. Stephen's Day. Then they distributed the coins it contained to the needy. This practice gave rise to the use of the term "box" to denote a small gift of money or a gratuity.

By the early seventeenth century the Church's St. Stephen's Day tradition had inspired working people to adopt the custom of saving whatever tips they had been given throughout the year in clay boxes which they broke open on December 26. By the late seventeenth century they began to solicit tips from all those who had enjoyed their services during the year. They collected the last of these "boxes" on December 26, after which they broke open these containers and used the money to buy Christmas treats. By the nineteenth century the custom of boxing had so colored the character of the day that many people began to refer to December 26 as Boxing Day rather than St. Stephen's Day. Like medieval New Year's gifts,

Christmas boxes took place in the context of unequal social relationships. Rather than express personal affection, Christmas boxes permitted the well-to-do to express appreciation for services rendered to them. The custom also presented working people with an opportunity to collect a little extra cash around the holidays.

German Christmas Gifts

The earliest historical records of Christmas gift giving come from **Germany**. As early as the sixteenth century some German children received "Christ-bundles" at Christmas time. These bundles contained an assortment of small gifts, such as coins, **sugarplums**, nuts, apples, dolls, clothing, lesson books, religious books, or writing materials. Some scholars suggest that the traditional Christmas bundle contained at least five things: a coin, an article of clothing, a toy, something tasty to eat, and a pencil box or other scholastic item. Parents also included a small stick in these bundles, which some writers have interpreted as a reminder that chastisement still awaited those who misbehaved. Parents told their children that the *Haus-Christ* had brought them their gifts (*see also* **Christkindel**). Two other German customs encouraged the preparation of simple gifts for the family. The **Christmas tree** and the Christmas **pyramid**, decorated with edible treats, such as nuts, apples, cookies, and candy, provided everyone with holiday sweets.

The Christ Child, also brought Christmas gifts to children in sixteenth-century **Norway**. Children left a plate or a bowl in an obvious place so that the visiting Christ Child could leave them a present. Moreover, in Norway, Christmas gift exchanges among friends and adult family members began as early as the sixteenth century.

Julklapp

Another old tradition of Christmas gift giving comes from Sweden. The Swedes called these gifts **Julklapp**, which means "Christmas knock." This name comes from an old Swedish custom whereby Christmas gift givers would knock on doors, toss in their gift, and run away. Recipients then tried to guess who had delivered the gifts. In addition, Julklapp usually arrived in some form of trick packaging. These surprise gifts added a dash of humor to the **Christmas season**.

Santa Claus, Christmas Trees, and Gifts

The custom of exchanging Christmas gifts among friends and family became widespread during the nineteenth century. In this same era Europeans and Americans began to adopt the German Christmas tree. At the same time **Santa Claus** became a popular mythological figure associated with Christmas in the United States. Both of these innovations encouraged the growth of Christmas gift giving—the tree by providing a beautiful location to display the gifts, and Santa Claus by serving as a new Christmas gift bringer. Unlike the medieval New Year's gift, or the English Christmas box, the nineteenth-century Christmas gift circulated between family and friends and expressed the affection of the sender.

Although charity had for centuries been a theme of Christmas celebrations, it became increasingly important in the nineteenth century. Charitable gifts linked Christmas gift giving with the spiritual celebration of the holiday. Finally, in the twentieth century many American companies adopted the custom of distributing **Christmas bonuses** to their workers at Christmas time. Reminiscent of the English Christmas box, these gifts of cash rewarded employees for their hard work in the past year.

Conclusion

The midwinter gift has passed through many transformations in its two-thousand-year history. These gifts served different purposes in different times and places. They might symbolize good wishes for the coming year, affirm one's social rank, generate fun and excitement, redistribute wealth from richer to poorer, demonstrate affection, or serve as a means of honoring the spiritual significance of the holiday. The gifts themselves have changed along with their significance. The sweaters, neckties, and toys of today's American Christmas seem far removed from the twigs that the Romans exchanged with one another in honor of Kalends. Finally, several midwinter holidays developed gift-giving traditions over the centuries, the most recent being Christmas. In spite of its relatively short history the Christmas gift has become a central element of contemporary Christmas celebrations (*see also* **Commercialism**).

Further Reading

Henriksen, Vera. *Christmas in Norway.* Oslo, Norway: Johan Grundt Tanum Forlag, 1970.

Hutton, Ronald. *The Rise and Fall of Merry England.* Oxford, England: Oxford University Press, 1994.

———. *The Stations of the Sun.* Oxford, England: Oxford University Press, 1996.

Miles, Clement A. *Christmas in Ritual and Tradition.* 1912. Reprint. Detroit, Mich.: Omnigraphics, 1990.

Pimlott, J. A. R. *The Englishman's Christmas.* Atlantic Highlands, N.J.: Humanities Press, 1978.

Restad, Penne. *Christmas in America.* New York: Oxford University Press, 1995.

Schmidt, Leigh Eric. *Consumer Rites: The Buying and Selling of American Holidays.* Princeton, N.J.: Princeton University Press, 1995.

Waits, William B. *The Modern Christmas in America.* New York: New York University Press, 1993.

Gingerbread

The term "gingerbread" encompasses a variety of sweet, spicy cookies, cakes, and breads. These foods originated in medieval **Europe** at a time when ginger was an especially popular spice. Europeans have celebrated special occasions with gingerbread for centuries. From an earlier association with medieval fairs, gingerbread evolved into a favorite Christmas treat.

Uses and Recipes

The ancient Romans greatly esteemed ginger for both its culinary uses and curative powers. They used it to flavor sauces as well as to treat upset stomachs and to induce bowel movements. Roman traders bartered with Asian merchants to acquire this useful root. After the fall of the Roman Empire the trade routes established and maintained by the Romans dissolved, making ginger hard to get in Europe. In medieval times spice merchants charged high prices for ginger. Well-to-do medieval Europeans paid these prices, because they prized the relatively rare root.

Medieval cooks had discovered that ginger lent a preservative effect to pastries and breads. Some of the early recipes for these sweet, spice breads seem a bit crude by modern standards. One simply recommended mixing dry bread crumbs with spices and honey. Another combined bread crumbs with cinnamon, aniseed, ginger, licorice, and red wine. Cooks molded the pasty dough resulting from these recipes into various decorative shapes (*see also* **Christmas Cake**). This kind of gingerbread survived until the seventeenth century, when a more cake-like gingerbread, composed of flour, sugar, butter, eggs, molasses, ginger, cinnamon, and chopped fruits, began to replace it. "White gingerbread," which mixed ginger with marzipan, also became popular around this time. Bakers often pressed this kind of gingerbread into molds and then covered it in gilt.

Fairs and Bakers

At the close of the eleventh century gingerbread flourished throughout northern Europe. Gingerbread vendors sold their goods at fairs across **England, Germany, France**, and Holland. These fairs served as traveling, medieval shopping malls providing people with opportunities for commerce as well as entertainment. In England gingerbread was such a popular fairground treat that people began to refer to gingerbread cookies or pastries as "fairings." In addition, gingerbread became such a common item at many fairs that people began to call these commercial gatherings "gingerbread fairs." Several English gingerbread fairs survived into the twentieth century.

Many gingerbread vendors cut their cookies into fanciful shapes, some associated with the time of year, others purely decorative. For example, gingerbread sold at spring fairs might be cut into the shape of a flower. Other popular shapes included windmills, kings, queens, and various animals. Gingerbread sellers delighted in decorating their creations both by cutting them into exquisitely detailed shapes and by adding fancy embellishments. By the eighteenth century gingerbread makers had developed their art to such an extent that English speakers adopted the term "gingerbread work" to refer to fancy, carved, wooden trim on colonial seaport houses or to the gilded, carved prows of ships.

German Traditions

In German-speaking lands shaped and decorated gingerbreads appeared at autumn fairs and **Christmas markets**. In fact, the gingerbread of contemporary American Christmas celebrations probably came down to us from old German traditions. German cooks often cut their gingerbread dough into the shape of gingerbread men and houses which they baked, cooled, and decorated. The traditional German gingerbread house plays a prominent role in the famous German fairy tale, "Hansel and Gretel." The witch featured in this story built and lived in a house made out of gingerbread decorated with candy and icing. This tasty exterior tempted children, such as Hansel and Gretel, to venture inside. The Scandinavians also create miniature houses from gingerbread at Christmas time. In the United States gingerbread men are the more common Christmas treat. Sometimes these cookies briefly serve as **ornaments** for the **Christmas tree** before they are eaten.

Further Reading

Stellingwerf, Steven. *The Gingerbread Book*. New York: Rizzoli International Publications, 1991.

Wilson, C. Anne. *Food and Drink in Britain*. Chicago: Academy Chicago Publishers, 1991.

Glastonbury Thorn

The tale of the Glastonbury Thorn has woven itself around some of the most romantic legends ever to have emerged from the British Isles. The thorn takes its name from Glastonbury, **England**, a location that has hosted many legendary characters and mystical events over the centuries. In the Middle Ages monks from Glastonbury Abbey claimed to have discovered King Arthur's remains buried in their cemetery. Indeed, Celtic mythology identifies Glastonbury as "Avalon," the enchanted island from which came Arthur's famous sword, Excalibur, and to which the fatally wounded king was carried by fairy queens. Moreover, Christian legends proclaim that Joseph of Arimathea came to Glastonbury in the first century A.D. According to these tales, Joseph brought with him the Holy Grail, a sacred relic sought by many of King Arthur's knights centuries later. Subsequent stories add that Joseph established the Glastonbury Thorn, a mysterious bush that blooms when most others are barren — at Christmas time.

Life and Legends of Joseph of Arimathea

The Gospels identify Joseph of Arimathea as a "good and upright man," a member of the Sanhedrin (the Jewish high court) who disagreed with their decision to turn **Jesus** over to the Roman authorities (Luke 23:50-52). After Jesus' death, Joseph asked Pilate for permission to remove the body for burial. With Pilate's consent, Joseph took Jesus' body from the cross, wrapped it in linen, and sealed it in the tomb.

Later legends added to this sparse biblical account of Joseph's deeds. By the Middle Ages Joseph had become both an important saint and an acclaimed hero. Legends declared that Joseph of Arimathea was the first keeper of the Holy Grail, the vessel Jesus used in the Last Supper. The tales added that Joseph used the chalice to collect the blood that dripped from Christ's wounds.

Years after Jesus' death Joseph journeyed to Britain as a Christian missionary, bringing the Grail with him (many legends give 63 A.D.

as the year of his arrival). A few tales also state that Joseph carried a staff made of hawthorn wood from the Holy Land. Some say it was Christmas Eve when Joseph's ship finally pulled in to the harbor at Glastonbury. Joseph and his companions disembarked and began the climb up steep Wearyall Hill. Finally, cold and tired, the old man thrust his staff into the ground in despair. To his amazement it not only rooted itself, but burst into leaf and bloom. Joseph perceived this miracle as divine confirmation of his faith and his mission of evangelization. Thereafter, the hawthorn bush bloomed every year at Christmas, distinguishing itself from native English hawthorns. Joseph's miraculous tree became known as the Glastonbury Thorn.

Although no solid historical evidence exists to support this tale of Joseph's journey to England, a winter-blooming hawthorn tree did flourish in Glastonbury for many years. Descendants of this plant have been identified as *Crataegus mongyna biflora*, a species of hawthorn native to the Middle East.

The History of the Glastonbury Thorn

The earliest appearance of the Glastonbury Thorn in written records dates back to an account of the life of Joseph of Arimathea written in the early 1500s. By the early 1600s firsthand descriptions of Glastonbury's hawthorn noted that the plant was suffering from the many carvings made in its trunk and the many cuttings taken from its branches. One Sir William Brereton, after carving his initials in the tree and collecting several branches for his own keeping, thought fit to criticize the people of Glastonbury for neglecting to care for the tree! The Glastonbury thorn reached its yearly peak of popularity around Christmas time, when crowds assembled to witness the tree's miraculous blooming.

Many believed that the buds and flowers had healing powers. These beliefs and customs eventually aroused the ire of the increasingly vocal **Puritans**, who scorned what they saw as evidence of popular belief in magic and superstition. It is said that during the reign of Elizabeth I (1558-1603), the tree met its fate at the hands of an irate Puritan who assaulted it with an axe. After he had destroyed half of the enormous tree, a splinter flew into his eye, blinding him in some versions of the tale and killing him in others. Having avenged itself, the tree lingered another thirty years before finally succumbing to this fatal attack. Other accounts of the tree's demise differ. One simply states that the tree was demolished in 1653 during England's Civil War.

Nevertheless, by this time a number of cuttings from the original plant flourished in Glastonbury and other locations. They continued to bloom on or around Christmas until the calendar reform of 1752, when Britain finally adopted the Gregorian calendar (*see also* **Old Christmas Day**). As a consequence the nation leaped forward eleven days overnight. Many ordinary people resisted this change. In fact, some explained their allegiance to the old calendar by pointing to the unchanged blooming habits of the Glastonbury Thorn. Two clippings from a 1753 issue of *The Gentleman's Magazine* illustrate this sentiment:

> *Quainton in Buckinghamshire, December 24, 1752.* Above 2,000 people came here last night, with lanthorns and candles, to view a black thorn which grows in the neighbourhood, and which was remembered (this year only) to be a slip from the famous Glastonbury Thorne, that it always budded on the 24th, was full blown the next day, and went all off at night; but the people, finding no appearance of a bud, 'twas agreed by all, that 25 December, N.S. [new style], could not be the right Christmas Day, and accordingly, refused to go to Church and treating their friends on that day, as usual; at length the affair became so serious that the ministers of the neighbouring villages, in order to appease the people, thought it prudent to give notice that the old Christmas Day should be kept in as holy as before [Muir, 1977, 102-3].

> *Glastonbury.* A vast concourse of people attended the noted thorns on Christmas Eve, New Stile; but, to their great disappointment, there was no appearance of its blowing, which made them watch it narrowly on the 5th of Jan., the Christmas Day, Old Style, which it blow'd as usual [Coffin, 1973, 58].

The Glastonbury Thorn in the United States

At the turn of the twentieth century, the once-renowned abbey at Glastonbury lay in ruins (*see also* **Mincemeat Pie**). Stanley Austin, son of England's reigning poet laureate, owned the abbey property. (The abbey has since passed into the hands of the Church of England.) In 1901, when Austin heard of the plans to build the National Cathedral in Washington, D.C., he sent a clipping of the Glastonbury Thorn to the bishop of Washington, the Right Rev. Henry Yates Satterlee. He also sent a sufficient quantity of stones from the ruined abbey to build a bishop's chair in the new American cathedral. Bishop Satterlee saw the English plant established on the Cathedral grounds, where it does occasionally bloom on Christmas Day.

Christmas at Glastonbury

A descendent of the old tree lives on in Glastonbury today. Each year on Old Christmas Eve, January 5, the keepers of Holy Thorn clip a branch of the tree and send it to the reigning monarch. The sprig serves both as a symbol of respect and as a public affirmation of the town's Christian heritage. This custom dates back about four hundred years.

Further Reading

Coffin, Tristram P. *The Book of Christmas Folklore*. New York: Seabury Press, 1973.

Foley, Daniel J. *The Christmas Tree*. Philadelphia, Pa.: Chilton Company, 1960.

Hadfield, Miles, and John Hadfield. *The Twelve Days of Christmas*. Boston, Mass.: Little, Brown and Company, 1961.

Howard, Alexander. *Endless Cavalcade*. London, England: Arthur Baker, 1964.

Leach, Maria, ed. *Funk and Wagnalls Standard Dictionary of Folklore, Mythology, and Legend*. New York: Harper and Row, 1984.

Metford, J. C. J. *Dictionary of Christian Lore and Legend*. London, England: Thames and Hudson, 1983.

Muir, Frank. *Christmas Customs and Traditions*. New York: Taplinger, 1977.

Web Site

A site sponsored by *Britannia Internet Magazine*, contains an article by historian Geoffrey Ashe, "Magical Glastonbury": http://www.britannia.com/history/glaston1.html

Gold

No other metal is named as frequently in the Bible as gold. The Bible most often refers to gold as a form of worldly wealth, but gold also serves as a symbol of spiritual wealth. In biblical times, gold was rarer than today. For the most part, only kings or the very wealthy possessed it. Gold was one of the three gifts that the **Magi** offered to the baby **Jesus**. Therefore, the Magi's **gift** of gold is most often interpreted as recognition of Jesus' kingship or his spiritual authority.

Until the mid-1700s tradition dictated that the British monarch offer gifts of **frankincense**, gold, and **myrrh** at the Chapel Royal on **Epiphany**. Heralds and knights of the Garter, Thistle, and Bath accompanied the king on his royal pilgrimage. Under the unstable King George III (1760-1820) the procession was abandoned, although the monarch's gift of gold, frankincense, and myrrh is still sent to the Chapel Royal by proxy. A similar royal offering was at one time customary in **Spain**.

Gold has been considered rare, valuable, and beautiful throughout history. In addition to its beauty and brightness, gold has some unusual properties. It is nearly indestructible, and yet it is also the most malleable of metals. A single ounce of gold can be beaten into a sheet of gold leaf that measures approximately 200 feet on each side. Gold does not tarnish or corrode, and is extremely resistant to wear. Finally, it is often found in a nearly pure state. These qualities enhance its value, versatility, and mystery.

Further Reading

Coughenour, Robert A. "Gold." In Paul J. Achtemeier, ed. *HarperCollins Bible Dictionary*. Revised edition. San Francisco, Calif.: HarperSanFrancisco, 1996.

Crippen, Thomas G. *Christmas and Christmas Lore*. 1923. Reprint. Detroit, Mich.: Omnigraphics, 1990.

Peattie, Donald Culross. "Gold, Frankincense, and Myrrh." *Saturday Evening Post* 264, 6 (November 1992): 56.

Gospel Accounts of Christmas

The Christian Bible provides two accounts of the birth of **Jesus**. One account appears in the first two chapters of the **Gospel according to Matthew**, and the other in the first two chapters of the **Gospel according to Luke** (*see also* **Jesus, Year of Birth**). A quick review of these accounts reveals a number of broad similarities as well as some striking differences.

Similarities

Jesus' parents, **Joseph** and **Mary**, figure in both accounts. Both Matthew and Luke assert that Joseph was a descendant of the Old Testament hero, David. They also agree that Mary was a virgin when she became pregnant with Jesus by the power of the Holy Spirit. An **angel** appears in order to explain the nature of Mary's pregnancy, according to both writers. Both accounts affirm that Jesus was born in **Bethlehem** during the reign of **Herod** the Great. Finally, Matthew and Luke both tell of strangers called by God to witness and worship the birth of the Savior.

Differences

If probed more closely, a few of these similarities turn out to be only partial, however. Both Matthew and Luke state that Joseph is a descendant of David, but Matthew takes Joseph's lineage back to

Abraham, while Luke takes it all the way back to **Adam**. Moreover, Matthew includes five women in Jesus' genealogy, while Luke mentions no women at all. In Luke the angel Gabriel, who explains the nature of Mary's pregnancy, appears to Mary herself, while in Matthew the angel appears to Joseph. Although both writers agree that Jesus was born in Bethlehem, Matthew implies that Jesus' family lived in Bethlehem, while Luke states that Jesus' parents lived in Nazareth and came to Bethlehem only to comply with a Roman census. While Luke's account describes the events that took place on the night of Jesus' birth, Matthew's account leaves vague the issue of whether Jesus was a newborn infant or already a toddler on the night when the **Magi** arrived to worship him.

Some elements of Matthew's story have no parallel whatever in Luke's account. Matthew tells of learned men called the Magi who bring Jesus expensive **gifts** fit for a king. They find him by following a star which suddenly appeared in the heavens to signal his birth (*see* **Star of Bethlehem**). Moreover, in Matthew's account the Magi inadvertently alert Herod to the existence of the newborn king. As a result, Herod sends soldiers to kill all of Bethlehem's male infants (*see* **Holy Innocents' Day**). Finally, an angel visits Joseph warning him of Herod's intentions and telling him to escape with his family into **Egypt** (*see* **Flight into Egypt**). After Herod's death the family returns from Egypt, but decides to settle in Galilee, far from Herod's brutal successor.

Turning now to Luke's account of Jesus' birth, we can identify a number of elements that don't appear in Matthew's Gospel. According to Luke, humble **shepherds**, rather than noble Magi, witness Jesus' birth. Moreover, the shepherds learn of the Savior's birth from an angel instead of by studying the stars. In Luke's story Mary and Joseph must search for lodging because they don't live in Bethlehem. The innkeepers cannot accommodate them, so they end up spending the night in a stable, where Mary gives birth to Jesus.

Folklore

Scholars have attributed much significance to both the similarities and the differences contained in these accounts. Although these differences may perplex researchers, they do not appear to have inhibited the representation of Jesus' birth in folklore. Around Christmas time **Nativity scenes, store window displays**, and Christmas pageants present us with colorful images of Jesus' birth (*see also* **Nativity Play**). Often these scenes mix together shepherds, wise men, stars, angels, animals, and other figures. These happy scenes suggest that Matthew's and Luke's accounts of Jesus' birth have merged together to form a single story in the popular imagination.

Further Reading

Brown, Raymond E. *The Birth of the Messiah*. New updated edition. New York: Doubleday, 1993.

Horsley, Richard A. *The Liberation of Christmas: The Infancy Narratives in Social Context*. New York: Crossroads, 1989.

Porter, J. R. *The Illustrated Guide to the Bible*. New York: Oxford University Press, 1995.

Gospel According to Luke

The third book of the Christian Bible, the Gospel according to Luke, offers an account of the events surrounding **Jesus'** birth. This account, which appears in chapter two, verses one through twenty, has been reprinted below. It begins with the Roman emperor's call for an enrollment, which today we would call a census. Another, slightly different version of the events surrounding Jesus' birth may be found in the **Gospel according to Matthew** (*see also* **Angels; Bethlehem; Gabriel; Gospel Accounts of Christmas; Jesus, Year of Birth; Joseph; Mary; Shepherds**).

The Birth of Jesus According to Luke:

In those days a decree went out from Caesar Augustus that all the world should be enrolled. This was the first enrollment, when Quirinius was governor of Syria. And all went to be enrolled, each to his own city. And Joseph also went up

from Galilee, from the city of Nazareth, to Judea, to the city of David, which is called Bethlehem, because he was of the house and lineage of David, to be enrolled with Mary, his betrothed, who was with child. And while they were there, the time came for her to be delivered. And she gave birth to her first-born son and wrapped him in swaddling cloths, and laid him in a manger, because there was no place for them in the inn.

And in that region there were shepherds out in the field, keeping watch over their flock by night. And an angel of the Lord appeared to them, and the glory of the Lord shone around them, and they were filled with fear. And the angel said to them, "Be not afraid; for behold, I bring you good news of great joy which will come to all the people; for to you is born this day in the city of David a Savior, who is Christ the Lord. And this will be a sign for you: you will find the babe wrapped in swaddling cloths and lying in a manger." And suddenly there was with the angel a multitude of the heavenly host praising God and saying,

> Glory to God in the highest
> and on earth peace among men with whom he is
> pleased!

When the angels went away from them into heaven, the shepherds said to one another, "Let us go over to Bethlehem and see this thing that has happened, which the Lord has made known to us." And they went with haste, and found Mary and Joseph, and the babe lying in a manger. And when they saw it they made known the saying which had been told them concerning this child; and all who heard it wondered at what the shepherds told them. But Mary kept all these things, pondering them in her heart. And the shepherds returned, glorifying and praising God for all they had heard and seen, as it had been told them. [Taken from *The Holy Bible*, Revised Standard Version. New York: Thomas Nelson and Sons, 1953.]

Gospel According to Matthew

The first book of the Christian bible, the Gospel according to Matthew, offers an account of the events surrounding **Jesus'** birth. This account, which appears in chapter two, verses one through eighteen, has been reprinted below. Another, slightly different version of these events may be found in the **Gospel according to Luke** (*see also* **Bethlehem; Flight into Egypt; Gospel Accounts of Christmas; Herod; Jesus, Year of Birth; Joseph; Magi; Mary; Star of Bethlehem**).

The Birth of Jesus According to Matthew:

Now when Jesus was born in Bethlehem of Judea in the days of Herod the king, behold, wise men from the East came to Jerusalem, saying "where is he who has been born king of the Jews? For we have seen his star in the East, and have come to worship him." When Herod the king heard this, he was troubled, and all Jerusalem with him; and assembling all the chief priests and scribes of the people, he inquired of them where the Christ was to be born. They told him, "In Bethlehem of Judea; for so it is written by the prophet:

And you, O Bethlehem, in the land of Judah
are by no means the least among the rulers of Judah;
for from you shall come a ruler
who will govern my people Israel."

Then Herod summoned the wise men secretly and ascertained from them what time the star appeared; and he sent them to Bethlehem, saying, "Go and search diligently for the child, and when you have found him bring me word, that I too may come and worship him." When they had heard the king they went their way; and lo, the star which they had seen in the East went before them, till it came to rest over the place where the child was. When they saw the star they rejoiced exceedingly with great joy; and going into the house they saw the child with Mary his mother, and they fell down and worshiped him. Then, opening their treasures, they offered him gifts, gold and frankincense and myrrh. And being warned in a dream not to return to Herod, they departed to their own country by another way.

Now when they had departed, behold, an angel of the Lord appeared to Joseph in a dream and said, "Rise, take the child and his mother, and flee into Egypt, and remain there till I tell you; for Herod is about to search for the child, to destroy him." And he rose and took the child and his mother by night, and departed to Egypt and remained there until the death of Herod. This was to fulfil what the Lord had spoken by the prophet, "Out of Egypt have I called my son."

Then Herod, when he saw that he had been tricked by the wise men, was in a furious rage, and he sent and killed all the male children in Bethlehem and in all that region who were two years old or under, according to the time which he had ascertained from the wise men. Then was fulfilled what was spoken by the prophet in Jeremiah:

A voice was heard in Ramah,
wailing and loud lamentation,
Rachel weeping for her children;
she refused to be consoled,
because they were no more.

But when Herod died, behold, an angel of the Lord appeared in a dream to Joseph in Egypt, saying, "Rise, take the child and his mother, and go to the land of Israel, for those who sought the child's life are dead." And he rose and took the child and his mother, and went to the land of Israel. But when he heard that Archelaus reigned over Judea in place of his father Herod, he was afraid to go there, and being warned in a dream he withdrew to the district of Galilee. And he went and dwelt in a city called Nazareth, that what was spoken by the prophets might be fulfilled, "He shall be called a Nazarene." [Taken from *The Holy Bible*, Revised Standard Version. New York: Thomas Nelson and Sons, 1953.]

Grandfather Frost

Dyed Moroz

During the era of Communist rule (1917-91), Grandfather Frost became **Russia**'s official winter season **gift** bringer. Known in Russian as *Dyed Moroz*, Grandfather Frost symbolizes the piercing cold of Russia's winters. Accompanied by his grandchild, the **Snow Maiden**, he travels across Russia bringing gifts to children on **New Year's** Eve.

History

Grandfather Frost existed long before the Communists came to power. In those days, however, he brought his gifts on Christmas Eve rather than on New Year's Eve. Grandfather Frost probably evolved from rural folk beliefs about a spirit known as "the Frost." Country folk did not have an image of what the Frost looked like, but they well knew his rigid and aloof personality. In the nineteenth century, rural people did not dress up like the Frost and did not believe that he brought Christmas gifts. Instead they left gifts of food for the Frost, hoping to satisfy his hunger so that his icy touch would not whither their crops.

By the nineteenth century, a very different image of the Frost had developed in the cities. There, the winter spirit acquired a kindly name, "Grandfather Frost," as well as a kindly reputation. Urban folktales cast Grandfather Frost as a bringer of gifts to well-behaved children at Christmas time. Unlike some of his harsher counterparts in western Europe, Grandfather Frost ignored rather than threatened poorly behaved children (*see also* **Befana; Berchta; Black Peter; Cert; Jultomten; Knecht Ruprecht; St. Nicholas's Day**). City dwellers pictured Grandfather Frost as an old man with a long white beard who wore a red hat and long, red robe edged with white fur. Their tales told that he lived deep in the forest and rode about on his sleigh.

Before the Communists came to power, Russian children might receive gifts from Grandfather Frost at Christmas or from **Baboushka** on **Epiphany** Eve. A Russian folktale tells how Baboushka rejected the **Magi**'s invitation to accompany them on their journey to worship the newborn **Jesus**. She has wandered the world ever since, bringing gifts to children on Epiphany Eve. The religious content of Baboushka's story made Communist leaders uneasy, since they opposed religion and the celebration of religious holidays on principle. To counteract this story the government promoted the idea that Grandfather Frost alone brought children their presents. Moreover, they changed the date of his arrival from Christmas Eve, a religious holiday, to New Year's Eve, a secular holiday. Grandfather Frost survived the transition to a democratic, capitalist form of government in the 1990s, but now he faces competition from a new, Western import: **Santa Claus**.

Customs

Some say that Grandfather Frost makes his home in Veliki Ustyug, a town about 500 miles northeast of Moscow. Nevertheless, during the holiday season he makes many public appearances in other towns and cities. He usually wears a full white beard, dresses in a long red, white, or blue robe, and supports himself with a staff. In this eye-catching garb he may be glimpsed at department stores or at public events. For a fee, parents can hire Grandfather Frost and the Snow Maiden to come to their homes as a special treat for the children. More than a thousand Grandfather Frosts crisscross Moscow on New Year's Eve, performing this service for children and parents.

Further Reading

Christmas in Russia. Chicago: World Book, 1992.

Del Re, Gerard, and Patricia Del Re. *The Christmas Almanack*. Garden City, N.Y.: Doubleday, 1979.

MacDonald, Margaret Read, ed. *The Folklore of World Holidays*. Detroit, Mich.: Gale Research, 1992.

Naythons, Matthew. *Christmas Around the World*. San Francisco, Calif.: Collins San Francisco, 1996.

Greece, Christmas in

The Greek **Christmas season** contains three distinct holidays: Christmas, **St. Basil's Day** (or **New Year's Day**), and **Epiphany**. In spite of the festivities that surround it, Christmas is a much less important holiday than is Easter for the Greeks.

Advent

In Greece devout Orthodox Christians prepare for Christmas with "Christmas Lent," a fast lasting from November 15 to December 24 (*see also* **Advent**). During this period those who observe the fast eat no meat, eggs, dairy products, fish, olive oil, or wine. The less observant may participate in a shortened fast period, beginning a week before Christmas.

Carols

On December 24 young people go door to door in small groups singing **Christmas carols**. Called *Kalanda*, these songs tell the story of the birth of Christ. The singers accompany the carols with music made from folk instruments such as harmonicas, drums, and triangles. Many also carry a small, hollow ship made from cardboard, wood, or metal (*see also* **Christmas Symbols**). Householders toss sweets or coins inside the ship in return for the carolers' serenade. In Greece the ship is said to represent St. Basil, who sails to Greece to bring presents to children on St. Basil's Day.

Christmas Dinner

In Greece some families eat Christmas dinner after church services on Christmas Eve. Other families wait until Christmas Day. The meal begins with the head of the family blessing the Christmas loaf and making the sign of the cross over it. This bread is called *Christopsomo*, or "Christ's bread." Christopsomo consists of rich, sweetened bread dough studded with nuts and, perhaps, also dried fruit.

The dough is shaped into a large, round loaf, sprinkled with sesame seeds and decorated with a dough cross. Each person at the table receives a piece of the blessed bread and the meal begins. Greek families often serve roast pork for Christmas dinner.

Name-Day Celebrations

Greeks celebrate name-days with greater festivity than they do birthdays. One's name-day occurs on the feast day of the saint or holy figure after whom one was named. According to this custom, Greeks not only celebrate the birth of **Jesus** Christ on Christmas Day, but also may honor people who share related names. The English variants of some of these names include Christopher, Christine, Emmanuel, and Emmanuela.

Superstitions

Although the Greeks celebrate Christmas with joy, old superstitions warn that trouble may not be far behind. According to Greek folklore, pesky demons known as the **kallikantzari** roam the earth during the **Twelve Days of Christmas**. These imps pull mischievous pranks, often while keeping out of sight. Luckily for the Greeks, the holy rites performed by the priests on Epiphany chase them back into their underground dens for another year.

St. Basil's Day

The Greeks open their holiday **gifts** on January 1 rather than on Christmas. Since January 1 is observed as St. Basil's Day in Greece, children view St. Basil as the Christmas gift bringer. Other St. Basil's Day customs include sharing a special loaf of bread called *vasilopita*, or "St. Basil's Bread." Often this takes place at midnight on New Year's Eve, but it may also take place on the following day. Some families observe a special ceremony when cutting and distributing the holiday bread. The head of the family blesses the bread and makes the sign of the cross over it. The bread is sliced, and the first piece is offered to Christ, the second to the Virgin **Mary**, the third to St. Basil, and the fourth to the poor. The next piece goes to the head of the family. The rest of the family receive their pieces according to age, the eldest first. The bread contains a small token, such as a coin. Whoever finds the token in their slice of bread will have good luck in the coming year (*see also* **Christmas Cake; King of the Bean**).

Greek folklore teaches that the first person to enter the house in the new year symbolizes the fortunes of the household (*see also* **First-footing**). Some Greeks prefer a healthy, strong person to enter first, others prefer an icon (a religious image) to enter first, held in someone's outstretched arms. Householders often welcome the first person to cross their threshold in the new year with sweets and coins.

Epiphany

Epiphany closes the Christmas season in Greece. Church services include the blessing of water. These services may take place outdoors, alongside natural bodies of water. They may also take place inside churches into which a large vessel of water has been brought. Parishioners receive small bottles of holy water to take home with them.

Further Reading

Del Re, Gerard, and Patricia Del Re. *The Christmas Almanack*. Garden City, N.Y.: Doubleday, 1979.

Rouvelas, Marilyn. *A Guide to Greek Traditions and Customs in America*. Bethesda, Md.: Nea Attiki Press, 1993.

Spicer, Dorothy Gladys. *The Book of Festivals*. 1937. Reprint. Detroit, Mich.: Omnigraphics, 1990.

Greenery

Christmas trees, wreaths, and other seasonal decorations made out of greenery ornament our homes, streets, and churches at Christmas time. Ancient peoples also celebrated winter festivals with decorations of greenery. Over the centuries Christmas appears to have absorbed some of these ancient customs.

Ancient Beliefs and Customs

Evergreen plants, such as **holly, ivy, mistletoe, laurel** (or bay), yew, fir, spruce, and pine stay green all year round (*see also* **Rosemary**). For many ancient peoples, this special property converted these plants into seasonal symbols of the promise of new life or eternal life. Holly, ivy, and mistletoe may have been especially revered, since they not only stay green in winter, but also bear fruit during this harsh season. The pagan peoples of northern Europe garlanded their homes with greenery during their winter festival, **Yule.** Perhaps they wished to honor and imitate the triumph of these living greens over the cold and darkness of winter. Further south, the Romans also decorated their homes with greenery during their winter festivals, **Saturnalia** and **Kalends.** In addition, friends exchanged sprigs of holly as tokens of good will and good wishes for the upcoming new year (*see also* **New Year's Day**).

Christianity and Winter Greenery

For hundreds of years, Christian officials waged a campaign against the old pagan European practices. Tertullian, a third-century Christian writer, admonished those followers of the new religion, Christianity, who practiced these old customs. He thundered: "Let those who have no Light burn their (pagan) lamps daily. Let those who face the fire of hell affix laurels to their door-posts. . . . You are a light of the world, a tree ever green; if you have renounced the pagan temple, make not your home such a temple!" A sixth-century

Church council (the Second Council of Braga) forbade Christians the use of green boughs in home decoration. This edict implies that many Christians were still adorning their homes with greenery at that time.

In southern Europe such criticism extinguished this practice, but further north—especially in **Germany** and **England**—it continued. In medieval and Renaissance times, many English songs still depicted holly and ivy as special plants associated with the winter season. These songs may indicate that earlier beliefs about winter greenery dimmed but never completely died out, in spite of Church opposition.

Unable to completely destroy this custom, the Church eventually set about reinterpreting these seasonal symbols. Christian legends developed over time, explaining the connection between these evergreens and the **Christmas season** (*see also* **Nativity Legends**). Laurel, for example, represented the triumph of **Jesus** Christ. Holly became a symbol of the Virgin **Mary**'s love for God. Its spiky leaves and blood-red berries also served to remind Christians that Jesus would end his days wearing a crown of thorns.

Not only did the use of greenery persist in seasonal home decorations but the practice also crept into church decorations. One sixteenth-century observer of English customs commented that parishioners bedecked both home and church with ivy, holly, bay and other greenery at Christmas time. Some authorities claim that mistletoe was seldom adopted for English church decorations, however, due to its strong associations with the pagan past. One notable exception to this trend occurred at York Cathedral during medieval times. A branch of mistletoe was placed on the high altar on Christmas Eve, signaling a general pardon for all wrongdoers for as long as it remained there.

The Green Branch as a Symbol

For many centuries green branches symbolized hospitality or the reconciliation of differences. During the Middle Ages messengers, negotiators, and heralds carried them in times of battle to signify their peaceful intentions. Taverns and inns hung green boughs, especially

ivy, above their doors in lieu of printed signs. Even after literacy spread and lettered signs came into common use, many pubs retained related names, such as The Ivy Bush or The Greenwood Tree.

Christmas Greenery

Many English folk beliefs suggested that the evergreens most closely connected with Christmas possessed subtle powers. Holly offered protection against witches, and rosemary against evil spirits. Ivy granted good luck to women, while holly bestowed good luck on men. Special customs developed in order to harness the beneficial powers of these plants and deflect the harmful ones. For instance, some believed that winter greenery should not be brought into the house before Christmas Eve or Christmas Day lest it carry ill luck with it. From Christmas to **Epiphany**, however, garlands of greenery inside the home might bring good luck. According to others, a mischievous wood sprite hid behind each sprig of greenery carried into the house for decoration. During the **Twelve Days of Christmas** these sprites kept their peace, but afterwards they might begin to vex the occupants of the household with their pranks (*see also* **Elves**).

In some parts of England, people dismantled their decorative greenery on Twelfth Day. In other parts of the country, the **ornaments** were left until **Candlemas**. The seventeenth-century English poet Robert Herrick reminded others of the importance of removing winter greenery by Candlemas with these lines, "For look how many leaves there be / Neglected there maids trust to me / So many goblins you shall see." In many cases, folk beliefs cautioned that the withered greens should not simply be tossed away when taken down, but disposed of ceremoniously. Some believed that they should be burned. Others thought that burning them drew bad luck and that feeding them to cattle might preserve their good luck. Still others felt that they should simply be left to decay on their own. Sometimes a sprig of holly or mistletoe was saved for the following year. These sprigs might be used to light the fire under the next year's Christmas pudding (*see* **Plum Pudding**).

Although seasonal decorations of greenery have festooned centuries of Christmas celebrations, the style and components of these decorations have changed over time. In Britain, the custom of hanging up a bit of mistletoe, often in the form of a **kissing bough,** reached the height of its popularity in the eighteenth century and began to fall from favor in the nineteenth. The nineteenth century saw other changes in British Christmas decorations as well. Before that time the English trimmed their homes with laurel, rosemary, ivy, holly, box, and yew. In the nineteenth century holly rose from the ranks to become the favorite plant of English Christmas decorations, replacing, to some extent, the wider variety of winter greenery used. Finally, the British and the Americans adopted the German custom of bringing a **Christmas tree** into their homes in the nineteenth century. Today the Christmas tree reigns supreme over all other forms of Christmas greenery and has become a widely recognized symbol of the holiday.

Further Reading

Auld, William Muir. *Christmas Traditions*. 1931. Reprint. Detroit, Mich.: Omnigraphics, 1992.

Baker, Margaret. *Christmas Customs and Folklore*. Aylesbury, Bucks, England: Shire Publications, 1968.

Crippen, Thomas G. *Christmas and Christmas Lore*. 1923. Reprint. Detroit, Mich.: Omnigraphics, 1990.

Drury, Susan. "Customs and Beliefs Associated with Christmas Evergreens." *Folklore* 98, 2 (1987): 194-99.

Hole, Christina. *Christmas and Its Customs*. New York: M. Barrows and Company, 1958.

Segall, Barbara. *The Holly and the Ivy*. New York: Clarkson Potter, 1991.

Weiser, Francis X. *The Christmas Book*. 1952. Reprint. Detroit, Mich.: Omnigraphics, 1990.

Guatemala, Christmas in

Guatemalan Christmas celebrations combine Spanish and German customs. Native American influences may also be seen in Guatemalan Christmas foods and decorations.

Fires and Housecleaning

In Guatemala the Devil runs wild during the first week or so of **Advent**. In highland villages and towns local men in devil costumes appear on the streets and pursue children, who flee from the strange figures. The Devil's reign ends on December 7 with a folk ritual known as *La Quema del Diablo,* or "The Burning of the Devil." People rummage through their homes for things that they no longer want or deem useless. They pile these objects together in front of their houses, scatter some firecrackers on top of the heap, and set fire to it. This act not only chases away the Devil, but also symbolizes the housecleaning of the heart done in preparation for the coming of the infant **Jesus**. Other **Christmas season** preparations also touch on the theme of housecleaning. For example, many repair and paint their homes at this time of year.

Decorations

Due to the influence of Guatemala's large German community, many people have adopted the **Christmas tree** as one of their seasonal decorations. Since it is illegal to cut down trees in Guatemala, however, many people create Christmas trees out of tree branches. As Christmas nears, vendors line the streets and plazas offering these trees and many other colorful Christmas trinkets for sale.

Posadas

On December 16 Las **Posadas** begins. In this nine-day ritual, people reenact **Mary** and **Joseph's** search for shelter in **Bethlehem**. Las Posadas concludes on Christmas Eve with a large party for all who have participated in the event.

Christmas Eve and Day

Many Guatemalans choose to spend December 24 at home with their families. Others participate in public festivities. In the city of Antigua the clanging of church **bells** at midday kicks off the Christmas Eve celebrations. As the afternoon wears on, the air begins to ring with the sound of firecrackers and other explosives. Men wearing the traditional costumes and oversized pasteboard heads of the *gigantes* and *cabezudos* ("giants" and "big-heads") march through the main streets accompanied by folk musicians. In the evening performers dressed as bulls with fireworks strapped to their backs entertain the crowds. When the fuses are lit these men, called *toritos* ("little bulls"), charge through the streets like their namesakes. A formal fireworks display follows. At night a procession wends its way towards the cathedral for the celebration of **Midnight Mass**.

Traditionally, Guatemalans waited until after Midnight Mass to enjoy their Christmas dinner, although nowadays some people dine earlier. Children open their presents on Christmas Eve after dinner. Parents and other adults generally wait until **New Year's Day** to exchange **gifts**. A traditional Christmas dinner includes *tamales*, bundles of corn dough wrapped around a filling of meat and sauce, and *ponche*, or "punch," a sweet made from plums, raisins, dates, brown sugar, and liquor. According to folk beliefs, Jesus was born at the stroke of twelve on Christmas Eve (*see also* **Misa de Gallo**). Therefore, fireworks explode at midnight, commemorating the moment of the holy birth. On Christmas Day fireworks and celebrations begin again at noon.

Further Reading

Clynes, Tom. *Wild Planet!* Detroit, Mich.: Visible Ink Press, 1995.

Del Re, Gerard, and Patricia Del Re. *The Christmas Almanack*. Garden City, N.Y.: Doubleday, 1979.

MacDonald, Margaret Read, ed. *The Folklore of World Holidays*. Detroit, Mich.: Gale Research, 1992.

Wakefield, Charito Calvachi. *Navidad Latinoamericana, Latin American Christmas*. Lancaster, Pa.: Latin American Creations Publishing, 1997.

Hanukkah

Feast of Dedication, Feast of Lights

Hanukkah is a Jewish holiday that is unrelated to Christmas. Because it often falls in the month of December, however, some people have mistakenly assumed that Hanukkah is the "Jewish Christmas." In spite of the difference between the two holidays, many American Jewish families have adapted certain Christmas customs, such as cards and **gifts** for children, for Hanukkah celebrations.

What Is Hanukkah?

The Hebrew word *Hanukkah* means "dedication." The holiday is also known as the Feast of Dedication or the Feast of Lights. Hanukkah commemorates an historical event, the Jewish victory in 162 B.C. over the Syrians in the Maccabean War. At this time Judea was part of the Syrian empire, in which Greek culture predominated. Some Jews began to adopt Greek ways of life and thought. A small group of

Jews, led by the Maccabee family, resisted this process of assimilation by taking up arms against the Syrian political authorities. After their victory, they cleansed and rededicated the Jewish temple in Jerusalem, which their opponents had occupied and used to offer sacrifices to pagan gods. One record states that those present at the dedication witnessed a miracle. A small amount of oil, enough to keep the temple lamp lit for one day, lasted a full eight days.

Today's Hanukkah celebrations often downplay the military history behind the festival. Instead, they emphasize the rededication of the temple in Jerusalem, the victory over religious persecution, and the survival of Judaism. The celebrations last for eight days. They feature a special candleholder, known as a *menorah*, with room for nine candles. The middle candle, the *shamash*, or "server," is used to light the other eight. On the first evening of Hanukkah one candle is lit and special prayers are said. On the second evening two candles are lit, and so on. The rest of the evening is spent singing songs, playing games, telling Hanukkah stories, and enjoying special holiday foods.

Hanukkah and Christmas

Because the Jewish calendar is based on the lunar rather than the solar year, the date of Hanukkah moves about on our calendar. The first day of Hanukkah falls on the twenty-fifth day of the Jewish month of Kislev, which means that it can fall anywhere between November 25 and December 26. In the United States this proximity to Christmas has affected the way in which Hanukkah is celebrated. Originally a minor holiday, Hanukkah has assumed greater importance in the Jewish calendar in order to counter the pervasive presence of Christmas themes and images in the general culture. The old custom of distributing Hanukkah gelt (coins) to children has been expanded to include gifts as well. Many Jewish parents give their children one present for each of the eight nights of Hanukkah. In addition, some people now exchange Hanukkah cards with Jewish friends and family members.

In recent years American presidents have added Hanukkah-related activities to their round of holiday duties. In 1979 Jimmy Carter became the first president to participate in a menorah-lighting ceremony (*see also* **White House, Christmas in the**).

Further Reading

Edidin, Ben M. *Jewish Holidays and Festivals*. 1940. Reprint. Detroit, Mich.: Omnigraphics, 1993.

Henderson, Helene, and Sue Ellen Thompson, eds. *Holidays, Festivals, and Celebrations of the World Dictionary*. Second edition. Detroit, Mich.: Omnigraphics, 1997.

Strassfeld, Michael. *The Jewish Holidays: A Guide and Commentary*. New York: HarperCollins, 1993.

Herod, King

According to the Bible **Jesus** was born in the land of Judea. The **Gospel according to Matthew** tells us that King Herod ruled Judea at the time of Jesus' birth. Historians cannot confirm the treacherous deeds attributed to Herod in Matthew's Nativity story. Nevertheless, these barbarities resemble the kinds of brutal acts historians know him to have committed.

Herod in the Gospel of Matthew

In chapter two of Matthew we learn that **Magi** from the east have arrived in Jerusalem. They inquire about the birthplace of the newborn king of the Jews whose Nativity has been foretold by the rising

326

of a miraculous star (*see also* **Jesus, Year of Birth; Star of Bethlehem**). Herod is disturbed by their questions, seeing in the coming of a great Jewish leader only a potential rival for power. Herod assembles the Jewish priests and scribes, and finds out that prophecy dictates that the Messiah will be born in the town of **Bethlehem**. He passes this news on to the Magi, requesting that they first go to Bethlehem and find the child, and then report back to Jerusalem. The Magi journey on to Bethlehem, identify Jesus as the newborn king, and pay him homage. A dream warns them that Herod intends to kill the child they identify as the king of the Jews so they return to their own countries without going back to Jerusalem. Herod is furious with their failure to return and orders soldiers to kill all the male children in the town of Bethlehem under the age of two. In the meantime, however, an **angel** warns **Joseph**, Jesus' father, of Herod's bloody plan. The angel instructs Joseph and his family to flee into **Egypt** (*see* **Flight into Egypt**). Herod's massacre of Bethlehem's male children is commemorated on **Holy Innocents' Day**, December 28.

The Historical Herod

Herod was the family name of a line of kings who ruled Judea at the time of Jesus' birth. Although they were kings in Judea, they were not themselves of Jewish descent. They were Idumeans, a people from outside the land of Judea, many of whom had been forced to convert to Judaism. Some commentators note that Matthew's account of his meeting with the Magi demonstrates Herod's unfamiliarity with Jewish teachings; in order to answer the Magi's questions, he had to consult those who knew Jewish scripture. The Herod who ruled at the time of Jesus' birth was known as Herod the Great (73 B.C. to 4 B.C.).

Herod the Great became King of Judea in 40 B.C. He rose to power by collaborating with the Roman conquerors of Judea. King Herod was hated and feared by his Jewish subjects. He ruthlessly crushed all political opposition, going so far as to execute a wife and several sons whom he suspected might be plotting against him. He impoverished the people with oppressive taxes in order to fund numerous building projects and other lavish expenditures. Finally, he ordered that a number of well-known Jews be executed on the day of his death in order to ensure that the people would actually mourn on

327

that day. Although no historical evidence exists for the massacre of Bethlehem's children reported by Matthew, the act is not inconsistent with the record of Herod's known deeds.

Herod's Sons

After the death of Herod the Great, the Romans divided his former kingdom among his remaining sons. Herod Archelaus became ruler of Judea, and Herod Antipas ruler of Galilee. The Gospel of Matthew states that after Herod the Great's death, an angel told Joseph that it was safe to return to Israel. When Joseph discovered that the brutal Archelaus had become king of Judea he was too afraid to return there, so he moved his family to Galilee. Thus, the King Herod that interviewed Jesus shortly before his crucifixion (Luke 23) was Herod Antipas, ruler of Galilee.

Further Reading

Garcia-Treto, Francisco O. "Herod." In Paul J. Achtemeier, ed. *The Harper Collins Bible Dictionary*. Revised edition. San Francisco, Calif.: HarperSanFrancisco, 1996.

Henderson, Yorke, et al. *Parents' Magazine Christmas Holiday Book*. New York: Parents' Magazine Press, 1972.

Horsley, Richard A. *The Liberation of Christmas: The Infancy Narratives in Social Context*. New York: Crossroad, 1989.

Hogmanay

The people of Scotland refer to their **New Year's** Eve celebrations as Hogmanay. For centuries New Year's Eve was the most important midwinter holiday in Scotland, far outstripping Christmas in its importance. Even though Christmas gained a good deal of popularity in the late twentieth century, the Scots still celebrate a festive new year that attracts many visitors to their country.

History

In the sixteenth century a religious reform movement, the Protestant Reformation, blossomed in northern Europe. In Scotland John Knox (1513-1572), leader of the Scottish Reformation and founder of the Presbyterian Church, opposed all church festivals, as did many of the new Protestant religious leaders. In **England** and Scotland, a certain group of Protestants known as the **Puritans** came into political power during the seventeenth century. In their attempt to reform British society they tried to abolish its Christmas celebrations, which they viewed as a disgrace to the Christian religion. After the Puritans fell from power the English returned to many of their old Christmas customs. The people of Scotland, however, took many of the Puritan criticisms of Christmas to heart and never really revived their old Christmas celebrations. Instead, New Year's Day became the main midwinter holiday. In fact, Christmas didn't become a legal holiday again until the second half of the twentieth century.

Daft Days

In Scotland the days surrounding Christmas and New Year's were once called the "daft days" (*see also* **Twelve Days of Christmas**). Indeed, the University of Glasgow holds an annual all-night ball on the last Friday of the Christmas term, which is called the "Daft Ball." Some reserve the "Daft Days" as a name for the last day of the old year and the first day of the new year, in reference to the lively customs and sometimes zany behavior that characterize Scottish New Year celebrations.

Origins of the Word "Hogmanay"

The most popular name for the New Year's festival in Scotland, however, is Hogmanay. No one can explain for certain the origins of this word. Linguists suspect that it evolved from the old French term, *aguillaneuf*, which means New Year's **gift**, the last day of the year, or the celebration at which New Year's gifts are exchanged. A related Spanish word, *aguilnaldo*, means Christmas tip, New Year's gift, or, in Latin America, "**Christmas carol**" (*see also* **Boxing Day**).

Many more colorful, but less plausible, origins have been advanced over the years. One early explanation suggested that the word came from the Greek phrase, *hagia mana*, meaning "holy month." Since it is a bit difficult to explain how the Scots, in the far north of Europe, came to be so influenced by a Greek phrase, another scholar proposed that Hogmanay comes from an old Saxon phrase, *halig-monath*, meaning "holy month." The difficulty with this theory is that according to the Anglo-Saxon scholar, St. Bede (673?-735), the Saxon holy month fell in September.

Yet another far-fetched theory attributes both Hogmanay and the nonsense word "trololay," which often follows it in song and verse, to a French couplet:

> *Homme est né*
> *Trois rois allois.*

It means, "A man is born, three kings are come." Little evidence exists to support the idea that the Scots used or were influenced by this phrase, however.

While some strive to find a Christian meaning for the word, others search for pagan roots. One writer bases his explanation for the phrase on the contention that the ancient Scots worshipped the Scandinavian sun god Thor at the **Yule** festival that took place around this time of year. He continues by suggesting that they named all sorts of feasts "oels" (or "ales") and that they called the cup of remembrance drunk at the Yule festival "minne." Thus Hogmanay Trololay could have come from an old Scots phrase like,

> *Hogg minne!*
> *Thor oel, oel!*

which he translates as, "Remember your sacrifices; The feast of Thor, the Feast!" The problem, again, seems to be finding evidence to support such a claim. Along these same lines, some have suggested that the French word *aguillaneuf* comes from the phrase *au gui l'an neuf*, "to the **mistletoe** the new year," again linking Hogmanay to pagan celebrations. Nevertheless, most scholars reject this explanation of the word.

Visits and Treats

Gift giving, as well as good-luck charms, figured prominently in traditional Scottish New Year celebrations. In past eras children used to go door to door asking neighbors to give them their Hogmanay, which in this context meant gifts of cheese and oat cakes. They chanted old folk rhymes, such as:

> Get up good wife and shake your feathers
> And dinna think that we are beggars,
> For we are guisers come out to play
> Get up and gie's our hogmanay.

This rhyme usually accompanied the recitation of a bit of a mummer's play (*see also* **Mumming**). Another rhyme works on the listener's sympathy as a means of soliciting a treat:

> Ma feet's cauld
> Ma shoon's thin,
> Gies ma cakes
> An' let me rin.

In some places groups of boys called the *Gillean Callaig*, or Hogmanay Lads, went from door to door carrying sticks, a sack, and an old hide. They recited an old Gaelic folk verse at each house they visited while they used their switches and sticks to beat the animal hide. Then they circled the dwelling place, taking care to move in the same direction as the sun. Householders were then expected to invite the boys in for a treat. Some people added another twist to the custom by bringing the boys inside, singeing a bit of the hide, and wafting the smoke over each family member. All who inhaled the pungent fumes of this purification ritual were supposed to enjoy good health in the coming year, while the boys received a bit of bannock (a coarse oatmeal cake) to take away in their sack. This custom died out in the early twentieth century.

Firstfooters

Scottish folklore teaches that the **firstfooter**, the first person to set foot over the threshold after midnight, determines the household's luck in the new year. Lucky firstfooters possess certain physical qualities. In most regions, a dark-haired, healthy, adult male is considered the luckiest firstfooter. In some places local lore even specifies that he not be flat-footed. Rather than leave the luck of the household to fate, some families arrange for a person with the lucky characteristics to visit them just after midnight.

Firstfooters often bring gifts of food, drink, fuel, or money to the homes they visit. These are considered lucky gifts that help to attract the same goods to the household throughout the year. Some people follow a tradition whereby family members remain silent until the firstfooter enters, places his gifts of food and drink on the table, stirs up the fire, and wishes the household and all its members well.

Other Superstitions

Traditional folk beliefs warned that the conditions prevailing in the home on New Year's Eve would be likely to persist throughout the coming year. Therefore, people prepared for New Year's Eve by paying off their debts, returning borrowed items, tuning musical instruments, washing and mending clothes, sheets and blankets, polishing silver and metal goods, winding clocks, cleaning their fireplaces, and emptying out the ashes. Since superstitions warned that stray dogs were portents of evil to come, people often chased away any strays lingering about their homestead.

Other beliefs advised people to collect the "cream of the well," or the "flower of the well." This water, contained in the first bucket to be drawn from the well after midnight on New Year's Eve, was said to be especially sweet and pure. In some places people competed to be the first person to draw it from the well and to gain the luck it was said to impart. People not only drank this water for their health, but also saved some with which to bless their homes and barns.

Many Scots also enacted purification rituals—known as *saining*—on New Year's Eve or New Year's Day. These rituals involved censing house, barn, family members, and animals with smoke, often juniper smoke. Another common good-luck ritual consisted of opening the door at the stroke of midnight on New Year's Eve to let the old year out and the new one in. Many people accompanied this action by ringing **bells** and banging on pots and pans. The noise chased away any evil spirits or influences lurking about the house.

On the island of Orkney, local lore boasts that Stane O'Quoybune, a 4,000-year-old, 12-foot-tall standing stone, walks down to Boardhouse Loch in the early hours of New Year's morning to drink its icy water. Few stay up past midnight to watch for the event, however, since local lore also insists that those who see the stone move will die in the year to come.

Foods

The Scots also celebrate the new year by indulging in special foods. One traditional drink, called a *het pint*, resembles **wassail**. It is made by mixing ale, spirits, sugar, cloves, nutmeg, coriander, cinnamon, and other spices. Another New Year's Eve concoction, *athole brose*, is made from oatmeal, cream, honey, and whiskey. Scotch whiskey or tea may also be served. *Sowen*—oat and bran gruel sweetened with honey or molasses and spiked with whiskey—constitutes a special dish connected with the holiday. Other New Year's foods include oatcakes, cheese, shortbread, black bun (a cake made with dried fruit, almonds, spices, and spirits), and *ankersocks* (**gingerbread** made with rye.)

Parties

Today many Scots celebrate Hogmanay with parties. These may take place in people's homes, in pubs, or on the streets. In 1993 the city of Edinburgh began its open-air Hogmanay Festival. It has become the largest New Year's Eve party in Europe and it attracts many foreign visitors. This festival has become so popular that the city had to issue passes limiting the number of those who can attend the events to about 180,000. The celebration takes place over the course of three days and includes pop, rock, and folk concerts, dances, street parties, and a torchlight procession ending in a bonfire.

Noise and Song

At midnight on New Year's Eve Scots link arms with the people surrounding them and sing "**Auld Lang Syne.**" This song, whose title means, "Days of Long Ago," is credited to Scotland's most famous poet, Robert Burns (1759-1796). Much noisemaking also takes place at midnight, especially the firing of guns.

Torches, Dancing, and Sports

People all over Scotland celebrate the new year with torchlit processions (*see also* **Up Helly Aa**). These usually take place on December

30. People often observe New Year's Eve by attending *ceilidhs* (pronounced kay-lees), dance parties featuring Scottish bagpiping and other kinds of Celtic music. New Year's Day is frequently marked by a variety of sporting events, including traditional Highland activities such as wrestling, tossing the caber (throwing a long pole) and putting the stone (throwing a heavy disk). Other popular sports include *shinty*, a **game** similar to hockey, and curling, a game which involves moving a puck over ice. Group walks are another common New Year's Day activity.

Further Reading

Edwards, Gillian. *Hogmanay and Tiffany, The Names of Feasts and Fasts.* London, England: Geoffrey Bles, 1970.

Gaster, Theodor. *New Year, Its History, Customs, and Superstitions.* New York: Abelard-Schuman, 1955.

Griffin, Robert H., and Ann H. Shurgin. *Junior Worldmark Encyclopedia of World Holidays.* Volume 4. Detroit, Mich.: UXL, 2000.

Hutton, Ronald. *The Stations of the Sun.* Oxford, England: Oxford University Press, 1996.

Livingstone, Sheila. *Scottish Festivals.* Edinburgh, Scotland: Birlinn, Ltd., 1997.

Mackie, Albert. *Scottish Pageantry.* London, England: Hutchinson, 1967.

Miles, Clement A. *Christmas in Ritual and Tradition.* 1912. Reprint. Detroit, Mich.: Omnigraphics, 1990.

Tober, Bruce. "Hogmanay." *British Heritage* 20, 1 (December 1998-January 1999): 46-50.

Web Site

The city of Edinburgh, Scotland, has posted a web site on its Hogmanay Festival at: http://www.edinburghshogmanay.org

Holly

Holly springs up all around us at Christmas time. It ornaments to-day's **Christmas cards**, **wreaths**, **wrapping paper**, and other Christmas decorations. Although holly serves as a very contemporary symbol of the season, folklorists trace holly's association with Christmas back to ancient times.

Ancient Beliefs and Customs

Evergreen plants, such as holly, **ivy**, and pine, stay green all year round. For many ancient peoples, this special property converted these plants into seasonal reminders of the promise of rebirth or eternal life. Many writers believe that the pagan peoples of northern Europe decorated their homes with **greenery** during their winter festival, **Yule**. Perhaps they wished to honor and imitate holly's triumph over the dark and the cold, for the plant not only remains green during the winter but also bears bright red fruit during this harsh season. Further south, the Romans also decorated their homes with greenery during their winter festival, **Saturnalia**. In addition, friends exchanged sprigs of holly and other evergreens as tokens of friendship and good wishes for the upcoming new year.

Christianity and the Significance of Holly

Some folklorists think that holly and ivy represented the male and female principles in nature to the pagan peoples of northern Europe. These old beliefs may have lingered on in song and folklore long after Christianity conquered the northern lands. A good number of English songs from the Middle Ages and Renaissance depict a rivalry between holly and ivy in which holly represents masculinity and ivy, femininity. In early Christian times, the Church resisted the pagan European custom of making seasonal decorations out of winter greenery. The sixth-century second Council of Braga forbade Christians the use of green boughs in home decoration.

As time went on, however, Christianity adopted the holly and ivy of pagan winter celebrations, molding their significance to fit Christian beliefs. One authority states that early northern European Christians interpreted holly as a symbol of the Virgin **Mary**'s love for God. Its spiky leaves and blood-red berries also served to remind Christians that **Jesus** would end his days wearing a crown of thorns. The words to the **Christmas carol** titled "The Holly and the Ivy" illustrate similar Christian reinterpretations of these seasonal symbols. After the older beliefs about the plant had faded, some Christian authorities suspected that the word "holly" must be related to the word "holy," a belief that would support their interpretations of its connection with the **Christmas season**. They were mistaken. The modern English word "holly" comes from the older terms for the plant — *hollin, holin,* and *holme* — and before that, from the Anglo-Saxon word for holly, *holegn.*

Folklore and Customs

Old British folklore attributed a variety of special powers to holly. In medieval times, practitioners of folk medicine used holly to treat many conditions, including fever, rheumatism, gout, and asthma. (Holly berries are poisonous, however.) Picking holly on Christmas Day could enhance its medicinal properties. In addition, holly warded off evil spirits. A medieval traveler who had lost his way might shelter under a holly tree for protection against unseen dangers. Placed on doors and around windowsills, holly's spiny leaves would snag any evil spirit that tried to enter the house. One custom advised unmarried women to place a sprig of holly beside their beds on Christmas Eve as protection against witches or goblins. A sprig of holly inside the house might also shield the householders from fire and storms. Holly that had been used in church decorations was believed to be especially powerful. It could confer luck, peace, or happiness, according to English folk beliefs, and protect against lightning, according to German folk beliefs.

Traces of the old association with masculinity and the battle of the sexes lingered on in holly lore. English folklore deemed prickly holly "male" and non-prickly holly "female." (Holly plants are indeed sexed, but the sex difference does not manifest itself in this way). If male holly was brought into the house first, the husband would rule during the upcoming year, and if female holly entered first, the wife would rule. Several hundred years ago, English folk custom still connected competing figures known as the "holly boy" and the "ivy girl" with a number of wintertime observances. During this same period, the Welsh observed "Holming Day" on December 26 with another customary battle of the sexes in which men hit women's bare arms with holly branches (*see also* **St. Stephen's Day**). According to folk belief, holly dealt good luck to men, while ivy granted good luck to women.

Careless dealings with holly could turn good luck into bad, however. Some believed that cutting holly at any other time than Christmas brought bad luck. Bringing holly into the house for Christmas decorations also required special care. Some thought it unlucky to bring it in before Christmas Eve or Christmas Day. The withered greens must also be disposed of respectfully. Some believed that they should be burned. Others thought that burning them drew bad luck and that feeding them to cattle might preserve good luck. Still others felt they should simply be left to decay on their own. Sometimes a sprig of holly was saved for the following year, when it was used to light the fire under the next year's Christmas pudding (*see also* **Plum Pudding**).

Holly, often alongside its mate, ivy, served as an important **Christmas symbol** during the nineteenth century. The Victorians wove it into **kissing boughs**, greenery swags, and other seasonal home adornments, and embellished many a Christmas card with its image. Today, some Americans still hang a wreath of holly on their front doors at Christmas. In Britain many people place similar wreaths on the graves of the family dead at this time of year. In addition, holly continues to trim contemporary holiday decorations, symbolizing for many the mirth of the season. The old yet still popular Christmas carol, "Deck the Halls," expresses this connection between holly and revelry.

Further Reading

Leach, Maria, ed. *Funk and Wagnalls Standard Dictionary of Folklore, Mythology, and Legend.* New York: Harper and Row, 1984.

Segall, Barbara. *The Holly and the Ivy.* New York: Clarkson Potter, 1991.

Holy Innocents' Day

Childermas, Feast of the Holy Innocents, Innocents' Day

In chapter two of the **Gospel according to Matthew**, the birth of **Jesus** is followed by a massacre from which the Holy Family narrowly escapes. An **angel** warns Jesus' father **Joseph** that King **Herod** intends to kill the child, whom the **Magi** have identified as the newborn king of the Jews. The angel instructs Joseph to flee with his family into **Egypt** (*see* **Flight into Egypt**). Herod's soldiers arrive in **Bethlehem** after the Holy Family has departed. They slaughter all the male children in the town and surrounding region who are under two years of age. This event is known as "the slaughter of the Innocents." Holy Innocents' Day, observed on December 28, mourns this act of cruelty.

Church History

Three Christian festivals follow in close succession upon Christmas. **St. Stephen's Day** occurs on December 26, **St. John's Day** on December 27, and Holy Innocent's Day on December 28. These commemorative days were established in western Europe by the late fifth century. The individuals they honor share two things in common. Stephen, John, and the Innocents all lived during the time of Jesus and were martyred for him. In addition, Stephen, John, and the Innocents represent all possible combinations of the distinction between martyrs of will and martyrs of deed. The children slaughtered at King Herod's orders in Bethlehem did not choose their fate, but suffered it nonetheless, and so were considered martyrs in deed. St. John willingly risked death in his defense of the Christian faith, but did not suffer death, and so was considered a martyr of will. St. Stephen risked and suffered death for his faith, and thus became a martyr of will and of deed.

Around the year 1000, Holy Innocent's Day acquired a new name. The English began to refer to the observance as "Childermas," a contraction of *childern* (an archaic form of the word "children") and "mass." In the past, if Innocents' Day fell on a Sunday, the liturgical color was red, signifying martyrdom. If the feast fell on any other day of the week, the liturgical color was purple, signifying penitence. This difference reflected the doubt of some early theologians concerning the fate of the children's souls. Although they had died in Christ's place and so might be considered martyrs, they had not been baptized. In 1960 the Roman Catholic Church eliminated this variation in liturgical colors, assigning the red of martyrdom to all observances of the feast.

Folk Customs

Many of the customs associated with Holy Innocents' Day assign a special role to children. Moreover, a number of Innocents' Day customs encourage activities that reverse power and authority between the older and younger generations. Centuries ago in **England, boy bishops** held sway in some churches on Childermas (*see also* **Feast of Fools**). On December 28 the boy bishop was expected to deliver a public sermon before stepping down from office. In medieval times boy bishops could also be found in **Germany** and **France**. Another old English custom encouraged older family members to swat younger ones with switches on Childermas. Although one writer suggests that the practice served to remind young people of the sufferings of Bethlehem's Innocents, most folklorists view this practice as a remnant of an old, pre-Christian custom intended to drive out evil spirits, ill health, or other harmful forces.

Innocents' Day whipping customs were also popular at one time in central Europe. In some areas groups of children marched from house to house whipping girls and women with twigs and branches. A folk verse which accompanied this practice reveals that it was viewed as a means of imparting health, fertility, abundance, and good luck:

> Many years of healthy life,
> Happy girl, happy wife:
> Many children, hale and strong,
> Nothing harmful, nothing wrong,
> Much to drink and more to eat;
> Now we beg a kindly treat [Weiser, 1952, 133].

Childermas customs in some regions of Germany permitted children to strike anyone they passed with their whips of twigs and branches. The children demanded coins in exchange for this service, which was known as "whipping with fresh greens." In Hungary boys and men whipped women and girls with switches in order to endow them with health and beauty. In Yugoslavia mothers switched children, hoping to promote their health and strength. Afterwards the children circulated through the neighborhood, smacking adults with switches and receiving treats and coins in exchange.

In Belgium children seized control of the house on December 28. Early in the morning the children would collect all the keys in the house. Later, when any adult ventured into a room or closet for which they had the key, the child would lock him or her in. In order to gain their release the adults promised the child a treat, such as money, candy, fruit, or a toy. The children referred to these ransomed adults as their "sugar uncle" or "sugar aunt." In Austria old folk traditions also allowed children to play tricks on their parents on Holy Innocents' Day and to usurp their parents' authority by sitting in their chairs.

This playful, topsy-turvy spirit also runs through Innocent's Day customs in **Mexico, Ecuador**, and other Latin countries (*see also* **Spain, Christmas in**). Mexicans celebrate the day in much the same way we celebrate April Fools' Day—by playing practical jokes on one another. The one who gets fooled is referred to as an "innocent."

Folklore

Another, more ominous theme also runs through the lore and customs associated with Innocents' Day, however. Because the feast commemorates such a despicable deed, it came to be viewed as an extremely unlucky day, according to old European folk beliefs. Any undertaking begun on Childermas was bound to fail, according to these superstitions. The Irish called December 28 "the cross day of the year" for that reason. Those who married on that day ran especially high risks of future misery. According to some sources, King Louis XI of France (ruled 1461-83) absolutely refused to conduct or discuss affairs of state on Holy Innocents' Day. It is also believed that the English monarch Edward IV (ruled 1461-70, 1471-83) postponed his own coronation ceremony, originally scheduled for December 28, for fear of tagging his reign with bad luck.

Further Reading

Chambers, Robert. "December 28—Innocents' Day." In his *The Book of Days.* Volume 2. 1862-64. Reprint. Detroit, Mich.: Omnigraphics, 1990.

Cowie, L. W., and John Selwyn Gummer. *The Christian Calendar.* Springfield, Mass.: G. and C. Merriam Company, 1974.

Henderson, Helene, and Sue Ellen Thompson, eds. *Holidays, Festivals, and Celebrations of the World Dictionary.* Second edition. Detroit, Mich.: Omnigraphics, 1997.

Hole, Christina. *British Folk Customs.* London, England: Hutchinson and Company, 1976.

Hutton, Ronald. *The Stations of the Sun.* Oxford, England: Oxford University Press, 1996.

Joyce, E. J. "Innocents, Holy." In *New Catholic Encyclopedia.* Volume 7. New York: McGraw-Hill, 1967.

MacDonald, Margaret Read, ed. *The Folklore of World Holidays.* Detroit, Mich.: Gale Research, 1992.

Miles, Clement A. *Christmas in Ritual and Tradition.* 1912. Reprint. Detroit, Mich.: Omnigraphics, 1990.

Spicer, Dorothy Gladys. *The Book of Festivals.* 1937. Reprint. Detroit, Mich.: Omnigraphics, 1990.

Urlin, Ethel. *Festivals, Holy Days, and Saints' Days.* 1915. Reprint. Detroit, Mich.: Omnigraphics, 1992.

Weiser, Francis X. *Handbook of Christian Feasts and Customs.* New York: Harcourt, Brace and World, 1952.

Hopping John

Hopping John is a traditional **New Year's Day** food in the American South. The dish consists of black-eyed peas and rice, seasoned with onions, a bit of pork, and some salt and pepper. It developed among rice plantation slaves in South Carolina and eventually spread to the surrounding black and white communities. Recipes for hopping John appear in cookbooks written by white Southerners as early as the latter half of the nineteenth century (*see also* **Slaves' Christmas; America, Christmas in Nineteenth-Century**).

Cookbook author Karen Hess speculates that in making hopping John slaves were recreating the familiar dishes of their African upbringing. This kind of dish, a rice and bean pilaf, can be found throughout the rice-growing regions of Asia and Africa. Hess believes the name "hopping John" in fact derives from the Malay word *kachang*, referring to a certain type of bean, and the Hindi word *bhat*, which means cooked rice.

Food writer John Thorne suggests another origin for hopping John. He suspects that Caribbean slaves first invented the dish and brought it with them to the United States. He proposes that the name "hopping John" comes from the French word used by these Caribbean slaves to describe the beans that make up the mainstay of the dish: *pois a pigeon*, or pigeon peas. When English speakers were told that the dish consisted of pois a pigeon, pronounced in the Creole dialect as "pwaah-peeJON," they might easily have dubbed the dish "hopping John." African slaves brought pigeon peas with them to the Caribbean, where they thrived. Pigeon peas never really took root in the United States, where other types of beans and peas have replaced them in dishes like hopping John.

Over the years ordinary people have come up with a variety of imaginative explanations for the dish's unusual name. One such explanation suggested that the name of the dish went along with a peculiar custom requiring children to hop around the dining room table before it was served. Another wraps a bit of a folktale around the name, proposing that there once was a man named John who loved the dish so much that he always came "a-hopping" when his wife set it on the table.

No one knows exactly how hopping John — originally the humble fare of slaves and poor folk — became attached to New Year's Day, or why consuming it on this date brings good luck. Folk wisdom suggests that by "eating poor" on New Year's Day, one becomes a magnet for rich foods during the rest of the year. An old, southern folk rhyme confirms this theory:

> Those black-eyed peas are lucky
> When et on New Year's Day;
> You'll always have sweet 'taters,
> And possum come your way [Kane, 1998, 155].

Other superstitions have also attached themselves to the dish. For example, some say that on New Year's Day hopping John should always be served with a side dish of greens so as to attract greenbacks, that is, paper money. Still others believe that the luck-bringing effects of the dish can be enhanced by adding side dishes of sweet potatoes and cornbread.

Further Reading

Hess, Karen. *The Carolina Rice Kitchen*. Columbia, S.C.: University of South Carolina Press, 1992.

Kane, Harnett T. *The Southern Christmas Book*. 1958. Reprint. Detroit, Mich.: Omnigraphics, 1998.

Selbert, Pamela. "A Good Start?: Southerners Ring In a Lucky New Year with Hopping John." *St. Louis Post-Dispatch* (December 16, 1994): 1.

Thorne, John. *Serious Pig*. New York: North Point Press, 1996.

Web Site

"The Story of Hopping John," posted by noted food writer John Thorne on his web site at: http://www.outlawcook.com/Page0102.html

How the Grinch Stole Christmas

Acclaimed children's writer Dr. Seuss, born Theodor Geisel, published *How the Grinch Stole Christmas* in 1957. This story tells how the grumpy Grinch tries to prevent the sweet-tempered citizens of Whoville from celebrating Christmas. He steals the trappings of Christmas — the **Christmas trees**, decorations, **gifts**, and special foods — but discovers that he cannot steal the spirit of Christmas. This realization transforms the Grinch, who then returns the stolen loot.

Book, Cartoon, and Movie

In Dr. Seuss's Christmas story, the spirit of Christmas converts a Scrooge-like main character into a joyful soul. Viewed in this light, Dr. Seuss's story might be seen as a children's cartoon version of Dickens's classic holiday tale, *A Christmas Carol*. Its immense appeal to children led to its being transformed into an animated television special in 1966. Geisel adapted the script from his book, while director and animator Chuck Jones turned Dr. Seuss's drawings into moving cartoon characters. Actor Boris Karloff, famous for his roles in horror films, dubbed in the voice of the Grinch. The show proved an immediate hit, and was rerun year after year. In 1971 Geisel received a Peabody Award for his work on the animated version of *How the Grinch Stole Christmas*. In the years to come, further Grinch television specials brought him two Emmy Awards — *Halloween Is Grinch Night* (1977) and *The Grinch Grinches the Cat in the Hat* (1982).

How the Grinch Stole Christmas — both the book and the cartoon — imprinted itself in the minds of millions of American youth. So much so that in the year 2000 Universal Studios, hoping to cash in on the phenomenon, released a live-action movie version of the story entitled *Dr. Seuss's How the Grinch Stole Christmas*. Directed by Ron Howard, the film featured Jim Carrey in the title role. Realizing that the story told in the short book would have to be expanded if it were to become a full-length movie, Howard began adding scenes that developed the characters.

The designers labored to take Dr. Seuss's two-dimensional drawings and recreate a three-dimensional Seussian world for the movie set. Rather than duplicate the exact look of Dr. Seuss's Grinch book, they decided that the sets would reproduce a blend of environments depicted in the books. Dr. Seuss's fantastical settings, buildings, and furniture, often drawn without right angles or much regard for the laws of physics, proved a great challenge to the design team. Make-up artist Rick Baker faced an equally difficult challenge, that of turning Jim Carrey into the Grinch and scores of other actors into the Whos of Whoville. Each morning before filming began, Carrey endured a three-and-a-half-hour makeup session, which included applying makeup over three foam rubber facial pieces as well as inserting false teeth and yellow contact lenses.

In the end the effort proved worth the trouble. *Dr. Seuss's How the Grinch Stole Christmas* won an Academy Award for Best Makeup and was nominated for two additional awards — Best Art Direction-Set Decoration and Best Costume Design.

Dr. Seuss

Dr. Seuss was the pen name of Theodor Geisel (1904-1991). His love for doodling and drawing expressed itself at an early age. It continued throughout his formal education at Dartmouth College and Oxford University. Never a particularly dedicated student, he lost patience with the obscurity of advanced academic study while attending Oxford and returned to the United States, where he began to make his living as a cartoonist. As the years went by, Geisel became increasingly fascinated with language and rhyme, and began to work on wedding his rhymes to drawings. Some years later he prepared his first manuscript for a children's book, eventually titled *And to Think That I Saw It on Mulberry Street*. Twenty-seven different publishers rejected it. As Geisel walked the streets of New York, looking for the 28th publisher, he ran into an old college friend, Marshall McClintock, who had just become the children's book editor for Vanguard Press. McClintock gave him the break he needed. Vanguard Press published Geisel's book in 1937.

And to Think That I Saw It on Mulberry Street, written in verse, was a success. Though Dr. Seuss's next books were written in prose, he eventually returned to the rhyme schemes for which he became famous.

Over 200 million copies of Dr. Seuss's books have been published in 20 different languages. The enormous popularity of these stories propelled Dr. Seuss and his books into the role of cultural icons. He liked to think of himself as the man who had single-handedly rid American classrooms of the boring "see Dick run" style of early reader. In 1985 the senior class of Princeton University paid a humorous tribute to his role in forming generations of young readers, when they stood in unison and recited the entire text of *Green Eggs and Ham* as Seuss mounted the stage to receive an honorary doctorate.

Further Reading

Fensch, Thomas. *The Man Who Was Dr. Seuss*. The Woodlands, Tex.: New Century Books, 2000.

Lipschultz, Andy. *How the Grinch Stole Hollywood*. New York: Random House, 2000.

Seuss, Theodor Geisel. *How the Grinch Stole Christmas*. New York: Random House, 1957.

Web Site

The web site for the Dr. Seuss National Memorial Sculpture Garden, located in the author's hometown of Springfield, Massachusetts, offers a brief biography of Geisel, images of previously unpublished art work, and a listing of local Seuss-related events: http://www.catinthehat.org/index.html

Iceland, Christmas in

The first Europeans settled in Iceland in the ninth century. They were from Scandinavia and the Celtic lands, and some researchers believe that they brought with them a midwinter festival called **Yule**. They also imported a rich collection of stories, beliefs, and folklore concerning **elves**, fairies, trolls and other unseen, magical peoples. In the year 1000, Iceland adopted Christianity. This religion called for a new, midwinter holiday called Christmas. Over the years the beliefs and practices associated with Christmas began to eclipse those associated with the earlier pagan feast. Nevertheless, old folk beliefs continued to link this time of year with supernatural creatures and various kinds of heightened paranormal activity (*see also* **Ghosts**).

Past Preparations

In past times, Icelanders busied themselves in the week before Christmas preparing for the holiday. Women made candles, baked, cooked, washed clothes, and knit **stockings** and mittens. The folk-lore of Iceland abounds in tales of hard-hearted bosses who worked their domestic servants so far into the night during this week that they had to place sticks between their eyelids to keep them propped open. For this reason, Icelanders dubbed the week preceding Christmas "Stick Week." Snacks eaten during this week were named "stick bites." Those who did their share of the work received at least one article of woolen clothing as a Christmas present.

According to Icelandic folklore, the Christmas cat would pursue those who had nothing new to wear on Christmas. This fearsome creature was the pet of Gryla, the ogress who spawned the **Christmas Lads**. Presumably, fear of falling prey to this hungry, magical cat motivated people to work hard in preparing for the Christmas festival.

St. Thorlak's Day

Icelanders observe December 23 as St. Thorlak's Day. St. Thorlak—an Icelandic monk, as well as the bishop of Skaholt—won fame for his efforts to reform the church, but was murdered in 1193. According to tradition, intensive preparations for the coming Christmas festival took place on this day. People washed clothes, prepared the Christmas feast, and cleaned their homes. Stores stayed open late and people did their Christmas shopping. Today many people mark the day by consuming a simple meal in the evening, often skate hash, a dish similar to the Norwegian *lutefisk* (*see also* **Norway, Christmas in**). In addition, many people wait until St. Thorlak's Day to de-corate their **Christmas tree**.

Christmas Eve and Day

Icelanders begin their Christmas celebrations on Christmas Eve. Many people attend Christmas church services on this day. A large festive meal is prepared for 6 p.m., when Icelanders consider Christmas to begin. Traditional Christmas dishes include *hangikjot* (smoked meat), halibut, dried fish, sausages, an Icelandic bird called rock ptarmigan, *laufabraud* (leaf-bread, a type of cookie) and a kind of rice pudding. The rice pudding contains a single almond. Whoever finds the al-mond in their serving of pudding gets an extra **gift**. Nowadays many imported foods are available in addition to the traditional Icelandic

Christmas fare. In past times custom frowned on the consumption of alcohol at Christmas time, though nowadays people may lubricate their festivities with **Christmas ale** or other alcoholic beverages.

Families open their presents after dinner on Christmas Eve. When this has been completed some families join hands around the **Christmas tree** and sing **Christmas carols**. Icelandic television stations shut down between 5 and 10 p.m. on Christmas Eve, affirming the high value that Icelanders place on having this time together with their families.

On Christmas Day people stay at home with their families, go visiting, attend parties, and continue to enjoy special Christmas foods.

Gift Bringers

The people of Iceland invented their own unique Christmas gift bringers called the Christmas Lads. In past centuries Icelanders imagined this band of thirteen brothers as fearsome trolls. Over the years they shrank in stature and their appetite for troublemaking diminished. Nowadays images of the Christmas Lads often depict them as elf-like beings, dressed in a manner that resembles **Santa Claus**. The first Lad arrives thirteen days before Christmas. Another comes on the following day and so on, until the household hosts all thirteen elves on Christmas Eve. On Christmas Day the first elf leaves. One leaves each day thereafter, until the last Lad departs on **Epiphany**.

Some Icelanders wish to popularize the idea that Santa Claus lives in Iceland. At one point the government-run Iceland Board of Tourism answered the thousands of **children's letters** to Santa that arrived in Iceland. After funding cuts decimated this program a private foundation stepped in to answer these letters.

Gifts

In past centuries, each member of an Icelandic household received an article of woolen clothing as a Christmas gift. In the twentieth century Icelanders began to give each other more and different gifts. For example, candles, books, and packs of playing cards became popular gifts. In the second half of the twentieth century a new custom evolved. Children place a **shoe** on the windowsill in the weeks

351

that precede Christmas. If they have been good, the Christmas Lads will fill the shoe with candy. If not, they might leave a potato there instead. Researchers believe that this custom was imported from **Germany** some time around the 1920s.

Decorations

Burning candles have long served as important Christmas decorations in Iceland. This makes sense in a land that sees only about four hours of daylight around Christmas time (*see also* **Winter Solstice**). Many Icelanders also decorate their homes with **Advent wreaths**, a custom most likely adopted from **Denmark**. Trees are relatively scarce in Iceland and most people would never dream of cutting one down merely to use it for a week or two as a Christmas decoration. As a result, the Christmas tree didn't become popular until the second half of the twentieth century, when imported spruce trees became available. Before that time, however, some people constructed homemade artificial trees out of colorful sacks and poles.

New Year's Eve

Icelanders celebrate New Year's Eve with fireworks, bonfires, and "elf dances." The bonfires can be traced back to the eighteenth century, when they began as a means of getting rid of holiday trash. Icelanders continue to enjoy dressing up as elves, trolls, or imps on New Year's Eve. This custom reflects a long-standing belief that magical creatures are out in force on this evening.

According to Icelandic folklore, all manner of supernatural events may occur on New Year's Eve. The dead may rise from their graves, animals may speak, and seals may transform themselves briefly into human beings. What's more, elves are believed to be especially active on Christmas and New Year's Eve. Until recently many people left at least one light burning on these nights as a way of welcoming the elves.

According to Icelandic folklore, elves move their homes on New Year's Eve. This same lore taught that those who catch the elves in the middle of their move might gain an elvish blessing for good luck and wealth. To this end, it recommended that those who dared risk an encounter with these magical beings sit at a crossroads on New Year's

Eve. If an elf traveling on either road wanted to get by, he or she would try to lure the human to move with promises of money, treasure, food, and other tempting things. Those who stood their ground and spoke no word until morning would gain all the promised treasures. On the other hand, if their mood turned sour, the elves could wish ill fortune on the humans who had interrupted their journey.

In past times many people offered the elves hospitality on New Year's Eve by performing special house cleanings and leaving food and lights burning in an out-of-the-way nook or corner. Some walked about their house three times and announced a welcome to the elves, promising them safe usage of the premises for the evening.

Another bit of old lore claimed that frost that drifted into the house through an open pantry window on this night was especially sweet and that it brought with it the promise of abundance. The only difficulty was that in order to collect this "pantry drift," a housewife had to stay awake all night in a dark pantry with the window open to the stern cold of an Icelandic winter night, while the drift slowly collected in a pot on the floor. Once this task was completed, a design made up of crosses was traced over the pot, which prevented the prosperity from escaping. No statistics exist to tell us how many women took up this icy challenge.

Twelfth Night and Epiphany

The last of the Christmas Lads departs on Epiphany. People hold parties on this day to mark the end of the **Christmas season**, and some people costume themselves as one of the Christmas Lads or their troll parents. In addition, Icelanders often mark the day with bonfires into which they throw the trash that has accumulated over the holidays.

Further Reading

Bowler, Gerry. *The World Encyclopedia of Christmas*. Toronto, Ontario, Canada: McClelland and Stewart, 2000.

Griffin, Robert H., and Ann H. Shurgin, eds. *The Folklore of World Holidays*. Second edition. Detroit, Mich.: Gale, 1999.

Osmond, Stephen. "Long Night of Dreams: Midwinter Celebrations in Iceland." *The World and I* 11, 1 (January 1996): 206(12).

India, Christmas in

Christians make up just over two percent of the population in India. Nevertheless, Christmas is a national holiday and many Indians who are not Christian still observe some of its folk customs. These include the lighting of many oil lamps along the perimeter of one's courtyard or the edge of one's roof. Indian Christians borrowed these lamp-lighting customs from a Hindu holiday known as Dewali. The task of filling and lighting the lamps often falls to children. Some families also paint **Christmas symbols** and images on the walls of their whitewashed homes with powdered dyes. These pictures may include the **Star of Bethlehem**, the **Magi**, or **shepherds**. The cooking and sharing of special foods is another widespread Christmas custom, although the dishes may vary from place to place. **Gift** giving and carol singing also take place in many Indian communities at Christmas time (*see also* **Christmas Carol**).

Bengal

Christians in Bengal focus their anticipation on Christmas Day church services. Boys and men gather regularly to practice the music for the Christmas program. Women clean the home. This cleaning includes giving the walls a fresh coat of whitewash or clay, and decorating the house with marigolds, leaves, and brightly colored paper. Girls make decorations for the church, such as paper chains and chains of marigolds.

On Christmas Eve boys and young men gather at the church, festooning it with palm branches, **wreaths**, garlands of marigolds, and paper chains. Then they set up a **Christmas tree** just outside the building. Afterwards they go caroling.

On Christmas Day Bengali Christians enjoy special foods, such as fruitcake, dates, oranges, raisins, coconut-filled rice cakes, fried rice, and meat with curry sauce. Children often deliver plates of these special Christmas foods to their friends.

Worshipers, decked out in new clothes if possible, pack Christmas Day church services. Services generally include a sermon and choral music. After the conclusion of the service the congregation crowds around the Christmas tree for the distribution of gifts. Poorer members of the congregation can expect gifts of new clothes, and children receive trinkets from the Sunday school.

Many Santals live in the state of Bengal. These tribal people celebrate Christmas for five days. Girls dance up and down the streets and sing songs. Boys also take to the streets, entertaining the public by playing instruments. Onlookers often treat the boys and girls to fried rice and tea after their performances.

Kerala

In the southwestern state of Kerala many Christians belong to Eastern churches, like the Syriac Orthodox Church, the Egyptian Coptic Church, the Armenian Orthodox Church, and the Abyssinian Church. Others are Roman Catholic. The Eastern churches observe somewhat different rites than those observed by Western Christians, that is, Roman Catholics and Protestants. For example, those belonging to the Syriac Orthodox Church observe **Advent** by fasting. For the four weeks preceding Christmas they abstain from eating meat, fish, and milk products.

In the last week before Christmas, many Christian children in Kerala spend an evening singing Christmas carols from door to door. They carry with them candle-lit lanterns hanging from the ends of poles (*for a similar custom, see* **Star Boys**). These beacons, raised aloft, cast a warm glow on the band of roving musicians who visit the homes of those who work at the church schools. Many decorate the outsides of their homes with oil lamps during this week.

People gather at churches on Christmas Eve, where celebrations begin, accompanied by ringing **bells**, exploding firecrackers, and pipe and drum music. They go home after the services, but gather again at around three in the morning for religious processions honoring the birth of **Jesus**. Worshipers carry crosses, torches, flags, lit candles, and richly decorated ceremonial umbrellas. Priests in formal robes also march in the procession. They chant religious verses in the

Syriac language, covered by canopies held aloft on poles by devout believers. The processions end at the church. Then everyone files inside for a Christmas morning service that concludes at dawn.

On Christmas Day people leave off fasting and celebrate with rich and delicious foods, including meat curry and bread made with rice flour and coconut paste. Visits to the homes of relatives also take place.

Further Reading

Griffin, Robert H., and Ann H. Shurgin, eds. *The Folklore of World Holidays.* Second edition. Detroit, Mich.: Gale, 1999.
Tucker, Cathy C. *Christmas Worldwide.* Philadelphia, Pa.: Xlibris, 2000.
Wernecke, Herbert H. *Celebrating Christmas Around the World.* 1962. Reprint. Detroit, Mich.: Omnigraphics, 1999.

Web Site

Kerala Journal has posted "A Boy's Easter, and Christmas too," an essay by Thomas Palakeel, a professor of English literature at Bradley University. It describes a boy's Christmas in Kerala, India: http://www.shelterbelt.com/KJ/eastchrist.html

Iran, Christmas in

Ninety-nine percent of the citizens of Iran, or Persia, are Muslims. Christians, members of the Bahai faith, Jews, and others make up the remaining one percent. The very small number of Christians means that Christmas celebrations in Iran generally revolve around quiet church and home observances. Nevertheless, in the capital city of Tehran, shops located in the Armenian quarter of the city display **Nativity scenes** in their windows as the holiday draws near and Christian families shop for the upcoming festival (*see also* **Armenia, Christmas in**). Many Iranian Christians are of Armenian and Assyrian descent. Most are members of some branch of the Eastern Church, which is composed of Christians whose traditions of worship developed in the Middle East, eastern Europe and north Africa. Eastern Christians fast during **Advent**. Iranian Christians call this period of spiritual preparation for the coming of Christ at Christmas time the "Little Fast." This name distinguishes it from the Easter festival's Lenten fast, which they call the "Great Fast."

On Christmas Eve Iranian churches hold special services, which usually include a **Nativity play** that retells the story of **Jesus'** birth. Iranians end their Christmas fast with the bread and wine taken during the rite of Holy Communion (Eucharist) at this service. Church services also take place on Christmas Day.

Iranian Christians have incorporated two western Christmas traditions into their celebrations: the **Christmas tree** and the gift giver *Baba Noel*, a Middle Eastern version of **Father Christmas** or **Santa Claus**. On Christmas Day children delight in opening the presents they discover under the tree. In past times most children received one modest, homemade **gift**—often new clothing—slipped gently under their pillow. Delighted with this practical gift, they paraded about in their new clothes all week long. Now they scamper to the tree on Christmas morning to find a number of gifts waiting for them. Adult family members also give one another presents. In addition, friends and family visit one another on Christmas Day. Visiting children are offered packets of sweets. Iranian children sometimes celebrate Christmas with egg-tapping **games** similar to those played by children around the world at Easter time.

Iranian Christians traditionally enjoy a kind of chicken stew, called *harisa*, for their Christmas dinner, as well as a pastry dessert called *kada*. Iranian Christians sometimes refer to the festival as the "Little Feast." This name distinguishes it as a holiday of less importance than Easter, which is known as the "Great Feast."

Though today their numbers are few, Christians of Assyrian, Armenian, and Chaldean descent have lived in Iran since the fourth and fifth centuries. The country's association with Christmas dates back even further, however. Some writers believe that the **Magi**, the wise men who brought the infant Jesus gifts of **gold**, **frankincense** and **myrrh**, came from this ancient land.

Further Reading

Bowler, Gerry. *The World Encyclopedia of Christmas*. Toronto, Ontario, Canada: McClelland and Stewart, 2000.

Griffin, Robert H., and Ann H. Shurgin, eds. *The Folklore of World Holidays*. Second edition. Detroit, Mich.: Gale Research, 1999.

Wernecke, Herbert H. *Celebrating Christmas Around the World*. 1962. Reprint. Detroit, Mich.: Omnigraphics, 1999.

Iraq, Christmas in

The vast majority of Iraqis are Muslims. Christians make up less than five percent of the population of this Middle Eastern nation. The majority of them embrace some form of Eastern Christianity, that is, traditions of Christian worship and belief that developed in the Middle East, north Africa, and eastern Europe. Some come from minority ethnic groups, such as the Assyrians and Chaldeans, and represent remnants of ancient Christian communities. Iraqi Christians belong to many different denominations, including the Syrian, Greek, and Armenian Orthodox and Catholic churches, the Coptic Church, the Assyrian (or Nestorian) Church, and the Chaldean Church. A few Western Christians, that is, Roman Catholics and Protestants, live in Iraq as well.

Christmas observances among the many Christian denominations vary. Yet everyone goes to religious services on Christmas Eve or Day. Iraqi Christians also celebrate the holiday by sharing a sumptuous dinner with family members and friends. Moreover, they exchange **gifts** said to come from the Iraqi gift bringer, *Baba Noel*—an adaptation of **Father Christmas** or **Santa Claus**. Offering holiday hospitality to friends and neighbors is an Iraqi Christmas tradition. In the capital city of Baghdad, people visit one another's homes in the week between Christmas and **New Year's Day**, giving and receiving lavish welcomes. In the countryside village residents may sit down together to a communal Christmas meal, often featuring roast lamb.

Many Iraqis celebrate Christmas by putting up a **Christmas tree** in their home. This custom is not limited to Christians, however. Many Muslims, too, have embraced this tradition as a means of enjoying a bit of holiday fun and as a way of decorating their home for the new year.

Further Reading

Bowler, Gerry. *The World Encyclopedia of Christmas.* Toronto, Ontario, Canada: McClelland and Stewart, 2000.

Kaplow, Larry. "Holidays Are Muted in Iraq: But Muslims, Christians Share Their Celebrations, and Baba Noel Will Visit Many Homes Despite Bleak Economy and Recent U.S. Air Strikes." *The Atlanta Journal and Constitution* (December 24, 1998): A08.

Wernecke, Herbert H. *Celebrating Christmas Around the World.* 1962. Reprint. Detroit, Mich.: Omnigraphics, 1999.

Ireland, Christmas in

In Ireland families prepare for Christmas by baking cakes and buying candles. The roads and bus stations are crowded on Christmas Eve as people journey home to spend Christmas with their families.

Christmas Preparations

Women bake the **Christmas cake** as early as October or November. This rich caramel cake, studded with dried fruits and nuts and fortified with brandy, mellows and improves as it ages. Most people living in Ireland are Roman Catholics, and many observe special devotions during **Advent**, a four-week period of spiritual preparation before Christmas. In addition, many people give their homes a thorough cleaning and write their **Christmas cards** in the weeks before Christmas. As Christmas Day draws near, people begin shopping for food and **gifts**. Nowadays this may include buying a **Christmas tree**, an imported Christmas custom which became popular in recent years. The Irish also preserve the more traditional **Nativity scene**. Many families set up their Nativity scene a few days before Christmas.

Christmas Candles

On Christmas Eve most Irish families place a lighted candle in the front window. The largest front window gets the largest candle, a white, red, green, or blue candle as much as two feet tall. Many families illuminate all the windows in their homes with **Christmas candles**. In past eras most families fashioned holders for these candles out of turnips. Today many people buy candleholders for this purpose.

One old tradition suggests that the youngest child in the house named Mary light the candles. Many families walk about their neighborhood on Christmas Eve, admiring the sight of so many illuminated windows. Legend has it that this custom began hundreds of years ago, at a time when Ireland's stern, English Protestant rulers forbade priests to celebrate the Catholic mass. People placed lighted candles in windows as a signal to Catholic clergy that priests would be welcome to say mass in their home.

Another legend attributes the practice to an old folk belief. According to this belief, each year on Christmas Eve **Mary** and **Joseph** once again roam the earth, reenacting their search for shelter in **Bethlehem**. A lighted candle acts as a beacon, drawing the Holy Family to homes where they will be warmly welcomed. Irish immigrants brought the tradition of placing a lighted candle in the window at Christmas time to other countries, including the United States.

Christmas Eve in Times Past

In past eras the Irish observed December 24 as a fast day, eating no food except a meatless meal in the evening. They spent Christmas Eve at home, telling stories and singing songs. Many believed spirits walked abroad on Christmas Eve and deemed it wiser not to venture outdoors after dark. At about an hour before midnight, church **bells** all over Ireland began to ring. This tolling, known as the "Devil's funeral" or the **Devil's knell**, announced the death of the Devil, who was believed to expire annually on Christmas Eve with the birth of **Jesus** Christ. On Christmas morning many people attended a very early church service, known as "First Light" mass.

Christmas Eve Today

Today many people still sit down to a meatless meal on Christmas Eve, often some combination of fish, potatoes, and vegetables. Some people also observe an old custom whereby the man of house prepares the potato soup for the family in a ceremonial way. Irish children customarily hang up their Christmas **stockings** on Christmas Eve. In recent years it has become popular to attend **Midnight Mass** later that evening. Before going to bed some families put more wood on the fire, place some food on the table, and make sure the candles in the windowsills are still lit. Some may also leave a door unlocked, another symbolic gesture welcoming the Holy Family to enter and refresh themselves.

Christmas Day

The Irish like to spend Christmas Day with their immediate family. The day's events revolve around Christmas dinner, the most festive meal of the year. Before sitting down to their own dinner, many families send hot meals or foodstuffs to less fortunate people living nearby. The Irish view these acts of charity as central to the celebration of Christmas. In past times a traditional Irish Christmas dinner usually featured spiced, boiled beef. Nowadays many families prefer roast turkey or goose. The meal closes with the long-awaited Christmas cake and, often, **plum pudding** as well.

St. Stephen's Day

December 26, **St. Stephen's Day**, is a national holiday in Ireland. The **wren hunt** and forms of **mumming**, such as mummers' plays, entertain many people on that day. The wren hunters often contribute part of their earnings to fund the St. Stephen's Day dances popular throughout Ireland on the evening of December 26. Other traditional St. Stephen's Day pastimes include sporting events, especially steeplechasing and fox hunting.

New Year's Day

In past times **New Year's Day** wasn't much celebrated in Ireland. On New Year's Eve, however, many people employed folk charms to ward off hunger in the coming year. Some recommended eating a big meal on New Year's Eve to set a pattern of consumption for the new year. Others suggested knocking a loaf of bread or a cake against house or barn doors, and reciting a bit of verse that welcomed happiness and plenty and rejected hunger and want. **First-footing**, another old New Year's custom, is still practiced in Ireland. In recent years the government made New Year's Day a holiday. Now, more and more people celebrate New Year's Eve by staying up late, drinking, and going to parties.

Epiphany

Epiphany, which falls on January 6, is the last day of the **Christmas season** in Ireland. Epiphany is also called **Twelfth Night**, "Little Christmas," or even "Women's Christmas." This last name reflects the old custom of serving a light dinner on Epiphany, featuring sherry and dainties, foods thought to be particularly appealing to women. Many people put three candles in their windows on Epiphany, one for each of the Three Kings, or **Magi**. The figurines representing the Three Kings finally arrive in Irish Nativity scenes on this day. The next day Christmas decorations are removed and stored until the following Christmas season.

Further Reading

Moran, Rena. *Christmas in Ireland*. Chicago: World Book, 1995.

Italy, Christmas in

Italians favor the **Nativity scene** above all other Christmas decorations. As Christmas approaches, they appear in churches, homes, shops, and public places of all kinds. These images of the Holy Family illustrate two important themes in Italian Christmas celebrations: religious observance and family togetherness.

Christmas Markets

As the **Christmas season** draws near, families began to frequent the **Christmas markets** that spring up in cities and towns across Italy. Here they find all manner of Christmas merchandise, including sweets and other foods, flowers, Christmas decorations, clothes, toys, and more. Balloon sellers, musicians, and other entertainers amuse shoppers as they wander through the stalls.

Pre-Christmas Celebrations and Observances

Along Italy's Adriatic coast many people celebrate **St. Nicholas's Day** on December 6. Religious processions are held and adults give sweets to children. The remains of this fourth-century saint now rest in the cathedral in Bari, Italy (*see also* **St. Nicholas**).

Sicilians celebrate **St. Lucy's Day** on December 13. Children leave their **shoes** outdoors hoping that the saint will fill them with treats during the night.

In some Italian cities, such as Rome, the unlikely sound of bagpipes announces that Christmas is near. Following an old custom, **shepherds** from the surrounding mountainous areas visit the cities with their bagpipes around mid-December. Called *zampognari,* they make music in the markets, in front of churches, and alongside Nativity scenes. In the past they would sometimes go door to door, playing in front of the family's Nativity scene in exchange for tips.

Between December 16 and December 24 many Italians participate in Christmas novenas, special prayer services held on nine consecutive days. The novenas end with **Midnight Mass** on Christmas Eve.

Nativity Scenes and Ceppos

Many writers believe that St. Francis (c. 1181-1226), born in Assisi, Italy, created the first Nativity scene. According to legend, he staged a living Nativity scene in 1224 in a cave near the Italian village of Greccio. Francis hoped that the scene would impress viewers with the wonder of Christ's birth. The custom quickly caught on. Today, Italians still cherish their Nativity scenes. Churches and homes throughout Italy display these scenes in the weeks before Christmas. In some Italian villages, people create living Nativity scenes on Christmas Eve. Costumed villagers and visitors make a pilgrimage to the life-sized stable, where a living **Mary, Joseph,** and baby **Jesus** await them. Nativity scenes are so popular in Italy that they may even be found in gas stations, city squares, airports, post offices, railway stations, and shop windows. Italians place the baby Jesus figurine in his crib on Christmas Eve. The Three Kings, or **Magi,** often do not reach the manger until **Epiphany**.

Although the Nativity scene is the focus of home Christmas decorations in Italy, many families also construct a *ceppo,* or Christmas **pyramid**. Ceppo means "log" in Italian, and some researchers believe that it acquired that name because it replaced the once-popular **Yule log**. This pyramidal arrangement of shelves may be used to display **Christmas symbols**, sweets, cards, candles, and small **gifts**.

Christmas Eve

Many Italians begin Christmas Eve with a sumptuous meal. The meal is all the more satisfying for those who follow the Roman Catholic custom of fasting on Christmas Eve. Traditionally, the Christmas Eve meal is meatless, although many delicious seafood, grain, and vegetable courses may be served. Eel is a favorite main course for this meal. As midnight draws near, many Italians leaves their homes to attend Midnight Mass. One lucky group will be able to attend mass at St. Peter's Church in the Vatican, where the pope himself conducts the service. Television stations all over the world broadcast this service live from the Vatican.

Christmas Day

Italians usually spend Christmas Day enjoying the company of their families. The Italians eat Christmas dinner at midday on December 25. In Italy the menu varies from region to region. Both roast turkey and ham are popular main courses, and a bowl of lentils with sausage is often served as a side dish. In addition, many Italians serve *panettone*, a sweet Christmas bread originally from Milan, as a Christmas dessert (*see also* **Christmas Cake**). *Amaretti*, almond cookies, *cannoli*, tubes of pastry filled with sweetened ricotta cheese and candied fruit, and *strufoli*, fried dough balls, often appear on the dessert table. Sometimes children write letters to their parents, which they place next to their father's plate. The letters usually offer an apology for past misbehavior and a promise of better behavior to come. The letters also provide the children an opportunity to show off their handwriting.

New Year

Italian folklore teaches that the first person one encounters after midnight on **New Year's** Eve determines one's luck for the year to come (*see also* **Firstfooting**). The luckiest person to encounter is a young, healthy man. Meeting a priest means you will attend a funeral, perhaps your own, whereas meeting a child means you may die young. If the first person you encounter is a woman, you will have bad luck in the coming year.

Epiphany

La **Befana**, the traditional Italian gift bringer, arrives on January 6, Epiphany. Many children write letters to La Befana in the weeks preceding Epiphany, describing the kind of gifts they would like to receive (*see also* **Children's Letters**). On Epiphany Eve they leave their **stockings** by the fire, and the next morning they find them filled with presents. Many young people celebrate Epiphany by gathering in the streets and welcoming Epiphany and La Befana with horn blasts and other forms of noisemaking. In some parts of Italy **Santa Claus** now competes with La Befana for the affections of Italian children.

In some Italian cities people give gifts to traffic policemen on Epiphany. As the day wears on, mounds of presents, such as fruit baskets, wine, and food, pile up around the stands from which they direct traffic. This practical custom probably offers those who practice it the hope that small traffic infractions will be ignored in the coming year.

Further Reading

Del Re, Gerard, and Patricia Del Re. *The Christmas Almanack*. Garden City, N.Y.: Doubleday, 1979.

Ross, Corinne. *Christmas in Italy*. Chicago: World Book-Childcraft International, 1979.

Spicer, Dorothy Gladys. *The Book of Festivals*. 1937. Reprint. Detroit, Mich.: Omnigraphics, 1990.

It's a Wonderful Life

Many Americans view the 1946 movie *It's a Wonderful Life*, directed by Frank Capra, as the definitive American Christmas story. Some even call it the American version of Charles Dickens's classic Christmas tale, *A Christmas Carol*. The movie tells the story of a responsible but ambitious young man, George Bailey, who never realizes his dream of leaving his hometown for adventure and a big career. Aware of how his departure will hurt the fortunes of others, he decides instead to stay home in order to serve his family and his community. The story begins on a Christmas Eve after World War II, when a crisis enters George's life and causes him to reconsider the value of all he's done. The final, happy ending celebrates the worth of George's achievements and the importance of friendship.

The Greatest Gift

Frank Capra based his movie on a short story called "The Greatest Gift" by Philip Van Doren Stern. The main character, George Pratt, despairs over the boredom and triviality of his life. On Christmas Eve he decides to commit suicide by throwing himself over the edge of a bridge. Suddenly a man whom he didn't realize was there begins to talk to him. George tells this stranger that he wishes he had never been born. The stranger, an **angel**, grants this wish. George returns to town and visits his family and place of business, finding things and people changed for the worse. He comes back to the bridge and begs the angel for the opportunity to live again. The angel restores everything as it was, and George returns home, realizing that any life, no matter how seemingly unimportant, is a great **gift**.

Stern penned the brief story in 1938. Unable to find a publisher, he printed up 200 copies of the story as a 24-page pamphlet and sent them to his friends at Christmas time in 1943. His agent Shirley Collier thought the story would make a good film. She convinced Stern to let her try to sell the story to a Hollywood studio. In 1944 RKO Pictures bought the film rights to "The Greatest Gift." In that same year *Good Housekeeping* magazine published the short story under the title "The Man Who Never Was." RKO thought the story would provide a suitable lead role for Cary Grant, but was not satisfied with the ideas their screenwriters came up with for turning the short story into a movie script.

The Story Becomes a Script

In 1945 director Frank Capra, just back from his World War II stint in the armed services, bought the screen rights to Stern's story from RKO. His first concern was to flesh out the brief and thinly developed original story. Capra worked on developing the material himself, but also hired screenwriters Albert Hackett and Frances Goodrich to come up with a script. In the end, the film lists Hackett, Goodrich, and Capra as the authors of the screenplay, and notes that additional scenes were added by Jo Swerling.

Capra loved the new, expanded story. He thought the plot's exploration of the dark themes of despair and contemplated suicide as well as the uplifting themes of love and service to others would be perfect for his first postwar movie.

The Script Becomes a Film

As Hackett and Goodrich worked on the script, Capra sought the needed actors. He wanted, and got, Jimmy Stewart to play the lead role of George Bailey. Jean Arthur, his first choice to play the role of Mary Bailey, turned him down, however. He considered several more actresses for the part, including Olivia De Havilland, before offering the role to Donna Reed, who accepted. Capra, a meticulous planner, thought as deeply about the casting of the film's small roles as he did its starring roles. When he had finally assembled the perfect cast, he was ready to begin making the movie.

The film's original budget totaled $1,700,000, but the final cost came in at over $3,000,000. A good portion of this money went to building sets and creating special effects. Set designers recreated several sections of Bedford Falls, the town in which the action takes place, at RKO's Encino Ranch. Covering four acres of land, this was among the longest sets that had yet been created for a movie filmed in the United States. The Main Street set stretched three blocks in length and included 75 buildings and shops. The center of the street was lined with 20 real oak trees, uprooted elsewhere and replanted on the set. The special effects crew labored for three weeks in order to produce the snowstorm that takes place on the night that George Bailey decides to commit suicide. In the process they devised a new way of generating artificial snow, for which they were given a Certificate of Honorable Mention at the 1947 Academy Awards. Although the beautifully filmed wintertime scenes convinced movie viewers, the thermometer on the set registered temperatures in the 80s and 90s on the day they were shot.

It's a Wonderful Life

The film was released on December 20, 1946. It was not a box office hit, nor did it inspire an unbroken string of rave reviews. Some commentators think that the film's unusual blend of romance, comedy, and dark emotional drama may have confused viewers, thereby contributing to a less than stunning box office return. Moreover, some of America's most prestigious periodicals panned the movie as cloyingly sentimental and unrealistic. Nevertheless, the film charmed scores of other reviewers, and perhaps more importantly, thousands of fans. In addition, it won five Academy Award nominations: Best Actor, Best Picture, Best Director, Best Film Editing, and Best Sound. Though *It's a Wonderful Life* did not receive any Academy Awards, Capra did take home a "Golden Globe" award for best director of the year from the Hollywood Foreign Correspondents Association.

It's a Wonderful Life was the first movie Capra made with Liberty Films, an independent studio formed by Frank Capra, George Stevens, William Wyler, and Sam Briskin after World War II. Financial difficulties soon downed the fledgling company, however. Capra and his partners sold it to Paramount Pictures in 1947, and along with it, the right to any future profits garnered by *It's a Wonderful Life*. The film languished under Paramount's care, and when its original copyright ran out in 1974, no one bothered to renew it. At this point television stations all over the country began to show *It's a Wonderful Life* at Christmas time, because they didn't have to pay for it. These showings revived the interest of older fans and introduced new audiences to the film. This once-forgotten film has now become a beloved Hollywood classic.

Looking Back

Many movie viewers can imagine no one else but Jimmy Stewart in the role of George Bailey. Although Stewart made over 75 films, *It's a Wonderful Life* remained his favorite. Moreover, he received more fan mail about that movie than any other he ever made.

Donna Reed recalled working harder for Capra than she had for any other director. Still, she later described her days on the set as fun and inspired.

369

Most of the cast and crew fondly remember their participation in *It's a Wonderful Life*. The same cannot be said of music director Dimitri Tiomkin. Tiomkin had chosen "Ode to Joy" as the song for the last scene in the movie. Capra overruled him and substituted **"Auld Lang Syne"** instead. He also cut some of the tunes Tiomkin had written specially for the film and replaced them with music written by other composers. Furious, Tiomkin never worked with Capra again. Screenwriters Hackett and Goodrich, too, grew to dislike Capra, who they felt did not respect their contribution to the film.

Though he made scores of movies over his lifetime, Capra loved *It's a Wonderful Life* best of all his creations. He explained his preference in the following way:

> *It's a Wonderful Life* sums up my philosophy of filmmaking. First, to exalt the *worth* of the individual. Second, to champion man — plead his causes, protest any degradation of his dignity, spirit, or divinity. And third, to dramatize the viability of the individual — as in the theme of the film itself.
>
> I wanted *It's a Wonderful Life* to say what Walt Whitman said to every man, woman, and babe in the world: "The sum of all known reverences I add up in you, whoever you are. . . ." I wanted it to reflect the compelling words of Fra Giovanni of nearly five centuries ago: "The gloom of the world is but a shadow. Behind it, yet within reach, is joy. There is a radiance and glory in the darkness, could we but see, and to see we have only to look. I beseech you to look." . . . For myself, I can only say . . . it was my kind of film for my kind of people [Basinger, 1986, ix].

Further Reading

Basinger, Jeanine. *The It's a Wonderful Life Book*. New York: Alfred A. Knopf, 1986.

Cahill, Marie. *It's A Wonderful Life: A Hollywood Classic*. New York: Smithmark, 1993.

Hawkins, Jimmy. *It's a Wonderful Life: The Fiftieth Anniversary Scrapbook*. Philadelphia, Penn.: Courage Books, 1996.

McBride, Joseph. *Frank Capra: The Catastrophe of Success*. New York: Simon and Schuster, 1992.

Munby, Jonathan. "A Hollywood Carol's Wonderful Life." In Mark Connelly, ed. *Christmas at the Movies*. New York: I. B. Tauris and Company, 2000.

Scherele, Victor, and William Turner Levy. *The Films of Frank Capra*. Secaucus, N.J.: Citadel Press, 1977.

Stern, Philip Van Doren. *The Greatest Gift*. New York: Penguin Studio, 1996.

Ivy

From the **Christmas tree** to the **kissing bough**, decorations made of **greenery** have adorned our Christmas celebrations for centuries. Of all the evergreens used to represent the season, ivy's connection to Christmas is perhaps the most obscure. Known to botanists as *Hedera helix*, ivy has enjoyed a long association with the **Christmas season** and, before that, with various pagan myths and celebrations.

Ancient Beliefs and Customs

Evergreen plants, such as ivy, **holly**, and pine, stay green all year round. For many ancient peoples, this special property converted these plants into reminders of the promise of rebirth and eternal life. The pagan peoples of northern Europe decorated their homes with evergreens such as ivy for their winter festival, **Yule**. Perhaps they wished to honor and imitate ivy's triumph over the cold and darkness, for the plant not only remains green during winter but also bears fruit during this harsh season. The ancient Egyptians associated ivy with Osiris, a god who died and was resurrected. To the Greeks ivy symbolized Dionysus, the god of wine. The Greeks told a legend that explained this connection. A nymph had once danced herself to death at the feet of Dionysus in a frenzy of adoration. In recognition of her devotion the god changed her body into the ivy plant, which casts an adoring embrace around all it encounters.

Further to the south, the ancient Romans also decorated their homes with greenery during their winter festival, **Saturnalia**. In addition, they exchanged branches of ivy, holly, and other evergreen plants as symbols of their good wishes for the upcoming new year. Ivy also became the symbol of the Roman god of wine, Bacchus. Wine sellers in ancient Rome sometimes used ivy as a symbol of their trade. A bush or bunch of evergreens, usually ivy or box, tied to the end of a pole was a generally recognized symbol of a wineshop. Pliny the Elder, a famous scholar of ancient Rome, believed that consuming ivy berries before drinking wine or ivy leaves with one's wine could prevent drunkenness. Modern researchers, however, have discovered ivy to be toxic when ingested in large enough quantities.

Medieval Beliefs and Customs

As literacy was uncommon in the Middle Ages, people continued to use ivy and images of ivy or other greenery to signify a tavern or wineshop. In Britain the decorated pole used by the Romans became known as an alepole or an alestake. Long after lettered signs replaced these old icons, many British taverns retained related names, such as The Ivy Bush or The Greenwood Tree. Ivy not only represented wine, but also was believed to cure drunkenness. Likewise, imbibing from a bowl of ivy wood was thought to cancel out the effects of alcohol.

Some folklorists believe that holly and ivy represented the male and female principles in nature to pagan peoples of northern Europe, and that these early beliefs lingered on in the songs and folklore of later eras. Many medieval and Renaissance songs and **Christmas carols** tell of a rivalry between holly and ivy, in which holly represents masculinity, and ivy femininity.

In early Christian times, the Church resisted the pagan custom of making seasonal decorations out of greenery. The sixth-century second Council of Braga forbade Christians the use of green boughs in home decoration. As time went on, however, Christianity adopted the holly and ivy of pagan winter celebrations, bending their significance to Christian ends. The clinging ivy plant became a reminder of the soul's dependence on God. The words to the Christmas carol "The Holly and the Ivy" depict another Christian reinterpretation of these seasonal symbols. Due to its continuing association with drunkenness, however, some Christians thought it disrespectful to incorporate ivy into Christmas decorations.

Later Beliefs and Customs

Many diverse, and sometimes conflicting, beliefs and customs concerning ivy have been recorded during the last two centuries. Because it often grew in cemeteries, ivy acquired an association with death. Some people believed it was therefore unlucky to bring ivy plants indoors. Its persistent association with drunkenness also fueled this belief, especially in continental Europe. Nevertheless, because of its decorative potential, ivy became a favorite houseplant in the Victorian age (*see also* **Victorian England, Christmas in**).

In the "language of flowers" (a set of meanings attributed to flowers and plants which became popular in the eighteenth and nineteenth centuries), the encircling vines of the ivy plant represented fidelity and undying love. Many attributed magical properties to the plant, especially the ability to reveal the identity of future mates. In **England** an ivy leaf dropped into a dish of water on **New Year's** Eve, covered and left until **Twelfth Night**, could reveal one's own fortune for the upcoming year. If the leaf remained green, one would enjoy good health, but if the leaf spotted, illness threatened. Overall deterioration of the leaf signaled death.

Traces of the old association with femininity and the battle of the sexes echo through the folklore associated with ivy. According to some, holly dealt good luck to men, while ivy bestowed good luck to women. As late as several hundred years ago, English folk customs still connected competing figures known as the "holly boy" and the "ivy girl" with a number of wintertime observances. Ivy, often alongside holly, continued as a symbol of Christmas festivities during the nineteenth century. The Victorians wove it into kissing boughs, greenery swags, and other seasonal adornments, and embellished many a **Christmas card** with its image.

Although less popular than in Victorian times, ivy has gently entwined itself around the edges of contemporary Christmas celebrations. Images of this ancient seasonal favorite still trim our Christmas cards, **wrapping paper**, and other holiday decorations.

Further Reading

Segall, Barbara. *The Holly and the Ivy*. New York: Clarkson Potter, 1991.

Jesse Tree

The Jesse tree gets its name from a prediction made by the Old Testament prophet Isaiah describing the rise of a great, new Jewish leader as "a branch" growing "from the stock of Jesse" (Isaiah 11:1). In reference to this prophecy, medieval artists frequently painted portraits of **Jesus** and his ancestors on the limbs of a tree, with Jesus at its crown and Jesse at its root. This image was called a "Jesse tree." The identity of Jesus' ancestors played an important role in establishing his identity as the Messiah. In recognition of this fact, both Gospel Nativity stories included an account of Jesus' genealogy. Chapter one of the **Gospel according to Matthew**, which directly precedes Matthew's account of Christ's birth, begins by listing Jesus' ancestors. The **Gospel according to Luke** (3:23-38) offers a slightly different account of Jesus' ancestry (*see also* **Gospel Accounts of Christmas**).

The Jesse tree has long served as a symbol of Jesus' ancestry in Christian art. In recent times, however, people have begun to use the image of the Jesse tree to adapt the modern **Christmas tree** to specifically Christian ends. **Ornaments** representing events in the lives of Jesus' ancestors are hung on an evergreen tree or tree branch. Some people add symbols for other biblical figures and events as well. For example, Moses may be represented by stone tablets, David by a six-pointed star, Jonah by a whale, and Judith by a sword. Decorated this way, the evergreen becomes a living Jesse tree.

Further Reading

Augustine, Peg, comp. *Come to Christmas.* Nashville, Tenn.: Abingdon Press, 1993.

Metcalfe, Edna. *The Trees of Christmas.* Nashville, Tenn.: Abingdon Press, 1969.

Jesus

Christians view Jesus of Nazareth as the founder of their faith. He spent his adult life as a spiritual teacher and healer who moved from place to place, teaching people about God. In one Bible passage Jesus describes himself as "anointed" by God to "preach good news to the poor . . . proclaim release to the captives and recovering of sight to the blind, to set at liberty those who are oppressed," and "to proclaim the acceptable year of the Lord" (Luke 4:18-19). Christian scripture also describes Jesus as the Son of God whose sacrificial death renewed humanity's relationship with God and conferred the forgiveness of sins.

The Easter festival commemorates the life, death, and resurrection of the adult Jesus. The Christmas festival, by contrast, celebrates his coming into the world. Theologians call this event the Incarnation, a word that literally means "to be made flesh."

The Incarnation

"Incarnation" refers to the idea that Jesus was both human and divine, and that in him God came to earth in human form. The joy and hope inspired by this event has found a multitude of expressions in the world's Christmas celebrations.

In the **Gospel according to Matthew** and the **Gospel according to Luke**, the accounts given of Jesus' birth state that his mother, **Mary**, conceived Jesus by the power of God's Holy Spirit while still a virgin. Thus Jesus was both human and divine, an idea also expressed in two of his biblical titles, "Son of God" and "Son of Man."

Commentators have remarked that the stories of Jesus' birth reveal something of the nature of the Christian God. The stories show that God is not distant and unmoved by human suffering, but rather cares about particular people in particular places and so enters into the world to effect good. Indeed, Mary is directed by the **angel Gabriel** to name her son Jesus, which means "God saves" or "God heals." Christian scripture expresses Jesus' care for his followers by describing him as a **shepherd**.

In recent years, some theologians have begun to question traditional views of the Incarnation and the Virgin Birth. They point out that "son of God" was a title that the ancient Hebrews gave to people who played a special role in bringing God's help to humanity. The title did not imply divine identity, but rather service rendered to God. These thinkers suggest that the Christian notion of a divine Son of God came about after Jesus' death, as people struggled to understand the nature of Jesus' spiritual authority and to define his identity. The Virgin Birth has similarly been questioned. Some theologians today accord it greater symbolic than literal significance, suggesting that the story of the Virgin Birth was invented to symbolize Jesus' divine origins to a first-century audience. Others interpret Mary's virginity as a symbolic representation of her spiritual wholeness.

Jesus the Christ

Jesus' followers also gave him the title "Christ," which comes from the Greek word for "anointed." Among the ancient Jews high religious leaders underwent a ceremony in which they were anointed with oil. Jesus' followers viewed him as the one chosen and anointed by heaven to reconcile humanity with God and so came to call him Jesus Christ.

Jesus' Birth According to John

Although most people refer to the accounts of Jesus' birth given in Matthew and Luke as the Bible's two Infancy Narratives, the Gospel according to John offers another, more philosophical account of Jesus' coming into the world. It, too, emphasizes Jesus' divine nature and explains that God came into the world through Jesus that humans might come to know God. In this poetical passage Jesus' divine essence is referred to as "the Word" and as "light":

> In the beginning was the Word, and the Word was with God, and the Word was God. He was in the beginning with God; all things were made through him, and without him was not anything made that was made. In him was life, and the life

was the light of men. The light shines in the darkness, and the darkness has not overcome it.

There was a man sent from God, whose name was John. He came for testimony, to bear witness to the light, that all might believe through him. He was not the light, but came to bear witness to the light.

The true light that enlightens every man was coming into the world. He was in the world, and the world was made through him, yet the world knew him not. He came to his own home, and his own people received him not. But to all who received him, who believed in his name, he gave power to become children of God; who were born, not of blood nor of the will of the flesh nor of the will of man, but of God.

And the Word became flesh and dwelt among us, full of grace and truth; we have beheld his glory, glory as of the only Son from the Father [John 1:1-14].

Creeds and Councils

John's passage concerning Jesus' birth raises theological issues not addressed in the other two Gospel accounts. Several hundred years after the birth of Jesus, theologians were still debating the exact nature of Jesus' identity and the mechanics of how he came into being and into the world. Christian leaders decided that they needed to settle these debates once and for all. So they held councils in which they hammered out a general consensus on these matters, creating in the process various creeds and doctrines of the church. Especially important were the Nicene Creed, formulated at the Council of Nicea in 325, and the doctrines that came out of the Council of Chalcedon in 451.

The Festival of Jesus' Birth

The holiday devoted to the celebration of Jesus' birth, which we call Christmas, dates back to the year 336. It was set for **December 25,** an already important date in the ancient world. Centuries later, Christians would become concerned with establishing the year of Jesus' birth, which had not been recorded in scripture or other early Christian writings (*see* **Jesus, Year of Birth**).

The debate over when Jesus was born continues to this day, as does discussion concerning the appropriate way in which to celebrate Jesus' birth. Five hundred years ago, the **Puritans** objected to celebrations that revolved around eating, drinking, masquerading, and **game** playing. More recently some Americans have begun to question the degree of **commercialism** that has invaded the festival. Some feel, like the Puritans of old, that contemporary American Christmas celebrations have become so divorced from the story of Jesus' birth that the holiday is more a secular than a religious one. Many are searching for ways to link the spiritual teachings contained in the story of Jesus' birth to their own Christmas celebrations. Indeed many devotional books advise Christians of various denominations on how to prepare their own heart and spirit to receive the Christ Child (*see also* **Advent**). Some who do not identify themselves as Christians are looking for ways to celebrate the holiday's secular themes and its universal spiritual themes, while disregarding specific Christian doctrines. These themes include generosity and **gift** giving, the celebration of birth and new life, the joys of winter, and the return of the sun (*see also* **Winter Solstice**).

Further Reading

Brown, Raymond E. *An Adult Christ at Christmas*. Collegeville, Minn.: Liturgical Press, 1988.

———. *The Birth of the Messiah*. Updated edition. New York: Doubleday, 1993.

Burns, Charlene P. E. *Divine Becoming*. Minneapolis, Minn.: Fortress Press, 2002.

Cross, F. L., and E. A. Livingstone, eds. "Incarnation, the." In their *The Oxford Dictionary of the Christian Church*. Second edition, revised. Oxford, England: Oxford University Press, 1983.

Gregg, D. Larry. "Incarnation." In David Noel Freedman, ed. *Eerdmans Bible Dictionary*. Grand Rapids, Mich.: William B. Eerdmans Publishing Company, 2000.

Hick, John. *The Metaphor of God Incarnate*. Louisville, Ky.: Westminster/John Knox Press, 1993.

Horsley, Richard A. *The Liberation of Christmas: The Infancy Narratives in Social Context*. New York: Crossroad, 1989.

Maier, Paul L. *In the Fullness of Time*. Grand Rapids, Mich.: Kregel, 1991.

Matera, Frank J. "Incarnation." In Paul J. Achtemeier, ed. *The HarperCollins Bible Dictionary*. Revised edition. San Francisco, Calif.: HarperSanFrancisco, 1996.

Raya, Joseph. *Abundance of Love*. West Newton, Mass.: Educational Service Department, Melkite Greek Catholic Diocese of Newton, 1989.

Weis, E. A. "Incarnation." In *New Catholic Encyclopedia*. Volume 7. New York: McGraw-Hill, 1967.

Jesus, Year of Birth

Christians celebrate the birth of Jesus on **December 25**. A quick look at the biblical accounts of the Nativity, however, reveals the fact that neither story mentions the year or the date of **Jesus'** birth (*see also* **Gospel According to Matthew; Gospel According to Luke;** and **Gospel Accounts of Christmas**). Over the centuries many scholars have tried to match details given in the two Gospel accounts of the Nativity with known historical events in order to establish the year and date of Jesus' birth. Although debate continues, most scholars now believe that Jesus was born sometime between 7 and 4 B.C.

The Date

The biblical accounts of Jesus' birth in **Bethlehem** provide only one clue as to the date of this event. Luke's Nativity story mentions **shepherds** who were spending the night with their flocks in the fields. In those days shepherds might well have spent the night with their flocks during the spring lambing season in order to aid the newborn lambs and their mothers. Historians believe that it is much less likely that shepherds would be sleeping in the fields with their flocks during the winter. This detail from Luke's account would seem to suggest that Jesus was born sometime in the spring. Nevertheless, the first celebrations of the Nativity took place in January. During the second and third centuries, a number of Christian communities began to commemorate Jesus' birth on January 6 as part of their **Epiphany** celebrations. In the middle of the fourth century,

Church officials in Rome established a separate festival to honor the Nativity. They chose to celebrate this festival on December 25, and successfully promoted it throughout the Christian world.

The Year

The scriptural accounts of the Nativity offer more, but somewhat conflicting, clues to those searching for the year of Jesus' birth. They agree in one regard, though. Both Luke's and Matthew's Nativity stories assert that Jesus was born during the reign of **Herod** the Great, king of Judea (73 B.C.-4 B.C.). The Gospel of Matthew offers an additional clue, implying that Herod died not long after Jesus' birth. Most historians agree that Herod died in the year 4 B.C., since archeological evidence points to the fact that his successors began their reigns in that year. Taken together these indications suggest that Jesus was born sometime between 7 and 4 B.C. Luke also mentions that Jesus was born during the reign of the Roman emperor Caesar Augustus (63 B.C.-14 A.D.). Augustus ruled the Roman Empire from around 42 B.C. to 14 A.D., so this information fits with the assumption that Jesus was born during the reign of Herod the Great, possibly near the time of Herod's death.

A closer look at Luke's account of the Nativity complicates matters, however. Luke declares that Jesus' birth coincided with a Roman census called for by Emperor Augustus and administered locally by Quirinius, the governor of Syria. Historians know that Quirinius became governor of Syria in 6 A.D. Furthermore, they confirm that he conducted a census of Judea around 6-7 A.D. This information fits with the claim that Jesus was born in the days of Caesar Augustus, but contradicts the claim that he was born during the reign of Herod the Great, who presumably died in 4 B.C.

Although scholars have put forward a number of ingenious proposals to reconcile the date of Quirinius's census with the date of Herod's death, most researchers agree that Luke must have erred when he wrote that Jesus was born during the time of the census. Some scholars suggest that Luke may have included the story of the census as a way of locating the birth of Jesus in Bethlehem, since Jewish scripture claimed that the Messiah would be born there. Historians who find Luke's description of the Roman census somewhat unconvincing tend to support this view. They argue that a Roman census would not require people to return to their ancestral homeplaces, since the Romans were interested in where people lived, not where their ancestors came from.

The Gospel of Luke provides another clue to the year of Jesus' birth in a later passage describing the beginning of Jesus' ministry. In chapter three Luke informs us that Jesus was about thirty years old in the fifteenth year of the reign of the Roman emperor Tiberius (42 B.C.-37 A.D.; Luke 3:1, 23). The fifteenth year of Tiberius's reign occurred between the years 27 to 28 A.D. This data fits well with the proposal that Jesus was born sometime between 7 and 4 B.C., but conflicts with a birth date of 6 to 7 A.D.

The Star

The Gospel of Matthew offers one final bit of information some scholars have used to determine the year of Jesus' birth. According to Matthew, the rising of an unusual star heralded the birth of Jesus. Many ancient peoples studied the night skies and recorded any unusual occurrences. A number of scholars have studied these ancient records in an attempt to identify possible candidates for the Christmas star and so determine the year of Christ's birth (*see also* **Star of Bethlehem**).

Most of these scholars identify the triple conjunction of 7 B.C. as the most likely candidate for the Christmas star, but recently some writers have switched their allegiance to the triple conjunction of 3-2 B.C.

In order to reconcile a Christmas star that appeared in 3-2 B.C. with the claim that Jesus was born during the reign of Herod the Great, they reject the idea that Herod died in 4 B.C. They argue instead that Herod died in 1 B.C. They point to the writings of the ancient Jewish historian Josephus to back up their claim. According to Josephus, in the year Herod died a lunar eclipse preceded Passover. Josephus also recorded a number of events that took place between the eclipse and Herod's death. In the year 4 B.C. ancient astronomers indeed recorded the occurrence of a partial lunar eclipse one month before the Jewish holiday of Passover. In the year 1 B.C., however, a full lunar eclipse occurred three months before Passover. Some scholars argue that Josephus was referring to this eclipse, reasoning that the full eclipse was the more dramatic event and therefore more likely to have impressed historians. Furthermore, because the 1 B.C. eclipse occurred approximately three months before Passover, there was time for all the events that Josephus claimed happened between the eclipse and Herod's demise to play out. This line of reasoning leads to the conclusion that Jesus was born in the years 3 to 2 B.C.

Continuing Controversy

To date scholars have not been able to reconcile every detail in Matthew's and Luke's Nativity stories with known historical events in a way that everyone can agree on. Debates over the correct date and year of Jesus' birth are nothing new. They can be traced as far back as the third century. In addition, some modern scholars now believe that Matthew and Luke intended their Nativity stories to serve as spiritually, rather than historically, accurate accounts of Jesus' birth. If so, the attempt to correlate the details reported in these stories with historically documented events is somewhat unlikely to provide us with the correct year and date of Jesus' birth.

B.C. and A.D.

Although scholars cannot agree on the year of Jesus' birth, our calendar system assumes that Jesus was born in the year 1 B.C. It divides recorded history into two eras, labeled "B.C." and "A.D." B.C. stands for "before Christ" and A.D. stands for *Anno Domini*, a Latin phrase that means "in the year of the Lord." This method of reckoning was devised in the early sixth century by a monk named Dionysus Exiguus (c. 500-c. 560). At that time people still relied upon the old Roman system for numbering years. This system reckoned the year in which Diocletian (c. 245-c. 313) was proclaimed emperor of Rome, 284 A.D., as year one. This methodology distressed Dionysus, who declared that Christians should no longer perpetuate a calendar system associated with Diocletian since he was a noted persecutor of Christians. Instead, he proposed that the birth of Jesus serve as the landmark event from which to date the dawn of a new era. Dionysus accepted the then-established date of Christmas, December 25, and the Roman date for the beginning of the new year,

January 1. He calculated the year of Jesus' birth to the best of his abilities and declared that year to be 1 B.C. Dionysus then proclaimed that the new, Christian era began seven days later on January 1, 1 A.D.

St. Bede (c. 672-735), a scholarly Anglo-Saxon monk, began the practice of dating historical events from the birth of Christ, and other writers followed his lead. This system of reckoning time gained near universal acceptance over the centuries. In recent years, however, people who object to the Christian bias implicit in this system have replaced the initials B.C. with "B.C.E.," which stands for "before common era." Accordingly, the initials A.D. are replaced with "C.E.," which stands for "common era."

Further Reading

Achtemeier, Paul J., ed. *The HarperCollins Bible Dictionary*. Revised edition. San Francisco, Calif: HarperSanFrancisco, 1996.

Begley, Sharon. "The Christmas Star—Or Was it Planets?" *Newsweek* 118, 27 (December 30, 1991): 54.

Brown, Raymond E. *The Birth of the Messiah*. New updated edition. New York: Doubleday, 1993.

Cross, F. L., and E. A. Livingstone, eds. *The Oxford Dictionary of the Christian Church*. Second edition, revised. Oxford, England: Oxford University Press, 1983.

Keck, Leander, ed. *New Interpreter's Bible: Luke, John*. Volume IX. Nashville, Tenn.: Abingdon Press, 1996.

Krupp, E. C. *Beyond the Blue Horizon*. New York: HarperCollins, 1991.

Mosley, John. *The Christmas Star*. Los Angeles, Calif.: Griffith Observatory, 1987.

Porter, J. R. *The Illustrated Guide to the Bible*. New York: Oxford University Press, 1995.

Jonkonnu

John Canoe, John Kooner, Junkanoo

At the beginning of the eighteenth century a new Christmas custom arose in the British West Indies. Called Jonkonnu, this Caribbean Christmas celebration blended African and English masquerade and **mumming** traditions. At one time Jonkonnu celebrations spread as far as the southern United States. The festival survives today in Jamaica, the Bahamas, Belize, St. Kitts-Nevis, Guyana, and Bermuda.

Jonkonnu in Jamaica

The origins of Jonkonnu reflect Jamaica's colonial history. The British seized control of Jamaica from the Spanish in 1660 and established a colonial outpost there. Although some African **slaves** already lived on the island, in the late seventeenth century the English colonists began to import slaves from west Africa in great numbers to work on their sugar plantations. The English colonists brought many cultural traditions with them to Jamaica, including the celebration of Christmas with music, dancing, masquerades, and mumming. The African slaves retained their own music, dance, and masquerade traditions, for which they, too, sought an outlet. These two cultural streams flowed together in Jamaican Christmas celebrations, giving rise to Jonkonnu.

Jamaican Jonkonnu celebrations take place on December 26 (*see also* **St. Stephen's Day**). Most of the Jonkonnu performers are male. Bands of dancers prepare homemade costumes that identify them as specific characters associated with the festival masquerade. Some of these characters, such as "cowhead," clearly reflect African imagery. Others, like "the king" and "the queen," show remnants of British influence. Small bands of musicians accompany these dancers as they briefly parade to some public location. The bands are composed of both African instruments, like the gumbay drum, and European instruments, such as the fife. The dancing that takes place when the group arrives at the chosen site also illustrates this Afro-European cultural blend. The participants combine African dance movements with old European dance steps, such those from the quadrille. African cultural influences appear to dominate Jonkonnu dancing, probably because Jamaicans of African descent developed and kept the custom alive over the centuries.

No one knows for sure where the name "Jonkonnu" comes from. Some say it refers to an early eighteenth-century west African king, John Canoe. Others believe it represents a sloppy English pronunciation of a French phrase, *gens inconnu*, meaning "unknown people." They suggest that early observers gave that name to the ritual because they could not recognize the masked and costumed dancers.

Jonkonnu in the Caribbean

As Jonkonnu spread throughout the Caribbean, the people of different islands varied the costumes, parades, dances, festival name, and festival date. Belize dancers call their tradition "John Canoe" and perform it on Christmas and December 26, **Boxing Day**. In the Bahamas the festival is called "Junkanoo" and is celebrated between December 26 and January 1, **New Year's Day**. Bahamians use strips of colored paper to create dazzling costumes for Junkanoo. Today, with government sponsorship of the parade and costume competition, the elaborate costumes worn by top competitors resemble those of Trinidad's fabulous Carnival celebrations.

Jonkonnu in the United States

During slavery times American blacks in North Carolina also carried out the Jonkonnu ritual at Christmas time. They called the custom "John Kooner" and spoke of going "John Canoeing" or "John Kunering" on Christmas morning. Like their Caribbean counterparts, most participants in American Jonkonnu celebrations were men. They prepared homemade costumes embellished with strips of colorful cloth and also wore masks, some of which sported horns. Thus garbed, and armed with simple musical instruments such as drums, triangles, violins, and jew's harps, they made their way across town. The masqueraders stopped at the houses of the well-to-do, sang and danced for the occupants, and asked for money in return. They also entertained the people they met on their way. Some reports depict plantation slaves celebrating Jonkonnu on the grounds of the estate. The plantation owners enjoyed the music, dancing, and masquerading, and often rewarded the participants with small **gifts**, such as coins or scarves. Some slaveowners convinced themselves that the happiness the slaves enjoyed during this yearly festival justified the institution of slavery.

The nineteenth-century American version of Jonkonnu strongly resembles the Christmas mumming practices common in **England** at the time. Nevertheless, the custom probably arrived in the United States via Jamaica and the Bahamas. In past centuries, much trade from these areas entered the United States through the port town of Wilmington, North Carolina. Caribbean slaves familiar with Jonkonnu probably passed the custom on to American blacks via this trade route. After the Civil War African Americans began to abandon Jonkonnu. Oddly enough, as the tradition declined among African Americans, white youths began to adopt it. They called the seasonal masquerade "coonering" and kept it going from the 1890s until it finally died out in the early 1900s. (*See also* **America, Christmas in Nineteenth-Century**.)

Further Reading

Cohen, Hennig, and Tristram Potter Coffin, eds. *The Folklore of American Holidays*. Detroit, Mich.: Gale Research, 1987.

Kane, Harnett T. *The Southern Christmas Book*. 1958. Reprint. Detroit, Mich.: Omnigraphics, 1998.

Nissenbaum, Stephen. *The Battle for Christmas*. New York: Alfred A. Knopf, 1996.

Nunly, John W., and Judith Bettleheim, eds. *Caribbean Festival Arts*. Seattle, Wash.: University of Washington Press, 1988.

Restad, Penne. *Christmas in America*. New York: Oxford University Press, 1995.

Web Site

The Bahamas Tourism Office provides information on Jonkonnu at:
http://www.bahamas.com/culture/junkanoo/index.htm

Joseph

Jesus' earthly father was a man named Joseph. The Bible implies that he made his living as a carpenter (Matthew 13:55). In the **Gospel accounts of Christmas** Joseph emerges as a righteous man of faith who dutifully observes the rituals of his religion.

Joseph plays a relatively large role in the story of Jesus' birth recorded in the **Gospel according to Matthew** (chapters 1 and 2). When he finds out that his betrothed wife, **Mary**, is pregnant, he decides that he will follow Jewish law by breaking his engagement to her. Instead of doing so publicly, however, he looks for some way to call it off quietly. Many commentators have read his desire not to inflict unnecessary shame upon Mary as a sign of Joseph's righteousness. Then an **angel** visits Joseph, informing him that Mary is pregnant by God's Holy Spirit and asking that he take her as his wife. Joseph demonstrates his faith and trust in God by continuing his engagement to Mary and eventually marrying her. In Matthew's account the angel appears once more to Joseph after Jesus' birth. The angel warns him to leave **Bethlehem** immediately, as **Herod** is planning to kill all the town's male babies in an effort to rid himself of the "newborn King of the Jews" (*see* **Holy Innocents' Day**). Once again, Joseph places his trust in the angel's message and hurries his family away to **Egypt**.

Joseph plays a much smaller role in the story of Jesus' birth reported in the **Gospel according to Luke**. In this account, the angel appears to Mary with the message of Jesus' divine father. Yet in this version, too, Joseph trusts the divine message and continues his engagement with Mary. Luke says nothing of the **Flight into Egypt**. Instead, he mentions Jesus' circumcision and naming ceremony, which took place eight days after Jesus' birth, according to Jewish law (*see* **Feast of the Circumcision**). Once again, Joseph is portrayed as a pious man who carefully observes the teachings of his religion.

Joseph does not appear in the gospel accounts of Jesus' adult life. This has led many commentators to assume that Joseph died before

Jesus became an adult. Many Christian artists have portrayed Joseph as an old man in accordance with this interpretation.

As the centuries rolled by, Christians became more and more interested in Joseph. Perhaps because the Bible has so little to say about him, an apocryphal, or legendary, literature sprang up, adding further detail to his life and personality. In Roman Catholicism, he became the patron saint of workers, fathers, and happy deaths, as well as the patron saint of Canada, **Mexico**, **Russia**, Peru, Korea, Belgium, Vietnam, Austria, and Bohemia.

Feast Days

Western Christians began to observe March 19 as St. Joseph's Day in the Middle Ages. Researchers have yet to unearth the reason for the selection of that particular date. Orthodox and other Eastern Christians honor St. Joseph on the first Sunday after Christmas. In 1955 Pope Pius XII declared May 1 to be St. Joseph the Worker's Day, in an effort to add religious overtones to workers' celebrations that took place in various communist countries on that date.

Christmas Customs

Joseph, along with his wife Mary and the baby Jesus, are the central characters in most **Nativity scenes**. **Nativity plays**, including the Hispanic folk play called Las **Posadas**, accord him an important role. He is also mentioned in a number of **Christmas carols**, such as "Joseph Dearest, Joseph Mine" and the "Cherry Tree Carol."

Further Reading

Coats, George W., and Paul J. Achtemeier. "Joseph." In Paul J. Achtemeier, ed. *The HarperCollins Bible Dictionary*. Revised edition. San Francisco, Calif.: HarperSanFrancisco, 1996.

Cross, F. L., and E. A. Livingstone, eds. "St. Joseph." In their *The Oxford Dictionary of the Christian Church*. Second edition, revised. Oxford, England: Oxford University Press, 1983.

Filas, F. L. "Joseph, St." In *New Catholic Encyclopedia*. Volume 7. New York: McGraw-Hill, 1967.

———. "Joseph St., Devotion to." In *New Catholic Encyclopedia*. Volume 7. New York: McGraw-Hill, 1967.

McBrien, Richard P. *Lives of the Saints*. New York: HarperCollins, 2001.

Yang, Seung Ai. "Joseph." In David Noel Freedman, ed. *Eerdmans Bible Dictionary*. Grand Rapids, Mich.: William B. Eerdmans Publishing Company, 2000.

Julklapp

Julklapp is the Swedish term for a Christmas **gift**. The term "Julklapp" literally means "Christmas knock." This name comes from an old Swedish custom whereby Christmas gift givers would knock on doors, toss in their gift, and run away. These mysterious packages might also be delivered by the **Yule goat**.

In previous eras, Scandinavians exchanged important gifts on **New Year's Day**. They treated Christmas Eve as an occasion only for small or token gifts. In Sweden these small gifts, or Julklapp, became vehicles for seasonal fun and **games**. The gift giver tried to keep his or her identity a secret by hurrying away. Nevertheless, givers often wrote a dedication on the **wrapping paper**, which could offer clues to their identity. These dedications teased recipients in a few lines of rhyming verse. Sometimes gift givers hid the real gift inside something of lesser value. For example, they might insert a gold ring inside a small cake.

At other times they confounded recipients with trick packaging. A series of boxes might be wrapped one inside the next. The final box might contain directions to the location of the actual present. The more time people spent on figuring out the puzzles presented by the Julklapp, the more successful the gift was considered to be.

The Swedes still refer to Christmas presents as Julklapp. Even though most of the old customs surrounding the gifts have disappeared, they still enjoy sending rhymed verse along with their Christmas gifts. The rhymes usually needle the recipient about some past action or character flaw. Sometimes they take the form of a riddle about the gift itself. The good humor generated by these rhymes is an integral part of the Christmas gift. (*See also* **St. Nicholas's Day.**)

Further Reading

Del Re, Gerard, and Patricia Del Re. *The Christmas Almanack.* Garden City, N.Y.: Doubleday, 1979.
Ross, Corinne. *Christmas in Scandinavia.* Chicago: World Book, 1977.

Jultomten

Joulutonttuja, Julenissen, Julnissen

In Sweden, Christmas **gifts** are brought by the Jultomten. The word *Jultomten* combines the Swedish word for Christmas, *Jul,* with the word *tomten,* which means household fairy or **elf**. The Jultomten is often depicted as a portly gnome with a white beard and a pointed red cap. During most of the year this creature hides under the staircase, in the attic, or in any other dark corner of the house. The Jultomten emerges on Christmas Eve, tucking small gifts into unlikely locations about the house. Capricious by nature, the Jultomten may reward or punish householders depending on his mood. Old customs suggest that the family leave small offerings of porridge and milk, or even liquor and tobacco, about the house to appease him.

Each family or neighborhood may elect a member to dress up as the Jultomten. After assuming a disguise that will hopefully hide his or her identity from the children, the Jultomten knocks on the door with a sack of presents. When the door opens the Jultomten asks, "Are there any good children here?" and distributes presents accordingly.

Denmark, Norway, and Finland

In **Denmark** these Christmas elves are known as *Julnissen*, and in **Norway** as *Julenissen*. Although similar to the Jultomten in appearance, the Danish Julnissen does not distribute gifts. Instead, he lurks about the dark corners of the house, perhaps assuring himself that the family cares properly for the homestead. The Norwegian Julenissen takes after his Swedish cousin and does bring gifts. These Danish and Norwegian sprites become more active during the dark midwinter season. Like the Jultomten, they, too, must be placated with porridge on Christmas Eve if the householders wish to escape their pranks. Finland also has its version of the Christmas gnomes, called the *Joulutonttuja*. Unlike the other Scandinavian Christmas gnomes, the Joulutonttuja are cheerful, helpful creatures. They watch children to find out what they'd like as presents and help Santa make these gifts in his workshop.

History

In ancient times Scandinavian householders thought that the spirits of the land's past inhabitants lingered on, jealously watching over their old domain. During **Yule**, when the dead were believed to return, the thoughtful, and perhaps fearful, made offerings of food and drink to these **ghosts**. Folk belief gradually transformed these spirits into the Scandinavian household fairies known as *nissen* or *tomten*. These peevish elves guarded household and barn. When unsatisfied with the family's behavior, they punished them with small pranks, like making the milk go sour.

The figure of the Jultomten developed in the late 1800s. Before that time the **Yule goat** brought Swedish families their Christmas presents. The traditional Swedish tomten, or household sprite, is not associated with any particular season. By contrast, the Jultomten not only appears around Christmas time, but also delivers presents. The importation of German Christmas decorations in the late nineteenth century, featuring the gift-giving **St. Nicholas**, may have suggested the assignment of this function to the Jultomten. The English gift giver **Father Christmas** may also have influenced this shift. Some writers suggest that the Scandinavian Jultomten, Julnissen, and Joulu-tonttuja, in turn, inspired the invention of the helpful elves who became **Santa Claus**'s assistants in the frozen **North Pole**.

Further Reading

Cagner, Ewert, comp. *Swedish Christmas*. New York: Henry Holt and Company, 1959.

Christmas in Denmark. Chicago: World Book, 1986.

Ross, Corinne. *Christmas in Scandinavia*. Chicago: World Book, 1977.

Web Site

A site sponsored by the Royal Norwegian Ministry of Foreign Affairs: http://odin.dep.no/ (Click on "Language," "English," "History, culture, geography, recreation," then scroll down to "Christmas in Norway.")

Kalends

Calends

Kalends, the Roman new year festival, began on January 1 and lasted until January 5. The Romans celebrated Kalends in much the same way they did **Saturnalia**. Early Christian writers condemned the carousing crowds. Nevertheless, some of the customs associated with Kalends were eventually absorbed into the celebration of Christmas.

In 45 B.C. the Roman emperor Julius Caesar introduced a new calendar (called the Julian calendar) which shifted the date of the Roman new year from March 25 to January 1. The Romans called the festival that began on this day "kalends" (or "calends"). They also used this word to refer to the first day of each month. On this day Roman officials posted the calendar for each month. The English word "calendar" comes from the old Latin term "kalends."

Customs

The Romans celebrated Kalends by decorating their homes and temples with lights and **greenery**. They exchanged **gifts** with one another as well. A sprig of greenery taken from the groves dedicated to the goddess Strenia was considered a very traditional gift. Later the Romans added cakes and honey (symbolizing a "sweet" new year), and coins (symbolizing wealth) to the roster of traditional new year gifts. The Romans called these gifts *strenae*, after Strenia. This Latin word finds echo in the modern French word for new year's gift, *étrenne*. In addition to exchanging gifts with friends and family, many Romans offered gifts and *vota*, wishes for prosperity, to the emperor. The mad emperor Caligula (12 A.D.-41 A.D.) went so far as to require these gifts and good wishes, and stood outside the palace to collect them in person.

Other Kalends customs included fortune-telling and informal masquerades in which men cavorted through the streets dressed as animals or as women. Their bold and sometimes rude antics entertained some onlookers and outraged others. Some researchers trace the origins of **mumming** back to this Kalends custom. During the Kalends festival slaves enjoyed time off and even sat down with their masters to play dice. Feasting, drinking, and merrymaking rounded out the festival. Certain superstitions also attached themselves to the holiday. The Romans believed bad luck would follow any who lent fire or iron to a neighbor at this time.

Kalend's Eve celebrations resembled our own New Year's Eve festivities. A fourth-century Greek scholar named Libanius (314-393 A.D.) wrote that almost everyone stayed up on Kalend's Eve to usher in the new year with drinking, singing, and revelry. Instead of spending the evening at home, crowds of people roamed through the streets, returning to their houses near daybreak to sleep off the night's overindulgence. Coins were distributed among the people on the first day of the new year. Indeed, all Kalends gift giving took place on the first of January. On January second most people stayed at home and played dice. Races entertained the populace on the third of January. Kalends festivities wound down on the fourth of January and finally came to a close on the fifth.

Similarity to Christmas

Libanius left future generations a lengthy description of the attitudes and activities that characterized the celebration of the Roman new year. This description reveals many striking similarities between Kalends and contemporary Christmas celebrations:

> The festival of Kalends . . . is celebrated everywhere as far as the limits of the Roman Empire extend. . . . Everywhere may be seen carousals and well-laden tables; luxurious abundance is found in the houses of the rich, but also in the houses of the poor better food than usual is put upon the table. The impulse to spend seizes everyone. He who the whole year through has taken pleasure in saving and piling up his pence, becomes suddenly extravagant. He who erstwhile was accustomed and preferred to live poorly, now at this feast enjoys himself as much as his means will allow. . . . People are not only generous towards themselves, but also towards their fellow-men. A stream of presents pours itself out on all sides. . . . The highroads and footpaths are covered with whole processions of laden men and beasts. . . . As the thousand flowers which burst forth everywhere are the adornment of Spring, so are the thousand presents poured out on all sides, the decoration of the Kalends feast. It may justly be said that it is the fairest time of the year. . . . The Kalends festival banishes all that is connected with toil, and allows men to give themselves up to undisturbed enjoyment. From the minds of young people it removes two kinds of dread: the dread of the schoolmaster and the dread of the stern pedagogue. The slave also it allows, so far as possible, to breath the air of freedom. . . . Another great quality of the festival is that it teaches men not to hold too fast to their money, but to part with it and let it pass into other hands [Miles, 1990, 168-69].

Christian Opposition

Many of the customs and attitudes associated with Kalends and Saturnalia gradually attached themselves to the celebration of Christmas. Ironically, this transfer took place in spite of the overwhelming rejection of these holidays and their customs by Christian officials. For centuries Christian authorities condemned the drunkenness, disorder, fortune-telling, gambling, and masquerading associated with the celebration of Kalends. Nevertheless, these customs proved remarkably difficult to stamp out, even after Christianity became the dominant religion and Christmas an important winter holiday. One researcher has counted at least forty separate Church documents containing official denunciations of the kinds of midwinter masquerades associated with Kalends. These documents range from the fourth to the eleventh centuries and come from authorities in many European lands as well as north Africa and the Near East.

Church officials urged their followers to abandon riotous pagan practices and instead to observe the day with thoughtfulness and sobriety. In 567 the second provincial Council of Tours tried to counteract the still popular festivities surrounding Kalends by ordering Christians to fast and do penance during the first few days of the new year. In the seventh century Church officials made a new effort to reclaim the day from pagan celebrations. They introduced a new Christian holy day, the **Feast of the Circumcision**, to be celebrated on January 1. By the time Kalends finally withered away, however, the peoples of **Europe** had already transferred many of its customs to the **Christmas season**.

Further Reading

Henisch, Bridget Ann. *Cakes and Characters: An English Christmas Tradition.* London, England: Prospect Books, 1984.

Miles, Clement A. *Christmas in Ritual and Tradition.* 1912. Reprint. Detroit, Mich.: Omnigraphics, 1990.

Kallikantzari

Callicantzari, Kallikantzaroi

According to traditional Greek folklore, the kallikantzari rampaged across **Greece** during the **Twelve Days of Christmas**. These diminutive demons spent the rest of the year deep inside the earth gnawing at the tree that supports the world. The tree renewed itself each year during the season of Christ's birth. Thus thwarted, the enraged kallikantzari swarmed up to the surface of the earth to bedevil humanity. The holy ceremonies occurring on **Epiphany** drove them back underground. Belief in the kallikantzari was especially strong in the region of Mt. Parnassos.

Appearance

Reports concerning the appearance of these demons varied. According to some, the kallikantzari appeared half human and half animal. Many claimed to have caught a glimpse of long, curved talons, red eyes, hairy bodies, or donkey's ears. Others told frightening tales of tiny imps who rode astride lame or deformed chickens.

Activities

According to Greek folklore, the kallikantzari knew many ways of vexing human beings. Some reports said that they entered homes by the door or the chimney, relieved themselves in any open containers of food and drink, upset furniture, and extinguished the fire. Others credited them with direct attacks on human beings. For example, they hopped on peoples' backs and drove them to dance until they collapsed. The presence of the kallikantzari during the Twelve Days of Christmas posed special problems for expectant mothers. Children born at this time of year ran the risk of becoming kallikantzari themselves. From sunset to dawn the demons roamed the countryside looking for opportunities to harass humanity. They tended to retreat into hiding places at daybreak, however.

Remedies

Just as traditional beliefs warned of the dangers presented by the kallikantzari, they also offered methods for warding off these attacks. Keeping a fire burning in the hearth during the Twelve Days of Christmas prevented the demons from entering the home through the chimney. In addition, the kallikantzari found the smell of burning shoes, salt, wild asparagus, or other substances that produced a foul smoke especially repugnant. Of course, so did human beings. Greek folklore apparently did not address the subject of whether this method of repelling the kallikantzari also repelled family, friends, and neighbors. Traditional lore also recommended hanging a pig's jaw bone by the door as a method of preventing the kallikantzari from crossing the threshold. To protect babies born during the Twelve Days of Christmas from becoming kallikantzari, mothers wrapped their infants in garlic or straw, or scorched their toes in the fire.

The religious ceremonies associated with Epiphany offered the most effective method of driving off the malicious pranksters. According to Greek custom, priests visited homes on Epiphany, filling them with the scent of burning incense and sprinkling them with holy water. Greek folklore insisted that the kallikantzari fled before this onslaught of holiness, retreating to their underground lair until the following Christmas.

Parallels

According to various European folk traditions, demons, spirits, and magical creatures of all kinds roamed the earth during the Twelve Days of Christmas. Some of these demons served as the unlikely companions of **St. Nicholas** (*see also* **St. Nicholas's Day**). The good saint somehow tamed the Czechoslovakian **cert**, the Dutch **Black Peter**, and the German **Knecht Ruprecht**. Yet many other supernatural creatures still wandered freely through the dark nights. In some parts of northern Europe traditional lore asserted that werewolves, bears, or trolls prowled for victims during the Twelve Days of Christmas. Legends from some countries warned that the fearsome spirits known as the **Wild Hunt** raced across the night skies at this time of year. German lore cautioned that the supernatural figure known as **Berchta** toured the countryside with her entourage during these cold, dark days. Often, **Frau Gaude**, too, appeared to German villagers at this time of year. Other folklore told of frolicking **elves** and fairies, such as the Swedish **Jultomten** and the Icelandic **Christmas Lads**.

Further Reading

Arrowsmith, Nancy, and George Moorse. *A Field Guide to the Little People*. New York: Pocket Books, 1977.

Del Re, Gerard, and Patricia Del Re. *The Christmas Almanack*. Garden City, N.Y.: Doubleday, 1979.

MacDonald, Margaret Read, ed. *The Folklore of World Holidays*. Detroit, Mich.: Gale Research, 1992.

Miles, Clement A. *Christmas in Ritual and Tradition*. 1912. Reprint. Detroit, Mich.: Omnigraphics, 1990.

King of the Bean

Bean King, Epiphany King

A long succession of mock kings have ruled over winter holiday merrymaking in **Europe**. In ancient times they presided over feasts held in honor of the Roman festival of **Saturnalia** (*see also* **Zagmuk**). In the Middle Ages the **boy bishop** and the **Lord of Misrule** directed certain Christmas festivities (*see also* **Feast of Fools**). Twelfth **Night** celebrations, however, came under the special supervision of another mock ruler: the King of the Bean.

In past centuries the English, French, Spanish, German, and Dutch celebrated Twelfth Night, or **Epiphany** Eve, with a feast. The Twelfth Night cake not only provided dessert, but also helped to facilitate an old custom (*see also* **Christmas Cake**). While preparing the cake the cook dropped a bean, coin or other small object into the batter. The man who found this object in his slice of cake was declared "King of the Bean." If a woman received the bean, she became queen and appointed a man as king.

The king presided over the rest of the evening's activities. In some areas the king chose his own queen. In others, a pea was also added to the cake batter and the woman who found the pea in her serving of cake enacted the role of "queen." Everyone else became a member of the royal court. At some parties the courtiers carried out their role by announcing the mock ruler's every action. Cries of "the king drinks" or "the king coughs" cued others to follow suit. The mock rulers might also give silly commands that the court was expected to carry out. The French saying, *il a trouvé la fève au gâteau*, which means "he found the bean in the cake," comes from this Twelfth Night custom and means "he's had some good luck."

History

Christmas season mock kings sprouted up regularly in the courts of medieval Europe. Records indicate that in late medieval **France**

these kings were selected by a kind of edible lottery. All candidates received a piece of a special cake into which a bean had been baked. Whoever found the bean in their slice of cake became the king of the feast. The title conferred upon these mock monarchs, "Bean King" or "King of the Bean," referred back to this custom. It may also have alluded to their lack of real power. In the sixteenth century, ordinary Dutch and German households celebrated Twelfth Night by baking a coin into a cake and acknowledging whoever received the coin in their slice of cake as king of the feast. In the next century, this Twelfth Night custom spread to **England**, France, and **Spain**.

The following poem by English poet Robert Herrick (1591-1674) describes a seventeenth-century English Twelfth Night feast. These lines capture the merriment surrounding the selection of the bean king and bean queen:

> Now, now the mirth comes
> With the cake full of plums,
> here bean's the king of sport here;
> Beside we must know,
> The pea also
> Must reveal as queen in the court here.
>
> Begin then to choose
> This night as ye use,
> Who shall for the present delight here
> Be a king by the lot,
> And who shall not
> Be Twelfth-day queen for the night here.
>
> Which known, let us make
> Joy-sops with the cake;
> And let not a man then be seen here,
> Who unurg'd will not drink,
> To the base from the brink,
> A health to the king and the queen here [Miles, 1990, 338].

The English added an innovation of their own to the Twelfth Night feast. In 1669 English diarist Samuel Pepys (1633-1703) described his enjoyment of a new custom whereby Twelfth Night merrymakers drew slips of paper from a hat on which were written the names of characters found at the bean king's court. They were expected to impersonate this character for the rest of the evening. In this way everyone present at the celebration, not just the king and queen, got into the act.

The King of the Bean continued to preside over English Twelfth Night celebrations until the nineteenth century. In this era people began to substitute metallic objects for the bean and pea embedded in earlier Twelfth Night cakes. These objects stood for future fortunes rather than for characters. For example, a ring might foretell marriage, and a thimble spinsterhood. The importance of Twelfth Night declined throughout the nineteenth century. Rather than fade into oblivion, however, this fortune-telling custom transferred itself to Christmas. The tokens found a new home inside the **plum pudding** so popular at English Christmas dinners. By the end of the nineteenth century the English had all but abandoned the Twelfth Night king. The custom of baking a bean into the Twelfth Night cake survived into the twentieth century in the southern French region of Provence. In **Germany** the bean king and his cake still appear at Epiphany celebrations.

Further Reading

Chambers, Robert. "January 6 — Twelfth-Day." In his *The Book of Days*. Volume 1. 1862-64. Reprint. Detroit, Mich.: Omnigraphics, 1990.

Hadfield, Miles, and John Hadfield. *The Twelve Days of Christmas*. Boston, Mass.: Little, Brown and Company, 1961.

Henisch, Bridget Ann. *Cakes and Characters: An English Christmas Tradition*. London, England: Prospect Books, 1984.

Hole, Christina. *British Folk Customs*. London, England: Hutchinson and Company, 1976.

Hutton, Ronald. *The Stations of the Sun*. Oxford, England: Oxford University Press, 1996.

MacDonald, Margaret Read, ed. *The Folklore of World Holidays*. Detroit, Mich.: Gale Research, 1992.

Miles, Clement A. *Christmas in Ritual and Tradition*. 1912. Reprint. Detroit, Mich.: Omnigraphics, 1990.

Kissing Bough
Kissing Ball, Kissing Bunch, Kissing Ring

During the nineteenth century a kissing bough hung from the doorway, ceiling, or chandelier of many English homes at Christmas time. Families fashioned this homemade decoration by winding Christmas **greenery** around a circular wire frame. Sometimes a spherical frame was formed by placing one hoop inside another. Householders often embellished this basic design with ribbons, apples, oranges, colored paper, candles, and other **ornaments**.

The most important element in the kissing bough was **mistletoe**. Mistletoe might cover the frame or, if only a small quantity was available, a bunch of mistletoe might hang from the center of the frame. By the time the kissing bough became popular in the late eighteenth century, the English had already adopted the custom of

407

stealing kisses from those who passed by, or stood beneath, a sprig of mistletoe. Placed where guests and family members were certain to walk under it, the kissing bough provided an opportunity to exercise this custom. In the nineteenth century the English began to decorate their homes with **Christmas trees**. As the tree became the focal point of English Christmas decorations, the kissing bough declined in popularity.

Further Reading

Del Re, Gerard, and Patricia Del Re. *The Christmas Almanack*. Garden City, N.Y.: Doubleday, 1979.

Hadfield, Miles, and John Hadfield. *The Twelve Days of Christmas*. Boston, Mass.: Little, Brown and Company, 1961.

Harrowven, Jean. *Origin of Festivals and Feasts*. London, England: Kaye and Ward, 1980.

Hole, Christina. *British Folk Customs*. London, England: Hutchinson and Company, 1976.

Hutton, Ronald. *The Stations of the Sun*. Oxford, England: Oxford University Press, 1996.

Muir, Frank. *Christmas Customs and Traditions*. New York: Taplinger, 1977.

Pimlott, J. A. R. *The Englishman's Christmas*. Atlantic Highlands, N.J.: Humanities Press, 1978.

Knecht Ruprecht

Aschenklas, Belsnickel, Bullerklas, Butz, Hans Muff, Hans Trapp, Klaubauf, Krampus, Pelz Nicholas, Pulterklas, Ru-Klas, Schimmelreiter

According to old European folklore, a variety of frightening figures lurk in the long, dark nights of the **Christmas season**. They range from the ghostly personnel of the **Wild Hunt** to mysterious wanderers such as **Berchta** and **Frau Gaude**. Many folklorists interpret these figures as remnants of old pagan spirits that blended into the emerging Christian folklore of the Christmas season. The folklore associated with **St. Nicholas's Day** offers a clear example of this dynamic. **St. Nicholas,** a fourth-century bishop from Asia Minor, became the Christmas time **gift** bringer in much of northern and central **Europe**. According to folklore, however, this clearly Christian figure travels about with a variety of somewhat sinister companions. In Czechoslovakia, a demon called a **cert** accompanies the good Nicholas. In Holland the devilish **Black Peter** aids Nicholas in his virtuous work. And in the German-speaking lands scruffy Knecht Ruprecht trails behind St. Nicholas, meting out punishment to naughty children. Some folklorists trace Knecht Ruprecht's roots back to ancient times.

Ruprecht's Many Names

St. Nicholas's German helper goes by many different names. In Austria and some areas of **Germany**, many children know him as Knecht Ruprecht, which means "Knight" Ruprecht or "Servant" Ruprecht. Some Austrian tales name him as Krampus or Bartel, while German folklore also records the names *Hans Muff, Butz, Hans Trapp, Krampus, Klaubauf, Bullerklas, Pulterklas*, and *Schimmelreiter*. Some of the names assigned to this bogeyman reveal that somewhere along the line his identity merged with that of St. Nicholas. Some know him as *Ru-Klas*, or "Rough Nicholas," while others identify him as *Pelz Nicholas*, or "Fur Nicholas." Still others call him *Aschenklas*, or

"Ash Nicholas." In some areas a figure known as *Pelzmartin,* or "Fur Martin," blended the identity of St. Martin with the Christmas season bogey (*see also* **Martinmas**). The Pennsylvania Dutch brought Pelz Nicholas with them to America when they began to settle in Pennsylvania in the eighteenth century. There the name "Pelz Nicholas" eventually slurred into *Belsnickel* (sometimes written as "Bellsnickle," "Bellschniggle," or "Pelznichol"; *see also* **America, Christmas in Colonial**).

Folklore

The appearance and activities of these folk figures vary in a number of details, but a rough composite image does emerge. Knecht Ruprecht startles onlookers with his menacing demeanor and unkempt appearance. He wears clothing made of rags, straw, or furs, and often adds a soot-blackened face, beard, or a frightening mask. In past times he sometimes sported devil's horns. In addition, he carries one or more of the tools of his trade: a whip, stick, **bell**, or sack. The bell warns of his approach. He cows all children into good behavior and punishes badly behaved children with his whip or stick. The sack contains treats for well-behaved children and items that serve as symbolic warnings to wrongdoers that their misbehavior has not gone unnoticed.

According to folklore St. Nicholas and his companion visit homes on St. Nicholas's Eve, often entering through the chimney. They leave treats, such as nuts, fruit, and cookies for good children, and ashes, birch rods, or other warnings for naughty ones. In some areas the pair make their rounds on Christmas Eve instead of St. Nicholas's Eve.

For the most part, Knecht Ruprecht and his various aliases tag along behind St. Nicholas, serving as an ever-present reminder of the fate awaiting the poorly behaved. Although most often found serving St. Nicholas, in the past Knecht Ruprecht has also accompanied other saintly figures, such as St. Peter and St. Martin (*see also* **Martinmas**). In some areas of Germany he followed the **Christkindel**, or "Christ Child," on his gift-bringing journey. In other areas, however, this Christmas bogey appears to have struck out on his own. Belsnickel seems to have emigrated to America's Pennsylvania Dutch country without a companion saint.

Origins

Few historical records mention Knecht Ruprecht or his counterparts. A seventeenth-century document notes the appearance of Knecht Ruprecht in a Christmas procession in Nuremberg, Germany. In addition, nineteenth- and early twentieth-century folklorists observed that people dressed as Ruprecht, St. Nicholas, and St. Martin visited homes during the Christmas season in Germany. Still, the lack of historical records has not prevented folklorists from guessing about Ruprecht's origins. Many believe that Ruprecht in all his guises represents some remnant of a pagan spirit or deity. One writer suspects that Ruprecht evolved from the Teutonic god Odin. Another proposes that Ruprecht represents a relatively modern interpretation of the "wild man," an ancient, archetypal figure representing the forces of nature. She suggests that as Christianity spread throughout Europe, Christian authorities campaigned against folk representations of the wild man, likening him to the Devil. After many centuries his role in folk celebrations dwindled to that of the scruffy servant who follows behind the Christmas season saints.

European Customs

Until the early part of the twentieth century, men dressed as Knecht Ruprecht and St. Nicholas visited homes on St. Nicholas's Eve in German-speaking lands. St. Nicholas quizzed the children on their behavior, their prayers, and their lessons, while Ruprecht posed threateningly in the background. In some areas the Christmas bogey worked alone and arrived on other dates during the Christmas season, such as Christmas Eve. Although Knecht Ruprecht's looks and manners often intimidated, his brash and erratic behavior entertained. Children still prepare for his visit by leaving their **shoes** by the fireplace, on the doorstep, or in some other place where the gift bringer was sure to notice them. In the morning well-behaved children find their shoes filled with treats, while those whose behavior needs improvement find birch rods, ashes, or other warnings.

Belsnickeling in the United States

In the early years of the United States people from different countries adopted elements of each other's lore and traditions, giving rise to new customs. By the nineteenth century the English custom of **mumming** had grafted itself onto the Pennsylvania Dutch figure of the Belsnickel to create the custom of belsnickeling.

Groups of young men or single individuals dressed themselves in rags, overcoats, or furs, and hid their faces behind beards, hats, or masks, or covered them with soot. They carried whips, bells, and sacks as they marched from house to house. After gaining entrance to a neighbor's home they entertained the householders with their comic antics and horseplay while family members tried to guess their identities. In return for their visit the belsnickelers expected to receive hospitality in the form of food and drink. The belsnickelers took nuts and sweets out of their pockets and tossed them onto the floor, cracking their whips over the heads of any children bold enough to retrieve them. Sometimes they also pulled pranks on their neighbors under the cover of their disguise.

Although Belsnickel was originally associated with St. Nicholas's Day, Pennsylvania belsnickelers shifted the dates of their activities closer to Christmas, visiting their neighbors in masquerade on the dark nights between Christmas and **New Year's Day**. Belsnickelers also plied their trade in Canada's Nova Scotia province.

Opposition

Christmas season masquerading met with some resistance by the more subdued groups who made up Pennsylvania's population. In the eighteenth century, Quakers in Philadelphia vigorously opposed this custom. Court records indicate that some masqueraders were brought before juries for their unruly behavior. In the early nineteenth century the Pennsylvania House of Representatives formally outlawed Christmas season masquerading. Those who dared to flaunt this edict faced fines of between $50 and $1,000, and prison sentences of up to three months. A Philadelphia ordinance forbade Christmas Eve masquerading and noisemaking in 1881. Nevertheless, belsnickelers continued their seasonal activities in rural areas settled by people of Germanic descent who were friendly to the custom.

Decline

Belsnickeling died out in the early twentieth century, about the time when authorities ceased to oppose it. In 1901 Philadelphia issued its first permit for a New Year's Day mummers' parade. This parade developed out of the mumming and noisemaking traditions of a variety of Philadelphia's immigrant groups, among them the German-American tradition of belsnickeling. Philadelphia's New Year's Day **Mummers Parade** continues to this day. Today's parade, however, revolves around a competition between highly organized groups wearing elaborate and expensive costumes. (*For more on Christmas in Pennsylvania, see* **America, Christmas in Nineteenth-Century; Amish Christmas; Barring Out the Schoolmaster; Bethlehem, Pennsylvania, Christmas in**).

Further Reading

Barrick, Mac E. *German-American Folklore.* Little Rock, Ark.: August House, 1987.

Crippen, Thomas G. *Christmas and Christmas Lore.* 1923. Reprint. Detroit, Mich.: Omnigraphics, 1990.

MacDonald, Margaret Read, ed. *The Folklore of World Holidays.* Detroit, Mich.: Gale Research, 1992.

Miles, Clement A. *Christmas in Ritual and Tradition.* 1912. Reprint. Detroit, Mich.: Omnigraphics, 1990.

Russ, Jennifer M. *German Festivals and Customs.* London, England: Oswald Wolff, 1982.

Sansom, William. *A Book of Christmas.* New York: McGraw-Hill Book Company, 1968.

Shoemaker, Alfred L. *Christmas in Pennsylvania.* Kutztown, Pa.: Pennsylvania Folklore Society, 1959.

Siefker, Phyllis. *Santa Claus, Last of the Wild Men.* Jefferson, N.C.: McFarland and Company, 1997.

Thonger, Richard. *A Calendar of German Customs.* London, England: Oswald Wolff, 1966.

Web Site

A site sponsored by the Philadelphia Recreation Department on the Mummers' Parade: http://www.phila.gov/recreation/mummers/index.html

Knocking Nights
Anklopfnächte, Klöpfelnachte, Klopfelnächte, Klöpfleinsnächte

In past times, German folk beliefs alleged that evil spirits and witches accomplished many acts of mischief on Thursday nights during **Advent**. This belief may have faded, but the German Knocking Nights remain. *Klöpfelnachte*, or "Knocking Nights," takes place on one or all of the last three Thursday nights during Advent. In parts of Upper and Lower Bavaria and rural zones of south **Germany**, groups of costumed children parade through the streets of town on these nights, ringing cowbells, cracking whips, rattling tin cans, and tossing pebbles against windows (*see also* **Mumming**). They march from house to house knocking on doors, reciting rhymes, and asking for **gifts** in return. Sometimes this request takes the form of shoving a pitchfork through the open doorway and singing a song that praises the householders. Family members then place a gift, such as an item of food, on one of the tines of the pitchfork.

In other cases, the knockers toss a small present in through the open door and dash away, leaving the occupants to guess the sender's identity. These anonymous gifts, called *Klöpfelscheit*, resemble the **Julklapp** tossed through open doors and windows in Scandinavia. The noisemaking element of this traditional celebration finds echo in numerous other European Christmas customs.

Further Reading

Russ, Jennifer M. *German Festivals and Customs*. London, England: Oswald Wolff, 1982.

Sansom, William. *A Book of Christmas*. New York: McGraw-Hill Book Company, 1968.

Thonger, Richard. *A Calendar of German Customs*. London, England: Oswald Wolff, 1966.

Kriss Kringle

*See **Christkindel; Santa Claus***

Kwanzaa

Kwanzaa is an African-American holiday that is unrelated to Christmas. Nevertheless, its founder, Dr. Maulana Karenga, a University of California at Los Angeles professor from Nigeria, placed the seven-day holiday between Christmas and **New Year's Day**. He did so in order to provide an African-American alternative to Christmas, which he viewed as a European holiday. He also wanted to make Kwanzaa easy to celebrate by placing it during a week when many people were already celebrating and had time off from work or school. Kwanzaa begins on December 26 and lasts until January 1.

Dr. Karenga hoped that the new holiday, based on principles and symbols associated with African harvest festivals, would provide an ethnic celebration all African Americans could observe, regardless of religious affiliation. He also sought to create a holiday that emphasized communal and spiritual values, rather than the materialism he found rampant in American Christmas celebrations (*see also* **Commercialism**).

Karenga created the word "Kwanzaa" from the Swahili phrase *matunda ya kwanza*, which means "first fruits." Many African first fruits celebrations, or harvest festivals, last between seven and nine days. Accordingly, Karenga decided to have the new American festival continue for seven days. He added the extra "a" to the Swahili word *kwanza* so that the name of the new holiday, Kwanzaa, would contain seven letters.

Karenga selected seven principles from among the values most commonly held in high esteem by the peoples of Africa and honored in their harvest celebrations. One of the seven principles of Kwanzaa is celebrated on each of the seven days of the festival. The seven principles include *umoja* (unity), *kujichagulia* (self-determination), *ujima* (collective work and responsibility), *ujamaa* (cooperative economics), *nia* (purpose), *kuumba* (creativity), and *imani* (faith). Kwanzaa celebrations also feature a seven-branched candleholder called a *kinara*. The kinara holds red, green, and black candles — colors symbolic of African identity. One candle is lit on each of the seven nights. On December 31 celebrants participate in a communal feast. On January 1, the last day of the festival, modest **gifts** are exchanged.

Since its founding in 1966 Kwanzaa has steadily grown in popularity. One researcher has estimated that over 18 million Americans observe Kwanzaa each year. Millions more are thought to celebrate the festival in Africa, Canada, the Caribbean, and Europe.

Further Reading

Henderson, Helene, and Sue Ellen Thompson, eds. *Holidays, Festivals, and Celebrations of the World Dictionary*. Second edition. Detroit, Mich.: Omnigraphics, 1997.

Karenga, Maulana. *The African-American Holiday of Kwanzaa*. Los Angles, Calif.: University of Sankore Press, 1988.

Santino, Jack. *All Around the Year*. Urbana, Ill.: University of Illinois Press, 1994.

Thompson, Sue Ellen, ed. *Holiday Symbols*. Detroit, Mich.: Omnigraphics, 1998.

Lamb's Wool
Wassail

If you ever attend a traditional English Christmas feast you might find lamb's wool on the menu. This oddly named English Christmas beverage combines sugar, spice, wine or ale, and a number of other ingredients. Over the years English cooks have varied the recipe in many ways. Most recipes include roasted, chopped apples. The soft, whitish chunks of apple float to the top and give the surface the appearance of lamb's wool, hence the name of the drink. Some variations substitute crumbled toast for roasted apple chunks. Other recipes include cream, milk, or beaten eggs. These give the beverage a creamy, whitish appearance suggestive of lamb's wool. (*See also* **Eggnog**.)

Lamb's wool dates back to the Middle Ages. Since lamb's wool traditionally filled the **wassail** bowl at Christmas time, some people also refer to the beverage as "wassail." The English poet Robert Herrick (1591-1674) describes the preparation of the wassail bowl for a seventeenth-century Christmas party:

> Crown the bowl full
> With gentle lamb's wool—
> Add nutmeg, sugar, and ginger,
> With store of ale too;
> And this ye must do
> To make the wassail a swinger [Crippen, 1990, 100].

Recipes

The following recipes, used in **England**'s royal kitchen in the early seventeenth century, offer somewhat more specific instructions for concocting the mixture:

> Set ale on the fire to warm, boil a quart of cream with two or three whole cloves, add the beaten yolks of three or four eggs, stir all together, and pour into the ale: add sops or sippets of fine Manchet or French bread; put them in a basin, and pour on the warm mixture, with some sugar and thick cream on that; stick it well with blanched almonds, and cast on cinnamon, ginger, and sugar, or wafers and comfits [Crippen, 1990, 101].

> Boil three pints of ale; beat six eggs, the whites and yolks together; set both to the fire in a pewter pot; add roasted apples, sugar, beaten nutmegs, cloves, and ginger; and, being well brewed, drink it while hot [Crippen, 1990, 101].

A contemporary recipe adapts the beverage for today's tastes by omitting the eggs and cream and adding wine:

> In a large pot combine one bottle of sweet white wine with six and one half cups of brown ale. Add one teaspoon each of cinnamon, nutmeg, and ginger. Place over medium low heat. Peel and chop two roasted apples. When wine and spice mixture is warm, add the chopped apples and brown sugar to taste. Serve warm.

Further Reading

Cosman, Madeleine Pelner. *Medieval Holidays and Feasts*. New York: Charles Scribner's Sons, 1981.

Crippen, Thomas G. *Christmas and Christmas Lore*. 1923. Reprint. Detroit, Mich.: Omnigraphics, 1990.

Latvia, Christmas in

The vast majority of Latvians are Christians. Most are Lutherans but sizeable Roman Catholic and Orthodox minorities exist. In past times Latvians often gathered together during the long evenings that surround the **winter solstice** to do needlework and other crafts, as well as to tell stories, guess riddles, dance, and sing. Though today Latvians honor Christmas as the birthday of **Jesus** Christ, their ancestors celebrated the winter solstice as the birthday of the sun maiden.

Preparations

Latvians anticipate Christmas with **Advent wreaths** and **Advent calendars**. They also prepare for the coming of the Christmas holiday by baking, cleaning, and decorating. Many people construct three-dimensional **ornaments** out of bent straws, which are used to dress up rooms. Decorations are also made from **greenery**, colored cloth, and other natural substances. **Christmas trees** constitute another important decoration, whose use in Latvia can be traced back several hundred years.

Christmas Eve

Christmas Eve is the highlight of the **Christmas season**. Latvians enjoy an elaborate dinner on this day, usually featuring roast pork, sausage, bacon, or even pig's head (*see also* **Boar's Head**). Another prominent dish, a barley mash called *koca, kukis,* or *kikas,* gave rise to a Latvian nickname for Christmas Eve, which may be referred to as "Kukis Evening." Other typical Christmas Eve dishes include beans, peas, sauerkraut, beer, **gingerbread**, cookies, and fruit. Some say that the beans and peas became midwinter favorites because their round shape symbolized the longed-for sun. After dinner Latvians exchange their Christmas presents. In some homes **Father Christmas** arrives in time to distribute **gifts** and ask the children how well they have behaved during the year.

Latvian Christmas Traditions

The **Yule log** once played an important role in traditional Latvian Christmas celebrations. Villagers felled an oak tree from which they obtained their logs. They pulled these logs round their properties and then set fire to them. Several families might share a single log, which was burned after it had been dragged round the last homestead. Latvian lore offers two different explanations for this custom. One interprets the log as a kind of sponge that absorbs all the ill luck that clings to the household. Burning it permits the family to begin the new year with a clean slate. Another suggests that the logs signify life and burning them entices the sun to spend more time in the sky.

Mumming was another traditional practice associated with the midwinter holidays. Called *kekatas, kujenieki, budeli, cigani, preili* or *kaladnieki,* these masked and costumed wanderers might appear anytime from **Martinmas** to Carnival (the festival that precedes the start of Lent). They were most active at Christmas time, however. Popular mummers' disguises included those of wolves, horses, bears, cranes, goats, short men, tall women, haystacks, Death, dead people, and fortune-tellers. Under the direction of a "father," they traveled from house to house singing songs and telling fortunes. One frequently used fortune-telling method involved ladling molten lead or wax into a pail of icy water and reading the twisted shapes as signs of future events. Their visits were thought to scare off harmful spirits, to promote fertility, and to bless (*see also* **Ghosts**). In exchange for all these favors, householders offered the mummers food and drink.

Repression and Revival

Between the years 1940 and 1991 the Russian-led U.S.S.R. (Union of Soviet Socialist Republics) occupied Latvia. This government forbade the celebration of religious holidays. Latvians restored these holidays as soon as the occupation ended.

Further Reading

Bowler, Gerry. *The World Encyclopedia of Christmas.* Toronto, Ontario, Canada: McClelland and Stewart, 2000.

Web Site

"Latvian Seasonal Holidays," an article written by Mera Mellon of the University of Latvia's Center for Ethnic Studies and posted to the web by the Latvian Institute, located in Riga, Latvia: http://www.latinst.lv/seasonal_holidays.htm

Laurel
Bay

Seasonal decorations of **greenery** have embellished European Christmas celebrations for centuries. Laurel's association with the season can be traced back even further, however. The Romans celebrated their new year festival, **Kalends**, by adorning their homes and temples with evergreen branches. Both the Greeks and the Romans crowned the victors of their athletic and other contests with wreaths of laurel, since the laurel branch served as a symbol of victory. In later times northern Europeans gathered laurel, or bay, for their Christmas garlands. In the seventeenth century the English poet Robert Herrick (1591-1674) noted that, according to local custom, "**Rosemary** and baies [bays] that are most faire were stuck about the houses and the churches as Christmas decorations." Christian authorities explained this use of laurel with reference to its ancient association with victory, declaring that when used in Christmas trimmings the fragrant leaves represented the triumph of **Jesus** Christ.

Further Reading

Crippen, Thomas G. *Christmas and Christmas Lore.* 1923. Reprint. Detroit, Mich.: Omnigraphics, 1990.

Lebanon, Christmas in

Lebanese Christians celebrate Christmas with **Christmas trees**, outdoor light displays, **Christmas carols**, special church services, holiday foods, and **gift** exchanges.

Although no recent, accurate census has been taken, most experts believe that Muslims constitute more than fifty percent of the population of this Middle Eastern nation. The vast majority of those remaining are Christians. Most of these people belong to the Maronite Church or various Orthodox churches. A very small percentage of people adhere to other religions. Strife between Muslims and Christians fueled a civil war that lasted from 1975 to 1990. In spite of this recent conflict, in the past several years, when Christmas fell during the Muslim holy month of Ramadan, some Muslims honored the eve of **Jesus'** birth with special gatherings and gift exchanges. Others hung shooting star decorations on the tents where they assembled to celebrate their own festival (*see also* **Star of Bethlehem**).

Preparations

Many Eastern Christians, such as the Maronites and the Orthodox, fast for some or all of **Advent**, a period of spiritual preparation for the coming of Christ at Christmas time. Eastern Christians fast by avoiding meat, dairy products, fish, and eggs.

As the holiday draws near, numerous Lebanese families buy and decorate Christmas trees. Many Lebanese Christians also construct **Nativity scenes** to place next to the tree. Housewives prepare for a sumptuous Christmas dinner, some buying a live turkey as early as November in order to ensure a plump, juicy, fresh bird for the Christmas table. Christmas preparations also include shopping trips to buy gifts for family members and friends. Shopping areas take on a festive appearance in many Lebanese towns at Christmas time. Christmas trees glitter with **ornaments** and strings of electric lights twinkle in the dark but mild winter nights. Images of *Papa Noël*, or **Fa-**

ther **Christmas**, remind shoppers of their mission. For many people this Lebanese **Santa Claus** has replaced the camel as Lebanon's traditional Christmas gift bringer. Gifts may also be purchased at church bazaars, which usually feature homemade foods and crafts.

Christmas Eve and Day

People celebrate Christmas Eve by lighting firecrackers, ringing church **bells**, and shooting guns off into the air (*for similar customs, see* **Shooting in Christmas**). Many attend special religious services, such as **Midnight Mass**. Some churches also hold special concerts featuring Christmas carols on this evening.

Children enjoy a special privilege on Christmas Day. Custom permits them to approach any adult with the cry, "*Editi 'aleik*," meaning, "You have a gift for me!" In this way they hope to add to the presents they have already received on Christmas morning. Nevertheless, a Lebanese Christmas emphasizes family togetherness over gift giving. Lebanese Christians often go visiting on Christmas Day, paying their respects first to older relatives and then visiting with other family members and friends. Guests are usually offered holiday treats, such as sugared almonds. Dried, sugared fruit is another favorite holiday sweet. Dishes of nuts, seeds, and fresh fruit provide additional snacks. Christmas dinner often features turkey or chicken, but people also enjoy many special pastries at Christmas time. In addition to *baklava*, a pastry made from phyllo dough, nuts, spices and sugar syrup, many Lebanese prepare *knafi*, a baked dessert made from cheese, shredded wheat, and sugar syrup.

New Year's Eve and Day

Both Muslim and Christian Lebanese celebrate New Year's Eve on December 31. Some people go out to elegant restaurants and night clubs. Among the more traditionally minded, families visit each other on New Year's Eve, sitting up late to sing, dance, tell jokes and stories, and to play **games**, especially cards and other games of chance. Superstition hints that these games may reveal one's fortune for the coming year. Fathers sometimes distribute a small sum of money to their children on New Year's Eve. These gifts express their hope to provide well for them in the coming year. Some Lebanese children receive presents on **New Year's Day** rather than on Christmas.

Epiphany

Lebanese Christians celebrate **Epiphany** on January 6, a holiday which, for these Eastern Christians, honors the occasion of Jesus' baptism. According to Lebanese folklore, the trees still bow down at midnight on Epiphany eve in honor of this great event. In past times, children who lived in the cold, mountainous regions of Lebanon would venture forth the next morning looking for brush marks in the snow. These disturbances revealed where the crowns of trees had grazed the ground.

Further Reading

Marston, Elsa. *Lebanon: New Light in an Ancient Land.* New York: Dillon Press, 1994.

Sheehan, Sean. *Lebanon. Cultures of the World.* Tarrytown, N.Y.: Marshall Cavendish, 1997.

Walker, Richard Kennedy. *Lebanon: A Portrait of the Country Through Its Festivals and Traditions.* Danbury, Conn.: Grolier Education, 1999.

Web Site

An article titled "Lahhoud Attends Christmas Mass at Bkirki," published in Beirut, Lebanon, on December 26, 1998, posted on news@Lebanon.com: http://www.lebanon.com/news/local/1998/12/26.htm

Lithuania, Christmas in

Lithuanian folk tradition treats the **Christmas season** as a time of religious mystery and folk magic. In past times Lithuanians associated many old superstitions and folk charms with the season. Though no longer taken seriously, these magical formulas may still be practiced as a form of entertainment. In this predominantly Roman Catholic country, people once observed **Advent** with fasting. This tradition has left its mark on the customary Lithuanian Christmas Eve dinner, which is meatless. Today Lithuanians observe Christmas Eve with a ceremonial evening meal, fortune-telling **games**, and attendance at **Midnight Mass**, which is referred to as the Shepherd's Mass (*see also* **Shepherds**).

In the twentieth century Lithuanians adopted certain Christmas customs more familiar to Americans and western Europeans. These include the exchange of Christmas **gifts**, the decorated **Christmas tree**, and the nighttime visit of **Santa Claus** who sometimes makes a personal appearance in Lithuanian homes on Christmas Eve to distribute gifts. Many Lithuanian families like to gather around the tree after leaving the Christmas Eve dinner table and sing **Christmas carols**. In some families children are expected to recite a poem, sing a song, or offer some other kind of performance before receiving their gifts.

The Christmas season closes on January 6, with **Epiphany**, or Three Kings Day. On this day people write the letters KMB over their doorway in chalk as a reminder of the kings who came to visit the baby **Jesus** (*see also* **Magi**). The letters stand for the names assigned to the kings in folklore: Kaspar, Melchior, and Balthasar.

Christmas Eve Preparations and Ceremonies

Lithuanians make every effort to return home for Christmas Eve, even if it means traveling long distances. People prepare for the evening's festivities by bathing, putting on their best clothes, and giving their homes a thorough cleaning. They also cook both the

Christmas Eve meal and the Christmas Day meal, since according to custom, no work should be done on **December 25**. The family strews the dining table with straw over which is placed a white tablecloth. The hay reminds everyone that **Mary** gave birth to Jesus in a stable (*see also* **Yule Straw**). Plates are often set for family members who could not attend. Plates with a candle in the center are also set for those who have recently died. Some people observe the tradition of waiting until the first evening star appears in the sky to begin the meal (*see also* **Star of Bethlehem**).

In Lithuania both Christmas Eve and the Christmas Eve meal share the same name: *Kucios*. Before eating the meal Lithuanians say a prayer and observe a ceremonial blessing involving the use of wafers. The father begins by offering his wafer to his wife and wishing her a joyful Christmas. She breaks off a piece and says "God grant that we are all together again next year." Then she extends her wafer to her husband and they repeat the words and actions. Afterwards everyone at the table exchanges wafers and greetings with every other person present. This ceremony also gives people a chance to play a game of luck. In breaking the wafer, whoever is left with a bigger piece in their hand will have better fortune in the coming year. Naturally, people try to manipulate this exchange so that they will be left with the larger piece of wafer.

Adam and Eve Day

Lithuanians observe December 24 as the feast day of **Adam and Eve**. In some parts of the country people set apples on the table in their honor. Some people observe another short ceremony with the apples. The lady of the house cuts an apple into pieces. Then she offers the man of the house the first slice and passes them around until everyone receives his or her piece. These apple slices remind diners of Adam and Eve's act of disobedience in the Garden of Eden. Mary's obedience to God's will, and the resulting birth of the Savior celebrated on Christmas Day, provides an instructive contrast to this story.

Christmas Eve Foods

In past times many families thought it unlucky if an odd number of people sat down to dinner on Christmas Eve. If faced with an odd number of family members the head of the house invited a solitary neighbor or even a beggar to join the family's Christmas Eve supper. Today many people still observe a folk custom that requires everyone at the table to eat at least a little bit of every dish. An old folk belief claimed that those who neglected to do so would die before the next Christmas Eve. Custom dictates that the family serve twelve dishes said to represent either Jesus' twelve disciples or the twelve months of the coming year. Traditional Christmas Eve dishes omit meat, eggs, and dairy products. Many Lithuanian families still observe these customary restrictions. Foods often found on the Christmas Eve table today include herring and other kinds of fish, *kisielius* (a kind of cranberry pudding), fruit soup or compote, *slizikai* or *kuciukai* (a kind of biscuit), poppy seed milk, oat pudding, beet soup, mushrooms, salad or dried vegetables, sauerkraut, potatoes, and bread.

Fortune-Telling

Fortune-telling is a popular Christmas Eve activity. Events that occur on this day are generally thought to predict trends in the coming year. For example, those who quarrel on Christmas Eve will most likely quarrel all year long. Therefore people do their best to pay their debts, avoid gossip and idleness, prepare a bountiful feast, and, in general, to behave in an exemplary fashion. The weather on Christmas Eve foretells the weather for the coming year. If the night is clear and starry, the weather will be good.

Hundreds of little Christmas Eve formulas and charms offer Lithuanians ways in which to use the events of this evening to predict the future. For example, if someone rises to leave the Christmas Eve dinner table before everyone has finished eating, then that person will be the first in the family to die. The shadows cast on the wall give further indications of one's health and fate. If one's shadow is clear, definite, and shows both the head and body, one can expect a pleasant year. If the shadow quivers, is small or lacks definition, trouble is brewing. If one's head appears not to cast a shadow, terrible misfortune lies ahead.

One fortune-telling charm requires everyone seated at the table to reach under the tablecloth and pull out a straw. For an unmarried person, a short, fat straw predicts a short, fat boyfriend, girlfriend, or spouse. A long, thin straw assures one of attracting a tall, thin partner. Married people interpret the same signs in a different fashion. The long, thin straw means a year of hardship while a fat straw indicates abundance. Girls would also try to predict their marital future by picking up a large number of fence posts, sticks of firewood, matches, candy, or other items. Then they would count them. If they picked up an even number it meant that they would marry within the year. An odd number indicated another year as a maiden. If these techniques did not appeal, Lithuanian girls could avail themselves of dozens of other methods of learning about their future mates.

Return of the Dead

When the family leaves the dinner table on Christmas Eve, they make no effort to clear the food. They leave it out all night long in accordance with an old folk belief that the spirits of the family's dead return to earth on Christmas Eve (*see also* **Ghosts**). In this way the dead may refresh themselves before returning to heaven.

Increasing Crop Yields and Protecting Animals

Lithuanian folklore presents farmers with many Christmas Eve charms to foretell or improve the health of farm animals and crops. In some parts of Lithuania people placed little piles of wheat, rye, barley, and oats on the floor and then brought in a hen. The hen's choice of grain indicated which crop would flourish in the coming year. Other charms taught householders how to enhance their crops. For example, wrapping one's fruit trees in straw was thought to increase their production. Scattering cooked peas in the orchard would achieve the same effect. Sprinkling a mixture of peas and wheat in the barn, on the other hand, would ensure the well-being of one's animals. Washing the doorknobs and windows of one's house and then giving the wash water to the animals protected them from evil eyes. Beekeepers observed a number of superstitions on this day, including placing a communion wafer in the beehive to bless the bees.

Miracles

Lithuanian folklore asserts that on Christmas Eve many miracles may occur. It was once widely believed that animals gain the power of speech on this magical evening. Creeping into the barn to listen to them was perilous, however. Their favorite topic of conversation was the death of their masters and they seemed to have foreknowledge of when these deaths would come. At the exact stroke of midnight the animals knelt and prayed out loud using human speech. Another folk teaching proclaimed that at midnight on Christmas Eve, all water turns briefly into wine.

Christmas Day

In past times people honored Christmas Day—*Kaledos* in Lithuanian—by scrupulously avoiding all forms of work. This meant that Christmas dinner had to be prepared the day before. In times past many householders slaughtered their pigs at Christmas time, and pig's head was a customary dish for Christmas dinner (*see also* **Boar's Head**). Upon waking, family members would take the straw that had lain on the table during the Christmas Eve feast and give it to their cows, sheep, and oxen—all animals that might have been present in the stable where Jesus was born. Before they distributed the hay they examined it. If it had shed most of its grain, then that meant the family could expect a bountiful harvest in the year to come.

The weather on Christmas Day was thought to predict the weather on Easter Day. If snow covered the ground on Christmas Day, Easter Day was sure to be green. On the other hand, if snow hadn't yet fallen by Christmas, then Easter Day was bound to be snowy.

In the nineteenth century groups of men went door to door on Christmas Day, singing hymns and dragging a **Yule log** behind them. Householders rewarded the men with Christmas treats. The carolers later set fire to the log outside the village.

In past times Christmas festivities involving parties and dancing began on the second day of Christmas, that is, **St. Stephen's Day** (*see also* **Twelve Days of Christmas**). Many people thought Christmas Day too holy for these kinds of activities and waited until the day after Christmas to gather together with their neighbors. People also took their oats to church to be blessed on this day.

In more recent times Christmas festivities began on Christmas Day. The celebrations lasted for several days, during which time custom forbade most types of work. Sometimes bands of revelers in costume went door to door during the Christmas season wishing householders abundant crops in the coming year (*see also* **Mumming**). This group included *Kaledu Senis*, the Lithuanian **Father Christmas**. People thanked these well-wishers with Christmas treats. Kaledu Senis gave nuts to children and blessed homes by sprinkling grain in a special corner of the family's dining area.

Today many Lithuanian families decorate their Christmas trees with geometrically shaped **ornaments** made from bent straws. These ornaments, once used by Lithuanian peasants to beautify their homes for weddings and feast days, were adapted to the Christmas tree by Lithuanians living in the United States. In past times Lithuanians decorated their trees with glass ornaments, candies, cookies, apples, and little toy figurines. When Christmas was over children consumed the edible ornaments.

Christmas under Soviet Rule

Between the years 1940 and 1991 the Russian-dominated U.S.S.R (Union of Soviet Socialist Republics) occupied Lithuania. Religious holidays were forbidden during these years and some Christmas customs transferred to **New Year's Day**, a secular holiday. For example, the government renamed Christmas trees "New Year's trees" and promoted a New Year's gift bringer, **Grandfather Frost** (*see also* **Russia, Christmas in**).

New Year's Eve and Day

Lithuanians nicknamed New Year's Eve "Little Christmas Eve." The holidays are celebrated in comparable ways. Lithuanians prepare similar dishes on the two days, although meat dishes are allowed on New Year's Eve. After eating dinner Lithuanians sit up to welcome the start of the new year. Like Christmas Eve, New Year's Eve furnishes Lithuanians with an important opportunity for fortune-telling.

Many New Year's Eve superstitions offered young men and women yet another batch of charms that could reveal something of their future mates. One such method required a girl to write twelve different male names on twelve pieces of paper and put them under her pillow on New Year's Eve along with a blank slip of paper. When she awoke she reached her hand under the pillow and pulled out the first slip of paper her hand touched. The name she saw there was the name of her future husband. If she received the blank slip it meant that she would not find a boyfriend that year. Boys worked the same fortune-telling trick by sleeping with twelve female names under their pillow. Another fortune-telling charm called for a group of boys and girls to gather in a dark room on New Year's Eve. They lit a candle with a match, and waited for the match to burn all the way out. Then someone asked aloud, "Who loves me?" and blew out the candle. The direction in which the candle smoke drifted answered the question. If the candle smoke went straight up, then no one present cared for the questioner; if it went straight down, then someone there disliked him or her.

People watched the weather on New Year's Day carefully, as it was seen to predict the weather for the coming year. Snow on New Year's Day indicated a year of bad weather. If it snowed in the morning it meant that lots of young people would die in the year to come. Snow in the evening signified that many older people would die. A clear day, on the other hand, signaled a bountiful harvest. Cold weather on New Year's Day foretold a warm Easter.

Human activities were also viewed as indicators of future events. People tried to smile and be kind to one another, as this meant that they could expect much of the same throughout the year. People hoped to hear good news when they rose on New Year's Day. The first piece of news they heard, whether good or bad, revealed the kind of news they would receive in the year to come.

Further Reading

Brazyte Bindokiene, Danute. *Lithuanian Customs and Traditions*. Third edition. Chicago: Lithuanian World Community, 1998.

Web Sites

The Lithuanian Folk Culture Center, located in Vilnius, Lithuania, offers excerpts from two books on Lithuanian folk customs, *Lithuanian Roots*, edited by Rytis Ambrazevicius, at: http://www.lfcc.lt/publ/roots/node1.html and *The Lithuanians: An Ethnic Portrait*, by Juozas Kurdirka, at: http://www.lfcc.lt/publ/thelt/node1.html

The *Anthology of Lithuanian Ethnoculture* contains an article entitled "Lithuanian Customs and Traditions" at: http://ausis.gf.vu.lt/eka/customs/christmas.html

Lord of Misrule

Abbot of Unreason, Christmas Lord,
Master of Merry Disports

In late medieval and Renaissance **England**, towns, colleges, noble houses, and the royal court often chose a mock king to preside over their Christmas festivities. Temporarily elevated from his ordinary, humble rank to that of "king," he was known by a variety of names, including the Lord of Misrule, the Abbot of Unreason, the Christmas Lord, and the Master of Merry Disports. These colorful titles reflect the kind of madcap revelry associated with these parties.

Activities

The Christmas festivities over which the Lord of Misrule presided might include feasts, dances, **mumming**, musical entertainments, plays, and **masques**, as well as good deal of general merriment. According to an irate **Puritan** of the sixteenth century, Christmas Lords sometimes led their retinue of giddy followers through the streets of the town and into churches while services were being held. Perhaps in imitation of the **Feast of Fools**, the motley band careened down the aisle, dancing, singing, jingling **bells**, and brandishing their hobbyhorses. Many worshipers laughed at the spectacle and stood on their pews to get a better view. Apparently, the Puritans did not find the interruption at all amusing.

Of course, the noble and wealthy enjoyed the most elaborate Christmas celebrations, and also left the best records of the Lord of Misrule and his activities. One of the earliest records of an English Christmas celebration presided over by a mock king dates back to the time of King Edward III (1312-1377). In 1347 Edward enjoyed a number of extravagant Christmas masques and dances prepared for him by his "Master of Merry Disports." King Henry VIII (1491-1547) found the Lord of Misrule and his diversions vastly entertaining. His enthusiasm for the custom was such that in a few cases he ordered

others to follow suit. For example, when he founded Cambridge University's Trinity College he mandated that a Lord of Misrule preside at its Christmas festivities.

Term of Office and Duties

The duties of the Lord of Misrule varied from place to place, as did the type of entertainment offered and the duration of the Christmas holiday. The Lord of Misrule's most fundamental duty, however, was to attend the Christmas festivities in the character of a mock king. His temporary elevation of status permitted him to command all present, but he was primarily expected to foster a **merry** atmosphere. One wealthy estate owner has left us a written record of the authority granted to his chosen Lord of Misrule. It states:

> I give free leave to Owen Flood, my trumpeter, gentleman, to be Lord of Misrule of all good orders during the twelve days. And also, I give free leave to the said Owen Flood to command all and every person or persons whatsoever, as well as servants as others, to be at his command whensoever he shall sound his trumpet or music, and to do him good service, as though I were present myself, at their perils. . . . I give full power and authority to his lordship to break up all locks, bolts, bars, doors, and latches, and to fling up all doors out of hinges, to come at those who presume to disobey his lordship's commands. God save the king! [Chambers, 1990, 2: 741-42].

In some cases the Lord of Misrule also helped to plan the various **Christmas season** entertainments. At this time Christmas celebrations in wealthy households usually lasted throughout the **Twelve Days of Christmas**. In some places, though, Christmas festivities began as early as All Hallow's Eve (Halloween), October 31, with the selection of the Lord of Misrule. Indeed, the period between Halloween and **Twelfth Night** coincided with the theater season in London, a period of parties and entertainments of all sorts for the well-to-do. The Lord of Misrule's tenure might or might not end with **Epiphany** on January 6, however. In 1607 the Christmas Lord serving St. John's College at Oxford University began offering Christmas entertainments on November 30, St. Andrew's Day (*see also*

Advent). Followers enjoyed his program of festivities so much that they extended his term of office until **Candlemas**, February 2, and, after that, prolonged it until Lent.

Rise and Decline

The Lord of Misrule was known in England as early as the fourteenth century. The custom reached the height of its popularity in the fifteenth and sixteenth centuries and declined in the seventeenth century. Some writers believe he evolved out of the mock bishops associated with the Feast of Fools. Others guess that the **King of the Bean**, already popular in parts of continental Europe, may have inspired the creation of this custom. Whatever his origins, the Lord of Misrule did resemble these and other temporary kings of the Christmas season, including the **boy bishop** and the mock kings associated with **Saturnalia**.

Further Reading

Chambers, E. K. *The Mediaeval Stage.* Volumes 1 and 2. Oxford, England: Clarendon Press, 1903.

Chambers, Robert. "December 24—The Lord of Misrule." In his *The Book of Days.* Volume 2. 1862-64. Reprint. Detroit, Mich.: Omnigraphics, 1990.

Del Re, Gerard, and Patricia Del Re. *The Christmas Almanack.* Garden City, N.Y.: Doubleday, 1979.

Hutton, Ronald. *The Stations of the Sun.* Oxford, England: Oxford University Press, 1996.

Leach, Maria, ed. *Funk and Wagnalls Standard Dictionary of Folklore, Mythology, and Legend.* New York: Harper and Row, 1984.

Muir, Frank. *Christmas Customs and Traditions.* New York: Taplinger, 1977.

Pimlott, J. A. R. *The Englishman's Christmas.* Atlantic Highlands, N.J.: Humanities Press, 1978.

Lovefeast

The lovefeast is a special kind of Moravian church service. The Moravians are Protestant Christians whose denomination was established in 1457 in what is now the Czech Republic. Heavily persecuted in the early years of their existence, they moved from Bohemia to **Germany**, and from there sent members to establish Moravian communities in the American colonies. The denomination's official name is the Unity of the Brethren, or *Unitas Fratrum* in Latin. Moravians hold lovefeasts on holidays and other special days, such as Christmas Eve, Good Friday, church anniversaries, or mission occasions.

Moravian lovefeasts revolve around a small communal meal. The meal, usually composed of a sweet roll and coffee, should not be confused with the Christian sacrament of Holy Communion. Rather, the sharing of food and drink is intended to foster the growth of love and connectedness among members of the congregation. Moravian church officials trace the origins of the lovefeast back to the year 1727, when a group of Moravians attending a communion service in Germany felt an outpouring of the Holy Spirit. Grudges melted away and arguments over religious doctrine gently resolved themselves, leaving participants with renewed feelings of love and appreciation for one another. Afterwards people celebrated with communal meals in one another's homes. These historical events inspired the Moravian lovefeast. Some writers also note that these incidents recalled the fellowship displayed by the first Christians who shared their meals in common after experiencing the marvelous power of the Holy Spirit (Acts 2:46).

The Central Moravian Church in **Bethlehem, Pennsylvania**, celebrates two lovefeasts at Christmas time. The first occurs on the first Sunday in **Advent**. The service begins with a hymn sung by the entire congregation and a prayer. Then several women pass through the church, distributing buns to the congregation. Dressed in old-fashioned lace caps called *haubes*, they are referred to as *deiners*, the German word for "servers." The women are followed by male servers, who distribute mugs of coffee to the worshipers. When all have been served, the choir sings anthems and the congregation eats. More hymn singing follows the meal of bread and coffee.

The second lovefeast takes place on the afternoon of December 24. The Church gears this service towards children and their families. Sugar cookies and chocolate milk replace the buns and coffee at this service. The congregation and the choir alternate in singing **Christmas carols** and hymns. The singing of an old Moravian hymn titled "Morning Star" constitutes the highlight of the musical program. Each year a child is chosen to sing portions of this hymn as a solo. To be entrusted with this role is considered a great honor. The congregation also chimes in on portions of this hymn. Then the servers distribute a lighted beeswax candle to every member of the congregation and everyone sings the closing hymn, "How Bright Appears the Morning Star" (*see also* **Christingle**).

Further Reading

Sawyer, Edwin. A. *All About the Moravians*. Bethlehem, Pa.: The Moravian Church in America, 2000.

Sweitzer, Vangie Roby. *Christmas in Bethlehem*. Bethlehem, Pa.: Central Moravian Church, 2000.

Web Site

The New Philadelphia Moravian Church in Winston-Salem, North Carolina, maintains a page on the Moravian lovefeast at: http://www.everyday counselor.com/np/lovefea.htm

Luminarias

Luminarias (pronounced "loo-mee-NAR-ee-yahs") means "lights" or "illuminations" in Spanish. The word also refers to the small bonfires that illuminate the dark nights of the **Christmas season** throughout the American Southwest (*see also* **Farolitos**). These bonfires are made from piñon pine logs that have been stacked in log-cabin fashion to form a box about three feet in height. Although one may spot luminarias throughout the Christmas season, they are most common on Christmas Eve. On that evening the little bonfires blaze in front of churches, homes, and in public plazas guiding worshipers to mass, enlivening public and family celebrations, and welcoming the coming of the Christ child.

Some believe that the custom of celebrating Christmas Eve with luminarias can be traced all the way back to the fires that warmed the **shepherds** to whom the birth of **Jesus** was announced in the **Gospel according to Luke**. Others say the custom came from Native American traditions, which Spanish missionaries later incorporated into the celebration of Christmas. Still others think that Spanish missionaries brought the custom with them to **Mexico.** They note that the Spanish custom evolved out of various pagan European practices (*see also* **Advent Candle; Christmas Candles; Martinmas; Yule**). Whatever its origins, the earliest historical record of the practice in the New World dates back to the sixteenth century. Spanish missionaries, sent to evangelize the native peoples of Mexico, wrote that on Christmas Eve the people celebrated by singing, drumming, and lighting bonfires on church patios and on the roofs of their flat-topped houses.

Today, the custom of lighting luminarias on Christmas Eve continues in New Mexico. Although city conditions sometimes make the lighting of outdoor fires difficult, many people and organizations strive to continue this old custom. In Albuquerque, New Mexico, organized tours guide interested viewers through the neighborhoods that tend to offer the best displays.

Further Reading

Christmas in the American Southwest. Chicago: World Book, 1996.

Ribera Ortega, Pedro. *Christmas in Old Santa Fe.* Second edition. Santa Fe, N.M.: Sunstone Press, 1973.

Macy's Thanksgiving Day Parade

For many Americans Macy's Thanksgiving Day Parade, which takes place in **New York City**, symbolizes the start of the holiday season (*see also* **Christmas Season**). It also announces the beginning of the Christmas shopping season. Macy's, a department store chain that began in New York City, launched the yearly parades in 1924 as a means of advertising its stores at the start of the year's busiest shopping season. In 2001 the parade celebrated its seventy-fifth anniversary. It featured 30 giant balloons, 28 floats and falloons (float and balloon combinations), 12 marching bands, 14 music and dance ensembles, over 20 groups of clowns, and performances from four Broadway shows. The Radio City Rockettes, a group of New York City dancers, also appeared in the parade, in addition to a number of celebrities. Four thousand Macy's employees helped to stage the two-and-one-half-mile parade, which takes place between 9:00 a.m. and noon on Thanksgiving Day. Although similar Thanksgiving Day parades — also sponsored by department stores — take place in Detroit and Chicago, national television coverage has helped to make the New York parade an American institution.

Store-sponsored Thanksgiving Day parades developed in the 1920s as a means of attracting Christmas season shoppers. In the nineteenth-century many cities instead hosted military parades on Thanksgiving Day. In addition to the military parade, the citizens of New York City celebrated Thanksgiving Day with a few unique customs that may have helped to inspire the format of Macy's parade.

Thanksgiving Day in Nineteenth-Century New York

In the late nineteenth century many New Yorkers celebrated Thanksgiving Day with public masquerades. Bands of working-class men dressed in costume and paraded around the streets. Known as "fantasticals," they often lubricated their costumed hijinks with liberal amounts of alcohol. Their parades began early in the morning and were accompanied by blaring horns, much to the annoyance of those who preferred to sleep in. They usually ended their march about town with a meal in one of the city's parks and in the evening often attended costumed balls.

Children who participated in Thanksgiving Day masquerades were called ragamuffins. They did not march with the adults but rather begged for coins or treats under the cover of costume, much in the way children do today at Halloween. Frequently, boys dressed as girls and girls dressed as boys. White children blackened their faces with soot while black children whitened their faces with powdered talc. The sight of children dressed up in old clothes and make-up was so common that some New Yorkers called Thanksgiving "Ragamuffin Day."

The Target Companies provided another Thanksgiving Day public spectacle for nineteenth-century New Yorkers. These bands of young men, most of whom belonged to a slightly higher social class than did the fantasticals, enjoyed being soldiers for a day. They gave their "company" a name, dressed in boots and military costumes, and marched to a city park to practice target shooting. Since most practiced only once a year, there were not many good shots among them. Proper military parades also took place in New York and other U.S. cities on Thanksgiving Day.

Some commentators believe that the November antics of the raga-muffins and fantasticals began as celebrations of the final withdraw-al of British troops from the city, which took place on November 25, 1783. Others view them as Carnival customs that somehow migrat-ed from early spring to autumn. Researcher Diana Karter Appel-baum suggests that they might instead have grown out of early Guy Fawkes Day celebrations — commemorated by the British on No-vember 5 — which moved to Thanksgiving Day as the city's inhabi-tants began to think of themselves less as British and more as Ameri-cans. As the twentieth century dawned and rolled on, fewer and fewer people celebrated Thanksgiving Day as fantasticals or raga-muffins, however. These customs died out around the time of World War II.

Macy's Thanksgiving Day Parade Begins

Thus, when Macy's launched its first parade in 1924 the sight of peo-ple marching through the streets of New York in costume on Thanks-giving Day was nothing new. Though the organizers of Macy's pa-rade may have found inspiration in New York's old parade and mas-querade customs, the most immediate influence was likely to have been the parades sponsored by Gimbel's department store in Phila-delphia in 1921 and Hudson's department store in Detroit in 1923. These stores had used the parades to convince the public that the Christmas shopping season began as early as Thanksgiving and to draw shoppers into their store. Macy's thought the gimmick a good one and followed suit.

The first parade featured Macy's employees dressed in costumes, animals on loan from the Central Park Zoo, and **Santa Claus**, who unveiled Macy's **store window display** as the finale of the parade. The parade was a hit with New Yorkers and a great boost for the store. In fact, Macy's estimated that the parade contributed to bringing 5,000 children per day to visit the Santa who held court at the store. A few years after the parade's installation, however, devout citizens be-gan to complain that the popular event drew people away from morn-ing church services held in honor of the day. The complaint led Macy's to change the parade from the morning to the afternoon hours. Several years later, however, Macy's reinstated the morning parade. Parade administrators didn't want their event to conflict with the increasingly popular afternoon **football** games that were beginning to draw even bigger audiences than the church services.

Balloons

The first few parades did not include the gigantic balloons that characterized the event in later years. These first appeared in 1927 and were the invention of Tony Sarg, an expert puppeteer and designer that Macy's hired to help jazz up their show. Sarg got rid of the wild zoo animals, because they frightened away the little children, and replaced them with papier mâché creatures. Finding inspiration in the dirigible and zeppelin — the helium-inflated flying devices of his day — and drawing on his experience as a puppeteer, he designed a number of huge airborne balloons shaped like a dragon, a toy soldier, an elephant, and a cartoon character named Felix the Cat. Sarg viewed his creations as enormous, upside-down marionettes, manipulated by ropes from below, rather than by strings by above. He called them "balloonatics."

Making the balloonatics required the help of expert manufacturers. Sarg sent his designs to the Goodyear Tire & Rubber Company in Akron, Ohio. Goodyear executed the designs in rubber and fabric and sealed them with airship cement.

In the early years, the public not only loved the sight of the tethered giants careening down broad city streets, but also thrilled to the sport of hunting them down afterwards. At the end of the parade the balloon wranglers simply let the big behemoths go, knowing that they would eventually deflate and sink to earth. Macy's gave a cash reward to anyone who found and returned the deflated balloons. In 1931 world-class pilot Clarence Chamberlin caught sight of the unleashed Jerry the Pig balloon bobbing over Brooklyn's Prospect Park on Thanksgiving Day. He roped the balloon and towed it back to the ground, winning not only Macy's cash reward but also a good deal of publicity. Nevertheless, the policy of releasing the balloons with cash rewards for their return caused unexpected problems. Some people shot the balloons down, damaging them for future use. The most alarming incident occurred in 1932, however, when a student pilot and her instructor nearly collided with a giant cat balloon that had ascended to 5,000 feet. After that, Macy's quietly deflated the balloons at the end of the parade route.

The big balloons have continued to cause problems over the years. A Santa Claus balloon exploded during inflation in 1941. High winds took out all but one balloon during the 1956 parade. A helium shortage in 1958 meant that the balloons had to be filled with air and then suspended from cranes for the duration of the parade. In 1971 strong winds led to the cancellation of the parade balloons.

Nevertheless, the big balloons are the most noted feature of the parade. One of the biggest balloons in the 2001 parade, representing Thommy, Chuckie, and Spike from the Rugrats cartoon series, measured 48 feet high, 60 feet long, and 28 feet wide. Sixteen thousand seven hundred eighty cubic feet of helium filled out the balloon while 46 handling lines assured wranglers of some control over the enormous cartoon characters. Since the big balloons are capable of lifting over 600 pounds, wranglers must work the giant, inflatable puppets in groups at all times. Each wrangler must weigh at least 125 pounds.

World War II

The Thanksgiving Parade was cancelled in 1942, 1943, and 1944, due to World War II. In 1942, Macy's surrendered its balloons to wartime officials in response to the government's call for citizens to donate rubber to the military. Making a spectacle out of the event, parade officials inflated one of the balloons — a giant, green dragon — and escorted it to city hall. When they arrived, Mayor Fiorello La Guardia, also head of the Office of Civilian Defense, took a long knife and "slew" the beast. By handing over its balloons, Macy's contributed 650 pounds of rubber to the war effort.

National Popularity

The parade resumed in 1945, drawing a crowd of two million as well as attracting its first television coverage. In 1948 television coverage went nationwide, expanding the parade's potential viewing audience from coast to coast. The 1947 Christmas film *Miracle on 34th Street* generated further publicity for the event by setting the opening scenes of the story at the Macy's Thanksgiving Day parade. By the 1950s the opportunity to ride in the parade drew well-known celebrities. In 1957, the first high school marching band participated. The marching bands, as well as other groups of young entertainers, would become a regular feature of the parade, with hopeful candidates auditioning yearly before Macy's judges. The 1970s saw the first falloons — part float, part balloon — enter the parade.

Commercial Effects and Influences

From its modest beginnings, the parade has grown to become big business for the Big Apple. In the late 1990s the mayor's office estimated that the parade generated just over $24 million of economic activity annually in New York City. But the economic effects of the parade are also felt far away from New York. About 60 million people watch the parade each year, either in person or on television. This enormous audience, glued to television sets right at the start of the Christmas shopping season, creates plenty of opportunity for what some have termed holiday **commercialism**. For example, many companies pay Macy's for putting a balloon in the parade that will promote one of their products. Quite a number of the characters represented by the Macy's parade balloons are licensed images. In the late 1990s companies were paying about $350,000 to have their character represented as a balloon in the Macy's Thanksgiving parade.

In the year 2001 some of the "commercial" balloons included Jimmy Neutron (sponsored by Nickelodeon), Snoopy (sponsored by United Feature Syndicate), Arthur (sponsored by the Learning Company), Cheesasaurus Rex (sponsored by Kraft Macaroni and Cheese), Pikachu (sponsored by the Pokémon Company), Ronald McDonald (sponsored by McDonald's Corporation), Barney the purple dinosaur (sponsored by HIT Entertainment), Big Bird (sponsored by Sesame Workshop), Jeeves (sponsored by Ask Jeeves, Inc.) and the Honey-Nut Cheerios Bee (sponsored by Honey-Nut Cheerios). Non-commercial balloons in 2001, billed as novelty balloons, included an **elf**, a flying fish, Chloe the Holiday Clown, Harold the Fireman, a hippopotamus, an ice cream cone, and a toy soldier.

Where and When

The parade begins at 9:00 a.m. at the intersection of 77th Street and Central Park West. It ends around noon at the Macy's store in Herald Square. Located at 34th Street and Sixth Avenue, this, Macy's flagship branch, bills itself as the largest department store in the world. Just as he did in the early days, Santa Claus still brings up the rear of the parade. Promoters bill his arrival at Herald Square as the official start of the holiday season in New York.

Further Reading

Appelbaum, Diana Karter. *Thanksgiving: An American Holiday, An American History*. New York: Facts on File, 1984.
Pool, Daniel. *Christmas in New York*. New York: Seven Stories Press, 1997.

Web Site

The New York Historical Society maintains a web exhibit on the parade at: http://www.nyhistory.org/macyday/index.html

Madagascar, Christmas in

The people of Madagascar, a large island nation off the coast of southern Africa, enjoy a summertime Christmas (*see also* **Winter Solstice**). Just over forty percent of the Malagasy people are Christians, about seven percent are Muslims, and the rest practice traditional religions.

Christians in Madagascar celebrate Christmas with church services and **gift** giving. In spite of the summer heat, their Christmas gift bringer wears a red suit edged with white fur, much like **Santa Claus**. In Malagasy his name is *Dadabenoely*. In French he is called *le Bonhomme Noël*, which may be translated as **Father Christmas**.

New Year's Celebrations

The traditional Malagasy **New Year's Day** falls months after Christmas. This lunar festival takes place in March, at the time of the first new moon of the Malagasy year. Both New Year's Eve and Day are important occasions in Madagascar. In the capital city of Antananarivo people celebrate both days. On the first day people put on their brightly colored holiday clothes and assemble at Ambohimanga, the holy hill on top of which the queen once had her palace. Once there they listen to energetic music and take part in rituals designed to honor and communicate with their ancestors. People attend these ceremonies in bare feet as a sign of humility. Some attendees fall into trances during which time they can convey messages and prayers to those who have died. Once these ceremonies have concluded people head for home where families gather together for special meals. On this occasion many people eat *romaza*, a dish made from meat, rice, herbs and leaves. A kind of wine, distilled from sugar cane and rice, may also be served. People begin New Year's Day with a Christian hymn. In this country most people are perfectly comfortable mixing together Christian and indigenous customs and rituals. Later, two zebu, a humpback kind of African cattle, are sacrificed and people are anointed with the blood, which is thought to enhance the power of prayers.

Further Reading

Ellis, Royton, and John R. Jones. *Festivals of the World: Madagascar*. Milwaukee, Wis.: Gareth Stevens, 1999.

Heale, Jay. *Cultures of the World: Madagascar*. Tarrytown, N.Y.: Marshall Cavendish, 1998.

Magi
Three Kings, Three Kings of Cologne, Wise Men of the East

Christian lore and tradition assigns several different titles to the Magi, sages from the East who traveled to **Bethlehem** to pay tribute to the baby **Jesus**. They are referred to as the Wise Men of the East, the Three Wise Men, the Three Kings, the Three Kings of Cologne, or by the names most commonly associated with them in legend — Melchior, Caspar (or Gaspar), and Balthasar. Their association with Christmas begins in Christian scripture. Of the two **Gospel accounts of Christmas** recorded in the Bible, the **Gospel according to Matthew** is the only one to mention the Magi and their pilgrimage. However, this brief account of their actions neither reveals their identities nor elaborates on the source of their prophetic knowledge. Over time, tangled vines of legend have grown up around the slender trunk of Matthew's account, creating a rich heritage of story, custom, and celebration around these mysterious witnesses of the first Christmas.

The Magi in Matthew's Gospel

In chapter two of the Gospel according to Matthew, Magi from the East, led by a **star**, journey to Jerusalem. They arrive at the court of King **Herod** asking for the whereabouts of the newborn king of the Jews. Herod, secretly troubled by news of a potential rival, consults Jewish priests and scribes. He discovers that prophecy dictates that the Messiah will be born in Bethlehem. Herod relays this information to the Magi, asking them to return with news of the child's identity. The Magi then continue on their journey, again guided by the star. They find Jesus in Bethlehem, worship him, and offer him costly **gifts: gold, frankincense,** and **myrrh**. A dream warns the Magi not to return to Herod, who is planning to kill the child they identify as the king of the Jews, and they set off for their own country by another route.

451

The Magi in History

Although the Gospels give no further information about these prophets from the East, scholars of ancient history can tell us something about the people known in biblical times as magi. The word "magi" comes from the ancient Greek term μαγοι (*magoi*, plural of *magos*) and from the Old Persian word *magu*. Both terms referred specifically to a class of scholar-priests originally from the ancient land of Media (Medes), now part of Iran. In biblical times, magi could be found throughout Persia and in many other Near Eastern countries.

The magi were famed for their knowledge of astronomy, astrology, dream interpretation, philosophy, and religious ritual, hence the translation often given for the term magi is "wise men." They often served as councillors to kings and as tutors to princes. Their teachings were studied and recorded by some of the most renowned thinkers of ancient Greece, including Plato, Aristotle, Pythagoras, and Herodotus. The magi were also associated with what we today would call magical or occult practices, such as divination. Indeed, the English word "magic" comes to us from the ancient word "magi." Because of the magi's strong association with magic, the term magi was sometimes used more loosely and negatively by ancient Greek and biblical writers to refer to anyone who claimed occult knowledge from Eastern lands.

When Media was conquered by Persia in the sixth century B.C., the magi adopted many of the ideas of Persian Zoroastrianism, an ancient religion. They became important proponents and developers of Zoroastrian ideas, spreading their influence beyond Persia. One of these beliefs corresponds well with their role in the Christmas story. Like the ancient Jews, Zoroastrians believed in the coming of a savior, a *saoshyant*. Zoroaster had been the first saoshyant. The last of the three saoshyants, who would be born to a virgin mother, was to be the greatest. He would have the power to defeat the forces of evil, resurrect the dead, banish old age and decay from the world, and would usher in a new age for humanity.

Early Christian Interpretations

This historical background helps to explain the presence of magi in Matthew's account of Jesus' birth. As believers in the coming of a saoshyant, they would be expecting the birth of a savior. Since they were skilled in divination practices, they might be keenly interested in predicting this event. As astrologers, they might expect that the prophet's birth would correspond with a heavenly event, such as the rising of an unusual star. As astronomers, they would know and watch the night sky and notice immediately any such event. As scholars and religious experts, they might be interested in making the journey to Judea to discover the identity of the child and to worship him. Finally, as experts in the study of dreams, they would understand the dream imagery warning them of Herod's evil intent. Because of the intellectual and occult prestige of the magi in the ancient world, readers of Matthew's account would be likely to interpret their recognition of Jesus' birth as confirmation of his identity as the Messiah.

Although we do know something of the activities and beliefs of magi in ancient times, we know literally nothing about the individuals who appear in Matthew's account. He states that the Magi journeyed to Bethlehem from the East, but he does not mention their names, their nationalities, or their exact number. They could have been from any number of countries, such as Arabia, Persia (or **Iran**), Mesopotamia, or even **India**. The lack of detail given in the scriptures led to speculation about the Magi by religious figures, as well as much embellishment of the story in folk tradition. Early Christian artwork depicts two, three, four, or more Magi. Eastern Christians believed that there were twelve Magi. By the sixth century A.D., the idea that there had been three Magi became firmly established among Western Christians. This belief was probably based on the three gifts mentioned in the scriptures, which became associated in folk tradition with three individuals.

By the end of the second century A.D., Christians began to celebrate a special holiday, called **Epiphany**, in honor of the Magi's pilgrimage. The word "epiphany" means "manifestation," "appearance," or "showing forth." The feast of Epiphany thus celebrates the first manifestation of Jesus' divinity, as witnessed by the Magi. Epiphany predates Christmas by well over a century, illustrating its importance to early Christians.

Folk Beliefs and Legends

By the early Middle Ages, folk and Church tradition had converted the enigmatic wise men of Matthew's Gospel into three kings. Some scholars attribute this transformation to the influence of prophetic writings in the Old Testament (Psalms 72; Isaiah 60:3-6) linking the future conversion of the gentiles with the homage of foreign kings and gifts of gold and frankincense.

The most widespread Western legend about the Magi assigns them the following identities: Melchior, king of Arabia; Caspar (or Gaspar), king of Tarsus (located in southern Turkey); and Balthasar, king of **Ethiopia** or king of Saba (in modern-day Yemen). Not only did legend assign them names and nationalities, but they were also assigned various characteristics. Melchior is most often described as an elderly, light-complexioned man with white hair and beard who bears the gift of gold. Caspar, a young and beardless man of "ruddy" complexion, offers frankincense. Balthasar, a middle-aged African man, brings the infant Jesus a gift of myrrh. (Sometimes the ages of Balthasar and Caspar are switched).

Once these identities became firmly established in the folk imagination, they, too, began to excite speculation. St. Bede (c. 672-735) suspected that the diverse kings represented the continents of Europe, Africa, and Asia. Others believed that the ethnic and racial diversity of the three kings represented the belief that Jesus' teachings were to spread to all nations. The gifts of the Magi also acquired symbolic meanings. The gold was said to represent Jesus' kingship, the frankincense his divinity, and the myrrh his early death or his ability to heal.

In addition to providing answers about the names, ages and fates of the Magi, folk tales also speculated about their ancestry and origins. One legend affirms that they were descendants of Balaam, a Mesopotamian seer from the Old Testament, who some also called a magus. Balaam predicted that "a star out of Jacob" (Numbers 24:17) would foretell the birth of a great Jewish leader. The legend suggests that Balaam kept watch for the appearance of the star, passing the search to his sons, who in turn passed it on to their descendants. Another account, again credited to St. Bede, speculates that the Magi were descended from Noah's sons, Shem, Ham, and Japheth.

Yet another tale declares that the kings of Persia and Chaldea sent the twelve wisest men of their courts to follow the star.

Magi Tales from the East

In the late thirteenth century, Venetian explorer Marco Polo (1254-1324) returned to Italy from his years of travel in central and east Asia. He brought with him many exciting, foreign tales, including some Eastern stories concerning the Magi. In one, Melchior, the eldest, first entered the shelter where Jesus lay. There he encountered an old man who spoke with the wisdom of many years. The middle-aged king went next, and found Jesus to be a learned man of his own age. When the youngest stepped over the threshold he discovered a young man full of passion and inspiration. After comparing and marveling over their varied experiences, the kings entered the shelter together bearing their gifts and found Jesus to be an infant.

Another tale of Eastern origins suggests that the Magi's gifts were meant to test the baby Jesus. If he chose the gold, he was a king; if he chose the incense he was a priest; and if he chose myrrh he was a healer. The child took them all, and the Magi concluded that Jesus was all three things at once.

One more story states that the Magi received a small gift in return for their pilgrimage, some say from **Mary**, others say from the infant Jesus. When the Wise Men opened the box, they found only a stone inside. The stone was meant as a sign that their faith should be as firm as a rock. The Magi did not understand this, however, and, thinking the stone worthless, they tossed it down a well. As they did so, fire streamed down from heaven towards the well (or, some say, ascended from the well towards heaven). The amazed Wise Men transported the fire back to their own countries where it was worshiped. This tale presents us with an interesting link back to Zoroastrianism. In the Zoroastrian religion, fire represents the divine. In Zoroastrian fire temples, flames are kept burning perpetually and are used in religious ceremonies and worship.

The Fate of the Magi

Many legends suggest that, after returning to their own lands, the Magi devoted the rest of their lives to good works and to spreading the news of Christ's birth. One tale declares that they were baptized by **St. Thomas** the Apostle and later became Christian priests and bishops. Another suggests that the Star of Bethlehem appeared to them once more, shortly before their deaths. Some believed that they died in the city of Sewa, now in Iran. Marco Polo, who visited that city during his thirteenth-century travels, declared that the inhabitants showed him the tombs of the three ancient kings, called Melchior, Caspar, and Balthazar, who in their lifetimes had made a great journey to worship a newborn prophet.

Relics

In the tenth century the citizens of Milan, **Italy**, turned to the well-known legends concerning the Three Kings to interpret an unusual discovery. The embalmed bodies of three men, one young, one middle-aged, and one old, had been found in the church of St. Eustorgius. These remains were quickly assumed to be those of the Three Kings. The emperor Frederick Barbarossa had the relics transferred to Cologne, **Germany**, in 1164, where a special shrine was built to house them in the city's cathedral. In this way, the Magi acquired yet a new name: the Three Kings of Cologne.

But how did the three Middle Eastern kings end up buried in Italy? It was believed that the Empress Helena (St. Helena, c. 248-c. 328) had originally retrieved the bodies from the East during her travels to the Holy Land. Legend had it that she brought the remains to Constantinople, and that later they were moved to the city of Milan. The bodies appeared not to have aged since the Magi's momentous meeting with Jesus, but it was not difficult for people to believe that, in death, the bodies of the kings had been preserved as they had been during that holy encounter. The long tale of the Magi's bones took a final turn in 1903, when the Cardinal of Cologne approved the return of some of the relics to Milan.

Enduring Popularity

The story of the Magi's quest has kindled the imaginations of Christians for centuries. The Magi's journey was one of the most popular images depicted by early Christians in the Roman catacombs. The Magi often appear as characters in medieval **Nativity plays**. A multitude of artists, including the famous painters Diego Velázquez (1599-1660), Sandro Botticelli (1445-1510), and Leonardo da Vinci (1452-1519), have created memorable images of the adoration of the Magi. Gian Carlo Menotti's twentieth-century opera, *Amahl and the Night Visitors*, revolves around a small boy's encounter with the Magi. Both the Italian La **Befana** and the Russian **Baboushka** were believed to have met the Three Kings on their journey towards Bethlehem. The Magi are the central figures in such familiar **Christmas carols** as "We Three Kings of Orient Are." The initials of each of the three kings, CMB, are still inscribed over the doors of houses during the **Christmas season** in Germany, Austria, **Poland**, **Lithuania**, and Czechoslovakia in order to protect the house. Roman Catholic priests sometimes bless the homes of their parishioners at Epiphany by writing the initials CMB inside the door with blessed chalk, surrounded by the numbers representing that calendar year. In the year 1999, for example, the priest would write 19 CMB 99. Finally, the Magi are often represented in the **Nativity scenes** that Christians all over the world assemble during the Christmas season.

Significance

For close to two millennia, folk tales and legends have embroidered additional details around Matthew's spare outline of the Magi's pilgrimage to Bethlehem. For some, however, Matthew's original text is rich in spiritual significance. The Magi's journey may be said to represent the universal search for God. Some Christians see the Magi's story as a demonstration of an active faith; the Magi act on the inspiration and understanding that they have while others, who presumably also see the star, do nothing. The story's assertion that the non-Jewish Magi are the first people inspired to worship Jesus is also believed to be significant by many Christian commentators. It symbolizes that seekers of all ethnic and religious backgrounds will be drawn to Jesus, that his message is to be offered to all peoples, and that his teachings will spread throughout the entire world.

Further Reading

Chambers, Robert. "December 25—The Three Magi." In his *The Book of Days*. Volume 2. 1862-64. Reprint. Detroit, Mich.: Omnigraphics, 1990.

Gnoli, Gherardo. "Magi." In Mircea Eliade, ed. *The Encyclopedia of Religion.* Volume 9. New York: Macmillan, 1987.

———. "Saoshyant." In Mircea Eliade, ed. *The Encyclopedia of Religion.* Volume 13. New York: Macmillan, 1987.

Grigson, Geoffrey. "The Three Kings of Cologne." *History Today* 41, 12 (December 1991): 28-34. Reprint of 1954 article.

Hackwood, Frederick W. *Christ Lore.* 1902. Reprint. Detroit, Mich.: Gale Research, 1969.

Hadfield, Miles, and John Hadfield. *The Twelve Days of Christmas.* Boston, Mass.: Little, Brown and Company, 1961.

Hottes, Alfred Carl. *1001 Christmas Facts and Fancies.* 1946. Reprint. Detroit, Mich.: Omnigraphics, 1990.

Keck Leander, ed. *The New Interpreter's Bible.* Volume VIII. Nashville, Tenn.: Abingdon Press, 1995.

Lehane, Brendan. *The Book of Christmas.* Chicago: Time-Life Books, 1986.

Manger Scene. *See Nativity Scene*

Marshall Islands, Christmas in the Republic of the

The Marshall Islands are located in the Pacific Ocean, about 3,000 miles southwest of the Hawaiian Islands. The Marshallese adopted Christianity with the coming of European colonists and Christian missionaries in the late nineteenth and early twentieth centuries. The people of this 34-island nation have created a celebration of Christmas that is all their own, by blending Christian beliefs with their own cultural traditions and values. On Christmas Day huge baskets of food are exchanged and the entire day is spent watching various local groups, called *jeptas*, perform original songs, dances, and skits. Preparations for the great day begin months in advance. In fact, the Marshallese enjoy a holiday season that stretches from September through December. The activities of this long season of preparation, as well as those of the Christmas festivities that crown it, illustrate Marshallese concepts of well-being, abundance, love, generosity, prestige, beauty, and play. The following description of the **Christmas season** in the Marshall Islands summarizes the celebrations that take place on Ujeland and Enewetak atolls.

The Christmas Season

People begin to think about Christmas shortly after Easter, and start to set aside food and other resources during the summer. What's more, composers and choreographers begin dreaming up new Christmas ditties and dances during the summer months, basing them on bits and pieces of the tunes and dance movements used in past holiday performances, Western church hymns, and Pacific Islands songs and dances. The real work begins in the fall, however. Indeed, *Kurijmoj*, the word for Christmas, is used to refer not only to **December 25**, but also to the several months that precede it, when preparation for Christmas becomes a part of one's daily occupation.

Jeptas

When Christmas is still a few months away, the islanders divide them-selves into jeptas, which may be thought of as teams. These teams begin practicing the new songs and dances that will be performed from memory on Christmas Day. Each group may perform as many as fifteen to twenty songs. Before Christmas Day, the jeptas visit one another, engaging in competitive songfests in order to show off their skills and assess the competition. In these "surprise attacks" one jepta drops in on another bearing **gifts** of food and other small items, such as bars of soap and books of matches. The generosity, musical polish, and skill of each group's chosen orators will be judged and the pres-tige of each jepta will rise or fall accordingly.

The women also take part in another form of playful competition between the jeptas, known as *karate*. The preparations made by the jeptas include stockpiling gifts of food that will be distributed to other islanders on Christmas Day. When the women of one jepta spy some men from a rival jepta coming back from a food-collecting mis-sion, the women surround them and steal their food. Nevertheless, the women always leave the men with a meal of some kind. These encounters have become an occasion for much good-natured banter between the sexes and islanders find them extremely amusing.

During **Advent**, the jeptas perform their songs in front of the church. Each jepta also builds a piñata-like construction, called a *wojke*, which serves as a kind of **Christmas tree**. It may take on many shapes, including that of a ship, plane, or bomb. It contains numer-ous little presents "for God," such as bars of soap, matches, and money. The teams explode the piñatas at the end of their Christmas Day performances. The gifts are usually collected by the local pastor.

Last-Minute Preparations

During the last few days before Christmas, the islanders prepare by giving their homes, streets, and church a thorough cleaning. They also prepare gifts for the performers who will sing and dance on Christmas Day, including bottles of coconut oil, bags of copra (co-conut), and various handmade items. Men slaughter pigs, prepare fish, and gather coconuts. Women make rice, doughnuts, bread, and put the final touches on their breadfruit paste and other foods. In addition, they sew costumes for the jeptas and weave mats and food baskets. Young boys take special responsibility for cleaning pathways and disposing of trash. Young girls help the older women with their cooking and weaving and provide childcare. At last, after months of preparation, the Christmas foods are packed into baskets which will be given away—to members of another family, cookhouse, or jepta —on Christmas Day.

In the last few days before Christmas the jeptas make special visits to the minister's home. They sing for him and his family and give them food and presents. The minister often responds with a polite speech and gifts of coffee or tea.

Christmas Day

Christmas Day celebrations begin with an early morning church service. Then the baskets of food are exchanged. These hefty gifts, which weigh 25-40 pounds, elicit hearty thanks. People eat some of the choicest foods on the spot and take the rest home for later. At around 10:00 a.m. the people return to the church to watch the performances of the jeptas, which last the rest of the day. When a particular song, dance, or speech especially pleases members of the audience, they may run up to the stage area and grab the performer's headdress, flower necklace, watch, or clothing. The performer lets them take everything but necessary pieces of clothing; modesty dictates that these be delivered later that evening. Rushing the stage to douse the performers with sweet-smelling substances such as baby powder, cologne, or pomade is another spontaneous tribute paid to thrilling acts. The performances end with a short skit at the conclusion of which the wojke explodes, scattering money and other party favors among the crowd. The festivities end with prayers and the singing of a hymn.

The day's performances are talked about for months. The singing, dancing, speeches, costumes, skits, and gift giving will be exhaustively analyzed, and the members of the jepta that made the best display will gain status in the community.

Some United Church of Christ Christmas services include a tree-lighting ceremony that links the Christmas tree with the traditional Christian symbol of the cross. A Christmas tree is concealed inside a large, hollow cross. While the congregation sings **Christmas carols**, the tree rises out of the cross. The congregation greets this sight with exploding firecrackers. Then the tree descends back into the cross, while the singers hush their voices. After the singing, the cross splits open down the middle, revealing the tree standing inside.

New Year Celebrations

Feasting and gift giving also take place on New Year's Eve, but to a much lesser degree. Children stay up late on New Year's Eve. At midnight they go door to door, singing songs and receiving in exchange treats and trinkets. Islanders make every attempt to attend early morning church services on **New Year's Day**, as good behavior on the first of the year is thought to honor the new year and to steer it in a good direction. Hotly contested softball matches take place later on New Year's Day.

Further Reading

Carucci, Laurence Marshall. *Nuclear Nativity: Rituals of Renewal and Empowerment in the Marshall Islands*. Dekalb, Ill.: Northern Illinois University Press, 1997.

Henderson, Helene, and Sue Ellen Thompson, eds. *Holidays, Festivals, and Celebrations of the World Dictionary*. Second edition. Detroit, Mich.: Omnigraphics, 1997.

Martinmas

Funkentag, Martinalia, Martinsfest, Martinstag, St. Martin's Day

Martinmas, or St. Martin's Day, falls on November 11. This Christian feast day honors St. Martin of Tours (c. 316-397 A.D.), but many of the popular customs that have been associated with it over the centuries resemble those connected to a much earlier pagan autumn festival. In medieval **Europe**, the arrival of Martinmas signaled the beginning of winter. In early medieval times, the festival marked the beginning of **Advent** in some parts of Europe.

Life and Legends of St. Martin

Born into a pagan family in Hungary in the late fourth century A.D., St. Martin became interested in Christianity and a monastic life at an early age. His military father forced him to become a soldier, however. Many tales about the saint's life illustrate his generosity. In the most famous of these, Martin, while stationed in Amiens, **France**, as a soldier, encountered a beggar shivering miserably in the cold. Martin quickly removed his cloak, cut it in half with his sword, and covered the beggar with the cloth. That night **Jesus** appeared to Martin in a vision declaring, "Martin the catechumen hath clothed me in this garment." Shortly afterwards Martin was baptized. At the age of forty he left the army and began a life of religious devotion. He was elected bishop of Tours in 371 A.D.

One legend tells that when the retiring saint heard the news of his election, he was so flustered that he ran away and hid in a barn, but the squawking of a goose soon announced his presence. The goose thereafter became a symbol of the saint. As bishop of Tours, Martin gained a reputation for religious fervor by converting his entire diocese to the new religion of Christianity and replacing the pagan temples with Christian churches. St. Martin eventually became one of the most popular saints of the medieval era.

Precedents

In pre-Christian times the Germanic peoples of north-central Europe celebrated a great autumn festival. As pastures thinned with the coming of cold weather, they slaughtered the animals that could not be kept alive and preserved most of their meat for the winter. At this time the people gathered together, feasted on fresh meat, and drank. They may also have honored the dead and lit ceremonial bonfires at these celebrations. This festival probably marked the end of the old year and the beginning of the new year in pre-Christian times. According to several scholars, some of the customs associated with medieval **Yule** celebrations were actually transferred to that season from earlier celebrations of this great autumn festival. At least one researcher has identified the date of this ancient Germanic new year festival as November 11 or 12.

History

The Christian festival of Martinmas developed in the several hundred years that followed the saint's death in the late fourth century. In 490 A.D. Bishop Perpetuus of Tours called for a forty-day period of partial fasting in preparation for Christmas. This period began on November 11, a day already associated with the veneration of St. Martin, and was known as the "Forty Days' Fast of St. Martin," or "St. Martin's Lent." In later times these weeks of spiritual preparation for Christmas came to be called Advent. Pope Martin I (d. 655) established Martinmas as a great Church festival. He may have been attempting to provide a Christian rationale for the celebrations that pagan northern Europeans still held around this time of the year. In the Middle Ages some referred to Martinmas by the Latin name *Martinalia*.

The customs associated with medieval celebrations of Martinmas closely resemble those connected with earlier pagan celebrations. In the Middle Ages the feast of Martinmas marked the beginning of winter. Customs in some regions suggest that it may have been treated as a kind of new year as well. In areas of **England**, France, and **Germany**, leases ended at Martinmas, rents were due, and servants left households in search of new employment. In his eighth-century chronicles, St. Bede (c. 672-735) noted that the Anglo-Saxon term for November was *Blot Monath*, or "Blood Month," in reference to the customary slaughtering of animals that took place during that month. Not only did this old custom attach itself firmly to Martinmas, but so also did the feasting and drinking of earlier November celebrations. In medieval times Martinmas may have served as a kind of thanksgiving festival during which the people rejoiced at the close of the harvest and their full barns and larders. In Germany St. Martin became the patron saint of the harvest, as well as the champion of the poor.

The sixteenth-century Protestant Reformation created a new rationale for this traditional November festival. Rather than forbid the celebration of the day because it venerated a Roman Catholic saint, Protestant authorities dedicated the celebrations to Martin Luther, the German founder of the Protestant movement who was born on November 10, 1483. In some areas of Germany the celebrations were shifted to November 10; in others the people continued to celebrate on November 11 in the belief that the Protestant reformer was baptized on that day. In Germany the holiday acquired the name *Martinsfest* or *Martinstag*, meaning "Martin's Festival" or "Martin's Day."

Martinmas Fires

In Germany and the Netherlands, great bonfires roared on Martinmas or Martinmas Eve in past times. In the fifteenth century, the festival acquired the nickname *Funkentag* (Spark Day) in Germany, due to the many fires that blazed in honor of the occasion. In the centuries that followed, people in Austria, Germany, **Denmark**, and Belgium, also participated in lantern parades on Martinmas Eve, marching through the darkened streets of town with lanterns or jack-o'-lanterns fashioned out of turnips or pumpkins.

Martinmas Feasts

The central and enduring customs of Martinmas feature the preparation and consumption of meat and drink. The date at which the holiday falls in the agricultural cycle anchored these customs to it. In Britain the customary slaughter of cattle on Martinmas produced

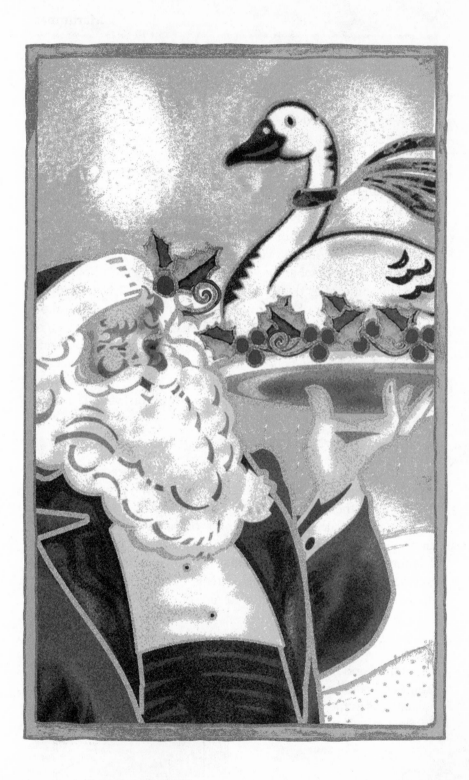

"Martlemas Beef," the salted and dried meat that sustained people throughout the lean winter months. In Germany, Denmark, **Ireland**, and Scandinavia goose became the traditional Martinmas feast, perhaps in reference to the Christian legend connecting the saint with a goose. Another possible explanation for this association between Martinmas and geese arises from an old German agricultural custom; in past centuries people fattened geese for the fall season, when they could be used to pay the taxes due on Martinmas. Not every European country favored roast goose for their Martinmas feast, however. In Portugal the traditional St. Martin's Day feast featured roast pig.

According to old German and Italian traditions, the year's new wines were sampled for the first time on Martinmas. People who got drunk on Martinmas were often called "Martinmen," as were people given to spending their money on short-lived good times. Indeed, so important was this association between Martinmas and wine that St. Martin became the patron saint of tavernkeepers, wine makers, and drunkards. Indulging in large quantities of meat and drink persists as a perennial feature of the holiday. In France the upset stomach that often follows the consumption of too much food and drink is known as *mal de Saint Martin,* or "Saint Martin's sickness." St. Martin's Day is still observed in Europe with traditional festive meals, most commonly of roast goose.

Martinmas Folklore

Long after pagan European religions disappeared, early November retained its association with the commemoration of the dead. Old Scottish and Irish folk beliefs declared that the **ghosts** of the dead returned to their old homes on Martinmas. In the twentieth century, the festivals of early November still link the season to the remembrance of the dead. On November 5, Guy Fawkes Day, the British commemorate the capture and execution of a group of men who tried to blow up the Houses of Parliament. In Britain and North America many celebrate October 31 as Halloween, a folk festival associated with spirits of the dead. Christians in many countries observe All Saints' Day on November 1 and All Souls' Day on November 2. Even the secular calendar retains November 11 as a date sacred to the memory of the dead. After World War I, November 11 was established as Armistice Day and dedicated to the memory of the soldiers who died in that war. (In Britain and Canada the day is known as Remembrance Day). In 1954 Armistice Day became Veterans Day in the United States, and its purpose broadened to include the recognition of all those who have served in the United States armed forces.

In some European countries St. Martin became a gift-bearing folk figure, much like **St. Nicholas**. He was often depicted as a bishop garbed in red robes riding a white horse. In Belgium and other European countries he distributes sweets to well-behaved children on St. Martin's Eve, but badly behaved youngsters may receive a rod instead.

A variety of folk beliefs and sayings link Martinmas with the weather. In Europe the temperate days that often surround Martinmas may be referred to as "St. Martin's Summer." Legend has it that God first sent mild weather at this time of year to shield St. Martin from the cold, since he had just given half of his cloak to a beggar. An English folk belief suggests that if Martinmas is mild, the coming winter will be severe, whereas if frost occurs before Martinmas, the winter will be gentle.

Martinmas in Contemporary Germany

In the twentieth century Martinmas Eve fires still blazed along the banks of the Rhine and Moselle rivers in Germany. Although fire safety has become an issue in recent decades, the fires burn on in some parts of Germany. Excited children collect cardboard, tree branches, and other tinder for weeks in anticipation of the event. Lantern parades continue to be celebrated in Germany, although they have become primarily a children's custom. Children fashion elaborate lanterns from paper or recreate the traditional turnip lanterns. The finished lanterns dangle from a wooden pole. In some areas the lantern processions end with a reenactment of St. Martin's most famous deed, sharing his cloak with a beggar. Afterwards the children disperse, singing songs (*Martinslieder*) and reciting rhymes for neighbors and shopkeepers. In return, they are given small **gifts** (*Martinswecken*), such as nuts, candies, apples, cookies, and coins.

Further Reading

Christmas in Germany. Second edition. Lincolnwood, Ill.: Passport Books, 1995.

Hole, Christina. *British Folk Customs*. London, England: Hutchinson and Company, 1976.

Leach, Maria, ed. *Funk and Wagnalls Standard Dictionary of Folklore, Mythology, and Legend*. New York: Harper and Row, 1984.

MacDonald, Margaret Read, ed. *The Folklore of World Holidays*. Detroit, Mich.: Gale Research, 1992.

Russ, Jennifer M. *German Festivals and Customs*. London, England: Oswald Wolff, 1982.

Spicer, Dorothy Gladys. *Festivals of Western Europe*. 1958. Reprint. Detroit, Mich.: Omnigraphics, 1994.

Thompson, Sue Ellen, ed. *Holiday Symbols*. Detroit, Mich.: Omnigraphics, 1998.

Tille, Alexander. *Yule and Christmas: Their Place in the Germanic Year*. London, England: David Nutt, 1899.

Urlin, Ethel L. *Festivals, Holy Days, and Saints' Days*. 1915. Reprint. Detroit, Mich.: Omnigraphics, 1992.

Mary, Blessed Virgin

Jesus was born to a human father named **Joseph** and a human mother named Mary. The Bible tells that Mary conceived the child by the power of God's Holy Spirit before the couple was married, however. For this reason she is known as the Virgin Mary, or the Blessed Virgin Mary. Although she is present at various events recorded in Christian scripture, Mary figures most prominently in the biblical passages describing the events surrounding Jesus' birth. In Roman Catholic and Orthodox Christianity, Mary is the most revered of all the saints, honored both as the mother of the Lord and for her own spiritual attributes: purity, faith, humility, love, steadfastness, and introspection. Artists have often pictured Mary in blue robes, as the color blue symbolizes truth, love, fidelity, and constancy in Christian art.

The Annunciation

The **Gospel according to Luke** gives the most detailed portrait of Mary's miraculous pregnancy. In an event that later became known as the **Annunciation**, she receives a visit from **Gabriel**, an **angel** who greets her with the phrase "Hail, O favored one, the Lord is with you" (Luke 1:28). He then tells her that she is to bear a son, conceived by the Holy Spirit, whom she will name Jesus and who shall be acclaimed as "the Son of the Most High" (Luke 1:32). Generations of Christians have interpreted the angel's greeting, along with heaven's selection of Mary to be Jesus' mother, as signs of her great purity and virtue. She demonstrates her steadfast faith in God and her humility by assenting to the decree delivered by the angel, saying, "Behold, I am the handmaid of the Lord; let it be to me according to your word" (Luke 1:27).

The Visitation

After receiving the angel's visit Mary hurries to see her kinswoman Elizabeth, who is also pregnant with a son who will become the prophet called John the Baptist. During the meeting between the two women, often referred to as the Visitation, Elizabeth honors Mary as the mother of the Lord. Mary exults in the fulfillment of God's promise to bring both mercy and justice to those on earth in a long speech known as the Song of Mary, or the Magnificat (Luke 1:46-56). The title Magnificat, which means "it magnifies," comes from the first word of the Latin version of the hymn:

> My soul magnifies the Lord,
> And my spirit rejoices in God my Savior,
> For he has regarded the low estate of his handmaiden.
> For behold, henceforth all generations will call me blessed;
> For he who is mighty has done great things for me,
> And holy is his name.
> And his mercy is on those who fear him
> From generation to generation.
> He has shown strength with his arm,
> He has scattered the proud in the imagination of their hearts,
> He has put down the mighty from their thrones,
> And exalted those of low degree;

He has filled the hungry with good things,
And the rich he has sent empty away.
He has helped his servant Israel,
In remembrance of his mercy,
As he spoke to our fathers,
To Abraham and to his posterity for ever [Luke 1:47-55].

Various branches of the Christian church have incorporated this beautiful hymn of praise into the liturgy of daily religious services. In addition, numerous composers have set it to music. Mary's hymn not only underscores her faith and humility, but also reveals her love of God, her gratitude for the gift God has made to her, and her joy at the prospect of seeing God come to the rescue of the needy and downtrodden.

Jesus' Birth

In both the Gospel according to Luke and the **Gospel according to Matthew**, Mary and Joseph receive visitors around the time of Jesus' birth. Matthew's account implies that the Holy Family lived in **Bethlehem**. He tells of a mysterious **star** that guided a number of learned men from Eastern lands, the **Magi**, to the site of Jesus' birth in order to pay him homage.

By contrast, Luke's story has the couple journeying to Bethlehem in order to comply with a Roman census. Since the Bethlehem inn was full the couple spent the night in a stable, where Mary gave birth to Jesus. **Shepherds** received notice of the holy birth from angels and came to Bethlehem to worship the newborn Son of God. The shepherds explain to Mary and Joseph how they came to know of the child's birth, and Mary "kept all these things, pondering them in her heart" (Luke 2:19). Thus Luke's account also shows Mary to be a seeker of spiritual wisdom. Because of her faith and her heart's inclination to "ponder" God's ways, many Christians view Mary as a model of contemplation and the contemplative life.

The Flight into Egypt and the Circumcision

The Gospel according to Luke and the Gospel according to Matthew also differ in their accounts of the events following Jesus' birth.

Matthew fails to mention Mary's role in these events. Nevertheless, Luke's account gives us one more clue as to Mary's character. Matthew reports that King **Herod** ordered soldiers to kill all the male infants in Bethlehem so that he might rid himself of the child the Magi identified as the King of the Jews (*see* **Holy Innocents' Day**). The Holy Family escapes the slaughter because an angel warned Joseph about what was soon to occur. Following the angel's mandate the family journeys to **Egypt**. This event, called the **Flight into Egypt**, is not reported in Luke's gospel. Luke instead says that eight days after his birth, Jesus' parents had him circumcised and gave him the name Jesus. These events illustrate Mary's obedience to Jewish law and her continuing cooperation with the divine plan announced to her by the angel Gabriel.

Early Christian Ideas

Early Christian writers and teachers, such as Justin Martyr (c. 100-c. 165), Irenaeus (c. 120-140 to c. 200), and Tertullian (c. 155-160 to after 220) compared Mary to Eve, the first woman, whose story is told in the Bible's Book of Genesis. Eve heard God's command and disobeyed, but Mary listened to the angel Gabriel and gave her assent to God's plan. Thus Mary was cast as a "second Eve," the woman who would bring a savior into the world to undo the damage done by **Adam and Eve**'s disobedience. This comparison was heightened by the medieval calendar of Christian holy days, in which Adam and Eve were commemorated on December 24, and Jesus' birth on **December 25**.

Early Christian leaders sometimes disagreed on the nature of the role Mary played in the birth of the Savior and the degree of veneration that should be accorded to her. They resolved some of these issues in the year 431 at the Council of Ephesus. The Council declared that Mary was the *Theotokos*, or "God bearer," paving the way for greater devotion to be dedicated to her.

Feast Days

Over the centuries many festivals evolved to pay tribute to the important events in Mary's life. The first festival scheduled in honor of

Mary was called the Commemoration of St. Mary and dates back to the fifth century. Some researchers report that it was scheduled for the Sunday before Christmas, others believe that it was held on December 26 or even on January 1. It celebrated Mary's death, which was viewed as her birth into heaven. This observance eventually evolved into the Feast of the Assumption, and the date was changed to August 15.

Other Marian festivals still celebrated today commemorate events related to the Nativity. The **Feast of the Circumcision** (January 1), for example, honors the fact that Mary and Joseph complied with Jewish law by taking their son to be circumcised on the eighth day after his birth. In the Roman Catholic Church the day celebrates Mary's role as the mother of God. **Candlemas** (February 2) commemorates Mary's purification in the temple 40 days after Jesus' birth. The Annunciation (March 25) recalls the angel Gabriel's visit to the Virgin Mary and her acceptance of the mission with which God entrusted her.

Other important Marian festivals include the Birthday of the Blessed Virgin Mary (September 8) and a Roman Catholic observance called the Feast of the Immaculate Conception (December 8). In addition, many people celebrate Marian festivals particular to their community. Mexicans, for example, honor the Virgin of Guadalupe on December 12. All told, the major feasts dedicated to Mary, plus those feasts celebrated only in certain places or observed by certain monastic communities, numbered about 1,000 by the early twentieth century. This number reflects the love and respect accorded to the Blessed Virgin Mary by generations of Christians.

New Views

In recent decades feminist theologians have begun to question some of the traditional doctrines concerning Mary. Some of these views are critical, suggesting, for example, that in upholding Mary as both virgin and mother, religious authorities have encouraged both women and men to view female sexuality as dirty and shameful. Others object to the emphasis placed on Mary's humility in her role as exemplary woman, noting that church officials have used this image of Mary to support the subordination of women in society. Nevertheless, for many people Mary models a deeply faithful Christian spirituality to be adopted by all those who follow the teachings of Jesus, both men and women.

Further Reading

Ceroke, C. P. "Mary, The Blessed Virgin, I (in the Bible)." In *New Catholic Encyclopedia*. Volume 9. New York: McGraw-Hill, 1967.

Clement, Clara Erskine. *A Handbook of Christian Symbols*. 1886. Reprint. Detroit, Mich.: Gale Research, 1971.

Cross, F. L., and E. A. Livingstone, eds. "Mary, The Blessed Virgin." In their *The Oxford Dictionary of the Christian Church*. Second edition, revised. Oxford, England: Oxford University Press, 1983.

Cuneen, Sally. *In Search of Mary*. New York: Ballantine Books, 1996.

Hulme, F. Edward. *The History, Principles and Practice of Symbolism in Christian Art*. 1891. Reprint. Detroit, Mich.: Gale, 1969.

McManus, Jim. *All Generations Will Call Me Blessed*. New York: Crossroad, 1999.

Maier, Paul L. *In the Fullness of Time*. Grand Rapids, Mich.: Kregel, 1991.

Metford, J. C. J. *The Christian Year*. London, England: Thames and Hudson, 1991.

Munro, Winsome. "Mary, the Virgin." In Paul J. Achtemeier, ed. *The Harper Collins Bible Dictionary*. Revised edition. San Francisco, Calif.: HarperSanFrancisco, 1996.

Warner, Marina. *Alone of All Her Sex*. New York: Alfred A. Knopf, 1976.

Web Site

The Marian Library/International Marian Research Institute of the University of Dayton, a Roman Catholic university with a Marian focus, has set up a page of questions and answers about Mary:
http://www.udayton.edu/mary/ (Click on "Questions")

Masque
Disguising

Around the time of the Renaissance, **England**'s elite celebrated the **Christmas season** with roving, costumed entertainments known as masques. The English borrowed the French word *masque*, meaning "mask," to describe these events because the costumes were often designed around elaborate and sometimes bizarre masks.

Early Masques

Early English masques, sometimes called "disguisings," probably evolved out of such popular Christmas folk customs as **mumming** and **Nativity plays**. Early masques resembled mumming in that bands of costumed revelers dropped in on friends and family and startled them with their unexpected entrances and entertaining antics. Unlike the mummers, however, masquers wore elaborate costumes, often traveled about with musicians, and amused the assembled company with flowery speeches and courtly dances. For example, in 1347 some of the masquers who appeared at King Edward III's Christmas celebrations wore masks resembling **angels'** faces surrounded with haloes. Other more unusual masks looked like mountaintops or a collection of legs swinging wildly though the air. Yet another group of masquers came dressed as dragons, peacocks, and swans.

Although the noble and well-to-do might enjoy a masque at any season of the year, they were often performed during the Christmas season and were particularly popular on **Twelfth Night**. The young King Henry VIII once surprised his wife, Katherine of Aragon, by presenting her with a Twelfth Day masque. He burst unannounced into her apartments dressed as Robin Hood. His companions followed, dressed as Robin's merry men.

The fact that masked and costumed bands of men were a fairly common sight during the Christmas season eventually gave a few individuals the idea of adopting the mummer's or masquer's disguise in order to commit crimes. In the early 1400s London officials passed a law against nighttime plays, mummings, and disguisings, excepting those that took place at private homes. The city of Bristol also adopted ordinances that curbed one's rights to ride through the street in mask and costume during the Christmas season.

Although these decrees may have decreased public mummings and disguisings to some extent, courtly masques continued to flourish. King Henry VIII introduced an Italian custom whereby masquers interacted with bystanders, selecting dance partners from the audience. The presentation and narration of short dramatic scenes also became an important part of the masque. On the whole, however, masques remained short, simple, and frivolous works designed to stimulate the senses by providing an amusing, colorful spectacle.

Height of Popularity

The English masque reached its artistic height in the early seventeenth century. During this era the famous writer Ben Jonson (1572-1637) wrote several masques. He created one of these specifically as a

Christmas entertainment. Titled *Christmas His Masque* (1616), it featured **Father Christmas** as a main character. The characters presented in Jonson's masque embodied popular Christmas foods, symbols, and customs. They included Misrule, Caroll, Minc'd Pie, Gamboll, Post-and-Paire, New-Year's-Gift, Mumming, Wassal, Offering, and Baby Cake (*see also* **Lord of Misrule; Mincemeat Pie; Wassail**). The innovative scenery contributed by designer and architect Inigo Jones (1573-1652) also enriched the masques of this era. Masques began to fall out of favor in the second half of the seventeenth century, eventually disappearing altogether as a Christmas entertainment.

Further Reading

Banham, Martin, ed. *The Cambridge Guide to World Theatre.* Cambridge, England: Cambridge University Press, 1988.

Crippen, Thomas G. *Christmas and Christmas Lore.* 1923. Reprint. Detroit, Mich.: Omnigraphics, 1990.

Henisch, Bridget Ann. *Cakes and Characters.* London, England: Prospect Books, 1984.

"Masque." In Phyllis Hartnoll, ed. *The Oxford Companion to the Theatre.* Fourth edition. Oxford, England: Oxford University Press, 1983.

Muir, Frank. *Christmas Customs and Traditions.* New York: Taplinger, 1977.

Pimlott, J. A. R. *The Englishman's Christmas.* Atlantic Highlands, N.J.: Humanities Press, 1978.

Masquerades

For Christmas customs involving the use of masks and costumes, *see* **America, Christmas in Nineteenth Century; Berchta; Black Peter; Boy Bishop; Ecuador, Christmas in; Feast of Fools; Guatemala, Christmas in; Jonkonnu; Kalends; King of the Bean; Knecht Ruprecht; Knocking Nights; Lord of Misrule; Masque; Mummers Parade; Mumming; Nativity Play; Nigeria, Christmas in; Pantomime; Paradise Tree; Pastores; Plough Monday; Posadas; St. Barbara's Day; St. Lucy's Day; St. Nicholas's Day; Saturnalia; Star Boys; Twelfth Night; Yule Goat; Zagmuk**

Merry

In contemporary English the word "merry" means "jolly," "cheerful," "lively," or "happy." Few people realize, however, that it once meant something slightly different. At the time the English coined the phrase "**Merry Christmas**," merry meant "pleasant," "delightful," or "joyful." Thus, at that time, the well-known phrase "merry England" did not mean "jolly England," but rather "pleasant" or "delightful" England. When used to describe a holiday, the word "merry" signaled that it was a time of festivity or rejoicing.

In greeting one another with the phrase "Merry Christmas," the English were wishing each other a festive and joyful holiday. The sixteenth-century English **Christmas carol**, "God Rest You Merry, Gentlemen," offers another example of this usage. Contemporary English speakers often interpret the title of this song to mean something like "God Rest You, Jolly Gentlemen." In fact, the comma separating "merry" from "gentlemen" in the original phrase tells us that in this context "merry" does not function as an adjective describing the gentlemen in question. In the sixteenth century, "God Rest You Merry, Gentlemen" meant "God Rest You Joyfully, Gentlemen" or, as contemporary English speakers might be more likely to say, "God Keep You Joyous, Gentlemen" (*for the phrase "Merry Christmas" in different languages, see* **Merry Christmas and Happy New Year**).

Further Reading

Weiser, Francis X. *The Christmas Book*. 1952. Reprint. Detroit, Mich.: Omnigraphics, 1990.

Merry Christmas and
Happy New Year

Here's how to say "Merry Christmas and Happy New Year" in languages from around the world.

Afrikaans	Geseknde Kersfees en 'n Gelukkige Nuwe Jaar
Brazilian Portuguese	Boas Festas e Feliz Ano Novo
Bulgarian	Vesela Koleda i Chestita Nova Godina
Catalan	Bon Nadal i un Feliç Any Nou
Chinese (Cantonese)	Sin Dan Fae Lok. Gung Hai Fat Choi.
Chinese (Mandarin)	Shen Dan Kuai Le. Xin Nian Yu Kuai.
Croatian	Sretan Bozic. Sretna Nova Godina.
Czech	Stastne a Vesele Vanoce a Stastny Novy Rok
Danish	Glaedig Jul Og Godt Nytår Gelukkige Nieuwjaar
Dutch	Vrolik Kerstfeest en een Gelukkig Nieuw Jaar
Esperanto	Felican Kirstnaskon Kaj Bonan Novjaron
Estonian	Rõõmusaid Jõulupuhi ja Head Uut Aastat
Faeroese	Gledhilig Jol Og Eydnurikt Nyggjar
Finnish	Hyvaa Joulua ja Onnellista Uutta Vuotta
Flemish	Zalig Kerstfeest en Gelukkig Nieuw Jaar
French	Joyeux Nöel et Bonne Année
Gaelic (Scots)	Nollaig Chridheil Agus Bliadhna Mhath Yr
German	Fröhliche Weihnachten und ein Glückliches Neues Jahr
Greek	Kala Christougenna kai Evtichismenos o Kainourious Chronos
Hausa	Barka ka Kirsimatikuma Barka da Sabuwar Shekara
Hawaiian	Mele Kalikimaka Ame Hauoli Makahiki Hou
Hebrew	Hag ha-Molad Sameah. Shanah Tovah.

Hungarian	Boldog Karácsonyi Üennepeket Es Boldog Ujévet
Icelandic	Gledhileg Jol Og Farsflt Komandi Ar
Indonesian	Selemat Hari Natal Dan Selamat Tahun Baru
Inupik (Eskimo)	Jutdlime Pivdluarit Ukiortame Pivdluaritlo
Italian	Buon Natale e Felice Anno Nuovo
Japanese	Meri Kurisumasu Soshite Akemashite Omedeto
Korean	Sungtanul Chukaheyo. Sehae Bok Mani Baduseyo.
Latin	Natale Hilare et Annum Faustum
Latvian	Priecigus Ziemsvetkus un Laimigu Jaungadu
Lithuanian	Linksmu kaledugnenna. Laimingu Najuju Metu.
Norwegian	God Jul Og Godt Nytt År
Pennsylvania German	En Frehlicher Grischtdaag un en Hallich Nei Yaahr
Persian	Krismas-e Shoma Mubarak. Sal-e no Mobarak.
Polish	Wesolych Swiat i Szczesliwego Nowego Roku
Portuguese	Feliz Natal e um Prospero Ano Novo
Romanian	Craciun Fericit Si Un An Nou Fericit
Russian	Vesëlogo Rozhdestva. Schastlivogo Novogo Goda.
Serbian	Hristos se Rodi. Srecna Nova Godina.
Slovak	Vesele Vianoce i na Ndravie v Novom Roku
Slovenian	Vesele Bozicne Praznike in Srecno Novo Leto
Spanish	Feliz Navidad y Próspero Año Nuevo
Swedish	God Jul Och Ett Gott Nytt År
Tagalog	Maligayang Paskó. Maligayang Bagong Taon.
Turkish	Neseli Noel. Mutlu Yilbasi.
Vietnamese	Chuc Mung Giang Sinh. Chuc Mung Nam Moi.
Yiddish	Fraylekhn Krimes. A Git Yor.
Yoruba	E Ku Odun, e Ku Iye'dun

Web Sites

The Donnell Library Center of the New York Public Library maintains a web site listing common phrases in 26 different languages. For "Merry Christmas," see: http://www.nypl.org/branch/central_units /d/f/expressions/list/merryc.htm

For "Happy New Year," see: http://www.nypl.org/branch/central_units/d/f/expressions/list/happyn/htm

Travelang.com, a commercial web site dedicated to providing products and services useful to travelers and students of foreign languages, offers a page that translates the phrase "Merry Christmas" and "Merry Christmas and Happy New Year" into a wide variety of foreign languages: http://www.travlang.com/languages/christmas.html

Messiah

George Frideric Handel's (1685-1759) *Messiah* is perhaps the most popular piece of classical music associated with the **Christmas season**. Two common misconceptions have spread along with its fame. Although many call the work "*The Messiah*," Handel named his oratorio simply "*Messiah*." These days most performances of the piece take place around Christmas. Nevertheless, Handel never intended *Messiah* to be connected with the Christmas season. In fact, he wrote the oratorio in the late summer of 1741 and premiered it around Easter of the following year. Subsequent performances during Handel's lifetime also took place around Easter.

Composition of Messiah

Although he composed the music for *Messiah*, Handel did not select the biblical texts that make up the libretto. His friend Charles Jennens compiled a collection of biblical verses outlining the birth and death of **Jesus** and the redemption of humankind. Jennens's compilation delighted and inspired Handel. He sat down to write the music for these texts on August 22, 1741. Composing with lightning speed, he completed the oratorio about three weeks later, on September 14. Some say that Handel once remarked about the work's creation, "I did think I did see all Heaven before me, and the great God himself." The approximately two and one-half hours of music is divided into three parts, often referred to as the "Nativity," "Passion," and "Redemption" sections because of the themes developed in each.

Handel scored *Messiah* as an oratorio. An oratorio is a long choral work made up of arias, duets, trios, and choruses. Oratorios attempt to tell a story, usually a religious one. The music must convey all, since no dialogue, scenery, or costumes are used. Some experts believe that oratorios evolved out of the medieval mystery plays (*see also* **Nativity Play**). Indeed, early oratorios included dance and dramatic representations, as well as church hymns, and were usually performed in churches. Handel's *Messiah* differed significantly from the first oratorios written in the early 1600s. *Messiah* consists of nothing other than music, beautiful and sometimes difficult music. Handel often employed opera singers to perform the challenging solo parts of his oratorios and staged the performances in theaters rather than churches.

First Performance of Messiah

Although the German-born Handel was living and working in London at the time he composed *Messiah,* the first public performance of the oratorio took place in Dublin, **Ireland**. Handel brought several principal singers over from **England,** including noted operatic soprano Signora Avoglio and singer-actress Mrs. Susannah Cibber, who sang the alto parts. He engaged Dublin musicians to present the other solo parts. The choir consisted of singers from both Dublin cathedrals, although the premiere performance took place in a music hall on Fishamble Street. The cantankerous dean of St. Patrick's Cathedral, who was none other than Jonathan Swift (1667-1745), the author of *Gulliver's Travels,* at first refused to permit his choristers to participate in an event held in such a secular setting. Luckily for the audience, and for the history of music, he eventually relented.

In order to increase the number of people who would fit in the available seating, newspaper advertisements kindly requested that ladies who planned to attend refrain from wearing hoops under their skirts. Gentlemen were asked to leave their swords at home.

Handel's *Messiah* premiered on April 13, 1742, and was warmly received. Mrs. Cibber's rendition of "He Was Despised" so moved one member of the audience, Dr. Patrick Delaney, a friend of Jonathan Swift's, that he cried out, "Woman, for this thy sins be forgiven thee!" Delaney may have had some very specific sins in mind since rumors concerning Susannah Cibber's amorous affairs had made her the talk of London. In the days that followed, several Dublin newspapers printed the following review:

> On Tuesday last Mr. Handel's Sacred Grand Oratorio, the Messiah, was performed in the New Musick Hall in Fishamble-street; the best Judges allowed it to be the most finished piece of Musick. Words are wanting to express the exquisite Delight it afforded to the admiring crowded Audience. The Sublime, the Grand, and the Tender, adapted to the most elevated, majestick and moving Words, conspired to transport and charm the ravished Heart and Ear.

The review also praised Handel for donating the proceeds from this performance to three Dublin charities.

Later Performances of Messiah

Encouraged by Dublin's warm reception Handel returned home to London and arranged for performances to take place in that city. London rewarded his best efforts with rejection. Church officials objected to staging a work on a sacred theme in the profane space of a public theater. In spite of these objections, Covent Garden Theater hosted the first London performance of *Messiah* on March 23, 1743. The audience and the critics responded with indifference. In addition, Handel's friend Jennens, who had supplied the libretto for *Messiah*, faulted the composer in a letter to a friend. With blind conceit Jennens wrote, "His Messiah has disappointed me, being set in great hast, tho' he said he would be a year about it, & make it the best of all his Compositions. I shall put no more Sacred Works into his hands thus to be abused" (Jacobi, 1982, 41-42).

Apparently, King George II attended one of the early performances of *Messiah*. Some writers believe this occasion gave birth to the tradition whereby the audience stands during the "Hallelujah" chorus. (Others believe that King George III started this tradition). In any case, one of these kings rose from his seat at this point in the piece. Whether he was reacting to the exuberance of the music or simply attempting to stretch his legs cannot now be determined. In those days etiquette demanded that no one remain seated when the king stood up. As a result, the entire audience rose to its feet, creating a tradition still observed today.

During the decade of the 1740s Handel aired *Messiah* only a few more times. The work teetered on the edge of obscurity until 1750 when Handel began to perform it in a series of annual concerts to benefit charity. Over the next nine years the work achieved widespread popularity.

Handel's Death

On April 6, 1759, two days before Palm Sunday, Handel conducted what was to be the last performance of his life, a presentation of *Messiah* at Covent Garden. He collapsed upon leaving the theater and had to be carried home. In the days that followed, Handel passed in and out of consciousness. The elderly composer recognized the seriousness of his condition. In one of his clear moments he expressed his wish to die on Good Friday, as did Jesus, "in the hope of rejoining the good God, my sweet Lord and Savior, on the day of his Resurrection." On Good Friday, April 13, 1759, seventeen years to the day from the premiere performance of *Messiah* in Dublin, Handel lay dying at his home in London. He passed away quietly sometime between that evening and the following morning.

A few days before his death Handel requested that he be buried in Westminster Abbey and set aside money to pay for his funeral monument. The artist who created the monument depicted the composer at work on one of the arias from *Messiah*. Visitors to Westminster Abbey may note that the monument dedicated to the composer's memory misspells the word "messiah."

Handel's Personality and Legacy

Although later generations attributed a kind of milktoast piety to the famed composer of *Messiah*, Handel's friends and contemporaries described him as a somewhat gruff yet amiable man. He rejoiced in the consumption of large quantities of food and drink, earning himself a reputation for gluttony. Stubborn, arrogant, and irritable when it came to the correct interpretation of music, he acquainted many musicians with the rough edge of his tongue. He could, and often did, swear fluently in four languages. On the other hand, Handel possessed an excellent sense of humor combined with a flair for telling funny stories. He won a reputation for honesty in financial dealings, so much so that musicians accepted his occasional IOUs without a qualm. Finally, friends, family, musicians in his employ, and charities all benefited from his generosity.

Although *Messiah* stands as perhaps the composer's best-known work, Handel himself did not count it as his greatest achievement. He judged the chorus "He Saw the Lovely Youth" from his oratorio *Theodora* to be far superior to the "Hallelujah" chorus from *Messiah*. Neither proud nor self-effacing, Handel evaluated his own accomplishments fairly and was capable on occasion of belittling some of his less-distinguished pieces of music. Later composers paid tribute to his brilliance. Ludwig von Beethoven (1770-1827) once exclaimed "He was the greatest composer that ever lived. I would uncover my head and kneel before his tomb." Franz Joseph Haydn (1732-1809), after hearing *Messiah* for the first time, reportedly exclaimed of Handel, "He was the master of us all."

Further Reading

Barber, David W. *Getting a Handel on Messiah*. Toronto, Ontario, Canada: Sound and Vision, 1994.

Buxton, David, and Sue Lyon, eds. *Baroque Festival*. Volume 4 of *The Great Composers, Their Lives and Times*. New York: Marshall Cavendish, 1987.

Dean, Winton, and Anthony Hicks. *The New Grove Handel*. New York: W. W. Norton, 1983.

———. "Handel, George Frideric." In Stanley Steele, ed. *The New Grove Dictionary of Music and Musicians*. Volume 8. London, England: Macmillan, 1980.

Del Re, Gerard, and Patricia Del Re. *The Christmas Almanack*. Garden City, N.Y.: Doubleday, 1979.

Jacobi, Peter. *The Messiah Book*. New York: St. Martin's Press, 1982.

Weinstock, Herbert. *Handel*. Second edition, revised. New York: Alfred A. Knopf, 1959.

Mexico, Christmas in

Mexicans ornament their homes, churches, and streets in joyous anticipation of Christmas. These festive decorations may include bright *piñatas*, multicolored **Nativity scenes**, scarlet **poinsettias**, and twinkling light displays. Religious observance and family merrymaking are also important elements of Mexican Christmas celebrations.

Decorations

The **Christmas season** in Mexico begins in mid-December when many families retrieve their Nativity scenes from storage. Old pieces are cleaned and new figurines may be added to the family collection. In Mexico Nativity scenes are called *nacimientos*, which literally means "births." The central figures of **Joseph**, **Mary**, and the baby **Jesus** are referred to as *misterios*, or "mysteries." Along with Nativity scenes, piñatas, and poinsettias, some families now add a **Christmas tree** to their home decorations.

Posadas, Pastores, and Novenas

Many families assemble their Nativity scenes on December 16. This date coincides with a number of other Christmas customs. It marks the beginning of the nine-night Christmas novena, a series of prayer services in preparation for Christmas. These services are called *misas de aguinaldo*, which means "Christmas gift masses" (*see also* **Misa de Gallo**). Las **Posadas**, a reenactment of Joseph and Mary's journey to **Bethlehem** and search for shelter, also begins on December 16. Performances of Los **Pastores**, a humorous folk play recounting the story of the **shepherds'** journey to Bethlehem, begin in the latter part of December as well.

Piñatas

As Christmas draws near, markets begin to fill up with colorful Christmas goods such as children's toys and figurines for Nativity scenes. Merchants also display a wide variety of *piñatas,* a special kind of Mexican toy popular at celebrations involving children. The traditional way of making a piñata calls for filling a clay pot with treats, such as candy, nuts, fruit, and small toys. Artisans then cover the pot with a combination of papier mâché, colorful tissue or crepe paper, paint, tinsel, and sequins. Nowadays, many artisans leave out the pot and form the piñata out of paiper mâché alone, shaping it into any form that strikes their fancy. Children may choose from a nearly infinite variety of shapes, including animals, cartoon characters, flowers, vegetables, suns, moons, stars, comets, electrical appliances, and vehicles of all kinds. During the Christmas season, homes, plazas, shops, schools, churches, and other institutions display piñatas as seasonal decorations.

What's more, children play **games** with piñatas at holiday season parties, such as those that follow Las Posadas. The piñata hangs from a rope which is suspended over a pulley in the ceiling. Each child is blindfolded in turn and given a chance to break open the piñata with a big stick. An adult spins the blindfolded child around several times and then takes hold of the rope. While the rest of the children call out instructions to the blindfolded youngster, an adult raises or lowers the piñata to keep it away from the swinging stick.

Eventually, a child succeeds in striking the piñata, breaking it open and spilling all of its treats onto the floor. The children rush forward to gather up the sweets and toys.

Christmas Foods

Mexicans serve Christmas dinner on Christmas Eve. This meal usually features roast turkey. This dish is especially appropriate to Mexican celebrations. Turkey is native to the Americas, and it was first imported to Europe by the Spanish colonists who conquered Mexico in the sixteenth century. *Ensalada de la Nochebuena,* or "Christmas Eve Salad," is another typical Christmas dish. It usually includes sliced fruits, beets, and nuts. Tamales, tortillas, fish, steak, punch, hot chocolate, and a special kind of doughnut often appear on the Christmas menu as well.

Christmas Activities

On Christmas Eve many families finally place the Christ child figurine into the Nativity scene. The figurines representing the shepherds, who have been inching their way towards the stable sheltering the Holy Family, also arrive on Christmas Eve. Mexicans celebrate Christmas Eve by attending the Misa de Gallo, or **Midnight Mass**. Often the air crackles with the sound of exploding firecrackers as worshipers approach the church. After church families return home to large, festive meals. The next morning the children may receive a small **gift** from their parents. They will have to wait until **Epiphany** to receive the rest of their gifts. Mexicans spend Christmas Day visiting with family members and friends.

Innocents' Day, Epiphany, and Candlemas

In spite of the gruesome deed it commemorates, Mexicans celebrate *Día de los Inocentes,* or **Holy Innocents' Day**, December 28, with high spirits. Tradition calls for the playing of practical jokes and tricks on the unwary. The one who is tricked is referred to as an *inocente,* or an "innocent."

In Mexico children traditionally receive their Christmas presents on Epiphany, which they call *Día de los Reyes,* or Three Kings' Day. The

Three Kings, or **Magi**, serve as Mexico's gift bringers. According to Mexican folklore, the Three Kings journey around the world on the eve of Epiphany, rewarding well-behaved children with Christmas presents. In anticipation of these treats children place their **shoes** near the family Nativity scene or just outside a door or window. Often they leave straw and a dish of water to refresh the Wise Mens' camels. In the morning they find the water and straw gone and their shoes spilling over with gifts. Three Kings' Day celebrations usually feature a special ring-shaped bread or cake called *La Rosca de los Reyes*, or "Three Kings' Cake." Bakers insert a tiny doll in the batter for each cake. Whoever finds the doll in their slice of cake will have good luck in the coming year. Lastly, Mexicans finally complete their Nativity scenes on Epiphany, moving the figurines representing the Three Kings into the stable that shelters the Holy Family.

The Christmas season ends with **Candlemas** on February 2. On this day many families take down their Nativity scenes and store them until the following year.

Further Reading

Christmas in Mexico. Chicago: World Book, 1976.

Marcus, Rebecca, and Judith Marcus. *Fiesta Time in Mexico*. Champaign, Ill.: Garrard Publishing Company, 1974.

Sechrist, Elizabeth Hough. *Christmas Everywhere*. 1936. Reprint. Detroit, Mich.: Omnigraphics, 1998.

Silverthorne, Elizabeth. *Fiesta! Mexico's Great Celebrations*. Brookfield, Conn.: Millbrook Press, 1992.

Wakefield, Charito Calvachi. *Navidad Latinoamericana, Latin American Christmas*. Lancaster, Pa.: Latin American Creations Publishing, 1997.

Web Site

A site sponsored by *Mexico Connect*, a web magazine published by Conexión México S.A. de C.V.: http://www.mexconnect.com/mex_/feature/xmasindex.html

Midnight Mass

The Roman Catholic Church honors Christmas with three separate masses, each with its own distinctive liturgy. The first of these masses takes place in the middle of the night on Christmas Eve and is called Midnight Mass. In Spanish-speaking countries, Midnight Mass is known as the **Misa de Gallo,** or the rooster's mass (*see also* **Plygain**).

The first Christmas masses were celebrated at St. Peter's Basilica in Rome on Christmas morning. In the fifth century Roman officials added another mass to be celebrated in the middle of the night. Rules in effect from about 400 to 1200 A.D. prescribed that this mass be held *ad galli cantum,* that is, when the rooster crows. Roosters begin to crow at about three in the morning. Eventually, however, the scheduling of the mass shifted to midnight. Perhaps the popular belief that **Jesus** was born at midnight influenced this shift. A fourth-century Latin hymn expresses this belief:

> When the midnight, dark and still,
> Wrapped in silence vale and hill:
> God the Son, through Virgin's birth,
> Following the Father's will,
> Started life as Man on earth [Weiser, 1990, 52].

In the fifth century a third mass, held at daybreak, was added to the first two. Each of the three masses, however, emphasized a different aspect of the Nativity. The first mass at midnight celebrated the mystery of the relationship between the Father and the Son, the second rejoiced at the birth of the Son on earth, and the third commemorated the birth of the Son in human hearts. Folk tradition translated these three themes into descriptive names for each of the masses. Thus, the Midnight Mass was known as the "**Angels** Mass," the dawn mass became the "**Shepherds** Mass," and the morning mass was called the "Mass of the Divine Word."

Until the eleventh century, the pope alone held the privilege of conducting three masses in honor of Christmas. After that time the custom spread throughout the Church. Today Roman Catholic churches and cathedrals throughout the world offer Midnight Mass on Christmas Eve. In addition, television stations in seventy nations transmit live broadcasts of the pope's Midnight Mass from St. Peter's Basilica in Rome.

Further Reading

Baldovin, John F. "Christmas." In Mircea Eliade, ed. *The Encyclopedia of Religion.* Volume 3. New York: Macmillan, 1987.

Del Re, Gerard, and Patricia Del Re. *The Christmas Almanack.* Garden City, N.Y.: Doubleday, 1979.

Weiser, Francis X. *The Christmas Book.* 1952. Reprint. Detroit, Mich.: Omnigraphics, 1990.

———. *Handbook of Christian Feasts and Customs.* New York: Harcourt, Brace and World, 1952.

Web Site

A site sponsored by the French Ministry of Culture and Canadian Heritage: http://www.culture.fr:80/culture/noel/angl/mesminu.htm

Mincemeat Pie
Christmas Pie

The name "mincemeat" may puzzle many of those who have come across a meatless recipe for this dish in their cookbooks. Mincemeat pie is an old English Christmas favorite. The dish got its name from what used to be its main ingredient, minced meat. Over the centuries, however, meat gradually dropped out of many recipes. Today the dish gets most of its flavor from fresh and dried fruits, spices, and sugar.

Medieval Christmas Cookery

In pre-industrial times people slaughtered the animals that were to provide them with their winter meats in late autumn. At this time of the year domesticated animals could no longer find enough to eat by grazing. Since most of the family's grain was needed for feeding human beings throughout the lean winter months, the animals that were not kept for breeding purposes were killed (*see also* **Martinmas**). In medieval times this meant that cooks could expect a large quantity of meat to prepare for the feasting that took place during the **Twelve Days of Christmas**.

Food preservation, however, challenged medieval cooks since they did not have access to preservatives or reliable refrigeration. Instead, people employed sugars and spices to preserve meats and fish. Fresh and dried fruits were less expensive and easier to obtain than sugar or honey, so they were often used to flavor dishes. In **England** medieval cooks prepared large fruit, meat, and butter pies for wealthy families entertaining many guests at Christmas. Some researchers believe that the sugary fruit helped to preserve the meat, others contend that its function was to cover the flavor of the aging meat. Enclosing the ingredients in a tough, airtight crust also helped to preserve them. Medieval diners apparently possessed a rather blunt sense of humor about their foods. They sometimes called these sturdy enclosures "coffins." Not only could these hard-crusted meat pies be prepared well ahead of time, but also their rich ingredients served as a special Christmas treat.

The dish we know today as mincemeat pie was so popular during the **Christmas season** that, in earlier times, it was also called Christmas pie. During the Middle Ages the presentation of the Christmas pie was just as important as its ingredients, since medieval feasts aimed at offering diners a spectacle as well as a meal. A late fourteenth-century recipe for Christmas pie describes a manner of both preparation and presentation:

> Take a Pheasant, a Hare, a Capon, two Partridges, two pigeons, and two Conies; chop them up, take out as many bones as you can, and add the livers and hearts, two kidneys of sheep, forcemeat made into balls with eggs, pickled mushrooms, salt, pepper, spice, and vinegar. Boil the bones in a pot to make a good broth; put the meat into a crust of good paste "made craftily into the likeness of a bird's body"; pour in the liquor, close it up, and bake well; "and so serve it forth with the head of one of the birds at one end and a great tail at the other, and divers of his long feathers set cunningly all about him" [Crippen, 1990, 122-23].

Another popular way of presenting the Christmas pie required the cook to mold the pie into the shape of a manger and place a dough image of the baby **Jesus** on top.

Jack Horner's Christmas Pie

Mincemeat pies have played a prominent role in several episodes of English political and religious history. In 1532 King Henry VIII (1491-1547) began a campaign to reduce the political and economic power of the Roman Catholic Church in England. He started to dissolve England's monasteries and to claim their wealth for the crown. Some say that Richard Whiting, the last abbot of Glastonbury, tried to protect his abbey from this fate by freely offering the monarch the deeds to twelve of the abbey's richest estates (*see also* **Glastonbury Thorn**). He attempted to tickle the king's fancy as well as satisfy his greed by inserting the deeds into the crust of a Christmas pie which was to be presented to the king as a Christmas **gift**. The abbot asked one of his trusted agents, Thomas Horner, to deliver the pie to the king. Along the way, however, Horner reportedly pulled out the deeds for himself. Some writers claim that an old English nursery rhyme commemorates this Christmas theft in what are now veiled images:

> Little Jack Horner
> Sat in a corner
> Eating a Christmas pie
> He put in his thumb
> And pulled out a plum
> And said, "What a good boy am I!"

In this instance, crime did pay. Henry VIII dissolved Glastonbury Abbey and seized its possessions, Horner took possession of Mells Manor, and Abbot Richard Whiting was brutally executed on a trumped-up charge of treason. It is only fair to add that Horner's descendants, still living at Mells Manor, deny much of this story. They claim that Thomas Horner bought Mells from the king and that the rhyme has nothing to do with their ancestor. The full truth of the matter may never be known.

Puritan Opposition to Mincemeat

In the following century Christmas pie once again landed in the middle of England's political and religious controversies. In the seventeenth century mincemeat pie, along with **plum pudding**, raised the ire of an increasingly powerful Protestant sect known as the **Puritans**. Some writers claim that the manger-shaped pies and dough images of Jesus scandalized the Puritans' sense of religious decorum. Others suggest that the Puritans viewed the consumption of mincemeat pie as an act of gluttony that did not befit the season of the Nativity. An anonymous writer of the time parodied the Puritans' objection to traditional English Christmas fare in the following lines of verse:

> The high-shoe lords of Cromwell's making
> Were not for dainties — roasting, baking;
> The chiefest food they found most good in,

> Was rusty bacon and bag pudding;
> Plum-broth was popish, and mince-pie —
> O that was flat idolatry! [Chambers, 1990, 2: 755]

The Puritans condemned mincemeat pie and those who feasted on it at Christmas time. Another writer mimicked their thundering denunciations of the dish in the following lines:

> Idolatrie in crust! Babylon's whore
> Rak'd from the grave, and bak'd by hanches, then
> Sew'd up in Coffins to unholy men;
> Defil'd, with superstition, like the Gentiles
> Of old, that worship'd onions, roots, and lentiles!
> [Pimlott, 1978, 46]

Catholics and Anglicans defended the traditional Christmas pie against Puritan attackers. As Protestants and Catholics strove with one another to dominate England's political life, the consumption or avoidance of mincemeat pie at Christmas time became a sign of religious and political loyalties. One writer mocked the views of his more extreme Puritan contemporaries in the following lines of verse:

> All plums the prophet's sons deny,
> And spice-broths are too hot;
> Treason's in a December pie,
> And death within the pot [Chambers, 1990, 2: 755].

In spite of this controversy both plum pudding and mincemeat pie survived the brief period of Puritan rule in the seventeenth century. They emerged once again in the following centuries as English Christmas favorites. In 1728 one foreigner who had experienced an English Christmas noted that at this time of year, "Everyone from the King to the artisan eats [plum] soup and Christmas pies."

Changing Recipes

Over the years mincemeat pie recipes began to call for less meat and more fruit and sugar. A sixteenth-century pie described by English poet Robert Herrick (1591-1674) contained beef tongues, chicken, eggs, orange and lemon peel, sugar, and various spices. As sugar became more affordable and, therefore, more widely available, a division between sweet and savory dishes arose in English cooking. Mincemeat pie gravitated towards the galaxy of sweet foods. In fact, many later recipes for mincemeat pie omit meat entirely. Nevertheless, most of these meatless pies still call for suet, or beef fat.

Today's Christmas baker can choose between meat and meatless recipes. For example, one recipe calls for sliced apples, chopped lean beef or ox hearts, suet, sugar, cider, sour cherries, raisins, citron, candied orange and lemon peel, mace, cinnamon, cloves, nutmeg, salt, pepper, and nuts. More common, however, are recipes that omit the meat and add additional fruits to the mixture, such as figs, prunes, cherries, pears, dried apricots, raisins, or currants. Sherry, brandy, or molasses may be added as well. Mincemeat ages well and may be made several weeks in advance in order to allow the flavors to blend and mature.

Further Reading

Bett, Henry. *Nursery Rhymes and Tales*. Second edition. 1924. Reprint. Detroit, Mich.: Singing Tree Press, 1968.

Black, Maggie. "The Englishman's Plum Pudding." *History Today* 31 (December 1981): 60-61.

Chambers, Robert. "December 25—Old English Christmas Fare." In his *The Book of Days*. Volume 2. 1862-64. Reprint. Detroit, Mich.: Omnigraphics, 1990.

Crippen, Thomas G. *Christmas and Christmas Lore*. 1923. Reprint. Detroit, Mich.: Omnigraphics, 1990.

Del Re, Gerard, and Patricia Del Re. *The Christmas Almanack*. Garden City, N.Y.: Doubleday, 1979.

Opie, Iona, and Peter Opie, eds. *The Oxford Dictionary of Nursery Rhymes*. Oxford, England: Oxford University Press, 1997.

Pimlott, J. A. R. *The Englishman's Christmas*. Atlantic Highlands, N.J.: Humanities Press, 1978.

Weiser, Francis X. *The Christmas Book*. 1952. Reprint. Detroit, Mich.: Omnigraphics, 1990.

Miracle on 34th Street

Miracle on 34th Street (1947) has become one of America's best-loved Christmas movies. Based on a book of the same name, it tells the story of Susan Walker (a little girl who doesn't believe in **Santa Claus**), her mother Doris Walker (an independent career woman), neighbor Fred Gailey (a lawyer who has fallen in love with Doris), and an elderly gentleman who calls himself Kris Kringle. Doris Walker works at Macy's in **New York City**. She hires Kris Kringle to play Santa Claus for **Macy's Thanksgiving Day Parade**. Seeing that he is a natural in the role, she convinces him also to work as a store Santa. Kringle's unconventional philosophy of sending customers to rival stores if Macy's does not carry the item they're looking for boosts Macy's sales. Nevertheless, his belief that he really is Santa Claus raises difficulties. Kringle remains unaware of these difficulties for quite a while, as he works on inspiring Susan's belief in Santa Claus and aiding Doris's handsome neighbor in his campaign to win her heart. By the end of the movie, the girl has found faith in Santa, her mother has fallen in love with the neighbor, and Kris Kringle has returned home.

The Author of the Book

Valentine Davies grew up in New York City. He attended the University of Michigan and Yale Drama School and went on to write plays, novels, and, eventually, screenplays. He and director George Seaton became pals and, during a vacation that the two of them took with their wives in Nevada, he shared with Seaton his idea for *Miracle on 34th Street*. Seaton set to work on creating a screenplay and finished his first draft about a year and a half later. Davies's short novel was published in the same year that the film was released. For his part in the film, Davies won an Academy Award for best original story. Davies and Seaton worked together on other projects, including the films *Chicken Every Sunday* (1949) and *The Bridges at Toko-Ri* (1955).

The Director and Screenwriter

George Seaton began his theatrical career as a stage actor and producer. In 1933 he began to write screenplays. He did double duty on *Miracle on 34th Street*, both writing the script and directing the film. His ability to translate Davies's novel into the more visual medium of a movie script garnered him an Academy Award for best screenplay. Though it did not win, the movie also received an Academy Award nomination for best picture of the year.

The Actors

Little Natalie Wood, who played Susan Walker, made her motion picture debut in 1943 at the age of five. She had appeared in three other movies before *Miracle on 34th Street*. Her naturalness on camera adds much appeal to the film and made her a child star. She continued her career on into adulthood and picked up three Academy Award nominations along the way for her roles in *Rebel Without a Cause* (1955), *Splendor in the Grass* (1961), and *Love With a Proper Stranger* (1963). She is also remembered for her tragic death in a drowning accident off the California coast in 1981.

Miracle on 34th Street charms audiences by pairing 8-year-old Natalie Wood with 72-year-old Edmund Gwen, who played Kris Kringle. While Wood was a relative newcomer, both to life and to the world of film, the elderly Gwen had achieved the status of veteran in the world of the dramatic arts. Born in Wales in 1875, he appeared in his first movie in 1916, after a successful London stage career. *Miracle on 34th Street* won him the acclaim of his peers. He received an Academy Award for best supporting actor for his portrayal of Kris Kringle.

The film's romantic angle often takes a back seat to its comedic bits and its touching treatment of a mother and child's journey towards the capacity to imagine, hope, and trust. Maureen O'Hara, who plays Doris Walker, and John Payne, who plays her boyfriend Fred Gailey, were well paired as a subdued romantic couple. Just as she did in *Miracle on 34th Street*, O'Hara often played independent, strong-willed women who go it alone in a world where men have the upper hand. John Payne played many romantic leads in the 1940s. In the

1950s his career turned towards action and western films. He also starred in the western-themed television show, *The Restless Gun.*

Facts about the Film

Seaton had originally planned to use the false names "Tracy's" and "Trimballs" for the two famous New York stores that appear in the film. After both stores gave permission to use their proper names, however, he changed them back to Macy's and Gimbel's. A good portion of the movie was shot on location in New York City. Seaton was even permitted to range freely about the 34th Street store during the **Christmas season**, in order to film Macy's real holiday rush. During the movie's opening scenes, viewers are treated to actual shots of Macy's famous Thanksgiving Day Parade.

Although *Miracle on 34th Street* appears incredibly sweet to today's audiences, the Roman Catholic Church voiced moral objections to the film at the time of its debut. Church officials disapproved of the movie because the leading lady plays a divorced woman.

When the film first came out, publicity experts played up the romantic aspects of the film rather than its connection to Christmas. In fact, instead of opening during the holiday season the film premiered in June of 1947.

Remakes

The enduring popularity of the 1947 film inspired Twentieth-Century Fox to authorize a remake in 1994. The new, color version of the film stars child actress Mara Wilson as Susan Walker, and Richard Attenborough as Kris Kringle. This time around, however, Macy's refused to let the filmmakers use its name. After shooting a few parade shots in New York City—not Macy's real parade but rather a movie version of the yearly event—production moved to Chicago. In this version of the story, Susan's mother works for a fictional department store called Cole's, which faces stiff competition from its arch-rival, Shopper's Express.

The story was also adapted as a made-for-television movie in 1973. Barely remembered television versions of the story aired in 1955, 1956, and 1959, the first two airing under the title *Meet Mr. Kringle.*

Further Reading

Danielson, Sarah Parker. *Miracle on 34th Street: A Hollywood Classic*. New York: Smithmark, 1993.

Davies, Valentine. *Miracle on 34th Street*. New York: Harcourt, Brace and Company, 1947.

Galbraith, Jane. "Now the Miracle Is Off 34th Street, Macy's Says 'No Thanks' to a Remake of the Classic, so the Film Moves to Chicago." *Newsday* (April 18, 1994): B13.

Werts, Diane. "A 'Miracle' in the Making/Behind the Scenes of a Christmas Classic." *Newsday* (November 21, 2001): B27.

Misa de Gallo

Misa de Aguinaldo, Missa do Galo

Misa de gallo (pronounced MEE-sah day GAH-yoh) means "rooster's mass" in Spanish. Both the Spanish- and Portuguese-speaking peoples of the world refer to **Midnight Mass** on Christmas Eve as the rooster's mass. The Portuguese term for "rooster's mass," *missa do galo*, closely resembles its Spanish cousin.

This curious name for Midnight Mass comes from a bit of old European folklore. According to a traditional tale **Jesus** was born at the stroke of midnight. The task of announcing this miraculous event fell to the roosters. The first rooster fluttered to the roof of the stable and proclaimed in a human voice, "Christ is born!" The second followed, crying out, "In **Bethlehem**!" Since the rooster was the first creature to call humankind to worship on the eve of Jesus' birth, people throughout the Spanish- and Portuguese-speaking worlds honor the animal by referring to Midnight Mass on Christmas Eve as the "rooster's mass."

Perhaps elements of this legend inspired the scheduling of Midnight Mass itself. Since early medieval times Roman Catholic priests have celebrated three Christmas masses. Rules dating back to the fifth century A.D. ordained that the first Christmas mass be celebrated *ad galli cantum,* that is, when the rooster crows (*see also* **Plygain**). Few roosters crow as early as midnight. Instead, the belief that Jesus was born at midnight determined the hour at which the first mass was held.

The Philippines

Roman Catholic churches in the **Philippines** offer nine rooster's masses on the nine nights preceding Christmas. This practice remains from colonial times. In the Philippines and other areas colonized by the Spanish, missionaries instituted a special novena for the nine days before Christmas. A novena is a prayer service offered on nine consecutive days. The missionaries deemed the novena necessary in order to impress upon the recent converts the importance of the upcoming feast day. In the Philippines the Christmas novena is called *Simbang Gabi,* a Tagalog phrase which means "night mass." The Filipinos also use Spanish terms for these masses, referring to them as *misas de gallo,* "rooster's masses," or *misas de aguinaldo* (MEE-sahs day ah-ghee-NAL-doh), which means "Christmas present masses" or "**gift** masses." The "gifts" refer to the **shepherds'** offerings to the infant Jesus. These nine early morning masses are also celebrated in some parts of Central America and the Caribbean.

In the Philippines the rooster's masses begin on December 16 and usher in the **Christmas season**. A festive rather than solemn mood pervades these observances, in spite of the fact that the masses begin at four in the morning. At four a.m. church **bells** ring, marching bands play, and fireworks explode, rousing anyone who is still in bed and reminding everyone to attend mass. Young people who went to parties the night before may stay out long enough to attend the masses before returning home. After the service many stay to socialize with one another and share the traditional breakfast of *salabat* (ginger tea) and *puto bum-bong* (sweetened rice cakes). Although the last of these nine masses occurs in the early morning hours of December 24, Roman Catholic churches in the Philippines still offer Midnight Mass on Christmas Eve.

Further Reading

Christmas in Brazil. Chicago: World Book, 1991.
Christmas in Mexico. Chicago: World Book, 1976.

Christmas in the Philippines. Chicago: World Book, 1990.

Henderson, Helene, and Sue Ellen Thompson, eds. *Holidays, Festivals, and Celebrations of the World Dictionary*. Second edition. Detroit, Mich.: Omnigraphics, 1997.

MacDonald, Margaret Read, ed. *The Folklore of World Holidays*. Detroit, Mich.: Gale Research, 1992.

Weiser, Francis X. *The Christmas Book*. 1952. Reprint. Detroit, Mich.: Omnigraphics, 1990.

Mistletoe

The parasitic plant known as *Viscum album* to botanists has attached itself in a mysterious way to the celebration of Christmas. More commonly known as mistletoe, this plant frequently makes its home on the branches of apple trees, but may also be found on poplars, hawthorns, limes, maples, and even, occasionally, on oak trees. According to an old English custom, sprigs of mistletoe may be hung over doorways and from ceilings around Christmas time; anyone may kiss a person who passes beneath the mistletoe. How did this plant and this custom come to be associated with Christmas? Perhaps no definitive answer to this question can be given, but we can review the history of the plant from ancient times to the present. Over the centuries a variety of European beliefs and customs have linked mistletoe to the winter season, magic, good will, and flirtation.

Evergreens in Ancient Times

Mistletoe is an evergreen, a plant that stays green throughout the winter. Like **holly** and **ivy**, mistletoe even bears fruit during this cold, dark season. The ancient Romans as well as the pagan peoples of northern Europe adorned their homes with evergreen boughs for their winter festivals (*see also* **Kalends**; **Yule**). These plants, which continue to thrive as others around them appear to wither and die, may have symbolized the promise of new life or of eternal life to these ancient peoples. The custom of decking homes and temples with **greenery** during the heart of winter passed on into later northern European Christmas celebrations.

Celtic Customs and Beliefs

Over a century ago the famous anthropologist and classics scholar Sir George Frazer (1854-1941) suggested that mistletoe was an especially sacred plant to both the ancient Romans and the ancient peoples of northwestern Europe (sometimes referred to as the Celts). He proposed that the mistletoe plant, which not only lives without roots in the ground but also stays green in winter, baffled these ancient peoples. Therefore, they assigned mistletoe a special role in their religious beliefs.

Frazer claimed that the pagan peoples of ancient **France**, Britain, and **Ireland** held mistletoe to be sacred, and they harvested it in special ceremonial ways. These peoples believed that mistletoe possessed magical powers and that the rare plants that grew on oak trees were the most powerful of all. Mistletoe gained its power in part from its ability to live halfway between heaven and earth. Therefore, when the Druids, or pagan priests, harvested the plant, they cut it with golden sickles and were careful never to let it touch the ground. The Druids called the plant "all-healer" and thought it had the power to cure many ills, including infertility, nervous diseases, and toothaches. (Today we know that mistletoe berries are highly poisonous, however). Mistletoe was also thought to attract good luck and to ward off witchcraft. Frazer asserted that the European folklore of his day still contained traces of these ancient beliefs. He noted that in some modern Celtic languages the word for mistletoe translates to "all-healer."

Norse Mythology

The ancient Norse also reserved a special place for mistletoe in their mythology. Balder, the Norse god of sun and summer, was beloved in heaven and on earth. His mother, Frigga, the queen of the Norse gods, loved Balder so much she set about extracting a promise from every thing on the earth to refrain from harming her son. She disregarded the puny mistletoe, however, thinking it powerless to damage the sun god.

This omission provided an opportunity for the evil god Loki to scheme against Balder. Loki obtained some mistletoe and fashioned it into a spear. Then he brought it to Hodur, Balder's blind brother, the god of night. The other gods were amusing themselves by tossing all sorts of objects at Balder and watching them turn aside at the last minute, bound by their promise not to harm the god. Loki offered Hodur the spear, assuring him that it, too, would turn aside before it could hurt the sun god. Hodur threw the mistletoe spear at his brother. It pierced Balder's chest and killed him. According to one version of the myth, the father of these two brothers, Odin, eventually sent someone to kill Hodur, thus avenging Balder's death.

At least one writer has suggested that the Norse attached this myth to the turning of the seasons, viewing the summer solstice as the time of Balder the sun god's death, and the **winter solstice** as the time of Hodur the night god's death.

Mistletoe as an Emblem of Good Will

This Norse myth suggests that the ancient Scandinavians believed that mistletoe possessed unseen powers—in this case, put to evil purposes. At some point, though, mistletoe became a symbol of peace and good will in pagan Scandinavia. Enemies who happened to meet beneath it in the forest declared a day's truce from fighting. In Scandinavia a branch of mistletoe hung above a threshold thus came to signify the offer of hospitality and friendship within. Some claim that, after the coming of Christianity, mistletoe was seldom incorporated into church Christmas decorations, due to its strong association with the pagan past. Others disagree with this claim. If such a ban did exist, then York Cathedral in **England** defied it. During medieval times Church officials placed a branch of mistletoe upon the high altar on Christmas Eve, signaling a general pardon for all wrongdoers for as long as it remained there.

Kissing under the Mistletoe

The custom of kissing under the mistletoe appears to be of English origin. Although in recent centuries the British have earned a reputation for being physically reserved, this was not always the case. In the sixteenth century the visiting Dutch scholar Erasmus (1466?-1536) wrote that the English were so fond of kissing at meeting and parting that it was impossible to avoid being constantly kissed. It is difficult to say with certainty when the British adopted the custom of kissing under the mistletoe at Christmas time. A seventeenth-century document speaks of the transport and sale of mistletoe at Christmas, but none mentions the custom of kissing under the mistletoe until the eighteenth century, when some writers suggest that it became a common practice.

The custom attracted a number of somewhat contradictory folk beliefs. According to one belief, each time a boy kissed a girl under the mistletoe, he must pluck one of the berries. When no berries remained, no more kissing could occur under that branch. Some claimed that to refuse a kiss under the mistletoe meant that one would not marry in the next twelve months. Others claimed that no marriage was possible after such an offense. Another folk belief advised householders to burn their mistletoe branches after **Twelfth Night** in case the boys and girls who kissed under them never married. Still another recommended that a sprig of mistletoe be kept in order to drive evil away from the house during the coming year. The sprig might also be used to light the fire under next year's Christmas pudding, or **plum pudding**. Finally, some thought it unlucky to cut mistletoe at any other time than Christmas.

The English often displayed mistletoe in the form of a **kissing bough**, a circular, or even spherical, configuration of greenery woven around hoops of wire or wood. One expert claims that the kissing bough reached the peak of its popularity in the eighteenth century and began to decline in the nineteenth century. In *The Pickwick Papers*, British writer Charles Dickens (1812-1870) offers a charming description of the fun and flirtation that occurred under the mistletoe in his day:

> From the centre of the ceiling of this kitchen, old Wardle had just suspended with his own hand a huge branch of mistletoe, and this same branch of mistletoe instantaneously gave rise to a scene of general and most delightful struggling and confusion; in the midst of which, Mr. Pickwick, with a gallantry that would have done honour to a descendent of Lady

Tollimglower herself, took the old lady by the hand, led her beneath the mystic branch, and saluted her in all courtesy and decorum. The old lady submitted to this piece of practical politeness with all the dignity which befitted so important and serious a solemnity, but the younger ladies, not being so thoroughly imbued with a superstitious veneration for the custom — or imagining that the value of a salute is very much enhanced if it cost a little trouble to obtain it — screamed and struggled, and ran into corners, and threatened and remonstrated, and did everything but leave the room until some of the less adventurous gentlemen were on the point of desisting when they all at once found it useless to resist any longer and submitted to be kissed with a good grace. Mr. Winkle kissed the young lady with the black eyes, and Mr. Snodgrass kissed Emily, and Mr. Weller, not being particular about the form of being under the mistletoe, kissed Emma and the other female servants just as he caught them. As to the poor relations, they kissed everybody, not even excepting the plainer portions of the young-lady visitors, who, in their excessive confusion, ran right under the mistletoe as soon as it was hung up, without knowing it! Wardle stood with his back to the fire, surveying the whole scene with the utmost satisfaction; and the fat boy took the opportunity of appropriating to his own use, and summarily devouring, a particularly fine mince-pie that had been put carefully by for someone else.

Today many people still enhance their Christmas festivities with mischievous sprigs of mistletoe. The custom is typically found in Britain, France, or countries where the British have settled, such as Canada and the United States.

Further Reading

Baker, Margaret. *Christmas Customs and Folklore*. Aylesbury, Bucks, England: Shire Publications, 1968.

Cooper, Quentin, and Paul Sullivan. *Maypoles, Martyrs and Mayhem*. London, England: Bloomsbury, 1994.

Del Re, Gerard, and Patricia Del Re. *The Christmas Almanack*. Garden City, N.Y.: Doubleday, 1979.

Frazer, James. *The New Golden Bough*. Theodor Gaster, ed. New York: S. G. Phillips, 1959.

Guerber, H. A. *Myths of Northern Lands*. 1895. Reprint. Detroit, Mich.: Singing Tree Press, 1970.

Hole, Christina. *British Folk Customs*. London, England: Hutchinson and Company, 1976.

Weiser, Francis X. *The Christmas Book*. 1952. Reprint. Detroit, Mich.: Omnigraphics, 1990.

Mummers Parade

For more than one hundred years, the people of Philadelphia, Pennsylvania, have lined the streets on **New Year's Day** to watch the Mummers Parade. Marching string bands, fancy and funny floats, and thousands of extravagantly costumed mummers dazzle onlookers brave enough to risk the winter weather. Although participants in Philadelphia's first officially sanctioned parade strutted up Broad Street in 1900, local people established the custom of parading in costume on New Year's Eve and Day way back in the first half of the nineteenth century (*see* **America, Christmas in Nineteenth-Century**).

Parade Forerunners

Many of those who celebrated Christmas in early nineteenth-century America did so by shooting off guns (*see also* **Shooting in Christmas**). This custom was popular in the West, the South, and in many areas settled by Germans. Those who didn't own guns, such as children, found other ways to make loud noises, like popping inflated hog bladders, the nineteenth-century equivalent of a balloon. On occasion a gang of especially rowdy frontiersmen blew up a stash of gunpowder, so as to create an especially deafening noise with which to usher in Christmas. In some American towns and cities boys and men took to the streets at Christmas and New Year's, blowing on tin horns, ringing fire **bells**, firing guns, shouting, drinking, cussing, fighting, and generally disturbing the peace.

In areas where the English had settled, some of their descendants kept up a version of Christmas time **mumming**. Groups of boys or young men would dress in rude, homemade costumes, and go door to door, reciting some garbled folk verse and partaking of the household's hospitality in the form of food and drink. The Scotch Irish practiced similar customs on New Year's Eve, or **Hogmanay**. In Pennsylvania, some Americans of German descent developed a distinctive custom called belsnickling *(for more on belsnickling, see* **Knecht Ruprecht***)*. Young men and boys disguised their identities by covering their faces with a mask or low-slung hat or by darkening them with burnt cork, soot, or redwash. Then they dressed in rags, furs, or baggy overcoats and armed themselves with bells, whips, and sacks. Thus arrayed they trouped about town or village, playing tricks on neighbors and frightening children by cracking their whips while tossing them sweets and nuts. They received food and drink at homes where they succeeded in amusing householders with rhymes and horseplay.

Pre-Civil War Holiday Masquerades in Philadelphia

In nineteenth-century Philadelphia all these traditions collided and merged, creating pandemonium in the streets at New Year's and Christmas. By the 1830s and 1840s, people began to create slightly fancier disguises for their holiday frolics. Some dressed up as blacks or members of other ethnic groups in order to make fun of them, thereby using holiday mumming customs as a way of expressing their fear of or hostility towards certain groups. Others were less pointed in their actions and choice of dress. Costumed celebrants, dubbed "fantasticals," often converged downtown, engaging in lively horseplay and raising a ferocious din with firecrackers, horns, whistles, bells, hornpipes, or homemade instruments of various kinds. Some of these intrepid instrumentalists organized themselves into impromptu bands, marching up and down the street and churning out a discordant kind of music referred to as "callithumpian." A newspaper account from January 10, 1834, describes New Year's celebrations in the nearby town of Easton:

> The Fantasticals. On New Year's Day our borough witnessed a parade of the fantasticals — the immediate body guard of the lately elected redoubtable Col. Sheffler. It was a new and per-

haps an improved edition of the late parades in New York and Philadelphia. The corps including music (numbered) about one hundred. The Calithumpian band had been uniformed and pressed into service. These commenced their melody about 10 o'clock in the forenoon and made the circuit of the town, playing the most splendid and novel voluntaries and variations. Their dresses displayed taste and ingenuity. All the quarters of the earth appeared to have been ransacked to swell the ranks of the Enterpian band. Indians, Negroes, hunters, Falstaffs, Jim Crows and nondescripts, all displaying surprizing (sic) skill upon their several instruments . . . Conch-shells, old cracked instruments, stones, shingles, tin horns, speaking trumpets, here and there a bassoon, old kettles, pot-lids, dozens of cow-bells strung upon poles and iron hoops constituted their musical instruments. . . . [Welch, 1991, 29-30]

In the rest of the country these carnivalesque Christmas celebrations faded as the century rolled by. In Philadelphia, however, holiday noisemaking and masquerading customs grew in popularity. Philadelphia's first mummers club, a group organized solely for the purpose of parading together in costume on New Year's Day, was organized in 1846. Called the Chain Gang, the club survived into the twentieth century.

In the early days these masqueraders were referred to as "shooters." The name came from the old, established custom of shooting in Christmas. By the 1880s a few people began to refer to them as mummers and the new name stuck.

In the year 1861 the rowdy revelers succeeded in reducing the center of the city to chaos. Many of the city's leading citizens were not amused. Opposition to these disorderly practices can be traced back to the eighteenth century, when historical documents reveal that certain Christmas masqueraders were tried in courts of law for their unruly behavior. The Pennsylvania legislature passed a law against Christmas masquerading and masked balls in 1808, but in spite of the stiff penalties—up to three months in jail and fines of up to $1,000—the law was not really enforced. In 1868 and again in 1881 Philadelphia's city government attempted to outlaw Christmas noise-making, masquerading, and parading.

These laws failed to root out the deeply entrenched custom, however. Instead, these half-hearted restrictions, plus the growing, late-nineteenth-century consensus that Christmas was a domestic holiday, acted together to shift the holiday season masquerading away from Christmas and towards New Year's Day (*for more on the changing sentiments concerning Christmas, see* America, Christmas in Nineteenth-Century).

African-American cultural elements began to influence the parade in the second half of the nineteenth century. Many mummers paraded with a particular kind of strutting walk that some researchers believe may have been derived from the cakewalk, a nineteenth-century African-American dance that parodied and exaggerated the fancy steps popular in the formal balls of the time. The name came from the custom of awarding a cake to the couple with the best moves. The song "Oh, dem Golden Slippers," written by African-American composer James Bland in 1879, became very popular with the mummers and today it still serves as a kind of theme song for the parade.

Post-Civil War Parade

In the years following the Civil War, the Philadelphia Mummers Parade as we know it today took shape. The year 1876 witnessed the first, unofficial, New Year's Day Mummers Parade. The parade did not proceed in a direct manner down the street, however. Instead, participants meandered towards city hall, stopping frequently to eat, drink, and socialize. The leisurely paraders might take all day to arrive at their final destination. In that era many saloons offered free beer and food to the marchers. Paraders partook freely of these offerings. What's more, neighborhood women and local stores often baked cakes for their favorite clubs. The clubs stopped by to serenade the women or the storeowners, and received the cake in return. Some groups pulled a cake wagon along behind them, a vehicle specially designated to hold these offerings. These cakes provided refreshments at later New Year's parties.

By the 1880s many mummers clubs had been established. Members of these groups came primarily from the neighborhoods of South Philadelphia, still a stronghold of parade enthusiasts today. In 1888 the first cash prize was awarded to a mummers club for its performance in the parade.

Twentieth Century and Beyond

By 1900 city officials grew tired of trying to curtail the sprawling parade and decided to sponsor it instead. The city provided cash prizes for the best club performances in two divisions, fancy and comic. The fancy clubs focused their attention on creating beautiful and elaborate costumes. The comics dedicated themselves to making people laugh. In 1902 the first string band, named Trilby, marched in the official parade.

With the parade now an accepted event in Philadelphia's yearly calendar, participants began to put more and more effort into their costumes. By the 1920s the captains of fancy clubs wore long, magnificent trains along with their costumes. In 1929 the leader of the Silver Crown Club wore a satin train that stretched a city block in length. Dozens of page boys kept the train from dragging on the ground.

As the years went by old clubs died out and new clubs took over. Some old traditions, too, began to fade away. The old simple comic costume — often a coat turned inside out with a sign pinned to it — fell out of favor to be replaced with more elaborate efforts. Another old mummers' device, a walking stick with some dice attached to the top of it, was eliminated, perhaps out of fears that some might use it as a weapon. Female impersonators began to make regular appearances with the clubs beginning in the early twentieth century.

The need for coordination between mummers clubs gave rise to the Mummers' Association. This association, together with city hall officials, began to formulate rules governing parade participants and the awarding of prizes. With each decade the number of rules and restrictions grew, as what was once a spontaneous folk custom became a government-regulated event.

Nevertheless, it is family tradition, not prize money, that inspires a large percentage of the mummers to carry on the old New Year's Day customs. Many parade participants grew up watching their grandfathers, uncles, and fathers march in the parade.

Nowadays mummers compete with one another in four divisions: the comics, the fancies, the string bands, and the fancy brigades. The comic clubs organize their displays around humorous themes and dress like clowns. The string bands are marching, costumed musical ensembles, featuring the banjo and the saxophone. The fancy clubs wow the audience with their imaginative and lavish costumes and floats, and the fancy brigades—the largest of all the clubs—showcase spectacularly costumed performers in an elaborately choreographed performance.

Over the years both the number of participants and the value of the cash prizes has increased. In recent years about 15,000 costumed mummers have taken part in the parade. In 2002 the judges awarded a total of $375,000 among various winners.

Recent Controversies and Challenges

One initially unpopular parade rule was announced in 1963. It declared that marchers could no longer appear in blackface. The ruling was made in response to pressure from civil rights activists, who felt that the spectacle of white people disguising themselves as simple-minded blacks was degrading to African Americans. Many mummers were outraged at this interference. They pointed out that mummers had painted their faces black for hundreds of years as a kind of simple, homemade disguise. Activists countered that in spite of its origins, blackface had since become a method of poking fun at black people. The 1963 parade, monitored by hundreds of police, was tense and sullen, but only a small percentage of mummers defied the ban on blackface. The tension over this issue subsided after a few years.

During the 1960s, no predominantly African-American clubs marched in the parade. The last African-American club, the Octavius V. Cato Club, had put in its final parade appearance in 1929. Lingering suspicion and resentment over the blackface issue kept all but a few African Americans out of the parade again until the Octavius V. Cato string band marched with the Goodtimers Club in 1987. Since that time slowly increasing numbers of African Americans have joined the existing clubs.

Women, too, had been excluded from the parade until recent times, although over the years a few had succeeded in infiltrating the parade in mask and costume. The first women to openly march in the parade did so in 1975, as official members of the Dick Crean String Band. Slowly but surely, other clubs began to accept female members.

Some bystanders complain that with the advent of television coverage, the mummers perform less for the crowds and more for the camera. Perhaps in response to the convenience of being able to watch the parade on television, the crowds lining the streets have dwindled from a high of about two million people in the 1940s to about a quarter of a million people in recent years. In response to declining turnouts, the city has decreased the parade route from 2.5 miles to 10 city blocks.

The mummers themselves are preoccupied with the expense involved in maintaining their tradition. Costuming an entire club costs tens of thousands of dollars, money that must be raised by club members since no corporate sponsorship is allowed. The number of fancy clubs has decreased in recent years in response to the rising costs of these costumes. Only the top contenders in each division can expect to defray some of their club's expenses with prize money. The rest continue because of their pride in a Philadelphia tradition and their love for mumming.

Further Reading

Alison, James. "Struttin' in Style." *The World and I* 13 (January 1998): 178 (11).

Davies, Susan G. *Parades and Power*. Berkeley, Calif.: University of California Press, 1986.

Lange, Karen E. "Kings for a Day." *National Geographic* 199, 1 (January 2001): 58-65.

Restad, Penne. *Christmas in America*. Oxford, England: Oxford University Press, 1995.

Welch, Charles E. *Oh, Dem Golden Slippers*. Revised edition. Philadelphia, Penn.: Book Street Press, 1991.

Web Sites

The Philadelphia Recreation Department maintains a page on the Mummers Parade at: http://www.phila.gov/recreation/mummers/index.html

Parade results, route map, photos, and other information concerning Philadelphia mummery can be found at: http://mummers.com

Mumming

Geese Dancing, Guising, Masking, Mummering

Mumming is a form of folk entertainment in which bands of masked and costumed merrymakers roam the streets singing, dancing, acting out stories, or simply engaging in horseplay. In past centuries people throughout **Europe** celebrated the **Christmas season** by mumming or by hosting bands of mummers in their homes. In the United States today we allow children to practice a similar form of seasonal masquerading at Halloween.

Since mumming began as a folk rather than elite tradition, mummers usually wore simple, homemade costumes, often accompanied by masks or blackening of the face. Indeed, some scholars trace the origins of the English word "mumming" back to the ancient Greek term for "mask," *mommo*. In some cases, the mummer's costume represented a mythical figure whose character or behavior the mummer enacted in a kind of folk drama called a mummers' play. In other cases, mummers simply cavorted under the cover of disguise, engaging in playful but sometimes rather unruly behavior to the amusement or irritation of their neighbors. Christmas time mumming was particularly common in the British Isles, where it survived as a popular folk custom until the mid-nineteenth century.

Ancient Precedents

How did this custom attach itself to the Christmas season? Some would answer this question by pointing to the revels that took place during the ancient Roman feast of **Kalends**. During this midwinter new year festival, groups of young men ran through the streets dressed as women or animals and, under the cover of disguise, engaged in many behaviors that would normally have been frowned upon.

Although Christian authorities condemned these activities, they proved difficult to stamp out, even after Christianity became the dominant religion and Christmas an important winter holiday. One researcher has counted at least forty separate Church documents containing official denunciations of these kinds of midwinter masquerades. These documents range from the fourth to the eleventh centuries and come from authorities in many European lands as well as north Africa and the Near East.

Mumming in Britain

Some researchers believe that these ancient customs lingered on in a few places, eventually giving rise to Christmas time mumming practices. Others disagree, arguing that these ancient practices died out in all but a few places hundreds of years before medieval mumming customs were established. In any case, Christmas time mumming can be traced back to the late Middle Ages. The earliest documents referring to it date back to the thirteenth century. Although mumming sprang from the lower classes, by the fourteenth century King Edward III adopted an elaborate rendition of this practice as a Christmas season entertainment at court. Among the elite, these costumed Christmas revels eventually developed into **masques** or masquerades.

In some areas mumming was known as "masking" or "guising" (from the word "disguise"). In other areas the word "guising" eventually became "geese dancing." In fifteenth- and sixteenth-century **England** bands of mummers, also called "maskers" or "guisers," frequently appeared on the streets during the **Twelve Days of Christmas**. The following account of one such band in the fifteenth century illustrates the mixture of fun and fear that the revelers inspired:

> John Hadman, a wealthy citizen, made disport with his neighbors and friends, and was crowned King of Christmas. He rode in state through the city, dressed forth in silks and tinsel, and preceded by twelve persons habited as the twelve months of the year. After King Christmas followed Lent, clothed in white garments trimmed with herring skins, on horseback, the horse being decorated with trappings of oyster shells, being indicative that sadness and a holy time should follow the Christmas revelling. In this way they rode through the city, accompanied by numbers in various grotesque dresses, making disport and merriment; some clothed in armour; others, dressed as devils, chased the people, and sorely affrighted the women and children; others wearing skin dresses, and counterfeiting bears, wolves, lions, and other animals, and endeavoring to imitate the animals they represented, in roaring and raving, alarming the cowardly and appalling the stoutest hearts [Halpert and Story, 1969, 49].

For the most part, people engaged in mumming and welcomed mummers into their homes because it was fun. Mummers relished parading in costume and appreciated the protection it gave them to praise or tease their neighbors as they saw fit. The less well-off might also avail themselves of this opportunity to exact hospitality from their more prosperous neighbors. Indeed, mummers usually demanded and received food or drink from each household or locale they visited. No doubt many people liked the lively atmosphere created by the mummers and enjoyed their entertaining antics. Others probably resented being pestered for **gifts** of food and drink.

Mummers' Plays

In Great Britain and **Ireland** some mummers eventually began to entertain their hosts with short folk dramas called mummers' plays. Since mummers' plays were often passed down through oral traditions, they varied in many details. Nevertheless, three main story lines emerge, which experts have dubbed the hero-combat, the sword play, and the wooing ceremony. The hero-combat was the most popular of these stories. Some of the characters likely to appear in this play include St. George, **Father Christmas**, the king of **Egypt** or England, the king's daughter, a pompous doctor, and a Turkish knight. The story revolves around a fight between the hero, St. George, and the Turkish knight. One combatant kills the other. Afterwards, the bumbling doctor miraculously manages to revive the dead soldier. All of this takes place amidst a great deal of silly or garbled dialogue in which characters flatly announce their identities and narrate their actions. Father Christmas often serves as a kind of announcer for the play. In England women did not usually take part in mumming, so all the roles were played by men.

After presenting their play, the mummers collected coins from the audience in return for their dramatic efforts. Mummers performed these plays most frequently at Christmas time, but in some areas they were presented around Easter and All Souls' Day (November 2). Although some writers believe these plays, or at least the themes they touch on, to be ancient, others point out that the earliest written records of the plays date back to the eighteenth century.

Mumming in Europe

British and Irish mumming traditions have been well documented by generations of historians and folklorists. Although Christmas mumming was practiced in many parts of Europe, it is somewhat more difficult to find descriptions of the custom from other European countries (*see also* **Bulgaria, Christmas in; Latvia, Christmas in; Lithuania, Christmas in; Russia, Christmas in;** *for similar customs practiced outside of Europe, see* **Ecuador, Christmas in; Marshall Islands, Christmas in the Republic of the; Nigeria, Christmas in**). One of the best portraits of the practice outside of Great Britain and Ireland comes from the pen of Leo Tolstoy (1828-1910), the great Russian writer. The following excerpt from his novel *War and Peace* (1865-69) describes Christmas festivities in a well-to-do Russian household:

> The mummers (some of the house-serfs) dressed up as bears, Turks, inn-keepers and ladies — frightening and funny — bringing with them the cold from the outside and a feeling of gaiety, crowded, at first timidly, into the anteroom, then hiding behind one another they pushed into the ballroom where shyly at first and then more and more merrily and heartily, they started singing, dancing, and playing Christmas games. The countess, when she had identified them and laughed at their costumes, went into the drawing-room. . . . Half an hour later there appeared among the other mummers in the ballroom an old lady in a hooped skirt — this was Nicholas. A Turkish girl was Petya. A clown was Dimmler. An hussar was Natasha, and a Circassian was Sonya with burnt-cork mustache and eyebrows. After the condescending surprise, non-recognition, and praise from those who were not themselves dressed up, the young people decided that their costumes were so good that they ought to be shown elsewhere.

Mumming in North America

Mumming remained a popular Christmas season pastime in England until the mid-nineteenth century. After that time it faded away almost completely, being kept alive in only a few places by local enthusiasts. Long before its decline, however, English emigrants had carried this custom to the New World. In the seventeenth century the English established themselves in Newfoundland (now part of Canada). Local inhabitants there carried on a tradition of Christmas mumming, or "mummering," as they called it, until the 1960s.

In the United States English settlers introduced mumming to an ethnically diverse population. In Pennsylvania, English Christmas time mumming traditions combined with the German folk figure Belsnickel to create the custom of belsnickeling (*see* **Knecht Ruprecht**). When these influences collided with the holiday season noisemaking traditions of Scandinavians and the musical and dance heritage of African Americans, new traditions were born.

Although Philadelphia city officials periodically attempted to disband the noisy holiday revelers, they finally accepted these customs in an organized format, issuing the first official permit for the Philadelphia **Mummers Parade** in 1901. Philadelphians continue to stage this extravagant event every year on **New Year's Day**. Squads of elaborately costumed mummers, magnificent floats, and lively string bands all march through the city streets, and judges select the winning entries. In spite of its name the parade bears little resemblance to its ancestral English mumming traditions, except that participants wear costumes and, often, masks.

Related Customs

Mumming was only one of a number of old Christmas customs that authorized revelry, including unruly or forbidden behavior, under the cover of masks and disguises. These practices span many centuries and come from different lands. Examples include belsnickeling, the ceremonies surrounding the **boy bishop**, the customs associated with **Berchta**, **Black Peter**, Germany's **Knocking Nights**, the **Feast of Fools**, masques, **pantomimes**, Los **Pastores**, Las **Posadas**, **Plough Monday**, **St. Sylvester's Day**, and **Twelfth Night** celebrations. Although their historical and cultural roots vary, some authors identify in these customs a perennial return to the ancient theme of celebrating midwinter with costumed merrymaking.

Controversies

Although Christmas mumming no doubt entertained many participants and onlookers, mummers also caused many disturbances. Complaints against mummers ranged from excessive noisiness to malicious mischief and, even, criminal acts. Perhaps the excitement of shedding one's usual social role with the aid of a disguise, combined with a good deal to drink, tilted some mummers towards raucous behavior. In other cases, some who set out to steal, incite political disturbances, or simply settle old scores with a neighbor found it convenient to disguise themselves as mummers. This tendency toward disorder caused local authorities throughout the centuries to attempt to eradicate the practice. Indeed, the oldest document known to mention Christmas mumming records that it was forbidden in the French town of Troyes in 1263. In 1405 the practice was outlawed in London.

In the seventeenth century the **Puritans** railed against it. Throughout the nineteenth century Pennsylvania legislators attempted to abolish it. Ironically, legislators were never able to kill this form of folk entertainment. Mumming finally died a natural death at a ripe old age when the societies that gave birth to it had changed so much that ordinary people simply abandoned the practice.

Further Reading

Brody, Alan. *The English Mummers and Their Plays*. Philadelphia, Pa.: University of Pennsylvania Press, 1970.

Chambers, Robert. "December 24—The Mummers." In his *The Book of Days*. Volume 2. 1862-64. Reprint. Detroit, Mich.: Omnigraphics, 1990.

Halpert, Herbert, and G. M. Story, eds. *Christmas Mumming in Newfoundland*. Toronto, Ontario, Canada: University of Toronto Press, 1969.

Helm, Alex. *The English Mummers' Play*. Totowa, N.J.: Rowman and Littlefield, 1981.

Hutton, Ronald. *The Rise and Fall of Merry England*. Oxford, England: Oxford University Press, 1994.

————. *The Stations of the Sun*. Oxford, England: Oxford University Press, 1996.

Langstaff, John. *Saint George and the Dragon*. New York: Atheneum Press, 1973.

MacDonald, Margaret Read, ed. *The Folklore of World Holidays*. Detroit, Mich.: Gale Research, 1992.

Miles, Clement A. *Christmas in Ritual and Tradition*. 1912. Reprint. Detroit, Mich.: Omnigraphics, 1990.

Miller, Katherine. *Saint George, A Christmas Mummers' Play*. Boston, Mass.: Houghton Mifflin Company, 1967.

"Mummers' Play." In Phyllis Hartnoll, ed. *The Oxford Companion to the Theatre*. Fourth edition. Oxford, England: Oxford University Press, 1983.

Nissenbaum, Stephen. *The Battle for Christmas*. New York: Alfred A. Knopf, 1996.

Robertson, Margaret. "The Symbolism of Christmas Mummering in Newfoundland." *Folklore* 93, 2 (1982): 176-80.

Web Site

A site sponsored by the Philadelphia Department of Recreation on the Mummers Parade: http://www.phila.gov/recreation/mummers/index.html

Myrrh

The sap of the myrrh tree (*Commiphora myrrha*) dries into hard, reddish brown lumps of gum resin known as myrrh. Although unfamiliar to us today, in ancient times myrrh was a precious and much sought-after substance. The **Magi**, or Wise Men from the East, brought the baby **Jesus** a **gift** of myrrh.

History and Significance

In order to understand the significance of this gift, we must explore the uses of myrrh in biblical times. Ancient records tell us that it was perhaps most commonly employed as a medicine. The Romans, Greeks, Assyrians, and other peoples of the ancient Mediterranean and Near East prescribed myrrh in treatments for a wide variety of afflictions, including sores in the mouth, infections, coughs, and worms. It was also burned to fumigate the rooms of the sick. Myrrh appears at the beginning of Jesus' life as a gift and at the end of his life as a medicine. Shortly before his crucifixion, Jesus is offered a cup of wine mixed with myrrh (Mark 15:23). This suggests that myrrh was used as a painkiller. The ancient Egyptians used myrrh in the process of embalming corpses. The ancient Hebrews also treated the dead with myrrh; according to the Gospel of John, Jesus' body was treated with myrrh and aloes before being wrapped in cloth for burial (John 19:39).

Myrrh was also highly valued as a component of perfume and incense. Although myrrh has a pleasant smell, like many more familiar perfume products, it has a bitter taste. In fact, the English word "myrrh" comes from the Hebrew and Arabic terms for "bitter." Myrrh was especially prized as an ingredient in perfumed oils and lotions because of its enduring fragrance and long shelf life. The Hebrews made myrrh one of the primary ingredients of the holy oil with which they anointed their high priests and the sacred objects of their temples. It was also used to make incense, which many ancient peoples, such as the Egyptians, Greeks, Romans, Hebrews, Persians, and Babylonians, burned in home and temple worship. **Frankincense** was preferred over myrrh in the making of incense, however.

In ancient times, Arabia supplied the Mediterranean and Asia with most of their myrrh and frankincense. These products were so highly valued and so difficult to obtain outside of Arabia that they became a luxury affordable only by the rich.

The Magi's gifts of **gold**, frankincense, and myrrh have each been assigned a special significance in Christian lore and legend. Due to its bitterness, the gift of myrrh has often been interpreted as a symbol of the hardships that Jesus would suffer in his adult life: persecution and early death. The fact that myrrh was used in embalming has led some to assert that myrrh represents Jesus' humanity. Like us, he would die. Another interpretation suggests that because myrrh had many medicinal uses in biblical times, it must represent Jesus' role as a healer of body and spirit. Finally, it might be argued that the gift of myrrh symbolizes Jesus' role as a Jewish religious leader, since myrrh was a main ingredient in the holy oil used to anoint Jewish high priests.

Customs

Until the mid-1700s tradition dictated that the British monarch offer a gift of frankincense, gold, and myrrh at the Chapel Royal on **Epiphany**. Heralds and knights of the Garter, Thistle, and Bath accompanied the king on this reenactment of the Magi's royal pilgrimage. The procession was abandoned under the unstable King George III (1760-1820), although a proxy continues to deliver the monarch's gift of gold, frankincense, and myrrh to the Chapel Royal on Epiphany. A similar royal offering was at one time customary in **Spain**.

Myrrh Today

Today myrrh trees can be found in Saudi Arabia, **Ethiopia**, and Somalia. Myrrh is still used as a component of incense and perfume. It is also found in mouthwashes, gargles, and toothpastes. Interest in the medicinal properties of myrrh has been increasing in recent years. Herbalists recognize its antiseptic, antifungal and astringent qualities. Moreover, a recent scientific study has found that myrrh indeed does reduce pain, affirming ancient uses of the drug.

Further Reading

Crippen, Thomas G. *Christmas and Christmas Lore*. 1923. Reprint. Detroit, Mich.: Omnigraphics, 1990.

Groom, Nigel. *Frankincense and Myrrh: A Study of the Arabian Incense Trade*. London, England: Longman House, 1981.

Hutton, Ronald. *The Stations of the Sun*. Oxford, England: Oxford University Press, 1996.

Lehner, Ernst, and Johanna Lehner. *Folklore and Symbolism of Flowers, Plants and Trees*. 1960. Reprint. Detroit, Mich.: Omnigraphics, 1990.

Lipkin, R. "Myrrh: An Ancient Salve Dampens Pain." *Science News* 149, 2 (January 13, 1996): 20.

"Myrrh." In Allen C. Myers, ed. *Eerdmans Bible Dictionary*. Grand Rapids, Mich.: William B. Eerdmans Publishing Company, 1987.

National Christmas Tree

The National Christmas Tree stands on the lawn of the President's Park South—or Ellipse, as it is more commonly called—in Washington, D.C. Its ceremonial illumination each year in early December kicks off a festival called the Pageant of Peace. The pageant was established in order to "foster friendship and understanding among all peoples" and "to reflect the unity of purpose that emanates from the diversity of traditions and backgrounds of mankind." The festival lasts till January 6, **Epiphany**. Over the years, radio and then television coverage has made the National Christmas Tree an increasingly important symbol of Christmas celebrations in the United States.

The Early Years

Community trees illuminated with electric lights date back to the first years of the twentieth century. From California the idea spread to **New York City**, resulting in a tree-lighting ceremony in Madison Park (now known as Madison Square Gardens). In 1913 the first community tree in Washington, D.C., was erected on the East Plaza of the Capitol Building. Lighting ceremonies took place in 1913 and 1914, but folded due to lack of funds. The event resumed at the end of World War I.

In 1923 the Capitol tree was eclipsed by another community tree, however, this one standing on the Ellipse south of the **White House** and lit by the president himself. That year President Calvin Coolidge agreed to flip the switch that illuminated the 60-foot fir tree's electric lights. He did so at sundown on Christmas Eve, but showed little interest in the proceedings. The evening's activities also included a free concert at the tree by the Marine Band quartet, a 9:00 p.m. carol sing on the North Lawn, and a midnight reenactment of the journey of the **Magi** at the Washington Monument.

Several years later President Coolidge designated the General Grant tree, located in California's King's Canyon National Park, the **Nation's Christmas Tree**. Although this 267-foot-tall tree is never decorated with lights and **ornaments**, Christmas ceremonies have taken place at the foot of the tree since 1925.

Washington's first National Christmas Tree had come from Coolidge's home state of Vermont, a donation from Middlebury College. Between the years 1924 and 1933 the ceremony took place in Sherman Plaza using a living **Christmas tree**. During these years the event became increasingly popular. Radio announcers broadcast the ceremony in 1925. In 1926, a flare was sent up at the moment of the illumination. This signal alerted buglers dispersed throughout the city to proclaim the lighting of the tree in song. By 1929 the hot lights and heavy ornaments had so damaged the tree that it had to be replaced.

Between the years 1934 and 1938, the renovation of Sherman Plaza forced the lighting ceremony to move to Lafayette Park. Two living Christmas trees were used in alternate years, in order to avoid permanently harming either one.

World War II

In 1939 the tree-lighting ceremony returned to the Ellipse, but in 1941 President Franklin D. Roosevelt ordered it moved to the South

Lawn of the White House, a decision he felt would make the proceedings "more homey." The United States entered World War II in December of that year. On Christmas Eve the British Prime Minister Winston Churchill, who was in Washington to confer with Roosevelt about the war, appeared alongside President Roosevelt at the tree-lighting ceremony. Both gave brief speeches about the war and Christmas. In 1942 wartime blackout requirements led to the cancellation of the tree's illumination. Nevertheless, First Lady Eleanor Roosevelt insisted on an alternate ceremony. Schoolchildren collected ornaments for the tree and a ceremony featuring the ringing of chimes was substituted for the usual illumination. The blackouts continued in 1943 and 1944. In these years, tags bearing the names of men serving in the military were attached to each ornament.

Post-War Years

By Christmas of 1945 World War II was over and Washingtonians rejoiced anew as President Harry S. Truman pushed the button that illuminated the National Christmas Tree for the first time since 1942. Truman preferred to spend Christmas at home in Missouri and so missed a number of illumination ceremonies. Without an appearance by the President, the event's glamour and popularity sagged.

President Dwight D. Eisenhower and his wife Mamie breathed new life into the illumination ceremony, however. In 1954 they moved it back to the Ellipse, which permitted larger crowds to gather. In that same year the date of the ceremony was moved back to December 17 and a series of related activities lasting from December 17 to January 6 was added. This program of activities, named the "Christmas Pageant of Peace," was concocted by local businessmen to attract more tourists to the area at Christmas time (*see also* **Commercialism**). Twenty-seven foreign embassies participated in the pageant that year, sending performers to demonstrate the Christmas songs, dances, and traditions of their countries. A full-scale **Nativity scene**, featuring live animals, was also erected as part of the pageant. In addition, during the Eisenhower years the tree-lighting ceremony was televised to ever-expanding TV audiences, which helped make the tree a national icon of the holiday season.

Between the years 1954 and 1972, festival organizers scouted out beautiful, tall trees from various parts of the country, bought them, cut them down, and imported them to Washington to serve as the National Christmas Tree. In that era festival organizers thought that planting a living Christmas tree on the Ellipse would interrupt the area's usage during the rest of the year. As the festival became a more important part of the nation's Christmas celebrations, various states began to send smaller Christmas trees to stand alongside the "pathway of peace" that leads to the National Christmas Tree. Eventually all fifty states were represented.

Problems and Protests

The illumination ceremony was postponed until December 22 in 1963. President John F. Kennedy had been shot and killed on November 22, and the nation observed a thirty-day mourning period for him in which it was deemed inappropriate to light the tree.

The illumination ceremony became the site of political protests during Richard M. Nixon's presidency. Citizens who opposed American involvement in Vietnam used the occasion to voice their objections to the war, heckling the President during his speech. One year the police arrested nine people, charging them with disorderly conduct.

Another kind of objection was raised by the American Civil Liberties Union. On behalf of several plaintiffs, they charged that the Nativity scene that had become part of the display violated the constitutional guarantee against the government establishing or promoting a particular religion. The courts decided in their favor in 1973, and the Nativity scene was eliminated.

At the same time, the White House received numerous letters that criticized the continuing practice of cutting down a magnificent tree each year for the ceremony. In response to these concerns President Nixon requested that a living tree be planted on the Ellipse. In 1973 the National Arborist Association contributed a 42-foot Colorado Blue Spruce from Pennsylvania, which was uprooted and transplanted to Washington, D.C., to serve as the National Christmas Tree. The tree lasted only four years. In 1977 it was replaced with another Colorado Blue Spruce. This tree was knocked over by strong winds in January 1978. The following year it was replaced by yet another Colorado Blue Spruce, 39½-feet high, which was uprooted from the home of the Myers family of York, Pennsylvania, in exchange for $1,500.

In December of 1978, a new ritual was added to the illumination ceremony. Jimmy Carter's daughter Amy was lifted to the top of the Christmas tree by a cherry picker to place the last, topmost ornament on the tree. In the years that followed, this honor was generally reserved for a member of the president's or vice-president's family. In 1980 Penne Langdon, the wife of one of the American hostages being held in **Iran**, performed this task.

As a means of expressing America's solidarity with the hostages, President Carter ordered that the National Christmas Tree remain unlit in 1979 and 1980. The hostages were released on January 20, 1980, President Ronald Reagan's Inauguration Day. Even though Christmas had passed, Reagan had the tree decorated and illuminated in celebration of both events.

The Eighties and Beyond

The Reagans often invited children to assist them in the tree-lighting ceremony. One year a boy scout and a girl scout attended the ceremonies. Another year a child selected by the Make-a-Wish Foundation helped the President and his wife light the tree.

During the Reagan years, the President lit the Christmas tree by remote control from inside the White House. An assassination attempt on Reagan's life in 1981 in combination with other death threats led security advisors to insist on this change. His successor, President George H. W. Bush, once again strolled out to the Ellipse to light the tree. During Bush's presidency his wife Barbara Bush placed the topmost ornament on the Christmas tree four years in a row. As the wife of Reagan's vice-president, she had also performed this task, and so holds the national record for most cherry picker rides (twelve) to the top of the National Christmas Tree.

Over the years the Pageant of Peace expanded, thereby pushing the date of the illumination ceremony back into the early part of December. During the Clinton presidency it took place on various dates between December 5 and December 11. The crowds continued to grow as well. In 1993, approximately 9,000 people attended the event. In recent years over 75,000 electric lights have twinkled from the National Christmas Tree. The decorations on the tree vary from year to year.

Further Reading

Menendez, Albert J. *Christmas in the White House*. Philadelphia, Pa.: Westminster Press, 1983.

Seeley, Mary Evans. *Season's Greetings from the White House*. Tampa, Fla.: A Presidential Christmas, 1998.

Web Site

The National Park Service, which maintains the President's Park South (the Ellipse), sponsors a page on the National Christmas Tree and the Pageant of Peace at: http://www.nps.gov/whho/pageant/

Nation's Christmas Tree

King's Canyon National Park, located in east central California, is home to some of the largest trees in the world. These enormous redwood trees, called giant sequoias, or *Sequoiadendron giganteum*, can live for over 3,000 years. One of these behemoths, named the General Grant tree, serves as the Nation's Christmas Tree.

The General Grant tree is only the third largest sequoia in the park. Nevertheless, its dimensions impress. The tree reaches over 267 feet in height. It measures 40 feet in diameter and 107 feet in circumference around the base. The first branch extending off the trunk does so at about 100 feet from the ground. A sturdy young adult, the tree is estimated to be between 1,500 and 2,000 years old.

President Calvin Coolidge declared the General Grant tree to be the Nation's Christmas Tree in 1926. He did so at the request of Charles E. Lee of Sanger, California. Mr. Lee visited King's Canyon in 1924, and as he gazed up at the General Grant tree, he overheard a little girl next to him say that it would make a marvelous **Christmas tree**.

Inspired by this chance remark, he led a **December 25** Christmas program at the foot of the tree in 1925. He also wrote to the President, requesting that the chief executive officially designate the General Grant as the Nation's Christmas Tree. Coolidge did so on April 28, 1926. President Dwight D. Eisenhower established the tree as a national shrine in 1956, dedicating it to those who died while serving their country.

The yearly Christmas ceremony at the foot of the tree has continued since 1925. The event has been nicknamed the "trek to the tree." It attracted 450 celebrants in 2001. In addition to visitors from across the nation and around the world, many residents of nearby Sanger, California, make the yearly pilgrimage, led by members of the town's chamber of commerce. Park rangers traditionally place a large Christmas **wreath** at the base of the tree. The "trek" takes place on the second Sunday in December.

Alternative ceremonies take place all the way across the country in Washington, D.C. There a rival tree, located on the Ellipse (or President's Park South), serves as the **National Christmas Tree**.

Web Sites

The National Park Service furnishes a page on the Nation's Christmas Tree at: http://www.nps.gov/seki/xmastree.htm

"The Spirit of the Season Seen in the General Grant Sequoia, the Nation's Living Christmas Tree," a news release article from the United States Geological Survey, can be found at this address: http://www.usgs.gov/public/press/public_affairs/press_releases/pr1537m.html

The web site for the Sanger District Chamber of Commerce offers some information about the trek to the tree at:
http://www.sanger.org/events. html#trek

Nativity Legends

Folklorists define a legend as a short, oral narrative about a person, place, or incident. Legends purport to be true, which generally means that they stay within the boundaries of what's considered possible within the shared cultural assumptions of the tale tellers and their audience.

The English word "legend" comes from the Latin word *legere*, which means "to read." The term originated in the early Middle Ages in reference to accounts of the lives of the saints read aloud at religious services held on their feast days. As the Middle Ages wore on, these saints' tales became more and more numerous, and more and more fantastic. Gradually, the word legend came to mean an untrue or improbable story. Medieval people not only told legends about saints, but also about biblical events and characters. Indeed, scriptural texts gave so little information concerning important events like the Nativity that much room remained for ordinary people to embroider their fanciful designs around the bare outlines of the story.

Legends Concerning Jesus' Birth

The **Gospel according to Matthew** tells of a miraculous star that appeared in the heavens to herald the birth of **Jesus** (*see* **Jesus, Year of Birth; Star of Bethlehem**). Old European legends expanded on this theme, inventing other miraculous signs that occurred on the day of Jesus' birth. For example, many tales proclaimed that on the day Jesus was born, plants burst into bloom and rivers ran with wine.

Although the **Gospel accounts of Christmas** do not mention any animals at the scene of Jesus' birth, medieval legends not only declared their presence at the manger in **Bethlehem**, but also told of their marvelous deeds. According to one tale, the rooster was the first animal to respond to the miraculous birth. He fluttered up to the roof of the stable and cried in Latin, *"Christus natus est,"* which means "Christ is born" (*see also* **Misa de Gallo**). It probably did not seem too odd to western European Christians in the Middle Ages to imagine a rooster in ancient Judea crowing in Latin to honor Christ's birth, since Latin was the official language of the Western Church. When the raven heard the rooster's declaration, he rasped the question, *"quando,"* or when? The rook replied, *"hac nocte,"* this night. The ox murmured, *"ubi,"* where? The sheep bleated, "Bethlehem," and the ass bellowed, *"eamus,"* let's go! This clever tale assigns each of the animals a Latin phrase that mimics the sound of its own voice.

Other legends recounted the ways in which various animals paid tribute to the Christ child on the night of his birth. According to one such story, the **robin** stood near the flames of the Holy Family's meager fire, beating its wings all night to keep the fire alive and, as a result, singeing its breast red from the flames. The stork tore feathers from her own chest to make a downy bed for the newborn Jesus, and ever since has been honored as the patron of new births. The nightingale nestled near the manger and caroled along with the **angels**. As a result, her song still remains sweeter and more musical than that of other birds. The owl did not follow the other animals to the stable at Bethlehem. Shamed by its own irreverence, the owl has ever since hidden from the sight of other animals, appearing only by night to cry in a soft voice: "Who? Who? Who will lead me to the Christ child?"

Even plants honored and aided the newborn Jesus and his mother, **Mary**. Yellow bedstraw and sweet woodruff offered themselves as bedding for Mary and the baby, thereby earning the folk name "Our Lady's Bedstraw." Some tales assigned creeping thyme the same modest role and a similar folk name, "Mary's Bedstraw." When the Holy Family fled into **Egypt** (*see also* **Flight into Egypt**), the **rosemary** plant provided Mary with a clean place on which to hang Jesus' baby clothes after she had washed them. For rendering this small service to Jesus and his mother, the plant was blessed ever after with beautiful blue flowers and a sweet fragrance. In other versions of this tale Mary hung Jesus' clothes on a lavender bush, which afterwards produced delightfully fragrant flowers. She hung her own blue cloak on the rosemary plant, whose previously plain white flowers remained forever imprinted with its color and soothing fragrance.

Christmas Legends

Over the centuries Christmas and the customs connected with it have inspired a multitude of legends. Many related folk beliefs accompanied these legends. These folk beliefs frequently echoed the underlying premise of the Nativity legends recounted above, that is, that the whole of creation responds to the Savior's birth by acts of praise, adoration, and service.

One popular European legend declared that oxen knelt in their stables at midnight each year on Christmas Eve to honor the moment of Jesus' birth. Often animals were granted powers far beyond their normal capacities on Christmas Eve. English, French, and German folklore maintained that barnyard animals whispered among themselves in human language at that moment. The tales cautioned that these animals often spoke of the faults of their human masters or of impending deaths in the community, making it perhaps unwise to try to overhear them. The daring listener would probably find greater delight in creeping up to a beehive on Christmas Eve, since English folklore insisted that bees sang psalms, hymns, or symphonies in glorious harmonies to commemorate the Nativity.

Among Middle Eastern Christians, stories circulated about trees and plants, especially those growing along the banks of the Jordan River, that bowed towards Bethlehem at that same moment. Many European legends marveled at trees and plants that momentarily burst into fruit and flower on Christmas Eve. An old Russian folk belief hinted that water briefly turns into wine in honor of the occasion. French and German folklore declared that hidden treasures revealed themselves at midnight on Christmas Eve, and that mountains split open to display their hidden veins of precious metals and stones. Other tales told of buried or sunken **bells** that somehow tolled mysteriously at midnight on Christmas Eve. (For other Christmas legends, *see* **Berchta; Befana; Boar's Head; Cherry Tree; Christmas Rose; Christmas Tree; Flight into Egypt; Frau Gaude; Glastonbury Thorn; Jultomten; Kallikantzari; Lebanon, Christmas in; Poinsettia; Snow Maiden; Syria, Christmas in; Twelve Days of Christmas; Urban Legends; Wenceslaus, King; Wild Hunt.**)

Further Reading

Crippen, Thomas G. *Christmas and Christmas Lore*. 1923. Reprint. Detroit, Mich.: Omnigraphics, 1990.

Dégh, Linda. "Legend." In Thomas A. Green, ed. *Folklore: An Encyclopedia of Beliefs, Customs, Tales, Music, and Art*. Santa Barbara, Calif.: ABC-CLIO, 1997.

Foley, Daniel J. *The Christmas Tree*. Philadelphia, Pa.: Chilton Books, 1960.

Hackwood, Frederick W. *Christ Lore*. 1902. Reprint. Detroit, Mich.: Gale Research, 1969.

Leach, Maria, ed. *Funk and Wagnalls Standard Dictionary of Folklore, Mythology, and Legend*. New York: Harper and Row, 1984.

Lehane, Brendan. *The Book of Christmas*. Alexandria, Va.: Time-Life Books, 1986.

Miles, Clement A. *Christmas in Ritual and Tradition*. 1912. Reprint. Detroit, Mich.: Omnigraphics, 1990.

Palmer, Geoffrey, and Noel Lloyd. *A Year of Festivals*. London, England: Frederick Warne, 1972.

Weiser, Francis X. *Handbook of Christian Feasts and Customs*. New York: Harcourt, Brace and World, 1952.

Web Site

A site sponsored by the Marian Library and International Marian Research Institute at the University of Dayton, Ohio, on Mary's Flowers (part of The Mary Page): http://www.udayton.edu/mary/main.html

Nativity Play

Throughout the centuries people have celebrated Christmas by re-enacting the story of **Jesus'** birth in folk dramas known as Nativity plays. This tradition can be traced back to the liturgical dramas of the European Middle Ages. Today the Christmas pageant, the Hispanic customs of Las **Posadas** and Los **Pastores**, the **star boys**, and various living **Nativity scene** customs carry on this tradition.

Liturgical Dramas

The liturgical dramas of the Middle Ages provide us with the earliest documented examples of Nativity plays. These dramas began as simple reenactments of biblical stories spoken in Latin and performed by members of the clergy and choir during religious services.

One of the earliest recorded versions of a play of this sort was performed at the cathedral in Rouen, **France**, in the twelfth century. In this brief representation of the Nativity, a choirboy, playing the part of an **angel**, announced the birth of Christ from on high. The choir sang, "Glory to God in the highest," and the priests below answered, "and on earth peace to men of good will." Several of the cathedral's canons (clerical staff), dressed as **shepherds**, drew near the altar. Two priests, acting as midwives, stopped them and asked whom they sought. The shepherds replied, "Our Savior, who is Christ the Lord." The priests then pulled back a curtain revealing a stable that contained a statue of the Virgin and Child. The shepherds bowed and worshiped, then returned to their places singing, "Alleluia."

The clergy used liturgical dramas to introduce a mostly illiterate population to a range of biblical stories. These simple dramas proved quite popular and began to be embellished. Humorously exaggerated and outlandish events eventually slipped in. These innovations entertained the audience and were not, in those times, seen as inappropriate by the ordinary person. Church authorities disagreed, however. Some scholars believe that this controversy, plus the need for greater space to accommodate the growing audiences, nudged these brief dramas out onto the church steps and other public arenas in the eleventh and twelfth centuries.

By the thirteenth century these dramas developed into "mystery" or "miracle" plays performed by lay actors. Mystery plays presented biblical stories concerning God's or Christ's intercession in the world, while miracle plays presented religious stories not found in the Bible, for example, dramas concerning the lives of the saints. Some scholars argue that these plays developed from secular dramatic traditions that evolved alongside, and not from, liturgical traditions. Whatever their origins, the mystery plays took many of the same biblical stories and greatly expanded them so that the plots now included numerous legendary or fanciful events and characters. In addition, actors recited the often humorous and sometimes even ribald dialogue in the local language rather than in Church Latin.

Mystery Plays

From the thirteenth to the sixteenth centuries, mystery plays were performed in public plazas and other open-air settings across **Europe**. Ordinary citizens not only enjoyed these public performances, but also acted in them and financed them. In **England** various guilds produced the mystery plays most closely related to their trade. The goldsmiths, for example, took responsibility for the adoration of the **Magi**, one of the most popular Christmas plays. Other Christmas themes represented in these plays included the slaughter of the innocents (*see* **Holy Innocents' Day**), the **Flight into Egypt**, and the shepherds' pilgrimage to **Bethlehem**.

In the meantime, Church authorities continued to disapprove of the coarse and humorous elements that had crept into the liturgical dramas and mystery plays. Roman Catholic authorities finally forbade churches from presenting the dramas in the fourteenth and fifteenth centuries. The secular versions of the plays began to die out in the sixteenth century due to opposition by the Church as well as the influence of new religious perspectives brought about by the Reformation. In England, the **Puritans** opposed the plays as sacrilegious and worked towards their eradication.

539

Folk Dramas in the New World

Even as Europeans were abandoning the mystery and miracle plays, Spanish missionaries were introducing them in the New World. Once again the clergy found that simple, dramatic representations of Bible stories could teach elements of the Christian religion to the illiterate. In this instance the plays also helped to bridge the gap in language and culture between the Spanish missionaries and the native peoples. Two of these religious plays survive today in the form of folk dramas that have become Christmas traditions in **Mexico** and other Central American countries as well as the American Southwest. Los Pastores tells the story of the shepherds' pilgrimage to the Christ child. Las Posadas reenacts **Mary** and **Joseph**'s search for shelter in Bethlehem.

Folk Dramas in Europe

In spite of the waning of Nativity plays in Europe, the tradition of **Christmas season** folk dramas continued in other guises. Many writers credit St. Francis of Assisi (c. 1181-1226) with creating the first Nativity scene in the early thirteenth century. Using real people and animals, he recreated the scene at the manger in Bethlehem in a cave near the Italian village of Greccio. The custom of staging living Nativity scenes soon spread throughout Europe. It survives today as a Christmas Eve custom in southern France and an **Epiphany** custom in parts of **Italy**.

Medieval Europeans also donned costumes for another Christmas tradition: **mumming**. Although the masked merrymaking carried out by mummers may not qualify as a form of drama, in some areas mummers presented folk plays as well as simply cavorted under the cover of a disguise. Christmas season mumming practices survived until recent times in Europe and North America. Several Epiphany customs also contain dramatic elements. In many Spanish-speaking countries, people reenact the arrival of the Three Kings at Bethlehem with parades featuring costumed Wise Men riding through the streets on horseback. In central Europe, Epiphany triggers the appearance of the star boys, local lads who carol from house to house dressed as the Three Kings.

The American Christmas Pageant

Of all the Christmas customs involving elements of folk drama, the contemporary American Christmas pageant bears perhaps the closest resemblance to the early medieval Nativity plays. These pageants are usually performed by children or teens with the aid of adults. They frequently take the form of a simple drama depicting the events surrounding the birth of Jesus. Christmas legends or the "holiday spirit" provide alternative themes. Christmas pageants often include music, especially **Christmas carols**, and various kinds of recitations. One writer traces the history of the American Christmas pageant back to mid-nineteenth-century Boston. Parishioners of a German Catholic church sponsored a pageant in which the parish children, dressed as shepherds and singing Christmas carols, dramatized the shepherds' pilgrimage to Bethlehem. The pageant attracted the attention of people throughout the city. The custom eventually spread across the country to Catholic and Protestant churches alike.

Further Reading

Crippen, Thomas G. *Christmas and Christmas Lore*. 1923. Reprint. Detroit, Mich.: Omnigraphics, 1990.

Margetson, Stella. "Medieval Nativity Plays." *History Today* 22, 12 (December 1972): 851-57.

Miles, Clement A. *Christmas in Ritual and Tradition*. 1912. Reprint. Detroit, Mich.: Omnigraphics, 1990.

"Mystery Play." In Phyllis Hartnoll, ed. *The Oxford Companion to the Theatre*. Fourth edition. Oxford, England: Oxford University Press, 1983.

Weiser, Francis X. *The Christmas Book*. 1952. Reprint. Detroit, Mich.: Omnigraphics, 1990.

Nativity Scene

Bethlehem, Christmas Crib, Crèche, Krippe, Lapinha,
Manger Scene, Nacimiento, Pesebre, Portale, Presepio, Putz

Against the backdrop of a stable complete with straw and farm animals, figurines representing **Mary** and **Joseph** peer with wonder
into the cradle where the newborn **Jesus** lies. Dolls representing the
Three Kings, or **Magi**, approach with **gifts**, while **shepherds** kneel
in adoration of the child. This recreation of the **Gospel accounts** of
Jesus' birth is called a Nativity scene. Placed in churches, homes, or
outdoor locations, Nativity scenes enhance worship or simply delight onlookers with beautiful representations of Christ's birth.

Origins

The earliest uses of a crib in worship date back to fourth-century
Rome. Of the three masses observed at Christmas, one was called *Ad
Praesepe* (meaning "to the crib"). This mass took place in the basilica
of Santa Maria Maggiore, at a shrine built from boards believed to
have come from the original stable of the Nativity in **Bethlehem**.

Churches throughout **Italy** and **Europe** gradually adopted the custom of saying mass over a crib at Christmas time.

St. Francis of Assisi (c. 1181-1226) generally receives the credit for popularizing the Nativity scene as we know it. It is said that at Christmas time in 1224 he recreated the manger scene using real people and animals in a cave near the Italian village of Greccio. Mass was said in this novel setting and St. Francis preached about the humble birth of the newborn King. Onlookers enjoyed this reenactment of Christ's birth so much that the custom soon spread throughout Italy and Europe.

Reenactments of this sort still take place on Christmas Eve in some villages in the French region of Provence. Lengthy processions of costumed villagers solemnly file through the streets arriving finally at the manger of Christ's birth, where a living Mary, Joseph, and baby Jesus await them. In the towns of Les Baux and Séguret hundreds of people walk in candlelit Christmas Eve processions that end in the local church where a mass is said.

Living Nativity scenes are also reenacted yearly in Italy. In Abruzzi, Italy, the village of Rivisondoli sponsors a procession and living Nativity scene on **Epiphany** Eve that involves up to 600 people. Many wear traditional regional costumes and are accompanied by animals as they make their pilgrimage to the manger. Worshipers may also bring gifts for the Holy Child, such as fruit, lambs, chickens, or pigs. The Magi, played by local officials, ride horses. The Virgin Mary rides a donkey and Joseph walks by her side. The procession ends at a manger within a cave and is followed by singing.

Early Nativity Scenes

The popularity of these living Nativity scenes gave rise to another custom: recreating the birth scene with figurines. By the sixteenth century many churches throughout Italy and **Germany** presented a Nativity scene of this type at Christmas time. Some French churches adopted the custom as well.

In the seventeenth century families began to create their own Nativity scenes. These became more elaborate with time. The art form reached spectacular heights in eighteenth-century Naples, Italy. Families competed with each other to produce the most elegant and elaborate crib scenes. These scenes expanded far beyond the manger to include village backdrops, ordinary villagers, ruined Roman temples, **angels**, and even foreigners whom the families thought might have rushed to Bethlehem had they known of the miraculous birth. (*See also* **Christmas Village**.)

Rich and noble Italian families employed established artists and sculptors to create clay or wood heads and shoulders. The artists then attached these heads to flexible bodies fashioned out of cloth, string, and wire. Costumes cut of rich fabrics, some embellished with jewels, adorned each figure. The splendor of the backdrops, however, vied with the exquisitely detailed props and figurines for the viewer's attention. Some settings included real waterfalls, while others featured gushing fountains or even an erupting Mount Vesuvius. Today many of these marvelous works are preserved and displayed in Italy's museums and churches.

The Nativity scene also rooted itself firmly in French soil, especially in the southern region of Provence. The first manger scenes included only those figures most related to the story of the Nativity: Mary, Joseph, the baby Jesus, the shepherds, etc. In the eighteenth century, however, people began to display a multitude of characters in their home Nativity scenes. Some writers claim that Italian peddlers introduced these new figurines to southern **France**.

In 1803 small clay statuettes from Provence, called *santons* (or "little saints") appeared at the Christmas fair in Marseille. These santons became an essential element of the French Nativity scene. In addition to characters mentioned in the biblical accounts of the Nativity, the Provençal santons represented a wide variety of ordinary French townspeople, such as the baker, the mayor, the fishmonger, the village idiot, and others. One writer has identified many of these figures as stock characters in folk **Nativity plays** that circulated throughout the region as early as the Middle Ages. Like their Italian counterparts, French Nativity scenes depicted the birth of Christ taking place in a local setting, such as a village in Provence. French settlers brought the Christmas crib with them to Canada where another innovation occurred. The French Canadians of Quebec often set up their Nativity scenes under the **Christmas tree**.

Southern Europe

In southern Europe, where the Christmas tree never found much favor, home Christmas decoration focuses around the Nativity scene. The Spanish call the scene a *nacimiento* (meaning "birth") or a *belén* (meaning "Bethlehem"), the Italians call it a *presépio* (meaning "crib"), and the French call it a *crèche* (meaning "crib"). In the same way that many North Americans collect Christmas tree **ornaments**, many southern European families slowly build a treasured collection of Nativity figurines. Though the scene itself may be assembled beforehand, many await Christmas Eve or Christmas morning to place the baby Jesus in his crib. Some civic and church celebrations also center on manger scenes. In **Spain** Nativity scenes may be found in public plazas. On Epiphany several local men dressed as the Three Kings may visit the public Nativity scene, reenacting the adoration of the Magi.

In Italy Nativity scenes pop up everywhere in the weeks before Christmas. Shop windows display manger scenes made out of pastry, bread, fruit, seeds, shells, and even butter. Children make Nativity scenes out of cardboard or papier mâché. Many churches present crib scenes as well. The Basilica of Saints Cosmos and Damian in Rome houses one of the most famous. Twenty-seven-feet high, forty-five-feet long, and twenty-one-feet wide, it contains several hundred hand-sculpted wooden statues. Rome's Church of Santa Maria in Ara Coeli exhibits the most famous Christ child, however. An old custom encourages children to recite carefully memorized sermons in front of his crib. Folk beliefs credit the jewel-studded golden infant, known as "Santo Bambino," with the power to heal.

Latin America

Spanish colonizers brought the Nativity scene with them to the Americas. The Nativity scene enjoys widespread popularity throughout Latin America today, where it is known as a nacimiento, *pesebre*, *portale*, or in Portuguese-speaking Brazil, as a presepio or *lapinha*. Latin American manger scenes range from simple representations of the Holy Family to elaborate depictions of the manger, village, and surrounding countryside. This countryside may host characters more likely to be found in rural South America than in ancient Judea, including women making tortillas, Indians selling tropical fruit, and peasants leading heavily laden burros. The figurines themselves range from relatively crude clay representations to delicate antique figurines passed down from previous generations. In **Mexico** many families set up their Nativity scenes on December 16, a date that corresponds with the beginning of the nine-day Christmas novena.

Many Latin American families place the Jesus figurine in his cradle on Christmas Eve. The Magi, on the other hand, inch forward daily towards the manger, arriving on January 6, Epiphany. Throughout Latin America Nativity scenes may also be found in churches and public squares. Many of these traditions can also be found throughout the American Southwest, a region of the United States with a long history of Spanish and Mexican settlement.

Central Europe

In Germany, Switzerland, Austria, and other central European countries, the preparation of Nativity scenes still provides a delightful occupation for children and adults during **Advent**. The German Nativity scene, called a *Krippe* (meaning "crib"), may contain hundreds of figurines and many lovely details. In Czechoslovakia people call their manger scenes "Bethlehems." In some areas of the country the figures may be constructed from bread dough and later painted.

The United States

In the eighteenth century German Moravian immigrants brought this custom with them to the United States. The Moravian Nativity scenes, called *putz* (from the German word for "decorate"), spread out in extravagant detail. Dozens or hundreds of figurines might be placed amidst gardens, fountains, arbors, villages, streams, bridges, waterfalls, and other delightful scenery. These elaborate designs might take up an entire room. In Pennsylvania many German Americans, particularly those in areas settled by Moravians, maintain the custom of "putzing" and "putz-visiting." The town of **Bethlehem, Pennsylvania**, founded by Moravians, builds a community putz every year. On one occasion the builders used 800 pounds of sand, 64 tree stumps, 12 bushels of moss, 40 evergreen trees, and 48 angels in the creation of the community putz.

In past years many towns throughout the United States erected Nativity scenes at Christmas time. Recently these displays have provoked controversy. Questions regarding the separation of church and state, as well as vandalism, have led many towns to abolish public Nativity scenes. Nevertheless, many families and churches continue to enjoy this old Christmas custom.

Further Reading

Christmas in Mexico. Chicago: World Book, 1976.

Cohen, Hennig, and Tristram Potter Coffin, eds. *The Folklore of American Holidays*. Detroit, Mich.: Gale Research, 1987.

Del Re, Gerard, and Patricia Del Re. *The Christmas Almanack*. Garden City, N.Y.: Doubleday, 1979.

Foley, Daniel J. *Christmas the World Over*. Philadelphia, Pa.: Chilton Books, 1963.

———. *Little Saints of Christmas*. Boston, Mass.: Dresser, Chapman and Grimes, 1959.

Milne, Jean. *Fiesta Time in Latin America*. Los Angeles, Calif.: Ward Ritchie Press, 1965.

Ross, Corinne. *Christmas in France*. Lincolnwood, Ill.: Passport Books, 1991.

———. *Christmas in Italy*. World Book-Childcraft International, 1979.

Shoemaker, Alfred L. *Christmas in Pennsylvania*. Kutztown, Pa.: Pennsylvania Folklore Society, 1959.

Stevens, Patricia Bunning. *Merry Christmas!: A History of the Holiday*. New York: Macmillan, 1979.

Thompson, Sue Ellen, ed. *Holiday Symbols*. Detroit, Mich.: Omnigraphics, 1998.

Weiser, Francis X. *The Christmas Book*. 1952. Reprint. Detroit, Mich.: Omnigraphics, 1990.

Web Sites

A site sponsored by the French Ministry of Culture and Canadian Heritage: http://www.culture.fr/culture/noel/angl/noel.htm

A site sponsored by the "Creche Herald" newsletter: http://www.op.net/~bocassoc

New Year's Day

In many places people begin their New Year's celebrations on New Year's Eve. Oftentimes these celebrations include staying up to ring in the new year. These late-night festivities frequently involve food, drink, fortune-telling, good-luck charms, **games**—especially games of chance—and, at the stroke of midnight, noisemaking. Exchanging well-wishes for the year ahead is another widespread New Year's Eve and New Year's Day practice (*for the phrase "Happy New Year" in a variety of languages, see* **Merry Christmas and Happy New Year**). The passing of the old year and the beginning of the new one inevitably call attention to the passing of time, represented by the popular European and American New Year's symbols **Father Time** and the New Year's **baby**.

In **Europe** fortune-telling was once a widespread New Year's Eve custom. People used a wide variety of rituals and spells in order to divine who would marry, who would prosper, who would endure hardship, and who would die in the coming year. Lithuanian folklore provided young people with many formulas for discovering the name of an admirer or a future spouse. Many people continue to use these old folk charms as New Year's Eve games.

In many countries folklore decrees that certain objects or activities bring luck for the new year. In a number of European countries people practice **firstfooting**, a custom whereby the household's luck for the year is determined by the first person to step over the threshold after the clock strikes midnight on New Year's Eve. In **Germany** folk tradition teaches that people who encounter a pig or a chimney sweep on New Year's Eve or Day will have luck in the year to come. In the **Philippines**, round objects—from the polka dots on clothing to round-shaped foods—bring luck on New Year's Eve. In **Greece**, St. Basil's bread confers good fortune to those who consume it at the start of the year (*for more on New Year's in Greece, see* **St. Basil's Day**). In **Spain** eating twelve grapes in the last twelve seconds of the old year brings sweetness and good fortune in the new year.

One widespread folk belief asserts that events taking place on New Year's Eve and New Year's Day foretell future trends. Thus people refrain from hard work and hope for good weather and good news during these crucial first hours of the new year. Some Americans practice the custom of kissing their spouse, boyfriend, or girlfriend at midnight on New Year's Eve, presumably as a good-luck charm to insure that love and passion will continue throughout the year.

In some places, such as **Syria**, Greece, and **Lebanon**, seasonal **gifts** are exchanged on New Year's Day (*for a twentieth-century New Year's gift bringer, see* **Grandfather Frost**). This custom was once widespread in Europe and America, but shifted in the nineteenth century, when Christmas became the occasion for gift giving among friends and family.

Roman New Year Celebrations

Many contemporary New Year's celebrations, with their emphasis on fun and carousing, bear a striking resemblance to those hosted by the ancient Romans (*for another ancient New Year's celebration, see* **Zagmuk**). The Romans celebrated their new year holiday, called **Kalends**, by feasting, singing, drinking, staying up late, masquerading, gambling, gift giving, fortune-telling, and exchanging good wishes for the new year. What's more, after the institution of the Julian calendar in 45 B.C., the Romans shifted their new year celebrations from March 25 to January 1, a date we eventually inherited from them (*for more on the Julian calendar, see* **Old Christmas Day**).

Medieval New Year Celebrations

Although early Christian authorities chose to place Christmas between **Saturnalia**, a Roman midwinter festival, and Kalends, the Roman new year celebration, they strongly disapproved of the customs associated with these holidays. For centuries Church officials urged their followers to abandon what they viewed as the riotous pagan practices attached to these festivals. In 567 the second provincial Council of Tours tried to counteract the still-popular Kalends festivities by ordering Christians to fast and do penance during the first few days of the new year.

At the same time, however, they expanded Christmas from a feast day to a season. They declared the days that fall between Christmas and **Epiphany** to be a festal tide—a period of special observance and rejoicing following an important feast day. These twelve days, often called Christmastide, became better known as the **Twelve Days of Christmas**. Since this new festive period now included January 1, practices associated with the Roman new year could easily attach themselves to the **Christmas season**. In the seventh century Church officials made a new effort to reclaim the January 1 holiday from pagan celebrations. They introduced a new Christian holy day, the **Feast of the Circumcision**, to be celebrated on January 1.

In spite of opposition from Church officials the customs surrounding Kalends lingered on long after Christianity had become the dominant religion in Europe. Religious authorities disapproved of some of these customs more than others, however. For instance, they vehemently denounced masquerades, fortune-telling, excessive drinking, and boisterous behavior in the streets. One researcher has counted at least forty separate documents containing official denunciations of midwinter masquerades. These documents range in dates from the fourth to the eleventh centuries and come from Church authorities in many European lands as well as north Africa and the Near East.

Nevertheless, these criticisms do not appear to have affected ordinary people very much. Medieval new year celebrations continued as fun-filled occasions. Though officially a religious observance, lively folk customs marked the celebration of **St. Sylvester's Day**, also scheduled for January 1. In some countries low-ranking clerics let loose by observing the **Feast of Fools** on that same date.

In spite of Church denunciations of the magical practices associated with Christmas and New Year's Day, European folklorists have recorded a multitude of popular beliefs concerning fortune-telling and good-luck charms linked to the Twelve Days of Christmas. One such fortune-telling custom, called firstfooting, was particularly associated with New Year's Eve. Religious authorities appear to have ignored New Year's customs which they viewed as more benign, however, such as feasting and gift giving. Indeed, these two Kalends customs flourished in medieval new year celebrations.

New Year Customs Migrate to Christmas

Some researchers believe that a number of ancient new year customs survived the decline of paganism by simply attaching themselves to the Christmas holiday. For example, many writers trace the decoration of homes and churches with **greenery** back to Roman new year celebrations. Exchanging greetings and good wishes for the new year also dates back to Roman times. Some researchers speculate that late medieval Christmas **masques** and **mumming** practices may have represented the remnants of Roman new year masquerades.

The Puritans and the Protestant Reformation

In the sixteenth century a religious reform movement surged across Europe giving birth to Protestant Christianity. In **England** during that same century, a new body of religious officials began to complain about the high incidence of masking, mumming, drinking, feasting, dancing, gambling, and gaming associated with the Christmas season. These officials, members of a Protestant religious sect known as the **Puritans**, attempted to eradicate these practices by outlawing the celebration of Christmas. What's more, they argued, New Year's Eve was better spent in self-examination and prayer than in hard drinking and rowdy revelry.

After the Puritans fell from power the English returned to many of their old Christmas customs. The people of Scotland, however, took many of the Puritan criticisms of Christmas to heart and never really revived their old Christmas celebrations. Instead New Year's Day became the main midwinter holiday (*for more on New Year's celebrations in Scotland, see* **Hogmanay**). In fact, Christmas didn't again become a legal holiday in Scotland until 1958. The Scots referred to New Year's Day as "Hogmanay," a word of uncertain origins. Linguists suspect that it evolved from the old French term *aguillaneuf*, which means New Year's gift, the last day of the year, or the celebration at which New Year's gifts are exchanged. A related Spanish word, *aguilnaldo*, means Christmas tip, New Year's gift, or, in Latin America, **Christmas carol** (*see also* **Boxing Day**).

Changing Dates

Before the introduction of the Julian calendar in 46 B.C., the Romans began their new year in March. Some scholars believe that they celebrated New Year's Day on March 25. When Julius Caesar (100 B.C.-44 B.C.) decided to reform the Roman calendar system (resulting in the Julian calendar), he moved New Year's Day to January 1. According to the Julian calendar, **winter solstice** fell on **December 25** and spring equinox fell on March 25. These two dates eventually became feast days in the Christian calendar. Church officials placed the Feast of the Nativity on December 25 and the Feast of the **Annunciation** on March 25. During the Middle Ages the religious significance of the Annunciation inclined many European countries to begin the new year on that date. Others began their new year on Christmas Day. In spite of the widespread official recognition of March 25 as New Year's Day, many ordinary people continued the ancient tradition of ushering in the new year on January 1.

When Pope Gregory XIII (1502-1585) authorized the Gregorian calendar reform in 1582 he ordered the official observance of New Year's Day back to January 1 (*see also* Old Christmas Day). **Italy, France,** Luxembourg, Spain, and Portugal switched to the new calendar system in that same year. Other European nations dawdled over making this change, primarily for religious reasons. Many Protestant nations hesitated to adopt the calendar for fear of seeming to accept the authority of the Pope. Much of Orthodox eastern Europe viewed the proposed changes as out of step with their religious traditions. Nevertheless, over the next several centuries the European nations slowly began to adopt the Gregorian date for the beginning of the new year. Scotland switched New Year's Day to January 1 in 1660, Protestant Germany in 1700, and **Russia** in 1706. England and her colonies adopted the Gregorian calendar in 1752. Up until that time their new year officially began on March 25, in spite of the fact that many people actually celebrated the holiday on January 1.

From the Puritans to the Nineteenth Century

In seventeenth- and eighteenth-century Europe and America, New Year's Eve celebrations still bore a good deal of resemblance to the Roman holiday of Kalends. Many people celebrated the holiday by staying up late in order to indulge in some combination of heavy drinking, public carousing, gaming, masquerading, gambling, feasting, fortune-telling, or dancing. The Puritan campaign against this kind of New Year's celebration—a continuation of the critique launched centuries ago by the early Christians—enjoyed only limited success, mostly among devout Protestants. By the nineteenth century, however, some concerned Protestants began to promote alternative methods of celebrating New Year's Eve. They gathered together at **Watch Night** services to pray, sing, and worship. They also formed spiritual **resolutions** at the start of the year.

In the nineteenth century, Christmas was becoming an increasingly important holiday (*see also* **America, Christmas in Nineteenth-Century**). As a result, several ancient New Year's customs migrated towards Christmas and eventually attached themselves to this holiday. People began to send **Christmas cards** to one another, a greeting that often replaced the New Year's letter, visit, or formal exchange of good wishes. Similarly, the New Year's gift, which had been associated with the holiday since Roman times, transferred itself to Christmas. As Christmas grew in importance, New Year's was drawn into its orbit, becoming a satellite observance surrounding the emerging, major midwinter holiday.

Twentieth Century and Beyond

Meanwhile, in Soviet Russia (1917-91), government policy turned New Year's Day into the major midwinter holiday. The government actively discouraged the celebration of Christmas because it was a religious holiday, while promoting the observance of New Year's Eve and Day. This policy also affected holiday celebrations in countries under Soviet rule, such as **Bulgaria, Estonia, Latvia**, and **Lithuania**. Soviet officials even tried to encourage the transfer of popular Christmas customs, such as decorating **Christmas trees**, to New Year's. Since the fall of the Soviet regime in 1991, people have been celebrating Christmas more openly.

In America, Watch Night services declined in popularity throughout the twentieth century. Certain Protestant churches, however, especially those whose congregations are composed mostly of African Americans, still host these observances.

By the twentieth century the custom of making a New Year's resolution had spread beyond pious Protestant circles into the wider culture, losing its religious associations in the process. People began to mark the start of the new year with a determined effort to improve themselves in some way, often to better their health.

In the late twentieth century, yet another campaign to convert traditional New Year's celebrations got started. Unlike previous efforts, however, this one was secular rather than religious in nature. In 1976 a group of Boston citizens organized an alternative New Year's Eve celebration called **First Night**. This civic event, designed as an alcohol-free, family-oriented celebration, featured entertainment by local performing artists. Its success led to its eventual adoption by over 150 American cities, as well as various cities abroad.

Nevertheless, most Americans continue to associate New Year's Eve with parties. The nation's best-known party takes place in **New York City's Times Square**. Although event organizers will not permit those attending the Times Square event to carry in liquor, alcoholic beverages, especially champagne, are common at most American New Year's Eve parties. Singing the Scottish song **"Auld Lang Syne"** has also become a popular American New Year's Eve custom.

New Year's Day is a national holiday in the United States. Some African Americans also observe it as **Emancipation Day**. Those who attended late-night parties the night before may take advantage of the opportunity to sleep in. Many Americans watch televised **football** matches on New Year's Day. These "bowl" games mark the conclusion of the college football season and pit the best teams in the various conferences against one another.

Many southerners, especially African Americans, enjoy a dish called **hopping John** on New Year's Day. Eating this mixture of black-eyed peas, rice, and pork on New Year's Day is said to bring luck for the coming year.

Further Reading

Bellenir, Karen. *Religious Holidays and Calendars.* Second edition. Detroit, Mich.: Omnigraphics, 1998.

Edwards, Gillian. *Hogmanay and Tiffany, The Names of Feasts and Fasts.* London, England: Geoffrey Bles, 1970.

Gaster, Theodor. *New Year, Its History, Customs, and Superstitions*. New York: Abelard-Schuman, 1955.

Hutton, Ronald. *The Stations of the Sun*. Oxford, England: Oxford University Press, 1996.

Leach, Maria, ed. *Funk and Wagnalls Standard Dictionary of Folklore, Mythology, and Legend*. San Francisco, Calif.: Harper and Row, 1984.

Miles, Clement A. *Christmas in Ritual and Tradition*. 1912. Reprint. Detroit, Mich.: Omnigraphics, 1990.

Muir, Frank. *Christmas Customs and Traditions*. New York: Taplinger, 1977.

New York City, Christmas in

A number of New Yorkers and New York City customs have played an important role in the development of the American Christmas. Several nineteenth-century New Yorkers helped to bring **Santa Claus** into being. In more recent times New York City has become an important destination for Christmas shoppers and tourists. Finally, at least one of the city's Christmas traditions, **Macy's Thanksgiving Day Parade**, has become a nationally televised event announcing the start of the **Christmas season**.

Birth of Santa Claus

Most researchers agree that Santa Claus bears a suspicious resemblance to the European **gift** bringer **St. Nicholas**. This resemblance is no coincidence, in spite of the fact that Dutch and German immigrants to the American colonies don't appear to have brought with them much of their St. Nicholas folklore. The early American writer Washington Irving (1783-1859) gave St. Nicholas an important position in New York's Dutch community in his satirical book *A History of New York* (1809). In 1822 one of Irving's friends, Clement C. Moore (1779-1863), a languages professor at New York's General Theological Seminary, used elements of Irving's portrayal of St. Nicholas in a poem of his own. Entitled "A Visit from St. Nicholas," the poem describes a Christmas gift bringer who rides through the night skies on Christmas Eve in a magic sleigh pulled by flying **reindeer** and enters homes via the chimney. Though Moore called the gift bringer "St. Nicholas," the American public soon dubbed the pot-bellied, pipe-smoking man "Santa Claus." Moore's description suggests that St. Nicholas was smaller than life-sized, in fact, an **elf**. In the latter part of the nineteenth century *Harper's Weekly* illustrator Thomas Nast (1840-1902) published a series of prints depicting Santa Claus. Nast settled on depicting him as a life-sized, portly old man with a long, white beard and a pipe. This description seized the public's imagination and became part of Santa's official image.

In 1897 yet another New Yorker, this time an eight-year-old girl named **Virginia O'Hanlon**, helped Americans to settle some of their metaphysical questions concerning the national gift bringer. She wrote a letter to a local newspaper called the *New York Sun* asking the newspaper editor to tell her whether or not Santa Claus was real. Virginia's letter and the newspaper's response have become beloved bits of American Christmas lore. The often-quoted phrase, "Yes, Virginia, there is a Santa Claus," comes from the paper's editorial response, written by reporter Francis P. Church.

Macy's Parade

As Santa Claus became an important part of American Christmas folklore he was drafted into the service of many **commercial** ventures. For example, he plays an important role in Macy's Thanksgiving Day Parade, begun in 1924. Macy's started the parade as a means of attracting shoppers to its stores and extending the Christmas shopping season as far back as Thanksgiving. The classic Christmas movie *Miracle on 34th Street* (1947) boosted the parade's fame by showing shots of the parade during the movie's opening scenes. Nationwide television coverage followed. In this manner the parade worked its way from an event of local importance to a national icon of the start of the holiday season. The parade's trademark feature consists of a series of enormous balloons in a wide variety of fun shapes, including those of cartoon characters and animals. Traditionally Santa Claus brings up the rear of the parade. The parade begins at 77th Street and Central Park West and ends at Macy's, located in Herald Square at the intersection of Sixth Avenue and 34th

Street. For New Yorkers, Santa's arrival in Herald Square kicks off the start of the holiday shopping season.

Window Displays

In addition to their reputation for quantity and quality of goods, a number of New York stores are famous for their Christmas **store window displays**. The more well known department stores announce opening dates for their windows, which often pre-date Thanksgiving, and people trying to get the first glimpses of these magnificent tableaux may crowd the pavement outside the stores on these days. Indeed, thousands line up to see the windows at Lord and Taylor—located on Fifth Avenue at 38th Street—which often feature mechanized, moving displays.

Rockefeller Center

Other New York City Christmas sites and decorations that have become familiar to the public at large include the **Christmas tree** and skating rink at Rockefeller Center. Over the years Rockefeller Center has become an important destination for the city's Christmas tourists. In 1996, half a million people per weekend visited the site.

The first Rockefeller Center tree, erected in 1931, measured only 12 feet high. It was put up on the empty lot by the men at work constructing the new complex of buildings, some say out of gratitude for having a job during the Depression. In 1933 the owners of the completed Rockefeller Center decided to carry on the tradition of the yearly tree. The tradition has been going strong since then. Designers have tried various tree-decorating schemes over the years. In 1933, strings of blue and white lights ornamented the tree. Another year only floodlights were used. During World War II, **ornaments** took the place of lights, which were eliminated in order to meet wartime blackout requirements. The use of ornaments was discontinued, however, when it was discovered that high winds, enhanced by the wind tunnel effect created by the surrounding tall buildings, could easily dislodge them from the tree. Decorators realized the danger posed by ornaments the year they festooned the tree with aluminum icicles. During strong winds the tree menaced people passing below by discharging volleys of the spear-like icicles. These days approximately 30,000 electric lights adorn the ornament-free tree, which is topped by a 60-pound star.

Rockefeller Center's landscape and garden team search New York state and New England for potential Christmas trees throughout the year. In order to find a Norway Spruce — the preferred variety — that has grown to about 70 or 80 feet, the team may employ the services of a helicopter. The trees usually come from privately owned properties rather than forests, as this variety is not native to the region. Once the ideal tree is spotted, the owners are approached with an offer to sell their tree. Many feel it an honor to have their tree selected for Rockefeller Center. The final selection is made by mid-summer. At the end of the Christmas season, the tree is turned into mulch and recycled into the earth.

The first few Christmas trees at Rockefeller Center were erected in the middle of the sunken plaza. In 1936 the plaza was transformed into a winter ice-skating rink. Nowadays the tree is set up between the rink and the General Electric building (formerly the RCA building).

Other Decorations

A number of the city's well-known buildings and institutions decorate for the holidays. The corporation that owns the Empire State Building illuminates the upper floors of the building with red and green lights during the month of December. The Humanities and Social Sciences Library of the New York City public library system — located at Fifth Avenue between 41st and 42nd Streets — shows its holiday spirit by placing two 60-pound wreaths around the necks of the magnificent stone lions that adorn the steps to the building. New Yorkers have quickly become accustomed to the giant snowflake that dangles above the intersection of Fifth Avenue and 57th Street. The snowflake stands approximately two-and-one-half stories in height and contains 6,000 light bulbs. This seasonal decoration first appeared in 1984. Ritzy Park Avenue puts on its own show for Christmas, decking the trees planted in the Avenue's meridians with white and gold lights. The display stretches for about two miles, beginning around 48th Street and ending at 96th Street.

Events

Each Christmas season the Rockettes, a troupe of female dancers, put on a special Christmas show at Radio City Music Hall. This tradition dates back to 1933. The **Nativity scene** calls for real camels and donkeys, which don't always behave on stage as planned. Each year they perform their dance of the toy soldiers, which ends with the toy soldiers, all in a row, falling over backwards like a set of dominoes.

Since 1954 New Yorkers have also enjoyed yearly performances of *The Nutcracker* by the New York City Ballet Company. Those who prefer song to dance may attend the *Messiah* Sing-In at Avery Fisher Hall. At this event the audience takes a stab at singing Handel's oratorio themselves. This tradition dates back to the 1960s.

Many New Yorkers and out-of-towners celebrate Christmas by taking in a Broadway show. Indeed New York's justly famous theater district sells more tickets at Christmas time than at any other time of year.

New Year's Eve

Finally, many Americans close out the holiday season by tuning into another New York City event: the large street party at **Times Square** on New Year's Eve. The climax of the party comes at midnight, when a large, illuminated ball atop a pole standing on the roof of the former Times Building begins to drop. The fall lasts 60 seconds and marks the last minute of the old year and the exact beginning of the new year. This event has been broadcast on television since 1943. In recent years about half a million people have gathered in Times Square on New Year's Eve to wait for the magic moment when the ball drops.

Further Reading

Pool, Daniel. *Christmas in New York*. New York. Seven Stories Press, 1997.

Web Sites

The Rockefeller Center web site offers information about its Christmas tree and skating rink at: http://www.rockefellercenter.com

Radio City Music Hall's web site contains information about its Christmas-time attractions at: http://www.radiocity.com

Nigeria, Christmas in

The west African nation of Nigeria, once a colony of Great Britain, is the most ethnically diverse country in all of Africa. It hosts over 200 different cultural groups that speak 400 different languages. About fifty percent of Nigerians are Muslims. Approximately 40 percent embrace Christianity, and 10 percent adhere to traditional religions. Muslims predominate in northern Nigeria, while Christianity is strongest in the southern part of the country.

Nigeria's Christians celebrate Christmas by buying their children **gifts**, especially new clothes and shoes. In large cities children may be taken to department stores where **Father Christmas** will give them a trinket of some kind. Many shops and businesses decorate their premises for the holiday. Christmas Eve and Christmas Day are often observed with church services.

In Calabar, a city in southeastern Nigeria where many ethnic Ibibio live, wandering companies in colorful attire perform traditional folk dramas and masquerades at Christmas time. Children also don masks made from colored raffia, or hide their faces under heavy makeup, as they gather together in groups that compete with one another to put on the best masquerade combining song, dance, and drumming. Sometimes bystanders will pay them for their efforts with a coin or two.

Many Nigerians living and working far from their native towns and villages travel home to spend Christmas with their families. The added strain on Nigeria's transportation system often means terrible traffic jams and extreme delays in all modes of public transportation. What's more, the high concentrations of people on the roads and in the marketplaces inspires bandits, pickpockets, and all manner of thieves to increase their activities during this season of the year. So far these difficulties have not stopped Nigerians from celebrating Christmas with gifts and family reunions.

The Ibo (also spelled Igbo) people, who make up about 28 percent of the country's population, are especially well known for their devotion to spending Christmas with their families. Although their native lands lie in eastern Nigeria, economic conditions have forced many Ibo to look for work in other parts of the country. Nevertheless, Ibo migrants continue to prize their place in village social life and make every effort to return at Christmas to spend time with family members. These holiday visits also afford them the opportunity to follow the fortunes of friends and acquaintances, and to attend weddings. People often schedule weddings and other important social functions for the **Christmas season**, so as to include these once-a-year returnees.

Further Reading

"Behold, Today Is Christmas." Africa News Service (January 25, 2001). Available for a fee through elibrary.com.

Blauer, Ettagale, and Jason Lauré. *Enchantment of the World: Nigeria*. New York: Children's Press, 2001.

Griffin, Robert H., and Ann H. Shurgin, eds. *The Folklore of World Holidays*. Second edition. Detroit, Mich.: Gale, 1999.

Momodu, Shaka. "The Annual Eastward Drift." Africa News Service (January 10, 2002). Available for a fee through elibrary.com.

Nonyelum, Chris. "The Other Side of Christmas." Africa News Service (December 27, 2001). Available for a fee through elibrary.com.

Owhonda, John. *Nigeria: A Nation of Many Peoples*. Parsipanny, N.J.: Dillon Press, 1998.

Noel

Noël, Nowel, Nowell

Contemporary English dictionaries define the word "noel" (also spelled "nowel" or "nowell") as a cry of joy associated with the celebration of Christmas. In past eras English speakers also used the word to refer to the feast of Christmas itself. This usage never faded in the French language, where the word *Noël* still means Christmas, or, when spelled without a capital "n," means "**Christmas carol.**" Although the English word "noel" is now considered somewhat obsolete, a number of traditional Christmas carols retain this old expression.

Researchers differ in their explanations of the origin of the word "noel." Most trace it back to the Latin word for birthday, *natalis.* Indeed, in the fourth century Church authorities in Rome introduced Christmas as *Dies Natalis Domini,* the "Birthday of the Lord" (*see also* **December 25**). The more formal name for the holiday was *Festum Nativitatis Domini Nostri Jesu Christi,* the "Feast of the Nativity of Our Lord Jesus Christ." Over the centuries the Latin words *Natalis* and *Nativitatis* passed into local languages across western Europe giving birth to vernacular words for Christmas. For example, the Portuguese call Christmas *Natal,* the Italians refer to it as *Natale,* and the Spanish call it *Navidad*. Other modern words for Christmas that probably evolved from the Latin *natalis* include the Gaelic *Nollaig,* the Welsh *Nadolig,* and the Provençal *Nadal*. Most scholars also trace the English "noel" and the French "Noël" back to the Latin word *natalis*.

In contrast, other writers suggest that the English word "noel" evolved from the Latin word for "news," *novella*. They believe that this Latin term was used to tell the joyous news of **Jesus'** birth, and so became the jubilant cry of those celebrating the feast of Christmas, or even another term for the feast itself. One researcher who supports this theory notes that in the Middle Ages people greeted news of especially happy events with cries of "noel." Finally, another scholar has suggested that "noel" comes from the Hebrew word *Immanuel* (or Emmanuel). This word — which, in Christian scripture is used to refer to Jesus (Matthew 1:23) — means "God with us."

Further Reading

Crippen, Thomas G. *Christmas and Christmas Lore*. 1923. Reprint. Detroit, Mich.: Omnigraphics, 1990.

Duncan, Edmondstoune. *The Story of the Carol*. 1911. Reprint. Detroit, Mich.: Omnigraphics, 1992.

Miles, Clement A. *Christmas in Ritual and Tradition*. 1912. Reprint. Detroit, Mich.: Omnigraphics, 1990.

Stevens, Patricia Bunning. *Merry Christmas!: A History of the Holiday*. New York: Macmillan, 1979.

Noisemaking

For Christmas customs that call for noisemaking, *see* **America, Christmas in Nineteenth-Century; Befana; Denmark, Christmas in; Germany, Christmas in; Knecht Ruprecht; Knocking Nights; New Year's Day; Norway, Christmas in; Shooting in Christmas; Twelfth Night; Twelve Days of Christmas; Up Helly Aa; Wassailing the Fruit Trees; Williamsburg, Virginia, Christmas in Colonial**

North Pole

How did **Santa Claus** come to choose the North Pole as his home? He didn't. This address was chosen for him by American cartoonist Thomas Nast (1840-1902). In 1882 Nast depicted Santa perched on top of a crate bearing the label "Christmas box 1882, St. Nicholas, North Pole." Nast's vision apparently caught on. Several years later, another artist portrayed Santa returning to his North Pole home. Soon, it became standard lore that the jolly **gift** giver inhabited the polar north.

What inspired Nast to give Santa such a remote residence? The influential portrait of the Christmas gift giver, painted decades earlier by Clement C. Moore in "A Visit from St. Nicholas," described him wearing fur robes. This made it likely that he came from a cold climate. Nast may also have read Horatio Alger's 1875 poem entitled "St. Nicholas," in which Alger declared that this "patron saint of Christmas night" lived beyond the "polar seas." At the time when Nast was conjuring up his images of Santa, no explorer had yet reached the North Pole, although several expeditions had begun the perilous journey. This remote and mysterious place, which no human being had yet seen, must have seemed the perfect abode for that elusive and magical creature, Santa Claus (*see also* **Children's Letters**).

Further Reading

Bowler, Gerry. *The World Encyclopedia of Christmas.* Toronto, Ontario, Canada: McClelland and Stewart, 2000.

Del Re, Gerard, and Patricia Del Re. *The Christmas Almanack.* Garden City, N.Y.: Doubleday, 1979.

Restad, Penne. *Christmas in America.* New York: Oxford University Press, 1995.

Norway, Christmas in

When Christianity came to Norway, its inhabitants abandoned some old beliefs and practices and adapted others to the new religion. Over the centuries remnants of ancient pagan beliefs concerning midwinter magic entwined themselves with Norway's developing Christmas lore and customs.

Yule

Some researchers believe that the ancient Norwegians, along with the other peoples of northern and central Europe, celebrated a midwinter festival called **Yule**. Moreover, these writers propose that a number of midwinter customs connected with this festival lingered on for centuries after the coming of Christianity. For example, old European beliefs concerning visiting Christmas **ghosts** and other supernatural figures may have been rooted in ancient ideas about the return of the dead at Yule. The midwinter rides of the **Wild Hunt** may also have grown out of the lore surrounding Yule. Some writers trace the origin of the **Yule log** back to the great bonfires lit for the Yule festival. The brewing of **Christmas ale** may also date back to ancient times. Lastly, some writers suspect that the Scandinavian Christmas mascot, the **Yule goat**, first kicked up its heels during the old Yule festival.

Old Customs and Superstitions

A number of old Norwegian Christmas superstitions and customs come from the ancient belief that spirits haunt the long, dark nights of the **Christmas season**. According to one old folk belief, the spirits of the dead return to their families on Christmas Eve. Folk custom suggested that, upon retiring, living family members leave out a plate of food so that the spirits of the dead could also join in the Christmas feast. In past times Norwegians believed that evil spirits were particularly active on Christmas Eve. Men in rural areas banded together on that night to practice a custom known as **shooting in Christmas**. Together they tramped to each house in the village and saluted it with a volley of gunfire. According to old folk beliefs, the sudden, explosive noise frightened away evil spirits. Keeping a Yule log or a blessed candle burning in the hearth all night also warded away witches and other evil beings. Moreover, in past times rural Norwegians painted tar crosses over doors at Christmas time. These crosses kept evil spirits from entering.

Another old superstition warned against doing any work that involved the turning of a wheel during the days surrounding Christmas (*see also* **Twelve Days of Christmas**). For example, spinning with a spinning wheel or carrying loads in wheeled vehicles were both considered unlucky. Old folk beliefs taught that at the time of the **winter solstice** the circular actions involved in these tasks indicated an ill-fated impatience with the slow turning of the wheel of the sun. These old superstitions and customs faded away in modern times.

The Julenisse

The traditions and lore surrounding the *Julenisse*, or Christmas **elf**, can also be traced back to ancient times. Unlike many old Norwegian Christmas traditions, however, the Julenisse lives on in contemporary folklore and customs. Some folklorists suspect that the Julenisse evolved from ancient beliefs in ancestral spirits who visited their old homesteads at Christmas time. Contemporary lore teaches that the Julenisse lives in dark corners of Norwegian homes. For most of the year this magical being dozes and dreams, although when awake he keeps a watchful eye on household doings. The Julenisse becomes more active around Christmas time. Then he will use his magical powers to cause household mishaps if not appeased with a bowl of porridge. Like his Swedish cousin, the **Jultomten**, the Norwegian Julenisse brings the family's Christmas **gifts**.

Preparations

Many Norwegians incorporate **Advent calendars** and **Advent candles** into their Christmas preparations. Selecting the family **Christmas tree** is also an important element of Christmas preparations for many families, as is giving the home a thorough cleaning. Families often bake a wide variety of cookies and breads during the days preceding Christmas, and some even brew special Christmas beers (*see also* **Christmas Cake**). In past times people believed that all Christmas cleaning, baking, slaughtering, and brewing should be completed by **St. Thomas's Day**, December 21. In the old days people also prepared for Christmas by making batches of candles. Although modern Norwegians no longer need to rely on candles for light during the long winter nights, candlemaking is still a popular pre-Christmas activity.

In old Norway the **Peace of Christmas** began on St. Thomas's Day. Towns designated special watchmen to ensure that peace and friendliness reigned during the holiday season. The Peace of Christmas also extended to animals. Hunters and fishermen removed traps and snares during the holiday season. This kindliness towards animals lives on in the custom of erecting a **Christmas sheaf** for birds and other small animals to feast on.

Christmas Eve

Church services are held around five p.m. on Christmas Eve. Those who attend return home to a sumptuous Christmas dinner. Popular main dishes include roast pork, sausages, and mutton. Many people also serve *lutefisk* (boiled codfish previously preserved in lye), a tradition surviving from past times when Norwegians abstained from eating meat on Christmas Eve. Like the Danes, Norwegian families also serve a dish of rice pudding with a single almond in it. Whoever finds the almond in their serving of pudding will have luck in the coming year. Other favorite Christmas desserts include crème caramel and cloudberry cream.

After dinner, some families take out the Bible and listen to one family member read the Gospel passages describing the birth of **Jesus** (*see* **Gospel According to Luke; Gospel According to Matthew**). Then the family gathers around the Christmas tree, joins hands, and sings **Christmas carols**. To the relief of many impatient children, opening gifts comes next. Before going to bed many families make sure to leave out a bowl of pudding for the Julenisse.

Christmas Day

Church services are also held on Christmas Day. The day's main event, however, consists of a lavish Christmas buffet. The meal may include pork ribs, meat patties, a selection of cold meats, herring, trout, salmon, codfish, cheese, fruit, cloudberry cream, bread, and cake. Adults also enjoy beer and *aquavit*, a Scandinavian liquor, with the meal.

Some people practice an old custom called *Julbukk*, or "Christmas goat," on Christmas Day. Groups of costumed children and adults walk through their neighborhood entertaining householders with songs in exchange for treats. These groups may bring a goat with them, or someone may impersonate a goat and this animal's typically unruly behavior. Sometimes these costumed goats discipline misbehaving children by butting them. If two costumed goats meet, they often entertain onlookers by engaging in a play fight (*for similar customs, see* **Mumming**).

Related Days

In Norway the Christmas season is peppered with saints' days and other related celebrations. Many Norwegians celebrate **St. Lucy's Day** on December 13. In the past, however, most Norwegians understood the Christmas season to start on December 21, St. Thomas's Day.

Norwegians also celebrate **St. Stephen's Day**, December 26. In the past bands of men rose before dawn and galloped from village to village singing folk songs about the saint. These robust performances awakened householders, who then refreshed Stephen's men with ale or other alcoholic beverages. Today one can still see bands of young men, often in traditional costumes, singing folk songs from door to door on St. Stephen's Day. Many Norwegians spend the day visiting with friends and family members.

Norwegians greet **New Year's** Eve with a fresh round of noisemaking and parties. On January 6, **Epiphany,** the **star boys** roam the streets singing Christmas carols. The Christmas season ends on **St. Knut's Day**, January 13.

Further Reading

Henriksen, Vera. *Christmas in Norway*. Oslo, Norway: Johan Grundt Tanum Forlag, 1970.

Hubert, Maria, comp. *Christmas Around the World*. Stroud, Gloucestershire, England: Sutton, 1998.

MacDonald, Margaret Read, ed. *The Folklore of World Holidays*. Detroit, Mich.: Gale Research, 1992.

Patterson, Lillie. *Christmas in Britain and Scandinavia*. Champaign, Ill.: Garrard Publishing Company, 1970.

Sechrist, Elizabeth Hough. *Christmas Everywhere*. 1936. Reprint. Detroit, Mich.: Omnigraphics, 1998.

Web Site

A site sponsored by the Royal Norwegian Ministry of Foreign Affairs: http://odin.dep.no/ (Click on "Language," "English," "History, culture, geography, recreation," then scroll down to "Christmas in Norway.")

T_he Nutcracker

One of the best-loved and most widely known ballets of our time, *The Nutcracker*, tells the story of a young girl's enchanted Christmas Eve. German writer, illustrator, and composer E. T. A. Hoffmann (1776-1822) wrote the original story on which the ballet is based. Russian composer Pyotr Ilich Tchaikovsky (1840-1893) set the tale to music in the early 1890s. Some ballet companies present *The Nutcracker* every year at Christmas time. In addition, Tchaikovsky's "The Nutcracker Suite," a shorter, orchestral work that summarizes the music presented at length in the ballet, appears on many Christmas concert programs.

The Tales and the Making of the Ballet

Hoffmann would have been delighted to discover that his stories lived on to inspire the works of great composers. Hoffmann himself found tremendous inspiration in the works of Austrian composer Wolfgang Amadeus Mozart (1756-1791), so much so that he changed his own middle name to Amadeus. Years after Hoffmann's death, his life as a teller of tales fueled the musical imagination of French composer Jacques Offenbach (1819-1880). Offenbach's opera *The Tales of Hoffmann* spins a fantasy around the writer and a number of his works.

One of Hoffmann's stories, "The Nutcracker and the Mouse King" (1819), intrigued French writer Alexandre Dumas (1802-1870). Dumas published a translated and freely adapted version of this story in French. Dumas's "The Story of a Nutcracker" (1844) charmed the director of **Russia**'s Imperial Ballet, who decided to commission a work based on the story. He hired the French choreographer Marius Petipa and his Russian colleague Lev Ivanov to choreograph the dancing. Petipa and Ivanov outlined the stage action needed to tell the story. Then they handed over a specific set of instructions to the composer who had been commissioned to write the music for the ballet. Luckily for future ballet lovers they selected Pyotr Tchaikovsky, who at that time was already considered a rising star among Russia's composers.

Hoffmann's complicated and somewhat frightening tale can hardly be recognized in today's productions of *The Nutcracker*. Petipa and Ivanov presented *The Nutcracker* as a delightful children's fantasy. The ballet companies that have performed *The Nutcracker* since then have adjusted the story here and there as well.

The Story as Told in the Ballet

Basically, the tale unfolds as follows. The first act takes place at a Christmas Eve party in Nuremberg, **Germany**. Many guests and their children arrive at the home of the Stahlbaum family. While the adults decorate the **Christmas tree**, the children play with toys. The mysterious Drosselmeyer arrives bringing **gifts** for his godchildren, Clara and Fritz Stahlbaum. Clara immediately falls in love with one of the toys, a wooden nutcracker. When the careless Fritz takes possession of the toy he breaks it, upsetting Clara greatly. The guests depart and the children are sent to bed.

Shortly thereafter, Clara comes back to the drawing room to visit her nutcracker. Clara finds herself reduced to the same size as the nutcracker and her brother's toy soldiers. Dozens of mice come out of their holes and, led by their king, they attack the soldiers. The nutcracker rallies the toy soldiers against the mice. As the mouse king and the nutcracker fight one another, Clara throws her shoe at the mouse king, giving the nutcracker the chance to defeat him. The soldiers win, and the nutcracker turns into a prince. Out of gratitude for her help, the nutcracker prince takes Clara on a journey to the Kingdom of Sweets. They pass through a flurry of dancing snowflakes as they enter the magic kingdom.

In act two the citizens of the Kingdom of Sweets entertain Clara and the nutcracker prince. Exotic foodstuffs, such as Arabian coffee and Spanish hot chocolate, dance for them. Even flowers come to life and begin to waltz. Finally, the queen of this enchanted kingdom, the Sugarplum Fairy, dances with the nutcracker prince (*see also* **Sugarplums**). Most versions of the ballet end with Clara returning to her own world, while in others she remains in the Kingdom of the Sweets.

Tchaikovsky's Score

Although Tchaikovsky accepted the job of producing the musical score for *The Nutcracker*, the task proved somewhat troublesome for him. He began working on the score in the winter of 1891. His personality and life circumstances may have contributed to the difficulty he experienced in composing the lighthearted music for the ballet. Extremely sensitive by nature, he often fell into periods of deep gloom. Several months before he began work on *The Nutcracker*, his close friend and patron, Mrs. Nadezhda von Meck, abruptly severed both their financial and personal relationships for no apparent reason. This abandonment plunged Tchaikovsky into depression and deeply shook his faith in human relationships. This recent event may explain why the composer found himself uninspired by the task of setting the sweet, simple fairy tale to music. Moreover, the rigid framework given him by the choreographers, which specified the character and exact length of many musical passages, restricted the degree of creativity he could bring to the work.

Nevertheless, Tchaikovsky labored away at the project until two great life events interrupted his progress. In March he left Russia for the United States, where he had been engaged to conduct the concert that was to open **New York City**'s new music hall, known today as Carnegie Hall. His journey to the United States took him through Paris, **France**. There he learned that his sister Alexandra had died. In a letter to his brother Modest, the composer confessed, "Today even more than yesterday I feel the absolute impossibility of portraying the 'sugar-plum fairy' in music."

After a successful sojourn in the United States his return trip to Russia again took him through France. There he bought a newly invented musical instrument called a celesta to take back with him to Russia. Tchaikovsky would introduce Russian audiences to its haunting xylophone-like tones in "The Dance of the Sugarplum Fairy," one of the most famous passages from *The Nutcracker*. When Tchaikovsky arrived in Russia in June he once again took up his work on the score. In spite of all his efforts, he confided in a letter to a friend that he thought *The Nutcracker* music far inferior to the music he had composed for the ballet *Sleeping Beauty*.

Tchaikovsky's estimation of the value of *The Nutcracker* music gradually increased. He decided to write an orchestral suite based on the ballet music. This time it took him only twelve days to complete the work. "The Nutcracker Suite" premiered in March of 1892, before the ballet had ever been performed. The audience loved the evocative melodies and requested several encores. Even today, "The Nutcracker Suite" stands as one of Tchaikovsky's best-loved works.

First Performances

The first performance of *The Nutcracker* ballet took place on December 17, 1892, in St. Petersburg, Russia. The audience and critics reacted without enthusiasm. Some writers point out that audiences of Tchaikovsky's time were not used to the idea of ballets being performed to high-quality symphonic music. In fact, Tchaikovsky's three great ballet scores — *Swan Lake, Sleeping Beauty*, and *The Nutcracker* — raised the standard for ballet music, and opened the door for other important composers to enter the field. Early audiences of *The Nutcracker* may also have disliked the fact that children occupy center stage for most of the first act, and that the serious dancing does not really begin until the second act. Luckily for Tchaikovsky, however, Tsar Alexander III of Russia liked the ballet. With the Tsar's nod of approval, *The Nutcracker* became a standard work in the world of Russian ballet. Outside of Russia, however, the ballet remained unknown for many years.

At the height of his career, less than a year after the premiere of *The Nutcracker*, Tchaikovsky was dead. In the fall of 1893 a Russian nobleman, who had discovered that his nephew had an affair with the composer, threatened to expose Tchaikovsky as a homosexual. Alarmed by this development, a number of Tchaikovsky's associates and former college classmates met to decide the composer's fate. This so-called "court of honor" ruled that Tchaikovsky should commit suicide in order to protect his, and, by extension, their reputations. Tchaikovsky had long feared the scandal and complete social shunning that would engulf him and his family if the public discovered his sexual orientation. When the great composer was found dead two days later, his associates circulated the story that he had died from cholera contracted from drinking a glass of unboiled water at a restaurant during an epidemic of the disease.

International Fame

The first performance of *The Nutcracker* in the West took place in London in 1934. In 1944 the San Francisco Ballet became the first American company to present the ballet. In 1954 the New York City Ballet added the work to their repertoire. Since that time *The Nutcracker* has become a December favorite for many dance companies. The work naturally attached itself to the **Christmas season**, since all the action in the story takes place on Christmas Eve. The story's magical elements offer ballet companies the opportunity to entertain their audiences not only with wonderful music and dancing, but also with fabulous costumes and fantastic special effects. The razzle-dazzle appeals to children as well as adults. In fact, many parents bring children to see *The Nutcracker* as a special holiday treat. Due to its popularity with audiences, the ballet has become a relied-upon money-maker for many ballet companies. Box-office receipts from its performances must often finance a good portion of a company's season.

Further Reading

Brinson, Peter, and Clement Crisp. *The International Book of Ballet*. New York: Stein and Day, 1971.

Brown, David, Gerald Abraham, David Lloyd-Jones, and Edward Garden. "Tchaikovsky." In *The New Grove Russian Masters*. Volume 1. New York: W. W. Norton, 1986.

Buxton, David, and Sue Lyon, eds. *Pyotr Tchaikovsky*. Volume 3 of *The Great Composers, Their Lives and Times*. New York: Marshall Cavendish, 1987.

Del Re, Gerard, and Patricia Del Re. *The Christmas Almanack*. Garden City, N.Y.: Doubleday, 1979.

Lehane, Brendan. *The Book of Christmas*. Alexandria, Va.: Time-Life Books, 1986.

Reynolds, Nancy, and Susan Reimer-Torn. *Dance Classics*. Chicago: A Cappella Books, 1991.

Terry, Walter. *Ballet Guide*. New York: Dodd, Mead, and Company, 1976.

Watson, Marjorie R. *The Fairy Tales of Hoffmann*. New York: E. P. Dutton and Company, 1960.

Weinstock, Herbert. *Tchaikovsky*. New York: Alfred A. Knopf, 1959.

Old Christmas Day

When Pope Gregory XIII established the Gregorian calendar in 1582, he ushered in an era in which the people of Europe disagreed on what day it was. As a result, they celebrated Christmas on different days. Before the Gregorian reform Europe had adhered to the Julian calendar, which was a full ten days behind the newly instituted Gregorian calendar. Some nations and churches refused to adopt the Gregorian reforms. In these lands people continued to celebrate Christmas on **December 25**, but did so according to the Julian calendar. Their celebrations fell on January 5 according to the new Gregorian calendar. In past eras the English sometimes referred to January 5 or 6 as "Old Christmas Day."

Calendar Confusion

By the sixteenth century many learned Europeans realized that there was something seriously wrong with their calendar system. The calendar in use at that time was called the Julian calendar, named after the Roman emperor Julius Caesar (100 B.C.-44 B.C.), who authorized its adoption in 46 B.C. A small but important error marred this calendar system. The astronomers who designed the Julian calendar calculated the solar year to be 365.25 days long. In fact, it takes the earth 365.2422 days to complete its orbit around the sun. While this difference only amounts to 11 minutes and 14 seconds every year, each passing year compounded the error, increasing the gap between the dates on the Julian calendar and the astronomical events and seasonal changes of the solar year. For example, in 45 B.C. spring equinox fell on March 25 (*see also* **Annunciation**). By the time the Council of Nicea met in 325 A.D. to determine the date of Easter, spring equinox was falling on March 21.

As the centuries passed scholars debated the calendar problem, although nothing was done to correct it until the sixteenth century. In 1545 the Council of Trent empowered Pope Paul III to propose a solution to the dilemma. Investigators labored on the problem for forty years, until a Jesuit astronomer named Christoph Clavius submitted a viable program of calendar reform to Pope Gregory XIII. In 1582 Pope Gregory XIII officially adopted Clavius's proposed reforms, resulting in a new calendar system known as the Gregorian calendar.

The researchers who devised the Gregorian calendar knew the true length of the solar year and based the new calendar around it. In order to correct the errors that had compounded over the years from the use of the Julian calendar system, Pope Gregory XIII decreed that ten days be eliminated from the calendar year of 1582. Thus, in that year October 5 was followed by October 15 in all lands that had adopted the new calendar. This brought the spring equinox back to March 21, the date on which it had occurred at the time of the Council of Nicea. Medieval calendar systems had also been plagued by the fact that the nations of Europe began their new year on different dates. The Gregorian calendar also declared January 1 to be **New Year's Day** in an attempt to standardize the beginning of the European year.

Resistance to Reform

Although scholars agreed that the Julian calendar system was flawed, many European nations resisted the changes proposed by the Gregorian calendar. Religious controversies fueled this resistance. The Roman Catholic nations of **Italy**, **France**, Luxembourg, **Spain**, and Portugal switched to the new calendar system in the same year it was announced. Many Protestant nations hesitated to adopt the calendar for fear of seeming to accept the authority of the Pope. In addition, much of Orthodox eastern Europe viewed the proposed changes as out of step with their religious traditions. This meant that at the close of the sixteenth century, the nations that did adopt the Gregorian reforms were fully ten days ahead of those that did not.

Europe Adopts the New Calendar

By 1584 most of the Roman Catholic German states had adopted the calendar, along with Belgium and parts of the Netherlands. Hungary switched to the new calendar in 1587. Switzerland began making the changes in 1583 and completed them 229 years later, in 1812. More than one hundred years passed before the Protestant nations began to adopt the Gregorian calendar. **Denmark** and the German Protestant states did so around the year 1700. In 1752 Great Britain and her colonies converted to the Gregorian calendar system. Sweden followed suit in 1753. Japan joined the Gregorian system in 1873, and **Egypt** in 1875. Between the years 1912 and 1917 many of the eastern European states switched to the Gregorian calendar system, including Albania, **Bulgaria**, **Estonia**, **Latvia**, **Lithuania**, Romania, and the former Yugoslavia. China also embraced the Gregorian system during those years. **Russia** joined the club in 1918, just after the Revolution. **Greece** held out until the early 1920s, the last major European nation to adopt the sixteenth-century reforms.

Christmas Controversy

At the time of its creation, the ten-day gap between the new Gregorian calendar and the old Julian calendar created a situation in which the peoples of Europe celebrated Christmas on different days. By the time **England** adopted the Gregorian calendar in 1752, the gap had crept up to eleven days. With the stroke of a pen English legislators ordered that September 2, 1752, be followed by September 14, 1752.

Many ordinary people defied this change, fearful that it would adversely affect their livelihood in some way. Although many writers have reported that resistance to the new calendar took the form of riots and slogans, such as "Give us back our eleven days," recent research has failed to find convincing evidence of these events. Instead, it appears that people resisted the change in less dramatic, more personal ways. Some refused to celebrate the feast days on the new Gregorian schedule and clung instead to the old dates, now known by different names (*see also* **Glastonbury Thorn**). For example, under the Gregorian reform the day that had been December 25 instantly became January 5. Many called January 5 "Old Christmas Day" or Christmas Day "Old Style." Correspondingly, December 25 was known as Christmas Day "New Style." By the nineteenth century Old Christmas Day had crept a day further away from the Gregorian calendar, falling on January 6, **Epiphany**. As the Julian calendar continued to drift away from the Gregorian calendar throughout the twentieth century, Old Christmas Day shifted yet another day forward in the Gregorian calendar, falling on January 7.

Some branches of the Orthodox Church have never accepted the Gregorian calendar. Their festival dates are still set according to the Julian calendar. Therefore, they observe Christian festivals on different dates than do most Western Christians. In Russia, for example, Orthodox believers celebrate Christmas on January 7. Orthodox Ethiopians and Egyptians also observe Christmas on January 7. (*See also* **Ethiopia, Christmas in**.)

Further Reading

Bellenir, Karen, ed. *Religious Holidays and Calendars*. Second edition. Detroit, Mich.: Omnigraphics, 1998.

MacDonald, Margaret Read, ed. *The Folklore of World Holidays*. Detroit, Mich.: Gale Research, 1992.

Muir, Frank. *Christmas Customs and Traditions*. New York: Taplinger, 1977.

Poole, Robert. "'Give Us Back Our Eleven Days'." *Past and Present* 149 (November 1995): 95-140.

Ornaments

Snow-covered evergreens standing in the woods are merely trees. Once decorated, they become **Christmas trees**. Over the centuries people have adorned their Christmas trees with many different kinds of objects. The very earliest ornaments tended to recall the religious significance of the holiday. At one point people decorated their Christmas trees with good things to eat and **gifts** for one another. In more recent times Christmas ornaments have served primarily as pretty decorations for the tree.

Earliest Ornaments

The earliest known Christmas tree ornaments were apples. Medieval actors used them to decorate the **paradise tree**, the central prop of the paradise play, a medieval European mystery play often performed on December 24 (*see also* **Nativity Play**). The apples represented the temptation of **Adam and Eve** in the Garden of Eden. Later, unconsecrated communion wafers were added to the tree, representing the salvation offered to humankind by **Jesus** Christ. Cherries might also hang from the tree in honor of the Virgin **Mary** (*see also* **Cherry Tree**). Although these town-square dramas eventually fell out of favor with the populace, some writers suspect that people in parts of **France** and **Germany** kept the custom of celebrating Christmas with a decorated fir tree, which eventually became known as a Christmas tree.

The first detailed description of a decorated Christmas tree in someone's home dates back to 1605 and comes from Strasbourg, Germany. According to this account, early seventeenth-century Germans festooned their Christmas trees with roses made out of colored paper, apples, wafers, and decorations made of shiny bits of gold foil or sugar. Indeed, a wide variety of ornaments made from food dangled from early German Christmas trees. The Germans hung gilded nuts on their trees, and later, cookies. They shaped these cookies in the form of hearts, **angels**, **bells**, and stars (*see also* **Star of Bethlehem**). Fruits and vegetables molded out of marzipan and colored with vegetable dyes soon followed. Some people made ornaments out of eggshells, transforming them, for example, into tiny baskets which could be filled with candy. In fact, the traditional German Christmas tree was covered with so many good things to eat that it was nicknamed a "sugar tree." Children looked forward to dismantling the tree on January 6, **Epiphany**, because they were then allowed to gobble up all the treats that had tempted them throughout the **Christmas season**.

Early Nineteenth-Century Ornaments

German immigrants brought their tree-decorating ideas with them to the United States. Like their ancestors in the old country, the Pennsylvania Dutch covered their Christmas trees with apples, nuts, and cookies. Some of them had brought elaborately carved wooden cookie molds with them from Germany. Others devised new tin cookie cutters to transform their dough into birds, animals, flowers, and other fanciful shapes.

As other Americans adopted the Christmas tree in the nineteenth century, they continued the German tradition of decorating it with good things to eat (*see also* **America, Christmas in Nineteenth-Century**). With a needle and thread they created long strings of cranberries and popcorn to drape over its branches, thereby adding two native American plant products to the decorated tree. They also created cornucopias, small cone- or horn-shaped containers filled with hard candies, and dangled them from the tree. Some stuffed lace bags with tiny treats and hung these as ornaments. Lucky children might also find **sugarplums** tucked among the branches of the tree. Candy canes, too, whose shape recalled **shepherds'** crooks, might swing from the branches of the nineteenth-century tree. Inventive women also fashioned ornaments out of strings of beads, ribbons, gilt paper, and lace.

In addition, many Americans adopted the German custom of hanging gifts for children on the branches of the Christmas tree. This worked because parents gave their children lightweight, unwrapped trinkets rather than heavy, boxed gifts throughout most of the nine-teenth-century (*see also* **Commercialism; Wrapping Paper**). Some families, however, preferred to hang **stockings** by the fireplace as receptacles for gifts. As people began to give each other heavier gifts, they shifted them to the space beneath the Christmas tree.

Covered with cookies and candies, studded with nuts, gilded with glittering candles, and trimmed with trinkets of all sorts, the nine-teenth-century Christmas tree dazzled children and adults alike. In his short story "A Christmas Tree" (1850), English author Charles Dickens (1812-1870) captured the allure of the bountifully decorated tree of his era in the following lines:

> I have been looking, this evening, at a merry company of chil-dren assembled round that pretty German toy, a Christmas tree. The tree was planted in the middle of a great round table, and towered high above their heads. It was brilliantly lighted by a multitude of little tapers; and everywhere sparkled and glittered with bright objects. There were rosy-cheeked dolls, hiding behind green leaves; and there were real watches (with movable hands, at least, and an endless capacity of being wound up) dangling from innumerable twigs; there were French polished tables, chairs, bedsteads, wardrobes, eight-day clocks, and various other articles of domestic furni-ture (wonderfully made, in tin, at Wolverhampton), perched among the boughs, as if in preparation for some fairy house-keeping; there were jolly, broad-faced little men, much more agreeable in appearance than many real men — and no won-der, for their head took off, and showed them to be full of sugarplums; there were fiddles and drums; there were tam-bourines, books, work-boxes, paint-boxes, sweetmeat-boxes, peepshow-boxes, and all kinds of boxes; there were trinkets for the elder girls, far brighter than any grown-up gold and jewels; there were baskets and pin cushions in all devices; there were guns, swords and banners; there were witches standing in enchanted rings of pasteboard, to tell fortunes; there were teetotums, humming-tops, needle-cases, pen-wipers, smelling-bottles, conversation-cards, bouquet-hold-ers; real fruit, made artificially dazzling with gold leaf; imita-

585

tion apples, pears, walnuts, crammed with surprises; in short, as a pretty child, before me, delightedly whispered to another pretty child, her bosom friend, "There was everything, and more."

Dickens's enticing description leaves little room to wonder why the decorated Christmas tree soon became the focus of family Christmas celebrations.

Commercial Ornaments

Sometime around 1870 a new fad in Christmas tree decorations began. Instead of decorating the tree with gifts and things to eat, people began to buy commercially made decorations designed solely for use as ornaments. Most of these early commercial ornaments came from Germany.

Early German designers fashioned novel ornaments out of tin and wax. In the city of Dresden, artisans specialized in making ornaments out of embossed and painted cardboard. Only some of their designs featured **Christmas symbols**. They also crafted numerous ornaments shaped like fish, birds, ordinary and exotic animals, or recent inventions, such as the steamship and the motor car. In 1878 artisans from Nuremberg devised thin strips of silver foil that could be strewn over the tree's branches like icicles. They called the thin strips *engelshaar*, which means "angels' hair," but we know them today as "tinsel." German printers also adopted recently invented color-printing techniques to turn out thousands of color illustrations of Christmas themes. Popular designs included angels, **St. Nicholas**, and the **Weihnachtsmann**. People collected especially pretty images and began to use them to ornament their Christmas trees and, sometimes, even to decorate their Christmas cookies (*see also* **Christmas Cake**).

Glass Ornaments

The blown-glass ornaments that began to pour out of Lauscha, Germany, in the 1870s were the ones that really caught the public's fancy, however. Lauscha had been a center of German glassmaking for centuries. In the second half of the nineteenth century some of its artisans discovered that they could blow decorative shapes out of glass to adorn Christmas trees. Demand was so high that the entire town was quickly drawn into the ornament industry. Whole families worked side by side, with the adult men molding the glass, the adult women silvering and painting the ornaments, and children breaking the glass stems and attaching metal caps. Soon, buyers representing major American stores, such as F. W. Woolworth, were making trips to Lauscha to snap up these unique Christmas decorations.

These early buyers chose their stock from a profusion of glass apples, pears, pinecones, and icicles. As the market for their products expanded, the glassblowers began to diversify their output into a dizzying range of shapes. Soon buyers could choose between a myriad of vegetable shapes, including pickles, carrots and corn, angels, the Weihnachtsmann, St. Nicholas, cartoon characters, hot air balloons, zeppelins, fish, dogs, clowns, birds, trumpets, drums, violins, bells, hearts, houses, churches, and more. A great deal of handcrafting went into many of these early glass ornaments. Some artisans, for example, took the trouble to insert tiny whistles into the stems of their trumpet ornaments, so that they could sound a single note. Americans could not get enough of these German novelties.

Although World War I disrupted production in Germany and cut off America's supply, the ornament trade resumed in the post-war years. World War II, however, struck the German industry a blow from which it would never recover. Not only was Germany devastated by the war, but the town of Lauscha fell within the territory turned over to the Soviets afterwards, becoming part of East Germany. The Communist government frowned upon trade with the United States and the other Western nations. This policy severely limited the artisans' access to the once-worldwide market for Lauscha's goods. In addition, many children of glassblowers abandoned this sweaty, labor-intensive trade after the war.

During World War II the Corning Glass Company began to produce ornaments in the United States. Corning replaced the glassblowers with glass-blowing machines, however. Although the machines turned out uniform, round balls rather than the dazzling variety of shapes produced by the German artisans, a machine could produce in a minute the same number of ornaments it took a German glassblower all day to produce. Today, Corning still makes most of the ornaments produced in the United States.

Ethnic Ornaments

Just as Christmas symbols vary from country to country, so do typical Christmas ornaments. Some of these ornaments may strike Americans as quite unusual. For example, in the Ukraine, spiders and their webs dangle from the traditional tree. These symbols come from an old legend that tells of a poor woman who had no ornaments to hang on her tree on Christmas Eve. The next morning, however, the family awoke to see shining silver spider webs floating between the branches. A friendly spider had decorated the tree for the poor family. In the Scandinavian countries one might find straw goats hanging from the tree (*see also* **Yule Goat**). The Danes favor red and white hearts and strings of miniature red-and-white Danish flags (*see also* **Denmark, Christmas in**).

Lighting the Tree

The earliest description of an illuminated tree comes from southern Germany in the year 1660. The light was provided by candles. Since candles were relatively expensive in those days, humble folk often had to make do with devices such as miniature wicks floating in walnut shells filled with oil.

Most of our early accounts of illuminated trees date from the nineteenth century, when the Christmas tree was becoming popular in Britain and the United States. By the second half of the nineteenth century, candles had become an expected ornament on the American Christmas tree. People found the spell of the candle-covered tree nearly irresistible, in spite of the dangers it posed. The candles not only threatened to set the tree itself on fire, but also could consume flammable ornaments or ignite the clothing of anyone who brushed by them. Newspaper advice columns cautioned families to designate at least one person to keep a watchful eye on the lit tree at all times and to have a bucket or wet sponge handy to extinguish any accidental fire. Often the tree was lit for the first time on Christmas Eve. Excited children fidgeted outside the parlor doors while their parents painstakingly placed and lit the candles. Some were told that **Santa Claus** not only left the gifts but also decorated the tree. The magical sight of the glowing, gift-bestrewn tree enchanted children and adults alike.

In spite of the yearly newspaper reports of Christmas tree fire trag-edies, people continued to illuminate their trees with candles. So great was the desire for a safe, illuminated tree that in 1882, only three years after inventor Thomas Edison gave the world the first electric light, one of his associates figured out how to use the new invention to light up a Christmas tree. The new electric tree soon became a fashionable Christmas toy for the rich, who could afford to hire an electrician to come to their homes and wire the tree by hand. In 1895 electric lights appeared on the **White House** Christmas tree at the request of President Grover Cleveland.

In 1903 the Ever-Ready Company of New York brought electric Christmas tree lights nearer the reach of ordinary people by devising the first string of ready-made lights. Problems remained, however. Not only were these strings heavier than today's lights, but each light was connected to the next by "series" wiring. This meant that when one bulb burned out, the whole string refused to light. In ad-dition, during the first decades of the twentieth century, many Amer-ican homes still did not have electricity. Gradually, electricity spread throughout the country and the price of the strings of electric lights came down. Only after World War II did "parallel" wiring come into widespread use. In this wiring system the failure of one bulb did not affect the others. Tiny "midget" lights achieved widespread popular-ity in the 1970s.

Further Reading

Foley, Daniel J. *The Christmas Tree*. Philadelphia, Pa.: Chilton Company, 1960.

Metcalfe, Edna. *The Trees of Christmas.* Nashville, Tenn.: Abingdon Press, 1969.

Snyder, Phillip V. *The Christmas Tree Book*. New York: Viking Press, 1976.

Sterbenz, Carol Endler, and Nancy Johnson. *The Decorated Tree*. New York: Harry N. Abrams, 1982.

Stevens, Patricia Bunning. *Merry Christmas!: A History of the Holiday*. New York: Macmillan, 1979.

The Time-Life Book of Christmas. New York: Prentice Hall, 1987.

Pantomime

In **England** many families celebrate Christmas by attending a pantomime show. Although in the United States the word "pantomime" refers to dramas enacted without dialogue, the word has a different meaning in Britain. There, a pantomime show combines dialogue, music, dance, acrobatics, slapstick humor, colorful costumes, and special effects around the enactment of a simple story, often a fairy tale. Pantomime brings a bit of the circus to the theater, as the emphasis is on amusing the audience with as many flashy diversions as possible rather than telling the story in an economical way. While children enjoy the spectacle, adults are amused by the innuendo, camp humor, and satire laced throughout the performance.

Pantomime traces its roots back to the ancient world, although much more recent theater traditions have influenced it as well. Its ancestors include Roman and Greek mime traditions, Renaissance improvisational comedy, and musical theater.

Ancient Pantomime

The English word "pantomime" comes from the ancient Greek words for "all" (*panto*) and "mimic" (*mimos*). The ancient Romans were especially fond of pantomimes. Roman mimes used masks to distinguish various characters and were often aided by a chorus, which chanted the story, as well as by musical accompaniment. By the end of the fourth century Christianity had become politically powerful in the Mediterranean world. Church and state officials began to speak out against pantomime and other forms of theater, arguing that its actors portrayed and promoted immoral and indecent activities. This attitude of condemnation continued through the Middle Ages. Mimes and other actors faced excommunication for their participation in the kinds of drama frowned upon by the Church. Nevertheless, many forms of folk drama persisted throughout this period, including some associated with the **Christmas season**, such as **mumming**, and Christmas time mystery or miracle plays, folk dramas depicting events related to the birth of **Jesus** (*see also* **Nativity Play**).

Commedia Dell'Arte

In the sixteenth century commedia dell'arte, a kind of improvised burlesque comedy, began to re-popularize elements of pantomime in **Italy**. Although the plots varied, these dramas revolved around the interactions of a number of standard characters. These characters included Pantalone (or Pantaloon), a lecherous, scheming businessman, and Graziano, a pompous professor. Other important roles were filled by the *zanni*, or "servant" characters. These included Arlecchino (or Harlequin), a scamp; Colombina (or Colombine), a simple young woman; and Pucinella (or Punch), a slow-witted, hunchbacked fool. The madcap antics of these servants gave rise to the English word "zany." In commedia dell'arte actors expressed themselves with exaggerated gestures, masks, miming, dancing, music, and tumbling, in addition to dialogue. Because it did not rely heavily on language to communicate, commedia dell'arte crossed boundaries easily. It became popular throughout Europe in the sixteenth through eighteenth centuries.

British Harlequinade

Nineteenth-century British pantomime evolved from eighteenth-century commedia dell'arte influences. John Weaver of London's Drury Lane Theatre introduced a new kind of entertainment he called a pantomime in 1702. Weaver's pantomime placed commedia dell'arte characters such as Harlequin and Colombine in the midst of ancient myths enacted through song, dance, and mime. In 1717 John Rich, inspired by Weaver's success, presented a short funny scene between the acts of a regular play at Lincoln's Inn Fields Theatre. This scene featured the courtship of Harlequin and Colombine and was told in mime.

This addition to the regular bill of fare at the theater proved wildly popular, and before long other commedia dell'arte characters were introduced, such as Punch and Pantaloon. Although these additional characters spoke dialogue, the romance between Harlequin and Colombine continued to be presented in mime. These entertainments always starred the roguish Harlequin, and so they became known as harlequinade. Like commedia dell'arte, harlequinade combined music, dance, acrobatics, mime, and dialogue to create a comic, burlesque spectacle. It also added special effects (such as characters disappearing through trapdoors) and lavish costuming, which dazzled and delighted audiences.

The Birth of British Pantomime

In the early nineteenth century British harlequinade evolved into the art form now known as pantomime. Pantomime flourished as the century progressed, while harlequinade faded, disappearing sometime in the early twentieth century. Pantomime treated spectators to the same kind of circus atmosphere as did harlequinade, but differed in a number of important ways. In pantomime the role of the clown grew to be larger and more important than that of Harlequin.

In the latter half of the century pantomime shed the commedia dell'arte characters of Harlequin, Colombine, and Pantaloon, and gravitated toward the retelling of fairy tales, myths, and fables. A loose-knit plot based around one of these stories held the various elements of the pantomime together as the extravagant spectacle surged back and forth across the stage. Unlike its predecessor, pantomime assigned all characters dialogue. By the 1820s women were being cast in the role of the principal boy, an innovation that tickled the theater-going public. This innovation slowly developed into a tradition whereby the young male lover was played by a woman and the dame, a comical older woman, was played by a man. Finally, whereas harlequinade had always been a diversion from or addition to the main attraction, pantomime developed into an attraction in and of itself.

In the 1830s and 1840s pantomime attached itself to the Christmas season (*see also* **Victorian England, Christmas in**). It was deemed a suitable family activity, since the fairy tale themes enchanted children, and the spicy dialogue, which children failed to understand, amused adults. Pantomimes generally opened on **Boxing Day**, December 26, and the public flocked to theaters to see them during the **Twelve Days of Christmas**. In some places, pantomimes proved so popular they ran until March. Although pantomime found favor with the general public, many literary and other intellectual figures disdained it as a vulgar and disorderly display.

Christmas Themes

Some writers have commented on the underlying similarities between pantomime and other Christmas entertainments that featured unruly behavior under the cover of masks and disguises. Examples of these entertainments include belsnickeling (*see* **Knecht Ruprecht**), the customs associated with **Germany's Knocking Nights**, the **Feast of Fools**, **Feast of the Ass; masques**, mumming, **Plough Monday** customs, and **Twelfth Night** celebrations (*see also* **Kalends** and **Zagmuk**). By the time pantomime became popular in Great Britain, however, most of these practices had died out.

Although pantomime sprang from a different set of cultural and historical roots than did these earlier customs, it seems to represent a perennial return to the theme of celebrating midwinter with costumed revelry. One important distinction remains. While ordinary people banded together to carry out these earlier forms of folk entertainment, pantomime was produced by professionals. Consequently, while the earlier revels often took place in the streets or in private homes, pantomimes, offered to the public as a product for sale, could only be experienced in private theaters.

Established Tradition

Many believe that the heyday of pantomime occurred during the Victorian era. Indeed, the nineteenth century produced a number of pantomime stars including Joey Grimaldi, the celebrated clown of the early 1800s, and Dan Leno, the famous dame of the late 1800s. Nevertheless, during the twentieth century the British public continued to crowd the theaters that hosted pantomimes during the Christmas season. Although in the past many pantomimes premiered on Boxing Day, today the pantomime season runs from mid-December to mid-January. Moreover, while theater attendance throughout Britain continues to sag, pantomime brings in such large audiences that many theaters rely on box-office takings from these performances to substantially boost yearly revenues.

Further Reading

Baxter, Beverley. "Two Thousand Years of Pantomime." In Harry Ballam and Phyllis Dibgy Morton, eds. *The Christmas Book*. 1947. Reprint. Detroit, Mich.: Omnigraphics, 1990.

Chambers, Robert. "December 26 — Christmas Pantomimes." In his *The Book of Days*. Volume 2. 1862-64. Reprint. Detroit, Mich.: Omnigraphics, 1990.

Del Re, Gerard, and Patricia Del Re. *The Christmas Almanack*. Garden City, N.Y.: Doubleday, 1979.

Hadfield, Miles, and John Hadfield. *The Twelve Days of Christmas*. Boston, Mass.: Little, Brown and Company, 1961.

Hutton, Ronald. *The Stations of the Sun*. Oxford, England: Oxford University Press, 1996.

Muir, Frank. *Christmas Customs and Traditions*. New York: Taplinger, 1977.

"Pantomime." In Phyllis Hartnoll, ed. *The Oxford Companion to the Theatre*. Fourth edition. Oxford, England: Oxford University Press, 1983.

Pimlott, J. A. R. *The Englishman's Christmas*. Atlantic Highlands, N.J.: Humanities Press, 1978.

Walsh, William S. *The Story of Santa Klaus*. 1909. Reprint. Detroit, Mich.: Omnigraphics, 1991.

Paradise Tree

Christbaum

Few people today would recognize a fir tree decorated only with red apples and white, circular wafers as a paradise tree. The paradise tree developed as a prop for the paradise play, a medieval European mystery play performed around Christmas time. Indeed, with its early historical connection to the **Christmas season**, the paradise tree may well have been the forerunner of the **Christmas tree**.

Mystery Plays

In medieval western **Europe**, mystery or miracle plays taught biblical stories and Christian ideas to a largely illiterate populace (*see also* **Nativity Play**). At first, only clergy acted in these plays, which were spoken in Latin and presented inside churches. As audiences grew, performances were moved to the front steps of the church or to large open plazas. With this movement out of sacred space, lay people began to take part in the plays, and the dialogue slipped into local languages. What's more, frivolous, humorous, and ribald incidents were added to the basic plot. Church officials frowned on these changes, but the plays only increased in popularity. Small groups of actors traveled from town to town satisfying the popular demand for this form of entertainment.

Paradise Play

Mystery plays often rooted themselves in the seasons and feast days of the Church calendar. The paradise play, which recounted the story of **Adam and Eve**, attached itself to the **Advent** season. Although the play featured the story of the Creation and the disobedience of Adam and Eve, it closed with the promise of the coming of a Savior. This made it appropriate for the celebration of Advent and Christmas. Moreover, the medieval Church declared December 24 the feast day of Adam and Eve. Around the twelfth century this date became the traditional one for the performance of the paradise play.

Paradise Tree

The paradise tree served as the central prop for the paradise play. It represented the two important trees of the Garden of Eden: the Tree of the Knowledge of Good and Evil and the Tree of Life. Originally, only apples adorned the paradise tree. These symbolized the fall of humanity described in the Adam and Eve story. Perhaps because most other trees were barren and lifeless during December, the actors chose to hang the apples from an evergreen tree rather than from an apple tree. In the fifteenth century round, white communion wafers were added to the paradise tree. These wafers stood for the promise of reconciliation with God made possible through **Jesus Christ**. Sometimes cherries also served as tree **ornaments**, symbolizing faith and reminding audiences of **Mary** and the **Annunciation** (*see also* **Cherry Tree**). A circle of lit candles usually surrounded the paradise tree during performances. The play was performed within this circle.

Church authorities banned miracle plays in the fifteenth century, but these popular plays continued to be performed for at least another century. Before disappearing completely they bequeathed the custom of the paradise tree to the peoples of **France** and the Rhine River region of **Germany**. Some Germans adopted a new name for the tree, calling it a *Christbaum*, or "Christ tree." Over time white pastry dough ornaments cut into the shape of hearts, **angels**, stars, and **bells** replaced the communion wafers. Ornaments representing humans, lions, dogs, birds, and other animals were made out of brown dough. Blooming paper roses might also embellish the tree, a symbol of the birth of Jesus (*see also* **Christmas Rose; Christmas Symbols**). During the nineteenth century some German people still put figurines representing Adam, Eve, and the serpent under their trees at Christmas time. In some sections of Bavaria the Christmas evergreen, decorated with lights, apples and tinsel, is still called a paradise tree.

Further Reading

Metcalfe, Edna. *The Trees of Christmas*. Nashville, Tenn.: Abingdon Press, 1969.

Sterbenz, Carol Endler, and Nancy Johnson. *The Decorated Tree*. New York: Harry N. Abrams, 1982.

Weiser, Francis X. *The Christmas Book*. 1952. Reprint. Detroit, Mich.: Omnigraphics, 1990.

Pastores, Los
La Pastorela

Los pastores (pronounced lohs pah-STOH-rays) means "the shepherds" in Spanish. This is the name given to a Mexican folk drama that tells the story of the **shepherds'** pilgrimage to the newborn Christ child. The play is also referred to as *La Pastorela*, which means "the pastoral" or "the country story" in Spanish. Performances of this play usually take place in mid to late December.

The **Gospel according to Luke** (2:8-20) states that an **angel** announced **Jesus'** birth to a group of shepherds and encouraged them to make a pilgrimage to **Bethlehem**. The shepherds went to Bethlehem and found the Christ child, confirming the words of the angel. The story told in Los Pastores is loosely based on this Bible passage.

History

The roots of the Shepherds' Play can be traced back to the mystery or miracle plays of medieval **Europe** (*see also* **Nativity Play**). These plays began as brief interludes during church services in which the clergy enacted simple versions of Bible stories and religious doctrines. These liturgical dramas began sometime around the tenth and eleventh centuries. The clergy used them to teach elements of the Christian religion to a largely illiterate population. The plays proved popular and, eventually, folk performers began to stage them in public arenas. Many changes accompanied this shift. The new folk dramas embroidered the original plots, adding humorous and racy dialogue, characters, and events. These innovations caused the Church to ban these performances in the fifteenth century.

Many of these plays dealt with the stories behind the Christian holidays and were performed on those days. The Shepherds' Play was one of a number of stories enacted at Christmas time. During the fifteenth century several Spanish authors developed elaborate written versions of The Shepherds' Play, or Los Pastores. These plays featured coarse and comical shepherds who entertained audiences by responding to the great events surrounding the Nativity with fear, greed, and confusion. In fact, the amusing antics of the shepherds nearly eclipsed the solemn story of the Nativity.

In the sixteenth century Spanish missionaries came to **Mexico** to convert the native peoples to Christianity. The Native Americans not only came from very different cultural backgrounds than did the Spanish, but also spoke very different languages. In order to bridge this gap the missionaries decided to use mystery plays to teach them Bible stories. They introduced Los Pastores sometime during the sixteenth century.

Like the mystery plays of medieval Europe, Los Pastores eventually passed from the hands of the clergy and the church grounds to the hands of the people and the public plaza. This transition produced similar results. Although the basic outline of the story remained the same, the play continued to evolve along the same lines it had followed in Europe. Over time new characters and events were added to the play. The drama evolved into a comedy in which the Devil tries to distract the dull-witted shepherds from their quest and heaven's angels intercede to keep the oafish pilgrims on course.

Plot and Characters

Although the plots may vary somewhat according to local traditions, a number of main characters appear in every version of the play. The starring roles go to the shepherds. They are portrayed as lazy, thickheaded, and easily distracted from their quest by opportunities to eat, sleep, or flirt. In fact, these less-than-heroic shepherds must be coaxed and even argued into setting out on their pilgrimage. At some point they encounter an elderly though spunky hermit. The hermit helps keep the shepherds on their course and entertains the audience with his sharp tongue. A scheming Devil appears throughout the play, sometimes disguised to fool the shepherds and sometimes in a traditional red costume complete with horns and a tail. He and his minions attempt to lure the shepherds away from their pilgrimage by appealing to all their weaknesses.

Often, the play also includes the angel **Gabriel**, who announces Jesus' birth to the shepherds, and the archangel Michael, who descends from heaven to protect the shepherds from the Devil's temptations. Sometimes a host of angels must battle a squadron of devils in order to protect the boorish travelers. At last, however, the shepherds arrive in Bethlehem and present their **gifts** to the Holy Family. The play ends with the Devil conceding defeat.

Performances

Local townspeople, schools, and even semi-professional acting groups present versions of Los Pastores. The drama is usually staged in some public place, like a plaza or a church, but may also be presented at someone's home. It may last anywhere from half an hour to several hours. Actors use dialogue, song, dance, verse, costume, and melodramatics to convey the story.

This Mexican folk drama may be found in numerous towns and cities in the United States, especially in areas where many Mexican Americans live, such as the southwestern states. Some American folklorists point out, however, that fewer and fewer folk performances are given each year. Instead, the tradition is being carried on by professional and semi-professional actors. The city of San Antonio, Texas, at one point hosted dozens of amateur troupes dedicated to the presentation of Los Pastores. Today only one amateur group remains, bringing about twenty performances a year to churches, missions, or people's backyards between Christmas Eve and **Candlemas**, February 2. In addition, the San Antonio Conservation Society presents the public with a more formal, professional version of the play each year at the city's San José Mission.

Further Reading

Christmas in Mexico. Chicago: World Book, 1976.

Christmas in the American Southwest. Chicago: World Book, 1996.

Cohen, Hennig, and Tristram Potter Coffin, eds. *The Folklore of American Holidays*. Detroit, Mich.: Gale Research, 1987.

Flores, Richard R. *Los Pastores, History and Performance in the Mexican Shepherd's Play of South Texas*. Washington, D.C.: Smithsonian Institution Press, 1995.

Milne, Jean. *Fiesta Time in Latin America*. Los Angeles, Calif.: Ward Ritchie Press, 1965.

Ribera Ortega, Pedro. *Christmas in Old Santa Fe*. Second edition. Santa Fe, N.M.: Sunstone Press, 1973.

Peace of Christmas

The city of Turku, Finland, claims to be the only place in Scandinavia that has observed the old Scandinavian tradition of declaring the "Peace of Christmas" from medieval times to the present. Each year around noon on December 24 a crowd gathers in Old Square, the former center of city government. After the clock of the nearby Turku cathedral strikes twelve they sing "A Safe Stronghold Is Our God," an old hymn by Protestant reformer Martin Luther (1483-1546). Then, from a balcony overlooking the square, the city clerk reads the words of an old document in Finnish and Swedish, thus signaling the start of the Peace of Christmas. The proclamation advises people to attend to their devotions and behave peacefully towards one another. The document also warns that anyone who violates the Peace of Christmas will answer to the law. The declaration ends by wishing the assembled crowd a **Merry Christmas**. Afterwards the crowd sings the Finnish national anthem. Both Finnish and Swedish television stations broadcast the event.

The city of Turku, which has declared itself Finland's "Christmas city," hosts another important peace event during the **Christmas season**. Each year bishops from four denominations make an ecumenical appeal for world peace in a special service held in Turku's cathedral. The bishops represent the Evangelical-Lutheran Church of Finland, the Orthodox Church of Karelia and Finland, the Roman Catholic Church of Finland, and the Methodist Church of Northern Europe. The bishops' appeal is taped and broadcast along with the declaration of the Peace of Christmas.

In past times people took the Peace of Christmas quite seriously. In old **Norway** the Peace of Christmas began on **St. Thomas's Day**, December 21. So strong was the desire for harmony that appointed guards roved the towns to insure that peace reigned throughout the season. The penalties for violent crimes doubled during this period, adding extra incentive to comply with the seasonal declaration of peace.

Further Reading

Henriksen, Vera. *Christmas in Norway Past and Present*. Oslo, Norway: Johan Grundt Tanum Forlag, 1970.

Web Site

A site sponsored by the city of Turku, Finland: http://www.christmas city.com

Philippines, Christmas in the

The Philippines is the only nation in Asia where the majority of people are Christian. Since Spanish colonizers brought the Christian religion to the Philippines hundreds of years ago, most Filipino Christians are, like the Spanish, Roman Catholic. The Philippines has been called the "land of fiestas." For many Filipinos, Christmas is the most joyous fiesta of the year.

Rooster Masses

In the Philippines the **Christmas season** begins on December 16 with the first of nine early morning church services called the **Misa de Gallo**, or "rooster's mass." Known as *Simbang Gabi* in the Tagalog language spoken by many Filipinos, these services take place every day between December 16 and December 24. A festive rather than solemn mood pervades these observances in spite of the fact that the masses begin at four in the morning. At that early hour church **bells** ring, marching bands play, and fireworks explode, rousing anyone who is still in bed and reminding everyone to attend mass. In small towns the priest himself may knock on doors, calling parishioners for this early morning service. These services are well attended, since many Filipinos see them as an essential element of their Christmas celebrations. To many who attend, the socializing that takes place after the service is as important as the mass itself. Vendors sell breakfast foods outside, and people stop to chat with friends and neighbors in the fresh, early morning air.

Christmas Carols

Many Filipinos enjoy singing **Christmas carols**. Caroling often begins in earnest on December 16. Bands of young people and adults take to the streets, singing Filipino carols as well as a smattering of English carols they have come to know. Filipino custom encourages people to reward carolers with money or sweets. Some people carol as a way of raising money for civic organizations. Youngsters often want to keep the coins and treats for themselves, however. Others carol simply for the fun of it.

In some parts of the Philippines groups of folk performers, called **Pastores**, offer free entertainment on the nights before Christmas. *Pastores* means **"shepherds"** in Spanish. This Filipino custom comes from an old Spanish custom of the same name. Dressed in folk costumes, the performers sing Christmas carols and other traditional Filipino songs. Sometimes they act out scenes from the Nativity story as well.

Decorations

Decorating the home is an important part of the Christmas celebration in the Philippines. The most cherished Christmas decoration is the *parol*, a star-shaped lantern. Many families make their own. Children often learn how to make star lanterns in school by covering a bamboo frame with colored rice paper or cellophane. Tassels or streamers are usually attached to each of the five points on the star. In the old days people illuminated these lanterns by placing a candle within them. Nowadays an electric light is often deemed safer.

Many cities sponsor parol competitions in the days before Christmas. Judges award prizes to the most beautiful homemade lanterns. In the city of San Fernando, the lantern competition has become a spectacle that draws crowds from the surrounding areas. Each year the lanterns entered in the competition have grown in size. Many now have to be carried on flatbed trucks.

Other Christmas decorations include candles, **wreaths, Christmas trees, Nativity scenes**, and **Christmas cards**. Cards may be displayed by attaching them to a red or green ribbon which is then

strung across the room. Filipinos also incorporate fresh flowers into their Christmas decorations. Flowers are readily available in the month of December due to the country's warm climate.

During the holiday season Christmas decorations festoon shops, streets, and plazas as well as homes. Electric light displays, star lanterns, Christmas trees, and scenes from the Nativity story all appear in these public displays.

Christmas Trees

Many Filipino families have adopted the European custom of decorating their homes with a Christmas tree. In the Philippines Christmas trees are as likely to be found on a porch or balcony as they are in the living room. Since pine trees are quite expensive in the Philippines, some families buy an artificial tree instead. Others use palm trees, or make an artificial tree out of twigs and branches or out of cardboard. Filipinos decorate their trees with miniature star lanterns, bamboo or wood carvings, candies, ribbons, shells, and tiny boxes wrapped like Christmas **gifts**.

Nativity Scenes

Nativity scenes are another important element of Filipino Christmas decorations. In past times Nativity scenes were principally found in churches and were made to be life sized. Nowadays these scenes may be smaller. They usually appear for the first time in churches on December 16. Nativity scenes may be found in Filipino homes as well. Filipinos call the Nativity scene a *belén*, the Spanish word for **Bethlehem**. Like the people of many other nations, Filipinos place the infant **Jesus** figurine in his Nativity scene crib on the evening of December 24.

Christmas Eve

Filipinos prepare for Christmas Eve by giving their homes a thorough cleaning. Those who can afford it also buy new clothes, which they wear for the first time to **Midnight Mass** or to Christmas morning mass. Families also stock up on special holiday foods, since extensive visiting takes place over the holiday season.

Christmas Eve is a family affair in the Philippines. Often the extended family will gather at one of the grandparents' homes early in the evening. Filipinos are famous for their hospitality, so distant relatives and even friends of relatives are often welcome at this event. Very small children may be left at home to nap while most of the family attends Midnight Mass. Large numbers of people attend mass on this evening, so many people arrive early, hoping to secure a seat. Churches are often filled by 10:00 p.m.

After the mass most people return home for a bountiful Christmas Eve banquet. Hosts and hostesses of large gatherings may have prepared as many as fifteen or twenty different dishes for guests to choose from. These may include *arroz caldo* (chicken and rice soup), *lumpia* (spring rolls), *rellenong manok* (boned stuffed chicken), *rellenong bangus* (boned stuffed milkfish), and *calamay* (coconut rice pudding). Bands of carolers may arrive at the door during this festive meal, as well as neighbors and friends who stop by to wish everyone a **Merry Christmas**. Children sometimes sing, dance, or perform a little play for the adults. The party continues until four or five in the morning. Afterwards, bed rolls are spread out for the many houseguests who stay the night.

Christmas Gifts

Some people exchange Christmas gifts during the Christmas Eve party. Others wait until Christmas Day. As a rule, gifts are simple in the Philippines and often include homemade foods or useful items, such as new clothes. Although **Santa Claus** is known in the Philippines, he does not act as a gift bringer there. Most Filipino children know that their presents come from Mom, Dad, and the grandparents.

Christmas Day

Those who did not attend Midnight Mass on Christmas Eve often begin the day by attending Christmas morning mass. More family visits take place on Christmas Day. Families may call on aunts, uncles, godparents, and grandparents. The children usually receive a small trinket at each house, so they eagerly agree to these rounds of visits. It is especially important that children visit their godparents on Christmas Day. Sometimes the children perform a song, dance, or skit for their godparents. The godparents, in turn, offer a gift to each godchild.

Filipinos sit down to another lavish meal on Christmas Day. Christmas dinner, which usually takes place around midday, frequently features *lechon,* roast suckling pig. Options for those who cannot afford a suckling pig include ham and *lenong manok,* stuffed chicken. *Flan,* a caramel-flavored custard, is often served for dessert.

The Twelve Days of Christmas

Filipinos celebrate throughout the entire **Twelve Days of Christmas,** the days between Christmas and **Epiphany**. Performances, parties, exhibitions, and entertainments of all kinds take place during these days.

Holy Innocents' Day

Filipinos observe December 28, **Holy Innocents' Day,** by playing practical jokes on one another. According to custom one cannot complain if one is fooled by a friend. In addition, anyone who succeeds in borrowing something on this day is not expected to give it back.

New Year

Filipinos often celebrate **New Year's** Eve at parties, discos, and balls. Many sport the paper party hats sold by countless roadside vendors in the preceding days. Polka-dotted clothes are also popular on New Year's Eve, since Filipino folklore teaches that anything round brings good luck for the new year. Filipinos celebrate New Year's Eve by making noise. Those who cannot lay their hands on firecrackers will beat on pots and pans. The noisemaking comes to a head at midnight. After midnight, many settle down to a large meal. The menu often includes stuffed peppers, ham, and sweets. Cooks try to place as many round foods as possible on the table. Many Filipinos make sure to have grapes in the house on New Year's Eve. Following an old Spanish custom, they pop one grape into their mouth for each of the twelve chimes of the clock as it rings in the new year. Doing so ensures that they will have a sweet new year. Many also turn on every light in their home at midnight. According to Filipino folk belief, this will bring about a bright new year. Another folk belief teaches that those who stay home all day on New Year's Day will spend much time with their loved ones in the coming year. Many people take this advice and spend January 1 at home with their families.

Epiphany

Epiphany, January 6, signals the end of the Christmas season. In order to bring the holiday season to a close a little more quickly, however, the holiday is often observed on the first Sunday of January. Some families follow the Spanish custom of putting the children's **shoes** near a door or window on Epiphany Eve, so that the Wise Men, or **Magi**, can fill them with candies and trinkets. Others distribute candies and trinkets to the children themselves. Many towns sponsor parades that reenact the Three King's journey to Bethlehem. Riding on horseback in splendid costumes, the kindly kings often toss coins and sweets to the children who have come to see the parade. Churches, too, offer similar pageants portraying the arrival of the Three Kings at the manger in Bethlehem.

Further Reading

Christmas in the Philippines. Chicago: World Book, 1990.

MacDonald, Margaret Read, ed. *The Folklore of World Holidays*. Detroit, Mich.: Gale Research, 1992.

Plough Monday

In past centuries the people of rural **England** observed the **Twelve Days of Christmas** with rest and recreation. Daily tasks resumed after **Epiphany**. Women returned to their spinning the day after Epiphany, dubbed **St. Distaff's Day**. Men took up their ploughs again on the first Monday after Epiphany, which was called Plough Monday.

In earlier times Plough Monday marked the beginning of "Plough-tide," one of the four agricultural seasons recognized by both folk and Church custom. After having lain fallow during the coldest, darkest months of the year, the earth was ready to be turned over in preparation for the sowing of the spring harvest. In the sixteenth century English writer Thomas Tusser (1524-1580) commemorated this return to the plough in verse:

> Plough Monday, next after that Twelftide is past
> bids out with the plough, the worst husband is last
> [Hutton, 1996, 126].

History

The earliest records of Plough Monday date back to medieval times. In those days ploughmen organized themselves into guilds, associations of men working the same trade. Plough guilds or other farming associations often kept a light burning in front of an image in the local church, which was believed to confer blessings on all those who plied the trade. It appears that some groups stored a communal plough in the church as well. On Plough Monday bands of plough-men collected money to keep these "plough lights" burning. Some pulled a plough in procession throughout the community while others collected coins from the populace. In addition, some writers suggest that in medieval times ploughs were blessed on Plough Monday.

In the sixteenth century the changes in religious thinking brought about by the Reformation partially halted these practices (*see also*

Puritans). Many reformers condemned plough lights and plough blessings as a form of superstition and therefore forbade them. Plough processions persisted, however, as a way of celebrating the beginning of a new agricultural cycle. The parading ploughmen continued to collect offerings as well, only now they put them towards their own amusement instead of some communal or religious purpose.

In the eighteenth and nineteenth centuries, those participating in these processions still dragged a plough throughout the community. They referred to it as a "fool plough" and often decorated it. The young men who participated in these processions were known by a variety of names, such as the plough boys, plough lads, plough jacks, plough bullocks, plough witches, or plough stots. They often blackened their faces and wore some kind of homemade costume. Frequently, one lad dressed as a woman, called Bessy, and another as a fool or clown. These two stock figures engaged in playful banter while the others, their clothing embellished with ribbons, patches, straw or other fanciful items, played along. The plough boys accepted food and drink as well as money, but threatened the householder who refused to give anything with the prospect of having his or her garden ploughed under. In some areas the lads enticed greater generosity from their audiences by performing **mummers'** plays and folk dances, such as sword dances and other kinds of morris dances.

Contemporary Customs

These practices finally died out in the late nineteenth and early twentieth centuries. The mid-twentieth century, however, witnessed a curious revival of religious customs surrounding Plough Monday. With the founding of the Council for Church and Countryside in 1943, a number of agriculturally oriented services from the medieval era were reintroduced into local worship. Some churches now observe the Blessing of the Plough on the Sunday before Plough Monday. In this ceremony farmers and others whose work is related to agriculture carry a plough up to the chancel steps where they and the plough are blessed "that the people of our land may be satisfied with bread." The congregation prays for the ploughmen and for all who "offer the work of the countryside to the service of God." In some areas local people have also revived the various folk celebrations associated with this day, such as morris dances and mummer's plays.

Further Reading

Brewster, H. Pomeroy. *Saints and Festivals of the Christian Church*. 1904. Reprint. Detroit, Mich.: Omnigraphics, 1990.

Chambers, Robert. "January 11 — Plough Monday." In his *The Book of Days*. Volume 1. 1862-64. Reprint. Detroit, Mich.: Omnigraphics, 1990.

Hole, Christina. *British Folk Customs*. London, England: Hutchinson and Company, 1976.

Howard, Alexander. *Endless Cavalcade*. London, England: Arthur Baker, 1964.

Hutton, Ronald. *The Stations of the Sun*. Oxford, England: Oxford University Press, 1996.

Plum Pudding
Christmas Pudding, Figgy Pudding

The traditional Christmas dinner in **England** ends with a dessert called plum pudding. This dish features a blend of dried fruit, spices, and other flavorings, such as lemon and orange peel, sugar, eggs, flour, and butter or suet. In spite of its name, plum pudding may or may not contain prunes or plums. The origins of this English Christmas favorite lie in medieval cooking techniques in which sugars, fruits, and spices were used to preserve and enhance the flavor of meat.

Medieval Cookery

The task of food preservation severely challenged medieval cooks since they did not have access to preservatives or reliable refrigeration. Instead, people employed sugars and spices to preserve meats and fish. Fresh and dried fruits were less expensive and easier to obtain than sugar or honey, so they were often used to flavor dishes. In England medieval cooks prepared large fruit, meat, and butter pies for wealthy families entertaining many guests at Christmas. Some researchers believe that the sweetness of the fruit covered the flavor of the aging meat. Enclosing the ingredients in a tough, airtight crust also helped to preserve them. Cooks achieved the same effect by adding sugars and spices to a common medieval dish known as pottage or porridge. This stew-like dish resulted from simmering all one's ingredients in a single pot. The well-to-do combined meats, spices, and fruits in their pottages. If a more solid dish was desired, cooks could produce a stiff pottage by adding thickeners such as bread crumbs, egg yolks, and ground almonds.

Plum Pottage

Although the popularity of most pottage dishes declined by the seventeenth century, one variation continued to thrive. It was known by the somewhat mysterious name of "stewed broth." Cooks created this pottage dish by boiling together meat, currants (a raisin-like dried fruit), spices, bread crumbs, and sandlewood (for coloring). By the late sixteenth century, cooks were tossing dried plums into the cooking pot. This innovation became so popular that stewed broth acquired the name "plum pottage," "plum broth," or "plum porridge." One old recipe suggested boiling beef or mutton in broth thickened with brown bread. After this combination had cooked for some time raisins, currants, prunes, cloves, mace, and ginger were added and the entire concoction boiled again. Another recipe instructed the cook to boil some beef and veal together with sherry, lemon juice, orange juice, sugar, raisins, currants, prunes, nutmeg, cinnamon, cloves, brown bread, and cochineal (a red dye). The resulting stew could be made weeks ahead of time. Diners consumed it as a first course rather than as a dessert. It became a Christmas favorite and was sometimes called "Christmas porridge."

During the seventeenth century the **Puritans** spoke out against many traditional English Christmas festivities. Many of them condemned the eating of plum porridge and **mincemeat pie** at Christmas time. Some saw it as a symbol of disgraceful gluttony. For others, the act of eating these foods symbolized allegiance to the pope and to Roman Catholicism, and so smacked of heresy. According to the Puritans, one writer of the day quipped, "Plum-broth was Popish, and mince-pie — O that was flat idolatry!" Catholics and Anglicans defended traditional English Christmas fare against these Puritan attacks. As Catholics and Protestants strove with one another to dominate England's political life during the seventeenth century, the consumption or avoidance of plum porridge at Christmas time was viewed by some as a sign not only of religious but also of political loyalties. One writer parodied the views of his more extreme Puritan contemporaries in the following lines:

> All plums the prophet's sons deny,
> And spice-broths are too hot;
> Treason's in a December pie,
> And death within the pot [Chambers, 1990, 2: 755].

The English continued to consume plum porridge with relish in spite of the brief period of Puritan rule in the mid-seventeenth century. In 1728 one foreigner who had experienced an English Christmas wrote: "Everyone from the King to the artisan eats soup and

Christmas pies. The soup is called Christmas porridge, and is a dish few foreigners find to their taste."

Plum Pudding

Plum porridge disappeared from the ranks of English Christmas fare in the early nineteenth century, supplanted by plum pudding. In 1823 another foreign observer of the English at Christmas time wrote that "probably there is not a single table spread on Christmas Day throughout the land — from the King's to the lowest artizan's that can scrape together enough to buy him a dinner at all — that is not furnished with roast beef and plum pudding." The dish proved so popular in the Devon village of Paignton that its citizens concocted a giant, communal pudding in 1819. It contained one hundred twenty pounds of raisins, an equal amount of suet, or beef fat, and four hundredweights of flour. When finished, the enormous pudding weighed nine hundred pounds.

Plum pudding evolved out of plum porridge sometime in the seventeenth or eighteenth centuries. Unlike its predecessor, it contained no meat, but did call for beef suet, or fat, as a thickener. Sugar might be added as well, as this commodity had become much less expensive and easier to obtain than in previous times. The sauce designed to accompany the pudding, a syrup made of such ingredients as butter, sugar and brandy, further enhanced the dish's sweetness. Indeed, unlike plum pottage, plum pudding was conceived of as a dessert.

A mid-eighteenth-century recipe called for currants, raisins, eggs, bread crumbs, nutmeg, and ginger. As this ingredient list reveals, some plum puddings contained neither prunes nor plums. This omission can be explained by the fact that sometime around the seventeenth century the word plum had come to be used as a general term referring to any dried fruit. Other writers point out that the word plum also used to mean "to swell" or "to plump up." They argue that the "plum" in plum pudding refers to the expansion that the dish undergoes when baked. In some areas of England plum pudding was known as "figgy pudding." People from these districts called raisins "figs," hence the raisin-rich plum pudding was called figgy pudding. Finally, plum pudding was thought to improve with age. One custom encouraged housewives to prepare their Christmas pudding by **Stir-Up Sunday**, approximately five weeks before Christmas.

Although the English considered plum pudding a special holiday dish before the nineteenth century, it wasn't adopted as the most fitting closure to the Christmas feast until that time. By the late nineteenth century, fashionable Victorian cooks were referring to plum pudding as Christmas pudding. It is unclear exactly what influenced the English to promote the dish to its new status. Perhaps the Christmas stories of Charles Dickens (1812-1870), which did much to encourage the Victorian revival of Christmas, inspired this change (*see also* **Christmas Carol, A; Victorian England, Christmas in**).

Another change in the nineteenth-century English Christmas was the decline of **Twelfth Night** celebrations. These celebrations featured an elaborate cake into which a pea, charm, or coin was baked. As the Twelfth Day cake fell out of favor, these objects found their way into the Christmas pudding. Today some still insert a coin into the Christmas pudding batter. It brings good luck to the diner who receives it in his or her portion of the pudding. One writer reports a more elaborate custom in which the cook adds a coin, ring, and thimble to the pudding batter. The coin represents worldly fortune; the ring, marriage; and the thimble, blessings to whoever receives them.

Further Reading

Black, Maggie. "The Englishman's Plum Pudding." *History Today* 31 (December 1981): 60-61.

Chambers, Robert. "December 25—Old English Christmas Fare." In his *The Book of Days*. Volume 2. 1862-64. Reprint. Detroit, Mich.: Omnigraphics, 1990.

Crippen, Thomas G. *Christmas and Christmas Lore*. 1923. Reprint. Detroit, Mich.: Omnigraphics, 1990.

Del Re, Gerard, and Patricia Del Re. *The Christmas Almanack*. Garden City, N.Y.: Doubleday, 1979.

Hottes, Alfred Carl. *1001 Christmas Facts and Fancies*. 1946. Reprint. Detroit, Mich.: Omnigraphics, 1990.

Muir, Frank. *Christmas Customs and Traditions*. New York: Taplinger, 1977.

Pimlott, J. A. R. *The Englishman's Christmas*. Atlantic Highlands, N.J.: Humanities Press, 1978.

Sansom, William. *A Book of Christmas*. New York: McGraw-Hill Book Company, 1968.

Plygain

The Plygain is a Welsh carol service originally held early on Christmas morning (*see also* **Wales, Christmas in**). The Welsh word "Plygain" comes from the Latin phrase *pulli cantus*, which means "cockcrow song." Originally, the service was scheduled for three a.m. to coincide with the crowing of the first rooster on Christmas morning (*see also* **Misa de Gallo**).

The Plygain seems to have evolved from the Roman Catholic **Midnight Mass** on Christmas Eve. During the Reformation religious authorities throughout Great Britain eliminated many Roman Catholic customs (*see also* **Puritans**). Nevertheless, Welsh historical records indicate that early morning Christmas services, called Plygains, were still being held in the seventeenth, eighteenth, and nineteenth centuries. These services, conducted by candlelight, included prayers, **Christmas carols**, and the occasional sermon. A widespread custom required each person who attended to bring a candle to help illuminate the dark church. Often the entire population of the parish attended, regardless of religious affiliation. In some places the people processed to the church with lighted candles or torches. Sometimes young people would stay up all night on Christmas Eve rather than get up early in the morning. They often passed the middle of the night at a local farmhouse singing, dancing, and amusing themselves.

The Plygain began to die out in the twentieth century. One researcher claims that it was discontinued because of the increasingly unruly behavior of those who chose to attend. In the few places in which the service survived, the inconvenient starting time of three a.m. shifted forward towards the morning or backwards towards the previous evening. Eventually, even the date of the service was changed. Today the Plygain takes place in only a few locales and may be scheduled anytime between mid-December and early January. It consists entirely of unaccompanied carol singing and no longer retains any element of religious observance.

Further Reading

Hole, Christina. *British Folk Customs*. London, England: Hutchinson and Company, 1976.

Hutton, Ronald. *The Stations of the Sun*. Oxford, England: Oxford University Press, 1996.

Poinsettia

Flor de la Nochebuena

The poinsettia originally hails from **Mexico**. The leaves that crown the end of each poinsettia stalk undergo a seasonal color change in December, turning from green to red. As Christianity spread across Mexico during the colonial era, this color change turned poinsettias into a popular Christmas decoration. The Mexicans call the plant *flor de la Nochebuena*, or "Christmas Eve flower."

A Mexican folktale explains this name. Many years ago on Christmas Eve a poor girl sought a **gift** to offer to the Christ child. She realized, however, that she owned nothing beautiful enough to give the infant. She began to cry, but eventually her desire to pay tribute to the child overcame her shame. She plucked a branch of an ordinary green plant that grew beside the road and humbly brought it to the manger. As she laid it beside the crib the leaves of the plant burst into a brilliant red in recognition of the child's humility and **Jesus'** pleasure with the gift.

The poinsettia's popularity in the United States can be traced back to the initial interest of one man, Dr. Joel Roberts Poinsett. Appointed the first U.S. ambassador to Mexico, Dr. Poinsett also maintained an interest in botany. While stationed in Mexico in 1825 he noticed a plant whose ordinary green leaves turned a brilliant red in December. Intrigued by these tongues of fire he sent samples home to South Carolina where he maintained a greenhouse. Other horticulturists soon adopted the plant. Botanists named the plant *Euphorbia pulcherrima*, but the public called it "poinsettia" in honor of the man who first imported it to the United States. By the last quarter of the nineteenth century New York shopkeepers were offering poinsettias at Christmas time. By the twentieth century Americans had fully adopted the plant as a **Christmas symbol**. The current popularity of the poinsettia as a Christmas decoration can be measured in numbers. In 2000 Americans bought more than 65 million of these potted plants.

The leaves of the poinsettia are very sensitive to light. During the darkest weeks of the year the leaves at the end of each stalk react to the shortage of sunlight by changing color. Although people commonly refer to the poinsettia's scarlet blooms as "flowers," in fact only the yellow buds at their centers are flowers. The red halos that surround them are composed of a special kind of leaf known as a bract.

Americans seem to favor red poinsettias as Christmas decorations, but other less well known varieties of the plant sport leaves that change from green to white, yellow, or pink. A number of these varieties were developed by the Ecke family. In the early part of this century Paul Ecke, a flower farmer located near Los Angeles, California, played a major role in developing new varieties of poinsettias and championing these hardier and more attractive plants as Christmas decorations. His cross-country promotional tours eventually paid off. Not only has the poinsettia become a Christmas symbol, but also the Ecke family farm, now located in Encinitas, California, continues to supply a large percentage of America's demand for the potted plants and the cuttings from which they grow (*see also* **Urban Legends**).

Further Reading

Christmas in Mexico. Chicago: World Book, 1976.

Christmas in the American Southwest. Chicago: World Book, 1996.

Comfort, David. *Just Say Noel.* New York: Fireside Books, 1995.

Del Re, Gerard, and Patricia Del Re. *The Christmas Almanack.* Garden City, N.Y.: Doubleday, 1979.

Hottes, Alfred Carl. *1001 Christmas Facts and Fancies.* 1946. Reprint. Detroit, Mich.: Omnigraphics, 1990.

Web Site

"Poinsettia: The Christmas Flower," an article by D. Michael Benson, et al., through the American Phytopathological Society, located in St. Paul, Minnesota. Published in the December 2000–January 2001 issue of their online journal, *APSnet,* at: http:www.apsnet.org/online/feature/xmasflower/

Poland, Christmas in

The people of Poland celebrate Christmas with many old folk and religious customs. A number of Polish Christmas customs make reference to the **Star of Bethlehem**. Indeed, the star is Poland's most popular **Christmas symbol**.

Christmas Eve Fast

Traditionally, Poles, following Roman Catholic teachings, have fasted on December 24. The first meal of the day was a meatless supper. The Poles made up for this, however, by permitting the Christmas Eve meal to be composed of up to twelve different dishes. According to folk tradition, Poles did not sit down to eat on Christmas Eve until the first star appeared in the sky. Around sunset children dashed outdoors to scan the sky for the first star, eager to begin the evening's festivities. When sighted, the star was referred to as the Star of Bethlehem.

Oplatek

Upon sitting down to their Christmas Eve supper, many Polish families observe the old tradition of sharing an *oplatek* between them. These small white wafers resemble Roman Catholic communion wafers. The father bids family members to be at peace with one another and breaks the wafer. Everyone present eats a piece of the broken wafer. So significant is this custom that families may even send absent members a broken oplatek so that they, too, may partake of the blessed wafer.

Animals

Polish folk tradition acknowledges the important role played by animals at the birth of **Jesus**. One old custom recommends strewing straw on the Christmas Eve table, as a reminder that Jesus was born in a stable (*see also* **Yule Straw**). Another advises that crumbled oplatek wafers be fed to barn animals on Christmas Eve, as a way of including them in the Christmas blessing.

Christmas Dinner

In Poland the Christmas Eve supper has a special name. It is called *Wigilia*, which means "vigil" in Polish. It may also be called the "star supper." Traditional Christmas Eve foods include carp or pike, almond soup (made from almonds, raisins, rice, and milk), beet soup, cabbage, and other vegetable and grain dishes. Poppyseed cake, ginger cake, and other pastries may be served for dessert. Polish folk tradition suggests setting a place at the table for the Christ child as well as places for any absent family members. The unused place settings remind diners of the spiritual presence of these absent guests.

Gifts and Carols

Other Christmas Eve activities include singing *kolendy*, or **Christmas carols**, opening **gifts**, and attending **Midnight Mass**. Poland's gift bringer is known as the "Star Man." Polish folk tradition teaches that he brings presents to children on Christmas Eve. The **star boys**, a group of carolers dressed as characters from the Nativity story and carrying a star-shaped lantern before them, often accompany the Star

Man. In past times the village priest sometimes dressed up as the Star Man and visited homes on Christmas Eve. This strict Star Man might quiz children on their knowledge of the Catholic catechism before handing out gifts. The star boys continue their activities throughout the **Twelve Days of Christmas**, the days between Christmas and **Epiphany**. They appear on street corners and doorsteps, singing Christmas carols and hoping to be offered coins and treats in return.

Fortune-Telling

Christmas Eve, and indeed the entire Twelve Days of Christmas, were once thought to be especially powerful days for fortune-telling. Many superstitions and charms offered advice on how to read one's future during these days. For example, the events that take place on Christmas Eve were thought to set the pattern for the coming year. Therefore people tried to eat well, give and receive generously, and act kindly. One folk belief declared that a sunny Christmas Eve meant that the year to come would bring fair weather. By contrast, another folk belief stated that a warm Christmas foretold a chilly Easter. Numerous folk charms taught young girls ways to predict their marital futures on Christmas Eve. For example, girls could hide straws underneath the Christmas Eve tablecloth and draw them out randomly. A green straw signified marriage in the near future, a withered straw foretold a period of waiting, a yellow straw meant spinsterhood, and a very short straw warned of an early death (*for a similar custom, see* **Lithuania, Christmas in**).

Christmas Trees, Nativity Scenes, Nativity Plays

Both **Christmas trees** and **Nativity scenes** may be found in Polish homes at Christmas time. The Polish city of Krakow sponsors a Nativity scene competition, which began in 1937 as a way of preserving an old folk tradition. Contestants in this competition must first make a model of Krakow's Wawel Cathedral and then place the manger scene on its doorstep. The winning entries are displayed in the Museum of Ethnography.

In past eras groups of boys performed **Nativity plays**, or *szopka*, during the Twelve Days of Christmas. These youngsters roamed towns and villages with homemade puppet theaters, performing folk plays loosely based on the events surrounding the birth of Jesus. With the boys' help, the puppets not only acted, but also sang, the story. The stage and backdrop for the puppets were usually designed to represent the manger in which Christ was born, thus these performances served as animated Nativity scenes. In Krakow the backdrop for the puppet shows often depicted Wawel Cathedral.

Epiphany

In Poland the **Christmas season** ends with Epiphany on January 6. On this day people blessed their homes by writing the initials of the Three Kings, or **Magi**, over their front doors with blessed chalk. These initials, KMB, come from the names most often associated with them in folklore: Kaspar (or Caspar), Melchior, and Balthasar.

Further Reading

Del Re, Gerard, and Patricia Del Re. *The Christmas Almanack*. Garden City, N.Y.: Doubleday, 1979.

Hubert, Maria, comp. *Christmas Around the World*. Stroud, Gloucestershire, England: Sutton, 1998.

MacDonald, Margaret Read, ed. *The Folklore of World Holidays*. Detroit, Mich.: Gale Research, 1992.

Spicer, Dorothy Gladys. *The Book of Festivals*. 1937. Reprint. Detroit, Mich.: Omnigraphics, 1990.

Web Site

A site sponsored by Internet Polska, a web site administrator for Polish government and travel agencies: http://www.polishworld.com/christmas/

Posadas, Las

During the nine days before Christmas, many Hispanic communities host a nightly procession known as Las Posadas. In Spanish *las posadas* means "the inns" or "the lodgings." According to this old Mexican custom, groups of children and adults reenact **Mary** and **Joseph**'s search for shelter in **Bethlehem**. Staging Las Posadas requires the coordination of many people. The event may be organized by a group of neighbors, families and friends, churches, or community organizations.

The Procession and Celebration

Las Posadas begins on the evening of December 16. Participants gather at a prearranged time and place, sometimes offering prayers before the event begins. Two youngsters are selected to play the roles of Joseph and Mary. These roles may be carried out in a variety of ways. In many places they hold images of Joseph and Mary before them as they lead the procession out into the street. These images are called *misterios*, or "mysteries." In other places the children acting as Joseph and Mary dress the part, donning robes that evoke the biblical era. In rural villages Mary may ride upon a donkey. In some locales a child dressed as an **angel** clears the way for the Holy Couple. Participants file out in procession behind Mary and Joseph, carrying candles and singing Christmas songs.

The procession dramatizes Joseph and Mary's search for a place to spend the night in Bethlehem, an event suggested in chapter two of the **Gospel according to Luke**. In Las Posadas the couple must be refused shelter at least once before a kind innkeeper finally takes them in. Joseph and Mary lead the procession through the streets to the first house. Joseph knocks on the door and begs shelter for the night. He often chants this request in rhymed verse. The homeowner has agreed in advance to participate in the event, playing the role of the innkeeper. He or she comes to the door, but refuses Joseph's request. Joseph and Mary turn away into the night, leading the procession to another house. The organizers may arrange many refusals or only one. Sometimes the first innkeeper experiences a change a heart after Joseph explains their situation and reveals their identities. In any case, Joseph and Mary finally encounter a family that graciously welcomes them, and their entourage, into the house. This family will host the evening's entertainment.

Before the arrival of the procession the hosts prepare a **Nativity scene** or altar with room for the images that the children carry. When the entire procession has entered the house Mary and Joseph come forward, putting the statues in the places reserved for them. This act, and the accompanying prayer, concludes the procession and the party begins. The hosts offer traditional Mexican sweets, such as tamales, *bizcochitos* (sugar cookies) and such beverages as spiced hot chocolate to their guests. The evening's entertainments usually include music, dancing, a candy-filled *piñata* for the children, and sometimes fireworks.

Las Posadas may be enacted in a variety of ways, depending on local traditions as well as on limitations of time, space, money, and personnel. In the old days, processions took place on each of the nine nights preceding Christmas. Today, many groups stage only one procession on the last of the nine nights, Christmas Eve. Although traditionally the pilgrims marched through the streets, Las Posadas has been adapted to fit new living situations. In some areas, Mary and Joseph wend their way down the halls of apartment buildings. In others they graciously include the corridors of nursing homes in their trek.

History

In many ways Las Posadas resembles the old European custom of Christmas time **mumming**. Most writers trace its historical roots back to the medieval European mystery or miracle plays, however (*see also* **Nativity Play**). These plays taught Bible stories and religious doctrine to a largely illiterate people. They began sometime around the tenth and eleventh centuries as simple enactments of the liturgy performed in churches by the clergy. As the plays became more complex and entertaining, audiences grew. Eventually, folk performers began to stage them in public arenas. Many changes deemed undesirable by the clergy accompanied this shift. These innovations caused the Church to ban these performances in the fifteenth century.

Nevertheless, dramatizing biblical stories had proved an effective means of communicating religious ideas. In the sixteenth century two Spanish saints created a new kind of religious ceremony to accompany the Christmas holiday. St. Ignatius Loyola (1491-1556) proposed that special prayers be offered on each of the nine days before Christmas. This type of religious observance, known as a novena, found favor with St. John of the Cross (1542-1591), who added a religious pageant to the event. Spanish missionaries brought this custom to **Mexico** in the sixteenth century where they used it to teach the story of **Jesus'** birth to the native people they found there. As these ceremonies were organized by Church officials, they were at first very religious and quite somber. Gradually, the people themselves began to organize the event, and a lighter, more festive mood began to emerge.

Observances in U.S. Cities

From Mexico Las Posadas spread south to El Salvador, **Guatemala**, Honduras, and Nicaragua, and north to the United States. In the latter, many impressive observances of Las Posadas can be found throughout the southwestern states. In Albuquerque, New Mexico, a number of Roman Catholic churches organize traditional nine-night Posadas. Different families host the celebrations during the first eight nights, then the churches themselves hold the party on Christmas Eve. The city of San Antonio, Texas, stages a Posadas procession along the river that attracts thousands of people. Mariachi musicians, choral ensembles, and ordinary citizens follow behind Mary and Joseph. **Luminarias**, or small bonfires, light the parade route. The crowd rejoices when the Holy Family finally finds lodging. Afterwards the city hosts a party for children in a nearby plaza.

Further Reading

Bragdon, Allen D. *Joy Through the World*. New York: Dodd, Mead, and Company, 1985.
Christmas in Mexico. Chicago: World Book, 1976.

Christmas in the American Southwest. Chicago: World Book, 1996.

MacDonald, Margaret Read, ed. *Folklore of World Holidays.* Detroit, Mich.: Gale Research, 1992.

Milne, Jean. *Fiesta Time in Latin America.* Los Angeles, Calif.: Ward Ritchie Press, 1965.

Ribera Ortega, Pedro. *Christmas in Old Santa Fe.* Second edition. Santa Fe, N.M.: Sunstone Press, 1973.

Puritans

In the sixteenth century a religious reform movement surged across Europe. The leaders of this movement, known as the Reformation, sought to abolish Church practices they deemed inconsistent with scripture. The Reformation gave birth to Protestant Christianity and to the many different sects and denominations that fall under that heading. In Britain it inspired the formation of a number of sects, one of which was known as the Puritans.

The Puritans advocated a "purified" form of worship, stripped of traditional embellishments such as organ music, choir singing, ecclesiastical robes, and church decorations. Puritan ministers wore street clothes while presiding over simplified services in plain churches.

Throughout the sixteenth century British Puritans lobbied for Church reform. The majority of high-ranking officials in the Church of England opposed them, however, as did Queen Elizabeth I and her Stuart successors. In the early seventeenth century, small groups of English Puritans sought religious freedom by immigrating to America. There they founded Plymouth Colony and, later, Massachusetts Bay Colony (*see also* **America, Christmas in Colonial; England, Christmas in**).

By the mid-seventeenth century, Puritan forces had gained the upper hand in British politics and succeeded in ousting the king. During the years in which they dominated the political scene, the Puritans legislated a number of religious and social reforms forcing English society to conform to their beliefs. They directed some of these reforms toward the celebration of Christmas.

Campaign Against Christmas

Before coming to power Puritan leaders had preached against what they viewed as irreverent and excessive Christmas customs. For example, in 1583 Philip Stubbes published a pamphlet titled *Anatomie of Abuses*, detailing what he viewed as the offensive behaviors with which the English celebrated Christmas. To his mind, a season marked by masking, **mumming,** theater-going, **games**, gambling, feasting, and dancing, as well as by an increased number of sexual encounters and robberies could hardly be said to honor Christ (*see also* **Masques**). Puritans also objected to the drinking, gaming, fortune-telling, and carousing that characterized New Year's Eve celebrations, and declared prayer and self-examination to be the most appropriate ways to commemorate the holiday (*see also* **Resolutions; Watch Night**).

By the mid-1600s, however, Puritan critics had gone from attacking excesses associated with Christmas to attacking the holiday itself. Between 1644 and 1659 the Puritan majority in Parliament attempted to abolish the celebration of Christmas. They pointed out that the Bible neither gives the date of **Jesus'** birth nor requests that people honor it (*see also* **Jesus, Year of Birth**). According to their way of thinking, this meant that Christmas should be eliminated. Many Puritan leaders condemned those who disagreed with them as enemies of the Christian religion. For example, in 1656 one Hezekiah Woodward published a pamphlet whose title revealed, at length, his scorn for Christmas and those who observed it. It read:

> Christ-Mas Day, The old Heathens feasting Day, in honour to Saturn their Idol-God, the Papists Massing Day, the Prophane man's Ranting Day, the Superstitious man's Idol Day. The Multitudes Idle Day, Satans, that Adversarys Working Day, The True Christian Mans Feasting Day. Taking to Heart, the Heathenish Customes, Popish Superstitions, Ranting Fashions, Fearful Provocations, Horrible Abominations, committed against the Lord, and His Christ, on that Day and days following [Pimlott, 1978, 53-54].

Puritan leaders in Parliament did more than just speak out against Christmas. In 1642 they banned the performance of plays at Christmas. In the year 1644 Christmas fell on the last Wednesday in December. The law ordered that people fast and do penance on the last Wednesday in the month. The Puritans saw to it that no exception would be made for Christmas. In London people ignored the edict, and shops closed as usual for Christmas Day. The following year the Puritan Parliament outlawed the religious observance of Christmas altogether, forbidding special church services in honor of the day. This change led one observer to comment wryly: "O blessed Reformation! . . . the church doors all shut and the tavern doors all open!" Handfuls of the traditionally devout defied the ban and sought out priests who quietly continued to offer services on Christmas Day. Yet even such sober celebrations involved a calculated risk. On Christmas Day in 1657 soldiers burst into one London church in the middle of the Christmas service and arrested all present.

Active Resistance

In 1647 Parliament took the final step. It outlawed the secular celebration of Christmas and many other Christian feast days as well. This time the edict met with active resistance, leading in some instances to violent clashes with officers of the law. In an effort to enforce the ban, town criers were ordered to ride through the streets shouting, "No Christmas! No Christmas!" Some London shops ignored the new law and closed on Christmas Day. Others remained open, drawing angry crowds to their doorstep.

Officers of the law were summoned to remove the **greenery** from several London churches, and sullen crowds booed the Lord Mayor when he appeared before them. A riot in Ipswich resulted in the loss of life. Oxford mobs rioted as well, though they were somewhat luckier, reporting only broken skulls. In Canterbury men defied the ban by playing ball games in the street, thereby frustrating the mayor's attempt to open the market. Eventually, the mayor was tossed to the ground, and in the general mayhem prisoners were rescued from the town jail. Twelve shops did open their doors to do business on that day, but menacing onlookers tossed their wares roughly about, encouraging them to close. Ten thousand men of Kent and Canterbury resolved to defend their holiday in a public declaration threatening that if they could not observe Christmas Day under the current government, then they would see the king put back on his throne.

Passive Resistance

In spite of this outburst of opposition, subsequent Christmases saw few open confrontations. Historians believe, however, that behind closed doors many English families continued to celebrate a private Christmas, consisting of a day's rest, a festive meal, and family merriment. Indeed, throughout the period in which both the religious and secular observance of the day were banned, many London shops continued to close on Christmas Day. In 1656 attendance in Parliament dipped notably on December 25. Presumably the defaulters were at home, celebrating Christmas.

Even these private, home celebrations did not escape Puritan criticism. Not only did Puritans object to those who observed Christmas by not working, attending religious services, and enjoying traditional entertainments, some strongly disapproved of traditional Christmas foods as well. To extremists certain foods, such as **mincemeat pie** and **plum pudding**, took on political connotations. Resisting them signified one's loyalty to the current regime; indulging in them revealed royalist or Roman Catholic sympathies. These traditional Christmas treats proved difficult to resist, though, even for Puritans. In 1652 Puritan authorities accused one of their own, a preacher named Hugh Peters, of speaking against the celebration of Christmas in his sermons and then eating two mincemeat pies for supper.

Scotland

In Scotland Puritanism took greater hold of both the laity and clergy. John Knox (1513-1572), leader of the Scottish Reformation and founder of the Presbyterian Church, opposed all church festivals. In 1561 the Scottish national assembly eliminated Christmas along with many other Christian feast days. In the years that followed, local authorities attempted to enforce this law. Historical records show that in the year 1574 fourteen women from Aberdeen were arrested and tried for dancing and singing carols on Christmas Eve (*see also* **Christmas Carols**). A baker found himself before local authorities for having thrown a **New Year's** Eve party at which he reportedly cried, "**Yule,** Yule, Yule." Others were punished for not working on Christmas Day. Nevertheless, thirty years later, shortly after the turn of the seventeenth century, some people still resisted the elimination of the old festivities.

Religious authorities repeatedly condemned the little bursts of midwinter revelry that took place in their towns. In 1606 clergymen in Aberdeen felt again compelled to denounce those who at Christmas or New Year's donned costumes, wore the clothing of the opposite sex, or danced with **bells**, whether in the streets or in private homes. By the 1640s authorities began to turn their attention towards quelling home celebrations of the holiday. In 1659 one especially severe minister named Murdoch Mackenzie went to extreme lengths to enforce this ban. He undertook a house to house search on Christmas Day to make sure that none of his parishioners were enjoying a private Christmas goose.

The Return of the Monarchy

In 1660 Parliament restored the monarchy and King Charles II assumed the British throne. King Charles restored all the old holidays, including Christmas. Many historians believe, however, that English Christmas celebrations never quite recovered their former luster. Indeed, the British never revived a number of old Christmas traditions, such as masques and the raucous revelry associated with the **Lord of Misrule**. In Scotland the Puritan attempt to abolish Christmas succeeded more completely. New Year's Day replaced Christmas as the principal winter holiday in that region (*see also* **Hogmanay**).

Conclusion

American journalist H. L. Mencken (1880-1956) once defined Puritanism as "the haunting fear that someone, somehow, may be happy." After reviewing the history of the Puritan campaign against Christmas, many contemporary Americans might agree with him. In order to gain a fuller understanding of what motivated the Puritans to cancel Christmas, one must consider the religious and political climate of the times. Puritan leaders sincerely believed that they were restoring their country to the true Christian faith. Moreover, in Reformation Europe politics and religion fused together to form a single system of rule. Each country's leader customarily chose that nation's religion, making religious dissent tantamount to political rebellion. Political authorities could, and did, imprison, persecute, and execute citizens for their religious beliefs. Depending on who was in power, both Protestants and Catholics suffered from this climate of intolerance. Viewed in this context, the Puritan crusade against Christmas can be seen as one of the era's typical, if by our standards eccentric, attempts to compel ordinary citizens to adopt the religious beliefs of those in power.

Further Reading

Hutton, Ronald. *The Rise and Fall of Merry England.* Oxford, England: Oxford University Press, 1984.

———. *The Stations of the Sun.* Oxford, England: Oxford University Press, 1996.

Miles, Clement A. *Christmas in Ritual and Tradition.* 1912. Reprint. Detroit, Mich.: Omnigraphics, 1990.

Pimlott, J. A. R. *The Englishman's Christmas.* Atlantic Highlands, N.J.: Humanities Press, 1978.

Putz

A putz is a kind of **Nativity scene**, that is, a representation of the scene of **Jesus'** birth. Putzes are most often found in towns that harbor a community of Moravians. Moravians represent a very old branch of Protestant Christianity; they are also known as the Unity of Brethren or the *Unitas Fratrum.* This denomination traces its roots back to central Europe and, indeed, many of the Moravians who emigrated to the United States in the eighteenth century were German speakers from that region. Thus they called their Nativity scenes *putz* (pronounced "pootz"), from the German verb *putzen,* which means "to decorate." Many Moravians settled in eastern Pennsylvania. Thus, putzes are more common there than in other parts of the country.

Possible Origins

The Moravian American putz may have been inspired by the Christmas gardens erected by many central Europeans in the 1700s (*for more on Christmas gardens, see* **Christmas Village**). The Christmas garden, usually constructed underneath the **Christmas tree**, consisted of a miniature village enclosed within a fence. Families delighted in organizing a Lilliputian community under their tree, complete with miniature barns, houses, and shops. Some of these villages contained a Nativity scene within them; others did not. The Christmas garden was particularly popular in **Poland** and the German-speaking countries.

Moravian Putzes

Among American Moravians putz building can be traced back to the late eighteenth century. Moravians built putzes in their churches and their homes. They often constructed their putzes under the Christmas tree, but also set them up against a backdrop of evergreens or placed them on tabletops covered with **greenery**. Though the magical, miniature landscape usually contained a Nativity scene, the holy figures were often embedded among a wealth of other details, such as hills, streams, flocks of sheep, mill-houses, barking dogs, homes, shops, craftsmen and women plying their trades, carriages, churches, farms, barns, old men smoking pipes, glassy lakes, waterfalls, snow-capped mountains, caves, and all manner of fish, fowl, and animals. Noah's ark and the pairs of attendant animals often made their appearance in the putz as well. People who built putzes invested a lot of time and energy into giving their landscapes a life-like appearance. They gathered real moss and other greenery to cover the hills and fields, sprinkled sand along their lakefronts to create beaches, and illuminated their buildings from within with tiny candles. Some devotees created miniature mechanical devices to turn mill wheels and make water flow in streams.

In nineteenth-century Moravian homes children were not allowed to view the putz until Christmas Eve. The putz stayed up from Christmas to **Epiphany**. In the late nineteenth and early twentieth centuries, Moravian residents of **Bethlehem, Pennsylvania**, celebrated this period of time, the **Twelve Days of Christmas**, with parties and visits. Putz-viewing parties became popular by 1850. In eastern Pennsylvania, non-Moravians began to take an interest in putzes. According to an 1858 newspaper article describing Christmas in Lititz,

Pennsylvania (a town with a large Moravian community), complete strangers might show up on one's doorstep and ask to see the putz.

As the tradition of putz building developed, the putzes tended to get larger and larger, and people began to compete to see who could build the biggest and best. Some putzes took up entire rooms and contained dozens, if not hundreds, of figures.

Today both large and small putzes can still be found in Moravian churches and homes. Some church putzes contain figures representing the entire Christmas story, from the prophecies of Isaiah to the **Annunciation**, Nativity, and **Flight into Egypt**.

The town of Bethlehem, Pennsylvania—founded by Moravians— builds several community putzes each year at the town's Moravian churches. This custom came about in the 1930s after one particularly successful putz-building family, that of Edward Neisser, had 1,000 people knock on their door during the **Christmas season**, asking to see their putz. Neisser suggested that the town build a community putz for the public to enjoy and the chamber of commerce took him up on that suggestion in 1937.

Related Customs

During the 1940s and 1950s, when toy train sets were an extremely popular gift for boys, the custom of setting up a toy train under the Christmas tree attained a certain degree of popularity. Some folklorists view this practice as an outgrowth of putz building. They also recognize similarities between the old Moravian custom of putz building and the more recent hobby of collecting and displaying miniature, ceramic Christmas villages.

Further Reading

King, Constance. *Christmas Antiques, Decorations and Traditions*. Woodbridge, Suffolk, England: Antiques Collectors Club, 1999.

Marling, Karal Ann. *Merry Christmas!* Cambridge, Mass.: Harvard University Press, 2000.

Shoemaker, Alfred L. *Christmas in Pennsylvania*. Kutztown, Pa.: Pennsylvania Folklore Society, 1959.

Sweitzer, Vangie Roby. *Christmas in Bethlehem*. Bethlehem, Pa.: Central Moravian Church, 2000.

Web Sites

"The Putz," a page from the Moravian Church in America's web site at: http://www.moravian.org/faq/putz.html

An explanation of the Moravian Christmas putz offered by the East Hills Moravian Church, located in Bethlehem, Pennsylvania: http://easthillsmc. org/putz.html

Pyramid

Ceppo, Lichtstock, Lightstock, Weihnachtspyramide

A Christmas pyramid is a triangular or pyramidal structure made up of shelves of unequal lengths joined along their outside edges by supporting posts or poles. Christmas decorations are displayed on each shelf, with the lowest and longest shelf often reserved for a **Nativity scene**. Family and friends may arrange apples, cookies, nuts, small **gifts**, evergreen branches, **Christmas cards**, stars, figurines, candles, flags, and other embellishments across the other shelves according to their taste. A star or pinecone often adorns the apex of the pyramid. In one variation of the pyramid popular in central Europe several centuries ago, a propeller sits atop a pyramid shaped like a tall, round, layer cake. A central axis pole supporting the propeller runs through each of three circular shelves. Rising heat currents from the candles on the shelves below cause the propeller to spin, which in turn causes the axis to spin and the layers of the pyramid to rotate.

Several authors view the candles as the most important **ornaments** on the pyramid and suggest that the decorated pyramid serves as an elaborate candlestick. Indeed, one German name for this structure, *Lichtstock*, means "light stick." Some authorities maintain, however, that the Lichtstock was a simple pole covered with evergreens bearing a single candle. They offer *Weihnachtspyramide* as the German term for the Christmas pyramid. The Italians call the pyramid a *ceppo*, which means "log." Some explain this odd name by noting that the ceppo, with its glowing candles, replaced the burning of the **Yule log** in **Italy**.

The Christmas pyramid originated in **Germany** and became a popular Christmas tradition by the seventeenth century. In early times, the pyramid was hung from the ceiling. Families garnished their pyramids with candles and figurines, for example, of soldiers and **angels**. Along with the **paradise tree**, the pyramid stands as a possible ancestor to the modern **Christmas tree**.

From Germany the use of pyramids spread to central Europe, Italy, and **England**. German settlers brought the custom to America. As early as 1747 Moravian communities in Pennsylvania were celebrating Christmas with decorated pyramids. By contrast, the first American Christmas tree dates only as far back as the early 1800s (*see also* **America, Christmas in Nineteenth-Century; Bethlehem, Pennsyvania, Christmas in**).

In Germany the Christmas tree began to replace the pyramid in the seventeenth and eighteenth centuries. The exploding popularity of the Christmas tree in the nineteenth century contributed to the declining use of the Christmas pyramid in many countries. The Italians maintained the tradition of the Christmas ceppo, perhaps because they never adopted the Christmas tree.

In Erzgebirge, a region of Germany famous for its mining industry, miners began carving fancy wooden pyramids in the nineteenth century. The miners had already developed a tradition of carving wooden candlesticks in the shape of miners and angels. The miners represented the men of the region, while the angels represented the women. Families placed groupings of these candlesticks in their windows at Christmas time, displaying one miner for every boy child in the family and one angel for every girl child. Similar wooden figurines eventually began to populate the shelves of their Christmas pyramids. Miners, Christmas trees, and scenes from the Nativity story, whirled round and round on the propeller-topped shelves. Today villages in Erzgebirge build large, motorized community pyramids, vying with one another to see which locale produces the most impressive display.

Further Reading

Del Re, Gerard, and Patricia Del Re. *The Christmas Almanack*. Garden City, N.Y.: Doubleday, 1979.

Foley, Daniel J. *The Christmas Tree*. Philadelphia, Pa.: Chilton Company, 1960.

Russ, Jennifer M. *German Festivals and Customs*. London, England: Oswald Wolff, 1982.

Sterbenz, Carol Endler, and Nancy Johnson. *The Decorated Tree*. New York: Harry N. Abrams, 1982.

Web Site

The German Embassy in Washington, D.C., offers a page describing the Christmas pyramid on its web site at: http://www.germany-info.org/xmas/ch_15.html

Reindeer

The natural habitat of the reindeer, or Arctic deer, spans the northernmost reaches of **Russia**, Siberia, and the Scandinavian countries. Reindeer also roam across Canada, where they are known as caribou. Reindeer differ from other deer not only in their capacity to withstand cold, but also in the fact that both male and female animals grow antlers. Until the twentieth century an indigenous people of northern Scandinavia called the Sami made their living primarily as reindeer herders. These reindeer facts, however, cannot by themselves explain how these unfamiliar animals were drafted into contemporary American Christmas lore.

Santa's Reindeer

The idea that **Santa Claus** drives a sleigh pulled by flying reindeer is usually credited to one man's flight of fancy. In 1822 Clement C. Moore (1779-1863), a classics professor at General Theological Seminary, wrote a poem for children entitled "A Visit from St. Nicholas."

This poem, officially published in 1844, did much to establish the legend and lore of Santa Claus in the United States (*see also* **Elves** and **North Pole**). In it Moore assigns eight flying reindeer the task of pulling Santa's toy-laden sleigh. Moreover, he gave these animals names: Dasher, Dancer, Prancer, Vixen, Comet, Cupid, Donder, and Blitzen. Moore encoded his own private joke in these last two names. Donder means "thunder" in Dutch, and Blitzen means "lightning" in German.

How did Moore come up with this unusual reindeer imagery? Certainly **St. Nicholas**, who might be considered Santa's European predecessor, never resorted to such an unusual mode of conveyance (*see also* **St. Nicholas's Day**). No definitive answer can be given to this question, although researchers have made a number of speculations. One writer points out that the year before Moore wrote "A Visit from St. Nicholas," one William Gilley published a poem that depicts "santeclause" driving a sleigh pulled by flying reindeer. Moore may have read this poem and simply borrowed the idea from this little-known work. Others have suggested that Moore was inspired by an image from old Norse mythology in which Thor, the thunder god, rides a flying chariot pulled by the magical goats, Gnasher and Cracker. It may also be that Moore paired Santa with the exotic reindeer in order to suggest that he came from a remote land in the far northern reaches of the world.

Rudolph the Red-Nosed Reindeer

In the early twentieth century an ordinary department store worker added a new reindeer to Santa's team. Robert L. May, an employee at Montgomery Ward, wrote a poem entitled "Rudolph the Red-Nosed Reindeer" in 1939. The store printed the poem and distributed it to children as a sales gimmick.

Written to appeal to children, the poem tells the story of a young reindeer who was rejected by his playmates for being different. The rejected youth, named Rudolph, had a large, shiny, red nose while all the other reindeers had small black noses. One very misty Christmas Eve, however, Santa discovers that the shiny red nose gives off enough light to help him sail safely through the murky night skies. Once the other reindeer realize Rudolph's nose is a valuable asset they befriend the once lonely youngster.

Almost two and one-half million copies of the poem were sent home with shoppers in 1939, and more than three and one-half million in 1946, when Montgomery Ward reprinted May's work. The store then released the copyright on the poem back to the author, who published it in a book for children.

In 1949 a friend of May's named Johnny Marks composed a song based on the story told in the poem. In its first year on the market Rudolph fans bought two million copies of the song. Entitled, like the poem, "Rudolph the Red-Nosed Reindeer," it remains a popular, contemporary Christmas tune, which has now been recorded hundreds of times. In the decades following publication of the poem and the song, Rudolph's fame continued to spread. His story has been told in 25 different languages, and has even been made into a network television special. In addition, hundreds of Christmas knickknacks now bear his image.

Further Reading

Del Re, Gerard, and Patricia Del Re. *The Christmas Almanack*. Garden City, N.Y.: Doubleday, 1979.

Restad, Penne. *Christmas in America*. New York: Oxford University Press, 1995.

Resolutions

Many Americans begin the new year by resolving to change something about their lives. The most common resolutions seem to involve losing weight, quitting smoking, getting more exercise, spending more time with loved ones, improving one's finances, and lowering stress. Relatively few people manage to keep these resolutions. Many complain that the tradition of making **New Year's** resolutions compels them to start the year with a struggle likely to end in failure and corresponding feelings of guilt. How did such a stressful custom come to be associated with the celebration of the new year?

History

The New Year's resolution developed among the **Puritans**, an early Protestant Christian sect whose teachings emphasized the need for self-discipline, morality, self-examination, and religious conversion. Puritan leaders found fault with the way in which most people celebrated Christmas and New Year's. They criticized the heavy drinking, public carousing, gaming, masquerades, gambling, and dancing that took place on New Year's Eve. They urged their followers to abandon these coarse practices and to instead devote the occasion to self-examination and prayer. Devout Puritans observed the new year by searching their souls, pledging to change their ways, and putting themselves right with God. In the eyes of committed Puritans, the turning of the year—which seems to bring with it a heightened awareness of the passing of time and our eventual deaths—provided a natural occasion to review one's life and amend it for the better.

In the eighteenth and nineteenth centuries, evangelical Protestant groups that grew out of the Puritan movement continued to criticize excessive New Year's Eve festivities. Ardent members of these groups marked the arrival of the new year with pious resolutions. Religious studies professor Leigh Eric Schmidt has recorded several of these resolutions in his book *Consumer Rites*. On New Year's Eve in 1846 a woman named Frances Quick resolved to "begin the New Year with prayerful petitions." She continued:

> I feel firm, strong, resolute tonight. I will not seek to glean pleasure from the coming year, or reap selfish and mercenary advantage from it; but will go forth in the strength of God to conquer my own weaknesses, improve the powers which he has given me, and make it my daily study to find some avenue of usefulness to others [Schmidt, 1995, 118].

Evangelical Christians began to hold New Year's Eve **Watch Night** services to facilitate the formation of spiritual resolutions such as these and to provide an alternative to the frivolous and often drunken activities that continued to characterize the holiday. These two visions for the holiday, the one sober and religious and the other raucous and secular, contended with one another throughout the nineteenth century (*see also* **First Night**).

Modern Resolutions

According to Schmidt, the New Year's Eve resolution as we know it came about in the early twentieth century when the evangelical Christian custom of making a pious resolution moved out into the broader culture, stripped of its religious content. People began to resolve to improve themselves in various ways — not necessarily spiritual or religious — in the coming year. Often these resolutions had to do with improving one's health.

In the mid-nineteenth century Frances Quick called on "the strength of God to conquer [her] own weaknesses." The contemporary custom of making a New Year's resolution still revolves around the desire to conquer one's weaknesses, but does not necessarily retain the reference to God. Many interpret the practice instead as a challenge to their own individual willpower. Advertisers are quick to remind us of the dangers of relying on individual willpower alone, however. Weight reduction programs, gyms, and other companies whose services might help us attain our most common goals flood the market with advertisements each January, hoping to profit from our need for help in carrying out our New Year's resolutions (*see also* **Commercialism**).

Further Reading

Schmidt, Leigh Eric. *Consumer Rites: The Buying and Selling of American Holidays*. Princeton, N.J.: Princeton University Press, 1995.

Réveillon

The French celebrate Christmas Eve with an elaborate meal called *réveillon* (pronounced ray-veh-YON). *Réveillon* means "awakening" in French. This banquet usually takes place after attending **Midnight Mass** on Christmas Eve. In past times people may have savored réveillon even more than they do today because it signaled the end of the four-week **Advent** fast.

Réveillon in France

Although in **France** some people choose to celebrate réveillon in restaurants, most opt to feast at home. Many invite extended family members and guests to their table. To sustain themselves through the long church services, the family often takes a light snack in the early evening. Small children may be put to bed for a few hours before the evening's activities begin. When families dine at home, the women usually cook and serve the food. This may include washing dishes between courses in order to serve each on a clean plate.

Special preparations set the tone for an elegant celebration. The table sparkles with candles, polished silverware, and a Christmas centerpiece. The family's best tablecloth lies underneath. Much work in the kitchen must take place before the diners sit down, since the meal may consist of up to fifteen courses. Several wines accompany the meal, and toasts are offered throughout. The feast often begins with oysters or other shellfish. In Paris common réveillon dishes include goose liver pâté, roast turkey or roast goose stuffed with prunes and pâté, special preparations of potatoes and vegetables, cheese, fruit, nuts, and for dessert, *bûche de Noël* (Christmas log), a special chocolate, cream-filled cake shaped like a log.

Other regions maintain their own traditional Christmas Eve menus. In the southern region of Provence a choice of thirteen desserts greets diners at the end of the meal, one for **Jesus** and each of the twelve apostles. Typical desserts include fresh and dried fruits, such as figs, dates, pears, and oranges, marzipan, sweet bread, and cookies.

Réveillon in the United States and Canada

The tradition of the réveillon supper traveled with French colonists to the Americas. In the nineteenth century New Orleans's French population continued to celebrate Christmas Eve with attendance at Midnight Mass followed by réveillon dinners at home. Today many prominent New Orleans restaurants attract diners with sumptuous réveillon menus. The French Canadians of Quebec also inherited the tradition of coming home to réveillon supper after Midnight Mass. A traditional réveillon menu in Quebec consists of *la tourtière* (a meat pie), a stew of meat balls and pork, minced pork pie, oyster or pea soup, a variety of sauces and relishes, and several desserts. Traditional réveillon desserts include pastries, candies, fruitcake, sugar pie, cornmeal cake, doughnuts, ice cream, and bûche de Noël.

Further Reading

Christmas in Canada. Chicago: World Book, 1994.

Del Re, Gerard, and Patricia Del Re. *The Christmas Almanack*. Garden City, N.Y.: Doubleday, 1979.

Ross, Corinne Madden. *Christmas in France*. Lincolnwood, Ill.: Passport Books, 1991.

Robin

The robin appears on **Christmas cards, ornaments,** and other Christmas decorations. No one seems to know, however, just how the bird became a **Christmas symbol**. British and Irish folklore links the robin with the wren, another Christmas bird (*see also* **Wren Hunt**). Past folk beliefs assigned magical qualities and near sacred status to both birds.

Folklore

British and Irish folklore often paired the robin and the wren. Some folk verses painted the two as sweethearts, in spite of the fact that they represent different species. These verses always cast the robin as male and the wren as female. The following lines describe their romance:

> Cock robin got up early
> At the break of day,
> And went to Jenny's window
> To sing a roundelay.
> He sang cock robin's love
> To little Jenny Wren,
> And when he got unto the end,
> Then he began again [Lawrence, 1997, 38].

Traditional lore also paired robins and wrens according to their shared qualities. Several English and Irish folk verses express the following sentiment:

> The robin and the wren
> Are God Almighty's cock and hen [Armstrong, 1970, 168].

Perhaps the assumption that the birds were especially beloved by God gave rise to folk beliefs warning against harming robins or wrens. As the following folk verses teach, bad luck inevitably followed:

Cursed is the man
Who kills a robin or a wren.

Kill a robin or a wren
Never prosper, boy or man.

The robin and the redbreast
The robin and the wren
If ye tak' out of the nest
Ye'll never thrive again [Lawrence, 1997, 40].

According to various legends, one of these sacred birds once performed a heroic feat for humankind. Old tales from various parts of Europe lauded either the wren or the robin as the original fire-fetcher, the creature who delivered the first flames to humankind. In addition, English folklore assigned supernatural abilities to the robin. A fairly widespread belief credited the robin with a foreknowledge of death and illness. According to these beliefs, a robin tapping on the window or flying in or about the house meant that death, disease, or some other misfortune would visit the family. Along similar lines, English folklore also claimed that both the robin and wren pitied the dead. According to this belief, the two birds often covered the lifeless bodies of whatever dead creatures they encountered in the woods with moss or leaves. These gestures of compassion supported their reputation as kindly, holy creatures.

Christmas Symbol

Very little in the above account makes the robin a natural choice for a Christmas symbol. Nevertheless, in Victorian times the robin appeared frequently on Christmas cards as an emblem of the season (*see also* **Victorian England, Christmas in**). Perhaps the popularity of this image grew out of a general affection for this non-migratory bird, remembered especially at the time of year when nature presented the robin with its harshest conditions (*see also* **Christmas Sheaf**).

In addition, some connection can be drawn between the bird images printed on some nineteenth-century Christmas cards and elements of the folk beliefs explained above. For example, one illustration depicts a smartly dressed robin in top hat, jacket, and vest courting a wren in bonnet and shawl. Another shows a winter woodland scene in which a robin and wren drape moss and leaves over a doll (whose body resembles that of a dead child partially covered with snow). Other Victorian Christmas cards cast the robin as a symbol of the new year and the wren as a symbol of the old year.

Far more difficult to understand, however, is the popularity of Christmas cards depicting dead birds, especially robins, which peaked during the 1880s. Sentiments such as "Sweet messenger of calm decay," and "Peace divine" accompanied these perplexing pictures. Nowadays most people would agree that neither the sentiments nor the images evoke the spirit of Christmas. The Victorian fondness for that which evoked tender emotions, especially pity, may explain the popularity of these kinds of cards.

Few people today associate the robin with death. Instead, the image of the robin at Christmas time probably triggers kindly thoughts about animals enduring the cold of winter or about the promise of spring to come.

Further Reading

Armstrong, Edward A. *The Folklore of Birds*. Second edition, revised and enlarged. New York: Dover Publications, 1970.

Buday, George. *The History of the Christmas Card*. 1954. Reprint. Detroit, Mich.: Omnigraphics, 1992.

Ingersoll, Ernest. *Birds in Legend, Fable and Folklore*. New York: Longmans, Green and Company, 1923.

Lawrence, Elizabeth Atwood. *The Hunting of the Wren*. Knoxville, Tenn.: University of Tennessee Press, 1997.

Rosemary

Seasonal decorations of **greenery** have embellished European Christmas celebrations for centuries. Rosemary was at one time a popular element in these decorations. Between the fourteenth and the mid-nineteenth centuries, rosemary reigned as a favorite item in English Christmas garlands. In the seventeenth century the English poet Robert Herrick (1591-1674) noted that, according to local custom, "Rosemary and baies [bays] that are most faire were stuck about the houses and the churches as Christmas decorations" (*see also* **Laurel**).

Folk belief attributed a number of positive qualities to the plant, qualities that might be thought to justify its association with the season. Rosemary signified remembrance, as attested to by Ophelia in Shakespeare's play, *Hamlet*. In addition, evil spirits fled in the presence of rosemary. Finally, its name echoed that of **Mary**, mother of **Jesus**, one of whose symbols was the rose. Should these explanations be found wanting, many legends developed to offer a Christian explanation of the herb's connection with Christmas (*see also* **Nativity Legends**). Rosemary's popularity has since declined, however. Today we seldom twine this fragrant herb into our Christmas decorations.

Further Reading

Auld, Williams Muir. *Christmas Traditions*. 1931. Reprint. Detroit, Mich.: Omnigraphics, 1992.

Russia, Christmas in

Contemporary Russian Christmas celebrations mix traditional folk and religious customs with remnants of the secular celebrations instituted during the Communist era (1917-91). The traditional Russian **Christmas season**, called *Sviatki*, lasted from Christmas to **Epiphany**, and was marked by feasting, fortune-telling, merrymaking, and religious observance. Since the fall of the Communist government the observance of religious holidays has been increasing. Most Russians who claim a religious affiliation are Orthodox Christians, a branch of the Christian faith known for its ancient and elaborate rituals. Since the Russian Orthodox Church still follows the Julian calendar, Russians celebrate Christmas on January 7 rather than on **December 25** (*see also* **Old Christmas Day**). Exposure to and adoption of Western Christmas customs has also increased in recent years.

Christmas Customs in Old Russia

As far back as the Middle Ages Russians welcomed Christmas with the singing of *kolyadki*, or **Christmas carols**. Carolers worked their way through neighborhoods expecting to be given cookies or other sweets in return for their musical entertainment. **Mumming** is another old Russian Christmas custom. The famous Russian writer Leo Tolstoy (1828-1910) included a passage describing Russian mumming customs in his novel *War and Peace*. Russian mummers favored dressing up as animals, especially as goats, horses, and bears. Beggar costumes were also popular.

Russian folklore warned that magical spirits and forces waxed powerful during the Christmas season. The Russian people, therefore, developed numerous folk charms to protect their homes, farms, and families from evil spirits or misfortunes. They also searched nature for omens of things to come. Folk tradition suggested that Christmas weather could predict the next year's agricultural prospects. Starry skies meant one could expect a plentiful pea harvest, for example.

Many young women worked fortune-telling charms at Christmas time in the hopes of catching a glimpse of their future husbands. Many different spells existed. One encouraged young ladies to throw a boot of theirs into the street on Christmas Eve. The first young man to find the boot would be their future husband. Another custom suggested that unmarried women light a candle in front of a mirror at midnight on Christmas Eve. This charm was supposed to cause the face of their future husband to appear in the mirror.

Other popular Christmas season activities included eating and drinking with family and friends, and decorating **Christmas trees**. Most people made homemade **ornaments** out of fruit, nuts, foil, and carved wood. Finally, children in the cities eagerly awaited the Christmas Eve visit of **Grandfather Frost**, who brought gifts to well-behaved girls and boys.

Feasting and Fasting in Old Russia

Religious observances surrounding Christmas also flourished in Old Russia. These observances began with a fast that started 39 days before Christmas. Those who participated abstained from eating meat, dairy products, and eggs during this period. On December 24 some refrained from eating anything at all until the first star appeared in the sky, signaling the arrival of Christmas Eve. Then they enjoyed a twelve-course dinner. The twelve courses represented the **Twelve Days of Christmas**. The main course was usually fish instead of meat. Other traditional dishes included a *kissel* (a kind of berry pudding), *borsch* (beet soup), and *kutya*, a dessert made of boiled wheat berries, poppy seeds, and honey. A number of superstitious customs surrounded this dessert. Peasant families used to save a spoonful of kutya to throw at the ceiling. If the grains stuck to the ceiling, it signaled a good harvest to come. Many people also attended a lengthy church service on Christmas Eve.

The **Advent** fast finally ended on Christmas Day. People celebrated the end of the fast and the arrival of Christmas Day by feasting on roast meats, such as goose, ham, and duck. Roast suckling pig and pig's head were favorite Christmas dishes (*see also* **Boar's Head**). Other popular Christmas dinner dishes included *piroshki* (meat-stuffed pastries), *pelmeni* (beef and pork dumplings), and *blini* (thin buckwheat pancakes filled with caviar and sour cream). People washed down these heavy dishes with tea and vodka. In addition, many people attended special religious services on Christmas Day. The devout might attend special services held on each of the Twelve Days of Christmas.

Christmas under Communism

The Communist party, which came to power in 1917, opposed religion and religious holidays. The new Soviet government also adopted the Gregorian calendar already predominant in the West. Since the Russian Orthodox Church stuck with the old Julian calendar, this meant that Christmas now fell on January 7 and Epiphany on January 19. Although the Communists did not close all of Russia's churches, government officials often persecuted those who dared to attend religious services. Religious and folk celebrations of Christmas were suppressed and the day was no longer a legal holiday.

New Year's under Communism

The Communists realized, however, that people wanted to continue their wintertime festivities. So they made January 1, **New Year's Day**, a legal holiday and shifted many non-religious Christmas customs to that day. Under the Communist government Grandfather Frost brought children **gifts** on New Year's Eve instead of Christmas Eve. It is said that Joseph Stalin reincorporated the decorated tree into these winter celebrations by declaring it to be a New Year's tree instead of a Christmas tree. Likewise, the Christmas dinner became the New Year's dinner.

The government also instituted new holiday customs of its own. Communist officials created a "Festival of Winter" with special performances, parades, and children's activities during the last two weeks of December. On New Year's Day a fabulous children's party took place inside the Kremlin, the walled compound that served as the headquarters of the Soviet government. Extravagant decorations converted this usually formidable location into a child's fantasyland. Fifty thousand tickets were made available for this yearly event, which included the official arrival of Grandfather Frost and his entourage as well as a variety of entertainments provided by musicians, dancers, acrobats, clowns, and actors dressed as fictional characters.

During the Communist period Grandfather Frost was assigned two new companions, the **Snow Maiden**, and the New Year's boy. While the Snow Maiden was a character from an old Russian folktale, the New Year's boy was a new creation. At public events he was represented by a young boy in a costume with the numbers of the new year blazoned across it (*see also* **Baby**).

Ironically, New Year's Day became Russia's favorite holiday during the Communist era, partly because of the popularity of the old Christmas customs that resurfaced on that date and also because the occasion did not lend itself to political propaganda.

Christmas since 1991

Since the fall of the Communist government in 1991 and the re-establishment of the independent nation of Russia, the Russian people have begun to revive the celebration of Christmas. The most noticeable change is the increase in religious observance. In recent years Russian Orthodox churches have noted record attendances at Christmas services. According to a 2003 poll, 27 percent of Russians stated that they planned to go to Christmas services, and 18 percent indicated that they might go. Many fewer people, however — only 12 percent — observed the rigorous pre-Christmas fast.

A Westerner might find a Russian Orthodox Christmas Eve service both tiring and fascinating. The service starts at midnight and lasts until close to dawn. The only seats in the church are lined up against the walls and are generally reserved for the elderly, the sick, and pregnant women. All others stand during the services. The candle-light flickering off the religious paintings that cover the walls, the scent of burning incense, the singing of the choir, and the chanting of the priest and congregation combine to create an atmosphere of religious mystery. Christmas Eve services conducted by the head of the Russian Orthodox Church, Patriarch Alexi II, are now broadcast on Russian television.

Some of the old Soviet customs linger, however. Gala New Year's Eve celebrations, which include champagne and fireworks, continue to find favor with the people. Winter festivals still provide Russians with special holiday season entertainments. Grandfather Frost continues to bring presents to children on New Year's Eve. What's more, he still finds New Year's trees there to greet him. Some writers believe that these old Christmas customs will eventually gravitate back to the celebration of the Nativity. For the time being, however, the celebrations that take place on New Year's Eve and Day still constitute the major midwinter festival in Russia. A poll taken in 2003 indicated that 88 percent of Russians approved of giving gifts on New Year's Day, while only 9 percent viewed gift exchanges as an appropriate Christmas custom.

Some Russians have begun to include elements of Western Christmas celebrations in their holiday festivities. In recent years **Santa Claus**-shaped decorations and treats have appeared in many stores. Moreover, some people have begun to celebrate December 25, a day known as "Catholic Christmas" in Russia.

Further Reading

Associated Press. "Russians Mark Orthodox Christmas." *New York Times* (January 6, 2003).
Christmas in Russia. Chicago: World Book, 1992.
Clynes, Tom. *Wild Planet*. Detroit, Mich.: Visible Ink Press, 1995.

St. Barbara's Day

In parts of **France**, **Germany**, **Syria**, and **Lebanon** the **Christmas season** opens on St. Barbara's Day, December 4. Scholars now believe that St. Barbara never existed. Moreover, the Roman Catholic Church eliminated her feast day in 1969. Nevertheless, many people continue to enjoy the folk customs connected with the saint.

Legend of St. Barbara

According to legend, Barbara lived in a city of Asia Minor called Nicomedia (currently Izmit) sometime between the second and fourth centuries. Her father kept her shut up in a tower in order to shield her from outside influences. Somehow she developed a strong interest in Christianity. When her father was away, she installed three windows, representing the Holy Trinity, in the bath he was building for her. When he returned she confessed that she was a Christian.

Upon hearing this news her father flew into a rage and beat her. When she persisted in her faith against his wishes, he turned her over to the authorities. They sentenced her to death, since Christianity was still illegal at that time. Barbara's father resolved to carry out the sentence himself. In one version of the story he beheaded her and was struck by lightning on his way home. In another version the lightning kills him before he can behead his daughter.

Christians venerated Barbara as a saint from as early as the seventh century A.D. Many artists depicted her standing in front of a tower with three windows. She became the special patron of miners, forts, and artillerymen, as well as the patron of builders and architects. The role of lightning in her story, as well as her improvement of, and later imprisonment in, a tower, may have suggested these connections. People have also invoked the saint to protect them against lightning, storms, and sudden death.

European Customs

In Europe Barbara is associated with the cherry blossom, which symbolizes spiritual or feminine beauty. Germans, Czechs, Austrians, Poles, and other central and eastern Europeans begin Barbara branches on December 4. **Cherry tree** branches are broken off and kept in a pot of water near the stove. This premature warmth encourages the branch to blossom. If the buds blossom on Christmas Eve, then the girl who tended the branch will find a good husband within the year. Others interpret the flowers as signs that good fortune will visit the household. This old custom has regained some popularity among Western Christians. Instead of cherry branches, some people use apple, plum, almond, forsythia, jasmine, or horse chestnut branches.

Middle Eastern Customs

In Syria and Lebanon, Christians celebrate St. Barbara's Day with feasting and alms-giving. Parents often throw a special party for their children. They prepare special sweet dishes and set them on a table illuminated with candles. Wheat plays a double role in the composition of these treats, both as a main ingredient and as a symbol of the soul's immortality. Often, a family member or friend dons a white robe and crown in order to play the role of St. Barbara at the feast. When all is ready she ushers the children into the room and leads them in singing and other activities. The children may also bring these treats to the homes of needy families. They greet the household with the following sentiment: "May God bless you and bring you happiness throughout the year. Father and mother beg you to accept these **gifts** from us." Some children in these countries celebrate St. Barbara's Day with masquerades. Wearing rags and frightening masks, they knock on doors in their neighborhood and ask for "blessings." Householders respond by giving them candy, coins, or candles.

Weather and Crop Lore

Weather and crop lore have also attached themselves to St. Barbara's Day. In southern France, especially Provence, an old custom advises that dishes of water-soaked grain be placed on sunny windowsills on this day. If the "St. Barbara's grain" sprouts and grows, crops will flourish in the coming year. If the seeds in the little dish die, then crops will fail. After performing this test some people put St. Barbara's grain in their **Nativity scene** to represent the coming harvest. In **Poland** people watch the weather on St. Barbara's Day. Rain on December fourth means that cold and ice will arrive by Christmas Day. Cold and ice on St. Barbara's Day foretells a warm, rainy Christmas.

Further Reading

Cross, F. L., and E. A. Livingstone, eds. *The Oxford Dictionary of the Christian Church.* Second edition, revised. Oxford, England: Oxford University Press, 1983.

Delaney, John J. *Dictionary of Saints.* Garden City, N.Y.: Doubleday, 1980.

Harper, Howard. *Days and Customs of All Faiths.* 1957. Reprint. Detroit, Mich.: Omnigraphics, 1990.

Henderson, Helene, and Sue Ellen Thompson, eds. *Holidays, Festivals, and Celebrations of the World Dictionary.* Second edition. Detroit, Mich.: Omnigraphics, 1997.

Kirsch, J. P. "St. Barbara." In Charles B. Hervermann, ed. *Catholic Encyclopedia.* Nashville, Tenn.: T. Nelson, 1913. Available online at: http://www.newadvent.org/cathen/02284d.htm

Russ, Jennifer M. *German Festivals and Customs.* London, England: Oswald Wolff, 1966.

Spicer, Dorothy Gladys. *46 Days of Christmas.* New York: Coward-McCann, 1960.

Thompson, Sue Ellen, ed. *Holiday Symbols.* Detroit, Mich.: Omnigraphics, 1998.

Weiser, Francis X. *Handbook of Christian Feasts and Customs.* New York: Harcourt, Brace and World, 1952.

St. Basil's Day

Orthodox Christians recognize January 1 as St. Basil's Day. St. Basil (c. 329-379) was born in central Turkey and became famous for his intellectual brilliance, his care of the poor, and the rules he wrote to govern monastic life. Greeks celebrate St. Basil's Day with **gift** giving, carol singing, a special kind of bread, and a number of customs designed to attract good luck for the coming year.

New Year's Eve

The eve of St. Basil's Day coincides with **New Year's** Eve. On this long, dark night, relatives and friends gather together to wait for the beginning of the new year. Many people play cards or other **games** of chance on this evening, as old superstitions link New Year's Eve and Day with fortune-telling. When the clock strikes midnight people wish each other *"Chrónia pollá"* (many years) or *"Kalí chroniá"* (good year).

The first person to enter the home after midnight determines the household's luck in the coming year (*see also* **Firstfooting**). A strong, healthy person will bring good luck to the house. An icon (a religious image used in prayer and worship) can also bring good luck to a home if it is the first thing to come in from the outside. The person bearing the icon must carry it with outstretched arms, so it enters the house before he or she does. Greek families may observe other superstitions on New Year's Eve, such as opening windows at midnight to release any evil spirits hanging about the house.

Another old New Year's Eve tradition encourages children and adults to go from house to house, singing carols called *kalanda* (*see also* **Christmas Carols**). One such Greek carol, called "*Kalanda Protochronias*" honors the start of the new year and the arrival of St. Basil from Caesarea in what is now Turkey. Traditionally these carolers carried with them a paper star, a ship, an orange, an apple, and a green branch from the dogwood tree (*see also* **Christmas Symbols**). The singers would bestow a blessing on the families they visited by brushing them on the back with the branch. People also went caroling on New Year's Day, but sometimes added other symbolic acts thought to ensure the household's luck, such as tossing wheat into their backyard or prodding their fire.

St. Basil's Day, New Year's Day

On New Year's Day families gather together to share a loaf of *vasilópita*, "St Basil's bread." (Some families eat the vasilópita after midnight on New Year's Eve.) Bakers insert a coin into this sweet, braided bread (or cake, in some regions of **Greece**). Whoever gets the coin in their slice of bread will have good luck in the coming year. The bread is often distributed in a ceremonial way. The head of the household makes the sign of the cross over the bread and cuts the first slice, which is "for Christ." The second and third pieces are offered to St. Basil and the Virgin **Mary**. The next piece goes to the head of the household, and the remaining slices go to the rest of the household, with the eldest receiving theirs first and the youngest last. Some families also designate slices "for the house" and "for the poor." In rural areas farm animals, too, may be included in this custom.

An old Greek legend explains the origins of this custom. It claims that when St. Basil was acting as bishop of Caesarea, he was asked to return a sack of valuable items that had been collected from the people of the city (some say by over-greedy tax collectors, others by thieves). People began to argue over what belonged to whom. St. Basil received divine aid in sorting out these disputes. He asked some women to bake the treasures into a large loaf of bread. When he sliced and distributed the pieces everyone miraculously received only their valuables.

As January 1 is the feast day of St. Basil, special religious services are held in his honor. These services feature the recitation of the Divine Liturgy written by St. Basil. Instead of celebrating birthdays, Greeks celebrate their name-day, that is, the feast day of the saint after whom they were named. January 1 is the name-day for all those named Vasil, Vasili, Vasiliki, Vasilia, Basil, and its English equivalent William.

Traditionally Greek families open their holiday **gifts** on St. Basil's Day. Indeed, St. Basil, who visits Greek homes on New Year's Eve, is the traditional **Christmas season** gift bringer. In some places families left out little offerings of special foods—such as a glass of water and pomegranates, sweets, vasilópita, fish, or jellied pork pie—during the night for the saint to refresh himself. In recent years foreign influence has led some people to exchange presents on Christmas Day rather than on St. Basil's Day.

Over the years plenty of superstitions and folk charms have attached themselves to New Year's Day. People still observe some of them for fun. As one's activities on New Year's Day are thought to predict one's preoccupations in the coming year, people try to avoid arguing, sobbing, or losing anything on this day. They seek out happy news and avoid thinking about sad things. Some eat sweets as a means of insuring they will have a "sweet" new year. Some people put on new clothes as a charm guaranteeing that they will be well groomed all year long. When dinnertime comes, tables are set with plenty of food, insuring that the family will enjoy abundant provisions in the months ahead.

Further Reading

Griffin, Robert H., and Ann H. Shurgin, eds. *The Folklore of World Holidays.* Second edition. Detroit, Mich.: Gale, 1999.

Mikalis, Elena, and Odysseus Mikalis. "Celebrating Christmas and New Year's Day in Traditional Greek Style." *Business America* 117, 12 (1996): 6.

Rouvelas, Marilyn. *A Guide to Greek Traditions and Customs in America.* Bethesda, Md.: Nea Attiki Press, 1993.

St. Distaff's Day
Rock Day

In pre-industrial **Europe** many of the agricultural and household chores that marked the turning of the seasons attached themselves to saints' days. All across Europe, for example, people slaughtered animals and celebrated the harvest on St. Martin's Day (*see* **Martinmas**). In **England** folk tradition carried this tendency one step further, inventing St. Distaff's Day to mark women's return to work after the Christmas holiday.

St. Distaff's Day fell on January 7, the day after **Epiphany**. On this day folk tradition advised women to return to the daily chores they had put aside during the **Twelve Days of Christmas**. Before the invention of factory-made cloth, the task of spinning constituted perhaps the most representative of all female chores. Women of all ages, ranks, and incomes spun thread. Thus, English folk tradition commemorated women's return to work on the day after Epiphany by inventing a joke holiday called St. Distaff's Day. There never was a saint named Distaff. The word "distaff" refers to one of the principal tools women used in spinning, a rod upon which flax or wool was tied and out of which thread was pulled. This tool was also known as a "rock," hence the day was also known as "Rock Day."

Although English custom encouraged women to return to work, men remained at liberty until **Plough Monday**. This inequality became the subject of many Distaff Day customs, which encouraged a playful battle of the sexes rather than an earnest return to work. Robert Herrick's (1591-1674) poem, "St. Distaff's Day; or, the Morrow After Twelfth Day" records some of these practices:

> Partly worke and partly play
> Ye must on S. Distaffs day:
> From the Plough soone free your teame;
> Then come home and fother them.
> If the Maides a spinning goe,

> Burne the flax, and fire the tow:
> Scorch their plackets, but beware
> That ye singe no maiden-haire.
> Bring in pailes of water then,
> Let the Maides bewash the men.
> Give S. Distaffe all the right,
> Then bid Christmas sport good-night.
> And next morrow, every one
> To his own vocation [Chambers, 1990, 1: 68].

Herrick shows that as women returned to their spinning, custom encouraged men to tease the women by setting fire to their flax or wool. This act in turn allowed women the pleasure of dousing the men with buckets of water. If Herrick's account is accurate, it would seem that very little work was actually accomplished on St. Distaff's Day (*see also* **St. Knut's Day**).

Further Reading

Brewster, H. Pomeroy. *Saints and Festivals of the Christian Church*. 1904. Reprint. Detroit, Mich.: Omnigraphics, 1990.

Chambers, Robert. "January 7 — St. Distaff's Day." In his *The Book of Days*. Volume 1. 1862-64. Reprint. Detroit, Mich.: Omnigraphics, 1990.

Miles, Clement A. *Christmas in Ritual and Tradition*. 1912. Reprint. Detroit, Mich.: Omnigraphics, 1990.

St. John's Day

On December 27 the Christian calendar commemorates St. John the Evangelist, also called St. John the Divine. One of the twelve apostles of **Jesus**, John is known as "the disciple whom Jesus loved." Perhaps this explains why he was honored with a feast day that falls just two days after Christmas. Germans and Austrians observed the day with the blessing and drinking of wine. At an old ceremony known as the *Johannissegen*, Roman Catholic priests blessed wine brought in by parishioners. The people then took the wine home and toasted one another with it, saying, "Drink the love of St. John." According to folklore, the blessed wine also bestowed health on all who drank it. For this reason even babies were encouraged to take a sip of the holy liquid on St. John's Day. Folklore also claimed that the blessed wine warded off lightning, attracted a bountiful harvest, kept other wines from going sour, and banished many diseases.

History and Legends

St. John's Day is one of three Christian festivals that follow in close succession upon Christmas. **St. Stephen's Day** occurs on December 26, St. John's Day on December 27, and **Holy Innocents' Day** on December 28. These commemorative days were established by the late fifth century. The figures they honor share two things in common. Stephen, John, and the Innocents all lived during the time of Christ and were martyred for him. In addition, Stephen, John, and the Innocents represent all the possible combinations of the distinction between martyrs of will and martyrs of deed. The children slaughtered at King **Herod's** command in **Bethlehem** did not choose their fate, but suffered it nonetheless, and so were considered martyrs in deed. St. John willingly risked death in his defense of the Christian faith, but did not suffer death, and so was considered a martyr of will. St. Stephen risked and suffered death for his faith, and thus became a martyr of will and deed.

By the sixteenth and seventeenth centuries Europeans were celebrating St. John's Day with the consumption of large quantities of wine, blessed and otherwise. These celebrations may have been inspired by a legend in which John was offered a cup of poisoned wine by a pagan priest. In some versions of the story John drinks the wine with no effect, in others he detects the poison before drinking it.

Further Reading

Chambers, Robert. "December 27—St. John the Evangelist's Day." In his *The Book of Days*. Volume 2. 1862-64. Reprint. Detroit, Mich.: Omnigraphics, 1990.

Hadfield, Miles, and John Hadfield. *The Twelve Days of Christmas*. Boston, Mass.: Little, Brown and Company, 1961.

Harper, Howard. *Days and Customs of All Faiths*. 1957. Reprint. Detroit, Mich.: Omnigraphics, 1990.

Henderson, Helene, and Sue Ellen Thompson, eds. *Holidays, Festivals, and Celebrations of the World Dictionary*. Second edition. Detroit, Mich.: Omnigraphics, 1997.

MacDonald, Margaret Read, ed. *The Folklore of World Holidays*. Detroit, Mich.: Gale Research, 1992.

Miles, Clement A. *Christmas in Ritual and Tradition*. 1912. Reprint. Detroit, Mich.: Omnigraphics, 1990.

Weiser, Francis X. *The Christmas Book*. 1952. Reprint. Detroit, Mich.: Omnigraphics, 1990.

St. Knut's Day
St. Hilary's Day

St. Knut's Day falls on January 13, the twentieth day after Christmas, and marks the end of the **Christmas season** in Sweden and **Norway**. In Sweden the day is known as the Twentieth Day of Christmas. The Swedish Christmas season lasts longer than twenty days, however, since it begins on December 13, **St. Lucy's Day**.

Two Saints

While the Swedes and Norwegians honor St. Knut (also spelled "Canute") on January 13, the Roman Catholic and Anglican traditions acknowledge St. Hilary of Poitiers on this day. Canute Lavard, a Danish nobleman, lived in the twelfth century. Political rivals murdered Canute on January 7, 1131, in order to prevent him from becoming king. Legends say that many miracles occurred at Canute's tomb. These miracles catapulted the deceased Danish lord into sainthood. His feast day was eventually moved from January 7 to January 13. St. Knut shares this date with St. Hilary (also "Hilarius"), a fourth-century bishop famed for his religious writings and forceful personality.

Customs

An old Scandinavian saying proclaims, "Twentieth-day Knut, drives the **Yule** out." People took the saying quite literally in past times. They removed all Christmas decorations, flung open doors and windows, and swept all the dust and debris from their celebrations out of the house on this day. Folk belief also recommended that householders tap the walls with sticks in order to chase out any Christmas **ghosts**, trolls, or **Jultomten** that might be lurking there. In Sweden a man dressed as "Knut" in colorful rags sometimes appeared to help the household "sweep out Christmas."

Elements of these older practices can be seen in Sweden's contemporary St. Knut's Day traditions. On this day Swedes dismantle their **Christmas trees**. Children's parties centered around this event have become another special feature of the day. These parties offer the opportunity for one last bout of Christmas eating, drinking, singing, and dancing, as well as the pleasure of observing the last lighting of the Christmas tree. While the adults pack up the delicate Christmas tree **ornaments**, the children stuff themselves with the candy and cookies that have been used to decorate the tree. After the tree is stripped the assembled company throws it out onto the snow, often wishing it and the Christmas season a final farewell in song. Folk traditions suggest that the tree be thrown through a window. Swedes sometimes dispose of the trees by gathering several together and setting them ablaze as great outdoor bonfires.

Further Reading

Cagner, Ewert, comp. *Swedish Christmas*. New York: Henry Holt and Company, 1959.

Henriksen, Vera. *Christmas in Norway*. Oslo, Norway: Johan Grundt Tanum Forlag, 1970.

MacDonald, Margaret Read, ed. *The Folklore of World Holidays*. Detroit, Mich.: Gale Research, 1992.

Ross, Corinne. *Christmas in Scandinavia*. Chicago: World Book, 1977.

St. Lucy's Day
Santa Lucia

In Sweden the **Christmas season** begins on December 13, St. Lucy's Day. St. Lucy's Day celebrations feature girls who dress and act as the saint. Crowned with wreaths of **greenery** studded with glowing candles, they sing songs about St. Lucy and distribute **gifts** of food. In North America, some Swedish families, churches, schools, and institutions also celebrate St. Lucy's Day. **Italy**, the country of Lucy's birth, honors her feast day as well.

Life and Legends of St. Lucy

St. Lucy, or Santa Lucia, lived in Syracuse, a town on the Italian island of Sicily, during the late third and early fourth centuries. The many legends of her life vary somewhat, offering accounts of some or all of the following events.

Although Lucy was a Christian, her great beauty attracted the attention of a pagan nobleman. He pursued her but she rejected him. When he told Lucy that her beautiful eyes "haunted him day and night," she tore her eyes out and sent them to him, hoping to be left in peace. God restored them in recognition of her willing sacrifice, however. In another effort to escape marriage, Lucy distributed her dowry among the poor. This act so angered her suitor that he informed religious authorities of her adherence to the then-illegal Christian faith. The authorities demanded that she perform a sacrifice to the pagan gods. She refused and was sent to a brothel. When this attempt to punish her failed, she was taken to prison. She again refused to sacrifice to the pagan gods, whereupon she was condemned to death. The first attempts to execute her failed as God again intervened on Lucy's behalf. The guards sent to fetch the girl from her cell found they could not move her. In an effort to carry out their orders they put ropes around her, then set the floor on fire. When neither of these tricks enabled them to move the saint, they stabbed her in the neck. It is believed that she died in 303 A.D.

History

Scholars agree that the legend of St. Lucy contains more fiction that fact. Nevertheless, her cult flourished in Syracuse as early as the fifth century. In the sixth and seventh centuries it spread to the Italian cities of Rome and Ravenna. Eventually her fame stretched across **Europe**, and she became one of the most popular saints of the Middle Ages. Artists often depicted her carrying her eyes in a dish or holding the palm of martyrdom and a lamp. Some portrayed her with a sword thrust through her throat. People invoked the aid of St. Lucy for afflictions of the eyes and throat.

Although her feast day currently falls on December 13, before the sixteenth-century Gregorian calendar reform (*see also* **Old Christ-**

mas Day), St. Lucy's Day fell on the **winter solstice**. Legends claimed that the saint blinded herself on this, the shortest day of the year. In fact, her name, Lucia, comes from the Latin word for "light," *lux*. Thus, many old folk customs invoked Lucy as a symbol of light, especially the light that coincides with the lengthening of days after the winter solstice.

St. Lucy's Day is especially celebrated in the country of her birth, Italy, and in Scandinavia. How did this Italian saint develop a following in the land of the Vikings? When the people of the cold, dark North converted to Christianity around 1000 A.D., they acquired a special fondness for the saint whose feast day marked the return of the sun and whose name itself means "light." Over the centuries they kindled many flames and fires in her name. At one time people in northern Europe lit "St. Lucy's fires" on the evening of her feast day. They threw incense into the flames and bathed in the smoke, which was said to protect one from witchcraft, disease, and other dangers. While this was happening, others played music to accompany the sun's changing course. An old Scandinavian custom forbade all turning motions on St. Lucy's Day, including spinning, stirring, and working a grindstone. Superstitions warned that these circular motions might interfere with the sun's change of course.

Folk belief also hinted that miracles occurred at midnight on St. Lucy's Eve. The few souls awake and alert at this potent hour might hear cattle speaking or see running water turn into wine. In past times many believed that the saint had the power to shorten the winter season. This belief led to the custom of writing her name and drawing a picture of a girl alongside it on doors and fences in the hopes that the saint would hasten the end of winter. Another old custom encouraged people to keep a candle burning in their home all day long on her feast day.

St. Lucy's Day in Italy

In Italy St. Lucy is called Santa Lucia. St. Lucy's Day is observed throughout the country, but is especially honored in Sicily. The day has traditionally been celebrated with bonfires, processions, and other illuminations. In Sicily St. Lucy, dressed in a blue cloak showered with stars, brings **gifts** to children on the eve of her feast day.

Children leave their **shoes** outside on St. Lucy's Eve in order to collect her offerings. Sicilians also remember the miracle that St. Lucy performed when famine struck the island. According to legend, hunger had weakened so many that the people of Syracuse went as a group to the church to ask the saint to deliver them. While they were praying, a ship loaded with grain sailed into the harbor. For this reason Italians celebrate St. Lucy's Day by eating a boiled wheat dish called *cuccia* or *cuccidata*. Lucy is the patron saint of the Italian cities of Syracuse and Milan.

St. Lucy's Day in Sweden

In Sweden today, St. Lucy's Day, or *Luciadagen*, marks the beginning of the Christmas season. The family celebrates this day in a special way. One daughter acts as the "Lucy bride." She gets up very early and prepares coffee and buns for the family. These buns are called *Lussenkatter*, or "Lucy cats." She dresses in a white robe with a red sash and carefully places a **wreath** of ligon berry leaves and lit candles on her head. Attired thus as St. Lucy, she brings the simple breakfast to each bedroom, awakening family members with a song about the saint. According to old traditions, this St. Lucy's Day breakfast should be served very early in the morning, between one and four a.m.

Varying traditions suggest that the oldest, youngest, or prettiest girl perform this role. The other girls in the family may follow her, dressed in white robes and crowned with tinsel halos. The boys may participate as *starngossar*, or **star boys**. They also dress in white. In addition, they wear tall, pointed hats made of silver paper and carry star-topped scepters. These Swedish customs have spread to Finland, **Norway**, and **Denmark**.

Over the years many other folk beliefs and customs also attached themselves to St. Lucy's Day. Old folklore in rural areas advised farmers to thresh all the grain from the year's harvest by St. Lucy's Day. The season's spinning and weaving were also to be completed by that day. Other traditions suggested that farmers slaughter the Christmas pig (*see also* **Boar's Head**) on St. Lucy's Day and that cooks bury the *lutfisken,* a traditional Christmas fish, in beech ashes on St. Lucy's Day in order for it to be ready by Christmas. Folklore also advised housewives to finish their Christmas cleaning and decorating by this day.

Origins of Swedish St. Lucy's Day

No one knows exactly when and how Swedes came to revere St. Lucy in this way. Some compare the symbols connected with the Lucy bride to those associated with Freya, a goddess from Scandinavia's pagan past. The pagan god Frey, to whom sacrifices were offered at **Yule**, had a sister named Freya. The ancient Scandinavians associated Freya with love, fertility, war, and wealth. She wore a bright necklace and drove a chariot pulled by cats.

Other folklorists contend that Lucy and her story are thoroughly Christian. Historians suspect that the custom of the Lucy bride developed in the late eighteenth or early nineteenth centuries. Some connect it with a Swedish legend concerning the saint's miraculous intervention during a famine. This legend closely resembles the Sicilian tale told above. One winter a terrible famine ravaged Sweden. During the longest night of the year, when the sufferings caused by cold, dark, and hunger were at their peak, a mysterious ship suddenly appeared on Lake Vannern. A woman dressed in white, her face radiating light, stood at the prow of the ship. It was St. Lucy. She guided the ship into harbor and delivered the stores of food it contained to the poor and hungry.

Recent Traditions

Although originally part of a family celebration, the role of the Lucy bride has spread to offices, schools, and other public institutions. Like the Lucys of home celebrations, these public Lucys wear white gowns and a crown of candles. They and their followers bring gifts of food, song, and light to co-workers, neighbors, and fellow citizens. Students playing the role of Lucy sometimes surprise favorite teachers in the early morning. Lucy and her followers also visit hotel guests, hospital patients, and even early-morning commuters and policemen.

During the past thirty or forty years villages and cities all over Sweden began to select their own Lucy queens. Often they organize a parade for the winner, who may be accompanied by youths dressed as star boys, biblical figures, trolls (*see also* **Jultomten**), or other related characters. In Stockholm the judges must select their Lucy from among hundreds of competitors. Each year the honor of crowning Stockholm's Lucy bride goes to the winner of the Nobel Prize in literature.

Further Reading

Ekstrand, Florence. *Lucia Child of Light*. Seattle, Wash.: Welcome Press, 1989.

Foley, Daniel J. *Christmas the World Over*. Philadelphia, Pa.: Chilton Books, 1963.

Henderson, Helene, and Sue Ellen Thompson, eds. *Holidays, Festivals, and Celebrations of the World Dictionary*. Second edition. Detroit, Mich.: Omnigraphics, 1997.

Miles, Clement A. *Christmas in Ritual and Tradition*. 1912. Reprint. Detroit, Mich.: Omnigraphics, 1990.

Ross, Corinne. *Christmas in Italy*. Chicago: World Book-Childcraft International, 1979.

———. *Christmas in Scandinavia*. Chicago: World Book, 1977.

Ryan, E. G. "Lucy, St." In *New Catholic Encyclopedia*. Volume 8. New York: McGraw-Hill, 1967.

Spicer, Dorothy Gladys. *Festivals of Western Europe*. 1958. Reprint. Detroit, Mich.: Omnigraphics, 1994.

———. *46 Days of Christmas*. New York: Coward-McCann, 1960.

Thompson, Sue Ellen, ed. *Holiday Symbols*. Detroit, Mich.: Omnigraphics, 1998.

Weiser, Francis X. *Handbook of Christian Feasts and Customs*. New York: Harcourt, Brace and World, 1952.

St. Martin. *See* Martinmas

St. Nicholas

St. Nicholas lived in the late third and early fourth centuries. Very little is known about his life. By the Middle Ages, however, he had become one of **Europe**'s most venerated non-biblical saints. In **France** and **Germany** more than two thousand churches carry the saint's name, bearing silent testimony to the intensity of past devotions. St. Nicholas was the **Christmas season** gift bringer in parts of northern Europe. His legend and the customs surrounding it traveled to America with European immigrants. In the United States St. Nicholas was transformed into **Santa Claus**. His new American name evolved from his old Dutch name, *Sinterklass*. Although Nicholas's popularity has declined considerably since medieval times, some Europeans still celebrate his feast day, which falls on December 6 (*see* **St. Nicholas's Day**).

Life of St. Nicholas

Nicholas was born in Asia Minor, a region that later became the nation of Turkey. Most scholars believe he was born around 280 A.D. and died around 343. He pursued a religious career and eventually became bishop of Myra, a town in Asia Minor now called Demre. Some believe that he attended the Council of Nicea in 325 A.D. This important meeting of the leaders of the early Christian Church produced the Nicene Creed, a fundamental statement of the Christian faith. Other researchers point out that his name does not appear on the roster of those in attendance until the Middle Ages, when his cult was at the height of its popularity. Although next to nothing is known for certain about the saint's life, many legends credit him with miraculous deeds.

St. Nicholas and the Three Maidens

One of the oldest and most popular of these legends tells how young Nicholas saved three sisters from an evil fate. The sisters had all reached the age at which young women marry. Unfortunately, their father could not provide any of them with a dowry so he planned to sell them into prostitution. When Nicholas found out about this he took a small bag of **gold** to the family's house after it got dark and threw it in an open window (some say he threw it down the chimney). The father gratefully seized the gold and used it to pay for the dowry of the eldest girl. Nicholas provided dowries for the second and third daughters in the same fashion. The third time Nicholas pulled this trick the girls' father was waiting for him. When the bag of gold came flying into the house he ran outside, discovered Nicholas, and thanked him for his generosity. Nicholas asked the man not to tell others of his good deed.

Some writers believe this legend eventually gave rise to several Christmas season customs, including the tradition whereby St. Nicholas distributes **gifts** on his feast day. In addition, the custom of putting out **shoes** or hanging **stockings** by the fireplace to receive the saint's, and later Santa's, gifts might also have been inspired by this story. This legend achieved such widespread fame and popularity that the three bags of gold became an emblem of the saint. Sometimes artists simplified their images of the saint by depicting the bags of gold as three gold balls. Eventually, the three gold balls became the symbol for a pawnbroker's shop, perhaps because to those who knew the legend, the gold balls recalled the act of reclaiming something of worth.

St. Nicholas and the Three Students

While the above story tells of a good deed the saint did during his lifetime, other tales recount the miracles he worked after his death. One of the most popular of these sprouted up in twelfth-century France and describes how St. Nicholas aided three traveling students who fell into the hands of an evil innkeeper. While the students slept the innkeeper searched their bags and stole all their money. In an attempt to cover up his crime, he not only killed the sleeping students but also cut them up and hid the pieces of their bodies in his pickle barrels. The saint, outraged at this crime, caused the pieces of their bodies to come together again and restored the students to life. This story depicts Nicholas once again coming to the rescue of young people. Perhaps this inclination to aid the young

explains why later traditions identified Nicholas as a bringer of gifts to children.

St. Nicholas and the Unpaid Loan

Another medieval tale describing a miracle performed by the dead saint tells how he prevented an unscrupulous Christian from cheating a Jewish moneylender. The saint caused the Christian's death in such a way as to reveal the hiding place of the money he owed to the moneylender. Uncomfortable with this solution to his problem, the moneylender remarked that if the saint were truly good he wouldn't have let the guilty man die. Thereupon St. Nicholas brought the Christian back to life. The Christian then repented his attempt to cheat the moneylender and paid his debt. These events impressed the moneylender so much that he converted to Christianity. Thus, St. Nicholas acquired a reputation for imposing scrupulous honesty in financial transactions.

In **Italy** around the time of the Renaissance the Medici family, a wealthy and influential clan of bankers and politicians, placed three gold balls on their coat of arms. They probably hoped that this symbol of St. Nicholas would inspire confidence in the integrity of their financial dealings. Eventually, others in the financial trades began to use the gold balls as a symbol of their profession.

Patronages

Many other tales tell how the saint rescued sailors from storms at sea, returned the kidnapped, defended those falsely accused of crimes, and fought against evil spirits associated with such pagan deities as Artemis. Along with the story of the three dowryless maidens, these tales circulated with greater frequency in southern and eastern Europe. There Christians recognized Nicholas first and foremost as the patron of seafarers. Belief in the saint's concern for those at sea spread throughout Europe. Evidence of this belief can be found in the many churches in European port towns dedicated to the saint.

In northern and central Europe, however, where the tale of the three students achieved widespread popularity, people venerated St. Nicholas primarily as the patron of children. Indeed, over time illustrations depicting the story of the three students reduced their ages so that they began to appear as children rather than as young men. This trend can also be detected in northern European depictions of the three dowryless maidens. Furthermore, in northern Europe St. Nicholas acquired the reputation of being sympathetic to the prayers of those looking for marriage partners and those hoping for children. His association with fertility further supported his identity as a patron of children.

By the late Middle Ages people living in different regions of Europe held somewhat different images of the saint's concerns. These differences explain why Nicholas eventually became a bringer of gifts to children in northern and central Europe and not in southern and eastern Europe. As the popularity of his cult grew, Nicholas acquired many patronages. He became the patron saint of children, students, bankers, pawnbrokers, sailors, dock workers, brewers, coopers (barrel makers), travelers, pilgrims, thieves, undeserving losers of lawsuits, and the nations of **Greece** and **Russia**.

Bones of St. Nicholas

For centuries the Church of St. Nicholas in Myra guarded what were believed to be the saint's remains in a stone sarcophagus. Around the year 1000, some of the saint's relics were donated to the city of Kiev, an act that planted the saint's cult in Russia. In the eleventh century another, more dramatic move took place. In the year 1087 a ship from Bari, Italy, arrived at Myra. The men on board seized the remains of the saint and carried them back to Bari. It is unclear whether or not the custodians of the saint's relics in Myra consented to their removal. The Italians may have been motivated by fear that the Muslim Turks, who had invaded Asia Minor from the east, would desecrate the saint's tomb. Or the citizens of Bari may simply have coveted the privilege of housing the saint's relics, since in those days people held the bodily remains of saints in great honor.

Soon after Nicholas's bones were established in Bari a steady train of pilgrims began to visit the town, no doubt bringing new wealth and prestige to the city. To accommodate the bones as well as the tourists, the archbishop commissioned the building of a glorious new basilica in Bari. It was completed in 1108. Only afterwards did anyone recognize that the Muslim workmen who had built and decorated much of the church had incorporated an assertion of the Islamic faith onto the church walls. The phrase "There is no God but Allah, and Mohammed is His Prophet," written in Arabic calligraphy, was woven into the designs decorating the walls. Given the beauty of these designs, church officials decided not to remove them.

St. Nicholas in the Twentieth Century

The cult of St. Nicholas in western Europe reached its height during the Middle Ages. In the centuries that followed, interest in the saint slowly diminished, reflecting an overall decline in the veneration of saints. In 1969 the Vatican itself struck a blow at the saint's status when it removed Nicholas from the universal calendar of saints, making his veneration optional, rather than obligatory, for all Roman Catholics.

Perhaps this demotion explains why in 1972 the Roman Catholic Church willingly donated some of the saint's long-coveted bones and relics to the Greek Orthodox Church of **New York City**. One might also recall that the Orthodox and Roman Catholic churches split apart from one another in 1054, shortly before the seizure of St. Nicholas's bones from their tomb in Orthodox Asia Minor by sailors from Roman Catholic western Europe. Viewed in this light, the transfer of a portion of St. Nicholas relics back to the Orthodox Church appears as something of a belated apology for this questionable act. In any case, the gift was presented as a token of the growing good will between the Roman Catholic and Orthodox churches. The Greek Orthodox Cathedral in New York kept some of the relics, but the majority of them are now housed in the Shrine of St. Nicholas in Flushing, New York.

In recent years the citizens of Demre, Turkey, have begun to lobby for the return of the bones to their original resting place. Their group, called the "Santa Claus Foundation," sent a letter to the archbishop of Bari requesting the return of the relics. Since Turkey is a predominantly Muslim country, some grumble that the group is not motivated by religious beliefs but rather by the desire to secure a lucrative tourist attraction for their town. Demre already hosts a yearly celebration on St. Nicholas's Day. The sixteen-year-old event, which began as a religious symposium, now includes a festival featuring the awarding of a "Father Christmas Peace Prize."

Further Reading

Del Re, Gerard, and Patricia Del Re. *The Christmas Almanack*. Garden City, N.Y.: Doubleday, 1979.

Ebon, Martin. *Saint Nicholas, Life and Legend*. New York: Harper and Row, 1975.

Jones, Charles W. *Saint Nicholas of Myra, Bari, and Manhattan*. Chicago: University of Chicago Press, 1978.

McKnight, George. *St. Nicholas*. 1917. Reprint. Williamstown, Mass.: Corner House Publishers, 1974.

Newland, Mary Reed. *The Saint Book*. New York: Seabury Press, 1979.

St. Nicholas's Day

During the Middle Ages **St. Nicholas** was one of the most venerated saints in western **Europe**. Although his popularity has since declined, his feast day, December 6, is still celebrated in the Netherlands and other European countries. Immigrants brought the legends and customs surrounding St. Nicholas with them to the United States. There the saint was transformed into the American **Christmas season** gift bringer called **Santa Claus**.

Shoes, Stockings, and Gifts

In Austria, the Netherlands, Belgium, Czechoslovakia, and parts of **Germany**, folk tradition cast St. Nicholas in the role of a Christmas season gift bringer. Folk representations of St. Nicholas usually portray him as an elderly white-bearded man who carries a bishop's staff and dresses in a red bishop's robe and miter. This kindly saint distributes presents to others in honor of his feast day. On the night of December 5 he brings fruit, nuts, cookies, candy, and other small **gifts** to well-behaved children. Those who have misbehaved too often during the year might receive a stick, warning them of punishment to come.

Children expecting presents on St. Nicholas's Eve helpfully provide small receptacles in which the saint may deposit his gifts. In the Netherlands children leave their **shoes** by the fireplace. In Czechoslovakia children attract the saint's attention with **stockings** hanging on the window frame. In Austria Nicholas knows to look for children's shoes on the windowsill. Perhaps inspired by legends of pagan spirits descending into homes via the smoke from the hearth, St. Nicholas often enters homes through the chimney (*see also* **Berchta**).

St. Nicholas's Helpers

The powerful saint does not have to carry out his gift-giving activities alone. According to some folk traditions, he can compel a minor demon to aid him in his mission. In Czechoslovakia this devil is known as a **cert**. In parts of Germany, Austria, and Switzerland a shaggy demon called Klaubauf, or Krampus, serves St. Nicholas. He frightens children with his blackened face, scarlet eyes, horns, and clanking chains. Incidentally, the name "Klaubauf" is a contraction of the German phrase *Klaub auf!*, which means "pick 'em up." This is an especially appropriate name since St. Nicholas and his helper often toss their goodies on the floor. In other parts of Germany a rough fellow named **Knecht Ruprecht**, or "Knight Ruprecht," sometime aids the saint. In the Netherlands a menacing character called **Black Peter** tags along behind Nicholas. These sinister figures often carry a heavy sack of gifts, the book in which the saint has recorded the children's behavior, and a stick with which to smack misbehavers.

History

As early as the tenth century, St. Nicholas's Day was observed with liturgical dramas retelling the story of the saint. By the twelfth century these dramas had evolved into "St. Nicholas Plays," which were usually produced by choirboys in honor of the saint's feast day (*see also* **Nativity Plays**). These plays retold some of the most widely known legends concerning St. Nicholas and were quite popular during the late Middle Ages, when the cult of St. Nicholas reached its zenith in western Europe. They present us with some of the earliest surviving European plays that take as their subject matter something other than Christian scripture.

Some researchers think that the custom of giving gifts to children on St. Nicholas's Day started in the twelfth century. At that time nuns from central **France** started to leave gifts on the doorsteps of poor families with children on St. Nicholas's Eve. These packages contained nuts and oranges and other good things to eat. Some researchers believe that ordinary people adopted the custom, spreading it from France to other parts of northern Europe. Other writers suppose that the folklore surrounding St. Martin may have inspired the traditions that turned St. Nicholas into a gift giver. In past centuries St. Martin, another bishop-saint, was said to ride through the countryside delivering treats to children on the eve of his feast day (*see* **Martinmas**). In the Netherlands Nicholas's helper Black Peter wears sixteenth-century clothing, which may indicate that St. Nicholas was bringing gifts to Dutch children at least as far back as that era.

Western Europeans honored Nicholas as the patron saint of children. Some of the customs associated with his feast day gave children the opportunity to reign over adults. For example, in medieval times the festivities surrounding the **boy bishop** often began on St. Nicholas's Day. The boy bishop, a boy who assumed the rank of bishop for a short while, was one of the mock rulers who presided over Christmas season merrymaking in the Middle Ages (*see also* **King of the Bean; Lord of Misrule**). In the sixteenth century, schoolboys in the British Isles hit upon the idea of **barring out the schoolmaster** in order to gain a few days' vacation. This custom, which continued for several centuries, was often practiced on St. Nicholas's Day.

An early seventeenth-century document records a German Protestant minister's displeasure with the myth that St. Nicholas brings gifts for children. His sentiments echoed the concerns of many Protestant leaders of that era who wished to do away with the veneration of saints. In the centuries that followed, the **Christkindel**, or

"Christ Child," became the Christmas season gift bringer in most of Germany. This change indicates that Protestant leaders had achieved some success in their campaign against the saint.

St. Nicholas's Day in the Netherlands

The Netherlands hosts Europe's most extensive St. Nicholas Day celebrations. They begin with the official arrival of St. Nicholas in the Netherlands, weeks before his feast day. Each year the arrival of St. Nicholas and Black Peter from their home in far-off **Spain** is reenacted in Amsterdam, the capital of the Netherlands. A great crowd gathers to witness the arrival of the ship bearing the saint and his helper. A white horse, St. Nicholas's traditional mode of transport, stands ready to serve the saint. As the gift bringers descend from the ship, the crowd easily identifies Nicholas by his red bishop's robe, miter, crook, and long white beard. After greeting the mayor, the saint and his helper lead a parade to Amsterdam's central plaza. There the royal family officially welcomes Holland's Christmas season gift bringers. This event is broadcast on Dutch television.

In the weeks that follow, **store windows** display treats and gifts appropriate for St. Nicholas's Day. Meanwhile, children dream of the evening when they will put their shoes by the hearth to receive gifts from the kindly saint. Dutch folklore asserts that Nicholas and Black Peter, mounted on the saint's magical white horse, fly across Holland on St. Nicholas's Eve distributing gifts to children. Black Peter does the dirty work of slipping down the chimneys to deposit the children's gifts. He also collects the carrots, hay, and sugar that thoughtful children have left there for St. Nicholas's horse. If the two should find any children who misbehave frequently, they leave a rod or switch, warning of punishment to come.

Families begin celebrating St. Nicholas's Day on the evening of December 5 when they enjoy a special meal together. A traditional St. Nicholas's Day dinner features roast chicken or duck. In addition, many special sweets are served at this meal. Some cooks mark each person's place at the table with *letterbankets*, large, marzipan-filled pastries shaped like letters of the alphabet. Other St. Nicholas's Day treats include *speculaas*, spicy butter cookies, *oliebollen*, doughnuts with raisins in them, and *taai-taai*, honey cookies.

It is not unusual for St. Nicholas and his helper, Black Peter, to visit these parties. Sometimes they just open the door, throw candies into the room, and dash away (*see also* **Julklapp**). Other times they enter and deliver these treats to the children in person, along with advice and admonitions concerning future behavior. Adults know that friends or family members are impersonating these figures, but children are often astonished by the pair's detailed knowledge of their good and bad deeds during the past year.

Family members also exchange presents with one another at this time. In fact, St. Nicholas's Eve, *Sinterklaas-Avond* in Dutch, is sometimes called *Pakjes-Avond,* or "Parcel Evening." Attention falls less on the simple gifts themselves, however, than on the tricky way in which they are delivered and the rhyming verses that accompany them. Sometimes the package only contains a clue as to where the real gift is hidden. Other times small gifts are wrapped in a succession of much larger boxes. The Dutch take great care in composing humorous lines of verse to accompany these gifts. Everyone looks forward to hearing these short poems read out loud. Those who can't come up with something clever can hire one of the professional verse writers who ply their trade at department stores around St. Nicholas's Day. Indeed, rhyming verses can be found throughout Dutch society at this time of year. Visitors to the Dutch parliament may be surprised to find the nation's politicians occasionally delivering a short rhyming speech in honor of the holiday.

St. Nicholas's Day in Italy

St. Nicholas's Day festivities in **Italy** emphasize the saint's role as the patron of seafarers. In Italy St. Nicholas Day is observed on May 7 and May 8, dates that commemorate the arrival of the saint's relics from their original tomb in Myra (now Demre), Turkey. The town of Bari, where the saint's remains now rest, hosts a large celebration. Worshipers flock to the saint's tomb in the Church of San Nicola. A procession escorts a statue of the saint from his tomb down to the harbor. Followers place the image on the deck of a flower-strewn boat which is escorted out to sea by hundreds of small vessels carrying fishermen and pilgrims. After the day's festivities worshipers escort the image back to the Church of San Nicola.

Further Reading

Bragdon, Allen D. *Joy Through the World*. New York: Dodd, Mead, and Company, 1985.

Henderson, Helene, and Sue Ellen Thompson, eds. *Holidays, Festivals, and Celebrations of the World Dictionary*. Second edition. Detroit, Mich.: Omnigraphics, 1997.

Jones, E. Willis. *The Santa Claus Book*. New York: Walker and Company, 1976.

MacDonald, Margaret Read, ed. *The Folklore of World Holidays*. Detroit, Mich.: Gale Research, 1992.

McKnight, George. *St. Nicholas, His Legend and His Role in the Christmas Celebration and Other Popular Customs*. 1917. Reprint. Williamstown, Mass.: Corner House Publishers, 1974.

Miles, Clement A. *Christmas in Ritual and Tradition*. 1912. Reprint. Detroit, Mich.: Omnigraphics, 1990.

Walsh, William S. *The Story of Santa Klaus*. 1909. Reprint. Detroit, Mich.: Omnigraphics, 1991.

Web Site

A site sponsored by the Netherlands Board of Tourism, contains a page describing St. Nicholas Day celebrations: http://www.holland.com
(Search "Sinterklaas" and "St. Nicholas")

St. Stephen's Day

St. Stephen lived during the time of the Apostles and the founding of the Christian Church. The Book of Acts (chapters 6 and 7) describes Stephen as a man "full of grace and power," as well as a skilled speaker. He was stoned to death around 35 A.D. for his religious beliefs, becoming the first Christian martyr. His feast day falls on December 26, the second of the **Twelve Days of Christmas**.

History and Legend

Three Christian festivals follow in close succession upon Christmas Day. St. Stephen's Day occurs on December 26, **St. John's Day** on December 27, and **Holy Innocents' Day** on December 28. These commemorative days were established by the late fifth century. The figures they honor share two characteristics in common. These characteristics motivated Church authorities to schedule their commemorative days close together in the **Christmas season**. Stephen, John, and the Innocents all lived during the time of Christ, and each was connected in a special way to his life and teachings. In addition, all became martyrs for him. In fact, Stephen, John, and the Innocents represent all the possible combinations of the distinction between martyrs in will and martyrs in deed. The children slaughtered at King **Herod's** orders in **Bethlehem** did not choose their fate, but suffered it nonetheless, and so were considered martyrs in deed. St. John willingly risked death in defense of the Christian faith, but did not suffer death, and so was considered a martyr in will. St. Stephen risked and suffered death for his faith, thus becoming a martyr in will and deed.

During the Middle Ages many legends arose about beloved saints, especially when biblical or historical accounts of their lives failed to provide sufficient details. An old English **Christmas carol** about St. Stephen illustrates this tendency. The carol dates back to the year 1400 and depicts the saint as a kitchen servant in King Herod's castle at the time of **Jesus'** birth:

Stephen out of the kitchen came, with boar's head on hand,
He saw a star was fair and bright over Bedlem stand.

He cast down the boar's head and went into the hall,
I forsake thee, King Herod, and thy works all.

I forsake thee, King Herod, and thy works all.
There is a child in Bedlam born is better than we all
[Duncan, 1992, 63-64].

With his great hall and **boar's head** supper, the King Herod of this writer's imagination resembles a medieval English lord more closely than he does a king of ancient Judea.

European Customs

Perhaps Stephen's death at the hands of a stone-throwing mob explains how he later became the patron saint of stonecutters and bricklayers. It is somewhat more difficult to explain how he became the patron saint of horses in many European countries, since they play no role in the story of his life or death. Nevertheless, throughout central and northern Europe many old folk customs associated with St. Stephen's Day feature horses. In rural Austria people decked their horses with ribbons and brought them to the local priest to receive a blessing. Afterwards the horses fed on blessed oats in order to insure their health and well-being in the coming year. In past centuries English and Welsh folklore recommended the running, and then bleeding, of horses on St. Stephen's Day. In those days people believed that this practice, which consisted of making a small cut in the horse's skin and letting some blood drain out, promoted good health. Horses were also bled in parts of Austria and **Germany** on St. Stephen's Day. Various German folk customs also advocated the riding or racing of horses on St. Stephen's Day. In Munich men on horseback entered the church during St. Stephen's Day services and rode three times around the sanctuary. Hundreds of riders and their beribboned horses participated in this custom, which was not abandoned until 1876.

Other customs at one time associated with St. Stephen's Day include the **wren hunt** in **Ireland**, **Wales**, and **England**, and the blessing of fields and straw in southern **France**, where the day was also known as

"Straw Day." In past centuries the Welsh celebrated December 26 as "Holming Day." On this day men and boys struck each other on the legs with **holly** branches. In some areas men thrashed women and girls about the arms with the branches. The spiny holly leaves quickly drew blood. Although some people interpreted the custom as a reminder of the bloody death of St. Stephen, it may also have originated from the belief that periodic blood-letting ensured good health.

A few final customs associated with St. Stephen's Day reflect a somewhat closer connection to the saint. In **Poland** people confer St. Stephen's Day blessings by throwing handfuls of rice, oats, or walnuts at one another. This act symbolizes the stoning of St. Stephen. In past centuries the English gave small **gifts** of money to all those who provided them with services during the year. These tips were called "boxes," thus, St. Stephen's Day became known as **Boxing Day**. In a small way this practice served to redistribute wealth in the community. Since St. Stephen's role in the Christian community of which he was a member was to ensure the fair distribution of goods, perhaps this custom can be said to reflect the saint's earthly vocation.

Swedish Customs and Lore

Old Swedish and Norwegian traditions also encouraged the racing of horses on St. Stephen's Day (*see also* **Norway, Christmas in**). In past centuries, horse races sometimes followed St. Stephen's Day church services. Folk belief suggested that the man who won the race would be the first to harvest his crops. The Swedish historian Olaus Magnus (1490-1557) mentioned these races in his writings, and they are believed to date back to medieval times. In rural areas mounted men raced each other to the nearest north-flowing stream or ice-free spring in the early morning hours, believing that the horse that drank first would stay healthy throughout the year.

The most noted Swedish St. Stephen's Day custom, however, involved bands of men on horseback called "Stephen's men" or "Stephen's riders." On St. Stephen's Day they rose before dawn and galloped from village to village singing folk songs about the saint. These robust performances awakened householders, who then refreshed Stephen's men with ale or other alcoholic beverages. Today one can still see bands of young men, often in traditional costumes, singing folk songs from door to door on St. Stephen's Day.

Swedish folklore implies that the country's St. Stephen's Day customs do not honor the St. Stephen of the New Testament, but rather
a medieval saint of the same name who spread Christianity in
Sweden. According to legend, the medieval Stephen loved horses
and owned five of them. When one tired, he mounted another in
order to spare the beasts without interrupting his tireless missionary
efforts. The Stephen riders are thus thought by some scholars to represent the saint and his devoted followers.

Other scholars, however, doubt the existence of the medieval St.
Stephen. They propose instead that legends concerning the medieval saint arose to explain persistent pre-Christian customs associated with the day. These researchers note that horses were sacred to
the cult of Frey, the Scandinavian god of sunlight, fertility, peace, and
plenty (*see also* **Yule**). Other experts trace the origin of St. Stephen's
Day horse riding back to the ancient Roman custom of racing horses
around the time of the **winter solstice**.

Further Reading

Brewster, H. Pomeroy. *Saints and Festivals of the Christian Church*. 1904.
Reprint. Detroit, Mich.: Omnigraphics, 1990.

Chambers, Robert. "December 26 — St. Stephen's Day." In his *The Book of
Days*. Volume 2. 1862-64. Reprint. Detroit, Mich.: Omnigraphics, 1990.

Duncan, Edmondstoune. *The Story of the Carol*. 1911. Reprint. Detroit,
Mich.: Omnigraphics, 1992.

Hadfield, Miles, and John Hadfield. *The Twelve Days of Christmas*. Boston,
Mass.: Little, Brown and Company, 1961.

Henderson, Helene, and Sue Ellen Thompson, eds. *Holidays, Festivals, and
Celebrations of the World Dictionary*. Second edition. Detroit, Mich.: Omnigraphics, 1997.

Hole, Christina. *British Folk Customs*. London, England: Hutchinson and
Company, 1976.

MacDonald, Margaret Read, ed. *The Folklore of World Holidays*. Detroit,
Mich.: Gale Research, 1992.

Miles, Clement A. *Christmas in Ritual and Tradition*. 1912. Reprint. Detroit,
Mich.: Omnigraphics, 1990.

Murray, Alexander. "Medieval Christmas." *History Today* 36, 12 (December
1986): 31-39.

Ross, Corinne. *Christmas in Scandinavia*. Chicago: World Book, 1977.

Urlin, Ethel. *Festivals, Holy Days, and Saints' Days*. 1915. Reprint. Detroit, Mich.: Omnigraphics, 1992.

Weiser, Francis X. *Handbook of Christian Feasts and Customs*. New York: Harcourt, Brace and World, 1952.

St. Sylvester's Day
Sylvester Abend

On December 31 the Roman Catholic Church honors St. Sylvester, a Roman Christian who became pope in 314 and continued in that role until his death in 335. His feast day falls on December 31 and is celebrated in Austria, **Germany**, and Switzerland.

Life and Legends of St. Sylvester

Little is known about Sylvester's life. His tenure as pope took place during the reign of the Roman emperor Constantine I. Legend claims that Sylvester played an active role in the conversion of Constantine to Christianity, but historians reject this tale. As Pope Sylvester witnessed the divisions between Christians caused by the rise of Arianism, a doctrine concerning the nature of Christ, he sent two representatives to the Council of Nicea. Convened by Emperor Constantine, the Council debated and rejected Arianism. His feast day was established in 1227 by Pope Gregory IX. At least one writer has suggested that his feast day was placed on December 31 for symbolic reasons. Just as December 31 ushers in a new year, so, too, did the conversion of the emperor Constantine usher in a new epoch in the history of Christianity.

Customs

Since *Silvester Abend*, or "Sylvester's Eve," is also New Year's Eve, many Germans and Austrians hold late-night parties (*see also* **New Year's Day**). In Germany these festive gatherings may include drinking, eating, dancing, singing, and fortune-telling. The traditional method of St. Sylvester's Eve fortune-telling is called *Bleigiessen*. This technique involves melting a small lump of lead in a spoon held over a candle. The molten lead is cast into a bowl of cold water. It hardens into a distinctive shape which is then interpreted to represent some aspect of one's fortune for the coming year.

In at least one Swiss town — Urnäsch in Appenzell Canton — bands of **mummers** known as "Silvesterclausen" still parade through the streets in costumes, **bells**, and headdresses on December 31, as well as on St. Sylvester's Day Old Style, which falls on January 13 (*see also* **Old Christmas Day**). They visit homes, yodel three times, and are rewarded with wine by the occupants.

Some of the customs associated with St. Sylvester's Day cannot easily be connected with the life of the saint. In past eras the Germans celebrated St. Sylvester's Day with mumming and noisemaking. In some parts of Austria, a rather sinister figure called Sylvester haunted New Year's Eve gatherings. He wore a grotesque mask, flaxen beard, and a **wreath** of **mistletoe**. He lurked in some dark corner until someone foolishly walked under the pine boughs suspended from the ceiling. Then he leaped forward, seized them, and roughly kissed them. At midnight the guests drove him away as the last remnant of the old year. Although this custom bears little association with the saint's life, it can be connected to the saint's name. The name "Sylvester" comes from the Latin word for forest, *silva*. Nearby forests probably provided the mistletoe associated with the startling Austrian Sylvester.

Further Reading

Brewster, H. Pomeroy. *Saints and Festivals of the Christian Church*. 1906. Reprint. Detroit, Mich.: Omnigraphics, 1990.

Del Re, Gerard, and Patricia Del Re. *The Christmas Almanack*. Garden City, N.Y.: Doubleday, 1979.

MacDonald, Margaret Read, ed. *The Folklore of World Holidays*. Detroit, Mich.: Gale Research, 1992.

Miles, Clement A. *Christmas in Ritual and Tradition*. 1912. Reprint. Detroit, Mich.: Omnigraphics, 1990.

Stevens, Patricia Bunning. *Merry Christmas!: A History of the Holiday*. New York: Macmillan, 1979.

A site sponsored by German instructor Robert J. Shea, Missouri:
http://www.serve.com/shea/germusa/customs.htm

St. Thomas's Day

The Feast of St. Thomas the Apostle, established in the twelfth century, originally fell on December 21, the day of the **winter solstice**. Folk customs attached to the saint's day, therefore, reflected both the occurrence of the solstice and the closeness of Christmas. Although the Roman Catholic Church has since moved St. Thomas's Day to July 3, some Anglicans preserve the December date. The Greek Orthodox Church celebrates the saint's feast on October 6.

Life and Legends of St. Thomas the Apostle

Jesus selected Thomas as one of his twelve disciples. Although he appears in all four Gospels, he is perhaps best remembered as the apostle who questioned the truth of Jesus' resurrection because he had not seen the risen Jesus with his own eyes (John 20:25). In so doing he earned the nickname "Doubting Thomas." In the Greek used by the writers of the New Testament, his name means "twin."

According to legend, St. Thomas spread the gospel to the East, venturing as far as **India** in his quest. There he established a Christian community in the southwestern region known then as Malabar, currently part of the state of Kerala. One story claims that Thomas found and baptized the Three Kings (*see also* **Magi**). These three then became India's first bishops. Another tale reports that an Indian king commissioned Thomas to build an opulent palace. Instead, the saint took the money entrusted to him for the project and distributed it to the poor. He died a martyr's death and was buried in Mylapore, near the city of Madras.

Artists often depicted the saint kneeling by the side of the risen Christ, verifying Jesus' identity by touching his wounds. Artists have also portrayed him holding a carpenter's rule. In medieval times he was known as the patron saint of architects, masons, and stonecutters. St. Thomas also protects the aged.

English Begging Customs

St. Thomas's Day falls within the **Christmas season** in many European countries. Customs associated with the day reflect its proximity to the holiday. In past times in rural **England** children, the poor, and the elderly might go "Thomasing" on that day. The most typical participants in this old customary practice, however, were poor, elderly women. Also known as "mumping," "doleing," "corning," or "gooding," the custom permitted these folk to go door to door asking for small handouts in order to enjoy good things to eat at Christmas time. The elderly collected money, which helped them afford special Christmas foods. The words to an old English Christmas song describe this custom:

> Christmas is coming and the geese are getting fat,
> Please spare a penny for the old man's hat,
> If you haven't got a penny, a ha'penny will do,
> If you haven't got a ha'penny, God bless you
> [Muir, 1977, 35].

In lieu of money, prosperous households often distributed grain to their less-fortunate neighbors, who turned it into various **Christmas cakes**, breads, or sweets. Often it became frumenty, a dessert made of boiled wheat, milk, sugar, and cinnamon. In Worcestershire children begged for apples. The well-to-do not only presented these small **gifts**, but might also offer **Christmas ale** or other forms of seasonal cheer. In return for their charity, rich householders received a sprig of **holly** or **mistletoe**, which folk beliefs suggested would bring them good luck. In some regions of the country, the well-off contributed money to a local church fund known as "St. Thomas's Dole." The clergy and churchwardens distributed the money to the needy on the Sunday before St. Thomas's Day. Evidence suggests that the custom of begging door to door on St. Thomas's Day arose in the eighteenth century, peaked in the early nineteenth century, and died out in the early twentieth century.

School Customs

In England students of past eras raced to school early on St. Thomas's Day. If they succeeded in arriving before the teacher, they were allowed to lock him out and so escape their lessons (*see also* **Barring Out the Schoolmaster**). In Belgium children practiced this custom with both parents and teachers, exacting the promise of treats in return for unlocking the doors. In some areas students tied their teachers to a chair until their demands were met, which often required teachers to take them to a local tavern. In **Denmark**, some schools put students in charge on St. Thomas's Day. The students conferred fancy titles on themselves and issued documents proclaiming their scholastic achievements.

Germany, Holland, Austria, and Czechoslovakia

In central Europe many past St. Thomas Day practices focused on the short day and long night of the winter solstice. In **Germany** and Holland one custom encouraged especially early rising after this, the longest night of the year. The last to rise or arrive at work or school was called "lazybones" or *Domesesel* (Thomas ass). In Germany St. Thomas's Eve was also called "Spinning Night," in reference to the practice of some spinners who stayed at their task all night in order to earn extra money for Christmas. Dancing and singing helped to ease the toil and pass the long night hours. Another past custom encouraged charity in light of the coming Christmas holiday. On St. Thomas's Day German employers were expected to make small gifts to their employees in order that they might buy Christmas provisions.

Old Austrian traditions recommended driving out demons on St. Thomas's Day. According to folk belief evil spirits fled from loud noises, so people rang **bells**, cracked whips, and staged raucous parades in frightening masks. These noisemaking practices continued on during the following nights, a practice that earned them the nickname the "rough nights." Christian versions of this St. Thomas's Day exorcism also existed. In some households the head of the family would walk through the house, barn, and yard spreading incense and sprinkling holy water, while the rest of the family and servants gathered together in prayer. In this way the family protected itself from evil spirits and blessed the homestead for the coming Christmas festival. Similar "smoke blessings" were also practiced during the Christmas season in Czechoslovakia and Germany.

This turning point in the solar year also attracted many charms and divination practices. For example, old folk beliefs informed German girls that if they slept upside down on St. Thomas's Day, with their feet on the pillow and their head near the foot of the bed, they would dream of their future husbands. English girls achieved the same effect by wrapping a peeled onion in a handkerchief and sleeping with it under their pillow. Another German and Austrian custom connected St. Thomas's Day with the baking of *Kletzenbrot* or *Hutzelbrot*, a fruit bread. In Germany, if the cook interrupted the kneading process to dash out and hug all the trees in the orchard, the trees were bound to bear much fruit in the coming year.

Norway

St. Thomas's Day ushered in the Christmas season in old **Norway**. In past times Norwegian custom insisted that all Christmas preparations be completed by St. Thomas's Day, including the chopping of enough firewood to last throughout the two-week Christmas festival. All Christmas baking, slaughtering, and brewing should also have been finished by that day. For this reason Thomas the Apostle long ago acquired the humorous nickname, "St. Thomas the Brewer." In past times Norwegians visited each other on St. Thomas's Day in order to sample one another's Christmas ale.

In old Norway the **Peace of Christmas** began on St. Thomas's Day. Towns designated special watchmen to ensure that peace and friendliness reigned during the holiday season. Penalties for violent crimes doubled at this time of the year. So strong was the desire for harmony during the Christmas season that one folk tradition even discouraged mentioning the names of harmful animals, such as wolves, during this period.

Further Reading

Chambers, Robert. "December 21 — St. Thomas's Day." In his *The Book of Days*. Volume 2. 1862-64. Reprint. Detroit, Mich.: Omnigraphics, 1990.

Henderson, Helene, and Sue Ellen Thompson, eds. *Holiday, Festivals, and Celebrations of the World Dictionary*. Second edition. Detroit, Mich.: Omnigraphics, 1997.

Henriksen, Vera. *Christmas in Norway Past and Present*. Oslo, Norway: Johan Grundt Tanum Forlag, 1970.

Hole, Christina. *Christmas and Its Customs*. New York: M. Barrows and Company, 1958.

Hutton, Ronald. *The Stations of the Sun*. Oxford, England: Oxford University Press, 1996.

Metford, J. C. J. *Dictionary of Christian Lore and Legend*. London, England: Thames and Hudson, 1983.

Miles, Clement A. *Christmas in Ritual and Tradition*. 1912. Reprint. Detroit, Mich.: Omnigraphics, 1990.

Muir, Frank. *Christmas Customs and Traditions*. New York: Taplinger, 1977.

Russ, Jennifer M. *German Festivals and Customs*. London, England: Oswald Wolff, 1982.

Thonger, Richard. *A Calendar of German Customs*. London, England: Oswald Wolff, 1966.

Weiser, Francis X. *Handbook of Christian Feasts and Customs*. New York: Harcourt, Brace and World, 1952.

St. Wenceslaus. *See* Wenceslas, King

Salvation Army Kettles

The sight of a well-wrapped man or woman standing next to a red kettle and shaking a hand-held **bell** greets many an American **Christmas season** shopper upon entering or leaving a department store. For over one hundred years the Salvation Army has stationed these bell-ringers on street corners and at malls in order to collect money to feed the poor at Christmas time. For many, the red kettle and tinkling bell have become a holiday symbol and a reminder that the Christmas season is upon us.

The Salvation Army is a non-profit, religious organization dedicated to spreading the Christian faith and aiding the poor. It began in London, **England**, in the year 1865, when Methodist minister William Booth (1829-1912) decided that in order to reach social outcasts and poor people with the Christian message, he would have to leave his church and preach in the streets. Booth and his followers overcame early opposition and achieved a degree of success. In 1878 Booth changed his organization's name from the Christian Mission to the Salvation Army. In 1880 some of Booth's followers emigrated to the United States, founding a branch of the Salvation Army in **New York City**. The organization is now active in 99 countries and claims over three million members worldwide.

The first Salvation Army Christmas kettle appeared in San Francisco in 1891. In that year Joseph McFee, who had achieved the rank of captain within the Salvation Army, resolved to raise funds to provide Christmas dinners for those in need. The Englishman remembered having seen people with big pots collecting coins for charity back home in his native Liverpool. He decided the same strategy could work here. McFee obtained a kettle and permission to set it up at the foot of Market Street, where the Oakland ferry landed. His campaign was a success, and by 1895 thirty Salvation Army divisions in various towns and cities were using the Christmas kettles. The use of kettles to collect coins reminded donors that their money would be used to prepare meals for the poor. Indeed, in the early days the slogan "Keep the pot boiling" often appeared on the Salvation Army signs posted above the kettles. In 1897 the Salvation Army declared that donations made to kettles nationwide had provided 150,000 Christmas dinners for poor people. By 1898 the New York chapter of the Salvation Army was providing an enormous, sit-down Christmas dinner for the poor in Madison Square Garden.

The vision of Christmas as a season especially appropriate for charitable giving gained in popularity in the second half of the nineteenth century (*see also* **Christmas Carol, A; America, Christmas in Nineteenth-Century**). By the last decade of the nineteenth century, the idea of funding Christmas dinners for the poor had become particularly fashionable among the middle and upper classes. Rich donors often attended the dinners as well, which were held in arenas or theaters. The well-to-do were required to buy a ticket to the event, which entitled them to a spectator's seat inside the arena. There they witnessed first-hand masses of poor people sating their hunger, and, hopefully, expressing their gratitude to their benefactors. These trends in charitable giving may have contributed to the Salvation Army's sweeping success in their Christmas kettle campaign.

The Salvation Army still provides sit-down Christmas dinners for those in need, but today's kettle donations may also go towards providing the means for poor families to celebrate Christmas dinner at home or towards other social services. The Salvation Army aids seven million Americans each year from Thanksgiving to Christmas. Their success with the bell and kettle at Christmas time has inspired other charities to post their own volunteers on the sidewalk with similar equipment to collect charitable donations during the holiday season.

Further Reading

Nissenbaum, Stephen. *The Battle for Christmas*. New York: Alfred A. Knopf, 1996.

Pool, Daniel. *Christmas in New York*. New York: Seven Stories Press, 1997.

Web Site

For more on the history of the Salvation Army's kettle campaign, visit the Salvation Army's International Heritage web site: http://www.salvation army.org/heritage.nsf/AllSubCategories?openView&RestrictToCategory= Christmas_Kettle&main=Symbols

Santa Claus

Kriss Kringle, St. Nick

Born in the United States of mixed ethnic and religious heritage, Santa Claus embodies the American ideal of the nation as a great melting pot of cultural identities. Santa Claus became an important folk figure in the second half of the nineteenth century, about the time when Americans were beginning to celebrate Christmas in large numbers (*see also* **America, Christmas in Nineteenth-Century**). Santa Claus bears a good deal of resemblance to his closest relative, the old European gift bringer **St. Nicholas**. Indeed "St. Nick" serves as one of Santa's nicknames.

While the origins of many legendary figures remain obscure, researchers have traced the basic framework of the Santa Claus myth back to the creative works of three individuals: writer Washington Irving (1783-1859), scholar Clement C. Moore (1779-1863), and illustrator Thomas Nast (1840-1902). These men, in turn, drew on elements of European and Euro-American Christmas folklore in their portrayals of the Christmas gift bringer. Interestingly enough, Americans embraced this "ready-made" folklore in the late nineteenth century, a time when ready-made goods of all kinds became widely available due to the rise of industrial manufacturing.

Today Santa Claus reigns as an icon of American Christmas celebrations. Many Christmas decorations bear his image, and popular songs tell of his **North Pole** and Christmas Eve activities. Nearly every American child can tell you that Santa is a plump, old man with a white beard who wears a baggy red suit and cap trimmed with white fur. Many send letters to his North Pole workshop describing the **gifts** they would like to receive for Christmas (*see also* **Children's Letters**). They eagerly await Christmas Eve, when he loads his sled with toys for good girls and boys and flies around the world, sliding down chimneys to place the presents under decorated **Christmas trees**. As if to confirm this Christmas fairy tale, men in

Santa suits regularly appear on street corners, at office parties, and in department and toy stores around Christmas time.

Before Santa Claus

In spite of its contemporary popularity, Christmas was not widely celebrated in the United States at the turn of the nineteenth century (*see also* **America, Christmas in Colonial**). A few ethnic groups, however, clung to the Christmas customs inherited from their European ancestors. Before Santa Claus became a familiar gift bringer to most Americans, the Pennsylvania Dutch received Christmas gifts from the Christ Child, whom they called **Christkindel**, *Christ-kind-lein,* or *Christkindchen*.

The Pennsylvania Dutch were Swiss and German immigrants who settled in Pennsylvania during the eighteenth and nineteenth centuries. These German-speaking immigrants called themselves *Deutsche,* which means "German." Eventually, Americans turned "Deutsche" into "Dutch." Although the "Plain Dutch" (the **Amish,** Mennonites, and Brethren) did not celebrate Christmas, the "Gay Dutch" (Lutherans and Reformed) did.

The Gay Dutch brought their German Christmas folklore with them to the United States. This folklore included two Christmas gift bringers, the Christ Child and Belsnickel (*see* **Knecht Ruprecht**). These two figures were distributing gifts to people of German descent in Pennsylvania in the eighteenth century, decades before Moore wrote his famous Christmas poem, "A Visit from St. Nicholas," and a century before Thomas Nast's illustrations popularized Santa Claus. Belsnickel was also known in German communities in Michigan, Iowa, and New York.

The Christ Child in America

The Christ Child contributed very little to our contemporary image of Santa Claus. Unlike Santa Claus, who rides in a magical flying sleigh, the early American Christ Child traveled from house to house on a humble donkey. Children left out plates or baskets filled with hay for the Child's mount. The Christ Child exchanged the hay for nuts, candy, and cookies.

By the early 1800s, however, the image of the Christ Child began to blur together with that of another European gift giver, the elderly St. Nicholas. Moreover, the German words for Christ Child, *Christ-Kindel* or *Christ-Kindlein,* began to slur as more non-German speakers attempted to pronounce these words. "Christkindel" turned into "Krist Kingle," and later, into "Kriss Kringle." In 1842 the publication of *The Kriss Kringle Book* cemented this pronunciation error and compounded it by using the name to describe a gift giver who seemed suspiciously like Santa Claus. Eventually, all that remained of the German Christ Child was the Americanized name "Kriss Kringle." And even that was transformed into a nickname for Santa Claus.

Belsnickel in America

Belsnickel may have contributed to the image of Santa Claus in a more direct way. In **Germany** Belsnickel, or Knecht Ruprecht, accompanied St. Nicholas on his gift-giving rounds. Germans pictured him as a shaggy, soot-covered man who carried a whip, a **bell**, and a sack of treats. In Pennsylvania Dutch country, however, Belsnickel made his rounds without St. Nicholas. He brought nuts, candies, and cookies to children daring enough to brave a possible smack of the whip as they scrambled for the treats he tossed on the floor. Since Belsnickel often dressed in furs, at least one writer has speculated that his image may have inspired the fur-trimmed suit worn by Santa Claus. In the United States beliefs and customs surrounding Belsnickel survived somewhat longer than those surrounding the Christ Child, dying out in the early twentieth century.

St. Nicholas in America

Whereas Belsnickel and the Christ Child appeared around Christmas, St. Nicholas traditionally brought his gifts on the eve of his feast day, December 6 (*see also* **St. Nicholas's Day**). Historical evidence suggests that the gift-giving customs surrounding the saint were well known in the Netherlands during the eighteenth century. By contrast, only a few scattered references to beliefs and customs surrounding St. Nicholas can be found among Dutch and German immigrants to the United States during this same era. Apparently, folk traditions concerning St. Nicholas as a winter season gift giver did not cross the Atlantic with Dutch and German immigrants in any great force.

Washington Irving and St. Nicholas

The St. Nicholas we know today needed the help of writer Washington Irving to establish a toehold in this country. In 1809 Irving's satirical *A History of New York* raised St. Nicholas to a position of importance in New York's Dutch-American community, primarily as a symbol of ethnic identity. In doing so, he made a few changes to the traditional European image of the saint. Irving replaced the tall, somber, and commanding man in a red bishop's robe with a short, round, jolly Dutchman who smoked a long-stemmed pipe and dressed in colonial garb.

Clement C. Moore and St. Nicholas

Clement C. Moore, a professor at New York's General Theological Seminary, was a friend of Washington Irving's. In 1822 he wrote a poem about St. Nicholas that was destined to shape the American image of Santa Claus. Titled "A Visit from St. Nicholas," the poem begins with the familiar line, "'Twas the night before Christmas." Moore based the appearance of St. Nicholas partly on the image of him presented in Irving's *History* and partly on a plump Dutch man who lived near Moore's house. Moore's St. Nicholas also bears some resemblance to Irving's portrait of Wouter Van Twiller, the first governor of the New Netherlands colony in what is now New York.

Although the poem is about St. Nicholas, Moore shifted the traditional date of Nicholas's visit from the eve of his own feast day to Christmas Eve. In this way Moore transformed the saint into a Christmas gift bringer. In addition, Moore's poem promoted the European St. Nicholas's Day custom of using **stockings** as convenient receptacles for gifts. Moore also retained the old European idea that St. Nicholas enters homes through the chimney, an idea some writers ultimately trace back to the belief that pagan deities spiraled downwards into homes on the smoke of hearth fires (*see also* **Berchta**).

In spite of his reliance on Dutch folklore in portraying the image and activities of St. Nicholas, Moore eliminated **Black Peter**, St. Nicholas's faithful companion in the Netherlands. According to Dutch tradition, Black Peter usually did the dirty work of climbing down the chimney and so acquired a grimy appearance. In Moore's poem St. Nicholas himself descends the chimney and thus appears all "tarnished with ashes and soot." Moore may also have been patterning this aspect of St. Nicholas's appearance after Belsnickel, whom nineteenth-century German-American youth would impersonate by coating their faces and hands with soot.

Although Moore is sometimes credited with the invention of Santa's flying **reindeer**, scholars note that the image actually appeared in a little-known children's poem published a year before Moore wrote "A Visit from St. Nicholas." Moore did, however, assign the reindeer the names by which we still know them today: Dasher, Dancer, Prancer, Vixen, Comet, Cupid, Donder, and Blitzen. Moore's poem was first published under his own name in 1844.

More Confusion Over Names

By the time the next major contributor to the gift bringer's mythology came upon the scene, the St. Nicholas figure popularized by Moore and Irving had become known as Santa Claus. The Dutch phrase for St. Nicholas is *Sinterklaas*. Apparently, American English speakers found this word troublesome. Scholars have uncovered a number of early American renditions of the good saint's name, including "St. Aclaus," "St. Iclaus," "Santeclaw," "Sancte Klaas," "St. Claas," and "St. a claus." Eventually, Americans settled on "Santa Claus," a name which, for most English speakers, obscured the gift giver's link back to one of Europe's most popular saints.

Thomas Nast and Santa Claus

Nineteenth-century illustrations depicting Santa Claus reveal that people held widely varying views as to what the gift bringer looked like. Some imagined him as fat, others as thin. Some saw him as gnome-like, others as an adult human being. One magazine illustration even depicted him as a little girl, perhaps confusing him with another gift bringer, Christkindel. In the late 1800s illustrator Thomas Nast, a German-born immigrant, published a series of Santa Claus drawings that captured the public imagination and settled the issue of Santa's appearance.

In embellishing the mythic figure outlined by Moore and Irving, Nast may well have drawn on his knowledge of northern European customs surrounding Christmas gift givers. In a series of drawings published over the course of thirty years, Nast created the Santa Claus costume with which we are so familiar today: a long, white beard, black boots, and a red suit trimmed with white fur. At least one writer has speculated that Nast drew on popular German conceptions of a fur-clad gift giver, such as Belsnickel, in designing the costume. The fact that the costume was primarily red, however, suggests that Nast had the European St. Nicholas in mind, since the saint was traditionally depicted wearing the red robes of a bishop.

Nast expanded the Santa lore of his time by giving the gift bringer a home address, the North Pole, and some new helpers, **elves**. Furthermore, although Moore's poem suggested that Santa was an elf himself, Nast settled on portraying him as a fat, jolly, elderly man. Some speculate that Nast knew of the Scandinavian tradition whereby elves deliver Christmas gifts (*see* **Jultomten**). They suggest that knowledge of this folk custom may have inspired him to add elves to Santa's household.

Nineteenth-Century Developments

Although the folklore surrounding Santa Claus has for the most part remained remarkably stable since its creation, a few changes occurred over the course of the nineteenth century. The original Dutch St. Nicholas punished misbehaving children by leaving them only a rod or stick, which symbolized a beating. So did Knecht Ruprecht, Belsnickel, and, by some reports, Christkindel. As the century rolled by, however, Americans placed less and less emphasis on the punitive aspect of Santa's mission. Some researchers attribute this development to changing concepts of childhood and child rearing. By the late nineteenth century many Americans began to view children less as unruly creatures who needed to be controlled by threat of punishment and more as ignorant and innocent souls who needed to be taught through nurturance and good example. Apparently, Santa Claus changed his attitudes towards children along with the rest of the country.

Moore's poem makes no mention of a Christmas tree, and has the jolly gift giver fill the children's stockings instead. Nevertheless, Santa eventually adopted the old German custom of placing gifts under the Christmas tree. In 1845 a children's book titled *Kriss Kringle's Christmas Tree* presented American audiences with the idea that the Christmas gift bringer hangs his gifts on the Christmas tree. Throughout the nineteenth century the association between the tree and the gifts grew stronger as the custom of installing a decorated tree in one's house at Christmas time gained in popularity. As Americans began to give one another more and heavier gifts, they began to place them beneath the tree rather than hang them on the tree. And while stockings hung by the fireplace never completely disappeared from the American Christmas scene, they became a much less important component of the gift-giving ritual when Santa began to place gifts under the tree.

Promoting the Santa Claus Myth

At the turn of the twentieth century, the Santa Claus myth had become so well established that retailers, advertisers, and charities began to use it to promote their interests (*see also* **Commercialism**). Hired Santas began to appear on street corners and in department stores. In 1937 the first training school for professional Santas was established in Albion, New York. Its classes taught potential Santas how to act and dress the role and coached them in Santa mythology. By the mid-1950s **New York City** alone could boast of at least three such Santa schools.

In the first half of the twentieth century, however, some people worried whether the sudden proliferation of street-corner Santas would cause children to question the Santa Claus myth. In 1914 a group of concerned citizens in New York City formed the Santa Claus Association, a group whose self-appointed mission was to safeguard children's belief in Santa Claus. At Christmas time they busied themselves with collecting children's letters to Santa Claus from the post office and responding to the requests they contained. In 1929 post office officials themselves took over the task of responding to these letters. Other groups did their part to limit the overbooking of Santas. In 1937 the **Salvation Army** stopped hiring Santas to promote their cause. In 1948 the Boston city council recommended that the city host only one Santa per season to be headquartered on Boston Common.

While some worked to protect children's belief in Santa Claus, others wondered whether children should be taught the myth at all. Religious parents expressed concern that children would confuse Santa Claus with **Jesus**. Their concern echoed that of German Protestant reformers from centuries past who eventually succeeded in replacing St. Nicholas as the holiday season gift bringer with Christkindel.

Twentieth-Century Developments

Santa has become such a popular American institution that a multitude of training courses are now available for the thousands of people who play Santa Claus each year at public events. It has been estimated that about 20,000 "rent-a-Santas" ply their trade across the United States each year at Christmas time. Most of the training directed at these seasonal Santas teaches them how to maintain their jolly manner and appearance under pressure from the public. Practical advice, such as not falling asleep on the job, blends with bits of Santa etiquette, such as not accepting money from a parent while a child is looking on, and avoiding eating garlic, onions, or beans for lunch. Another typical teaching counsels seasonal Santas to keep their cool even if blessed by a "royal christening" from an over-excited child.

The twentieth century has witnessed only a few refinements to the basic Santa Claus myth. The most important of these was the addition of a new member to Santa's team of flying reindeer, a gawky, young, red-nosed creature named Rudolf. Young Rudolf enjoyed instant popularity with the American public, inspiring both a popular song and a children's television special. In addition, beginning in the 1920s the Coca-Cola Company commissioned artist Haddon Sunblom to draw a series of color illustrations of Santa Claus for an

advertising campaign. Like Nast's earlier illustrations, these drawings helped to define the image of Santa Claus in the minds of many
Americans.

During the twentieth century American pop culture reached almost
every part of the globe. People from all over the world can now identify the jolly, chubby, white-bearded man in the red suit as Santa Claus.
He competes with other Christmas gift bringers, such as **Grandfather
Frost** and La **Befana**, for the allegiance of people in many nations.

Further Reading

Barnett, James H. *The American Christmas*. New York: Macmillan, 1954.

Comfort, David. *Just Say Noel!* New York: Fireside Books, 1995.

Del Re, Gerard, and Patricia Del Re. *The Christmas Almanack*. Garden City, N.Y.: Doubleday, 1979.

Jones, Charles W. *Saint Nicholas of Myra, Bari, and Manhattan*. Chicago: University of Chicago Press, 1978.

Jones, E. Willis. *The Santa Claus Book*. New York: Walker and Company, 1976.

Nast St. Hill, Thomas. *Thomas Nast's Christmas Drawings for the Human Race*. New York: Harper and Row, 1971.

Nissenbaum, Stephen. *The Battle for Christmas*. New York: Alfred A. Knopf, 1996.

Restad, Penne. *Christmas in America*. New York: Oxford University Press, 1995.

Sansom, William. *A Book of Christmas*. New York: McGraw-Hill Book Company, 1968.

Shoemaker, Alfred L. *Christmas in Pennsylvania*. Kutztown, Pa.: Pennsylvania Folklore Society, 1959.

Siefker, Phyllis. *Santa Claus, Last of the Wild Men*. Jefferson, N.C.: McFarland and Company, 1997.

Waits, William. *The Modern Christmas in America*. New York: New York University Press, 1993.

Saturnalia

The ancient Romans honored the god Saturn in a midwinter festival known as Saturnalia. Many of the customs associated with Saturnalia reversed ordinary social rules and roles. Early Christian writers disapproved of this rowdy Roman revelry. Nevertheless, some of the customs associated with Saturnalia later attached themselves to the celebration of Christmas (*see also* **Kalends**).

Saturn and His Festival

Some scholars believe that the Romans borrowed Saturn from the Greeks by simply exchanging the deity's Greek name, *Kronos*, for the Roman name, *Saturn* (*for more on Kronos, see* **Father Time**). In addition, they assigned him a new, Roman history. Others believe that he evolved from a minor Etruscan god of agriculture. Scholars debate the meaning of the Roman god's name. Some believe the word "saturn" comes from the Latin verb for "to sow," whose root is *sat*. Others, however, think it evolved from *saturo*, which means "to fill" or "to satisfy." According to Roman mythology, Saturn ruled over the kingdom of Latium, the region surrounding Rome, as its first king during its golden age. He established the first laws and taught human beings agriculture. In this era of joy and plenty, people lived together in harmony and shared equally in the earth's bounty.

The Romans honored Saturn as the patron of agriculture and of civilized life. They held his festival at the end of the autumn sowing season when cold weather arrived in earnest. In the early years of the Roman Republic Saturnalia took place on December 17. At the close of the first century A.D., however, the celebrations had stretched into a full week of fun ending around December 23. Many of the customs associated with Saturnalia recalled the equality and abundance that characterized Saturn's reign on earth.

Equality

Lucian, a second-century Greco-Roman writer, drew up a set of rules summarizing proper conduct during Saturnalia. Chief among these rules was the decree that "all men shall be equal, slave and free, rich and poor, one with another." This temporary equality was especially apparent at the banquets characteristic of this Roman holiday. During the rest of the year the seating arrangements, portions, and service offered at Roman feasts reflected differences in wealth and social rank among the guests. Lucian's rules for Saturnalian banquets, however, neatly erased these inequalities. At a Saturnalian feast:

> Every man shall take place as chance may direct; dignities and birth and wealth shall give no precedence. All shall be served with the same wine. . . . Every man's portion of meat shall be alike. When the rich man shall feast his slaves, let his friends serve with him [Miles, 1990, 166-67].

Perhaps the slaves enjoyed the festival more than anyone else. They were exempted from their usual duties and from all forms of punishment. Furthermore, during the time of the festival they wore the felt cap given to freed slaves and could criticize and mock their masters without fear of reprisal. Moreover, at the feast held in honor of the holiday slaves sat down to eat first and were waited on by their masters.

Mock Kings

The mock kings who presided over the Saturnalian feasts offered one humorous exception to the general rule of equality. As these monarchs were chosen by lot, anyone might become king for the evening, even a slave. The king's commands had to be obeyed, no matter how outrageous. According to one observer, the king's orders might require "one to shout out a libel on himself, another to dance naked, or pick up the flute-girl and carry her thrice around the room." Christmas celebrations in medieval **Europe** also elevated a variety of mock authorities into temporary positions of power (*see also* **Boy Bishop; Feast of Fools; King of the Bean; Lord of Misrule**). Many researchers trace the origins of these figures back to the mock kings who presided over the Saturnalian banquets.

Leisure and Merrymaking

Slaves were not the only people enjoying free time during Saturnalia. Schools, stores, and courts of law closed their doors for the duration of the festival. No one worked during Saturnalia except those who provided the food that fueled the feasts. In fact, Lucian's rules mandated that people put all serious business aside and devote themselves to enjoyment:

> All business, be it public or private, is forbidden during the feast days, save such as tends to sport and solace and delight. Let none follow their avocations saving cooks and bakers. Anger, resentment, threats, are contrary to law. No discourse shall be either composed or delivered, except it be witty and lusty, conducing to mirth and jollity [Miles, 1990, 166].

In addition to feasting and drinking, the Romans enjoyed public gambling during Saturnalia, an activity that was against the law during the rest of the year. They expressed good will towards one another by exchanging small **gifts**, especially wax candles called *cerei*, wax fruit, and clay dolls called *signillaria*. Other popular customs included various kinds of informal masquerades in which men and women cavorted in the clothing of the opposite sex. More serious-minded Romans disapproved of the drunken excesses and the noisy, carousing crowds that wandered through the streets during the festival.

Echoes of this ancient Roman holiday remain in the English language. Today we use the word "Saturnalian" to refer to celebrations characterized by excess and abandon.

Further Reading

Henderson, Helene, and Sue Ellen Thompson, eds. *Holidays, Festivals, and Celebrations of the World Dictionary*. Second edition. Detroit, Mich.: Omnigraphics, 1997.

Henisch, Bridget Ann. *Cakes and Characters: An English Christmas Tradition*. London, England: Prospect Books, 1984.

Hutton, Ronald. *The Stations of the Sun*. Oxford, England: Oxford University Press, 1996.

James, E. O. *Seasonal Feasts and Festivals*. 1961. Reprint. Detroit, Mich.: Omnigraphics, 1993.

Leach, Maria, ed. *Funk and Wagnalls Standard Dictionary of Folklore, Mythology, and Legend*. New York: Harper and Row, 1984.

Miles, Clement A. *Christmas in Ritual and Tradition*. 1912. Reprint. Detroit, Mich.: Omnigraphics, 1990.

Room, Adrian. *Who's Who in Classical Mythology*. Lincolnwood, Ill.: NTC Publishing Group, 1996.

Scullard, H. H. *Festivals and Ceremonies of the Roman Republic*. Ithaca, N.Y.: Cornell University Press, 1981.

Shepherds

The **Gospel according to Luke** tells that an **angel** announced **Jesus'** birth to some humble shepherds who were spending the night in a nearby field. Many Bible commentators have remarked that this incident shows that God's favor rests with the poor, since they were the first to receive news of Christ's birth.

After receiving the angel's visit, the shepherds journey to **Bethlehem** in order to pay homage to Jesus, the newborn king. They find the Holy Family lodged in a stable. Since **Mary** had no crib, she laid the baby Jesus in a manger, or trough used to feed animals. Thus in Luke's account of Jesus' birth, the Holy Family lodges with the animals and is visited by shepherds.

The **Gospel according to Matthew** offers a different version of events (*see also* **Gospel Accounts of Christmas**). In that account, educated and well-to-do men from the East, the **Magi**, are the first to learn of Jesus' birth. Matthew's story implies that the Holy Family lives in Bethlehem. No shepherds appear in Matthew's account, just as no Magi appear in Luke's account.

Sheep and Shepherds in the Bible

In biblical times people relied on sheep and goats more than any other kind of domestic animal. Important figures from the Hebrew scriptures, or Old Testament, were shepherds—such as Abraham,

Moses, and David. Nevertheless, shepherds were considered very humble folk and were thus looked down on by some.

The Bible mentions sheep and shepherds hundreds of times. Most of these references are metaphorical rather than literal, however. Sheep require a good deal of care and the expert guidance of a shepherd to flourish. In order to illustrate God's care for his people, biblical writers sometimes described God as a shepherd and God's people as sheep. The Bible also compares good leaders to shepherds.

Jesus, who began his life among animals and those who care for them, would later be described as both lamb and shepherd. In explaining his mission as a teacher, healer, and leader, Jesus refers to himself as a shepherd (Luke 15:4-7, Matthew 15:24, John 10:3-30). The early Christians pictured Jesus in this way as well (Hebrews 13:20, 1 Peter 2:25). The Bible also portrays Jesus as a lamb (John 1:29). The ancient Jews sacrificed lambs as a means of reconciling themselves to God after having sinned. The first Christians came to see Jesus as a kind of sacrificial lamb, whose willing death for their sakes released them from the consequences of sin.

Christmas Customs

The shepherds' pilgrimage to Bethlehem has been reenacted in countless **Nativity plays**, including the Hispanic folk play known as Los **Pastores**. In some predominantly Catholic countries, people refer to the dawn mass on Christmas Day as the "Shepherds' Mass," in honor of their journey to visit the newborn Jesus. Pilgrims to Jesus' birthplace in Bethlehem can visit various "Shepherds Fields," sites promoted as the place where the shepherds received the angelic announcement of Jesus' birth.

Further Reading

Freedman, David Noel, ed. *Eerdmans Dictionary of the Bible*. Grand Rapids, Mich.: William B. Eerdmans Publishing Company, 2000.

Keck, Leander, ed. *New Interpreter's Bible: Luke, John*. Volume IX. Nashville, Tenn.: Abingdon, 1995.

Ryken, Leland, James C. Wilhoit, and Tremper Longman, III, eds. "Sheep, Shepherd." In their *Dictionary of Biblical Imagery*. Downers Grove, Ill.: InterVarsity Press, 1998.

Shoes
Boots

Most Americans are familiar with the Christmas custom of hanging up a **stocking** by the fireplace for **Santa Claus** to fill with **gifts**. In some countries, however, people use shoes or boots rather than stockings as gift receptacles.

In Sicily, children leave their shoes outdoors on the eve of **St. Lucy's Day**, December 13 (*see also* **Italy, Christmas in**). When the kindly saint passes by during the night, she deposits treats in the shoes, which the children discover the next morning.

In the Netherlands, children put shoes by the fireplace on the eve of **St. Nicholas's Day**, December 6. Dutch children sometimes also leave hay, carrots, or sugar for St. Nicholas's horse. In the morning they find their shoes filled with presents. German children also receive gifts from **St. Nicholas** on his feast day. They place their boots by the fireplace, a window, or the bedroom door on the evening of December 5. In the morning they feast on the sweets tucked inside the boots (*see also* **Germany, Christmas in**).

In **Iceland** the **Christmas Lads** fill children's shoes with candy. Youngsters help the Lads find the shoes by positioning them on a windowsill in the days preceding Christmas. A similar custom takes place in **Estonia**, where young people leave shoes out on a windowsill in the weeks before Christmas and wait for **elves** to come fill them with treats.

In **France** children set their shoes before the fireplace, underneath the **Christmas tree**, or near the **Nativity scene** on Christmas Eve. The French gift bringer, Père Noël, fills them with sweets and toys before morning comes.

In **Spain** the Three Kings, or **Magi**, stuff children's shoes with trinkets and sweets on **Epiphany**, which the Spanish also refer to as Three Kings Day. Spanish children deposit their shoes on the balcony, outside their front door, or near a fireplace on the evening of January 5. Many considerately leave straw for the Magi's camels as well. The next morning they race to recover trinkets and sweets left inside the shoes. The Three Kings also fill the shoes of Mexican, Brazilian, and Filipino children on Epiphany (*see also* **Brazil, Christmas in; Philippines, Christmas in the**). Filipino and Brazilian youngsters put their shoes near a window or door on Epiphany eve and in the morning find them overflowing with sweets and trinkets. In **Mexico** children place their shoes near the Nativity scene, or just outside a door or window that they might serve as handy baskets for gifts. They often offer water and straw for the Kings' camels as well.

Further Reading

Christmas in Germany. Second edition. Lincolnwood, Ill.: Passport Books, 1996.
Christmas in Mexico. Chicago: World Book, 1976.
McLenighan, Valjean. *Christmas in Spain.* Chicago: World Book, 1988.
Ross, Corinne. *Christmas in France.* Chicago: World Book, 1988.

Shooting in Christmas

In some areas of Europe, the United States, and **Lebanon** people celebrate Christmas Eve by making noise. One especially noisy custom comes from central and northern Europe and is called "shooting in Christmas." In **Germany** some people still follow this old folk tradition. Several hundred marksmen gather in Berchtesgaden, Germany, each year on Christmas Eve. As midnight approaches, they fire rifles and mortars for nearly an hour to usher in Christmas. Folklorists suspect that in past times people hoped that the sudden bangs produced by noisemaking customs such as these would frighten off evil spirits (*see also* **Ghosts; Twelve Days of Christmas**).

Emigrants brought this custom with them to the United States, where it sometimes migrated from Christmas Eve to New Year's Eve. In the eighteenth century bands of men tramped from house to house between midnight and dawn on New Year's Eve in Pennsylvania's German communities (*see also* **Mummers Parade**). They shot off their guns, recited folk rhymes, and partook of each household's hospitality. This noisy habit irritated some of their neighbors. In 1774 the Pennsylvania Assembly attempted to preserve the general peace by passing an act prohibiting any random firing of guns on or around **New Year's Day**.

In spite of this opposition, the custom of shooting in the new year lingered on in some German-American communities until well into the twentieth century. In the nineteenth century many southerners and westerners shot off guns to welcome in Christmas Eve and Christmas Day (*see also* **America, Christmas in Nineteenth-Century; Williamsburg, Virginia, Christmas in Colonial**). Southerners added to the din by setting off firecrackers as well.

Further Reading

Barrick, Mac E. *German-American Folklore*. Little Rock, Ark.: August House, 1987.

Henderson, Helene, and Sue Ellen Thompson, eds. *Holidays, Festivals, and Celebrations of the World Dictionary*. Second edition. Detroit, Mich.: Omnigraphics, 1997.

Kirchner, Audrey Burie, and Margaret R. Tassia. *In Days Gone By: Folklore and Traditions of the Pennsylvania Dutch*. Englewood, Colo.: Libraries Unlimited, 1996.

Slaves' Christmas

Slavery in the United States can be traced back to the early seventeenth century. Although some of these colonial era slaves included Native Americans and poor Europeans, the vast majority of people subjected to slavery in America were of African descent. Slavery never became as popular in the Northern states as it did in the Southern states. By the 1830s the Northern states had all but eliminated slavery, though it was still legal throughout the South. Slavery in the Southern United States ended with the close of the American Civil War in 1865.

How did the slaves celebrate Christmas? Though many belonged to well-to-do families, they themselves were poor and shared only a small fraction of the families' lavish festivities. Many, but not all, slaveowners granted their slaves a day or more of rest at Christmas time. Some also provided them with ample amounts of food, including the better cuts of meat, a form of nourishment that some scholars believe they rarely enjoyed during the rest of the year. Some also distributed passes to certain slaves, permitting them to visit relatives who lived in different places. Slaves relished these simple Christmas pleasures, activities that many slaveowners took for granted the year round. (*See also* **America, Christmas in Nineteenth-Century**.)

Leisure

Many slaveowners gave their slaves three days off at Christmas time. Some permitted fewer or no days of rest, and others allowed more than three days. On some plantations slaves were authorized to select a **Yule log** to burn in the main fireplace of the manor house. The slaves' holiday lasted as long as the log burned. Naturally the slave sent to fetch the Yule log from the woods exercised a great deal of care in choosing what he hoped would be a very slow-burning log. In this way the Christmas holiday could be extended to **New Year's Day**.

Not every slave got to rest at Christmas time. Since slaveowning families sometimes hosted elaborate Christmas dinners and parties, slaves who worked as household servants often found their workload increased at Christmas time. What's more, slaves could not count on time off at Christmas, since the master could always cancel their holiday. Indeed, some slaveowners withheld the privilege of celebrating Christmas from slaves who had displeased them during the year.

Most plantation slaves passed their Christmas holiday by taking part in some or all of the feasting, singing, dancing, music making, and storytelling that characterized Christmas in the slaves' quarters. Some slaves took advantage of the time off to hold quilting bees. Many of the quilts they made featured the color red, a favorite shade with many slaves. Both slave men and women participated in the craft of quilting. Other handicrafts were also produced and sold at Christmas time, because in many areas custom permitted slaves to keep all the money they earned during the Christmas holiday. (The rest of the year any money they earned belonged to their masters.) Some slaves may have devoted time to a more dangerous holiday hobby: studying. Studying was dangerous because many Southern states had strict laws forbidding the education of slaves.

Food and Drink

Some slaves never quite got enough to eat throughout the year. Rich, sustaining, and especially tasty foods, like choice cuts of meat, butter, eggs, and sugar almost never appeared on slaves' tables. Since most masters gave their slaves extra rations of high-quality food at Christmas time, the holiday not only represented a mouth-watering chance for slaves to eat their fill but also afforded them an opportunity to savor some of the tasty foods that their masters enjoyed year round. At Christmas time slaves might dine on a combination of meats, including roast chicken, ham, pickled pigs' feet, squirrel, or possum. Side dishes might include squash, greens cooked with ham hocks, salad greens and eggs, or ashcakes (boiled cornmeal sweetened with molasses and wrapped in cabbage leaves to bake). For dessert some slaves baked a cake or made sweet potato pie. On some plantations the mistress prepared a large Christmas banquet, which the master and mistress served to their slaves. (*For more on slaves' holiday foods, see* **Hopping John**).

Many of these Christmas feasts included homemade wine or generous servings of the masters' own liquor. This policy often resulted in drunkenness, as slaves were not permitted to drink at any other time of the year and thus were unaccustomed to the effects of alcohol. Former slave and abolitionist Frederick Douglass (1817-1895) believed that many slaveowners promoted this drunkenness as a means of discouraging slaves from seeking their own freedom. After the holidays were over slaveowners suggested to the slaves that if freed they would quickly slip into a life of laziness and alcoholic overindulgence. They pointed to the slaves' recent excesses as evidence for their argument.

Visits and Marriages

Slaves could never count on keeping their families together. Sometimes the master would sell a husband away from a wife, or a child away from his or her parents. Nevertheless, some slaveowners permitted slaves to visit nearby relatives at Christmas time. On Christmas Eve the master distributed passes permitting certain individuals to travel. Slaves welcomed the visitors warmly. Even if not a relative, the visitor would bring news from another part of the county and, perhaps, greetings from a relative. Slaves looked forward to these Christmas visits all year long. Nevertheless, this privilege could be withheld from slaves who displeased their masters.

Christmas was a popular time for slaves to marry. The joyous family reunions and rowdy revelry that characterized the "Big Times," as slaves sometimes referred to the Christmas holiday, inspired an increased number of romantic encounters leading to marriage.

Gifts

Many slaveowners gave **gifts** to their slaves at Christmas time. Typical gifts included hats, hair ribbons, tobacco, sugar, bandanas, collars, or coins. In addition, the master often offered as Christmas gifts the things he would have to supply for the slave anyway, such as warm clothing and shoes. Some wealthy plantation owners furnished slaves with gifts of money at Christmas time. They might also present them with the means to prepare a sumptuous banquet, offering them such luxury foodstuffs as beef, chicken, turkey, pork, duck, apples, oranges, cakes, pies, and biscuits.

Plantation slaves sometimes had to make a formal visit to the "big house" (the manor house) to receive these gifts. Many never entered the mansion during the rest of the year. They arrived dressed in their best clothing to perform the little ritual surrounding Christmas gift giving. Along with his gifts, the master offered Christmas greetings to the slaves, wishing each of them a happy holiday. Sometimes he gave them a glass of **eggnog** and proposed a toast. Upon receiving his or her gift the slave would extend Christmas greetings and good wishes to the master and his family. Sometimes the slaves would collectively present the master or mistress with a token gift, such as a homemade basket or a clutch of eggs.

At other plantations, the slaves did not receive their gifts in the big house. Instead, the master and mistress visited the slaves in their quarters to watch them sing and dance and to present them with gifts. Sometimes the white folks joined for a while in the slaves' festivities.

On Christmas Day, custom permitted slaves to ask a Christmas gift of any white person they saw. All they had to do was to approach them and shout out, "Christmas gift!" before the white person could speak to them. Slaveowners who considered themselves good-natured let themselves be bested, and stocked up on coins, sweets, and trinkets to give away in this little **game**.

In spite of their poverty, slave parents often gave their children a modest Christmas gift. These gifts consisted of things like homemade baskets, hats, aprons, or strip quilts.

Song and Dance

Temporarily relieved from the daily routine of hard work, plantation slaves celebrated by music making and dancing. Some records indicate that these Christmas Eve and Christmas Day revels lasted most of the night. Slave musicians played music with any kind of instrument they could get their hands on, including homemade drums, pipes, fiddles, and banjos. Those who could not find or play musical instruments could still sing songs to entertain one another and to accompany instrumental music.

In some parts of the South slaves practiced a Christmas masquerade known as **Jonkonnu**. Men dressed in tattered, makeshift costumes and masks. Thus attired they rambled from house to house playing music and dancing. Householders gave them coins or trinkets in exchange for their entertainment.

Slaves also sang religious music at Christmas time. In fact, African-American slaves developed their own style of religious songs known as "spirituals." Some well-known spirituals retell elements of the Christmas story. These include "Mary Had a Baby," "Go Tell It on the Mountain," "Rise up Shepherd and Follow," "Sister Mary Had-a But One Child," and "Behold That Star."

Religion

Slaves attended religious services and gathered together to pray at Christmas time. Some slaves belonged to conservative Christian denominations, such as the Baptists and Methodists, which forbade dancing. These people would avoid the Christmas parties and instead organize prayer meetings. Some of the meetings lasted for hours; others lasted all night.

Running Away and Rebelling

Christmas was a popular time of year to run away from one's master and to seek freedom in the North. Slaves reasoned that they were less likely to be missed at home or apprehended on the roads at Christmas time than at any other time of the year. They would not be expected to show up for their daily chores until after the holiday. Furthermore, whites were accustomed to seeing many black wayfarers on the streets and byways during the holiday season. The liberties allowed slaves at Christmas time may also have inspired a number of slave revolts. One historian has estimated that approximately one third of both documented and rumored slave rebellions occurred around Christmas. In the year 1856, slave revolts occurred in nearly every slave-holding state at Christmas time.

Christmas Legends, Lore, and Superstition

Throughout the South, both white and black children were told that **Gabriel** the **angel** sprinkled stardust on the earth in early winter. It turned into the first frost of the season as it hit the ground. Its sparkling beauty served to remind children of the coming of the Christ

Child. Slaves also passed along bits of old European Christmas lore, such as the belief that animals gain the power of human speech on Christmas Eve (*see also* **Nativity Legends**). If one crept quietly into the barn at just the right moment, one might overhear them murmur praises to God and the baby **Jesus**. Nevertheless, to do so would bring a mountain of bad luck down on one's head.

New Year

Some plantation slaves celebrated New Year's Day with a cakewalk (*see also* **Mummers Parade**). In this competitive dance, couples stepped side by side, moving around the dance floor in the form of a square. Their exaggerated movements amplified and made fun of the formal dances popular among white folk. The couple who exhibited the fanciest moves won a cake.

Southern slaves and their masters shared certain New Year's Day superstitions. Many believed that consuming a dish called hopping John, made from black-eyed peas and ham hocks, brought good luck for the coming year. Other popular beliefs included the notion that to argue on New Year's Day meant that one would be drawn into arguments throughout the coming year. Many invoked the superstition that to cut one's hair on New Year's Day was to divide one's wealth in two. Others held to the belief that to borrow or lend anything on New Year's Day would bring bad luck for the rest of the year.

The worst luck a slave could encounter on New Year's Day was to be separated from a close family member through work contracts arranged by the master. Those hired out to work for the year on other plantations left on New Year's Day. For this reason slaves sometimes called January 1 "Heartbreak Day."

On January 1, 1863, President Abraham Lincoln (1809-1865) signed the Emancipation Proclamation into law, granting immediate freedom to slaves in the Southern states. This event is still celebrated as **Emancipation Day** in some African-American communities.

Psychological Pressures

In addition to all the other deprivations experienced year-round by American slaves, they were also subjected to unusual kinds of psychological pressures at Christmas time. These pressures resulted from the role that Christmas played in justifying the institution of human slavery to slaveowners. For example, the slaves' own joy could be used against them, since some slaveowners pointed to the happy Christmas celebrations of their slaves to justify the institution of slavery. Others harped on their slaves' enjoyment of leisure and alcoholic beverages at Christmas time, suggesting to them that they had a natural inclination towards idleness and drunkenness and thus were better off as slaves. While slaves ran the risk of inspiring these thoughts in their masters if they indulged in Christmas pleasures, they skirted other dangers if they refused. The master might view those who grumbled at Christmas time as potential troublemakers (who would be watched closely and subjected to possible future punishments). As a result, slaves may have felt obligated to appear pleased with the Christmas celebrations allotted to them, even when they were in fact unhappy.

Some masters cynically promoted slave Christmas celebrations, believing that this once-yearly binge relieved just enough suffering and want to prevent slaves from openly rebelling against their inferior status. Others may have been less aware of the possibility that the simple pleasures they afforded their slaves at Christmas time played a role in the preservation of slavery.

Conclusion

In spite of all the pressures and deprivations they were subjected to, African-American slaves wrested some degree of holiday happiness out of the foods and freedoms allowed them at this time of year. Rising above their circumstances, they contributed a number of beautiful spirituals to the American repertoire of **Christmas carols**. Our Christmas celebrations today are still the richer for them.

Further Reading

Dipeiro, Diane. "Together at Christmas (Christmas Traditions of African-American Slaves)." *Colonial Homes* 20 (December 1, 1994): 28(2).

Genovese, Eugene D. *Roll, Jordan, Roll.* New York: Pantheon, 1974.

McKissack, Patricia, and Frederick McKissack. *Christmas in the Big House, Christmas in the Quarters.* New York: Scholastic, 1994.

Nissenbaum, Stephen. *The Battle for Christmas.* New York: Alfred A. Knopf, 1996.

Scheel, Eugene. "Recalling Joys of Christmas, Big and Small." *The Washington Post* (December 3, 2000): V03.

Snow Maiden

Snegurochka

Contemporary Russian folklore declares that the Snow Maiden is **Grandfather Frost**'s grandchild and assigns her the role of helping him distribute **gifts** to **Russia**'s children on **New Year's** Eve. The Snow Maiden is usually represented as a beautiful little girl or teenager with long blond braids. She dresses in a light blue robe and cap trimmed with white fur. She may wear a modern, knee-length robe and white boots or a more traditional ankle-length robe. An old Russian legend tells her story. Neither Christmas nor Grandfather Frost appear in this traditional tale. In the twentieth century, Communist officials linked the legend of the Snow Maiden with their chosen gift bringer, Grandfather Frost.

Legend of the Snow Maiden

Snegurochka is the Russian word for "Snow Maiden." Many different versions of her tale can be heard across Russia. The outlines of the story remain the same, however.

Once upon a time an old, peasant couple were watching their neighbors' children romp in the snow. The couple had always wanted children of their own but had reached old age without having any. As they watched the youngsters play, their longing inspired them to build a little girl out of snow. They rolled, patted, and shaped the snow, creating the image of a beautiful little girl with long braids. She was so life-like that they spoke to her, beseeching her to come to life and live in their house as their own daughter. Moments later the snow girl seemed to breathe, then her lips and cheeks blushed pink, and her braids turned from white to golden blond. Their wish had come true! The girl told them that she had come from the land of winter to be their daughter. The astonished couple hugged the girl and took her home with them.

The Snow Maiden was cheerful and good as well as beautiful. Everyone loved her. The old couple took great joy in making a home for her and in watching her frolic with the other children. But as spring approached the Snow Maiden began to change. Little by little, she lost her good spirits and seemed to grow tired or ill. One day she announced that the time had come for her to return to the far north, to the land of winter. The couple begged her not to go. The old woman hugged her daughter tightly and felt drops of water on the surface of the girl's skin and clothes. This alarmed the old couple, but neither knew what to do. In a few minutes the Snow Maiden had melted away completely.

Her disappearance broke their hearts. They mourned for her throughout the spring and summer. They tried to shut their ears to the laughter of children playing in the sunshine, since it only reminded them of the sweet Snow Maiden. The old couple passed a gloomy autumn, and, soon, winter returned to the land. One evening, as the snow swirled around the eaves of their house, they heard a knock at the door. The sound struck fear into their hearts because they could not imagine who would visit them on such an evening. Soon they heard a familiar high-pitched voice cry, "Mama, Papa, open the door! The winter snows have returned your daughter to you!" The old man flung open the door and there stood the smiling Snow Maiden. The old couple wept and embraced her. Just as before, the three of them passed a joyful winter together. As spring approached the old couple resigned themselves to the Snow Maiden's disappearance. They did not grieve for her when she melted, though. They knew that the winter snow would return their Snegurochka to them next year.

Further Reading

Christmas in Russia. Chicago: World Book, 1992.

South Africa, Christmas in

South Africa is located on the southernmost tip of the African continent. Because it lies in the Southern Hemisphere, South Africa celebrates a summertime Christmas (*for more on the difference between the Northern and Southern hemispheres, see* **Winter Solstice**). Many people head for the mountains or the beach at this time of year and thus celebrate Christmas with picnics, barbecues, sports, and other outdoor activities.

In spite of the heat Christmas shoppers often find shopping districts decorated with the typical trappings of a northern Christmas, including **Christmas trees** sprayed with false snow, and various depictions of sleighs, **reindeers**, and cold, dark, winter evenings. **Father Christmas**, dressed in red velvet and furs, often makes a sweaty appearance as well. Shoppers may further the illusion of a cozy, northern Christmas by purchasing **Christmas cards** picturing snowy, winter scenes. Or they may embrace the realities of a South African Christmas by choosing cards that feature the plants, animals, and landscape of a South African summer.

The English Christmas Heritage

Christmas celebrations in South Africa share much in common with those of Great Britain, as many white South Africans are descended from English settlers (*see also* **England, Christmas in**). Although Afrikaners outnumber South Africans of British descent, English-speaking South Africans have wielded much cultural influence due to their political dominance in the twentieth century. Moreover, many Afrikaners come from strict Protestant sects, such as Calvinism, that have not placed much importance on the celebration of Christmas.

Father Christmas, Christmas cards, Christmas dinners that begin with **Christmas crackers** and end with **plum pudding**, Christmas **stockings**, and family excursions to **pantomime** shows are among the Christmas traditions introduced to South Africa by its English settlers. Some South Africans, following the lead of their Australian colleagues, hang up pillow cases instead of stockings, thereby giving Father Christmas more room to be generous (*see also* **Australia, Christmas in**). Like the British, South Africans observe **Boxing Day** on December 26 by giving tips to workers who have served them throughout the year, such as garbage collectors.

The Afrikaner Christmas Heritage

Afrikaners trace their roots back to Dutch, German, and French settlers who came to South Africa in the seventeenth and eighteenth centuries. In the early part of the twentieth century, Afrikaners from rural South Africa celebrated Christmas by attending church and receiving Holy Communion (the Eucharist), or by reading from the Bible at home. Children might receive a few, simple gifts. Special cakes and jam tarts, rarely available in those days, were served with Christmas dinner, which often featured roast turkey or roast pork. In some families, however, these special desserts were served on **New Year's** Eve rather than Christmas. Families often went visiting on Christmas Day to exchange Christmas greetings in person. Over time many Afrikaners adopted the more festive Christmas customs of English South Africans.

Music

South Africans have embraced the custom of attending outdoor, candlelit, sing-along caroling concerts on Christmas Eve (*see also* **Christmas Carols**). These concerts, known as Carols by Candlelight, began as an Australian Christmas custom and later migrated to South Africa.

Music is an important component of Christmas festivities for many South Africans. Some go caroling from door to door on Christmas Eve. Others form Christmas bands that play in the streets during the last few days before the holiday. Traditionally only men and boys participate in this custom. The groups wear matching uniforms whose purchase is financed through their various fundraising activities.

Christmas Day

Christmas morning church services often feature special programs, such as Christmas pageants put on by the congregations' youth or special choir concerts. Many South Africans eat Christmas dinner around noon. This makes sense if, in spite of the summer heat, they keep the European custom of eating a heavy, oven-roasted meal. After an early afternoon nap, some head off to the beach or other cool, outdoor locations.

Black and Asian South Africans

Black South Africans compose about 75 percent of the nation's population. Until recently a political system known as apartheid insured that most black South Africans lived separately from whites and remained relatively poor and uneducated. Most black South Africans are Christians, but a sizeable percentage hold to traditional, tribal religious beliefs. Before the dismantling of apartheid in the early 1990s, the Christmas celebrations of black South Africans tended to revolve around family gatherings, festive meals, and simple gifts. Now black South Africans find themselves increasingly drawn into Christmas **commercialism**.

South Africa also hosts a small minority of Asians, many of whom are Hindus and Muslims and therefore do not celebrate Christmas.

Further Reading

Bowler, Gerry. *The World Encyclopedia of Christmas*. Toronto, Ontario, Canada: McClelland and Stewart, 2000.

Tucker, Cathy C. *Christmas Worldwide*. Philadelphia, Pa.: Xlibris, 2000.

Wernecke, Herbert H. *Celebrating Christmas Around the World*. 1962. Reprint. Detroit, Mich.: Omnigraphics, 1999.

Spain, Christmas in

In Spain, as in many other southern European countries, Easter is a more important holiday than Christmas. Nevertheless, the Spanish celebrate a joyous **Christmas season**, one that emphasizes food, family, and religious observance.

Feast of the Immaculate Conception

Some Spaniards consider the Christmas season to begin on December 8 with the Feast of the Immaculate Conception. This holiday honors the purity of **Mary, Jesus'** mother. In the city of Seville the festival is celebrated with the "Dance of the Sixes," which takes place in the city's cathedral. At the close of the service held in honor of the Immaculate Conception, elaborately costumed choirboys perform this dance in front of the altar, accompanied by a hymn.

Christmas Decorations

In early December **Christmas markets** appear in the main plazas of many Spanish cities. These markets sell Christmas decorations, **ornaments, Nativity scene** figurines, garlands of **greenery**, and **Christmas trees**.

The Spanish center their home celebrations of Christmas around the Nativity scene, which they call a *nacimiento* (literally, "birth") or a *belén* (which means "Bethlehem"). Nativity scenes also appear in churches and town squares around Christmas time. Children delight in recreating the home Nativity scene each year, often embellishing previous arrangements with new figurines, bits of moss, and other additions designed to add a touch of reality to the setting. In recent years Christmas trees also have become popular in some areas. Nevertheless, the Spanish cherish their Nativity scenes. True enthusiasts, called *belenistas,* join clubs dedicated to promoting and preserving Spanish crib-making traditions.

Christmas Foods

As Christmas draws nearer, Spanish housewives begin to stock up on various Christmas foods. Many people look forward to munching on roasted chestnuts during the Christmas season. Marzipan and *turrón*, a kind of nougat candy studded with nuts, are both favorite Christmas sweets.

All across Spain, housewives serve a variety of fish dishes on Christmas Eve. Many serve roast turkey for Christmas dinner on the following day. Spanish cooks sometimes bone the turkey before stuffing and cooking it. Turkey stuffing usually includes some kind of pork—either bacon, ham, or sausage—as well as mushrooms, nuts, and onions. Various kinds of wines, including sherry and champagne, may also be served with the holiday meal. Spanish cuisine varies from region to region, and so do traditional Christmas foods. In the northwestern region of Galicia, for example, Christmas dinner might feature a roast suckling pig.

Pardons

Some lucky prisoners have their offenses pardoned on Christmas Eve. Prison officials and lawyers tour penitentiaries on December 24, reviewing cases and releasing those prisoners whose offenses seem excusable in some way.

Christmas Eve and Day

Spaniards spend Christmas Eve at home with their families. As the sky darkens some families place a lighted lamp in the window. Many also place lighted candles around the Nativity scene or around the family's shrine to the Virgin Mary. As is typical in Spain, dinner is not served until nine or ten o'clock. Afterwards, many people attend **Midnight Mass**.

Family celebrations continue on Christmas Day. The baby Jesus figurine is finally placed in the Nativity scene crib. Some families have adopted the practice of exchanging **gifts** on Christmas Day. Traditionally, however, only children received Christmas gifts, brought to them by the Three Kings on January 6, **Epiphany**. Singing **Christ-**

mas carols is another favorite Christmas Day activity. Ordinarily, the main meal of the day is a late lunch served around two in the afternoon. Accordingly, Spaniards serve a large Christmas dinner in the middle of the afternoon on Christmas Day.

Holy Innocents' Day

Spaniards celebrate December 28, **Holy Innocents' Day**, in much the same way Americans celebrate April Fools' Day, by playing practical jokes on one another. Children's parties and **games** are also held on this day. Although Innocents' Day commemorates a bloody event, folk customs associated with this day are fun and frivolous.

New Year's Eve

Spaniards celebrate **New Year's** Eve a few days later, on December 31. Many families eat pork on New Year's Eve, since the pig is considered a good-luck symbol for the coming year. As family members wait for the clock to strike midnight, twelve grapes are distributed to each person present. Everyone then attempts to eat one grape for each stroke of the clock as it chimes midnight. Although eating twelve grapes in twelve seconds may be uncomfortable, the rewards are worth it. According to Spanish folk belief, each of the twelve grapes will sweeten the corresponding month of the new year. After the stroke of midnight many people go out on the town. The rest of the evening may be spent at bars, nightclubs, or parties that last until the wee hours of the morning.

Epiphany

The Spanish refer to Epiphany as *Día de los Tres Reyes*, or "Three Kings Day." In the weeks preceding Three Kings Day, children write letters to the Wise Men, or **Magi**, letting them know about the gift they would like to receive (*see also* **Children's Letters**). In the old days families would gather at the edge of town hoping to offer their children a glimpse of the Magi on their journey. Somehow, the townsfolk never guessed correctly which road the Wise Men would take. Upon returning to town, however, the disappointed children often discovered that the Wise Men had arrived by another route and were waiting for them at the Nativity scene in the town's central plaza.

Nowadays, many Spanish cities hold elaborate parades on Epiphany Eve to welcome the Three Kings as they pass through town on their way to **Bethlehem**. Parents take their children to these parades so that the little ones can see the splendidly robed Magi riding high atop an elaborate float. The Kings wave kindly to the crowd and, more importantly, toss sweets to the children.

Upon returning home from excursions such as these, children leave their **shoes** in a place where the Wise Men are sure to find them, often on a balcony, just outside the front door, or by the fireplace. They usually leave a bit of straw for the Magi's camels as well. In the morning they find the shoes filled with trinkets and sweets. One old tradition recommended that parents brush their children's cheeks with coal or ashes as they slept on Epiphany Eve. When the children discovered the mark in the morning, the parents told them it meant that Balthasar, the black king, had stooped down to kiss them while they were asleep.

The Three Kings only bring presents to children. In recent years **Santa Claus** has become increasingly popular in Spain, and so has the custom of adults exchanging Christmas presents with one another.

Further Reading

Del Re, Gerard, and Patricia Del Re. *The Christmas Almanack*. Garden City, N.Y.: Doubleday, 1979.

McLenighan, Valjean. *Christmas in Spain*. Chicago: World Book, 1988.

Spicer, Dorothy Gladys. *The Book of Festivals*. 1937. Reprint. Detroit, Mich.: Omnigraphics, 1990.

Star Boys
Starngossar

In parts of central Europe and Scandinavia troupes of costumed children, known as star boys, entertain their neighbors with **Christmas carols** and dramas on **Epiphany**. One member of the group carries a long pole from which a bright star, representing the **Star of Bethlehem**, dangles. Children dressed as the Three Kings, or **Magi,** follow the star, sometimes accompanied by a retinue of figures associated with the Nativity and other Bible stories. In some areas a child dressed as Judas collects the coins that onlookers offer in return for the children's performances. In recent years some charitable organizations have begun collecting money by sponsoring groups of star boys. In many areas, however, neighbors have traditionally offered the group food and drink, rather than money. In places where young adults take part in these performances, neighbors may invite the group to sample their Christmas cheer. In past times Swedish star boys, called *starngossar*, often arrived at their final destination slightly drunk.

The yearly trek of the star boys reminds onlookers of the journey of the Magi and their final arrival at the stable in **Bethlehem** on Epiphany. Researchers speculate that this custom evolved out of medieval **Nativity plays** that reenacted the story of Three Kings. This Epiphany tradition can be found in parts of **Germany, Poland,** Switzerland, **Norway,** and Sweden. (*For a similar custom, see* **India, Christmas in.**)

Further Reading

Cagner, Ewert, comp. *Swedish Christmas.* New York: Henry Holt and Company, 1959.

Foley, Daniel J. *Christmas the World Over.* Philadelphia, Pa.: Chilton Books, 1963.

Henricksen, Vera. *Christmas in Norway.* Oslo, Norway: Johan Grundt Tanum Forlag, 1970.

Russ, Jennifer M. *German Festivals and Customs.* London, England: Oswald Wolff, 1982.

Star of Bethlehem
Christmas Star

In the **Gospel according to Matthew** (2:2-14), we learn that the rising of an unusual star guided the **Magi** to Jerusalem. The Magi interpreted this star as a sign that a great person was about to be born. They treated the star as a beacon, following it to the place directly above which it shone. There, in **Bethlehem**, they recognized **Jesus** as the newborn king whose birth was foretold by the star.

Astrology in Biblical Times

The **Gospel according to Luke** says nothing of the Star of Bethlehem, yet the miraculous star plays an important role in Matthew's account of Jesus' birth (*see also* **Gospel Accounts of Christmas**). What could explain this difference? Perhaps it has something to do with beliefs the ancient Hebrews held about astrology.

Many peoples of the ancient Near East, such as the Greeks, Romans, and Mesopotamians, thought that the stars influenced human behavior. Furthermore, unusual stellar events were widely believed to announce the birth of great individuals. Astrologers, therefore, cultivated knowledge of the stars in order to predict human events.

The ancient Hebrews seemed to be influenced by these beliefs, although for the most part their leaders rejected astrology. The Hebrew Bible (the Christian Old Testament) reflects this ambivalence. On the one hand, certain passages denounce astrology as foreign and wrong. On the other hand, some passages suggest that unusual human events could be accompanied by the movement of heavenly bodies. One prophecy links the coming of the Messiah with the rising of a new star. It proclaims that "a star shall come forth out of Jacob, and a scepter shall rise out of Israel" (Numbers 24-17). In another prophecy, a rising star stands for the coming of the Messiah. The prophecy declares that "nations shall come to your light and kings to the brightness of your rising" (Isaiah 60:3).

The difference between Matthew's and Luke's accounts of Jesus' birth may reflect this same ambivalence towards astrology. Matthew wrote of the rising of an unusual star, implying that the birth of Jesus fulfilled certain Old Testament prophecies about the coming of the Messiah. Luke's exclusion of the story of the star is consistent with the strand of Jewish belief that rejected astrology as a foreign religious doctrine.

Scientific Explanations for the Star

Did a strange star appear in the heavens at the time of Christ's birth? The question intrigues many scholars, from Bible experts to astronomers. A definitive answer still eludes them, however, because the two most important pieces of information necessary to solve the mystery are themselves unclear. First, Matthew's gospel provides only a vague mention of the star. Second, the exact year of Jesus' birth remains in doubt (*see* **Jesus, Year of Birth**). So researchers scan astronomical records from the years around 1 B.C. searching for unusual happenings in the sky.

Matthew's description could fit any bright, irregularly occurring celestial phenomena. For instance, he might have been referring to a comet. Comets, however, were generally thought to herald disaster in ancient times. So it is unlikely that the appearance of a comet could have inspired the Magi to search for a newborn messiah. The Magi might have been spurred into action by a conjunction, which occurs when two or more planets appear to draw very near each other in the sky. Finally, they might have witnessed an exploding star, or nova.

The first European person to seek a scientific explanation of the Star was Johannes Kepler (1571-1630), the famous German astronomer and mathematician. He speculated that the Christmas Star might in fact have been a conjunction. By calculating the movements of the planets backwards in time, he determined that there had been a conjunction of Mars, Jupiter, and Saturn in 6 B.C. Since that time a variety of astronomical explanations for the Star have been proposed. Until recently, most scholars agreed that the triple conjunctions of 7 B.C. presented themselves as the best candidates for the Christmas Star. Jupiter and Saturn drew near to each other on three occasions in that year, very spectacularly on May 22, and again on October 5 and December 1. Triple conjunctions of this sort are very rare, and the Magi, wise men who watched the stars, would have known that.

In recent years, another set of conjunctions has also begun to interest the experts. On August 12 in the year 3 B.C., Jupiter and Venus approached each other in the sky. The Magi might also have noted that this unusually close conjunction took place in the constellation of Leo. Leo, the lion, symbolized the people of Judah. This close conjunction was surpassed less than a year later when the two stars appeared to overlap each other in the early evening sky on June 17, 2 B.C. This extremely rare event, called an occultation, would certainly have attracted the attention of the Magi. None of us has ever witnessed an occultation, since the last one occurred in 1818 and the next will take place in 2065. What's more, between the dates of these two conjunctions, another set of three conjunctions occurred. The planet Jupiter and the star Regulus passed close by one another on September 14, 3 B.C., again on February 17, 2 B.C., and yet again on May 8, 2 B.C. This triple conjunction may have had special significance to the Magi as well. Both Jupiter and Regulus were associated with kingship by ancient Babylonian astrologers.

How do researchers decide which of these known astronomical events comes closest to fitting the description of the Christmas Star? They attempt to reconcile the dates of these events with other events that were supposed to have happened near the time of Christ's birth. For example, both Gospel accounts of Christmas agree that Jesus was born during the reign of **Herod** the Great. Most historians believe that Herod died in 4 B.C. Therefore, Jesus must have been born during or before 4 B.C., an assumption that rules out the possibility that the conjunctions of 3-2 B.C. could have been the star observed by the Magi. Yet other scholars contest the arguments offered by these historians and claim instead that Herod probably died in 1 B.C. In that case, the conjunctions of 3-2 B.C. become the best candidate for the Christmas Star.

Religious Perspectives

Finally, many religious people feel that a scientific explanation for the Star of Bethlehem is not needed. Some feel that the story of the Star is a symbolic, rather than an historical, account, attempting to convey spiritual truths rather than material facts. Others believe that the Christmas Star really did rise over Bethlehem when Jesus was born. Some people who hold this opinion think that it was a naturally occurring phenomenon of some kind. Others believe that God caused this miraculous star to appear in order to proclaim the birth of the Savior. They do not expect anyone to find a logical, scientific explanation for the star.

Folklore

Centuries of fascination with the Star of Bethlehem have made stars an important **Christmas symbol** (*see also* **Philippines, Christmas in the; Poland, Christmas in**). They often top our decorated **Christmas trees** and appear in other Christmas decorations. Old Christmas customs, such as the cavorting of the **star boys**, also make use of this symbol. Finally, many planetariums present special programs exploring the many theories about the Star of Bethlehem around Christmas time. These programs offer a new, scientific way to celebrate this ancient Christmas symbol.

Further Reading

Aveni, Anthony. "The Star of Bethlehem." *Archeology* 51, 6 (November-December 1998): 34-38.

Branley, Franklyn M. *The Christmas Sky*. Revised and newly illustrated edition. New York: Thomas Y. Crowell, 1990.

Hultgren, Arland J. "Stars, Star of Bethlehem." In Paul J. Achtemeier, ed. *HarperCollins Bible Dictionary*. Revised edition. San Francisco, Calif.: HarperSanFrancisco, 1996.

Krupp, E. C. *Beyond the Blue Horizon: Myths and Legends of the Sun, Moon, Stars, and Planets*. New York: HarperCollins, 1991.

Mosley, John. *The Christmas Star*. Los Angeles, Calif.: Griffith Observatory, 1987.

Web Site

A site sponsored by the *Earth & Sky* radio series contains an article by Jeff Kanipe, "The 'Stars' of Bethlehem" (January 19, 1999): http://www.earth sky.com/Features/Articles/stars.html

Stir-Up Sunday

In **England** some people still refer to the Sunday before the beginning of **Advent** as "Stir-Up Sunday." The name comes from the traditional collect (or prayer) offered in Anglican churches on that day. It reads: "Stir up, we beseech Thee O Lord, the wills of thy faithful people; that they, plenteously bringing forth the fruit of good works, may of Thee be plenteously rewarded." In past times the words "stir up," however, also reminded people to begin preparing their Christmas puddings (*see also* **Plum Pudding**). Children chanted a rhymed verse on that day that mixed the words of the collect with requests for special Christmas fare: "Stir up, we beseech thee, the pudding in the pot, and when we do get home tonight, we'll eat it up all hot." Thus, the preparation of the Christmas pudding eventually became associated with this day. Folk beliefs advised each family member to take a turn stirring the pudding, an act that was believed to confer good luck. Another custom encouraged stirrers to move the spoon in clockwise rotations, close their eyes, and make a wish.

Further Reading

Henderson, Helene, and Sue Ellen Thompson, eds. *Holidays, Festivals, and Celebrations of the World Dictionary*. Second edition. Detroit, Mich.: Omnigraphics, 1997.

Howard, Alexander. *Endless Cavalcade*. London, England: Arthur Baker, 1964.

MacDonald, Margaret Read, ed. *The Folklore of World Holidays*. Detroit, Mich.: Gale Research, 1992.

Muir, Frank. *Christmas Customs and Traditions*. New York: Taplinger, 1977.

Stockings

The early nineteenth-century poem by Clement C. Moore, "A Visit from St. Nicholas," describes an old Christmas custom concerning stockings. The poem's narrator notes that his children's stockings "were hung by the chimney with care, in hopes that **St. Nicholas** soon would be there." Many American homes today present a similar scene on Christmas Eve. Children leave stockings near the fireplace expecting that **Santa Claus** will come and fill them with candy and toys during the night.

Some writers trace the roots of this stocking custom back to an ancient legend concerning St. Nicholas (*see also* **St. Nicholas's Day**). The legend tells of an anonymous act of kindness performed by the saint. Nicholas knew of a man who had three daughters of marriageable age for whom he could not afford dowries. Since the girls could not get married without dowries, their father was considering selling them into prostitution. One evening Nicholas came by their house and threw a small sack of **gold** through the window, thereby providing a dowry for the eldest girl. He donated dowries for the other two girls in the same manner. On the evening of the last gift, the man raced outside, caught Nicholas in the act, and thanked him for his generosity. In some versions of this story, Nicholas throws the sack of gold down the chimney and it lands in one of the daughter's stockings, which had been hung there to dry.

In medieval times people across **Europe** celebrated St. Nicholas's Day on December 6. In a number of northern European countries, folk traditions developed around the idea of St. Nicholas bringing treats to children on St. Nicholas's Eve. Adults instructed children to leave their **shoes** by the fire that evening so that the saint could pop down the chimney and fill them up with fruit, nuts, and cookies. In some parts of Europe families substituted stockings for shoes.

Eventually, the tradition of giving **gifts** to children began to gravitate towards Christmas. In **Germany** children began to hang stockings by the end of their beds on Christmas Eve so that the Christ Child (*see* **Christkindel**) could fill them with treats as she voyaged from house to house. This stocking custom migrated to the United States, **England, France,** and **Italy** during the nineteenth century (*see also* **America, Christmas in Nineteenth-Century**). In the twentieth century Santa Claus overpowered both the Christ Child and the saint, emerging as the dominant winter holiday gift giver. Some believe that the stockings children hang up today ultimately hark back to St. Nicholas's good deed. These days, however, Santa, not the saint, is expected to perform this Christmas miracle.

Further Reading

Del Re, Gerard, and Patricia Del Re. *The Christmas Almanack*. Garden City, N.Y.: Doubleday, 1979.

Ebon, Martin. *Saint Nicholas, Life and Legends*. New York: Harper and Row, 1975.

Henisch, Bridget Ann. *Cakes and Characters: An English Christmas Tradition*. London, England: Prospect Books, 1984.

Shoemaker, Alfred L. *Christmas in Pennsylvania*. Kutztown, Pa.: Pennsylvania Folklore Society, 1959.

Store Window Displays

Department stores present window displays to the public all year round. But the scenes displayed at Christmas time are different. More imaginative, more opulent, and tinged with fantasy or nostalgia, these scenes add to the enjoyment of many holiday shoppers. The enticing Christmas window display is as old as the contemporary Christmas, having established itself as an important seasonal tradition in the late nineteenth century.

Nineteenth-Century Beginnings

Historians trace Christmas window displays back to the 1820s. These first few displays featured nothing more than merchandise surrounded by a few flowers, some **greenery**, and patriotic symbols. Still, during the 1820s and 1830s many inhabitants of **New York City** spent some part of Christmas Eve making the rounds of the better toy and candy stores, admiring the modest displays of shop wares nestled among evergreens and lit by gaslights.

Christmas shop windows quickly evolved beyond serving as mere functional displays of goods and became a form of **commercial** entertainment. By the 1870s New York shop window displays had reached such artistic heights that they were being reported in the newspapers. In 1872 a toyshop called L. P. Tibbals tickled the public's fancy with a large display of toy trains and other mechanical, moving toys. Macy's became famous for its yearly display of dolls. In 1874 its designers created a miniature croquet party populated by $10,000 worth of dolls imported from Europe (*for more on Macy's, see* **Macy's Thanksgiving Day Parade**). In the same year reviewers lauded Lord and Taylor for their fine display of **Christmas trees** and garlands.

Each year window dressers at rival stores vied with one another to produce the most eye-catching and talked-about Christmas displays of the season. By the 1880s New York window dressers were treating the public to a series of mechanized, moving displays. When one store mounted a tableaux featuring scenes from Montreal's winter carnival—complete with sledders sliding down an icy hill—Macy's countered by creating a miniature reproduction of a scene from the popular novel *Uncle Tom's Cabin* (1851-52)—the one in which the character Eliza is chased by bloodhounds. Displays such as these tended to sacrifice the capacity of the store window to advertise goods for sale in favor of attracting attention by means of novelty. Nevertheless, such lavish and artistic displays offered a form of free holiday entertainment to the public and thereby added to the store's prestige.

Though people thought the store windows entertaining, storeowners were well aware of the commercial value of these displays. In 1895, the *Dry Goods Chronicle* advised businesses gearing up for the Christmas shopping season to:

> Fit up your place as it was never fitted before. Dress it in evergreens and bright colors. Make your store such an inviting bower of Christmas loveliness that people cannot stay away [Schmidt, 1995, 161].

These extravagant Christmas fantasies invited shoppers to treat the holiday as a season of material abundance and wish fulfillment. Shop owners hoped that this attitude would inspire purchases.

Twentieth-Century Trends

In the twentieth century store window displays continued to serve as a form of **Christmas season** entertainment. In many large cities, stores unveiled their holiday displays the day before Thanksgiving or on Thanksgiving Day itself. These "openings" sometimes attracted crowds. Families often made special trips downtown during the holiday season to admire the Christmas windows. In many cities one store emerged as the perennial favorite in the unofficial yearly competition in Christmas window dressing. In Chicago Marshall Fields grabbed the spotlight. In Cleveland Higbees and the May Company split the honors. In New York City Macy's, with its 75 feet of display windows along 34th Street, established a solid reputation for outstanding Christmas windows. In Minneapolis Dayton's won rave reviews, while in Philadelphia Wanamaker's wowed the public with its yearly Christmas extravaganzas.

These last two stores hit upon the strategy of moving their displays inside the building, so that customers would actually have to enter and walk past merchandise for sale in order to view the decorations. Wanamaker's offered the public religious displays, while Dayton's specialized in the secular aspects of Christmas. The "Grand Court" in Wanamaker's interior held what was at one time the largest pipe organ in the world, making it easy for window dressers to turn the court into an elegant "cathedral" at Christmas time. The store played up this theme by hiring its own musical director, who led **Christmas carol** sing-alongs for shoppers and organized Christmas concerts in the court. In 1966 Dayton's of Minneapolis recreated an entire "Dickens Village" in the interior of the store (*for more on Charles Dickens, see Christmas Carol, A*). The "village" contained 34 buildings, 150 characters (automatons and humans), and 25 vignettes, all built at three-quarters life size. The attraction took up 12,000 square feet of floor space and cost about a quarter of a million dollars. The village was a hit with the public. It drew 110,000 people into the store in its first week alone, and 20,000 a day thereafter. To defray the tremendous cost of the exhibit the store decided to use it again the following two years.

Some have predicted that holiday shoppers' increasing reliance on catalogs and the internet as a means of simplifying holiday shopping will hurt brick-and-mortar merchants, leading to the eventual decline of the Christmas window display. The rise of large suburban shopping malls, with common areas available for holiday decorations, may also influence how stores choose to spend their display dollar. Nevertheless, the tradition of extravagant Christmas window decor continues in many quarters, much to the delight of dedicated holiday shoppers.

The View from the Other Side of the Window

The public may forget the delights of decorated store windows as soon as January rolls around. By contrast, many professional window dressers working for big city department stores begin planning their next Christmas display as soon as the holiday season ends. Coming up with a workable new idea may take time. Concepts and budgets generally require executive approval, and some materials may need to be ordered well in advance, such as custom-made mechanized mannequins and the designer clothes they wear. Though store windows change year round, many designers consider their Christmas windows to be their most important effort of the year, a chance to show off their skills and to make a reputation for themselves in the world of window dressing.

Further Reading

Bellman, Sheryll. *Through the Shopping Glass*. New York: Rizzoli, 2000.

Marling, Karal Ann. *Merry Christmas!* Cambridge, Mass.: Harvard University Press, 2000.

Pool, Daniel. *Christmas in New York*. New York: Seven Stories Press, 1997.

Schmidt, Leigh Eric. *Consumer Rites: The Buying and Selling of American Holidays*. Princeton, N.J.: Princeton University Press, 1995.

Sudan, Christmas in

Sudan, the largest country in Africa, is an ethnically and religiously diverse society. About 70 percent of its citizens are Muslim and some claim Arab roots. They live mostly in the north. About 25 percent of Sudanese follow tribal religions and about five percent are Christians. These people, mostly black Africans from a variety of ethnic groups, live primarily in the south. The country has been embroiled in a civil war since the 1980s which has left two million people either dead or displaced from their homes. Disease, starvation, and terrible abuses of human rights, including the use of torture and the capture and sale of southern Sudanese as slaves, have also caused unfathomable misery.

In spite of all this suffering, Sudanese Christians still celebrate Christmas. Their celebrations might seem unfamiliar to many Americans, however. They never adopted the western European custom of decorating a **Christmas tree**. The American **Santa Claus** and other Christmas **gift** bringers are unknown to them. In much of war-torn southern Sudan, Christians simply hope to celebrate Christmas by attending church and sharing a good meal with their family. Christmas church services in Sudan include readings from the Bible as well as many hymns written in tribal languages such as Nuer, Dinka, Shilluk, Naban, Zande, Baria, and Tira. Hymn singing is often accompanied by drumming and sometimes by dancing. One foreign aid worker described a moving Christmas Eve service attended by many refugees in which the sermon pointed out that **Jesus** came into the world as a refugee, his parents forced to leave their homes to fulfill the demands of a hostile government (*see also* **Gospel According to Luke**). People who can afford it wear new clothes on Christmas Day. Dance parties, featuring traditional tribal dress and dancing, also take place at Christmas time.

Further Reading

Humphrey, Marj. "Herod Lives; The Story from Sudan." *Commonweal* 121 (December 16, 1994): 8(3).
Tucker, Cathy C. *Christmas Worldwide*. Philadelphia, Pa.: Xlibris, 2000.

Sugarplums

In Clement C. Moore's famous poem, "A Visit from St. Nicholas," the children lie "nestled all snug in their beds, while visions of sugarplums danced through their heads." Although today's children crave candy canes and chocolates at Christmas time, Moore's poem reminds us that over one hundred years ago children longed for sugarplums. In fact, sugarplums symbolized a child's Christmas joys to such an extent that Pyotr Ilich Tchaikovsky's late nineteenth-century Christmas ballet, *The Nutcracker*, features a character called the "Sugarplum Fairy," who rules over the Kingdom of Sweets.

What exactly are sugarplums, anyway? In past centuries people might call any kind of candied fruit a sugarplum. In addition, confectioners

used the term to refer to candied spices. Thus, dried and sugared plums, apricots, cherries, ginger, aniseeds, and caraway seeds might all go by the name "sugarplum." Traditional recipes suggest various preparations for this confection. Some sugarplum recipes called for coating dried fruit in sugar or sugary icing. Others recommend cooking it in sugar syrup. Nineteenth-century American cooks occasionally stewed greengage plums in a sugar and cornstarch syrup, calling the resulting sweets "sugarplums."

Today's cooks might find it confusing to lump so many different confections together under the name "sugarplum." In earlier times, however, the word "plum" served as a generic term for any kind of dried fruit (*see also* **Plum Pudding**). Given this definition, the term "sugarplum" might be said to offer an accurate description of these candies. Sugarplums, or "comfits" as confectioners sometimes called them, not only delighted children as special Christmas treats, but also enriched a variety of cakes and puddings during the seventeenth through nineteenth centuries.

Further Reading

Snyder, Phillip V. *The Christmas Tree Book*. New York: Viking Press, 1976.

Weaver, William Woys. *The Christmas Cook*. New York: HarperPerennial, 1990.

Syria, Christmas in

Christians make up just under 10 percent of the population of the Middle Eastern nation of Syria. Most are Eastern Christians, that is, Christians whose traditions of worship developed in the Middle East, north Africa, and eastern Europe. Among the many denominations represented in Syria are the Syrian, Greek, and Armenian Orthodox churches, the Maronite Church, the Assyrian (or Nestorian) Church, the Syrian Catholic Church, and the Melchite (or Greek Catholic) Church. Many Eastern Christians fast for some or all of **Advent**, a period of spiritual preparation for the coming of Christ at Christmas time. Eastern Christians fast by avoiding meat, dairy products, fish, and eggs.

Christmas Eve and Day

Church **bells** ring out on Christmas Eve and many Syrians attend evening religious services. They mark Christmas Day with a festive dinner and visits to family members and friends. Visitors are offered coffee, nuts, fruit, candy, and Middle Eastern sweets, such as *baklava*, *burma*, and *mulabas*.

Gift Bringer

In Syria, the camel is the **Christmas season** gift bringer. Legend elaborates that the youngest of the camels that carried the **Magi** to **Bethlehem** to worship the infant **Jesus** fell down exhausted at the end of its long journey. Jesus blessed the animal and bestowed upon it the gift of immortal life. Ever after it has traveled the world, bringing **gifts** to Syrian children on New Year's Eve.

New Year's Day

Syrians give presents on **New Year's Day**. Many people also go visiting on this day. Hosts offer their guests coffee and sweets. Women usually stay home to receive guests on New Year's Day, and go visiting themselves on January 2.

Epiphany

Syrian Christians also have many customs and folk beliefs concerning **Epiphany**. This holiday, falling twelve days after Christmas, is interpreted differently by Eastern and Western Christians. While Western Christians associate the day with the arrival of the Magi, Eastern Christians observe it as a commemoration of Jesus' baptism. According to the Bible, when Jesus was baptized in the River Jordan, the Holy Spirit of God, in the shape of a dove, flew down to him from heaven (Matthew 3:16, Mark 1:10 and 3:22, John 1:32). Inspired by this event, Syrian folk legends declared that the gates of heaven open each year on Epiphany eve, making it a night of mystical power and unlooked-for miracles. Syrian Christians call Epiphany eve *Lailat al-Qadr*, "the night of destiny." Muslims use the same name for a holiday of their own, which falls during the holy month of Ramadan and honors another opening of the gates of heaven. For Muslims Lailat al-Qadr commemorates the delivery of the Qur'an, the Muslim holy book, to the prophet Muhammad by **Gabriel**, the **angel** who also heralded Jesus' birth.

According to Syrian folklore, the trees bow down at midnight on Epiphany eve in honor of Jesus Christ. What's more, God blesses the especially devout with miracles of increase on this evening. Thus, the truly good might wake to find that a half-empty jug of wine is now brimming, or a pot of dough is now filled to overflowing. One old superstition advises housewives to push a silver coin into a small lump of dough, tuck it inside a towel and tie it to a tree on Epiphany eve. Overnight the dough becomes leaven. Families keep the miracle dough throughout the year.

Christians in Syria mark Epiphany day with church services. Among Orthodox Christians Epiphany is also known as "Blessing of the Waters Day." Some Syrians bring bottles of water to church for the priest to bless. In addition, priests visit Christian homes at Epiphany time, performing a house-blessing ceremony with holy water (specially blessed water). Children chase and splash each other with water on this day, perhaps inspired by these pious customs.

Further Reading

Henderson, Helene, and Sue Ellen Thompson, eds. *Holidays, Festivals, and Celebrations of the World Dictionary*. Second edition. Detroit, Mich.: Omnigraphics, 1997.

Sechrist, Elizabeth. *Christmas Everywhere*. 1936. Reprint. Detroit, Mich.: Omnigraphics, 1998.

Spicer, Dorothy G. *The Book of Festivals*. 1937. Reprint. Detroit, Mich.: Omnigraphics, 1990.

Times Square, New Year's Eve in

Many Americans spend the exact moment of midnight on New Year's Eve watching a highly illuminated ball slide down a pole perched atop a tall building facing **New York City**'s Times Square. How did this event, broadcast on television throughout the United States and around the world, come to symbolize New Year's Eve for so many people?

History

In 1896 a businessman named Adolph Ochs bought a nearly defunct New York newspaper and began to restore it to health. After a number of years, he decided to construct a new building to house this paper, the *New York Times*. The property he purchased lay along 42nd Street, facing Longacre Square. At eighteen stories high, the completed *Times* building was among the taller buildings in turn-of-the-century Manhattan. The owners of other tall buildings had celebrated their openings with fireworks so Ochs decided to follow suit. Ochs scheduled his celebration for New Year's Eve 1904. The event not only marked the opening of the building, but also the changing of the square's name from Longacre to Times Square. In those days, many New Yorkers gathered at Wall Street's Trinity Church to usher in the new year. Ochs's fireworks lured people away from the church's midnight **bell** ringing.

The success of Ochs's event, and the publicity it garnered for the *New York Times*, enticed Ochs to repeat the stunt in the years that followed. In 1907 the city of New York decreed rooftop fireworks a fire hazard. So Ochs cooked up another eye-catcher to call attention to his building (and his newspaper). An iron and wood ball weighing over 600 pounds was attached to the top of a pole standing on the roof of the building. The one hundred 25-watt light bulbs embedded in the ball glowed dimly in the dark. At the stroke of midnight the ball was released and slid down the pole, signaling the start of the new year.

Ochs may well have patterned this spectacle after a long forgotten daily occurrence. In those days, Washington D.C.'s Naval Observatory telegraphed the New York City Western Union building (later the site of the World Trade Center) each day precisely at noon. A flanged metal ball at the summit of a pole perched atop the building was released upon the arrival of this signal. This highly visible event helped people to set their watches accurately.

With the exception of the years 1942 and 1943, the ball-dropping ceremony has continued to this day. In those years, wartime blackout restrictions prevented the illumination of the ball. Those who gathered in Times Square instead observed a minute of silence followed by the recorded sound of ringing bells. The first radio broadcast of the Times Square festivities took place in 1929. The first television broadcast occurred in 1943. These broadcasts helped to turn a local New York event into a nationwide celebration (*see also* **"Auld Lang Syne"**).

The Ceremony Today

The ball still drops from the rooftop of the same building, though the paper is no longer headquartered there and its name has been changed from the New York Times Building to One Times Square. The owners of this building possess the current New Year's Eve ball, while a consortium of local business owners, known as the Times

Square Business Improvement District, and an organization called Countdown Entertainment, produce the event itself.

Event organizers suggest that those who wish to witness the ball-dropping ceremony in person arrive at Times Square as early as possible. The best areas from which to see the ball drop often fill up during the afternoon hours of December 31. The police begin blocking off streets to vehicles at 6:00 p.m. or earlier, depending on when the streets begin to fill up. The event has drawn about half a million people to the Times Square area in recent years.

Today's event boasts considerably more razzle-dazzle than Ochs's original entertainments. At 6:00 p.m. workers hoist the ball to the top of a 77-foot pole and flip the switch that lights it up. The ball used today, a geodesic sphere made from aluminum and plastic, weighs 1,070 pounds and measures 6 feet in diameter. It is covered with 504 crystal triangles that reflect and refract the light from hundreds of bulbs. Four hundred thirty-two light bulbs — clear, colored, and strobe — blaze from the interior of the sphere, while 168 halogen bulbs sparkle on the exterior. Rotating mirrors affixed to the surface of the ball reflect the ball's glow into the crowd. Loudspeakers provide continual musical entertainment from 10:30 p.m. until 11:59 p.m., when the ball begins its 60-second descent.

The 2001 New Year's Eve festivities featured some special additions made to honor the victims of the September 11 terrorist attacks. The New Year's Eve ball was fitted with special crystal triangles dedicated to the memory of all those who died in the attacks. Event organizers also created an evening bell-ringing ceremony. All over the city, church bells rang at 6:00 p.m. in memory of the victims. Individuals and places of worship as well as other institutions were also asked to participate by ringing bells.

Further Reading

Pool, Daniel. *Christmas in New York*. New York: Seven Stories Press, 1997.

Web Site

The Times Square Business Improvement District maintains a web page on its New Year's Eve festivities at: http://www.timessquarebid.org/new_year/

Timkat
Timqat, Timket

In **Ethiopia, Epiphany** is a far more important holiday than Christmas. Whereas Western Christians commemorate the journey of the **Magi** in their Epiphany celebrations, Ethiopian Orthodox Christians honor the occasion of **Jesus'** baptism. Accordingly, they call the festival *Timkat* (sometimes also spelled "Timqat" or "Timket"), which means "baptism." Since the Ethiopian Orthodox Church follows a different calendar than that commonly adhered to in the West, Ethiopians celebrate Timkat on January 19 (*see also* **Old Christmas Day**). The festivities spill over to the following day, when Ethiopians observe the Feast of St. Michael the Archangel.

Preparations

Adults prepare for Timkat by washing their cotton robes, called *shamma,* and restoring them to a brilliant whiteness. In addition, they brew special beers, bake bread, and slaughter a sheep in preparation for the Timkat feast. Children receive new clothes from their parents for this special occasion.

Religious Observances

Religious observances begin around sunset on Timkat Eve. Garbed all in white, parishioners wait outside their local church for the priests to emerge with the *tabot,* or holy ark. The ark contains the Tablets of the Law, which Jews call the Torah and Christians know as the first five books of the Old Testament. Ethiopians do not believe that the original Ark of the Covenant was lost. Instead they claim that the Cathedral of Axum in Ethiopia now guards this precious relic. Each Ethiopian Orthodox church has a blessed replica of that original. On Timkat Eve the priests and parishioners of each church form a procession bearing the tabot to a nearby body of water where an all-night celebration will take place. Processional crosses, incense censers, drums, trumpets, and **bells** set the mood as the congregation wends its ways towards the water. Priests in their bejewelled ceremonial robes and sequined velvet umbrellas show up as splashes of color amidst the sea of worshipers in white. In Ethiopia's capital, Addis Ababa, many congregations meet at Jan Meda, the old horse-racing arena.

Hours of drumming, dancing, eating and drinking precede the religious service, which begins at two in the morning. Around dawn the priests bless the stream or lake by submerging a gold cross and a consecrated candle in it. The priests scatter drops of water on those who want to rededicate themselves to their Christian faith. Some enthusiastic worshipers, not content with this mild gesture, immerse themselves completely in the water. Afterwards the crowd resumes the feasting, singing, and dancing. Later, jubilant processions, led by dancing and singing priests, escort the tabots back to their shrines.

Recreation

Many enjoy the afternoon by watching *feres gugs*. This event, held on many feast days, resembles medieval European jousting. Participants wear capes made out of lions' manes and headdresses made from baboon hair. Colorful brocades, velvets, and tassels adorn their horses. The game itself may have developed out of the military maneuvers practiced by the mounted warriors of past eras. One band of horsemen armed with bamboo lances tries to knock the members of the other band off their horses. The defenders must escape these blows by clever horsemanship or deflect them with shields made of rhinoceros or hippopotamus hides.

Well-attended public events such as these provide an opportunity to engage in another kind of sport, that is, the search for a mate. Many young men wander through the crowds hoping to spot an attractive, eligible young woman. The more bold among them may then approach the girl's father with inquiries.

Further Reading

Clynes, Tom. *Wild Planet!* Detroit, Mich.: Visible Ink Press, 1995.

Henderson, Helene, and Sue Ellen Thompson, eds. *Holidays, Festivals, and Celebrations of the World Dictionary.* Second edition. Detroit, Mich.: Omnigraphics, 1997.

Levine, Donald N. *Wax and Gold*. Chicago: University of Chicago Press, 1965.

MacDonald, Margaret Read. *The Folklore of World Holidays*. Detroit, Mich.: Gale Research, 1992.

Web Site

A site sponsored by the Ethiopia Tourism Commission: http://www.visitethiopia.org/cultatt.htm

Twelfth Night
Epiphany Eve, Old Christmas Eve

According to an old European form of reckoning, the **Christmas season** ended on the twelfth day after Christmas. People relaxed and celebrated during these dozen days known as the **Twelve Days of Christmas**. Twelfth Night marked the last evening of the Twelve Days of Christmas. Twelfth Night customs called for one final burst of feasting and revelry to commemorate the close of the Christmas season. Church custom, and some ethnic traditions, placed Twelfth Night on the evening of January 5. In certain places, however, people celebrated Twelfth Night on January 6.

Feasts, Cakes, and Kings

In past eras the English, French, Spanish, German, and Dutch commemorated Twelfth Night with feasts, special cakes, and a kind of masquerade presided over by the **King of the Bean** (*see also* **Christmas Cakes**). This mock king may have evolved from a similar figure popular during the Roman midwinter festival of **Saturnalia**. In medieval courts, mock kings, like jesters, served to entertain the assembled company during the Christmas season. Records from some English households indicate that they were chosen from among those with musical or other skills that lent themselves to entertainment. Moreover, they took charge of organizing the holiday season festivities. These mock kings acquired many other names, including the **Lord of Misrule**, the Master of Merry Disports, and the Abbot of Unreason. Records from late medieval **France** indicate that one method of choosing this mock ruler was to serve out pieces of cake into which a single bean had been baked. The one whose piece of cake contained the bean got the job. His title, *Rex Fabarum*, or King of the Bean, may have referred back to this manner of selection or to his lack of real power.

During the Renaissance this particular title and custom appear to have gravitated towards Twelfth Night. Ordinary people began celebrating Twelfth Night with feasts, cakes, and bean kings. These kings, along with their queens, directed the remainder of the feast. The rest of those attending the feast took up the role of courtiers. The following day, **Epiphany**, introduced the image of a different kind of king. Starting in the Middle Ages, western European Epiphany customs began to revolve around commemorations of the arrival of the Three Kings, or **Magi**, in **Bethlehem**.

Shakespeare's Twelfth Night

In or around the year 1600 William Shakespeare wrote a play called *Twelfth Night, Or What You Will*. Although the play does not refer to the holiday per se, it does weave a comedy around the actions of characters in disguise. Some literary researchers think that Shakespeare put the words "Twelfth Night" into the play's title in order to suggest a particularly appropriate time of year for the play's performance. Indeed, playgoing was a popular activity during the Twelve Days of Christmas.

Masques

During the Renaissance some of the most splendid feasts of the Christmas season occurred at the homes of the wealthy on Twelfth Night. In **England** King Henry VIII (1491-1547) appears to have introduced the Italian custom of celebrating Twelfth Night with **masques**. These elaborate costumed events featured the enactment of some simple scenes or tableaux using song, dance, flowery speeches, and fancy scenery. The custom might be thought of as an elite version of the **mumming** practices already established among the common people. The masques performed at court were short, simple, and sometimes frivolous works designed to raise as much laughter as possible while providing a colorful spectacle. These productions were very popular during the Christmas season, but were also performed at other times of year. The famous writer Ben Jonson (1572-1637) raised the artistic level of these works somewhat when he offered a Christmas masque — *Christmas His Masque* — to be performed at court in the year 1616. In England the Twelfth Night masque reached its zenith in the early seventeenth century and afterwards began to decline.

Characters

In the late seventeenth century the English diarist Samuel Pepys (1633-1703) described his enjoyment of a new custom whereby Twelfth Night merrymakers drew slips of paper from a hat on which were written the names of characters found at the bean king's court. They were expected to impersonate this character for the rest of the evening. In this way everyone present at the celebration, not just the king and queen, got into the act. By the end of the eighteenth century this innovation had almost completely replaced the earlier custom of planting a bean and a pea inside the Twelfth Night cake. In fact, it became so popular with ordinary folk that, by the end of the eighteenth century, shops sold packets of cards with names and drawings of characters printed on them. The absurd names given to these characters served to describe their exaggerated personalities. Examples include Sir Tunbelly Clumsy, Sir Gregory Goose, and Miss Fanny Fanciful.

In the early part of the nineteenth century, the English still celebrated Twelfth Night with parties, cakes, mock kings, and characters. The English writer Leigh Hunt (1784-1859) described the Twelfth Night festivities of his era in the following way:

> Christmas goes out in fine style, — with Twelfth Night. It is a finish worthy of the time. Christmas Day was the morning of the season; New Year's Day the middle of it, or noon; Twelfth Night is the night, brilliant with innumerable planets of Twelfth-cakes. The whole island keeps court; nay all Christendom. All the world are kings and queens. Everybody is

somebody else, and learns at once to laugh at, and to tolerate, characters different from his own, by enacting them. Cakes, characters, forfeits, lights, theatres, merry rooms, little holiday-faces, and, last not least, the painted sugar on the cakes, so bad to eat but so fine to look at, useful because it is perfectly useless except for a sight and a moral — all conspire to throw a giddy splendour over the last night of the season, and to send it to bed in pomp and colours, like a Prince [Miles, 1990, 337-38].

Pranks

By the early nineteenth century, the Twelfth Night cake had evolved into a large and complicated display of cake, icing, and other embellishments. Bakeries displayed these models of the confectioner's art in their windows, and people gathered outside to admire them. The playful atmosphere of Twelfth Night may have encouraged schoolboys to carry out the following Twelfth Night prank. Unnoticed among the throng of cake-admirers, they pinned the clothing of two adults together or nailed a gentleman's coattails to the windowsill. Then they stood back and enjoyed the confusion that arose when the pinned and nailed individuals attempted to leave the bakery window.

Decline of Twelfth Night

The importance of Twelfth Night as a holiday declined throughout the second part of the century. Some writers blame this on the rapid industrialization of the English economy, which in general resulted in the increase of the number of workdays and the decrease in the number of holidays. As Twelfth Night began to wane, so did its customs. One of them, however, the Twelfth Night cake, was kept alive in at least one place by a curious bequest. In the late eighteenth century an actor by the name of Robert Baddeley achieved some success playing at London's Drury Lane Theatre. In his will he left a sum of one hundred pounds to be invested in such a way as to provide the actors playing at Drury Lane Theatre on January 5 with wine and a Twelfth Night cake every year. The will also stipulates that in return for the feast the company drink to his health.

Old Christmas Eve

Some Twelfth Night customs may have been created indirectly by the acts of politicians. The British calendar reform of 1752 moved the calendar forward eleven days in order to synchronize the country with the continental European calendar (*see* **Old Christmas Day**). With the stroke of a pen, the day that would have been Christmas Eve became Epiphany Eve. This maneuver appears to have transferred several English Christmas customs, such as the **wassailing of fruit trees** and the viewing of the **Glastonbury thorn** to Twelfth Night.

Twelfth Night in Colonial America and the Early United States

When the British settled in colonial America, they brought their Twelfth Night celebrations with them. In the eighteenth century Twelfth Night parties frequently took place in regions where large numbers of English colonists had settled, such as Virginia, Maryland, Delaware, and Pennsylvania. They were especially popular with members of the Church of England (later the Episcopal Church) and among the wealthy, who celebrated Twelfth Night with formal balls. These balls featured a bountiful buffet table, loaded with such delicacies as Twelfth Night Cake (a kind of fruit cake), roasted meats, candied fruit, cookies, fritters, and New Year's pie. This last item was an elaborate dish prepared by placing a beef tongue into a boned chicken, wedging the chicken into a boned duck, stuffing the duck into a boned turkey, cramming the turkey into a boned goose and then roasting the stuffed goose in an oven. Just as in Europe, colonial and early American cooks placed a bean and a pea inside their Twelfth Night cakes as a means of selecting a Twelfth Night king and queen.

In colonial and early American times the Christmas season, capped by the celebration of Twelfth Night, was associated with romance and served as a favorite time of year for weddings (*see also* Twelve Days of Christmas). Twelfth Night balls offered young, single people the chance to meet and to interact freely, and thus, hopefully, to find a mate. This goal was facilitated by the fact that the parties usually featured dancing and some form of masking, as well as card and dice **games**. Indeed, some balls were designed exclusively as affairs for the young. One very famous colonial romance led to a marriage scheduled for Epiphany, the day after Twelfth Night. George Washington (1732-1799) and his bride, Martha Dandridge Custis (1732-1802), married on January 6, 1759.

Needless to say, those who did not celebrate Christmas deplored the idea of a Twelfth Night ball (*see* **America, Christmas in Colonial; Puritans**). One man, Mordecai Noah, who published a book on home economics in the year 1820, had this to say about the wasteful custom of Twelfth Night feasting:

> What a sum to be destroyed in one short hour! The *substantials* on this table, consisting of a few turkeys, tongues, hams, fowls, rounds of beef and game, all cold, could have been purchased for *fifty dollars*; the residue of this immense sum was expended for whips, creams, floating islands, pyramids of kisses, temples of sugarplums, ices, *blanc manges*, macaroons and plumb cake; and ladies of delicacy, of refined habits, of soft and amiable manners, were *at midnight*, cloying their stomachs, after exercise in dancing, with this trash [Weaver, 1990, 13-14].

Last of the Twelve Days of Christmas

Some Twelfth Night customs appear to have sprung from its position as the last night of the Twelve Days of Christmas. Old folk customs in France and the German-speaking countries encouraged noisemaking processions on Twelfth Night, designed to drive out the spirits that prowled the dark evenings of the Twelve Days of Christmas. Old German folk beliefs also suggested that **Berchta**, a frightening figure associated with the Twelve Days, appeared to people most often on Twelfth Night. In fact, the day took on her name in some German-speaking areas, becoming *Perchtennacht*, or "Berchta Night." Finally, other Twelfth Night customs arose from its status as the evening before Epiphany. On this evening Italian children expect La **Befana** to arrive bearing their Christmas season **gifts**. Likewise, children in the Spanish-speaking world await the arrival of the gift-bearing Three Kings (*see also* **Epiphany; Mexico, Christmas in; Philippines, Christmas in the; Spain, Christmas in**).

Further Reading

Christmas in Colonial and Early America. Chicago: World Book, 1996.

Crippen, Thomas G. *Christmas and Christmas Lore*. 1923. Reprint. Detroit, Mich.: Omnigraphics, 1990.

Hadfield, Miles, and John Hadfield. *The Twelve Days of Christmas*. Boston, Mass.: Little, Brown and Company, 1961.

Henisch, Bridget Ann. *Cakes and Characters: An English Christmas Tradition*. London, England: Prospect Books, 1984.

Hole, Christina. *British Folk Customs*. London, England: Hutchinson and Company, 1976.

MacDonald, Margaret Read, ed. *The Folklore of World Holidays*. Detroit, Mich.: Gale Research, 1992.

Miles, Clement A. *Christmas in Ritual and Tradition*. 1912. Reprint. Detroit, Mich.: Omnigraphics, 1990.

Muir, Frank. *Christmas Customs and Traditions*. New York: Taplinger, 1977.

Pimlott, J. A. R. *The Englishman's Christmas*. Atlantic Highlands, N.J.: Humanities Press, 1978.

Weaver, William Woys. *The Christmas Cook*. New York: HarperPerennial, 1990.

Twelve Days of Christmas
Christmastide, The Days of Fate, The Nights of Mystery, Smoke Nights, The Twelve Quiet Days

The Twelve Days of Christmas fall between **December 25** and January 6, that is, between Christmas and **Epiphany**. Church customs, as well as some folk traditions reckon the twelve-day period as beginning on Christmas and ending on the day before Epiphany. Other traditions recognize the day after Christmas as the first of the Twelve Days and Epiphany as the last. In past centuries Europeans experienced the Twelve Days as both a festive and fearful time of year.

Establishment of the Holiday

By the fourth century most western European Christians celebrated Epiphany on January 6. In the same century Western Church officials declared December 25 to be the Feast of the Nativity. In establishing these dates for the two festivals, the Church bracketed a twelve-day period during which a number of non-Christian celebrations were already taking place. For example, the Roman new year festival of **Kalends** as well as the Mirthraic festival commemorating the **Birth of the Invincible Sun** occurred during this period. What's more, the raucous Roman holiday of **Saturnalia** was just drawing to a close as this period began. Further to the north some researchers speculate that the Teutonic peoples may have been observing a midwinter festival called **Yule** at about this time of year. The establishment of Christmas and Epiphany during this cold, dark season provided further occasions for midwinter celebrations. In 567 the Council of Tours declared the days that fall between Christmas and Epiphany to be a festal tide. This decision expanded Christmas into a Church season stretching from December 25 to January 5. In English this period is known as Christmastide.

Early Church authorities condemned the riotous festivities that characterized the pagan holidays celebrated during this period, especially Kalends, which fell on January 1. Eventually, they declared January 1 to be a Christian holiday, the **Feast of the Circumcision**. They urged their followers to observe this and the other Christian festivals that took place at this time of year with a joyful sobriety rather than drunken gaming, masking, dancing, and revelry.

As Christianity became more firmly rooted in **Europe**, political leaders declared the Twelve Days to be legal holidays. Near the end of the ninth century King Alfred the Great of England (849-899) mandated that his subjects observe the Twelve Days of Christmas, outlawing all legal proceedings, work, and fighting during that time. The Norwegian King Haakon the Good (d. c. 961) established the Christian observance of the festival in **Norway** in the middle of the tenth century.

Feasting, Resting, Revelry, and Charity

In late medieval **England**, manor house records indicate that the gentry indeed exempted the peasants who worked their lands from labor during these days. Of course the weather also cooperated, late December presenting the farmer with little to do in the fields or barns. Custom also dictated that the lord provide a feast for all those working on his lands. In exchange, the workers, or villeins, were expected to bring **gifts** of farm produce to the manor house.

The well-to-do enjoyed a variety of diversions during the Twelve Days, including feasting, storytelling, hunting, playing and listening to music, and watching and participating in dances and tournaments. King Richard II of England (1367-1400) organized a Christmas tournament that drew knights from all over Europe. The jousting matches lasted nearly two weeks and were followed each evening by feasting and dancing. The late medieval tale *Sir Gawain and the Green Knight*, set in England during the **Christmas season**, offers a marvelous description of how the well-to-do entertained themselves during these festival days.

By the end of the Middle Ages both jousting and the manorial feast for those who worked on large estates disappeared as ways of celebrating the Twelve Days. Although some landowners continued to entertain the poor at this time of year, most preferred to feast with family and friends. Records from the time of the Renaissance indicate that the English continued to enjoy feasting, dancing, music-making, and performances of various kinds during the Twelve Days

769

(*see also* **Christmas Carol**; **Lord of Misrule**; **Nativity Play**). Play-going was another popular holiday diversion around the time of the Renaissance. Lastly, the courtly **masque** evolved out of the **mumming** and disguising practices already common at this time of year during this era.

The idea that the wealthy should make some special provision for the poor during the Twelve Days of Christmas lingered throughout the following centuries. As late as the nineteenth century some English farm laborers felt entitled to claim Christmas hospitality from the local landlord. The customs associated with **Boxing Day** also reflected the notion that the well-to-do should give generously around Christmas time. This noble ideal inspired the American writer Washington Irving (1783-1859) to write a story about an English squire who tried to maintain old-fashioned Christmas hospitality by keeping an open house during the Twelve Days. Irving's work influenced the English writer Charles Dickens (1812-1870). Dickens's famous work *A Christmas Carol* tells the story of a rich and greedy old man who learns compassion and charity one Christmas Eve.

Wealthy colonial Americans who celebrated Christmas observed the Twelve Days as a period of festivity, relaxation, and romance. Many parties took place during the twelve days. Young, single people found these occasions ideal for light-hearted flirting or serious scouting for a possible mate. Many weddings also took place during this period.

Other Holidays

A variety of holidays punctuate the Twelve Days of Christmas. The customs, stories, and festivities associated with these observances add additional color to the celebration of the Twelve Days. These holidays include **St. Stephen's Day** on December 26, which later became Boxing Day in England, **St. John's Day** on December 27, **Holy Innocents' Day** on December 28, **New Year's Day** and the Feast of the Circumcision on January 1, and **Twelfth Night** on January 5 or 6. These celebrations, along with the festivities associated with the Twelve Days themselves, declined as European societies became increasingly industrialized.

Ghosts and Spirits

Much of the lore and many of the customs associated with the Twelve Days suggest that ordinary people viewed the time as one in which supernatural forces and spirits roamed the earth. Indeed, in ancient times the pagan observers of the Yule festival believed that the spirits of the dead returned to earth during these few days.

Perhaps this belief eventually gave rise to the lore surrounding the **Wild Hunt**. In much of northern Europe this band of fierce spirits was believed to ride the stormy night skies during the Twelve Days of Christmas. In the German-speaking lands the witch-like figure of **Berchta** haunted the Twelve Days. In Scandinavia the mischievous **Jultomten** lurked about the house during this season. In **Iceland** the prankster spirits known as the **Christmas Lads** annoyed householders while keeping just out of sight. Greek folk beliefs suggested that small goblins known as the **kallikantzari** caused many a mishap during the Twelve Days. In parts of northern Europe folk beliefs warned that bears, werewolves, and trolls wandered about preying on the unwary. British folklore suggested that fairies and the Will o' the Wisp, a magical creature who appeared as a light or flame in the darkness, hindered those who traveled abroad on these dark nights (*see also* **Elves**). Perhaps the English custom of telling **ghost** stories at Christmas time can be traced back to the widespread European folk belief that ghosts and spirits are especially active at this time of year.

Folklore suggested many remedies for this situation. In **Germany** and Austria people burned incense in their homes and churches throughout the Twelve Days. They believed that the smoke drove out evil influences and spirits. In fact, some Germans referred to the Twelve Days as the "Smoke Nights," *Rauchnächte* in German, in reference to this custom. Moreover, German speakers sometimes referred to the Twelve Days as the "Nights of Mystery," perhaps in reference to the religious significance of the season as well as the heightened activity of the spirit world during these days. Other German folk customs associated with the Twelve Days included making loud noises, crossing oneself, wearing frightening masks and costumes, and burning bonfires as ways of scaring off harmful spirits. In spite of all this noise and activity, people from the German region of Bavaria called this period the "Twelve Quiet Days." This name reflects old folk beliefs found in parts of England, **Denmark**, and Germany prohibiting spinning, washing, cleaning, and baking during this time.

While Germans and Austrians tried to scare off the Christmas season goblins, the Scandinavians tried to appease their relatively harmless visitors. Scandinavian folk custom advised householders that supplying the Jultomten with a nightly bowl of porridge would put these household sprites in a better mood. The Greeks, on the other hand, approached the problem in much the same way as did the Germans. Greek lore warned householders to keep a fire burning in the hearth during the Twelve Days to ward off the kallikantzari (*see also* **Greece, Christmas in**).

Fortune-Telling

In some parts of central Europe, events that transpired during the Twelve Days were taken as omens of what would happen in the coming twelve months. For example, the weather that occurred during the Twelve Days foretold the year's weather patterns, according to folk belief. In German-speaking lands the Twelve Days were sometimes called the "Days of Fate," perhaps in reference to these kinds of beliefs. Folklore also suggested that dreams occurring during these days predicted coming events. In past eras girls employed magical formulas at this time of year to discover who their future husbands would be. One such silly exercise recommended throwing a shoe into a pear tree twelve times in a row. If the shoe stuck in the tree on any of these attempts, one could rest assured of marrying the man of one's dreams.

Further Reading

Christmas in Germany. Lincolnwood, Ill.: Passport Books, 1995.

Crippen, Thomas G. *Christmas and Christmas Lore.* 1923. Reprint. Detroit, Mich.: Omnigraphics, 1990.

The Glory and Pageantry of Christmas. Chicago: Time-Life Books, 1963.

Hadfield, Miles, and John Hadfield. *The Twelve Days of Christmas.* Boston, Mass.: Little, Brown and Company, 1961.

Henisch, Bridget. *Cakes and Characters: An English Christmas Tradition*. London, England: Prospect Books, 1984.

Hole, Christina. *British Folk Customs*. London, England: Hutchinson and Company, 1976.

Hutton, Ronald. *The Rise and Fall of Merry England*. Oxford, England: Oxford University Press, 1994.

———. *The Stations of the Sun*. Oxford, England: Oxford University Press, 1996.

Lehane, Brendan. *The Book of Christmas*. Chicago: Time-Life Books, 1986.

MacDonald, Margaret Read, ed. *The Folklore of World Holidays*. Detroit, Mich.: Gale Research, 1992.

Miles, Clement A. *Christmas in Ritual and Tradition*. 1912. Reprint. Detroit, Mich.: Omnigraphics, 1990.

Pimlott, J. A. R. *The Englishman's Christmas*. Atlantic Highlands, N.J.: Humanities Press, 1978.

Russ, Jennifer. *German Festivals and Customs*. London, England: Oswald Wolff, 1982.

United States of America, Christmas and New Year's Celebrations in the

For Christmas and New Year's Eve and Day in the United States of America, *see* **America, Christmas in Colonial; America, Christmas in Nineteenth-Century; Amish Christmas; Barring Out the Schoolmaster; Bethlehem, Pennsylvania, Christmas in; "Charlie Brown Christmas, A"; Children's Letters; Christmas Card; Christmas Carol; Christmas Seals; Christmas Tree; Christmas Village; Commercialism; Eggnog; Emancipation Day; Farolitos; Football Bowl Games; First Night; Hopping John;** *How the Grinch Stole Christmas; It's a Wonderful Life;* **Jonkonnu; Lovefeast; Luminarias; Macy's Thanksgiving Day Parade;** *Miracle on 34th Street;* **Mummers Parade; Nation's Christmas Tree; National Christmas Tree; New York City, Christmas in; Pastores, Los; Posadas, Las; Poinsettia; Putz; Reindeer; Resolutions; Salvation Army Kettles; Santa**

Claus; Shooting in Christmas; Slaves' Christmas; Store Window Displays; Times Square, New Year's Eve in; Urban Legends; Virginia O'Hanlon; Watch Night; "White Christmas"; White House, Christmas in the; Williamsburg, Virginia, Christmas in Colonial; Wrapping Paper

Up Helly Aa

In Great Britain the long **Christmas season** draws to a close with Up Helly Aa, a spectacular fire festival celebrated in Scotland's Shetland Islands. In the late nineteenth century Shetlanders celebrated the festival on January 29, or "Twenty-Fourth Night" Old Style, the twenty-fourth evening after **Old Christmas Day**. In recent times, however, the festival has been scheduled for the last Tuesday in January.

This celebration has changed significantly over the past 140 years. In the mid-nineteenth century the young men of Lerwick blew horns and dragged burning barrels of tar through the streets atop sledges on various dates surrounding Christmas. After the town had admired the din and the blaze, guizers, or **mummers**, emerged onto the streets and visited the homes of their friends. Local folklore taught that these visits brought good luck. In the 1870s the town council banned the burning of tar barrels in response to complaints from housewives that the burning tar spilled onto the streets and stuck to the boots of passersby, who eventually tracked it into their homes. The burning tar barrels also constituted a significant fire hazard. The guizers remained, however.

In the late nineteenth century a torchlit procession replaced the burning tar barrels. The procession climaxed with the burning of a replica of a Norse, or Viking, galley. The ship represented the six hundred years during which the Shetland Islands were under Norse rule. In 1899 the chief guizer, known as Guizer Jarl, posted the first Up Helly Aa "bill," a lengthy document poking fun at local events, people, and institutions. In subsequent years, this custom became a regular feature of the festival, along with the torchlit procession, the burning of the ship, and the visits of the guizers. These days, teams of guizers visit social halls and restaurants instead of homes, and present a short skit to those assembled there. Merrymaking continues until the early hours of the morning.

What could the festival's strange name, "Up Helly Aa," possibly mean? Some researchers believe it came from "Uphaliday," an old Scottish term for Twelfth Day or **Epiphany**. Uphaliday was the day on which the holidays were up, or over. These writers reason that Up Helly Aa means something like "up holidays all," a fitting name for the festival that marks the end of the long Christmas season in the Shetland Islands.

Further Reading

Edwards, Gillian. *Hogmanay and Tiffany, The Names of Feasts and Fasts*. London, England: Geoffrey Bles, 1970.

Hole, Christina. *British Folk Customs*. London, England: Hutchinson and Company, 1976.

MacDonald, Margaret Read, ed. *The Folklore of World Holidays*. Detroit, Mich.: Gale Research, 1992.

Urban Legends

In addition to traditional **Nativity legends**, Christmas has inspired a number of urban legends over the years. An urban legend is a story about some mundane aspect of contemporary life that is usually believed by its teller to be true even though it is, in fact, false. While traditional legends often concern magical or supernatural creatures and events, urban legends generally treat everyday situations and events familiar to both listener and teller. They often contain an implied warning or commentary on some aspect of contemporary life. Urban legends spread by word of mouth, e-mail, faxes, the media, and the World Wide Web.

Poisonous Poinsettias

One urban legend concerning an everyday aspect of the Christmas holiday takes the form of a dire warning about the leaves of the **poinsettia** plant. It claims that they contain a deadly poison. Each year, it declares, small tots die from sampling the enticing, bright red leaves. Apparently, this legend took shape in 1919 when a child in Hawaii died suddenly, and people simply assumed that the culprit was a poinsettia leaf. This myth acquired so much power that in 1975 a petition was submitted to the Consumer Products Safety Commission requesting that poinsettias be sold with a warning label. After looking into the facts of the matter, the Commission denied the request.

According to the POISINDEX®, a reference source used at most poison control centers, poinsettia leaves are not poisonous. The U.S. Department of Agriculture agrees, although some researchers suspect that consuming sufficient quantities of the plant's milky sap may cause abdominal pain, diarrhea, and vomiting. Poinsettia leaves taste terrible, however, making it extremely unlikely that anyone would consume enough to get sick. The myth of the poisonous poinsettia persists in spite of the evidence against it. A 1995 poll of American florists showed that about 66 percent of them still believed that poinsettias were poisonous.

Crucified Santa Claus

Another urban legend concerning Christmas tells of a tasteless holiday **store window display** in Japan. According to the legend, the personnel at a Japanese department store attempted to boost Christmas sales by setting up a cheery, crucified **Santa Claus** in their display window. One version of this legend claims that this event took place in 1945, others claim it happened in the 1990s. One variant describes the Santa as a billboard image, another claims that the department store in question prepared a number of doll-sized, crucified Santas. The location at which this event supposedly took place also varies from story to story.

The legend implies that there is something deeply wrong with the way in which the Japanese celebrate Christmas. The crucifix is the central symbol of the Christian religion, hence the image of the crucified Santa seems to suggest that, whether out of ignorance or

greed, the Japanese in question have made Santa Claus into the central figure of the Christian religion. Japan is a non-Western nation, and Christians constitute only a small minority of the population. Thus, the story seems to confirm the fears of those who suspect that non-Western, non-Christian foreigners like the Japanese simply cannot or will not grasp our cherished symbols and values. Or perhaps the legend serves to transfer guilt about the Western obsession with the **commercial** aspects of Christmas onto the Japanese. The legend implies that it is they, not we, who have replaced **Jesus** with Santa Claus in our holiday observances.

Candy Cane Symbolism

Another recent legend suggests that hundreds of years ago candy makers encoded Christian symbols into the red-and-white design on candy canes. The story asserts that the red stripes represent the blood of Christ, and the white background his purity. Some versions of the legend assert that the three thin red stripes on some candy canes stand for the Holy Trinity. Other versions of the tale add that the J-shape of the candy cane stands for Jesus, and that the hardness of the candy cane stands for the idea that Jesus' church is founded on a rock.

In fact, the history of the candy cane is uncertain. Some researchers believe that it was invented in Europe in the seventeenth century and that the shape was intended to resemble a **shepherd**'s crook rather than the letter "j." One tradition maintains that it was invented by clerics from the cathedral in Cologne, **Germany**, as a treat for children attending Christmas services held around the **Nativity scene**. The suckable candies also kept the children quiet during the services. The original candy cane was pure white. American candy manufacturers added the red stripes in the early twentieth century.

"Santa" Dies in Chimney

One final legend tells of a family's Christmas tragedy. A man regretfully informs his wife and children that he must go out of town on a business trip for the Christmas holiday. The wife and children resign themselves to celebrating Christmas without him. He finishes his business earlier than expected, however, and returns home on Christmas

Eve. He decides to surprise his children by dressing up as Santa Claus and coming down the chimney with a sack of toys. He gets stuck in the chimney and suffocates to death. Meanwhile, his wife and children decide to celebrate Christmas Eve by lighting a fire in the fireplace. The smoke refuses to be drawn up the chimney and pours into the living room, accompanied by a funny smell. The children investigate what is blocking the chimney and find the lifeless body of their father, dressed as Santa Claus.

The impact of this tale hinges on the contrast between the wholesome, family Christmas celebration and the macabre discovery of the father's dead body. Like other urban legends, many variations of this morbid tale circulate throughout the population. The exact reason for the man's return, the cause of his death, and clues that lead his family to investigate what's blocking the chimney may vary, but the outline of the story remains the same. No verified account of any such event exists. Nevertheless, there have been several documented instances of burglars and would-be Santas getting stuck in chimneys and having to be rescued by police and fire departments. The legend of the dead, smoked Santa lives on, however.

Further Reading

Brunvand, Jan Harold. *The Mexican Pet: More "New" Urban Legends and Some Old Favorites*. New York: W. W. Norton and Company, 1986.

———. "Urban Legend." In his *American Folklore: An Encyclopedia*. New York: Garland Publishing, 1996.

Comfort, David. *Just Say Noel!* New York: Fireside Books, 1995.

Ellis, Bill. "Legend, Urban." In Thomas A. Green, ed. *Folklore: An Encyclopedia of Beliefs, Customs, Tales, Music, and Art*. Volume 2. Santa Barbara, Calif.: ABC-CLIO, 1997.

Smith, Paul. "Legend, Contemporary." In Thomas A. Green, ed. *Folklore: An Encyclopedia of Beliefs, Customs, Tales, Music, and Art*. Volume 2. Santa Barbara, Calif.: ABC-CLIO, 1997.

Turkington, Carol. *The Home Health Guide to Poisons and Antidotes*. New York: Facts on File, 1994.

Web Site

A site sponsored by the San Fernando Valley Folklore Society, California, on urban legends: http://www.snopes.com (click on "Holidays," then "Christmas")

Victorian England, Christmas in

Queen Victoria ruled the British Empire from 1837 to 1901. Although she played little part in it herself, she presided over the revival of English Christmas celebrations. At the turn of the nineteenth century many English Christmas customs had disappeared or were in decline. By the 1840s, however, the English had begun to revive the splendor of the **Christmas season**. The Victorian Christmas mixed new customs, such as the **Christmas tree**, with old ones, such as the singing of **Christmas carols**. In this way the Victorians recreated the English Christmas as a festival of good will, charity, and domestic harmony.

Decline

By the early 1800s Christmas had fallen out of fashion in **England**. Historians find few mentions of Christmas in newspaper articles or advertisements from the early decades of the nineteenth century. Moreover, folklorists of the era lamented the decline of many old

Christmas customs. Indeed, Christmas withered along with the entire calendar of saints' days and feast days inherited from earlier times. Changes in the British economy severely curtailed the observance of these holidays in the late eighteenth and early nineteenth centuries. For example, in the year 1761 the Bank of England closed its doors for 47 holidays. By 1825 the number of observed holidays had declined to 40 and in 1830 it dropped to 18. By 1834 the number of holidays honored by the Bank of England had plummeted to four. Some of the holidays eliminated were those that fell in or around the **Twelve Days of Christmas**, including **Holy Innocents' Day** and **Epiphany**. In 1833 the Factory Act ruled that British workers had a legal right to only two holidays besides Sunday: Christmas and Good Friday.

Revival

During the second half of the nineteenth century the English reclaimed and transformed Christmas. What caused the turnaround in attitude? Some historians believe that the Oxford movement, a campaign for religious reform within the Church of England, generated renewed appreciation of Christmas traditions through its promotion of ritual, decoration, and the old holy days. In addition, images of Prince Albert and Queen Victoria celebrating Christmas with a decorated Christmas tree kindled widespread interest in this new Christmas custom. Finally, some writers credit Charles Dickens's influential portraits of Christmas charity in *A Christmas Carol* (1843) and Christmas cheer in *The Pickwick Papers* (1837) with inspiring Victorian appreciation of the Christmas season. Others disagree, arguing that Dickens captured the emerging Victorian attitude towards Christmas, rather than inspired it. Whatever his place in the chain of cause and effect, both British and American audiences hailed *A Christmas Carol*, and the tale became a cherished element of Victorian Christmas lore.

Christmas Dinner

Christmas dinner was one of the few English Christmas customs that had never really gone out of fashion. The Victorians relished their holiday feast, contributing two new dishes to the traditional Christmas dinner. **Plum pudding**, a dessert, replaced plum porridge as a first course. The Victorians also adopted roast turkey as a possible main course, in addition to the more traditional roast beef or roast goose. The renewed emphasis on the pleasures of the table, so ably promoted by Dickens, elevated the Christmas dinner into a centerpiece of the Victorian festival.

Christmas Charity

Changes in the treatment of the poor at Christmas time reveal the importance of Christmas charity in Victorian times. In 1847 a new law allowed Christmas dinners to be served in all workhouses for the poor. Charitable donations supplied much of the food for these dinners. During the Victorian era, performing acts of charity became an important part of the observance of Christmas for many middle-class people. Some visited workhouses on Christmas Day. Others distributed **gifts** of food and money, known as "boxes," among the poor of their parish on the day after Christmas. In Victorian times people called the twenty-sixth **Boxing Day** in reference to this custom. In past eras the English had observed December 26 as **St. Stephen's Day**. Parliament declared Boxing Day a public holiday in 1871.

Protestants Embrace Christmas

As the themes of charity and domestic harmony became dominant in Victorian Christmas celebrations and the disorderly, public revelry of past eras faded, those Protestant denominations that had once opposed the celebration of Christmas softened their attitudes toward it. This opposition dated from the time of the Reformation and found its strongest advocates in the **Puritans**. In late nineteenth-century America a similar process of reincorporation was underway as many Protestant churches in the United States also accepted Christmas back into the fold of legitimate observances (*see also* **America, Christmas in Nineteenth-Century**).

Christmas Trees and Gifts

At the beginning of the nineteenth century the English gave Christmas gifts, or boxes, to servants, the poor, and those who provided them with services during the year. Those who gave holiday season gifts to family and friends did so on **New Year's Day**. In the early part of the nineteenth century, however, New Year's gift giving appeared to be dying out. Two English folklorists writing in the 1830s remarked upon the ominous decline of the practice. In the Victorian era the English revived winter season gift giving, transferring the custom from New Year's Day to Christmas. The Christmas tree played an important role in this transfer and revival.

Historians credit German-born Prince Albert for importing this German custom to Great Britain (*see also* **Germany, Christmas in**). A well-known 1840s illustration depicting Queen Victoria, Prince Albert, and their children gathered around the Christmas tree motivated middle-class families to adopt this custom. (Fashionable Victorians often sought to imitate royal tastes.) Like the Germans, English families covered their Christmas trees with good things to eat and small gifts. Hence, the tree focused everyone's attention on giving and receiving. In addition, because it stood at the center of the household, the tree drew the exchange of Christmas gifts into the family circle. By the end of the century, Victorians customarily gave Christmas gifts to friends and family. New Year's gifts had become the exception rather than the rule. Queen Victoria remained loyal to the old custom, though, still sending New Year's, rather than Christmas, gifts as late as 1900.

While the Christmas tree grew in popularity among middle-class Victorians, many working-class families adopted the more affordable and convenient Christmas **stocking**. This custom, too, encouraged the exchange of small gifts within the family.

By the 1880s **Santa Claus** had arrived in England. Unlike the English **Father Christmas**, Santa Claus brought gifts to children at Christmas time. By the end of the century the popularity of this American gift bringer prompted retailers to begin using his image to boost Christmas sales.

Christmas Carols

In the early years of the nineteenth century several English folklorists predicted the approaching demise of the Christmas carol. Observers of English folk customs mourned that only a scattered handful of old people knew and sang the traditional songs. This timely handwringing may have inspired several important collections of Christmas carols, which were published in the early part of the century. With their renewed interest in Christmas and its traditions, middle-class Victorians welcomed these traditional songs back into their Christmas festivities. By the 1870s churches began to incorporate these almost-forgotten Christmas songs into their holiday services. In 1880 an Anglican bishop, Edward W. Benson, later archbishop of Canterbury, first devised the **Ceremony of Lessons and Carols,** a special Christmas service blending Bible readings with carol singing.

Christmas Greetings and Entertainments

By the 1860s Victorians had come to cherish seasonal greeting cards (*see also* **Christmas Card; Robin**). Many of these cards wished the recipient "Happy New Year" rather than "**Merry Christmas,**" but by the 1870s the increasing importance of Christmas led card makers to include Christmas greetings as well. Victorian Christmas card designers created colorful and elaborate cards, often enhanced with silk, cords, and tassels. The ingenious cards so enchanted the public that newspapers reviewed new designs and people carefully collected and displayed the cards they received.

At about mid-century **Christmas crackers** emerged as another Victorian Christmas novelty. These cardboard tubes, wrapped in decorative papers, contained a variety of tiny trinkets. When pulled on both ends, the party favors burst with a loud popping sound.

Other Christmas entertainments included parlor **games.** In the game called "Snapdragon," the hostess filled a bowl with currants (a raisin-like dried fruit), poured spirits on top of them, and set a lighted match to the mixture. Players dared one another to grab a currant out of the flaming bowl. When the family tired of Snapdragon they might move on to other parlor games, such as Blind Man's Bluff or charades, or they might entertain one another with recitations, magic tricks, or Christmas carols.

The **kissing bough** offered a different kind of entertainment to the lovelorn or to the adventurous who lingered nearby. According to custom, one could steal a kiss from anyone who passed beneath its branches of **mistletoe.** Victorian tastes in Christmas decorations called for plenty of **greenery,** in addition to the kissing bough, usually displayed in the form of ropes, **wreaths,** and sprays.

Victorians continued their Christmas fun on Boxing Day. On this day many families crowded into theaters to view a **pantomime**, a circus-like presentation of a folk or fairy tale.

Customs in Decline

Although many of the more boisterous English Christmas customs, such as **mumming**, had already deteriorated by Victorian times, a few more withered away under the spell of the new Victorian Christmas. **Twelfth Night**, which had been celebrated in the past with sumptuous cakes, costumed balls, and charades, faded throughout the Victorian period as Christmas Day grew in importance. In addition, the **waits**, bands of nighttime musicians who serenaded householders at Christmas time in exchange for food, drink, or tips, also fell out of favor during this era. Nevertheless, by the end of the nineteenth century, the Victorians celebrated Christmas more vigorously than their ancestors had at the beginning of the century.

Further Reading

Hutton, Ronald. *The Stations of the Sun*. Oxford, England: Oxford University Press, 1996.

Miall, Antony, and Peter Miall. *The Victorian Christmas Book*. New York: Pantheon Books, 1978.

Pimlott, J. A. R. *The Englishman's Christmas*. Atlantic Highlands, N.J.: Humanities Press, 1978.

Web Site

A site sponsored by Victoriana.com contains pages that offer images and text descriptions of Victorian Christmas celebrations: http://www.victoriana.com/christmas/default.htm

Virginia O'Hanlon

In 1897 an eight-year-old girl named Virginia O'Hanlon wrote a letter to a newspaper called the *New York Sun*. The letter asked the newspaper editor to tell her whether or not **Santa Claus** was real. Virginia's letter, and the newspaper's response, have become beloved bits of American Christmas lore. The often-quoted phrase, "Yes, Virginia, there is a Santa Claus," comes from the paper's editorial response, written by reporter Francis P. Church and published on September 21, 1897.

Virginia's Letter and the **Sun's** *Response*

Dear Editor:

I am 8 years old. Some of my little friends say there is no Santa Claus. Papa says "If you see it in The Sun it's so." Please tell me the truth, is there a Santa Claus?

Virginia O'Hanlon
115 West 95th Street
New York City

Virginia, your little friends are *wrong*. They have been affected by the skepticism of a skeptical age. They do not *believe* except they *see*. They think that nothing can be which is not comprehensible by their little minds. All minds, Virginia, whether they be men's or children's are little. In this great universe of ours man is a mere insect, an ant, in his intellect, as compared with the boundless world about him, as measured by the intelligence capable of grasping the whole of truth and knowledge.

Yes, Virginia, there *is* a Santa Claus. He exists as certainly as love, and generosity and devotion exist, and you know that they abound and give to your life its highest beauty and joy. Alas! how dreary would be the world if there were no Santa Claus! It would be as dreary as if there were no Virginias. There would be no childlike faith, then, no poetry, no romance to make tolerable this existence. We should have no enjoyment, except in sense and sight. The eternal light with which childhood fills the world would be extinguished.

Not believe in *Santa Claus*! You might as well not believe in fairies! You might get your papa to hire men to watch in all the chimneys on Christmas Eve to catch Santa Claus, but even if they did not see Santa Claus coming down what would that prove? Nobody sees Santa Claus. The most real things in the world are those that neither children nor men can see. Did you ever see fairies dancing on the lawn? Of course not, but that's no proof that they are not there. Nobody can conceive or imagine all the wonders there are unseen and unseeable in the world.

You tear apart the baby's rattle and see what makes the noise inside, but there is a veil covering the unseen world which not the strongest man, nor even the united strength of all the strongest men that ever lived, could tear apart. Only faith, fancy, poetry, love, romance, can push aside that curtain and view — and picture the supernal beauty and glory beyond. Is it all real? Ah, Virginia, in all this world there is nothing else real and abiding.

No Santa Claus? Thank God he lives, and he lives forever! A thousand years from now, Virginia, nay ten times ten thousand years from now, he will continue to make glad the heart of childhood.

Who Was Francis P. Church?

Francis Church, the child of a Baptist minister, was born in 1839. He graduated from Columbia College in 1859 and went on to cover the Civil War as a reporter for the *New York Times*. Some time after that he joined the staff of the *New York Sun*, where he covered religious matters.

When Virginia's letter arrived at the offices of the *Sun* in 1897, the editorial page chief assigned Church the chore of writing a response. Church, known for his bitter, sarcastic wit, was none too pleased with the assignment, but resigned himself to crafting a suitable reply. His response surpassed everyone's expectations. It was so popular that the *Sun* reprinted it every year at Christmas time, until the paper went out of business about fifty years later. Church died in 1906.

Whatever Happened to Virginia?

Virginia's early thirst for knowledge continued as she matured into adulthood. She graduated from New York's Hunter College in 1910 with a B.A., and went on to acquire an M.A. at Columbia University. She completed her studies with a Ph.D. from Fordham University. Dr. O'Hanlon served as an educator in **New York City**'s public school system, ending her career as principal of P.S. 401 in Brooklyn. She retired in 1959 and died in 1971.

Further Reading

Foley, Daniel J. *Christmas in the Good Old Days*. 1961. Reprint. Detroit, Mich.: Omnigraphics, 1994.

Pool, Daniel. *Christmas in New York*. New York: Seven Stories Press, 1997.

Snyder, Phillip V. *December 25*. New York: Dodd, Mead, and Company, 1985.

Waits

Two hundred years ago groups of instrumentalists and singers known as "the waits" roamed the nighttime streets of towns and villages across Britain during the **Christmas season**. They stopped in front of houses and performed folk songs, popular tunes, or **Christmas carols**. During the two weeks before Christmas the waits sometimes played well into the night, often awakening people asleep in their beds. In return for these seasonal serenades householders were expected to offer the musicians food, drink, or money. In some towns the waits collected these tips by returning at a more reasonable hour in the days that followed, **Boxing Day** being a logical choice. In Scotland the waits performed around **New Year's Day** rather than Christmas.

History

In medieval **England** the king required certain of his minstrels to wander through the city streets at night guarding the citizenry and calling out the hour. Collectively known as "the watch," these court pages gradually evolved into uniformed town employees known as "the waits." Several theories have been advanced as to the origin of the term "waits." Perhaps the most popular one claims that "the waits" simply developed from the phrase "the watch." Others suppose that the term "waits" came from *wayghtes*, an old English word for the oboe, one of the instruments played by these musical watchmen. Another writer suggests that the term derived from the old Scottish word *waith*, which means "to wander" or "to roam."

In the early 1500s the citizens of London recognized the waits by their blue tunics, red sleeves, red hats, and silver collars and chains. Their official duties included playing for the mayor and town officials at feasts and parades, as well as watching over London's darkened streets. Several accounts dating from around the turn of the eighteenth century report that local youth routinely badgered these town musicians into helping them court their sweethearts with nighttime serenades. Eventually, the night patrols performed by these watchmen were taken over by a regular police force. The waits survived for a time, however, as bands of nighttime singers and instrumentalists.

Perhaps influenced by other Christmas customs, such as wassailing and caroling, the waits eventually adopted the practice of performing songs around Christmas time in exchange for food, drink, or tips (*see also* **Wassail; Wassailing the Fruit Trees**). Some towns and cities issued licenses to the waits for this purpose. The Christmas time activities of the waits peaked in the eighteenth and early nineteenth centuries. To the dismay of the established members of the waits, however, impromptu groups, often of dubious musical accomplishment, also began to carol at Christmas time in hopes of cashing in on the customary tip. In the town of Westminister the leader of the officially recognized town waits complained to the city magistrate about the unofficial competition in 1820. Perhaps the dissonant musical offerings made by these amateurs helped to turn public attitudes against the waits. By the late nineteenth century public approval of this and many other seasonal begging practices declined. No longer wanted, either as watchmen or as musicians, the institution of the waits finally disappeared.

Further Reading

Chambers, Robert. "December 24—The Waits." In his *The Book of Days*. Volume 2. 1862-64. Reprint. Detroit, Mich.: Omnigraphics, 1990.

Duncan, Edmondstoune. *The Story of the Carol*. 1911. Reprint. Detroit, Mich.: Omnigraphics, 1992.

Palmer, Geoffrey, and Noel Lloyd. *A Year of Festivals*. London, England: Frederick Warne, 1972.

Pimlott, J. A. R. *The Englishman's Christmas*. Atlantic Highlands, N.J.: Humanities Press, 1978.

Wales, Christmas in

Wales has been called "the land of song." Indeed, its Christmas traditions reflect a deep love of singing. Many Americans are familiar with at least one Welsh Christmas song; musicologists believe the familiar **Christmas carol**,"Deck the Halls," to be of Welsh origin.

Music

Communities across Wales sponsor music and poetry festivals called *Eisteddfods* in honor of the holiday. These festivals include competitions for the best carols and poems written in Welsh, thus helping to create a large body of Welsh Christmas music and verse. The Royal National Eisteddfod, held each year in August, is the largest of this kind of festival. The Eisteddfod is an ancient Welsh tradition; historical records trace it as far back as the twelfth century.

The **Plygain**, or carol service, is another old Welsh Christmas tradition involving singing. These church services used to be held around three a.m. on Christmas morning. This tradition survives in a modified form in a few locales. The observances now consist entirely of carol singing and have been shifted to hours considered more reasonable by the participants.

Another old custom taught children to go caroling with *calenigs*. A calenig is a piece of fruit (usually an apple) studded with spices, garnished with sprigs of **greenery**, and set on stick legs. Sometimes villagers also stuck a candle into the center of the apple (*for a similar custom, see* **Christingle**). Children carried these good-luck charms with them while caroling and gave them away at households where they received a warm welcome. Some writers believe that the word "calenig" comes from the Latin word for "new year," **Kalends**. Indeed, sprigs of greenery, such as those which adorn the calenig, were typical new year's **gifts** among the Romans.

Mari Lwyd

The yearly visit of the Mari Lwyd called for verbal, rather than musical, skill. The Mari Lwyd is a kind of hobbyhorse made from a horse's skull covered over with a sheet and ornamented with bits of glass and ribbons. The horse's head is devised in such a way that someone hiding underneath the sheet can snap the horse's jaws open and shut. Around Christmas time the Mari Lwyd appears in the company of a band of local men. This band visits each house in town, knocking on the door and engaging in an informal contest of improvisational verse with the occupants. The contest is over when one or the other party cannot think of anything more to say. Usually the householders concede defeat, after which they are expected to let the Mari Lwyd party enter their home. Tradition dictates that the householders reward the Mari Lywd band with something to drink and perhaps some coins. A similar custom, known as hodening, also takes place in a number of locations in **England**. These hodening customs occur at several different times of the year, including Christmas.

Wren Hunt

In past centuries boys frequently participated in the **wren hunt** on **St. Stephen's Day**, December 26. This custom appears to have died out in the twentieth century, however.

Further Reading

Hubert, Maria, comp. *Christmas Around the World*. Stroud, Gloucestershire, England: Sutton, 1998.

Muir, Frank. *Christmas Customs and Traditions*. New York: Taplinger, 1977.

Patterson, Lillie. *Christmas in Britain and Scandinavia*. Champaign, Ill.: Garrard Publishing Company, 1970.

Wassail

The word "wassail" may sound unfamiliar to many Americans in spite of its long association with the **Christmas season** in Great Britain (*see also* **England, Christmas in**). There, the word has been used over the centuries to refer to a toast, a caroling custom, and a beverage (*see also* **Christmas Carol**).

The Toast

The English word "wassail" comes from the Middle English phrase *wes heil*, which means "be whole" or "be healthy." The contemporary English word "hale," meaning sound, healthy or vigorous, evolved from the second word in this phrase. Medieval Britons toasted each other with the cry, "Wes heil!" The proper response was *"Drinc heil!"* meaning "drink wholeness" or "drink health." The phrase first appears in this context in a twelfth-century document.

A fourteenth-century document reveals that in that era the toast "wes heil" accompanied the passing of a communal cup. Each person in the gathering received the cup along with a kiss, responded, "Drinc heil," sipped from the vessel, toasted the next person, and passed the cup to them. A document dating from the thirteenth century mentions a special wassail bowl designed for communal dunking of bread and cakes. By the end of the fourteenth century many wealthy English families possessed heirloom wassail bowls. Much ceremony could accompany the use of these bowls. When King Henry VII (1457-1509) called for his wassail bowl on **Twelfth Night**, the following protocol was observed. The chapel choir came into the hall and stood to one side. Next, the steward entered the hall with the royal bowl and cried, "Wassail" three times. Then the choir burst into song.

The Caroling Custom

Historical evidence suggests that sometime in the sixteenth century common folk began carrying wassail bowls from house to house during the Christmas season. They garnished the bowl with decorations such as ribbons, **holly**, **mistletoe** or other **greenery**, and colored paper. Crying, "Wassail, wassail," they brought the decorated bowl full of spiced ale to their well-off neighbors, hoping to exchange a cup of **Christmas ale** for a **gift** of food or a tip. Hence, the groups were called "wassailers," and the custom itself, "wassailing." In another variant of this custom the wassailers carried an empty bowl to their neighbors, bidding the householders fill it up for them. Some researchers believe that women upheld this tradition more frequently than men.

Often these wassailers sang carols as they stood in front of their neighbors' homes. A number of wassailing carols have survived to present times. The following verses of an old wassailing song show that these carolers maintained the practice of toasting another's health with the beverage donated to them:

> Wassail, wassail all over the town
> Our bread it is white, and our ale it is brown
> Our bowl it is made of the maple tree
> So here, my good fellow, I'll drink to thee.
>
> The wassailing bowl, a toast within
> Come, fill it up unto the brim
> Come fill it up that we may all see
> With the wassailing bowl I'll drink to thee.
>
> Come, butler, come bring us a bowl of your best
> And we hope your soul in heaven shall rest
> But if you do bring us a bowl of your small
> Then down shall go butler and bowl and all
> [Duncan, 1992, 107].

The following verses of another carol, usually sung by children, show that wassailers did not necessarily limit their requests to drink:

> Here we come a wassailing
> Among the leaves so green,
> Here we come a wandering
> So fair to be seen.
>
> Chorus: Love and joy come to you,
> And to you your wassail too,

And God bless you and send you a happy New Year,
And God send you a happy New Year.

We are not daily beggars,
That beg from door to door;
But we are neighbor's children
Whom you have seen before.

Call up the butler of this house,
Put on his golden ring,
Let him bring us up a glass of beer
And the better we shall sing.

We have got a little purse
Made of stretching leather skin,
We want a little of your money
To line it well within.

Bring us out a table,
And spread it with a cloth;
Bring us out a moldy cheese
And some of your Christmas loaf.

God bless the master of this house,
Likewise the mistress too,
And all the little children
That round the table go [Chambers, 1990, 1: 28].

In rural zones some wassailers sallied forth at night to salute their fruit trees with song and drink (*see* **Wassailing the Fruit Trees**). In a few areas these agricultural wassailers bestowed this ritualized blessing on farm animals, such as oxen.

Wassailing took place throughout the Christmas season, the most important dates being those surrounding Christmas, **New Year's**, and Twelfth Night. The practice began to die out in the late nineteenth century, along with other seasonal begging customs.

The Beverage

In spite of the decline of public wassailing practices in Victorian times, the British continued to drink from the domestic wassail bowl (*see also* **Victorian England, Christmas in**). They referred to the beverage it contained as "wassail." This drink consisted of sweetened wine or ale spiced with some combination of cinnamon, cloves, ginger, mace, allspice, or coriander. The beverage might also contain chopped apples, beaten eggs, milk, or cream, in which case it was sometimes referred to as **lamb's wool**.

Further Reading

Chambers, Robert. "January 1 — New-Year's Day Festivities." In his *The Book of Days*. Volume 1. 1862-64. Reprint. Detroit, Mich.: Omnigraphics, 1990.

Crippen, Thomas G. *Christmas and Christmas Lore*. 1923. Reprint. Detroit, Mich.: Omnigraphics, 1990.

Del Re, Gerard, and Patricia Del Re. *The Christmas Almanack*. Garden City, N.Y.: Doubleday, 1979.

Duncan, Edmondstoune. *The Story of the Carol*. 1911. Reprint. Detroit, Mich.: Omnigraphics, 1992.

Hutton, Ronald. *The Stations of the Sun*. Oxford, England: Oxford University Press, 1996.

Palmer, K., and R. W. Patten. "Some Notes on Wassailing and Ashen Fagots in South and West Somerset." *Folklore* 82 (winter 1971): 281-91.

Pimlott, J. A. R. *The Englishman's Christmas*. Atlantic Highlands, N.J.: Humanities Press, 1978.

Wassailing the Fruit Trees

In past centuries people in some parts of **England** bestowed a traditional, ritualized blessing on their fruit trees during the **Christmas season**. They sang and drank to the trees' health, hence the custom was known as "wassailing the fruit trees" or, more specifically, as "wassailing the apple trees" (*see also* **Wassail**). This practice took place on a variety of dates within the Christmas season, including Christmas Eve, **New Year's** Eve, and Old **Twelfth Night** (January 17). Most people who participated in this tradition, however, honored their trees on the evening of January 5. This day was known as Twelfth Night, **Epiphany** Eve, or Old Christmas Eve (*see also* **Old Christmas Day**).

Although each locale developed its own variations, the main features of the custom remained the same. Family members, farm workers, or neighbors gathered together in the evening and prepared a bowl of wassail punch. Then they carried the wassail outside to the fruit trees or orchard, filled each other's cups, drank, and sang to the trees. These wassailing songs encouraged the trees to produce bountifully in the coming year, as illustrated in the following verse in a song from Devon and Cornwall:

> Here's to thee, old apple tree,
> Whence to bud and whence to blow,
> And whence to bear us apples enow:
> Barn-fulls, bag-fulls, sack-fulls,
> Lap-fulls, hat-fulls, cap-fulls:
> Hurrah, hurrah, hurrah! [Crippen, 1990, 190].

Another song from Kent conveys similar sentiments:

> Stand fast, root, bear well, top;
> God send us a yowling crop,
> Every twig, apple big;
> Every bow, apples enow;
> Hats full, caps full, bushel bushel sacks full,
> And my pockets full too! Hooray! [Crippen, 1990, 191].

Shouts, horn blasts, and even shots aimed between the tree branches might accompany the singing. Some folklorists interpret the noise as additional encouragement to the trees to blossom and fruit as the days lengthened. In some areas the singers poured the remains of the wassail onto the roots of the fruit trees. They sometimes left a bit of cake and some salt in the crook of the tree as a **gift** for **robins** or other birds. In some areas groups of local men trooped from homestead to homestead blessing the trees in this fashion. Householders usually thanked them with food, ale, or money.

Some folklorists believe that the wassailing of fruit trees may have originated in pagan times. The earliest documented account of the custom, however, dates back only as far as the sixteenth century. In the seventeenth century the English poet Robert Herrick (1591-1674) wrote the following lines about the custom as it was practiced in Devon:

> Wassail the trees, that they may bear
> You many a plum and many a pear:
> For more or less of fruit they bring
> As you do give them wassailing [Crippen, 1990, 189].

The wassailing of apple and other fruit trees at Christmas time began to die out in the nineteenth century. By the beginning of the next century it had disappeared, though the twentieth century witnessed a few revivals of the custom. Herrick's advice notwithstanding, the practice resurfaced in these places less as an aid to agricultural prospects and more as an occasion for festivity and an attraction for sightseers.

Further Reading

Crippen, Thomas G. *Christmas and Christmas Lore*. 1923. Reprint. Detroit, Mich.: Omnigraphics, 1990.

Hutton, Ronald. *The Stations of the Sun*. Oxford, England: Oxford University Press, 1996.

Muir, Frank. *Christmas Customs and Traditions*. New York: Taplinger, 1977.

Palmer, Geoffrey, and Noel Lloyd. *A Year of Festivals*. London, England: Frederick Warne, 1972.

Palmer, K., and R. W. Patten. "Some Notes on Wassailing and Ashen Fagots in South and West Somerset." *Folklore* 82 (winter 1971): 281-91.

Watch Night
New Year's Eve Service

Some Americans refer to **New Year's** Eve as Watch Night. The name comes from the tradition of attending lengthy church vigils, called Watch Night services, on this evening. Watch Night services begin late in the evening on December 31 and continue through midnight. They usually feature singing, prayers and sermons. Attendees are encouraged to review their behavior in the year that has just passed, to renew their commitment to God in the year to come, and to pray for themselves, their families, and the world (*see also* **Resolutions**). New Year's Eve Watch Night services got their start in the Methodist and Moravian churches. Today they are most often found in evangelical Protestant churches, especially those whose congregations are composed primarily of African Americans.

Vigils

Vigils—church services held on the evening before an important feast day—can be traced back to early Christian times. The Watch Night service adapts this church custom to New Year's Eve, a secular holiday. The word "vigil" comes from the Latin term *vigilia*, which means "to watch." When English Methodists began holding late-night services in the eighteenth century, they called them Watch Night services.

Making New Year's Eve a Religious Holiday

In the sixteenth century a religious reform movement known as the Reformation gave birth to Protestant Christianity. A group of early Protestant Christians known as the **Puritans** found fault with many holiday celebrations, including those that took place on New Year's Eve. In particular they objected to the heavy drinking, masking (*see also* **Masque**; **Mumming**), gaming, gambling, dancing, and public carousing that characterized the celebration of the holiday. They found these customs coarse and viewed them as contrary to the behavior that they believed should characterize a Christian society.

In the eighteenth and nineteenth centuries evangelical Protestant leaders, such as those belonging to the newly formed Methodist denomination, took up the campaign to reform New Year's Eve celebrations. They tried to give the holiday a religious significance by urging their followers to use the occasion to examine their spiritual lives and to resolve to do better in the coming year. Watch Night services provided worshipers an opportunity to meditate and pray on these issues. The late-night services could easily be linked to biblical teachings by referring to passages from Christian scripture that admonish the faithful to be awake and alert for the hour of Christ's coming (for example, Matthew 25:1-13). Watch Night services became popular among American evangelical Christians in the nineteenth century.

Methodist Watch Night Services

John Wesley (1703-1791), the founder of the Methodist Church, first observed Watch Night services among Moravian Christians. These services inspired him to approve of similar observances for Methodists (*for more on Moravian Christmas customs, see* **Bethlehem, Penn-**

sylvania, Christmas in; Christingle; Lovefeast; Putz). He first met Moravians on his sea voyage to the American colonies, where he served from 1735 to 1737 as an Anglican priest in Georgia. He continued to have contact with Moravians upon his return to **England**, where he broke away from the Church of England to form the Methodist Church.

The first Watch Night services convened by British Methodists were held monthly on the night of the full moon and were often attended by those who sought an alternative to carousing at the local pub. The service emphasized renewal of one's commitment to Christ. The light of the moon permitted worshipers to walk home safely after midnight when the service had concluded. Later the Methodist Church added New Year's Eve Watch Night services, also presented as an alternative to the boisterous and alcohol-laden celebrations taking place on the streets and in the taverns.

English Methodists brought the Watch Night service with them to the American colonies. The first Watch Night services to be convened by American Methodists took place at Philadelphia's St. George's Methodist Church and at **New York City**'s Wesley Chapel in November of 1770.

In the nineteenth century monthly Watch Night services declined in popularity while New Year's Eve Watch Night services found favor in both British and American Methodist churches. During the twentieth century, however, the New Year's Eve Watch Night service began to fall out of favor in Methodist congregations composed primarily of European Americans. In recent years, a secular attempt to reform New Year's Eve has produced a new alternative to traditional New Year's Eve celebrations: the **First Night** festival.

African Americans

Among African Americans the Watch Night service has spread beyond Methodist congregations and into other Protestant churches. In some black churches Watch Night services take on a somber tone, as people consider the passing of time and their own mortality. Inspiring sermons, along with plenty of opportunities to sing and pray, round out the experience.

African-American slaves who attended Watch Night services on December 31, 1862, may have felt their prayers were answered the following day (*see also* **Slaves' Christmas**). On January 1, 1863, President Abraham Lincoln signed the Emancipation Proclamation, freeing over three million slaves. Some African-American communities still celebrate January 1 as **Emancipation Day**.

Moravians

A few Moravian congregations also continue to hold Watch Night services. According to Moravian tradition, the pastor should begin a sermon as midnight approaches. As the clock strikes midnight a trombone choir or other kind of band cuts the sermon off in midstream. The pastor abandons his or her unfinished speech and joins the congregation in singing the hymn, "Now Thank We All Our God." The interruption symbolizes the teaching that Christ could return at any minute and reminds everyone of the need for constant spiritual readiness. In another form of this tradition the congregation stands up and leaves the church at midnight, in the middle of the pastor's sermon. In past times Moravian Watch Night services also included a review of the year's most important events, but this custom has been abandoned.

Further Reading

Bowler, Gerry. *The World Encyclopedia of Christmas*. Toronto, Ontario, Canada: McClelland and Stewart, 2000.

Hogan-Albach, Susan. "Watch Night: It's an Age-Old New Year's Eve Tradition That's about Much More than Watching the Clock and Making Resolutions." *Minneapolis Star Tribune* (December 27, 1997): 05B.

Sawyer, Edwin A. *All About the Moravians*. Bethlehem, Pa.: The Moravian Church in America, 2000.

Schmidt, Leigh Eric. *Consumer Rites: The Buying and Selling of American Holidays*. Princeton, N.J.: Princeton University Press, 1995.

Web Site

"Meet the New Millennium Through Watch-Night Service," an article by the Rev. Diedra Kriewald, published by the United Methodist News Service and available online at: http://umns.umc.org/99/nov/608.htm

Weihnachtsmann

In **Germany** Christmas begins on Christmas Eve, which is called *Weihnacht*, or "watch night." A mythological figure known as the *Weihnachtsmann*, or the "Christmas man," ushers in the **Christmas season** there. The Weihnachtsmann resembles the English **Father Christmas** more than he does **Santa Claus**. Like Father Christmas, the Weihnachtsmann personifies the Christmas season.

Unlike his English counterpart, however, the Weihnachtsmann often appears as both old and tired. He is commonly depicted as a bearded old man trudging through snow-covered streets, shoulders drooping. Often he carries a small **Christmas tree** over his shoulder. Perhaps the image of the exhausted, elderly gift bringer is meant to represent the age of the year, which at Christmas time has nearly expired. The Weihnachtsmann is only one of several folk figures known to visit German-speaking lands in December. Others include **Berchta**, **Christkindel**, **Knecht Ruprecht**, and **St. Nicholas**.

Further Reading

Lehane, Brendan. *A Book of Christmas*. Alexandria, Va.: Time-Life Books, 1986.

Wenceslas, King

St. Wenceslaus, Vaceslav, Vaclav

The familiar **Christmas carol**, "Good King Wenceslas," tells of a virtuous deed performed by the noble King Wenceslas on the day after Christmas, **St. Stephen's Day**. Is King Wenceslas an historical or a legendary character? If historical, did he ever perform a deed similar to that described in the carol?

According to the carol, King Wenceslas spied a poor man scavenging wood outside his castle on St. Stephen's Day. Moved by the needy man's plight, King Wenceslas found out where he lived, and set forth with his page to bring the man food, drink, and fuel. The wind and cold nearly overcame the king's page but, with Wenceslas's encouragement, the page stumbled forward, treading in his master's footprints. Heat rose from the tracks of the saintly king, a sign of heaven's approval of his act of charity.

The story told in the song combines historical fact with pious speculation. The song's lyrics describe a tenth-century Bohemian duke who later became a saint. Known as St. Vaceslav or St. Vaclav in Czechoslovakia, his name is usually rendered as "Wenceslas" or "Wenceslaus" in English. He was born to a Christian father, Wratislaw, and a pagan mother, Drahomira, around the year 903. His grandmother, St. Ludmilla, educated him in the Christian faith.

When his father died his mother became the duchess of Bohemia. Drahomira resented the influence of Ludmilla over the young Wenceslas, and so arranged to have the older woman murdered. Horrified by this act and by her unscrupulous political dealings, Wenceslas eventually wrested power away from his mother and assumed the title of duke. Drahomira had hindered the spread of Christianity, but Wenceslas supported the new religion. Furthermore, Duke Wenceslas acquired a reputation for personal piety and charity to the poor. Drahomira still opposed him, however, and soon convinced Wenceslas's brother Boleslaw to murder the young Duke and take his place on the throne. Wenceslas died at the hands of his brother on September 28 in the year 935. Although he may have been deprived of earthly power at a young age, Wenceslas was elevated to sainthood after his death. He became the patron saint of Bohemia by the eleventh century. His feast day is September 28.

In the nineteenth century an Englishman named John Mason Neele (1818-1866) wrote the lyrics to "Good King Wenceslas." He based the story on legends concerning the saint's good deeds as duke of Bohemia. He paired these lyrics with a thirteenth-century tune he found in an obscure book of early songs. Although the sturdy melody may now automatically evoke images of the noble king trudging through the snow, the tune had earlier been used as a spring carol titled "Spring Has Now Unwrapped the Flowers." Neele's winning combination of words and music spread the legend of Wenceslas to listeners who otherwise would never have known of the saint.

Further Reading

Mershman, Francis. "St. Wenceslaus." In Charles B. Hervermann, ed. *Catholic Encyclopedia*. Nashville, Tenn.: T. Nelson, 1913. Available online at http://www.newadvent.org/cathen/15587b.htm

Papin, J. "St. Wenceslaus." In *New Catholic Encyclopedia*. Volume 14. New York: McGraw-Hill, 1967.

Studwell, William E. *The Christmas Carol Reader*. Binghamton, N.Y.: Haworth Press, 1995.

"White Christmas"

"White Christmas" is the most popular Christmas song ever recorded. Written by Irving Berlin (1888-1989) and featured in the 1942 movie *Holiday Inn*, it soon inspired a large and loyal following. Bing Crosby (1904-1977), one of America's most popular mid-century crooners, sang the tune in the motion picture and also recorded it as a single. It sold so many copies that the die press used to imprint the records literally wore out. Crosby recorded the song again in 1947, once more in 1952 — as part of the sound track for the movie *White Christmas* — and yet again in 1955. By 1968 listeners had snapped up 30 million copies of the song. For decades "White Christmas" reigned not only as the best-selling Christmas song ever recorded, but also as the best-selling single ever recorded. In 1997, pop star Elton John finally toppled this achievement with his musical tribute to Princess Diana, "Candle in the Wind."

The Composer

Irving Berlin was the stage name of Israel Baline, the youngest child of a Russian Jewish family that immigrated to the United States in 1893 and settled in **New York City**'s Lower East Side. Although his own family did not celebrate Christmas, the composer later fondly recalled childhood memories of scampering over to his neighbors, the O'Hara's, to enjoy their **Christmas tree** and share in their Christmas goodies. Perhaps he called on some of these memories when he composed his nostalgic, best-selling Christmas song. Musical success was no stranger to Irving Berlin, however. He published 800 songs in his lifetime, many of them hits, and wrote hundreds more. Berlin possessed a knack for capturing in song the spirit of the times, an event, or a holiday, even one that he didn't himself celebrate. In addition to "White Christmas," some of his timeless tunes include "Oh How I Hate to Get Up in the Morning," "(There's No Business Like) Show Business," and "God Bless America."

"White Christmas," the Song

In 1940 Berlin began work on a series of songs for a musical comedy about a man who retires from show business to run a country inn open only on holidays. While working on the show's Christmas song, he remembered a winter spent in sunny Hollywood, where it never quite felt "like Christmas." He realized that the very difficulties he recalled formed the basis of a song. He fixed in his mind an image of jaded Hollywoodites sitting around a southern California swimming pool at Christmas time, reminiscing about the Christmases of their childhoods, and then put pencil to paper. The song as originally composed includes a first verse that speaks of palm trees and mild weather. Later renditions of the song usually skip this verse.

Although it generally took Berlin days, weeks, or months to write a song, he completed "White Christmas" in a single, all-night work session. Berlin, never afraid to sing his own praises, was so pleased with "White Christmas" that the morning after he completed the song he told his transcriber, "It is not only the best song I ever wrote, it's the best song anybody ever wrote" (Glancy, 2000, 65).

Holiday Inn

Berlin succeeded in selling his songs and story idea to Paramount Pictures, which turned them into the 1942 musical *Holiday Inn*. The movie gave "White Christmas" the public exposure it needed to become a hit. It featured Bing Crosby, who played a singer and dancer who moves to the country to run an inn open only on holidays. He falls in love with an up-and-coming singer, played by Marjorie Reynolds, who must choose between the retiring innkeeper and a flashy Hollywood-bound dancer played by Fred Astaire. Berlin composed a song for each holiday featured in the movie. As he liked to exercise a great deal of control over the presentation of his songs, he worked closely with the director, technicians, and actors, advising the singers on appropriate phrasing and execution for each song. Perhaps irritated with this constant stream of advice, the director asked Berlin to leave the set while they filmed Bing Crosby singing "White Christmas." Berlin agreed, but then found that he couldn't resist hanging around. He hid himself behind some flats (panels used to dampen sound), but was discovered during the filming by a technician.

Although the cast predicted that the film's Valentine's Day song, "Be Careful, It's My Heart," would become the most beloved song from the show, "White Christmas" soon entranced audiences. It spoke powerfully to American soldiers fighting in World War II, who were also dreaming of other, happier times. They swamped their radio stations with calls requesting the song. Back home, "White Christmas" won the Academy Award for the best song in a motion picture released in 1942.

While the American public dreamed along with "White Christmas," the idea behind the story for *Holiday Inn* fueled the business imagination of Kemmons Wilson. When he opened a chain of family motels in the 1950s he named it after one of his favorite movies, "Holiday Inn."

White Christmas, the Movie

Meanwhile, back in Hollywood movie producers decided to capitalize on the popularity of "White Christmas" by filming a remake of *Holiday Inn* which would again feature the song. In order to make sure the public knew that the movie revolved around the tune, they named the film *White Christmas* (1954). Bing Crosby once more played the lead role, this time with actor Danny Kaye as his sidekick. The two play old army buddies who are also song and dance men. They meet and fall in love with two singing and dancing sisters, played by Rosemary Clooney and Vera Ellen. The foursome prepare a Christmas show for a rural Vermont inn run by a retired army general, Crosby and Kaye's former commander. Like *Holiday Inn*, *White Christmas* gives Crosby two opportunities to sing "White Christmas," one at the beginning and the other at the end of the story.

A Personal Tribute

In 1967 New York City composer and singer John Wallowitch and a group of his friends gathered on the sidewalk outside Irving Berlin's house to celebrate Christmas by serenading the retired composer with his famous holiday song, "White Christmas," and a love song called "Always." These devoted fans kept up this yearly Christmas time tribute until Berlin's death in 1989. In 1983, the singers actually rang the doorbell and were invited in. Berlin graciously told them that their visit and performance was the nicest Christmas present he had ever had.

Further Reading

Bergreen, Laurence. *As Thousands Cheer: The Life of Irving Berlin*. New York: Viking, 1990.

Crump, William D. *The Christmas Encyclopedia*. Jefferson, N.C.: McFarland, 2001.

Furia, Philip. *Irving Berlin, A Life in Song*. New York: Schirmer Books, 1998.

Glancy, H. Mark. "Dreaming of Christmas: Hollywood and the Second World War." In Mark Connelly, ed. *Christmas and the Movies*. London, England: I. B. Tauris and Co., Ltd., 2000.

Marling, Karal Ann. *Merry Christmas!* Cambridge, Mass.: Harvard University Press, 2000.

Menendez, Albert J., and Shirley C. Menendez. *Christmas Songs Made in America*. Nashville, Tenn.: Cumberland House, 1999.

Pool, Daniel. *Christmas in New York*. New York: Seven Stories Press, 1997.

White House, Christmas in the

The White House became the official residence of the president of the United States in 1800. Throughout the nineteenth century, it was referred to as the President's House, the President's Palace, or the Executive Mansion. President Theodore Roosevelt (1858-1919) dubbed it the White House in 1901. As Christmas became a more important holiday in the United States, White House Christmas celebrations expanded beyond family festivities to include public acts of charity, political functions, activities dedicated to enhancing public relations, and special observances, such as the **National Christmas Tree**-lighting ceremony.

White House Christmas Parties

Christmas was not a popular holiday in some regions of the United States during the early years of the Republic (*see* **America, Christmas in Colonial**). Nevertheless, a number of the early American presidents, such as George Washington (1732-1799), Thomas Jefferson (1743-1826), James Madison (1751-1836), and James Monroe (1758-1831), came from Virginia, a state whose inhabitants tended to keep the old English custom of celebrating a jolly Christmas (*see also* **Williamsburg, Virginia, Christmas in Colonial**). Yet it was the Massachusetts-born John Adams (1735-1826) and his wife Abigail (1744-1818) who first occupied the White House upon its completion in November of 1800 and who hosted the first White House Christmas party in that same year. According to the story that grew up about the party, Mrs. Adams could not get the newly constructed building properly heated, in spite of the huge amounts of wood she burned in its fireplaces. The shivering guests left as soon as they deemed it polite.

In 1811 noted hostess Dolley Madison (1768-1849) gave a sumptuous Christmas dinner party, over which she presided dressed in a gown of purple velvet adorned with pearls. Her serious-minded husband, President James Madison, wore his usual plain black clothing. Dolley's sisters Anna and Lucy attended, as did writer Washington

Irving (1783-1859) and many notable political figures, such as Secretary of State James Monroe, Henry Clay (1777-1852), and John Randolph (1773-1833). The Madisons served a Virginia-style feast, featuring turkeys, chickens, ducks, wild game, vegetables, and puddings (*see* **Plum Pudding**). After dinner guests and hosts entertained each other with **games**, singing, and dancing.

Some White House Christmas parties have served diplomatic purposes as well as social ones. In 1860 President James Buchanan (1791-1868) hosted a delegation of Pawnee Indians at a White House Christmas party. In 1874 President Ulysses S. Grant (1822-1885) and his wife welcomed the King of Hawaii to their Christmas party. Special decorations were devised for this important occasion.

Needless to say, many first ladies have been accomplished hostesses. In 1929 fire struck the White House on Christmas Eve. Lou Hoover kept the dinner party going in the formal dining room, while her husband President Herbert Hoover (1874-1964) rushed to the site of the fire in the West Wing. Although 16 fire engines answered the alarm, some of the President's guests stayed through the entire party without ever realizing that the building was on fire.

Throughout the late twentieth century the number of Christmas parties hosted at the White House grew. Some of these parties reflected the personal tastes of the president or first lady. For example, in 1957 Mamie Eisenhower threw a Christmas tea party for women reporters. Some parties, once instituted, were taken up by succeeding administrations. The Kennedys threw a variety of specialized Christmas parties, including one for the members of the diplomatic corps, and another for their children. The Johnsons maintained both of these events.

By the 1970s the first family was expected to entertain several segments of Washington society at Christmas time. In 1979 the Carters gave a Christmas ball for 1,000 people, in large part members of Congress and their spouses. White House chefs loaded the buffet tables with ham, roast beef, smoked salmon, crab claws, cheese rings, artichokes, mushrooms, and more. The very next night the Carters threw another Christmas party for 500 members of the Washington press corps. By the time the Clintons threw a Christmas party for the press in 1994, the guest list numbered 2,000.

A Child's Christmas in the White House

The very first White House Christmas party, held in 1800 by President John Adams and his wife Abigail, included special festivities for children. The White House's first children's Christmas party did not end on a happy note, however. Susanna, the Adams's grandchild, showed the other children the dolly dish set she had received for Christmas. One little girl became so envious that she broke the tiny dishes into pieces. At this provocation Susanna flew into a rage and bit the nose and cheeks off her companion's doll. The President himself had to exercise his diplomatic skills and executive authority to break up the fight and restore order.

In 1805 Thomas Jefferson threw a Christmas party for his six grandchildren. As he was a widower, Dolley Madison, the wife of his secretary of state, James Madison, acted as hostess. One hundred children attended and were entertained by the President himself, who churned out rollicking tunes on the violin.

In 1835 President Andrew Jackson (1767-1845) invited a large number of Washington children to a Christmas Day party in the White House. He treated them to a fancy feast, prepared by his French chef and served in the formal dining room. After dinner he supplied the children with cotton snowballs and permitted them to have a snowball fight in the East Room.

Teddy Roosevelt's wife Edith once threw a Christmas party for 600 children, the sons and daughters of administration officials. It included a special dinner in the state dining room, at which the President helped serve the children their food.

First Lady Nancy Reagan threw a Christmas party for 178 hearing-impaired children in 1981. She hired professional entertainers, also hearing-impaired, to lead the festivities and presented each child with a Christmas **gift**.

White House Charity

Giving to charity became an important aspect of nineteenth-century Christmas celebrations (*see also* **America, Christmas in Nineteenth-**

Century). According to certain popular stories, the generosity of some of the nineteenth-century presidents and their families reflected this trend. According to one account, President Andrew Jackson once brought sweets and toys to a local orphanage at Christmas time. The orphans' plight moved him, as his parents had both died by the time he was fourteen, leaving him without a home. When asked by the children about **Santa Claus**, he reminisced that as a child he had not known of him, nor had he celebrated Christmas.

Abraham Lincoln's (1809-1865) son Tad was reported to have a large heart at Christmas time. According to one story, in 1863 he insisted on shipping the books his parents bought him for Christmas to soldiers fighting the Civil War. His father agreed with the plan, requesting that food and blankets also be added to the box. On Christmas Day in 1864 Tad brought some poor children home with him to the White House. The cook refused to feed them, but Tad went over her head and appealed to his father, who, pleased with his son's generosity, ordered that each be fed a turkey dinner.

In 1883 the sons and daughters of some of Washington, D.C.'s leading citizens joined **Christmas clubs** dedicated to helping the needy at Christmas time. With the aid of adults, the clubs organized charitable Christmas dinners for some of the capital's poor children. Young Nellie Arthur served as president of district II, and, accompanied by her father President Chester A. Arthur (1829-1886), she presided over a dinner for 500 needy children.

Presidential Christmas charity continued throughout the twentieth century. Grace Coolidge, wife of President Calvin Coolidge (1872-1933) handed out gifts at the offices of the **Salvation Army**. President Hoover's wife Lou also gave to the needy, as did Eleanor Roosevelt (1884-1962), who personally visited poor neighborhoods on Christmas Day, bearing food and gifts. President Harry S. Truman (1884-1972) provided two needy families — one white and the other black — with Christmas gifts and dinner, a custom which he preferred not to publicize. In 1961 Jacqueline Kennedy brought gifts to 200 children at the District of Columbia's Children's Hospital. Nancy Reagan visited the same hospital at Christmas time twenty years later.

Greetings from the White House

Franklin (1882-1945) and Eleanor Roosevelt were the first presidential couple to send large numbers of cards at Christmas time. These cards were specially prepared by the White House engraver. During the time of the Eisenhower presidency, it became customary for the president to send an official, presidential **Christmas card** to the members of his cabinet, heads of state, senators, congressional representatives, and other government workers. Dwight D. Eisenhower (1890-1969) was an amateur artist, and during his administration some of his own paintings were featured on the White House Christmas card. His portrait of Abraham Lincoln, executed from a black-and-white photograph, appeared on the White House card one year. In another year the White House Christmas card featured one of his landscape paintings.

Since Eisenhower's time, White House Christmas cards have usually depicted the president and first lady, or offered views of the White House at Christmas time. Subsequent presidents often commissioned painters or photographers to produce images specially for the White House Christmas card.

Throughout the twentieth century ordinary Americans became increasingly fond of the custom of sending Christmas cards. The numbers of cards sent from the White House during each administration seem to reflect this overall trend. The Nixons sent 37,000 Christmas cards in 1969. In 1980 the Carters sent over 100,000 cards. During the 1990s President and Mrs. Clinton customarily ordered 300,000 specially designed White House Christmas cards from Hallmark Cards.

A Discontinued New Year's Custom

Beginning in 1800 and continuing throughout the nineteenth century, American presidents hosted a kind of **New Year's Day** reception at the White House called a levee. (A similar event was held on July 4). Members of the administration, government officials, and other distinguished guests came to the White House to offer the president their best wishes for the new year. Ordinary citizens, too, were welcome at these events. As Washington and the nation grew, more and more people attended the New Year's Day levee.

818

By the 1920s the event had become an ordeal for the president and his wife. In 1929 members of Congress, the Supreme Court, the diplomatic corps, military officers, and government officials began arriving at 11:00 a.m. President and Mrs. Herbert Hoover received their guests on the north portico, shaking each person's hand and exchanging a few words with them. They began to receive the general public at noon and greeted 6,300 people before the day was done. After that, they decided that the nation had simply grown too large for such a ceremony and discontinued it.

White House Christmas Firsts

President Franklin Pierce (1804-1869) set up the first **Christmas tree** in the White House in 1853. Mrs. Coolidge organized the first **Christmas carol** sing in 1923, with the help of choristers from the First Congregational Church. The ceremonies surrounding the lighting of the National Christmas Tree got their start in 1923 under President Calvin Coolidge. Coolidge also composed the first presidential Christmas message to the American people. The first official White House Christmas card dates back to the Eisenhower administration. Jimmy Carter was the first president to participate in a public menorah-lighting ceremony held in Washington, D.C.'s Lafayette Park in 1979 (*see* **Hanukkah**). Subsequent presidents also participated in menorah-lighting ceremonies. In a 1997 Oval Office ceremony, William Jefferson Clinton became the first president to light a menorah inside the White House.

Further Reading

Menendez, Albert J. *Christmas in the White House*. Philadelphia, Pa.: Westminster Press, 1983.

Seeley, Mary Evans. *Season's Greetings from the White House*. Tampa, Fla.: A Presidential Christmas, 1998.

Web Site

The White House maintains a web site with information about its holiday celebrations at: http://www.whitehouse.gov/holiday/

Wild Hunt

Asgardsreid, Furious Host, Furious Hunt, Gabriel's Hounds, Gandreid, Jolerei, Julereien, Raging Host, Yuletide Host

If one listens closely to the swirling winds of a stormy winter night, eerie voices seem to howl in the darkness. In past centuries much folklore from northwestern **Europe** interpreted these sounds as a sign that the Wild Hunt was abroad. People invented many names for this unruly procession of **ghosts**, goblins, and deities that stormed across the night skies. For the most part, the wailing spirits frightened listeners, but in some places they also aided human beings.

Belief in the Wild Hunt was especially strong between the ninth and fourteenth centuries. Historical records indicate that some medieval Europeans believed the Wild Hunt capable of rampaging through their dreams, carrying their spirits off on unwholesome adventures while their bodies slumbered. Folkloric records indicate that the Wild Hunt might appear in the skies at any time of year. Nevertheless, in many locales the ghostly riders were thought to be most active during the **Twelve Days of Christmas**, especially **Twelfth Night**.

The leaders, members, and purpose of the Wild Hunt varied somewhat from region to region. In **Wales**, Gwyn ap Nudd, king of the Underworld, led the hunt. In **Englan**d some believed the Wild Hunt was led by King Arthur. Others referred to the noises on the wind as the baying of Gabriel's Hounds. The phantom hounds represented the souls of unbaptized infants, and their passing signified a death to come. In **Norway** the Hunt was known as the *Gandreid*, which means "spirits' ride." According to Norwegian folklore, the spirits of those who had died during the past year charged across the night skies during the Gandreid, increasing the fertility of all the fields they passed over. The Gandreid was most active around **Epiphany**, or Twelfth Night.

In German-speaking and Scandinavian lands the Hunt was known as *Asgardsreid*, literally "Asgard's Ride," and was thought to occur most often during **Yule** or the Twelve Days of Christmas. Asgard was the home of the Scandinavian gods. Many believed that the fearsome, one-eyed king of the Scandinavian gods, Odin, led the wild ride across the skies to Asgard, mounted on his eight-legged steed. He and his riotous following were sometimes called the Wild Hunt, the Raging Host, the *Jolerei* or the *Julereien* (the Yuletide Host), and it was believed dangerous for Christians to see them. Nevertheless, some peasants left the last sheaf of grain in their fields as an offering for Odin's horse. In some locales Odin's wife Frigga headed the throng of spirits.

In other German-speaking areas the noises on the wind meant that the goddess **Berchta** and her following of wraiths, fairies, and the souls of small children rode abroad. Berchta roamed the world during the Twelve Days of Christmas, but was especially active on Twelfth Night. She rewarded the industrious and punished the lazy. In northern German lands the Furious Hunt or Furious Host was led by a similar goddess, Holde, who commanded a similar band of followers. The passing of Holde and her followers blessed the lands below, ensuring that crops would double during the coming year. (*See also* **Germany, Christmas in.**)

Further Reading

Guerber, H. A. *Myths of Northern Lands*. 1895. Reprint. Detroit, Mich.: Singing Tree Press, 1970.

Hutton, Ronald. *The Pagan Religions of the Ancient British Isles*. Oxford, England: Basil Blackwell, 1991.

Leach, Maria, ed. *Funk and Wagnalls Standard Dictionary of Folklore, Mythology, and Legend*. New York: Harper and Row, 1984.

Williamsburg, Virginia, Christmas in Colonial

The town of Williamsburg became the capital of colonial Virginia in 1699. In colonial times the town was the site of important political, social, and cultural events. When Richmond became the capital of Virginia in 1780, Williamsburg's importance declined. In 1926 John D. Rockefeller (1839-1937), a wealthy philanthropist, decided to renovate or rebuild many of the town's eighteenth-century buildings. The result was an historic zone of 120 colonial-style buildings that has become a major tourist attraction. Visitors during the **Christmas season** can enjoy many elements of a colonial Christmas in Virginia, including accommodations furnished in the style of the eighteenth century, special concerts, colonial-style Christmas feasts, bonfires, fireworks, and tours of the Christmas decorations of the historic district.

Christmas in Colonial Virginia

In colonial times, American Christmas celebrations varied considerably from region to region (*see also* **America, Christmas in Colonial**). These differences stemmed from the religious affiliation of the foremost religious or ethnic group in the region. While the stern **Puritans** that dominated much of New England frowned on the celebration of Christmas, the many Christmas-loving Anglicans who made their homes in Virginia relished the holiday. In Puritan-governed communities Christmas was treated like any other work day, but in Williamsburg and much of the rest of Virginia, Christmas kicked off the start of a **merry** season of feasts, parties, weddings, and relaxation (*see also* **Twelve Days of Christmas**).

Before Christmas

Devout Anglicans observed **Advent**, a period of spiritual preparation for the coming of Christ, in the weeks preceding Christmas. The very observant among them fasted, consuming only one full meal a day. They also meditated on their own shortcomings and on the biblical passages concerning the birth of **Jesus** and the second coming of Christ. The less observant found their thoughts drifting to the coming pleasures of Christmas. A week before Christmas in the year 1773, Philip Fithian, a young man who served as a tutor to the children of wealthy Virginia planter Robert Carter, wrote in his diary:

> Nothing is now to be heard of in conversation, but the Balls, the Fox-hunts, the fine entertainments, and the good fellowship, which are to be exhibited at the approaching Christmas [Lewis and Young, 1970, 12].

Many shared these preoccupations. In 1766 the *Virginia Almanack* of 1766 warbled:

> Now Christmas comes, 'tis fit that we
> Should feast and sing, and merry be:
> Keep open house, let fidlers play,
> A fig for cold, sing care away;
> And may they who thereat repine,
> On brown bread and on small beer dine
> [Lewis and Young, 1970, 26].

Feasts and Parties

For well-to-do Virginians the holiday season revolved around festive meals and parties. Foods available to colonial Virginians at Christmas time included turkeys and other wild game, ham and other kinds of farm-raised meat, oysters, bread, corn, winter vegetables like potatoes and turnips, dried fruit, and preserved fruits and summer vegetables. Fresh and candied fruit, puddings, and cakes were favorite holiday desserts (*see* **Plum Pudding** and **Christmas Cakes**). Virginians washed down these foods with wine, liquor, beer, or other alcoholic beverages like hard cider, rum punch, and **eggnog**.

Perhaps more important than the food was the opportunity to socialize. Family reunions, visits with friends and relatives, and parties both large and small were the hallmarks of the season. Perhaps because newcomers often brought word of new ideas and events in far-off places, hostesses were eager for strangers to join friends and family members in their celebrations. In 1746 the *London Magazine* applauded the open-handed Christmas celebrations of colonial Virginians:

> All over the Colony, an universal Hospitality reigns, full Tables and open Doors, the kind Salute, the generous detention. . . . Strangers are fought after with Greediness, as they pass the Country, to be invited [*Christmas in Colonial and Early America*, 1996, 12].

Music making and dancing were important activities at these holiday get-togethers. Philip Fithian bears witness to Virginians' love for Christmas-time dancing with a journal entry from December of 1773:

> After Breakfast, we all retired into the Dancing-Room. . . . There were several Minuets danced with great ease and propriety; after which the whole company Joined in country-dances, and it was indeed beautiful to admiration, to see such a number of young persons, set off by dress to the best Advantage, moving easily, to the sound of well performed Music, and with perfect regularity, tho' apparently in the utmost Disorder — The Dance continued til two, we dined at half after three — soon after Dinner we repaired to the Dancing-Room again . . . [until] it grew too dark to dance [Oliver and Theobald, 1999, 20].

Christmas parties might include the singing of **Christmas carols** as well as instrumental music for dancing. People welcomed Christmas morning with all sorts of noisemaking activities. Virginians, like many other southerners, shot off guns and banged on pots and pans to usher in the holiday (*see also* **Shooting in Christmas**).

Marriage and Romance

The Christmas season, especially the period between Christmas Day and **Twelfth Night**, was a time associated with weddings and romance. Several famous early American couples from Virginia wed at this time of year. Future first president George Washington (1732-1799) and his bride, Martha Dandridge Custis (1732-1802), married on January 6, 1759. In 1782 Thomas Jefferson (1743-1826), who later became the third president of the United States, married Martha Wayles Skelton (1748-1782) on **New Year's Day**.

Slaves and Free Blacks

Slaveowners generally gave their slaves a few days off at Christmas time (*see also* **Slaves' Christmas**). In addition to the slaves, Williamsburg was home to many free blacks who worked in the skilled trades or as laborers. Indeed, historical research suggests that African Americans, both slave and free, comprised over half the population of Williamsburg.

Men, Women, Children, and Gifts

Well-to-do men often rode out to hunt on Christmas morning while women supervised the preparation of the Christmas feast. In colonial Virginia, Christmas was more of an adult holiday than a children's festival. No special activities were planned to entertain children and few parents gave their offspring **gifts**. Instead, as was the custom in that age, gifts were given to social inferiors to thank them for their service over the past year. Some tradesmen observed the custom of Christmas boxing (*see* **Boxing Day**), and most slave masters gave gifts to their slaves. Some people gave small gifts to family members and close friends on New Year's Day. George Washington, one of the colony's wealthiest men, proved an exception to these gift-giving rules. In 1759 he recorded the fact that he bought the following items as presents for his stepchildren: a bird on bellows, a cuckoo, a turnabout parrot, a grocers shop, an aviary, a Prussian dragoon, a man smoking, six small books for children, six pocket handkerchiefs, and other toys.

Christmas Decorations

In colonial times Virginians decked the insides of their homes and churches with **greenery**. They made garlands of evergreens which they strung along banisters and railings, and wrapped around pillars. At home ropes of greenery might dangle from the fireplace mantel. In addition, some pressed sprigs of **holly** against their window panes, or displayed bouquets of holly and other winter greenery on their tables. They might also strew their homes with herbs, such as **rosemary**, bay (or **laurel**), lavender, and rose petals, in order to give rooms a fresh scent. Boys often shot down boughs of **mistletoe** from high tree branches so that it could be fashioned into **kissing boughs** and other **ornaments**. The making of these decorations was usually women's work.

Christmas in Contemporary Williamsburg

In 1934, after the partial restoration of colonial Williamsburg had been completed, some residents of the historic district began to decorate their homes, inside and out. The practice grew and flourished year after year. Now tourists have become accustomed to seeing **wreaths** featuring fresh fruit and other colorful, natural materials on the front doors of Williamsburg homes and shops. The first wreaths of this kind were created by historical researcher Louise Fisher, who was inspired by the designs of Italian Renaissance sculptor Luca della Robbia (1400-1482) and also by the work of English artist Grinling Gibbons (1648-1721). Della Robbia's garlands and wreaths included natural garnishes, such as lemons, apples, and pine cones. Fisher knew these natural materials to be available in the eighteenth century and began to produce front door wreaths along these designs. Soon all Williamsburg followed suit, and from there this style of wreath began to spread across the country. Some people know them as Williamsburg-style wreaths, while others call them Della Robia wreaths.

In 1937 the first contest for front door wreaths and decorations took place. Soon homeowners began to vie for the prestigious blue ribbon affixed to the most charming Williamsburg-style doorway decorations. The cash prize donated by the Colonial Williamsburg Foundation also tempted homeowners to participate. In response to interest from tourists, a popular Christmas decorations tour of the historic district was launched in 1969.

In recent years, concerned that contemporary doorway decorations may be giving tourists the wrong impression, colonial Williamsburg officials have begun to publicize the fact that there is no historical evidence that colonial Virginians decorated the outside of their homes at all at Christmas time. Moreover, historians agree that they would never have wasted fruit, a relatively rare and precious item, especially in the winter, on outdoor or indoor decorations of any kind. Sometimes colonial hostesses arranged fruit into a pyramid and set it at the center of their buffet table, where it served both as a colorful table decoration and as dessert.

Residents of colonial Williamsburg also developed the tradition of placing a lighted candle in their window during the Christmas season (*see also* **Bethlehem, Pennsylvania, Christmas in; Christmas Candles; Ireland, Christmas in**). Historians give a cool nod of approval to this custom, since colonists did put candles in their windows to honor a royal anniversary of some kind or a military victory. They didn't, however, light these candles at Christmas time. Nevertheless, contemporary residents of the town see the practice as a compromise between the demands of historical accuracy and their own desire to observe the modern custom of lighting up one's home for Christmas. Nowadays a ceremony called the Grand Illumination, which takes place in early December, kicks off the season of candlelit windows in Williamsburg. In the past the ceremony has included the singing of Christmas carols and a procession through the historical district led by a fife and drum corps, as well as a group of men in colonial costumes representing the night watch. As the procession passes each home, family members light their candles. The procession continues until the windows of the historical district twinkle with candles.

Beginning in 1957 Christmas celebrations in colonial Williamsburg have also included fireworks displays. Although colonists exploded fireworks in celebration of successful military campaigns and in honor of a monarch's birthday, they did not use them at Christmas time. Again, the use of Christmas fireworks in colonial Williamsburg represents a compromise between historical accuracy and the desire to celebrate. Special bonfires, another authentic colonial custom, also light up the night skies at Christmas time.

Further Reading

Christmas in Colonial and Early America. Chicago: World Book, 1996.

Kainen, Ruth Cole. *America's Christmas Heritage*. New York: Funk and Wagnalls, 1969.

Lewis, Jr., Taylor Biggs, and Joanne B. Young. *Christmas in Williamsburg*. Williamsburg, Va.: The Colonial Williamsburg Foundation, 1970.

Oliver, Libbey Hodges, and Mary Miley Theobald. *Williamsburg Christmas*. New York: Harry N. Abrams, Inc., in association with the Colonial Williamsburg Foundation, 1999.

Weaver, William Woys. *The Christmas Cook*. New York: HarperPerennial, 1990.

Web Sites

"Another Look at Christmas in the Eighteenth Century," an article by David DeSimone, assistant manager of religious studies and programs in the Department of Trades/Presentations and Tours at Colonial Williamsburg (originally published in *The Colonial Williamsburg Interpreter* 16, 4 (winter 1995-96): http://www.history.org/Almanack/life/xmas/xmasqa.htm

"Christmas Customs," an article by Emma L. Powers, an historian in Colonial Williamsburg's Department of Research (originally published in *The Colonial Williamsburg Interpreter* 16, 4 (winter 1995-96): http://www.history.org/Almanack/life/xmas/customs.htm

"Colonial Williamsburg Activities and Programs," a page sponsored by American Park Network: http://www.americanparknetwork.com/parkinfo/cw/activities.html

Winter Solstice

Winter solstice, the shortest day of the year, falls on December 21 or 22 in the Northern Hemisphere. Winter solstice marks that turning point in the year after which the days begin to lengthen and the nights begin to shorten. In the Northern Hemisphere the longest day of the year, summer solstice, falls on June 21 or 22. In the Southern Hemisphere this same day is observed as winter solstice. In the course of human history many peoples have honored the solstices with ceremonies and festivals. Early Christian authorities placed Christmas near the winter solstice in the hopes of replacing pagan holidays clustered on and around that date (*see also* **December 25**).

Solstice Astronomy

The word "solstice" comes from the Latin phrase *sol stitium*, which means "the sun stands still." A daily observer of the sunrise will notice that the sun comes up at a slightly different position along the horizon each day. In the Northern Hemisphere, as summer turns to winter, the sun rises a bit further to the south each day. The days grow shorter and the nights longer. Finally, the sun appears to rise over the same point on the horizon for several days in a row. This is the time of the winter solstice, the time when the sun appears to "stand still" along the horizon. In reality, the sunrise still moves on those days, but only very slightly. The actual day of the solstice occurs when the sun reaches its southernmost position along the horizon. This happens on the shortest day and longest night of the year. The following day the sun begins to move north along the horizon, and the days slowly begin to lengthen while the nights shorten. The days continue to grow longer until the summer solstice, after which they begin to shorten again as the sun once more turns southward.

The explanation for this yearly cycle lies in the mechanics of the earth's orbit around the sun. The earth's axis, the hypothetical line connecting the North and South Poles, does not meet the plane of the earth's orbit around the sun at a perpendicular angle. Instead, the earth is tilted 23 degrees to one side. This tilt causes the earth's exposure to the sun to vary throughout the year.

During one six-month period of the earth's yearly orbit, the tilt points the **North Pole** towards the sun. During this period the Northern Hemisphere gradually gains exposure to the sun, while the Southern Hemisphere loses exposure. In the north the days lengthen and the sun crosses the sky more directly overhead, hence the weather grows warmer. Three months after the winter solstice the Northern Hemisphere arrives at the spring equinox, the twenty-four hour period in which night and day are of equal lengths. Night and day are also of equal lengths in the Southern Hemisphere on that same date. There, since the days are growing shorter, the event is called the autumn equinox. In the north the days continue to lengthen and the nights to shorten until the very last day of this six-month period, summer solstice, the longest day of the year.

This situation reverses itself during the next six months. As the earth continues its orbit around the sun, the tilt begins to turn the South Pole towards the sun and the North Pole away from it. This decreases the Northern Hemisphere's exposure to the sun's warming rays while increasing the Southern Hemisphere's exposure. As a result, the days lengthen in the Southern Hemisphere, bringing spring and summer to that zone while the people of the Northern Hemisphere experience fall and winter. The solstices as well as the equinoxes are reversed. The same day on which northerners experience winter solstice, southerners experience summer solstice.

The effect of this yearly cycle increases as one moves away from the equator and is greatest near the Poles, which undergo months of unbroken light or darkness near the solstices. The prolonged darkness may strongly affect those who live in the far north (*see also* **Depression**). Only the people living along the earth's equator are not affected by this cycle, since the equatorial zones receive about the same exposure to the sun throughout the year. The length of the days and nights does not change at the equator, so seasonal differences all but disappear.

Winter Solstice in Ancient Rome

According to the Julian calendar used by the ancient Romans, winter solstice fell on December 25. Although for most of their long history the Romans did not celebrate the winter solstice per se, two important Roman festivals fell on either side of this date. **Saturnalia** was celebrated from December 17 to December 23. **Kalends**, the new year festival, began on January 1 and lasted until January 5.

In the late third century A.D., however, the Roman emperor Aurelian (c. 215-275) added a new celebration to the calendar, the **Birth of the Invincible Sun**. He chose December 25, the winter solstice, as the date for this festival honoring the sun god. In fact, by the late third century the solstice did not occur on December 25. A flaw in the design of the Julian calendar caused this error. The creators of the Julian calendar believed the year to be 365.25 days long. The actual length of the solar year is 365.242199 days. This tiny discrepancy caused the calendar to fall behind the actual sun cycle by one day every 128 years. In 46 B.C., when the Julian calendar was established, the winter solstice really did occur on December 25. By the late third century winter solstice was arriving two and one-half days early. Nevertheless, the twenty-fifth had engraved itself in the minds of the populace as the date of the solstice, and so was retained as the date of the new solstice holiday (*see also* **Old Christmas Day**).

Winter Solstice and the Date of Christmas

In the middle of the fourth century, when Christian officials in Rome chose a date for the celebration of the Nativity, they, too, selected December 25. Most scholars believe that they chose this date in order to draw people away from the pagan holidays celebrated at that time of year. In fact, a document written by a Christian scribe later in that century explains that the authorities chose December 25 for the feast of the Nativity because people were already accustomed to celebrating on that date. Moreover, some Christian leaders found celebrating **Jesus'** birth at the time of the winter solstice especially appropriate as they considered him "the sun of righteousness" (Malachi 4:2) and the "light of the world" (John 8:12). With the new festival date in place, Christian leaders exhorted the populace to dedicate their midwinter devotions to the birth of Jesus rather than to the birth of the sun.

Winter Solstice and Other Ancient Celebrations

The people of **Egypt** used a slightly different calendar than did the Romans, one in which winter solstice fell on January 6. Egyptians also honored the sun god on the day of the winter solstice. Other Egyptian festivals that took place on January 6 included the birthday of the god Osiris and the birth of the god Aeon from his virgin mother, Kore. As early as the second century Egyptian Christians adopted January 6 as one of their feast days, too. They began to celebrate **Epiphany** on that day.

Some researchers speculate that the ancient peoples of northern Europe celebrated a festival called **Yule** around the time of the winter solstice. Other researchers disagree, however, arguing that the festival took place in November.

People who lived in close contact with the natural world and who did not possess modern astronomical knowledge may well have viewed the gradual shortening of the days and the cooling of the weather with apprehension. It is easy to understand why many of these ancient peoples honored the gods on the shortest day of the year and gave thanks for the return of the sun.

Contemporary Celebrations

In recent years, renewed interest in pagan or "earth" religions in the developed countries has prompted some people to begin celebrating the solstices again. Although we now understand the astronomical mechanisms behind this cycle in the earth's seasons, our lives still depend on these celestial maneuvers and the seasonal rhythms they create. The new solstice celebrations honor these life-giving processes with ceremony and festivity.

Further Reading

Baldovin, John. "Christmas." In Mircea Eliade, ed. *The Encyclopedia of Religion.* Volume 3. New York: Macmillan, 1987.

Bellenir, Karen, ed. *Religious Holidays and Calendars.* Second edition. Detroit, Mich.: Omnigraphics, 1998.

Heinberg, Richard. *Celebrate the Solstice.* Wheaton, Ill.: Quest Books, 1993.

Henes, Donna. *Celestially Auspicious Occasions.* New York: Berkley, 1996.

Hutton, Ronald. *The Stations of the Sun.* Oxford, England: Oxford University Press, 1996.

Krupp, E. C. *Beyond the Blue Horizon.* New York: HarperCollins, 1991.

Matthews, John, and Caitlin Matthews. *The Winter Solstice.* Wheaton, Ill.: Quest Books, 1998.

Smith, C. "Christmas and Its Cycle." In *New Catholic Encyclopedia.* Volume 3. New York: McGraw-Hill, 1967.

Wise Men of the East. *See Magi*

Wrapping Paper

How would you feel if, instead of finding a pretty arrangement of wrapped **gifts** under the tree on Christmas morning, you discovered a naked jumble of store-bought merchandise with the price tags still on? What is it that turns an ordinary purchase into a Christmas gift? Nineteenth-century Americans found the answer to that question in decorative wrapping paper. Once encased in the paper, the individual identity and cost of each item disappeared. All that remained visible was the wrapping, a symbolic statement of the item's status as gift. Today we use the trick of wrapping paper to turn ordinary store-bought items into gifts for all sorts of occasions.

History

Christmas gift giving was an uncommon practice throughout most of the nineteenth century (*see also* **America, Christmas in Nineteenth-Century**). Moreover, those who gave gifts seldom bothered to wrap them. Parents deposited trinkets in their children's **stockings** as is, and adults exchanged small homemade items without bothering to disguise them. In the late nineteenth century the idea of exchanging Christmas gifts grew more popular, and some people began to shop for them in stores.

Around 1880 people began to wrap their purchases in decorative paper or decorated boxes. At the same time retailers were searching for a way to encourage people to give store-bought rather than homemade items as Christmas gifts. Many consumers objected that manufactured goods were too impersonal and **commercial** to serve as appropriate Christmas gifts. In the last decade of the nineteenth century, retailers began to wrap their customers' holiday purchases in paper decorated with **Christmas symbols**. They discovered that the special wrapping paper boosted sales enormously. Apparently, removing the price tag and encasing the item in wrapping paper transformed manufactured goods into acceptable gifts by disguising their true identity until the last moment and emphasizing instead their status as a gift.

At the turn of the century, manufacturers also adopted the new sales gimmick. They began to ship all kinds of wares in decorative holiday packaging. If consumers wondered whether these ordinary manufactured items could serve as appropriate gifts, the holiday packaging removed all doubt. By the 1920s manufacturers had added one more detail to this already successful strategy. Instead of shipping goods in special packaging they slipped special, decorative sleeves around standard packaging. Retailers could remove the holiday sleeve right after Christmas, thereby turning their special "Christmas stock" back into ordinary stock.

Further Reading

Waits, William. *The Modern Christmas in America*. New York: New York University Press, 1993.

Wreath

Americans recognize the evergreen wreath as a **Christmas symbol**. Many people hang them on their front doors at Christmas time or display them in other parts of the house. No one seems to know the exact history of this custom. Some speculate that the front door wreath evolved out of the older, German **Advent wreath**. Others suppose it to be an old Irish custom.

The English word "wreath" comes from the old Anglo-Saxon verb *writhan*, meaning "to writhe" or "to twist." Indeed, Christmas wreaths are made by bending or twisting branches of **greenery** into a circular shape.

Wreaths have served as powerful symbols for millennia. In ancient Greece and Rome wreaths of greenery worn as crowns sat on the brows of those believed to have won divine favor. Thus, wreaths adorned the heads of sacrificial animals, winners of athletic and artistic competitions, participants in religious festivals, and kings. The type of greenery used to make the wreath also sent a message. Winners of athletic and literary contests donned wreaths of **laurel**. Wreaths of **ivy** circled the brows of those honoring the wine god, Dionysus or Bacchus. Those whose achievements brought about military victories or peace wore wreaths of olive.

The Bible also makes frequent mention of wreaths, usually associating them with joy, triumph, and honor. As Christianity developed its own symbolic code, it turned the laurel wreath into a sign of the attainment of salvation. In more general terms, the wreath represents the same thing as the circle, often interpreted as a symbol of eternity.

Further Reading

Becker, Udo, ed. "Wreath." In his *The Continuum Encyclopedia of Symbols.* New York: Continuum, 1994.

Palmer, Geoffrey, and Noel Lloyd. *A Year of Festivals.* London, England: Frederick Warne, 1972.

Thompson, Sue Ellen, ed. *Holiday Symbols.* Detroit, Mich.: Omnigraphics, 1998.

Webber, F. R. *Church Symbolism.* Second edition, revised. 1938. Reprint. Detroit, Mich.: Omnigraphics, 1992.

Weiser, Francis X. *The Christmas Book.* 1952. Reprint. Detroit, Mich.: Omnigraphics, 1990.

Wren Hunt
Hunting of the Wren

In rural communities of **England, Ireland, France,** and **Wales,** the day after Christmas once witnessed a ritualized attack on one of the region's tiniest and most harmless birds: the wren. Although this practice declined to near extinction during the twentieth century, the wren still figures as a minor **Christmas symbol**, appearing on **Christmas cards, ornaments,** and other seasonal decorations.

Customs

In some locales early accounts of the "wren hunt" or "the hunting of the wren" give Christmas or Christmas Eve as the date of the ceremony. Eventually, however, these local traditions gravitated to the day after Christmas, **St. Stephen's Day**, which was the more commonly accepted date for the hunt. On this day bands of men and boys would range the countryside scouring the brush in search of a wren. After spotting one of the dainty brown birds the group flushed it out of the bushes using sticks or stones to stun and, eventually, kill it. The hunting party might chase the bird for hours before they succeeded in this task. In some areas the hunters used bow and arrows or even pistols to bring down their diminutive prey. Afterwards, the band trooped back to town displaying their trophy. The man or boy who succeeded in finally killing the bird was lauded as the hero of the day.

The second phase of the wren hunt began when the team returned to town. The group devised a decorative display for the tiny carcass. In some areas of France the bird was nailed to a pole decorated with ribbons and **greenery**. On the Isle of Man it was suspended from the intersection of two hoops entwined with greenery, ribbons, foil, and other decorative items. The finished display was known as a "wren bush." The Welsh typically built a wren house, a small wooden box, in which to carry the bird.

After securing the dead bird amidst these trappings, the wren boys then paraded through the streets of town. In some areas they wore masks and unusual apparel, often dressing in women's or girls' clothing (*see also* **Mumming**). At each house they visited they displayed their catch, sang songs about the wren hunt, and asked for coins, food, or drink in return. The following verses from various wren hunt songs were often included in these performances:

> The wren, the wren, the King of all birds
> St. Stephen's Day was caught in the furze;
> Although he is little, his family is great,
> I pray you good landlady, give us a treat [Hutton, 1996, 98].

> We hunted the wren for Robbin the Bobbin
> We hunted the wren for Jack of the Can,
> We hunted the wren for Robbin the Bobbin
> We hunted the wren for everyman [Buday, 1992, 104].

On the Isle of Man the wren boys gave householders a wren feather, thought to bring good luck for the coming year, in exchange for a donation of coins. In many places, however, if householders refused a small **gift** to the wren boys, the boys sang insulting songs at the doorstep before moving on. After the day's ceremonies were over, the wren boys usually took time to bury the wren. In some locales these burials took the form of mock funerals.

In a few places the traditional wren hunt did not demand the death of the bird. In Wales' Pembrokeshire region, the wren boys captured and displayed a live bird. In general, the Scots did not participate in the wren hunt, but in Galloway a ceremony known as the "Deckan of the Wren" occurred on the morning of **New Year's Day**. The men caught, rather than killed, a wren, decorated it with ribbons, then let it go.

Origins

Folklorists disagree about the origins of this custom. Some experts argue that the wren hunt derives from the beliefs and practices of ancient societies. A number of these thinkers propose that the custom grew out of old Celtic beliefs about wrens. They speculate that as Christianity entrenched itself in Britain and Ireland, the killing of the wren came to represent the killing of pagan religious practices. Some evidence suggests that the Celts associated the bird with wisdom and prophecy. In one old Irish text, the wren was referred to as the "magus bird," a bird whose actions served as omens of the future. In another, it is claimed that the Celtic word for wren can be traced back to a contraction of the old Celtic words for "druid's bird."

Others who believe in the ancient roots of the custom link it to a different set of beliefs and practices. They find similarities between the wren hunt and the ancient European and Near Eastern custom of sacrificing a king or other royal figure to the gods. When ordinary people took on this sacrificial role they were treated as kings for a brief while before their execution. Interestingly enough, European folklore concerning the wren often depicts the tiny creature as a king. Moreover, the image of the wren as king emerges as a persistent theme in wren hunt lore. The folk verses cited above provide an example.

Eighteenth and Nineteenth Century

None of these speculations can be proven, however. The fact that the earliest accounts of the tradition in Britain and Ireland date back to the early eighteenth century has led at least one researcher to conclude that the custom must be of relatively modern origin and cannot have been in continual practice since ancient times. Moreover, this writer reminds us that efforts of the wren boys were directed toward the end result of collecting money and food. He notes that the hunting of the wren began to decline in the late nineteenth century, along with other begging traditions such as boxing (*see* **Boxing Day**), mumming, and Thomasing (*see* **St. Thomas's Day**).

Many of the historical documents describing the wren hunt express concern over the cruel fate dealt to the innocent and inoffensive bird. The wren hunt was condemned in France after the Revolution, briefly reinstated, and then banned again around 1830. Irish and English authorities condemned the custom in the middle of the nineteenth century. In spite of this opposition, the wren hunt continued in some places. In Wales the custom lingered until around the turn of the century.

Twentieth Century

Throughout Ireland the practice persisted until the mid-twentieth century. It continued in southern Ireland, and in recent times has even enjoyed a bit of a revival. Some people continue to wear the traditional straw suits for the event, though a dummy wren is usually substituted for a dead bird. The Irish have made other changes to the ancient custom as well. Nowadays both boys and girls, and even adults, may join in the wren hunt. Often the boys dress as women and the girls as men. They perform folk songs, folk dances, or even bits of mummers' plays at each house on their route. In West Kerry, a **pantomime** horse, or hobby horse, leads the wren hunt procession. The wren hunters usually donate the money given to them by householders in return for these performances to a civic cause. Contributions may also be used to fund a St. Stephen's Day "Wren Dance" to which the neighborhood is invited.

On the Isle of Man the wren boys killed their last wren in the early twentieth century. The ceremony continued in at least one location

839

on the island, however, using token wrens. A recent revival of interest in Manx folk traditions has led to a renewal of this revised version of the old seasonal custom.

Legends and Lore

A number of legends purporting to explain the yearly persecution of the wren depict the little bird as a betrayer of various Christian leaders. In one legend **Jesus** is fleeing his persecutors, who are tracking him by the trail of blood dripping from his wounds. A **robin** sees the drops of blood and flutters down to erase these tracks. A field of wheat miraculously springs up in the barren field over which Jesus has walked. When the pursuing soldiers encounter this field they ask the robin if a man has walked through the field recently. The robin answers, "Not since the wheat was planted." This answer temporarily fools the soldiers until a wren tells them that the wheat was planted only yesterday. The soldiers then hurry forward and capture Jesus.

In another legend, a wren foils St. Stephen's escape from his captors. In one variation of the tale, the wren's song wakens the guards just as Stephen is about to break free. In another, chirping wrens give away the saint's hiding place.

An Irish legend depicts the bird as a traitor to the cause of Irish political freedom who enjoys warning foreign invaders of Irish military maneuvers. In one version of the tale, the wren hops up and down on a drum in order to alert the Danes that the Irish are about to attack. In another, the wren tells Oliver Cromwell's forces of the impending Irish attack.

In spite of the role played by the wren in these legends, European folklore generally portrays the wren in a positive light. In addition to a widespread designation as the king of birds, much lore depicted the wren as a clever animal who uses her intelligence to counteract the disadvantages of her small size. In many areas people thought the bird brought good luck, and folk traditions warned against disturbing or harming the wren in any way. In the British Isles, the wren was especially beloved. In "Auguries of Innocence" (1803) the English poet William Blake (1757-1827) wrote:

> He who shall hurt the little wren
> Shall never be beloved by men.

Why then did the wren become the object of this yearly hunt? Why did the hunt take place on St. Stephen's Day? Perhaps the stoning of the wren, a beloved bird, symbolized the stoning of Stephen, a beloved saint. Or perhaps the yearly lifting of sanctions against harming the wren served to reinforce these sanctions during the rest of the year. Over a century of research by folklorists has produced many fascinating speculations, but no definitive answers to these questions.

Further Reading

Armstrong, Edward A. *The Folklore of Birds*. Second edition, revised and enlarged. New York: Dover Publications, 1970.

Buday, George. *The History of the Christmas Card*. 1954. Reprint. Detroit, Mich.: Omnigraphics, 1992.

Hadfield, Miles, and John Hadfield. *The Twelve Days of Christmas*. Boston, Mass.: Little, Brown and Company, 1961.

Hole, Christina. *British Folk Customs*. London, England: Hutchinson and Company, 1976.

Hutton, Ronald. *The Stations of the Sun*. Oxford, England: Oxford University Press, 1996.

Lawrence, Elizabeth Atwood. *Hunting the Wren: Transformation of Bird to Symbol*. Knoxville, Tenn.: University of Tennessee Press, 1997.

Moran, Rena. *Christmas in Ireland*. Chicago: World Book, 1985.

Muir, Frank. *Christmas Customs and Traditions*. New York: Taplinger, 1977.

Web Site

Ireland's Dingle Peninsula hosts a web site containing an article by Peter Woods entitled, "Hunting the Wren," at:
http://www.dingle-peninsula.ie/wren.html

Yule

Many researchers believe that in the early Middle Ages, people in northern **Europe** celebrated a midwinter festival called Yule, *Juul*, or *Jol*. Although the history of the word remains uncertain, some authorities believe it comes from an Anglo-Saxon word, *geol*, meaning "feast." Others argue that it derives from an old Germanic word, either *iol*, *iul*, or *guil*, meaning "wheel." Thus, the festival is thought by some to have celebrated the turning of the wheel of the year and the lengthening of days after the **winter solstice**. In medieval times, Yule became another term for "Christmas" or "**Christmas season**."

Origins

Some scholars believe that the ancient Celtic and Teutonic peoples of northern and central Europe observed a great autumn festival sometime in November. The customs connected with this festival highlighted the contrasting themes of death and abundance. With the coming of cold weather many plants withered and died, including the grass that fed domesticated animals. Consequently, the people adopted this season for the slaughter of the herds and the preparation of preserved meat for the winter. The slaughter also furnished the festival tables with a feast of fresh meat. Special autumn beers may also have been brewed for this festival, and used to toast the gods (*see also* **Christmas Ale**). At this time of the year people lit ceremonial fires and honored their dead ancestors. Some authorities claim that this feast venerated the Germanic god Odin, others that it venerated the Norse god Thor. This festival probably marked the end of the old year and the beginning of the new year.

At least one scholar has suggested November 11 or 12 as the date of this festival. In medieval times, November 11 became St. Martin's Day, or **Martinmas**. Medieval Europeans celebrated Martinmas by feasting, commemorating the dead, slaughtering animals and preserving their meat, and enjoying the first taste of the year's wines.

Did these November celebrations evolve out of the practices of ancient Mediterranean peoples or were they native to the North? One group of experts argues for Roman origins. They note that the Germanic peoples and the Romans came into close contact as they battled each other for land and rule during the last centuries of the Roman Empire. As a result of this exposure, the Teutonic peoples adopted some Roman customs, such as the celebration of the new year around the time of the winter solstice. The festivities that characterized Roman midwinter festivals, such as decorations of **greenery**, fortune-telling, processions of singers and masqueraders, and the exchange of **gifts**, also infiltrated northern celebrations (*see also* **Kalends; Saturnalia**). The northerners combined these customs with those of their autumn celebration and shifted the date of the new festival to midwinter, creating a new holiday called Yule.

Other authors disagree with this line of reasoning, however. They believe that the northerners must have waited anxiously for the winter solstice and the lengthening of days, since the midwinter days are even shorter and colder in northern Europe than they are in the Mediterranean. These writers contend that the pagan peoples of northern Europe always celebrated around the time of the winter solstice, rejoicing in the return of the sun and the lengthening of days. According to these authors, the customs associated with medieval Yule originated in the north.

Yule in Medieval Scandinavia

Since the pagan Scandinavian peoples left no documents of their own, it is impossible to confirm any theory of the holiday's origin. Around the ninth century Christian missionaries introduced the art of writing with pen and paper to the region. The years from around 900 to 1300 A.D. produced a few additional records describing the customs, stories, and beliefs of the pagan Scandinavians. From these records, researchers have reconstructed a speculative picture of medieval Scandinavian Yule celebrations.

Some say the festival began on the longest night of the year (the winter solstice), a day that ushered in the month known as "Yule Month." The Yule celebration lasted over a number of days and involved feasting, fires, and sacrifices. Bonfires blazed in honor of the sun's struggle against, and eventual triumph over, the darkness and cold of winter. People gathered around the fires listening to ancient legends, singing songs, eating, drinking, and offering sacrifices to the gods. They might save a piece of the great logs used for the fires, called **Yule logs**, in order to start the next year's bonfire. During the Yule festival those who had died during the year were remembered. Their **ghosts** were thought to rise from the grave and attend the festivities. The boar, a symbol of the god Frey, who represented sunlight, fertility, peace, and plenty, formed an important part of the Yule feast. The king offered the largest boar in the land in sacrifice. It was considered a holy object, and when it was brought into the king's hall, men swore binding oaths before it (*see also* **Boar's Head**).

As Christianity gained momentum in Scandinavia, some Christian rulers attempted to mesh pagan and Christian observances. The tenth-century Norwegian king, Haakon the Good, ordered that Yule celebrations should be held around the time of Christmas. Nevertheless, he refused to participate in the full range of sacrifices that the pagan kings usually offered at this time. Eventually, customs compatible with the Christian seasonal observance, such as feasting and merrymaking, were absorbed into the celebration of Christmas. A trace of the old pagan festival lingers in the modern Danish, Norwegian, and Swedish word for Christmas: *Jul.*

Yule in Medieval Britain

Although the word "yule" eventually passed into the English language, some say that the Britons did not observe the festival in early medieval times. The earliest written use of the word "yule" in Britain occurs in a manuscript written by the scholarly English monk St. Bede (c. 672-735). Bede noted that the English people of his day (the Angles) used the word *Giuli*, an ancestor of the word "yule," as a name for both December and January. He continued, "The months *Giuli* get their names from the turning round of the sun towards the increasing of the day, because one of them precedes and the other follows it." Bede's evidence suggests that the word "yule" may indeed have derived from an old word that referred in some way to the concept of turning.

But did the English celebrate a special festival at this time? Bede claims that they did. He wrote that the Angles "began their year from the eighth day before the Calends of January [Dec. 25], on which we now celebrate the birthday of our Lord. And they called that night *Modranicht*, i.e., night of the mothers, as I suppose, because of the ceremonies which they performed in it, keeping watch all night." Bede speculates that this day was originally called "Giuli" and that the months of December and January derived their names from the festival, but he is not certain. No evidence exists to confirm this speculation. It is not until the eleventh century that we find other British manuscripts that refer to **December 25** as "Yule." Before that time old English manuscripts referred to December 25 as "midwinter," "midwinter's mass," or "Nativity." From the eleventh century onwards, "Yule" gained gradual acceptance as another term for Christmas or the Christmas season.

Some argue that the Scandinavian Vikings brought the term and the festival with them when they conquered and settled in parts of **England** in the ninth through eleventh centuries. Others claim that the Anglo-Saxon people of early medieval Britain, along with the Scandinavians and northern Germans, did celebrate a midwinter festive season, regardless of what it may have been called. They point out that the strategy of early Christian missionaries was to convert pagan populations by allowing them to practice most of their old customs, but attaching new, Christian meanings to their observances. They believe that many British customs associated with Christmas in later centuries, such as the burning of Yule logs, **mumming**, the **wassailing of fruit trees**, the hunting of small animals, and decorating with greenery, originated in this early winter festival.

Further Reading

Gelling, Peter, and Hilda Ellis Davidson. *The Chariot of the Sun and Other Rites and Symbols of the Northern Bronze Age*. New York: Frederick A. Praeger, 1969.

Guerber, H. A. *Myths of Northern Lands*. 1895. Reprint. Detroit, Mich.: Singing Tree Press, 1970.

Henderson, Helene, and Sue Ellen Thompson, eds. *Holidays, Festivals, and Celebrations of the World Dictionary*. Second edition. Detroit, Mich.: Omnigraphics, 1997.

Hutton, Ronald. *The Stations of the Sun*. Oxford, England: Oxford University Press, 1996.

James, E. O. *Seasonal Feasts and Festivals*. 1961. Reprint. Detroit, Mich.: Omnigraphics, 1993.

Leach, Maria, ed. *Funk and Wagnalls Standard Dictionary of Folklore, Mythology, and Legend*. New York: Harper and Row, 1972.

Pimlott, J. A. R. *The Englishman's Christmas*. Atlantic Highlands, N.J.: Humanities Press, 1978.

Tille, Alexander. *Yule and Christmas: Their Place in the Germanic Year*. London, England: David Nutt, 1899.

Urlin, Ethel L. *Festivals, Holy Days, and Saints' Days*. 1915. Reprint. Detroit, Mich.: Omnigraphics, 1992.

Yule Goat

Joulupukki, Julbock, Julbukk, Klapparbock

In **Norway** and Sweden the goat, rather than the **reindeer**, symbolizes Christmas and brings Christmas **gifts**. In Sweden straw goats constitute a staple Christmas decoration (*see also* **Yule Straw**), while in Norway the animal lends its name to a Christmas Day caroling custom.

Origins and History

Some authors contend that the Yule goat originated in pre-Christian **Yule** celebrations. They believe that the ancient Scandinavians dedicated their Yule festival to the god Thor, whose companion animal was the goat. According to legend, this Norse god rode in a chariot pulled by two billy goats. Others view the Yule goat as a medieval invention. They argue that the goat typically accompanied the Devil in medieval folk plays performed around Christmas time.

In medieval times the Yule goat frolicked at the center of Scandinavian Christmas festivities. Using a goat skin and head as a costume, two men would masquerade as a goat, sometimes with a third sitting astride them. Such displays and the raucous revelry that accompanied them alarmed Church authorities. In the sixteenth century they began to issue prohibitions against these kinds of events. Nevertheless, groups of young people in Sweden maintained the goat as a sort of mascot when they caroled and danced for their neighbors around Christmas time. In the eighteenth century the goat adopted a new Christmas role in Sweden: gift bringer. In the late nineteenth century, however, this task was taken over by the **Jultomten**.

The Yule goat also visited **Denmark** and Finland in past times, but not as a gift giver. The Danish *Klapparbock* and the Finnish *Joulupukki* frightened children and warned them to behave. Although the Finnish gift bearer of today resembles **Father Christmas**, he still bears the name "Joulupukki," which translates as "Yule buck."

Today

In Sweden the Yule goat, or *Julbock*, lives on as a favorite Christmas decoration. In Norway a contemporary Christmas custom took its name, *Julbukk*, from the ancient Yule goat. Groups of costumed children and adults walk through their neighborhood entertaining householders with songs in exchange for treats. These groups may bring a goat with them, or someone may dress as a goat and impersonate the animal's typically unruly behavior. Sometimes, costumed goats discipline misbehaving children by butting them. If two costumed goats meet, they often entertain onlookers by engaging in a play fight.

Further Reading

Del Re, Gerard, and Patricia Del Re. *The Christmas Almanack*. Garden City, N.Y.: Doubleday, 1979.

Ross, Corinne. *Christmas in Scandinavia*. Chicago: World Book, 1977.

Web Sites

A site sponsored by the Finnish Embassy: http://www.finland.org/xmas.html

A site sponsored by the Royal Norwegian Ministry of Foreign Affairs: http://odin.dep.no/ (Click on "Language," "English," "History, culture, geography, recreation," then scroll down to "Christmas in Norway.")

Yule Log

*Bouche de Noël, Calignaou, Chalendal, Christmas Block,
Christmas Log, Tréfoir, Yule Clog*

In past eras many European people burned Yule logs in their homes
at Christmas time. Often these enormous logs burned throughout
the **Twelve Days of Christmas**. The many customs and beliefs associated with these logs suggest that at one time they were thought
to have magical powers. According to a variety of folk beliefs, a
burning Yule log or its charred remains could not only protect a
household from evil powers, but also confer health, fertility, luck,
and abundance.

History

Many writers trace the Yule log back to the ancient pagan holiday of
Yule. Although little can be determined for certain regarding the
early history of this celebration, most authors agree that it included
the burning of great bonfires. The earliest historical record mentioning a Yule log for the fireplace, however, comes from medieval **Germany**. German documents from this time contain a number of references to such logs. At least one writer traces the French Yule log
back to a medieval tax that required peasants to bring an enormous
log to the local manor house each year on Christmas Eve (*see also*
Europe, Christmas in Medieval).

In **England**, however, the custom can only be traced back as far as
the seventeenth century. The English had a number of names for the
logs, including Yule log, Yule clog, Christmas log, and Christmas block.
The English poet Robert Herrick (1591-1674) wrote a poem in which
he described the customs and beliefs surrounding the Yule log in
Devonshire, England. Herrick's householders lit their "Christmas
log" using a fragment of the previous year's log. Moreover, they serenaded the burning log with music in order to coax good luck and
abundance from it. Lines from another of Herrick's poems advised
that the singed remains of the Yule log could protect the household

against evil during the coming year. By the nineteenth century the Yule log could also be found at Christmas celebrations in Germany, France, northern Italy, Serbia, and most of northern Europe.

Selection and Preparation

The Yule log was bigger than the usual chunk of wood tossed on the evening fire. In some places tree trunks or parts of tree trunks were used. The Scots preferred the trunk of a birch tree, dried and stripped of leaves and bark. Hence, the Scottish saying, "He's a bare as a birk on Yule e'en," meaning "He's very poor." The French had many names for the Yule log. In Provence it was known as a *calignaou*, but in other areas it was called a *chalendal* or a *tréfoir*. In Provence people believed that the best Yule logs were taken from fruit trees. The Serbs chose their log from green oak, olive, or beech trees. In some parts of England people scoured the countryside for a Yule log on **Candlemas**. They set it aside to dry during the warm weather, thereby preparing an evenly burning log for the following Christmas.

Ceremonies and Superstitions

The selection of the log and its entrance into the house were often accompanied by rituals and invocations. The Serbs poured wine on the log, sprinkled it with grain or other foodstuffs, made the sign of the cross over it, and officially welcomed it into the home with a blessing. In Provence, France, people sprinkled wine over the log and blessed it in the name of the Trinity. Moreover, as the Provençal family trooped out to get their log, they sang songs requesting that fertility and abundance grace their family and their farm. Before burning the log they drew a human figure on it in chalk. In other areas, a human figure was carved onto the log. In Brittany, France, the oldest and youngest family members lit the log together, while offering a prayer to **Jesus**. Another popular custom in many areas advocated decking the log with ribbons and **greenery**.

Many superstitions attached themselves to the Yule log. In England many people believed that maidens should wash their hands before touching it. If they didn't, the log would not burn well. Other English folk beliefs warned that if a barefoot or squinting person came into the house while the log was lit, ill luck was sure to follow. According to some folk beliefs, the shadows cast by the light of the Yule log could be read as omens.

Lighting the Log

In many places tradition demanded that the new Yule log be lit with a fragment of last year's log. In some areas people set flame to the Yule log on Christmas Eve, in other places on Christmas morning. Custom commonly dictated that the log be kept burning continuously on Christmas Day. If the fire went out, bad luck would dog the household during the coming year. In some parts of Italy and England the log was kept burning throughout the Twelve Days of Christmas. English families whose logs went out during the Twelve Days often found it difficult to relight them. In some areas folk beliefs warned that it was unlucky to lend fire to a neighbor during these days, a belief that can be traced back to the Roman celebration of **Kalends**. Some towns kept communal fires burning for the purpose of lending flame to the unlucky folk whose fires went out. Greek folklore also advised householders to keep a fire in the hearth every day between Christmas and **Epiphany**. According to Greek folk beliefs, the fires warded off the evil **elves** known as the **kallikantzari** (*see also* **Greece, Christmas in**).

Gifts and Blessings

In some places Christmas **gifts** were distributed around the Yule log. In past times parents in some parts of Italy lit the Yule log, blindfolded their children, and instructed the tots to hit the burning Yule log with sticks, thereby releasing magical sparks. While the children were doing so, the parents brought out the children's gifts. When their blindfolds were removed the delighted children fell upon the gifts magically provided by the log. Eventually, the Italians adopted the Christmas **pyramid** as a way of displaying Christmas decorations, foods, and gifts. Nevertheless, they call the pyramid a *ceppo*, which means "log" in Italian. Only the name remains as a clue to the existence of an earlier custom. A similar custom was once practiced in Burgundy, France. Parents instructed their children to say their prayers in another room while they hid some treats underneath the log. When the children returned they hit the log with a stick to make it bring forth its hidden treasures.

Widespread beliefs attributed special powers to the remains of the Yule log. Many people spread the ashes on their fields to increase the fertility of the land. In addition, families often guarded a charred chunk of the log in their homes in the belief that it deflected evil forces from the household and contained curative powers. Folk beliefs found across Europe attributed many powers to the ashes, including the power to prevent chilblains, cure toothaches, rid farm animals of parasites and disease, make cows calve and poultry lay, keep mice out of the corn, and protect the house from lightning and fire.

Decline

Yule logs fell out of favor in the nineteenth century. Their disappearance coincided with the decline in the importance of fires as sources of household light and warmth. This, in turn, led to the disappearance of large fireplaces. Indeed, today's tiny ornamental fireplaces cannot accommodate a proper Yule log. In France a trace of the Yule log remains in a popular log-shaped **Christmas cake** called a *buche de Noël*, or "Christmas log."

Further Reading

Bragdon, Allen D. *Joy Through the World*. New York: Dodd, Mead, and Company, 1985.

Del Re, Gerard, and Patricia Del Re. *The Christmas Almanack*. Garden City, N.Y.: Doubleday, 1979.

Frazer, James. *The New Golden Bough*. Thomas Gaster, ed. New York: S. G. Phillips, 1959.

Hole, Christina. *Christmas and Its Customs*. New York: M. Barrows and Company, 1958.

Hutton, Ronald. *The Stations of the Sun*. Oxford, England: Oxford University Press, 1996.

James, E. O. *Seasonal Feasts and Festivals*. 1961. Reprint. Detroit, Mich.: Omnigraphics, 1993.

Miles, Clement A. *Christmas in Ritual and Tradition*. 1912. Reprint. Detroit, Mich.: Omnigraphics, 1990.

Muir, Frank. *Christmas Customs and Traditions*. New York: Taplinger, 1977.

Ross, Corinne. *Christmas in Italy*. Chicago: World Book-Childcraft International, 1979.

Yule Straw

In **Norway**, Sweden, **Estonia**, and Finland decorations made out of straw appear in homes and shops during the **Christmas season**. These **ornaments** may represent the remnants of the old custom of sleeping on a straw bed at Christmas time. In **Poland** and **Lithuania** people do different things with Yule straw. There they use it to tell fortunes on Christmas Eve.

Straw Beds

In Norway the straw bed can be traced back to the Middle Ages. Medieval Europeans often scattered fresh straw on the floor for special occasions. This may have served to increase cleanliness and decrease odors, especially in dwellings with earthen floors. In Norway all members of a household would sleep on the straw-covered floor instead of in their beds at Christmas time. Several explanations have been offered for this custom. Christian interpretations suggest that the practice represented the pious desire that rich and poor should share the same conditions at Christmas time. Moreover, the custom reminded one of the only kind of bed that the Holy Family could find on the night **Jesus** was born. Medieval records contain complaints about the loose behavior of some of those practicing this pious custom, however. Other authors suggest that the custom survived from pagan fertility rituals. Still others connect it with old folk beliefs concerning Christmas **ghosts**. Belief in the seasonal appearance of the dead may itself date back to pagan **Yule** celebrations.

Whatever its origin, the belief in the yearly reappearance of the dead lived on until the nineteenth century in Norway. According to this belief, the ghosts of one's ancestors and others associated with the homestead returned during the Christmas season. Folk traditions warned of the actions unhappy ghosts might take and advised families on how best to placate the spirits. One tradition suggested that the family vacate their beds in order that the ghosts might rest comfortably.

Straw Magic

The straw spread on the floor for Christmas acquired certain magical properties from its role in the observance of the holiday. The dreams one had while sleeping on the Christmas straw were often held to be prophetic. The grains falling from the straw to the floor gave clues about the quality of the coming harvest and even about the fate of individual family members in the coming year. Out of respect for its mysterious powers, people did not simply discard the straw at the end of the Christmas season. Until as late as the nineteenth century people spread the Yule straw in the fields hoping to improve the coming harvest. They also fed it to sick cattle as medicine and twisted it into ornamental crosses.

Straw Decorations

Although the beliefs that supported the old practices have died out, the custom of decorating with straw at Christmas time remains throughout Estonia and Scandinavia. Popular shapes include mobiles, goats, stars, and **angels**. In past days the mobiles were known as "crowns." They consisted of several straw rings hung with a multitude of diamond-shaped straw ornaments. In some areas of Norway these mobiles were fashioned from the Yule straw. The straw goat originated in Sweden, where it survives as a reminder of the **Yule goat** who, in the past, brought children their Christmas **gifts**.

Straw Fortunes

Lithuanian families often strew their Christmas Eve table with straw, which they then cover with a white tablecloth before setting out plates and utensils. The hay reminds everyone that **Mary** gave birth to Jesus in a stable. After dinner Lithuanians enjoy telling fortunes. One old folk charm requires everyone seated at the table to reach under the tablecloth and pull out a straw. For an unmarried person, a short, fat straw predicts a short, fat boyfriend, girlfriend, or spouse. A long, thin straw assures one of attracting a tall, thin partner. Married people interpret the same signs in a different fashion. The long, thin straw means a year of hardship while a fat straw indicates abundance.

In Poland, too, people tuck Yule straw under the tablecloth on Christmas Eve. Girls can predict their marital fortunes by reaching under the cloth and drawing out a straw. Those who pick a green straw are sure to marry soon, while those who select a withered straw will continue to wait. Yellow straws mean a life without marriage, and short straws indicate an early death.

Further Reading

Foley, Daniel J. *Christmas the World Over*. Philadelphia, Pa.: Chilton Books, 1963.

Henriksen, Vera. *Christmas in Norway Past and Present*. Oslo, Norway: Johan Grundt Tanum Forlag, 1970.

Ross, Corinne. *Christmas in Scandinavia*. Chicago: World Book, 1977.

Zagmuk

Akitu, Babylonian New Year, Zagmug

Some writers trace elements of traditional European Christmas celebrations back to ancient Mesopotamian new year festivities. Indeed,
an examination of the Zagmuk, or Akitu, festivals of ancient Mesopotamia reveals some striking resemblances to European celebrations of **Twelfth Night** and the **Twelve Days of Christmas**.

Myths

Two thousand years before the birth of Christ, the Mesopotamians, a
people of the ancient Middle East, celebrated their new year festival
around the time of the spring equinox. The land once occupied by
the ancient Mesopotamians now lies within the modern nation of
Iraq. The Sumerians, who inhabited southern Mesopotamia, called
their version of the festival "Zagmuk," while the Babylonians called
it "Akitu." Experts believe that the festival lasted eleven or twelve

days. It honored the yearly renewal of the world by the sun god Marduk, who created the world out of chaos. The people viewed the last days of the year as a time of decay. The forces of life and order were weak, and the forces of death and chaos were strong. To prevent the god of chaos and destruction from gaining control, the sun god Marduk must again defeat him in battle.

Ceremonies

The ceremonies enacted during Zagmuk reflected these beliefs. Priests recited the lengthy epic describing the original victory of Marduk over the forces of disorder. The king also played a special role in new year observances. In the temple of Marduk, the high priest ceremonially stripped the king of power and rank, reinstating him only after the king had knelt and sworn to the god that he had always acted in accordance with the god's will. Some scholars propose that Mesopotamian beliefs dictated that the king die at the end of the year in order to descend into the underworld and aid Marduk in his yearly battle. Historical evidence suggests that a mock king was selected from among the ranks of criminals. During the time of the festival, he was given all the luxuries and privileges that the real king enjoyed. At the end of the festival, however, some scholars believe that the mock king was executed and sent to the underworld in place of the real king. Other scholars doubt that this occurred. According to another custom, the king and a woman from the temple reenacted the marriage of the god Marduk and his consort.

Popular Customs

Popular customs and festivities evoked not only the epic struggle between the forces of order and disorder, but also the joyful celebration of the birth of the new year. In anticipation of Marduk's victory, the people staged mock battles between the gods, watched the burning of ceremonial bonfires, gave **gifts**, paid visits, feasted, and paraded in masquerade (*see also* **Kalends; Saturnalia**).

Similarities

Some of the customs and folk beliefs associated with Zagmuk resemble those of medieval European celebrations of the Twelve Days of Christmas and Twelfth Night (*see also* **Europe, Christmas in Medieval**). Similar acts of revelry and topsy-turvy events characterized the observance of both festivals. During the Twelve Days of Christmas, mock kings and bishops assumed temporary authority, costumed figures masqueraded through the streets, and people feasted together and lit special fires (*see also* **Boy Bishop; Feast of Fools; Feast of the Ass; Lord of Misrule; Mumming; Yule; Yule Log**). Moreover, both Zagmuk and the Twelve Days of Christmas were celebrated at the end of the calendar year. Folk beliefs associated with both festivals warned that the waning of the year unleashed potentially destructive supernatural forces (*see also* **Berchta; Christmas Lads; Ghosts; Kallikantzari; Knecht Ruprecht; Wild Hunt; Yule**). Finally, the length of these festivals—eleven or twelve days—presents another interesting similarity. Because both festivals were observed at the end of the year, some experts suggest that these festival days represented a kind of intercalary period, the additional 11.25 days needed to reconcile the lunar year of 354 days to the solar year of 365.25 days.

Further Reading

Count, Earl W. *4000 Years of Christmas*. New York: Henry Schuman, 1948.

Gaster, Theodor. *New Year: Its History, Customs, and Superstitions*. New York: Abelard-Schuman, 1955.

Smith, Jonathan Z. "Dying and Rising Gods." In Mircea Eliade, ed. *The Encyclopedia of Religion*. Volume 4. New York: Macmillan, 1987.

Bibliography

This bibliography lists all books and articles consulted for this volume.

Bibliography

Abbas, Jailan. *Festivals of Egypt*. Cairo, Egypt: Hoopoe Books, 1995.

Achtemeier, Paul J., ed. *The HarperCollins Bible Dictionary*. Revised edition. San Francisco, Calif.: HarperSanFrancisco, 1996.

Alison, James. "Struttin' in Style." *The World and I* 13 (January 1998): 178 (11).

Ammon, Richard. *An Amish Christmas*. New York: Atheneum Books, 1996.

Ann, Martha, and Dorothy Myer Imel. *Goddesses in World Mythology*. Santa Barbara, Calif.: ABC-CLIO, 1993.

Appelbaum, Diana Karter. *Thanksgiving: An American Holiday, An American History*. New York: Facts on File, 1984.

Armstrong, Edward A. *The Folklore of Birds*. Second edition, revised and enlarged. New York: Dover Publications, 1970.

Arrowsmith, Nancy, and George Moorse. *A Field Guide to the Little People*. New York: Pocket Books, 1977.

Associated Press. "Egypt Makes Christmas a National Holiday." *New York Times* (January 6, 2003).

Associated Press. "Russians Mark Orthodox Christmas." *New York Times* (January 6, 2003).

Augustine, Peg, comp. *Come to Christmas*. Nashville, Tenn.: Abingdon Press, 1993.

Auld, William Muir. *Christmas Tidings*. 1933. Reprint. Detroit, Mich.: Omnigraphics, 1990.

———. *Christmas Traditions*. 1931. Reprint. Detroit, Mich.: Omnigraphics, 1992.

Aveni, Anthony. *Empires of Time: Calendars, Clocks, and Cultures*. New York: Basic Books, 1989.

———. "The Star of Bethlehem." *Archeology* 51, 6 (November-December 1998): 34-38.

Baker, Margaret. *Christmas Customs and Folklore*. Aylesbury, Bucks, England: Shire Publications, 1968.

Baldovin, John F. "Christmas." In Mircea Eliade, ed. *The Encyclopedia of Religion*. Volume 3. New York: Macmillan, 1987.

Ballam, Harry, and Phyllis Digby Morton, eds. *The Christmas Book*. 1947. Reprint. Detroit, Mich.: Omnigraphics, 1990.

Baly, Denis. "Bethlehem." In Paul J. Achtemeier, ed. *The HarperCollins Bible Dictionary*. Revised edition. San Francisco, Calif.: HarperSanFrancisco, 1996.

Banham, Martin. *The Cambridge Guide to World Theatre*. Cambridge, England: Cambridge University Press, 1988.

Barber, David W. *Getting a Handel on Messiah*. Toronto, Ontario, Canada: Sound and Vision, 1994.

Barnett, James. *The American Christmas*. New York: Macmillan, 1954.

Barnett, Mary. *Gods and Myths of Ancient Greece*. New York: Smithmark, 1996.

Barrick, Mac E. *German-American Folklore*. Little Rock, Ark.: August House, 1987.

Basinger, Jeanine. *The It's a Wonderful Life Book*. New York: Alfred A. Knopf, 1986.

Bassett, Paul M. "Epiphany." In Everett Ferguson, ed. *Encyclopedia of Early Christianity*. Volume 1. New York: Garland, 1997.

Baxter, Beverley. "Two Thousand Years of Pantomime." In Harry Ballam and Phyllis Dibgy Morton, eds. *The Christmas Book*. 1947. Reprint. Detroit, Mich.: Omnigraphics, 1990.

Becker, Udo, ed. *The Continuum Encyclopedia of Symbols*. New York: Continuum, 1994.

Begley, Sharon. "The Christmas Star—Or Was it Planets?" *Newsweek* 118, 27 (December 30, 1991): 54.

"Behold, Today Is Christmas." Africa News Service (January 25, 2001). Available for a fee through elibrary.com.

Belk, Russell. "Materialism and the Making of the Modern American Christmas." In Daniel Miller, ed. *Unwrapping Christmas*. Oxford, England: Clarendon Press, 1993.

Bellenir, Karen, ed. *Religious Holidays and Calendars*. Second edition. Detroit, Mich.: Omnigraphics, 1998.

Bellman, Sheryll. *Through the Shopping Glass*. New York: Rizzoli, 2000.

Bibliography

Bergreen, Laurence. *As Thousands Cheer: The Life of Irving Berlin*. New York: Viking, 1990.

"Bethlehem." In Allen C. Myers, ed. *The Eerdmans Bible Dictionary*. Grand Rapids, Mich.: William B. Eerdmans Publishing Company, 1987.

Bethlehem's Early History. Bethlehem, Pa.: Historic Bethlehem Partnership Educational Services, 1999.

Bett, Henry. *Nursery Rhymes and Tales*. Second edition. 1924. Reprint. Detroit, Mich.: Singing Tree Press, 1968.

Bevilacqua, Michelle, and Brandon Toropov, eds. *The Everything Christmas Book: Songs, Stories, Food, Traditions, Revelry, and More*. Holbrook, Mass.: Adams Media Corporation, 1996.

Bigelow, A. L. "Bells." In *New Catholic Encyclopedia*. Volume 2. New York: McGraw-Hill, 1967.

Bigham, Shauna, and Robert E. May. "The Time O' All Times? Masters, Slaves, and Christmas in the Old South." *Journal of the Early Republic* 18, 2 (summer 1998): 263-88.

Black, Maggie. "A Common's Room Christmas Dinner 1773." *History Today* 30 (December 1980): 63.

———. "The Englishman's Plum Pudding." *History Today* 31 (December 1981): 60-61.

Blauer, Ettagale, and Jason Lauré. *Enchantment of the World: Nigeria*. New York: Children's Press, 2001.

Bolz, Diane M. "Art Imitates Life in the Small World of Baroque Creches." *Smithsonian* 22, 9 (December 1991): 100.

Bowler, Gerry. *The World Encyclopedia of Christmas*. Toronto, Ontario, Canada: McClelland and Stewart, 2000.

Bragdon, Allen D. *Joy Through the World*. New York: Dodd, Mead, and Company, 1985.

Branley, Franklyn M. *The Christmas Sky*. Revised and newly illustrated edition. New York: Crowell, 1990.

Brazyte Bindokiene, Danute. *Lithuanian Customs and Traditions*. Third edition. Chicago: Lithuanian World Community, 1998.

Brewster, H. Pomeroy. *Saints and Festivals of the Christian Church*. 1904. Reprint. Detroit, Mich.: Omnigraphics, 1990.

Briggs, Katharine. *An Encyclopedia of Fairies*. New York: Pantheon Books, 1976.

Brinson, Peter, and Clement Crisp. *The International Book of Ballet*. New York: Stein and Day, 1971.

Brockett, Oscar G. *The History of the Theatre*. Boston: Allyn and Bacon, 1968.

Brockman, Norbert C. *Encyclopedia of Sacred Places*. New York: Oxford University Press, 1998.

Brody, Alan. *The English Mummers and Their Plays*. Philadelphia, Pa.: University of Pennsylvania Press, 1970.

Brown, David, Gerald Abraham, David Lloyd-Jones, and Edward Garden. "Tchaikovsky." In *The New Grove Russian Masters*. Volume 1. New York: W. W. Norton, 1986.

Brown, Raymond E. *An Adult Christ at Christmas*. Collegeville, Minn.: Liturgical Press, 1988.

————. *The Birth of the Messiah*. New updated edition. New York: Doubleday, 1993.

Bruno, Barbara. *Victorian Christmas Crafts*. New York: Van Nostrand Reinhold, 1984.

Brunvand, Jan Harold. *The Mexican Pet: More "New" Urban Legends and Some Old Favorites*. New York: W. W. Norton and Company, 1986.

————. "Urban Legend." In his *American Folklore: An Encyclopedia*. New York: Garland, 1996.

Buday, George. *The History of the Christmas Card*. 1954. Reprint. Detroit, Mich.: Omnigraphics, 1992.

Burns, Charlene P. E. *Divine Becoming*. Minneapolis, Minn.: Fortress Press, 2002.

Butterfield, Lee. "Christmas in the Community of the First Moravian Church, Bethlehem, Pennsylvania, U.S.A." In Maria Hubert, comp. *Christmas Around the World*. Stroud, Gloucestershire, England: Sutton, 1998.

Buttrick, George Arthur, ed. *The Interpreter's Bible: A Commentary in Twelve Volumes*. New York: Abingdon Press, 1951.

Buxton, David, and Sue Lyon, eds. *Baroque Festival*. Volume 4 of *The Great Composers, Their Lives and Times*. New York: Marshall Cavendish, 1987.

————. *Pyotr Tchaikovsky*. Volume 3 of *The Great Composers, Their Lives and Times*. New York: Marshall Cavendish, 1987.

Cagner, Ewert, comp. *Swedish Christmas*. New York: Henry Holt and Company, 1959.

Cahill, Marie. *It's a Wonderful Life: A Hollywood Classic*. New York: Smithmark, 1993.

Campanelli, Pauline. *Wheel of the Year: Living the Magical Life*. St. Paul, Minn.: Llewellyn Publications, 1989.

Carucci, Laurence Marshall. *Nuclear Nativity: Rituals of Renewal and Empowerment in the Marshall Islands*. Dekalb, Ill.: Northern Illinois University Press, 1997.

Cathcart, Rex. "Festive Capers? Barring-Out the Schoolmaster." *History To-day* 38, 12 (December 1988): 49-53.

Cathey, H. Marc, and Jacqueline Heriteau. "A Gift from Mexico." *The World and I* 8, 12 (December 1993).

Ceroke, C. P. "Mary, The Blessed Virgin, I (in the Bible)." In *New Catholic En-cyclopedia.* Volume 9. New York: McGraw-Hill, 1967.

Chambers, E. K. *The Medieval Stage.* 2 volumes. Oxford, England: Clarendon Press, 1903.

Chambers, Robert. *The Book of Days.* 2 volumes. 1862-64. Reprint. Detroit, Mich.: Omnigraphics, 1990.

Christmas in Brazil. Chicago: World Book, 1991.

Christmas in Canada. Chicago: World Book, 1994.

Christmas in Colonial and Early America. Chicago: World Book, 1996.

Christmas in Denmark. Chicago: World Book, 1986.

Christmas in Germany. Second edition. Lincolnwood, Ill.: Passport Books, 1995.

Christmas in Mexico. Chicago: World Book, 1976.

Christmas in Russia. Chicago: World Book, 1992.

Christmas in the American Southwest. Chicago: World Book, 1996.

Christmas in the Holy Land. Chicago: World Book, 1987.

Christmas in the Philippines. Chicago: World Book, 1990.

Clement, Clara Erskine. *A Handbook of Christian Symbols.* 1886. Reprint. De-troit, Mich.: Gale Research, 1971.

Clynes, Tom. *Wild Planet!* Detroit, Mich.: Visible Ink Press, 1995.

Coats, George W., and Paul J. Achtemeier. "Joseph." In Paul J. Achtemeier, ed. *The HarperCollins Bible Dictionary.* Revised edition. San Francisco, Calif.: HarperSanFrancisco, 1996.

Coffin, Tristram Potter. *The Book of Christmas Folklore.* New York: Seabury Press, 1973.

Cohen, Hennig, and Tristram Potter Coffin, eds. *The Folklore of American Holidays.* Detroit, Mich.: Gale Research, 1987.

Comfort, David. *Just Say Noel!* New York: Fireside Books, 1995.

Cooper, J. C. *The Dictionary of Festivals.* 1990. Reprint. London, England: Thorsons, 1995.

Cooper, Quentin, and Paul Sullivan. *Maypoles, Martyrs and Mayhem.* Lon-don, England: Bloomsbury, 1994.

Cosman, Madeleine Pelner. *Medieval Holidays and Feasts.* New York: Charles Scribner's Sons, 1981.

Coughenour, Robert A. "Gold." In Paul J. Achtemeier, ed. *HarperCollins Bible Dictionary*. Revised edition. San Francisco, Calif.: HarperSanFrancisco, 1996.

Count, Earl W. *4000 Years of Christmas*. New York: Henry Schuman, 1948.

Cowie, L. W., and John Selwyn Gummer. *The Christian Calendar*. Springfield, Mass.: G. and C. Merriam Company, 1974.

Cramer, Kathryn, and David G. Hartwell. *Christmas Ghosts*. New York: Arbor House, 1987.

Crawford, Deborah. "St. Joseph in Britain: Reconsidering the Legends, Part I." *Folklore* 104 (1993): 86-98.

Crippen, Thomas G. *Christmas and Christmas Lore*. 1923. Reprint. Detroit, Mich.: Omnigraphics, 1990.

Cross, F. L., and E. A. Livingstone, eds. *Oxford Dictionary of the Christian Church*. Second edition. Oxford, England: Oxford University Press, 1983.

Crump, William D. *The Christmas Encyclopedia*. Jefferson, N.C.: McFarland, 2001.

Cuneen, Sally. *In Search of Mary*. New York: Ballantine Books, 1996.

Danielson, Sarah Parker. *Miracle on 34th Street: A Hollywood Classic*. New York: Smithmark, 1993.

Davidson, Gustav. *A Dictionary of Angels*. New York: Free Press, 1967.

Davidson, H. R. Ellis. *Gods and Myths of Northern Europe*. Harmondsworth, Middlesex, England: Penguin Books, 1964.

Davies, Susan G. *Parades and Power*. Berkeley, Calif.: University of California Press, 1986.

Davies, Valentine. *Miracle on 34th Street*. New York: Harcourt, Brace and Company, 1947.

Davis, Paul. *Charles Dickens, A to Z*. New York: Facts on File, 1998.

Dean, Winton, and Anthony Hicks. *The New Grove Handel*. New York: W. W. Norton, 1983.

———. "Handel, George Frideric." In Stanley Steele, ed. *The New Grove Dictionary of Music and Musicians*. Volume 8. London, England: Macmillan, 1980.

Dearmer, Percy, R. Vaughan Williams, and Martin Shaw. *The Oxford Book of Carols*. London, England: Oxford University Press, 1965.

Dégh, Linda. "Legend." In Thomas A. Green, ed. *Folklore: An Encyclopedia of Beliefs, Customs, Tales, Music, and Art*. Santa Barbara, Calif.: ABC-CLIO, 1997.

De Hoghton, Charles. "Incense." In Richard Cavendish, ed. *Man, Myth and Magic: An Illustrated Encyclopedia of the Supernatural*. Volume 8. New York: Marshall Cavendish, 1970.

Delaney, John J. *Dictionary of Saints*. Garden City, N.Y.: Doubleday, 1980.

Del Re, Gerard, and Patricia Del Re. *The Christmas Almanack*. Garden City, N.Y.: Doubleday, 1979.

Dickens, Charles. *The Christmas Books*. Oxford, England: Oxford University Press, 1960.

———. *The Complete Ghost Stories of Charles Dickens*. Peter Haining, ed. New York: Franklin Watts, 1983.

Dipeiro, Diane. "Together at Christmas (Christmas Traditions of African-American Slaves)." *Colonial Homes* 20 (December 1, 1994): 28(2).

Douglas, J. D. *The New International Dictionary of the Christian Church*. Revised edition. Grand Rapids, Mich.: Zondervan Publishing House, 1978.

Drury, Nevill. *Dictionary of Mysticism and Esoteric Traditions*. Revised edition. Dorset, England: Prism Press, 1992.

Drury, Susan. "Customs and Beliefs Associated with Christmas Evergreens." *Folklore* 98, 2 (1987): 194-99.

Duncan, Edmondstoune. *The Story of the Carol*. 1911. Reprint. Detroit, Mich.: Omnigraphics, 1992.

Ebon, Martin. *Saint Nicholas, Life and Legend*. New York: Harper and Row, 1975.

Edidin, Ben M. *Jewish Holidays and Festivals*. 1940. Reprint. Detroit, Mich.: Omnigraphics, 1993.

Edwards, Gillian. *Hogmanay and Tiffany, The Names of Feasts and Fasts*. London, England: Geoffrey Bles, 1970.

Efird, James M. "Angels." In Paul J. Achtemeier, ed. *The HarperCollins Bible Dictionary*. Revised edition. San Francisco, Calif.: HarperSanFrancisco, 1996.

Ekstrand, Florence. *Lucia Child of Light*. Seattle, Wash.: Welcome Press, 1989.

Eliade, Mircea, ed. *The Encyclopedia of Religion*. Volumes 3, 9, 13, and 15. New York: Macmillan, 1987.

Ellis, Bill. "Legend, Urban." In Thomas A. Green, ed. *Folklore: An Encyclopedia of Beliefs, Customs, Tales, Music, and Art*. Volume 2. Santa Barbara, Calif.: ABC-CLIO, 1997.

Ellis, Royton, and John R. Jones. *Festivals of the World: Madagascar*. Milwaukee, Wis.: Gareth Stevens, 1999.

Emurian, Ernest K. *Stories of Christmas Carols*. Revised edition. Boston, Mass.: W. A. Wilde Company, 1967.

Evergreen Alliance. *The First Green Christmas*. San Francisco, Calif.: Halo Books, 1990.

Fallon, T. L. "Gabriel, Archangel." In *New Catholic Encyclopedia*. Volume 6. New York: McGraw-Hill, 1967.

Fears, J. Rufus. "Sol Invictus." In Mircea Eliade, ed. *The Encyclopedia of Religion.* Volume 13. New York: Macmillan, 1987.

Ferguson, Everett, ed. *Encyclopedia of Early Christianity.* Volume 1. New York: Garland, 1997.

Fertig, Terry. *Christmas in Denmark.* Chicago: World Book, 1986.

Fiesta! Brazil. Danbury, Conn.: Grolier Educational, 1997.

Filas, F. L. "Joseph, St." In *New Catholic Encyclopedia.* Volume 7. New York: McGraw-Hill, 1967.

———. "Joseph St., Devotion to." In *New Catholic Encyclopedia.* Volume 7. New York: McGraw-Hill, 1967.

Flores, Richard R. *Los Pastores, History and Performance in the Mexican Shepherd's Play of South Texas.* Washington, D.C.: Smithsonian Institution Press, 1995.

Fluehr-Lobban, Carolyn, and Richard Lobban. "The Sudan since 1989: National Islamic Front Rule." *Arab Studies Quarterly* (April 1, 2001): 1.

Foley, Daniel J. *Christmas in the Good Old Days.* 1961. Reprint. Detroit, Mich.: Omnigraphics, 1994.

———. *Christmas the World Over.* Philadelphia, Pa.: Chilton Books, 1963.

———. *The Christmas Tree.* Philadelphia, Pa.: Chilton Company, 1960.

———. *Little Saints of Christmas.* Boston, Mass.: Dresser, Chapman and Grimes, 1959.

Foley, R. L. "Circumcision of Our Lord." In *New Catholic Encyclopedia.* New York: McGraw-Hill, 1967.

Franklin, John Hope. *The Emancipation Proclamation.* Garden City, N.Y.: Doubleday, 1963.

Frazer, James. *The New Golden Bough: A New Abridgement of the Classic Work.* Theodor Gaster, ed. New York: S. G. Phillips, 1959.

Freedman, David Noel, ed. *Eerdmans Dictionary of the Bible.* Grand Rapids, Mich.: William B. Eerdmans Publishing Company, 2000.

Furia, Philip. *Irving Berlin, A Life in Song.* New York: Schirmer Books, 1998.

Galbraith, Jane. "Now the Miracle Is off 34th Street, Macy's Says 'No Thanks' to a Remake of the Classic, so the Film Moves to Chicago." *Newsday* (April 18, 1994): B13.

Garcia-Treto, Francisco O. "Herod." In Paul J. Achtemeier, ed. *The HarperCollins Bible Dictionary.* Revised edition. San Francisco, Calif.: HarperSanFrancisco, 1996.

Gaster, Theodor. *New Year, Its History, Customs, and Superstitions.* New York: Abelard-Schuman, 1955.

Bibliography

Gelling, Peter, and Hilda Ellis Davidson. *The Chariot of the Sun and Other Rites and Symbols of the Northern Bronze Age*. New York: Frederick A. Praeger, 1969.

Genovese, Eugene D. *Roll, Jordan, Roll*. New York: Pantheon, 1974.

Gigot, Francis E. "Joseph of Arimathea." In Charles B. Hervermann, ed. *Catholic Encyclopedia*. Nashville, Tenn.: T. Nelson, 1913. Available online at http://www.newadvent.org/cathen/08520a.htm

Glancy, H. Mark. "Dreaming of Christmas: Hollywood and the Second World War." In Mark Connelly, ed. *Christmas and the Movies*. London, England: I. B. Tauris and Co., Ltd., 2000.

The Glory and Pageantry of Christmas. Maplewood, N.J.: Time-Life Books, 1963.

Gnoli, Gherardo. "Magi." In Mircea Eliade, ed. *The Encyclopedia of Religion*. Volume 9. New York: Macmillan, 1987.

———. "Mithraism." In Mircea Eliade, ed. *The Encyclopedia of Religion*. Volume 9. New York: Macmillan, 1987.

———. "Saoshyant." In Mircea Eliade, ed. *The Encyclopedia of Religion*. Volume 13. New York: Macmillan, 1987.

———. "Zoroastrianism." In Mircea Eliade, ed. *The Encyclopedia of Religion*. Volume 15. New York: Macmillan, 1987.

Godwin, Malcom. *Angels: An Endangered Species*. New York: Simon and Schuster, 1990.

Goldwasser, Maria Julia. "Carnival." In Mircea Eliade, ed. *The Encyclopedia of Religion*. Volume 3. New York: Macmillan, 1987.

Gonza, Sam. "Reclaiming the True Meaning of Christmas." All Africa News Service, Nairobi, Kenya (December 21, 1998).

Graham-Barber, Lynda. *Ho Ho Ho!* New York: Bradbury Press, 1993.

Green, Marian. *A Calendar of Festivals*. Rockport, Mass.: Element Books, 1991.

Green, Thomas A., ed. *Folklore: An Encyclopedia of Beliefs, Customs, Tales, Music, and Art*. 2 volumes. Santa Barbara, Calif.: ABC-CLIO, 1997.

Gregg, D. Larry. "Incarnation." In David Noel Freedman, ed. *Eerdmans Bible Dictionary*. Grand Rapids, Mich.: William B. Eerdmans Publishing Company, 2000.

Griffin, Robert H., and Ann H. Shurgin. *Junior Worldmark Encyclopedia of World Holidays*. Volume 4. Detroit, Mich.: UXL, 2000.

Griffin, Robert H., and Ann H. Shurgin, eds. *The Folklore of World Holidays*. Second edition. Detroit, Mich.: Gale, 1999.

Grigson, Geoffrey. "The Three Kings of Cologne." *History Today* 41, 12 (December 1991): 28-34.

Groom, Nigel. *Frankincense and Myrrh: A Study of the Arabian Incense Trade.* London: Longman, 1981.

Guerber, H. A. *Myths of Northern Lands.* 1895. Reprint. Detroit, Mich.: Singing Tree Press, 1970.

Gulevich, Tanya. *Encyclopedia of Easter, Carnival, and Lent.* Detroit, Mich.: Omnigraphics, 2002.

Gwynne, Walker. *The Christian Year: Its Purpose and History.* 1917. Reprint. Detroit, Mich.: Omnigraphics, 1990.

Hackwood, Frederick W. *Christ Lore.* 1902. Reprint. Detroit, Mich.: Gale Research, 1969.

Hadfield, Miles, and John Hadfield. *The Twelve Days of Christmas.* Boston, Mass.: Little, Brown and Company, 1961.

Hallinan, Tim. *A Christmas Carol Christmas Book.* New York: International Business Machines Corporation, 1984.

Halpert, Herbert, and G. M. Story, eds. *Christmas Mumming in Newfoundland.* Toronto, Ontario, Canada: University of Toronto Press, 1969.

Hamilton, Edith. *Mythology.* Boston, Mass.: Little Brown and Company, 1942.

Harper, Howard. *Days and Customs of All Faiths.* 1957. Reprint. Detroit, Mich.: Omnigraphics, 1990.

Harrowven, Jean. *Origin of Festivals and Feasts.* London, England: Kaye and Ward, 1980.

Hartman, Tom. *Guiness Book of Christmas.* London, England: Guiness Books, 1984.

Hartnoll, Phyllis. *The Oxford Companion to the Theatre.* Fourth edition. Oxford, England: Oxford University Press, 1983.

Hawkins, Jimmy. *It's a Wonderful Life: The Fiftieth Anniversary Scrapbook.* Philadelphia, Pa.: Courage Books, 1996.

Heale, Jay. *Cultures of the World: Madagascar.* Tarrytown, N.Y.: Marshall Cavendish, 1998.

Heinberg, Richard. *Celebrate the Solstice.* Wheaton, Ill.: Quest Books, 1993.

Helm, Alex. *The English Mummers' Play.* Totowa, N.J.: Rowman and Littlefield, 1981.

———. "In Comes I, St. George." *Folklore* 75 (spring 1964): 118-36.

Henderson, Helene, and Sue Ellen Thompson, eds. *Holidays, Festivals, and Celebrations of the World Dictionary.* Second edition. Detroit, Mich.: Omnigraphics, 1997.

Henderson, Yorke, et al. *Parents' Magazine Christmas Holiday Book*. New York: Parents' Magazine Press, 1972.

Henes, Donna. *Celestially Auspicious Occasions*. New York: Perigree, 1996.

Henisch, Bridget Ann. *Cakes and Characters: An English Christmas Tradition*. London, England: Prospect Books, 1984.

Henriksen, Vera. *Christmas in Norway*. Oslo, Norway: Johan Grundt Tanum Forlag, 1970.

Hess, Karen. *The Carolina Rice Kitchen*. Columbia, S.C.: University of South Carolina Press, 1992.

Hick, John. *The Metaphor of God Incarnate*. Louisville, Ky.: Westminster/John Knox Press, 1993.

Highfield, Roger. *The Physics of Christmas*. Boston, Mass.: Little, Brown and Company, 1998.

Hogan-Albach, Susan. "Watch Night: It's an Age-Old New Year's Eve Tradition That's about Much More than Watching the Clock and Making Resolutions." *Minneapolis Star Tribune* (December 27, 1997): 05B.

Hogwood, Christopher. *Handel*. London, England: Thames and Hudson, 1984.

Hole, Christina. *British Folk Customs*. London, England: Hutchinson and Company, 1976.

———. *Christmas and Its Customs*. New York: M. Barrows and Company, 1958.

Holy Days in the United States. Washington, D.C.: United States Catholic Conference, 1984.

Hopko, Thomas. *The Winter Pascha*. Crestwood, N.Y.: St. Vladimir's Seminary Press, 1984.

Horsley, Richard A. *The Liberation of Christmas: The Infancy Narratives in Social Context*. New York: Crossroad, 1989.

Hottes, Alfred Carl. *1001 Christmas Facts and Fancies*. 1946. Reprint. Detroit, Mich.: Omnigraphics, 1990.

Houghton, Walter E. *The Victorian Frame of Mind*. New Haven, Conn.: Yale University Press, 1957.

Howard, Alexander. *Endless Cavalcade*. London, England: Arthur Baker, 1964.

Hubert, Maria, comp. *Christmas Around the World*. Stroud, Gloucestershire, England: Sutton, 1998.

Hulme, F. Edward. *The History, Principles and Practice of Symbolism in Christian Art*. 1891. Reprint. Detroit, Mich.: Gale, 1969.

Hultgren, Arland J. "Stars, Star of Bethlehem." In Paul J. Achtemeier, ed. *HarperCollins Bible Dictionary*. Revised edition. San Francisco, Calif.: HarperSanFrancisco, 1996.

Humphrey, Marj. "Herod Lives; The Story from Sudan." *Commonweal* 121 (December 16, 1994): 8(3).

Hutchinson Guide to the World. Third edition. Phoenix, Ariz.: Oryx Books, 1998.

Hutton, Ronald. *The Pagan Religions of the Ancient British Isles.* Oxford, England: Basil Blackwell, 1991.

————. *The Rise and Fall of Merry England.* Oxford, England: Oxford University Press, 1994.

————. *The Stations of the Sun.* Oxford, England: Oxford University Press, 1996.

Ingersoll, Ernest. *Birds in Legend, Fable and Folklore.* New York: Longmans, Green and Company, 1923.

Jacobi, Peter. *The Messiah Book.* New York: St. Martin's Press, 1982.

James, E. O. *Seasonal Feasts and Festivals.* 1961. Reprint. Detroit, Mich.: Omnigraphics, 1993.

Jameson, Anna. *Legends of the Madonna.* 1890. Reprint. Detroit, Mich.: Omnigraphics, 1990.

Johnson, Rheta Grimsley. *Good Grief: The Story of Charles M. Schulz.* Kansas City, Mo.: Andrews and McMeel, 1995.

Jones, Charles W. *Saint Nicholas of Myra, Bari, and Manhattan.* Chicago: University of Chicago Press, 1978.

Jones, E. Willis. *The Santa Claus Book.* New York: Walker and Company, 1976.

Joy Through the World. New York: Dodd, Mead, and Company, 1985.

Joyce, E. J. "Innocents, Holy." In *New Catholic Encyclopedia.* Volume 7. New York: McGraw-Hill, 1967.

Kainen, Ruth Cole. *America's Christmas Heritage.* New York: Funk and Wagnalls, 1969.

Kane, Harnett. *The Southern Christmas Book.* 1958. Reprint. Detroit, Mich.: Omnigraphics, 1998.

Kaplow, Larry. "Holidays Are Muted in Iraq: But Muslims, Christians Share Their Celebrations, and Baba Noel Will Visit Many Homes Despite Bleak Economy and Recent U.S. Air Strikes." *The Atlanta Journal and Constitution* (December 24, 1998): A08.

Karas, Sheryl Ann. *The Solstice Evergreen: The History, Folklore and Origins of the Christmas Tree.* Boulder Creek, Calif.: Aslan Publishing, 1991.

Karenga, Maulana. *The African-American Holiday of Kwanzaa.* Los Angeles, Calif.: University of Sankora Press, 1988.

Kasbarian, Lucine. *Armenia.* New York: Dillon Press, 1998.

Keck, Leander, ed. *The New Interpreter's Bible: Matthew, Mark*. Volume VIII. Nashville, Tenn.: Abingdon Press, 1995.

———. *The New Interpreter's Bible: Luke, John*. Volume IX. Nashville, Tenn.: Abingdon Press, 1996.

Kee, Howard Clark. *Medicine, Miracle and Magic in New Testament Times*. Cambridge, England: Cambridge University Press, 1986.

King, Constance. *Christmas Antiques, Decorations and Traditions*. Woodbridge, Suffolk, England: Antiques Collectors Club, 1999.

Kirchner, Audrey Burie, and Margaret R. Tassia. *In Days Gone By: Folklore and Traditions of the Pennsylvania Dutch*. Englewood, Colo.: Libraries Unlimited, 1996.

Kirsch, J. P. "St. Barbara." In Charles B. Hervermann, ed. *Catholic Encyclopedia*. Nashville, Tenn.: T. Nelson, 1913. Available online at http://www.newadvent.org/cathen/02284d.htm

Krupp, E. C. *Beyond the Blue Horizon*. New York: HarperCollins, 1991.

Krythe, Maymie. *All About Christmas*. New York: Harper and Brothers, 1954.

Lagerlöf, Selma. *The Legend of the Christmas Rose*. New York: Holiday House, 1990.

Lang, Judith. *The Angels of God*. London, England: New City Press, 1997.

Lange, Karen E. "Kings for a Day." *National Geographic* 199, 1 (January 2001): 58-65.

Langstaff, John. *Saint George and the Dragon*. New York: Atheneum Press, 1973.

Lawrence, Elizabeth Atwood. *Hunting the Wren*. Knoxville, Tenn.: University of Tennessee Press, 1997.

Leach, Maria, ed. *Funk and Wagnalls Standard Dictionary of Folklore, Mythology, and Legend*. San Francisco, Calif.: Harper and Row, 1984.

Lehane, Brendan. *The Book of Christmas*. Chicago: Time-Life Books, 1986.

Lehner, Ernst, and Johanna Lehner. *Folklore and Symbolism of Flowers, Plants and Trees*. 1960. Reprint. Detroit, Mich.: Omnigraphics, 1990.

Levine, Donald N. *Wax and Gold*. Chicago: University of Chicago Press, 1965.

Lewis, James R., and Evelyn Dorothy Oliver. *Angels A to Z*. Detroit, Mich.: Visible Ink Press, 1996.

Lipkin, R. "Myrrh: An Ancient Salve Dampens Pain." *Science News* 149, 2 (January 13, 1996): 20.

Lipschultz, Andy. *How the Grinch Stole Hollywood*. New York: Random House, 2000.

Livingstone, Sheila. *Scottish Festivals*. Edinburgh, Scotland: Birlinn, Ltd., 1997.

Lizon, Karen Helene. *Colonial American Holidays and Entertainments*. New York: Franklin Watts, 1993.

McArthur, A. Allan. *The Evolution of the Christian Year*. Greenwich, Conn.: Seabury Press, 1953.

McBride, Joseph. *Frank Capra: The Catastrophe of Success*. New York: Simon and Schuster, 1992.

McBrien, Richard P. *Lives of the Saints*. New York: HarperCollins, 2001.

MacDonald, Margaret Read, ed. *The Folklore of World Holidays*. Detroit, Mich.: Gale Research, 1992.

McGregor, Malcolm, ed. *Christmas in Australia*. Milsons Point, Australia: Hutchinson Australia, 1990.

McInnes, Celia. *An English Christmas*. New York: Henry Holt and Company, 1986.

Mackenzie, Neil. "Boy into Bishop." *History Today* 37, 12 (December 1987): 10-16.

MacKenzie, Norman, and Jeanne MacKenzie. *Dickens, A Life*. Oxford, England: Oxford University Press, 1979.

McKibben, Bill. *Hundred Dollar Holiday*. New York: Simon and Schuster, 1998.

McKissack, Patricia, and Frederick McKissack. *Christmas in the Big House, Christmas in the Quarters*. New York: Scholastic, 1994.

McKnight, George. *St. Nicholas*. 1917. Reprint. Williamstown, Mass.: Corner House Publishers, 1974.

McLenighan, Valjean. *Christmas in Spain*. Chicago: World Book, 1988.

McManus, Jim. *All Generations Will Call Me Blessed*. New York: Crossroad, 1999.

Mackie, Albert. *Scottish Pageantry*. London, England: Hutchinson, 1967.

Maier, Paul L. *In the Fullness of Time*. Grand Rapids, Mich.: Kregel, 1991.

Marano, Hara Estroff. "Surviving Holiday Hell." *Psychology Today* 31, 6 (November-December 1998): 32-36.

Marcus, Rebecca, and Judith Marcus. *Fiesta Time in Mexico*. Champaign, Ill.: Garrard Publishing Company, 1974.

Margetson, Stella. "Medieval Nativity Plays." *History Today* 22, 12 (December 1972): 851-57.

Marling, Karal Ann. *Merry Christmas!* Cambridge, Mass.: Harvard University Press, 2000.

Marston, Elsa. *Lebanon: New Light in an Ancient Land.* New York: Dillon Press, 1994.

Masani, Rustom. *Zoroastrianism: The Religion of the Good Life.* New York: Macmillan, 1968.

"Masque." In Phyllis Hartnoll, ed. *The Oxford Companion to the Theatre.* Fourth edition. Oxford, England: Oxford University Press, 1983.

Matera, Frank J. "Incarnation." In Paul J. Achtemeier, ed. *The HarperCollins Bible Dictionary.* Revised edition. San Francisco, Calif.: HarperSanFrancisco, 1996.

Matthews, John, and Caitlin Matthews. *The Winter Solstice.* Wheaton, Ill.: Quest Books, 1998.

Mendelson, Lee. *A Charlie Brown Christmas: The Making of a Tradition.* New York: HarperCollins, 2000.

Menendez, Albert J. *Christmas in the White House.* Philadelphia, Pa.: Westminster Press, 1983.

Menendez, Albert J., and Shirley C. Menendez. *Christmas Songs Made in America.* Nashville, Tenn.: Cumberland House, 1999.

Mercatante, Anthony. *The Magic Garden.* New York: Harper and Row, 1976.

Mershman, Francis. "St. Wenceslaus." In Charles B. Hervermann, ed. *Catholic Encyclopedia.* Nashville, Tenn.: T. Nelson, 1913. Available online at http://www.newadvent.org/cathen/15587b.htm

Metcalfe, Edna. *The Trees of Christmas.* Nashville, Tenn.: Abingdon Press, 1969.

Metford, J. C. J. *The Christian Year.* London, England: Thames and Hudson, 1991.

———. *Dictionary of Christian Lore and Legend.* London, England: Thames and Hudson, 1983.

Miall, Antony, and Peter Miall. *The Victorian Christmas Book.* New York: Pantheon Books, 1978.

Michaelson, Herb, and Dave Newhouse. *Rose Bowl Football Since 1902.* New York: Stein and Day, 1977.

Mikalis, Elena, and Odysseus Mikalis. "Celebrating Christmas and New Year's Day in Traditional Greek Style." *Business America* 117, 12 (1996): 6.

Miles, Clement A. *Christmas in Ritual and Tradition.* 1912. Reprint. Detroit, Mich.: Omnigraphics, 1990.

Miller, Katherine. *Saint George, A Christmas Mummers' Play.* Boston, Mass.: Houghton Mifflin Company, 1967.

Milne, Jean. *Fiesta Time in Latin America.* Los Angeles, Calif.: Ward Ritchie Press, 1965.

Molinari, Cesare. *Theatre Through the Ages*. New York: McGraw-Hill, 1975.

Momodu, Shaka. "The Annual Eastward Drift." Africa News Service (January 10, 2002). Available for a fee through elibrary.com

Moran, Rena. *Christmas in Ireland*. Chicago: World Book, 1995.

Mosley, John. *The Christmas Star*. Los Angeles, Calif.: Griffith Observatory, 1987.

Motz, Lotte. "The Winter Goddess: Perchta, Holda, and Related Figures." *Folklore* 95, 2 (1984): 151-61.

Muir, Frank. *Christmas Customs and Traditions*. New York: Taplinger, 1977.

"Mummers' Play." In Phyllis Hartnoll, ed. *The Oxford Companion to the Theatre*. Fourth edition. Oxford, England: Oxford University Press, 1983.

Munby, Jonathan. "A Hollywood Carol's Wonderful Life." In Mark Connelly, ed., *Christmas at the Movies*. New York: I. B. Tauris and Company, 2000.

Munro, Winsome. "Mary, the Virgin." In Paul J. Achtemeier, ed. *The Harper Collins Bible Dictionary*. Revised edition. San Francisco, Calif.: HarperSan-Francisco, 1996.

Murray, Alexander. "Medieval Christmas." *History Today* 36, 12 (December 1986): 31-39.

Myers, Allen C., ed. *Eerdmans Bible Dictionary*. Grand Rapids, Mich.: William B. Eerdmans Publishing Company, 1987.

"Myrrh." In Allen C. Myers, ed. *Eerdmans Bible Dictionary*. Grand Rapids, Mich.: William B. Eerdmans Publishing Company, 1987.

"Mystery Play." In Phyllis Hartnoll, ed. *The Oxford Companion Guide to the Theatre*. Fourth edition. Oxford, England: Oxford University Press, 1983.

Nast St. Hill, Thomas. *Thomas Nast's Christmas Drawings for the Human Race*. New York: Harper and Row, 1971.

Naythons, Matthew. *Christmas Around the World*. San Francisco, Calif.: Collins San Francisco, 1996.

New Catholic Encyclopedia. New York: McGraw-Hill, 1967.

Newland, Mary Reed. *The Saint Book*. New York: Seabury Press, 1979.

Nissenbaum, Stephen. *The Battle for Christmas*. New York: Alfred A. Knopf, 1996.

Nonyelum, Chris. "The Other Side of Christmas." Africa News Service (December 27, 2001). Available for a fee through elibrary.com

Norris, Frederick W. "Bethlehem." In Everett Ferguson, ed. *Encyclopedia of Early Christianity*. Volume 1. New York: Garland, 1997.

Nunly, John W., and Judith Bettleheim, eds. *Caribbean Festival Arts*. Seattle, Wash.: University of Washington Press, 1988.

Opie, Iona, and Peter Opie, eds. *The Oxford Dictionary of Nursery Rhymes.* Oxford, England: Oxford University Press, 1997.

O'Shea, W. J. "Advent." In *New Catholic Encyclopedia.* Volume 1. New York: McGraw-Hill, 1967.

Osmond, Stephen. "Long Night of Dreams: Midwinter Celebrations in Iceland." *The World and I* 11, 1 (January 1996): 206 (12).

Ostrowski, Jeff. "Companies Moving Away From Christmas Bonuses, Study Finds." *The Palm Beach Post* (December 24, 1999): 1D.

Owhonda, John. *Nigeria: A Nation of Many Peoples.* Parsipanny, N.J.: Dillon Press, 1998.

Palmer, Geoffrey, and Noel Lloyd. *A Year of Festivals.* London, England: Frederick Warne, 1972.

Palmer, K., and R. W. Patten. "Some Notes on Wassailing and Ashen Fagots in South and West Somerset." *Folklore* 82 (winter 1971): 281-91.

"Pantomime." In Phyllis Hartnoll, ed. *The Oxford Companion to the Theatre.* Fourth edition. Oxford, England: Oxford University Press, 1983.

Papin, J. "St. Wenceslaus." In *New Catholic Encyclopedia.* Volume 14. New York: McGraw-Hill, 1967.

Patterson, Lillie. *Christmas in Britain and Scandinavia.* Champaign, Ill.: Garrard Publishing Company, 1970.

Peattie, Donald Culross. "Gold, Frankincense, and Myrrh." *Saturday Evening Post* 264, 6 (November 1992): 56.

Peters, Celeste A. *Don't Be SAD.* Calgary, Canada: Script Publishing, 1994.

Philip, Neil, ed. *Christmas Fairy Tales.* New York: Viking, 1996.

Pimlott, J. A. R. *The Englishman's Christmas.* Atlantic Highlands, N.J.: Humanities Press, 1978.

Pool, Daniel. *Christmas in New York.* New York: Seven Stories Press, 1997.

Poole, Robert. "'Give Us Back Our Eleven Days'." *Past and Present* 149 (November 1995): 95-140.

Poole, Shona Crawford. *The Christmas Cookbook.* New York: Atheneum, 1979.

Pope, Hugh. "St. Gabriel the Archangel." In Charles B. Hervermann, ed. *Catholic Encyclopedia.* Nashville, Tenn.: T. Nelson, 1913. Available on the World Wide Web at: http://www.newadvent.org/cathen/06330a.htm

Porter, J. R. *The Illustrated Guide to the Bible.* New York: Oxford University Press, 1995.

Price, Percival. *Bells and Man.* Oxford, England: Oxford University Press, 1983.

Priestly, J. B. *Charles Dickens and His World.* New York: Charles Scribner's Sons, 1961.

Bibliography

Raya, Joseph. *Abundance of Love*. West Newton, Mass.: Educational Service Department, Melkite Greek Catholic Diocese of Newton, 1989.

Reader's Digest Association. *Mysteries of the Bible: The Enduring Questions of the Scriptures*. Pleasantville, N.Y.: Reader's Digest Association, 1988.

———. *The Reader's Digest Book of Christmas*. Pleasantville, N.Y.: Reader's Digest Association, 1973.

Resnick, Abraham. *Bulgaria. Enchantment of the World*. Chicago: Children's Press, 1995.

Restad, Penne. *Christmas in America*. New York: Oxford University Press, 1995.

———. "Christmas in Nineteenth-Century America." *History Today* 45 (December 1995): 13-19.

The Revised English Bible with the Apocrypha. Oxford, England; Cambridge, England: Oxford University Press and Cambridge University Press, 1989.

Reynolds, Nancy, and Susan Reimer-Torn. *Dance Classics*. Chicago: A Cappella Books, 1991.

Rhodes, Christine, ed. *Encyclopedia of Beer*. New York: Henry Holt and Company, 1995.

Ribera Ortega, Pedro. *Christmas in Old Santa Fe*. Second edition. Santa Fe, N.M.: Sunstone Press, 1973.

Robbins, Maria, and Jim Charlton. *A Christmas Companion: Recipes, Traditions and Customs from Around the World*. New York: Perigree Books, 1989.

Robbins, Ruth. *Baboushka and the Three Kings*. Berkeley, Calif.: Parnassus Press, 1960.

Roberts, Paul William. *In Search of the Birth of Jesus*. New York: Riverhead Books, 1995.

Robertson, Margaret. "The Symbolism of Christmas Mummering in Newfoundland." *Folklore* 93, 2 (1982): 176-80.

Robinson, Jo, and Jean Coppock Staeheli. *Unplug the Christmas Machine*. New York: William Morrow and Company, 1982.

Room, Adrian. *Who's Who in Classical Mythology*. Lincolnwood, Ill.: NTC Publishing Group, 1996.

Rose, Peter Q. *The Gardener's Guide to Growing Ivies*. Portland, Ore.: Timber Press, 1996.

Rosenthal, Norman. *Winter Blues*. New York: Guildford Press, 1993.

Ross, Corinne. *Christmas in Britain*. Chicago: World Book, 1978.

———. *Christmas in France*. Chicago: World Book, 1988.

———. *Christmas in Italy*. Chicago: World Book-Childcraft International, 1979.

———. *Christmas in Scandinavia*. Chicago: World Book, 1977.

Rouvelas, Marilyn. *A Guide to Greek Traditions and Customs in America*. Bethesda, Md.: Nea Attiki Press, 1993.

Russ, Jennifer M. *German Festivals and Customs*. London, England: Oswald Wolff, 1982.

Ryan, E. G. "Lucy, St." In *New Catholic Encyclopedia*. Volume 8. New York: McGraw-Hill, 1967.

Ryken, Leland, James C. Wilhoit, and Tremper Longman, III, eds. "Adam." In their *Dictionary of Biblical Imagery*. Downers Grove, Ill.: InterVarsity Press, 1998.

———. "Sheep, Shepherd." In their *Dictionary of Biblical Imagery*. Downers Grove, Ill.: InterVarsity Press, 1998.

St. James, Elaine. *Simplify Your Christmas*. Kansas City, Mo.: Andrews McMeel Publishing, 1998.

Salzman, Michele Renee. *On Roman Time*. Berkeley, Calif.: University of California Press, 1990.

Sammon, Paul. *The Christmas Carol Trivia Book*. New York: Citadel Press, 1994.

Samuelson, Sue. *Christmas: An Annotated Bibliography*. New York: Garland, 1982.

Sansom, William. *A Book of Christmas*. New York: McGraw-Hill, 1968.

Santino, Jack. *All Around the Year*. Urbana, Ill.: University of Illinois Press, 1994.

Sawyer, Edwin A. *All About the Moravians*. Bethlehem, Pa.: The Moravian Church in America, 2000.

Scheel, Eugene. "Recalling Joys of Christmas, Big and Small." *The Washington Post* (December 3, 2000): V03.

Scherele, Victor, and William Turner Levy. *The Films of Frank Capra*. Secaucus, N.J.: Citadel Press, 1977.

Schmelz, Abigail. "Xmas Dreams Dashed as Santa Letters Go Unopened." *Reuters* (December 19, 1996).

Schmidt, Leigh Eric. *Consumer Rites: The Buying and Selling of American Holidays*. Princeton, N.J.: Princeton University Press, 1995.

Scullard, H. H. *Festivals and Ceremonies of the Roman Republic*. Ithaca, N.Y.: Cornell University Press, 1981.

Sechrist, Elizabeth. *Christmas Everywhere*. 1936. Reprint. Detroit, Mich.: Omnigraphics, 1998.

Seeley, Mary Evans. *Season's Greetings from the White House*. Tampa, Fla.: A Presidential Christmas, 1998.

Segall, Barbara. *The Holly and the Ivy*. New York: Clarkson Potter, 1991.

Selbert, Pamela. "A Good Start?: Southerners Ring in a Lucky New Year with Hopping John." *St. Louis Post-Dispatch* (December 16, 1994): 1.

Seuss, Theodor Geisel. *How the Grinch Stole Christmas*. New York: Random House, 1957.

Shannon-Thornbury, Milo. *The Alternate Celebrations Catalogue*. New York: The Pilgrim Press, 1982.

Sheehan, Sean. *Lebanon. Cultures of the World*. Tarrytown, N.Y.: Marshall Cavendish, 1997.

Shoemaker, Alfred. *Christmas in Pennsylvania*. Kutztown, Pa.: Pennsylvania Folklore Society, 1959.

Siefker, Phyllis. *Santa Claus, Last of the Wild Men*. Jefferson, N.C.: McFarland and Company, 1997.

Silverthorne, Elizabeth. *Fiesta! Mexico's Great Celebrations*. Brookfield, Conn.: Millbrook Press, 1992.

Simmons, Adelma Grenier. *A Merry Christmas Herbal*. New York: William Morrow and Company, 1968.

Simpson, J. A., and E. S. C. Weiner. *Oxford English Dictionary*. Volume 9. Second edition. Oxford, England: Clarendon Press, 1989.

Simpson, Jacqueline. *Icelandic Folktales and Legends*. Berkeley, Calif.: University of California Press, 1972.

Slim, Hugo. *A Feast of Festivals*. London, England: Marshall Pickering, 1996.

Smith, C. "Candlemas." In *New Catholic Encyclopedia*. Volume 3. New York: McGraw-Hill, 1967.

———. "Christmas and Its Cycle." In *New Catholic Encyclopedia*. Volume 3. New York: McGraw-Hill, 1967.

Smith, Harold Ivan. *A Decembered Grief: Living with Loss While Others Are Celebrating*. Kansas City, Mo.: Beacon Hill Press of Kansas City, 1999.

Smith, Jonathan Z. "Dying and Rising Gods." In Mircea Eliade, ed. *The Encyclopedia of Religion*. Volume 4. New York: Macmillan, 1987.

Smith, Paul. "Legend, Contemporary." In Thomas A. Green, ed. *Folklore: An Encyclopedia of Beliefs, Customs, Tales, Music, and Art*. Volume 2. Santa Barbara, Calif.: ABC-CLIO, 1997.

Snyder, Phillip V. *The Christmas Tree Book*. New York: Viking Press, 1976.

———. *December 25th*. New York: Dodd, Mead, and Company, 1985.

Spicer, Dorothy Gladys. *The Book of Festivals*. 1937. Reprint. Detroit, Mich.: Omnigraphics, 1990.

————. *Festivals of Western Europe.* 1958. Reprint. Detroit, Mich.: Omnigraphics, 1994.

————. *46 Days of Christmas.* New York: Coward-McCann, 1960.

————. *Yearbook of English Festivals.* New York: H. W. Wilson, 1954.

Stander, Hendrik F. "Christmas." In Everett Ferguson, ed. *Encyclopedia of Early Christianity.* New York: Garland, 1997.

Stapleton, Michael, comp. *The Cambridge Guide to English Literature.* Cambridge, England: Cambridge University Press, 1983.

Stavreva, Kirilka. *Bulgaria. Cultures of the World.* Tarrytown, N.Y.: Marshall Cavendish, 1997.

Stellingwerf, Steven. *The Gingerbread Book.* New York: Rizzoli International Publications, 1991.

Sterbenz, Carol Endler, and Nancy Johnson. *The Decorated Tree.* New York: Harry N. Abrams, 1982.

Stern, Philip Van Doren. *The Greatest Gift.* New York: Penguin Studio, 1996.

Stevens, Patricia Bunning. *Merry Christmas!: A History of the Holiday.* New York: Macmillan, 1979.

Strassfeld, Michael. *The Jewish Holidays: A Guide and Commentary.* New York: HarperCollins, 1993.

Strauss, Mark L. "Gabriel." In David Noel Freedman, ed. *Eerdmans Dictionary of the Bible.* Grand Rapids, Mich.: William B. Eerdmans Publishing Company, 2000.

Street, Ed. "Tom Smith's Novelty—The English Christmas Cracker." *The World and I* 11, 12 (December 1, 1996): 190-95.

Studwell, William E. *The Christmas Carol Reader.* Binghamton, N.Y.: Haworth Press, 1995.

————. *Christmas Carols: A Reference Guide.* New York: Garland, 1985.

Stuhlmueller, C. "Annunciation." In *New Catholic Encyclopedia.* Volume 1. New York: McGraw-Hill, 1967.

Sullivan, Tim. "The Modern, Material Christmas Makes Headway in West Africa." Associated Press Online (December 21, 1998).

Sweitzer, Vangie Roby. *Christmas in Bethlehem.* Bethlehem, Pa.: Central Moravian Church, 2000.

Talley, Thomas J. *The Origins of the Liturgical Year.* Second, amended edition. Collegeville, Minn.: Liturgical Press, 1991.

Taylor, Charles A. *Juneteenth.* Madison, Wis.: Praxis, 1995.

Terjimanian, Hagop. *Feasts and Holidays of the Armenian People.* Santa Monica, Calif.: Abril Bookstore, 1996.

Terry, Walter. *Ballet Guide.* New York: Dodd, Mead, and Company, 1976.

Thompson, Sue Ellen, ed. *Holiday Symbols.* Detroit, Mich.: Omnigraphics, 1998.

Thonger, Richard. *A Calendar of German Customs.* London, England: Oswald Wolff, 1966.

Thorne, John. *Serious Pig.* New York: North Point Press, 1996.

Tille, Alexander. *Yule and Christmas: Their Place in the Germanic Year.* London, England: David Nutt, 1899.

The Time-Life Book of Christmas. New York: Prentice Hall, 1987.

Tober, Bruce. "Hogmanay." *British Heritage* 20, 1 (December 1998-January 1999): 46-50.

Toon, Peter. "Candle; Candlemas." In J. D. Douglas, ed. *The New International Dictionary of the Christian Church.* Revised edition. Grand Rapids, Mich.: Zondervan Publishing House, 1978.

Trexler, Richard C. *The Journey of the Magi: Meanings in History of a Christian Story.* Princeton, N.J.: Princeton University Press, 1997.

Tucker, Cathy C. *Christmas Worldwide.* Philadelphia, Pa.: Xlibris, 2000.

Turkington, Carol. *The Home Health Guide to Poisons and Antidotes.* New York: Facts on File, 1994.

Tyson, Ann Scott. "Christmas Without Shopping." *Christian Science Monitor* (Thursday, December 11, 1997): 1.

Urlin, Ethel. *Festivals, Holy Days, and Saints' Days.* 1915. Reprint. Detroit, Mich.: Omnigraphics, 1992.

Waits, William. *The Modern Christmas in America.* New York: New York University Press, 1993.

Wakefield, Charito Calvachi. *Navidad Latinoamericana, Latin American Christmas.* Lancaster, Pa.: Latin American Creations Publishing, 1997.

Walker, Richard Kennedy. *Lebanon: A Portrait of the Country Through Its Festivals and Traditions.* Danbury, Conn.: Grolier Education, 1999.

Walsh, William S. *The Story of Santa Klaus.* 1909. Reprint. Detroit, Mich.: Omnigraphics, 1991.

Ward, Theodora. *Men and Angels.* New York: Viking, 1969.

Warner, Marina. *Alone of All Her Sex.* New York: Alfred A. Knopf, 1976.

Watson, Marjorie R. *The Fairy Tales of Hoffmann.* New York: E. P. Dutton and Company, 1960.

Weaver, William Woys. *The Christmas Cook.* New York: HarperPerennial, 1990.

Webber, F. R. *Church Symbolism*. Second edition, revised. 1938. Reprint. Detroit, Mich.: Omnigraphics, 1992.

Weinstock, Herbert. *Handel*. Second edition, revised. New York: Alfred A. Knopf, 1959.

Weis, E. A. "Incarnation." In *New Catholic Encyclopedia*. Volume 7. New York: McGraw-Hill, 1967.

Weiser, Francis X. *The Christmas Book*. 1952. Reprint. Detroit, Mich.: Omnigraphics, 1990.

———. *Handbook of Christian Feasts and Customs*. New York: Harcourt, Brace and World, 1952.

Welch, Charles E. *Oh, Dem Golden Slippers*. Revised edition. Philadelphia, Pa.: Book Street Press, 1991.

Wernecke, Herbert H. *Celebrating Christmas Around the World*. 1962. Reprint. Detroit, Mich.: Omnigraphics, 1999.

Werts, Diane. "A 'Miracle' in the Making/Behind the Scenes of a Christmas Classic." *Newsday* (November 21, 2001): B27.

Whittingham, Richard. *Rites of Autumn*. New York: Free Press, 2001.

Whybrow, Peter, and Robert Bahr. *The Hibernation Response*. New York: Arbor House, William Morrow, 1988.

Wiggins, Williams H. *O Freedom! African-American Emancipation Celebrations*. Knoxville, Tenn.: University of Tennessee Press, 1987.

Wilson, C. Anne. *Food and Drink in Britain*. Chicago: Academy Chicago Publishers, 1991.

Yang, Seung Ai. "Joseph." In David Noel Freedman, ed. *Eerdmans Bible Dictionary*. Grand Rapids, Mich.: William B. Eerdmans Publishing Company, 2000.

Young, Joanne B. *Christmas in Williamsburg*. New York: Holt, Rinehart and Winston, 1970.

Young, Katherine. "Sailing with the Sun: The Return of Christmas." *Russian Life* 39, 1 (January 1996): 4.

Web Sites

This appendix furnishes addresses for web sites offering information on a wide variety of Christmas-related topics.

Christmas Around the World

International

This site provides links to pages describing Christmas celebrations around the world, sponsored by Coral Technologies, Inc.:
   http://www.santaclaus.com/world.html

Australia

The following web site, sponsored by the Australian government's Department of Communications, Information Technology and the Arts, offers information on Christmas celebrations in Australia:
   http://www.acn.gov.au/articles/1998/11/xmas.htm

The Australian National Botanic Gardens sponsors a page on native plants associated with Christmas. Gives photos as well as text from *Australian Native Plants* by John Wrigley and Murray Fagg (1996):
   http://www.anbg.gov.au/christmas/christmas.html

Bulgaria

"Wonderland Bulgaria," a web site maintained by Iliana Rakilovska, Irina Simeonova, Maria Nankova, and Kamen Minchev, furnishes information on the history, population, folklore, and geography of Bulgaria. For information on Bulgarian folk festivals, see:
   http://www.omda.bg/engl/ethnography/festivals.html

Canada

A site sponsored by the French Ministry of Culture and Canadian Heritage presents research on Christmas customs in Canada and France, with bibliography:
http://www.culture.fr:80/culture/noel/angl/noel.htm

Estonia

"Christmas Customs in Estonia," an article posted on the web by Estonia's Ministry of Foreign Affairs, is available at:
http://www.mfa.ee/estonia/kat_174/1191.html

Ethiopia

A site sponsored by the Ethiopia Tourism Commission:
http://www.visitethiopia.org/cultatt.htm

Finland

Christmas site sponsored by the Finnish Embassy in Washington, D.C.:
http://www.finland.org/xmas.html

France

A site sponsored by the French Ministry of Culture and Canadian Heritage presents research on Christmas customs in Canada and France, with bibliography:
http://www.culture.fr:80/culture/noel/angl/noel.htm

Germany

The German Embassy in Washington, D.C., maintains a number of pages describing German Christmas foods and customs on its web site. Go to the site listed below, click on "search," and enter the word "Christmas":
http://www.germany-info.org

German customs, holidays, and traditions page, offering information on many German holidays and festivals, including Christmas, posted by German instructor Robert J. Shea, Missouri:
http://www.serve.com/shea/germusa/customs.htm

Ghana

The following page, posted by the Rev. Peter E. Adotey Addo, a writer and United Methodist minister born in Ghana, describes Christmas celebrations in his native country:

http://www.addo.ws/afishapa.htm

For a short story by the Rev. Peter Addo describing a boy's Christmas in Ghana, see:

http://www.southerncrossreview.org/3/fireedit.html

India

Kerala Journal has posted "A Boy's Easter, and Christmas too," an essay by Thomas Palakeel, a professor of English literature at Bradley University. It describes a boy's Christmas in Kerala, India:

http://www.shelterbelt.com/KJ/eastchrist.html

Jamaica

Past and present Jamaican Christmas customs, sponsored by Xavier Murphy, Ft. Lauderdale, Florida:

http://www.jamaicans.com/culture/christ90.htm

Latvia

"Latvian Seasonal Holidays," an article written by Mera Mellon of the University of Latvia's Center for Ethnic Studies and posted to the web by the Latvian Institute, located in Riga, Latvia:

http://www.latinst.lv/seasonal_holidays.htm

Lebanon

An article titled "Lahhoud Attends Christmas Mass at Bkirki," published in Beirut, Lebanon, on December 26, 1998, posted on news@ Lebanon.com:

http://www.lebanon.com/news/local/1998/12/26.htm

Lithuania

The Lithuanian Folk Culture Center, located in Vilnius, Lithuania, offers excerpts from two books on Lithuanian folk customs, *Lithuanian Roots*, edited by Rytis Ambrazevicius:

http://www.lfcc.lt/publ/roots/node1.html

and *The Lithuanians: An Ethnic Portrait,* by Juozas Kurdirka:
http://www.lfcc.lt/publ/thelt/node1.html

The *Anthology of Lithuanian Ethnoculture* contains an article entitled "Lithuanian Customs and Traditions" at:
http://ausis.gf.vu.lt/eka/customs/christmas.html

Merry Christmas in Foreign Languages

The Donnell Library Center, of the New York Public Library, maintains a web site listing common phrases in 26 different languages. For "Merry Christmas," see:
http://www.nypl.org/branch/central_units/d/f/expressions/list/merryc.htm

Travelang.com, a commercial web site dedicated to providing products and services useful to travelers and students of foreign languages, offers a page that translates the phrase "Merry Christmas" and "Merry Christmas and Happy New Year" into a wide variety of foreign languages:
http://www.travlang.com/languages/christmas.html

Mexico

Explains Mexican Christmas customs, sponsored by *Mexico Connect,* a web magazine published by Conexión México S.A. de C.V.:
http://www.mexconnect.com/mex_ /feature/xmasindex.html

Mexico Online, online information and consulting service, offers page on Christmas in Mexico:
http://www.mexonline.com/xmas.htm

Norway

Portrait of Christmas in Norway, sponsored by the Royal Norwegian Ministry of Foreign Affairs:
http://odin.dep.no/ (Click on "Language," "English," "History, culture, geography, recreation," then scroll down to "Christmas in Norway")

Poland

Description of Polish superstitions and traditions surrounding Christmas, sponsored by Internet Polska:
http://www.polishworld.com/christmas/

Christmas Customs

Advent

Bernadotte School in Hallerup, Denmark, offers customs for each day of Advent, submitted by elementary school students around the world:
  http://www.algonet.se/~bernadot/christmas/calendar.html

Epicurious Foods (a division of CondeNet., Inc.) offers recipes from *Bon Appetít* and *Gourmet* magazines for each day in Advent:
  http://food.epicurious.com/c_play/c02_advent/advent.cgi

The German Embassy in Washington, D.C., offers a page describing Advent customs in Germany:
  http://www.germany-info.org/xmas/ch_16.html

Advent Wreath

This page, sponsored by the Evangelical Lutheran Church in America, offers an introduction to the use of the Advent Wreath in religious services:
  http://www.elca.org/dcm/worship/worship_planning/church_
  year/christmas_cycle.html

Amish Christmas

"An Amish Christmas," by Brad Igou, posted on the web site of *Amish Country News*, a monthly visitors guide to Lancaster, Pennsylvania's Amish Country:
  http://www.amishnews.com/amisharticles/amishChristmas.htm

"Auld Lang Syne"

The World Burns Club furnishes a history of the song "Auld Lang Syne" on its web site:
  http://www.worldburnsclub.com/newsletter/auld_lang_syne_
  what_about.htm

"Burns Country," a web site devoted to the promotion and enjoyment of the works of Robert Burns, includes the "Auld Lang Syne"

entry from the *Robert Burns Encyclopedia*:
http://www.robertburns.org/encyclopedia/AuldLangSyne.5.shtml

Ceremony of Lessons and Carols

Cambridge University's King's College Chapel maintains a web site which offers information on its famous Ceremony of Lessons and Carols service:
http://www.kings.cam.ac.uk/chapel/ninelessons/

"Charlie Brown Christmas, A"

The Charles M. Schulz Museum, located in Santa Rosa, California, offers a web site with information on Schulz and his achievements:
http://www.charlesmschulzmuseum.org

Children's Letters

North Pole, Inc., an Icelandic organization that sends out return letters to children who write to Santa Claus in Iceland:
http://www.santa.is

Christingle

The Moravian Church in America offers a page on the Christingle at its web site:
http://www.moravian.org/faq/christingle.html

The Royal School of Church Music, a non-profit organization dedicated to promoting all styles of church music in all denominations, offers information on Christingle services at its web site:
http://www.rscm.com/sundaybysunday/christingle_services.htm

Christmas Card

The Greeting Card Association's web site:
http://www.greetingcard.org/

Victoriana.com, a site dedicated to history buffs and antique hunters interested in the Victorian age, offers the following page, which furnishes color photos of Victorian Christmas cards:
http://www.victoriana.com/christmas/default.htm

A Christmas Carol

Introduction to and background for *A Christmas Carol* posted by the Dickens Project, an educational project of a consortium of University of California scholars:

http://humwww.ucsc.edu/dickens/dea/ACC/ACC.index.html

Christmas History and Folklore

Victoriana.com, a site aimed at history buffs and antique hunters interested in the Victorian era, provides pages that offer text and description of Victorian Christmas foods, decorations, toys, crafts, cards, and trees:

http://www.victoriana.com/christmas/default.htm

The magazine *History Today* maintains a website which offers users the ability to search past issues by subject. Several articles on historical aspects of Christmas are available, some on the web, some through back order only:

http://www.historytoday.com

Freetown Village, a living history museum located in Indianapolis, Indiana, offers a brief description of its reenactment of an 1870s Christmas in a settlement of newly freed African Americans. Go to its web site and click on "special events":

http://www.freetown.org/

About.com's Urban Legends and Folklore site provides information on many aspects of Christmas lore:

http://urbanlegends.about.com/msubxmas.htm

Christmas Markets

A site sponsored by the German Information Center in New York and the German Embassy in Washington, D.C., contains a page on the Christ Child Market:

http://Germany-info.org/ (Search "Christmas market")

The November/December 2001 Newsletter of the Scandinavia Tourism Board of North America offers information on holiday celebrations in Denmark, Finland, Iceland, Norway, and Sweden at:

http://www.goscandinavia. com/frnewsletter.html

Christmas Tree

The National Park Service's page on the National Christmas Tree in Washington, D.C.:
   http://www.nps.gov/ncro/PublicAffairs/NationalChristmasTree.htm

The National Christmas Tree Association's web site:
   http://www.realchristmastrees.org/

The National Park Service furnishes a page on the Nation's Christmas Tree at:
   http://www.nps.gov/seki/xmastree.htm

"The Spirit of the Season Seen in the General Grant Sequoia, the Nation's Living Christmas Tree," a news release article from the United States Geological Survey, can be found at this address:
   http://www.usgs.gov/public/press/public_affairs/press_releases/pr 1537m.html

The web site for the Sanger District Chamber of Commerce offers some information about the trek to the tree at:
   http://www.sanger. org/events.html#trek

Christmas Village

Department 56's web site offers a brief history of the company and its products:
   http://www.dept56.com/history.asp

"Christmas Villages," a page from the Christmas Traditions in France and Canada exhibit, sponsored by the Virtual Museum of Canada:
   http://www.virtualmuseum.ca/Exhibitions/Noel/angl/village.htm

Commercialism

A site sponsored by Alternatives, a Christian non-profit group advocating simpler living and less wasteful holiday celebrations:
   http://www.simpleliving.org

"Simplify the Holidays" pamphlet posted at the Center for a New American Dream web site:
   http://www.newdream.org/holiday/index.html

Web Sites

Epiphany

The following article by the Rev. Thomas Fitzgerald offers information on Greek Orthodox "Special Services and Blessings," including Epiphany. It appears on the Greek Orthodox Archdiocese of America's web site:

http://www.goarch.org/en/ourfaith/articles/article7113.asp

Glastonbury Thorn

"Magical Glastonbury," an article by Geoffrey Ashe, describes the history and legends associated with Glastonbury, England, posted by *Britannia Internet Magazine*:

http://www.britannia.com/history/glaston1.html

How the Grinch Stole Christmas

The web site for the Dr. Seuss National Memorial Sculpture Garden, located in the author's hometown of Springfield, Massachusetts, offers a brief biography of Theodor Geisel, images of previously unpublished art work, and a listing of local Seuss-related events:

http://www.catinthehat.org/index.html

Jonkonnu

The Bahamas Tourism Office provides information on Jonkonnu at:

http://www.bahamas.com/culture/junkanoo/index.htm

Macy's Thanksgiving Day Parade

The New York Historical Society maintains a web exhibit on the parade at:

http://www.nyhistory.org/macyday/index.html

Mumming

The Philadelphia Department of Recreation's page on the Philadelphia Mummers Parade:

http://www.phila.gov/recreation/mummers/index.html

Nativity Legends

The Marian Library and International Marian Research Institute, hosted by the University of Dayton, posts "The Mary Page." This

searchable site contains a summary of the flower legends associated with the Blessed Virgin Mary:
http://www.udayton.edu/mary/main.html

Nativity Scene

This site provides a wealth of information concerning Canadian and French Christmas traditions and contains pages treating the history of the Nativity scene, sponsored by the French Ministry of Culture and Canadian Heritage:
http://www.culture.fr/culture/noel/angl/noel.htm

The "Creche Herald" newsletter, a publication for Nativity scene enthusiasts:
http://www.op.net/~bocassoc/creche1.htm

Peace of Christmas

City of Turku, Finland, site:
http://www.christmascity.com

Putz

"The Putz," a page from the Moravian Church in America's web site at:
http://www.moravian.org/faq/putz.html

An explanation of the Moravian Christmas putz offered by East Hills Moravian Church, located in Bethlehem, Pennsylvania:
http://easthillsmc.org/putz.html

An official site of the Moravian Church in America that offers a variety of information about Moravian beliefs and practices:
http://www.moravian.org

Pyramid

The German Embassy in Washington, D.C., offers a page describing the Christmas pyramid on its web site:
http://www.germany-info.org/xmas/ch_15.html

St. Nicholas's Day

A site sponsored by the Netherlands Board of Tourism:
http://www.holland.com (Search "Sinterklaas" and "St. Nicholas")

Star of Bethlehem

"The 'Stars' of Bethlehem," a January 19, 1999, article by Jeff Kanipe, is available through the *Earth and Sky* magazine web site:
http://www.earthsky.org/Features/Articles/stars.html

Urban Legends

The Urban Legends Reference Pages, sponsored by the San Fernando Valley Folklore Society, collects and analyzes urban legends and offers a page on Christmas legends:
http://www.snopes.com/ (Click on "Holidays," then "Christmas")

Christmas Resources

Reader's Digest Christmas site gives recipes, stories, crafts, and shopping links:
http://www.rdchristmas.com

"A Holy Christmas," a site sponsored by United Church of Christ minister Richard Fairchild and his wife Charlene, offers links to mostly religious resources posted on the web, including Advent calendars, Advent candle-lighting liturgies, Advent preparations and meditations, Advent sermons, biblical accounts and studies, Christmas history and traditions, Christmas carols and customs from around the world, Christmas Eve and Day services, hymns, stories, poems, and much, much more:
http://www.rockies.net/~spirit/sermons/christmaspage.html

Lists movies with Christmas themes and gives cast, director, and release date:
http://www.auburn.edu/~vestmon/christmas_movie.html

New Year's Celebrations and Customs

First Night

First Night™ International hosts a web site at the following address:
http://www.firstnight.com

Football Bowl Games

The Tournament of Roses Association maintains its own web site with detailed information on the parade and football game:
http://www.tournamentofroses.com

Happy New Year in Foreign Languages

The Donnell Library Center, of the New York Public Library, maintains a web site listing common phrases in 26 different languages. For "Happy New Year," see:
http://www.nypl.org/branch/central_units/d/f/expressions/list/happyn.htm

Travelang.com, a commercial web site dedicated to providing products and services useful to travelers and students of foreign languages, offers a page that translates the phrase "Merry Christmas" and "Merry Christmas and Happy New Year" into a wide variety of foreign languages:
http://www.travlang.com/languages/christmas.html

Hogmanay

The city of Edinburgh, Scotland, has posted a web site on its Hogmanay Festival at:
http://www.edinburghshogmanay.org

Hopping John

"The Story of Hopping John," posted by noted food writer John Thorne on his web site at:
http://www.outlawcook.com/Page0102.html

Web Sites

Mummers Parade

The Philadelphia Recreation Department maintains a page on the Mummers Parade at:

http://www.phila.gov/recreation/mummers/index.html

Parade results, route map, photos, and other information concerning Philadelphia mummery can be found at:

http://mummers.com

Saints and Holy Figures

Gabriel

"Gabriel the Archangel," a page available through Catholic Forum, a web site affiliated with Liturgical Publications of St. Louis, at:

http://www.catholic-forum.com/saints/saintg03.htm

Mary, Blessed Virgin

The Marian Library/International Marian Research Institute of the University of Dayton, a Roman Catholic university with a Marian focus, has set up a page of questions and answers about Mary at:

http://www.udayton.edu/mary/ (Click on "Questions")

Associations

This appendix lists groups whose missions relate to Christmas in some way. A brief summary of the group's purpose, available publications, and full contact information accompanies each listing.

Alternatives for Simple Living

Address: 5312 Morningside Ave., P.O. Box 2787, Sioux City, IA 51106
Phone: 712-274-8875; **Toll-free:** 800-821-6153; **Fax:** 712-274-1402
Contact: Rose Ann Pridie, Office Manager
E-mail: alternatives@simpleliving.com
Web site: http://www.simpleliving.org
Founded: 1973
Publications: *The Alternative Wedding Book; Beyond a Consumer Lifestyle* (video); *Have Yourself a Merry Little Christmas* (video); *Simplify and Celebrate: Embracing the Soul of Christmas; Adventures in Simple Living; Simple Living 101; To Celebrate: Reshaping Holidays and Rites of Passage; Whose Birthday Is It, Anyway?* (Christmas annual).

Purpose: Promotes voluntary simplicity by educating members and the public on alternatives to materialistic lifestyles and celebrations. Runs National Alternatives Celebrations campaign, urging a reduced reliance on commercial modes of celebration and a return to the original meaning of holidays, especially Christmas. Suggests donating money saved to projects that promote human welfare. Also known as "Alternatives."

Christmas Philatelic Club

Address: 312 Northwood Dr., Lexington, KY 40505-2104
Contact: Linda Laurence, Secretary-Treasurer
E-mail: cpc@hwcn.org
Web site: http://www.hwcn.org/link/cpc
Founded: 1969
Publications: *Yule Log* (bimonthly bulletin)
Purpose: Facilitates the association of stamp collectors interested in materials relating to Christmas. Promotes the education of its membership regarding Christmas stamps and stamp collecting.

Christmas Seal and Charity Stamp Society (CS & CSS)

Address: 3606 S. Atherton St., State College, PA 16801-8301
Phone: 814-466-3469; **Fax:** 814-466 3469
Contact: Florence H. Wright, Secretary-Treasurer
E-mail: betsychuck@att.net
Founded: 1931
Publications: *Green's Catalog of the Tuberculosis Seals of the World; Mosbaugh's Red Cross Seals of the World Catalog; Mosbaugh's U.S. All Fund Seal Catalog; Seal News* (quarterly newsletter).

Purpose: Distributes the results of worldwide research on charity and fundraising seals so that members can improve their collections. Offers occasional lectures and slide shows.

Friends of the Creche

Address: 3619 N. Nelson Street, Arlington, VA 22207
Phone: 707-525-2016
Contact: James Govan
E-mail: JimGovan@aol.com

Web site: http://www.udayton.edu/mary/gallery/creches/creche
  friends/html
Founded: 1999
Publications: *Creche Herald* (quarterly newsletter)
Purpose: Gathers information about crèches (Nativity scenes) and
  publicizes this Christmas tradition. Encourages crèche exhibits and
  inspires artists to create crèches. Serves as a liaison to crèche associations in other countries and educates members on the history
  and cultural diversity of crèches. Hosts biennial convention.

Golden Glow of Christmas Past

Address: 6401 Winsdale Street, Golden Valley, MN 55427
Contact: Mary Morrison
E-mail: snowbaby@marymorrison.org
Web site: http://www.execpc.com/~gmoe/gg-web2
Founded: 1980
Publications: *The Glow* (bimonthly newsletter)
Purpose: Promotes the collection of antique Christmas ornaments,
  lights, and other decorative paraphernalia (especially those made
  before 1966). Collects and disseminates information about antique
  Christmas decorations. Facilitates networking among collectors and
  educates them through its annual convention and newsletter.

Holly Society of America, Inc.

Address: 309 Buck Street, Millville, NJ 08332-3810
Phone: 856-825-4300
Contact: Rondalyn Reeser, Secretary
E-mail: secretary@hollysocam.org
Web site: http://www.hollysocam.org
Founded: 1947
Publications: *A Guide to Identification of Cultivated Ilex; Holly Pyrenes
  (Seeds); Holly Society Journal* (quarterly); *Sources for Unusual Hollies;*

Holly and Air Pollution; How to Pick a Winner: A Guide to Competitive Exhibition of Holly Sprigs; The Coin-Leaved Japanese Hollies; International Checklist of Cultivated Ilex, Part 1; Diseases of Holly in the United States; Hollies of the Canary Islands; A Field Guide to Insect Pests of Holly; Tips on Choosing, Planting and Caring for Your Holly; International Checklist of Cultivated Ilex, Part 2; Hollies—Versatile Beauty for the Landscape; Hollies: A Gardener's Guide; Hollies for the Landscape in the Southeast; Ilex Cultivar Registration List, 1958-1993.

Purpose: Works to inspire interest in holly cultivation. Provides a medium for all enthusiasts—from beginners to professional botanists—to exchange information on hollies. Sponsors lectures and publications concerning hollies and encourages scientific research on the plant. Arranges tours of important holly collections and hosts an annual meeting for society members and other interested parties.

National Christmas Tree Association

Address: 1000 Executive Parkway, Ste. 220, St. Louis, MO 63141
Phone: 314-205-0944; **Fax:** 314-576-7988
Contact: Don Evanshanko, executive director
E-mail: info@realchristmastrees.org
Web site: http://www.realchristmastrees.org
Founded: 1955
Publications: *American Christmas Tree Journal* (5 per year)

Purpose: Promotes the interests of Christmas tree growers. Runs National Christmas Tree contest. Holds national convention for growers and provides services to them. Collects and distributes information on Christmas trees, makes referrals.

Noelophiles Club

Address: 12 Passage Bourgoin, F-75013 Paris, France
Phone: 011-33-1-68275416; **Fax:** 011-33-1-44249166
Contact: Jean-Claude Baudot, President
Founded: 1992
Publications: *Le Pere Noel Par Le Pere Noel* (book written in French).
Purpose: Promotes the collection of items related to Pere Noel
(Father Christmas), Santa Claus, and other Christmas folk figures.
Sponsors exhibits of these collections.

Index

The Index lists customs, symbols, legends, musical and literary works, historical figures and mythological characters, foods and beverages, religious groups and denominations, geographical locations, ethnic groups, keywords, alternate names, and other special subjects mentioned in the text.

"A Solis Ortus Cardine" 140
Abbot of Unreason.
   See Lord of Misrule
Aberdeen, Scotland 630, 631
Aborigines 42
Abraham (biblical) 304, 714
Abruzzi, Italy 543
Abyssinian Church 355
Acts, Book of. *See* Bible
A.D. 385-86
Adam (biblical) 1-3, 107, 304,
   583, 597, 598
Adam, Adolphe Charles
   (1803-1856) 144
Adam and Eve Day 1-3, 428,
   473, 597
Adams, Abigail (1744-1818) . . . 814,
   816
Adams, John (U.S. president,
   1735-1826) 814, 816
Addis Ababa, Ethiopia 759
Adonis 59

Advent 3-6, 100, 161, 235, 275,
   463, 464, 597
   in America (colonial) 822-23
   in Austria 546
   in Bulgaria 91-92
   in Ecuador 201
   in Egypt 205
   in England 4, 54, 741
   in Estonia 224
   in France 4, 644
   in Germany 4, 6, 7, 10, 11,
   154, 276-78, 414, 546
   in Ghana 284
   in Greece 312
   in Guatemala 320
   in India 355
   in Iran 357
   in Ireland 8, 359
   in Lebanon 424
   in Lithuania 427
   in the Marshall Islands 460
   Moravian 65, 67, 438
   in Rome 4
   in Russia 652
   in Spain 4
   in Switzerland 546
   in Syria 751

Index

Index

Index

Index

Index

Index

Index

Index

Index

Index

Index

Index

Index

Index

M

Index

Index

Index

Index

Index

Index

Index

Index

Index

Index

Index

Index